Handbook of Research on Intelligent Data Processing and Information Security Systems

Stepan Mykolayovych Bilan
State University of Infrastructure and Technology, Ukraine

Saleem Issa Al-Zoubi
Irbid National University, Jordan

A volume in the Advances in Information Security, Privacy, and Ethics (AISPE) Book Series

Published in the United States of America by
IGI Global
Engineering Science Reference (an imprint of IGI Global)
701 E. Chocolate Avenue
Hershey PA, USA 17033
Tel: 717-533-8845
Fax: 717-533-8661
E-mail: cust@igi-global.com
Web site: http://www.igi-global.com

Library of Congress Cataloging-in-Publication Data

Names: Bilan, Stepan Mykolayovych, 1962- editor. | Al-Zoubi, Saleem Issa,
   1975- editor.
Title: Handbook of research on intelligent data processing and information security systems / Stepan Mykolayovych Bilan
and Saleem Issa
   Al-Zoubi, editors.
Description: Hershey, PA : Engineering Science Reference, [2020] | Includes
   bibliographical references and index. | Summary: "This book examines
   theoretical developments and practical applications in the field of
   information protection and intellectual data processing"-- Provided by
   publisher.
Identifiers: LCCN 2019027736 | ISBN 9781799812906 (h/c) | ISBN 9781799812920 (eISBN)
Subjects: LCSH: Computer security. | Data protection. | Electronic data
   processing.
Classification: LCC QA76.9.A25 N4856 2020 | DDC 005.8--dc23
LC record available at https://lccn.loc.gov/2019027736

This book is published in the IGI Global book series Advances in Information Security, Privacy, and Ethics (AISPE) (ISSN:
1948-9730; eISSN: 1948-9749)

British Cataloguing in Publication Data
A Cataloguing in Publication record for this book is available from the British Library.

All work contributed to this book is new, previously-unpublished material. The views expressed in this book are those of the
authors, but not necessarily of the publisher.

For electronic access to this publication, please contact: eresources@igi-global.com.

Advances in Information Security, Privacy, and Ethics (AISPE) Book Series

Manish Gupta
State University of New York, USA

ISSN:1948-9730
EISSN:1948-9749

Mission

As digital technologies become more pervasive in everyday life and the Internet is utilized in ever in-creasing ways by both private and public entities, concern over digital threats becomes more prevalent.

The **Advances in Information Security, Privacy, & Ethics (AISPE) Book Series** provides cutting-edge research on the protection and misuse of information and technology across various industries and settings. Comprised of scholarly research on topics such as identity management, cryptography, system security, authentication, and data protection, this book series is ideal for reference by IT professionals, academicians, and upper-level students.

Coverage

- Network Security Services
- Tracking Cookies
- Electronic Mail Security
- Privacy Issues of Social Networking
- Risk Management
- Device Fingerprinting
- Telecommunications Regulations
- Technoethics
- Internet Governance
- Security Classifications

IGI Global is currently accepting manuscripts for publication within this series. To submit a pro-posal for a volume in this series, please contact our Acquisition Editors at Acquisitions@igi-global.com or visit: http://www.igi-global.com/publish/.

Titles in this Series

For a list of additional titles in this series, please visit: www.igi-global.com/book-series

Handbook of Research on Machine and Deep Learning Applications for Cyber Security
Padmavathi Ganapathi (Avinashilingam Institute for Home Science and Higher Education for Women, India) and D. Shanmugapriya (Avinashilingam Institute for Home Science and Higher Education for Women, India)
Information Science Reference • © 2020 • 500pp • H/C (ISBN: 9781522596110) • US $295.00 (our price)

Advanced Digital Image Steganography Using LSB, PVD, and EMD Emerging Research and Opportunities
Gandharba Swain (Koneru Lakshmaiah Education Foundation, India)
Information Science Reference • © 2019 • 201pp • H/C (ISBN: 9781522575160) • US $165.00 (our price)

Developments in Information Security and Cybernetic Wars
Muhammad Sarfraz (Kuwait University, Kuwait)
Information Science Reference • © 2019 • 351pp • H/C (ISBN: 9781522583042) • US $225.00 (our price)

Cybersecurity Education for Awareness and Compliance
Ismini Vasileiou (University of Plymouth, UK) and Steven Furnell (University of Plymouth, UK)
Information Science Reference • © 2019 • 306pp • H/C (ISBN: 9781522578475) • US $195.00 (our price)

Detection and Mitigation of Insider Attacks in a Cloud Infrastructure Emerging Research and Opportunities
T. Gunasekhar (Koneru Lakshmaiah Education Foundation, India) K. Thirupathi Rao (Koneru Lakshmaiah Education Foundation, India) P. Sai Kiran (Koneru Lakshmaiah Education Foundation, India) V. Krishna Reddy (Koneru Lakshmaiah Education Foundation, India) and B. Thirumala Rao (Koneru Lakshmaiah Education Foundation, India)
Information Science Reference • © 2019 • 113pp • H/C (ISBN: 9781522579243) • US $165.00 (our price)

Network Security and Its Impact on Business Strategy
Ionica Oncioiu (European Academy of the Regions, Belgium)
Business Science Reference • © 2019 • 289pp • H/C (ISBN: 9781522584551) • US $225.00 (our price)

Exploring Security in Software Architecture and Design
Michael Felderer (University of Innsbruck, Austria) and Riccardo Scandariato (Chalmers University of Technology, Sweden & University of Gothenburg, Sweden)
Information Science Reference • © 2019 • 349pp • H/C (ISBN: 9781522563136) • US $215.00 (our price)

Cryptographic Security Solutions for the Internet of Things
Mohammad Tariq Banday (University of Kashmir, India)
Information Science Reference • © 2019 • 367pp • H/C (ISBN: 9781522557425) • US $195.00 (our price)

701 East Chocolate Avenue, Hershey, PA 17033, USA
Tel: 717-533-8845 x100 • Fax: 717-533-8661
E-Mail: cust@igi-global.com • www.igi-global.com

Editorial Advisory Board

List of Contributors

Table of Contents

Section 1
Information Security

Chapter 1
Devaraju Sellappan, Sri Krishna Arts and Science College, Coimbatore, India
Ramakrishnan Srinivasan, Dr. Mahalingam College of Engineering and Technology,
Pollachi, India

Chapter 2
Muzafer H Saracevic, University of Novi Pazar, Serbia.
Aybeyan Selimi, International Vision University, North Macedonia
Selver Pepić, Higher Technical Machine School of Professional Studies in Trstenik, Serbia

Chapter 3
Sergii Bilan, Onseo Company, Ukraine

Chapter 4
Mykola Bilan, The Municipal Educational Institution Mayakskaya Secondary School,
Moldova
Andrii Bilan, The Municipal Educational Institution Mayakskaya Secondary School,
Moldova

Detailed Table of Contents

Section 1
Information Security

This section contains chapters devoted to research in the field of information security. The issues of analysis of attacks on information systems and on biometric identification systems are considered. Several chapters are devoted to issues of cryptography and steganography, as well as the construction of pseudorandom number generators based on cellular automata.

  Devaraju Sellappan, Sri Krishna Arts and Science College, Coimbatore, India
  Ramakrishnan Srinivasan, Dr. Mahalingam College of Engineering and Technology,
   Pollachi, India

Intrusion detection system (IDSs) are important to industries and organizations to solve the problems of networks, and various classifiers are used to classify the activity as malicious or normal. Today, the security has become a decisive part of any industrial and organizational information system. This chapter demonstrates an association rule-mining algorithm for detecting various network intrusions. The KDD dataset is used for experimentation. There are three input features classified as basic features, content features, and traffic features. There are several attacks are present in the dataset which are classified into Denial of Service (DoS), Probe, Remote to Local (R2L), and User to Root (U2R). The proposed method gives significant improvement in the detection rates compared with other methods. Association rule mining algorithm is proposed to evaluate the KDD dataset and dynamic data to improve the efficiency, reduce the false positive rate (FPR) and provides less time for processing.

Chapter 2

Muzafer H Saracevic, University of Novi Pazar, Serbia.
Aybeyan Selimi, International Vision University, North Macedonia
Selver Pepić, Higher Technical Machine School of Professional Studies in Trstenik, Serbia

This chapter presents the possibilities of applying cryptography and steganography in design advanced methods of medical software. The proposed solution has two modules: medical data encryption and medical data hiding. In the first module for the encryption of patient data a Catalan crypto-key is used combined with the LatticePath combinatorial problem. In the second module for hiding patient data, the Catalan stego-key and medical image is used. The objective of the second part is to explain and investigate the existing author's method to steganography based on the Catalan numbers in the design of medical software. The proposed solution is implemented in the Java programming language. In the experimental part, cryptanalysis and steganalysis of the proposed solution were given. Cryptanalysis is based on time and storage complexity, leaking information and machine learning-based identification of the encryption method. Also, steganalysis is based on the amount of information per pixel in stego image, approximate entropy and bit distribution in stego-images.

Chapter 3

Sergii Bilan, Onseo Company, Ukraine

The chapter analyzes modern methods for constructing pseudo-random number generators based on cellular automata. Also analyzes the influence of neighborhood forms on the evolution of the functioning of cellular automata, as well as on the quality of the formation of pseudo-random bit sequences. Based on the use of various forms of the neighborhood for the XOR function, the quality of generators was analyzed using graphical tests and NIST tests. As a result of experimental studies, the optimal dimension of cellular automata and the number of heterogeneous cells were determined, which make it possible to obtain a high-quality pseudo-random bit sequence. The obtained results allowed to formulate a method for constructing high-quality pseudo-random number generators based on cellular automata, as well as to determine the necessary initial conditions for generators. The proposed generators allow to increase the length of the repetition period of a pseudo-random bit sequence.

Chapter 4

Mykola Bilan, The Municipal Educational Institution Mayakskaya Secondary School,
Moldova
Andrii Bilan, The Municipal Educational Institution Mayakskaya Secondary School,
Moldova

The chapter describes investigations of steganographic methods of information protection, which use containers represented by files in AVI format. MP3 audio files are selected as data that is embedded in the used container. For the introduction of audio data, the video container was divided into control and information parts. Secret data were embedded in the information part of the video file, which did not lead to distortions when the container file is played. Studies have been conducted to find repetitive blocks in the structure of a video container. The chapter analyzed the determination of the amount of embedded data for containers with different parameters: color saturation, video file resolution, video file length, compression quality, and frames per second. An algorithm has been developed for the introduction and extraction of information represented by sound formats.

Chapter 5

Richa Gupta, University of Delhi, India
Priti Sehgal, University of Delhi, India

Security-related issues are creeping in almost every authentication problem. Even the secured systems may be exposed to unknown attacks. While addressing one aspect of security, one tends to forget how vulnerable our system is to other attacks. Therefore, it is necessary to understand the impact of these attacks completely and also to get a vision of the hazard they may put when combined together. In this chapter, the authors focus on two such attacks on iris biometric: replay attack and template attack. They provide a detailed analysis of current research work on each of it individually. The comparative study of solutions to these individual attacks is done with the techniques that aim at combining these two attacks. The authors clearly bring out the advantages of the latter approach, which is the driving force in need for a shift to more innovative ideas.

Section 2
Intellectual Data Processing and Information Security in Various Aspects of Human Activity

The chapters that describe research in the field of specific practical applications of modern methods of intelligent data processing and information security in industry and in various specific areas of human activity (banks, space, geographic information systems, ecology, medicine, transport, oil production, etc.) are collected.

Chapter 6

Alessandro Massaro, Dyrecta Lab srl, Italy
Angelo Galiano, Dyrecta Lab srl, Italy

The chapter analyzes scientific approaches suitable for industrial security involving environment health monitoring and safety production control. In particular, it discusses data mining algorithms able to add hidden information important for security improvement. In particular k-means and artificial intelligence algorithms are applied in different cases of study by discussing the procedures useful to set the model including image processing and post clustering processing facilities. The chapter is focused on the discussion of information provided by data mining results. The proposed model is matched with different architectures involving different industrial applications such as biometric classification and transport security, railway inspections, video surveillance image processing, and quarry risk evaluation. These architectures refer to specific industry projects. As advanced applications, a clustering analysis approach applied on thermal radiometric images and a dynamic contour extraction process suitable for oil spill monitoring are proposed.

Andrey Fedorchenko, *St. Petersburg Institute for Informatics and Automation of the Russian*
Academy of Sciences (SPIIRAS), Russia
Elena Doynikova, *St. Petersburg Institute for Informatics and Automation of the Russian*
Academy of Sciences (SPIIRAS), Russia
Igor Kotenko, *St. Petersburg Institute for Informatics and Automation of the Russian*
Academy of Sciences (SPIIRAS), Russia

The chapter discusses how the intelligent data processing techniques, namely, the event correlation, can be used for automated discovery of information system assets. The authors believe that solving of this task will allow more accurate and detailed construction of the risk model for cyber security assessment. This task is complicated by the features of configuration and operation of modern information systems. The chapter describes different types of event analysis, including statistical, structural, dynamic, applied to this task. The authors propose a technique that incorporates determining the types of object characteristics, the types of objects (system assets), and their hierarchy based on the statistical analysis of system events. Significant attention is given to the stage of source data pre-processing. In addition, the developed technique has the broad application prospects to discover the inappropriate, dubious, and harmful information. The case studies and experiments that demonstrate an application of the developed technique are provided and analyzed.

Sergii Bilan, *Onseo Company, Ukraine*

The chapter is devoted to the analysis of the object of the study and highlighted its features as a means of information processing. The review of the existing methods of processing images of the profiles of laser beams, the principles of the operation of systems on the basis of similar algorithms, an analysis of the accuracy of the determination of the energy and geometric centers of the beam of laser beam, its diameter, and the differences of laser radiation are carred out. On the basis of the introduced criterion for estimating the symmetry of the contour of an image of a laser profile, a method for finding the optimal center for such an image is proposed. A comparative software model of effective methods for analysis of laser radiation parameters, namely, the search for laser image contour centers and the determination of the diameter of a laser beam, was constructed.

Addepalli V. N. Krishna, *Christ University, India*
Shriansh Pandey, *Christ University, India*
Raghav Sarda, *Christ University, India*

In the banking sector, the major challenge will be retaining customers. Different banks will be offering various schemes to attract new customers and retain existing customers. The details about the customers will be provided by various features like account number, credit score, balance, credit card usage, salary deposited, and so on. Thus, in this work an attempt is made to identify the churning rate of the possible customers leaving the organization by using genetic algorithm. The outcome of the work may be used by the banks to take measures to reduce churning rates of the possible customers in leaving the respective bank. Modern cyber security attacks have surely played with the effects of the users. Cryptography is one such technique to create certainty, authentication, integrity, availability, confidentiality, and identification of user data can be maintained and security and privacy of data can be provided to the user. The detailed study on identity-based encryption removes the need for certificates.

Chapter 10
Protection of Information From the Influence of Noise on the Transmission of Video Data in a
Olga Galan, State University of Infrastructure and Technologies, Ukraine

The chapter describes parallel-hierarchical technologies that are characterized by a high degree of parallelism, high performance, noise immunity, parallel-hierarchical mode of transmission and processing of information. The peculiarities of the design of automated geoinformation and energy systems on the basis of parallel-hierarchical technologies and modified confidential method of Q-transformation of information are presented. Experimental analysis showed the advantages of the proposed methods of image processing and extraction of characteristic features.

Section 3
Image Processing and Recognition

This section contains chapters that describe new research in image processing and recognition. For this purpose, the parallel shift technology, cellular automata and retinal simulation tools are used.

Chapter 11
*Sergey Yuzhakov, Haisyn Department of the SFS General Directorate in Vinnytsia Region,
Ukraine*

Image processing is one of the important tasks of creating artificial intelligence. The methods for digital images processing are widely used by developers at this time. The parallel shift technology makes it possible to create alternative ways of describing and processing images. It involves the transformation of images not into a set of pixels, but into a set of functions that are organized in a certain way. The completeness of the system is determined by the ability to perform some basic tasks. Image processing includes image pre-processing, video data storage, various image manipulations, images restoration. This chapter discusses a mathematical model for the recovery of flat convex binary images. Images are restored on the basis of data generated by an image processing system based on parallel shift technology. Two methods are provided for determining the imaging area.

Chapter 12
Methods for Extracting the Skeleton of an Image Based on Cellular Automata With a Hexagonal
*Ruslan Leonidovich Motornyuk, PU "Kiev Department" Branch of the Main Information
and Computing Center of the JSC "Ukrzaliznytsya", Ukraine
Stepan Bilan, State University of Infrastructure and Technology, Ukraine*

The chapter describes a brief history of the emergence of the theory of cellular automata, their main properties, and methods for constructing. The image skeletonization methods based on the Euler zero differential are described. The advantages of using hexagonal coverage for detecting moving objects in the image are shown. The software and hardware implementation of the developed methods are presented. Based on the obtained results, a hexagonal-coated cellular automata was developed to identify images of objects based on the Radon transform. The method and mathematical model of the selection of characteristic features for the selection of the skeleton and implementation on cellular automata with a hexagonal coating are described. The Radon transform allowed to effectively extract the characteristic features of images with a large percentage of noise. An experiment for different images with different noises was conducted. Experimental analysis showed the advantages of the proposed methods of image processing and extraction of characteristic features.

Chapter 13

Methods for image identification based on the Radon transform using hexagonal-coated cellular automata in the chapter are considered. A method and a mathematical model for the detection of moving objects based on hexagonal-coated cellular automata are described. The advantages of using hexagonal coverage for detecting moving objects in the image are shown. The technique of forming Radon projections for moving regions in the image, which is designed for a hexagonal-coated cellular automata, is described. The software and hardware implementation of the developed methods are presented. Based on the obtained results, a hexagonal-coated cellular automata was developed to identify images of objects based on the Radon transform. The Radon transform allowed to effectively extract the characteristic features of images with a large percentage of noise. Experimental analysis showed the advantages of the proposed methods of image processing and identification of moving objects.

Chapter 14

The chapter considers principles of construction of retina of the eye. It proposed a system recognition of complex images that models the structure of the retina and the signals at its output. The system is capable of recognizing images and creating new classes. The time impulse description method of images using cellular automata is considered. Images are described by pulse sequences that are created with the help of specially organized cellular automata. The system allows the authors to recognize images of complex shape, which can have an arbitrary location in the field of the visual scene and can have a different scale.

There are tasks of automatic identification of the moving stock of the railway, one of which is the automatic identification of rail cars cars by their number plates. Different organizational, legal, moral and ethical, technical, and programmatic methods of automated identification are used to solve this problem. At present little attention is paid to the development of means of automatic identification of moving objects, which would be possible regardless of the orientation and shape of the figure, especially if it concerns the recognition of freely oriented images of number plates. Therefore, many new methods for recognizing of number plates are developing. In the chapter, the system of identification of objects by their number plates in real time is considered. On moving objects (moving stock of a railway), an identifier image is drawn, which is an ordered set of characters. As a rule, these are numbers. But there may be other characters. The work also discusses the method of identification images of number plates with a high percentage of noise.

This chapter presents image compression based on SOFM and vector quantization (VQ). The purpose of this chapter is to show the significance of SOFM with bandpass filter in process of image compression to increase compression ratio and to enhance image compression effectiveness. Image compression by SOFM model is presented and consists of three stages: The first is band-pass filter. The result experiments used Lena.bmp, girl256.bmp, and show compression in block image 16x16 given best compression ratio with a small signal-noise ratio (SNR).

Preface

The current state of society is characterized by the rapid development and use of information technologies, which have greatly simplified the possibilities of interaction between people at great distances, as well as helping people to automate many processes. Modern scientists are interested in research in three areas: space, society and the brain. The use of computers and computer networks has allowed scientists in around the world to solve problems with great acceleration and to achieve goals in a space exploration and improving a person's living standards.

It is no longer surprising for anyone that every person has a mobile phone that helps a person in quality communication with other people, as well as make decisions using information obtained through telephone and software. At the same time, there are tasks for which it is necessary to develop new methods and tools based on intelligent data processing. Such tasks now appear more and more. Indisputable is the fact that modern search for solutions of intellectual data processing in most cases is based on the analysis and study of the human brain, since it is the most universal independent intellectual system. Decision-making processes and adaptation to existing control functions in the brain are not described today. For example, the processes of transferring some functions of the damaged part of the brain to another healthy part of the brain are not disclosed. The principles of the functioning of a single neuron, the human visual channel and other processes are also not described.

In modern information systems, data are presented in digital format. Therefore, almost all transmission and intelligent data processing systems are digital and implemented on electronic and optical - electronic elemental base. Mostly, data mining is used in decision-making systems, in forecasting systems, and in many other automation systems.

As a result of data mining, a model is defined that helps to make decisions. At the same time, with the advent of big data, requests for building intelligent systems have increased. However, data may not always be represented by an ordered set. In real life, data can be presented in the form of images, video, audio and other forms. In this case, the data set represents the object by unique ordering and the presence of quantitative characteristics. Moreover, the same object can be represented by different quantitative characteristics (for example, an image).

Today there are a large number of methods and tools for intelligent data processing. Practically all of them are aimed at solving a specific applied problem represented by a specific database. For example, in the banking sector, the customer database is different from the customer database in medicine, etc. As a result of the intellectual analysis of the initial data, a search is made for the links between the data, which mainly provide the resulting conclusions.

For intelligent data processing and building the required model, preliminary data preparation is performed. Preliminary data preparation is characterized by combining and cleaning data that are defined as input data at the stage of problem statement. At this stage, both obvious and hidden data are selected, which are the input data for the model used. This data is the most informative. For this reason, already known methods of cleaning (filtering) and extracting data are often used, or new methods are being developed that can improve their efficiency. Methods of preliminary processing and data preparation are developed on the basis of individual tasks.

The main stage of data mining is the building of an appropriate model. Based on the developed model, software and hardware tools are developed that implement the developed algorithms. As a rule, the intelligent data processing system is first learned on the basis of some algorithm for the selected model. This allows to configure the system for further data processing. The reliability of the results obtained on the basis of the developed model is also important.

The book is aimed at describing new and advanced technologies in the intellectual processing of data of various formats, as well as on the description of modern information security technologies. The problems arising in modern data processing and information security technologies are described, as well as methods and means for their solution, which are based on modern advanced technologies of intelligent data processing, are presented. The book presents the results of many experiments in the field of intellectual data processing and information security and describes recommendations for solving problems in these areas of research.

The book is designed for a wide range of readers, which is determined by bachelors, masters and graduate students who study and conduct research in the field of computer science, artificial intelligence systems and information security. The book will be useful for professionals working in all areas of human activity, especially where the creation, storage and processing of data, as well as their effective protection against unauthorized access are used.

The book presents the results of research in the field of modern approaches to information security, based on improving the basic characteristics of encryption, steganography, as well as creating high-quality pseudo-random number generators. Much attention is paid to the description of methods of countering modern attacks on information systems and access systems. The issues of describing the results in the field of image processing and recognition are considered. Much attention is paid to the description of modern methods for the identification of moving objects, as well as to methods of pre-processing images and extracting characteristic features.

Also important is the effective application of the developed methods and tools in all areas of industry and human activity. The book presents the results of applying the described methods for different areas. Much attention is paid to areas such as banks, space, medicine, transport, biometric identification systems, ecology, geographic information systems, modeling, etc.

The book will help to scientific researchers to get good academic results and choose the right path for the decision of tasks they have.

IMAGE PROCESSING AND RECOGNITION

Automatic processing of visual information is one of the most important areas in the field of artificial intelligence. Interest in the problems of computer processing is determined by the expansion of the capabilities of both the computer systems themselves and the development of new technologies for processing, analyzing and identifying various types of images. Images in computer systems are an ordered set of data in raster or vector formats. Data is represented in binary codes that form an array. Image processing and recognition requires the special techniques and tools. If image processing is based on a methods developed by the developer based on his individual experience, then image recognition requires the use of intelligent data analysis methods for decision making. The image analysis can be based on top and bottom approaches. The top approach implements the functional analysis algorithms by the human visual channel, and the bottom approach uses the construction of systems based on the structural analogue of the human visual channel. To date, a large number of image processing and recognition methods have been developed for various areas of human activity (space, medicine, transport, robotics, etc.), but none of them can claim to be universal. From this point of view, the fact that image recognition is based on the use of methods and means of intelligent data processing is obvious.

In addition, image processing and recognition is widely used in data access and data protection systems based on the biometric personal identification. This method is more reliable, since a key information can be transferred to another person, and the biometric characteristics make it possible to identify a person with high reliability and it is rather difficult to fake them. As biometric characteristics, the various images of faces, the fingerprints, palm, ear, the finger vein pattern, etc. are used.

A universal system for processing and recognition of images of various structures has not yet been created, which makes this book relevant for modern science and technology.

The book describes modern approaches for building methods and means of image preprocessing, as well as methods for their effective identification. Particular attention is paid to finding approaches to the development of methods for the efficient extraction of characteristic features. Efforts are aimed at reducing the number of the characteristic features and increasing their informativeness.

INFORMATION SECURITY

Currently, ensuring information security is one of the priorities of many countries. Information security is becoming one of the characteristics of system efficiency. At each point in time, the system must have a measured level of security, and ensuring the security of the system must be a continuous process throughout the entire life cycle of the system. The increase in data volumes requires their effective storage, processing and protection from external influences and unauthorized access. Currently, the most vulnerable link for transmitting symbolic and graphic information are digital communication channels. Anyone who is even slightly familiar with the computer and the Internet knows how unpleasant it is when your information falls into the wrong hands. Loss of confidentiality - a serious psychological blow. Modern methods and means of organizing data transfer along with efficient storage should use effective methods to protect them. Without knowledge and qualified use of modern technologies, standards, protocols and information security tools, it is impossible to achieve the required level of information security of computer systems and networks. Methods of unauthorized access to data are constantly being improved and therefore the challenge remains to counter such attacks. To do this, you need to study and compare known and new attacks on data. Every company has confidential information. Often this information is expensive. In this regard, the resources that store it may be subject to unauthorized interventions. Leakage or destruction of confidential information can lead to a complete shutdown of the entire company. In modern information systems, each of its elements can be exposed to external influences, which can lead to the cessation of data exchange and their destruction.

In this regard, the tasks in the field of information security require the creation of a comfortable mode and concentration of efforts to increase the level of protection against perceived threats. At the same time, the complexity and distribution of information systems requires the creation of methods and means of protecting data based on intellectual approaches of their organization.

From this point of view, the book is relevant and is devoted to the coverage of modern research in the field of information security. In this plan, modern studies are widely described in defining and combating attacks on information systems, and also covers security issues based on access systems. Much attention is paid to the research and construction of modern systems of the steganographic information protection.

ORGANIZATION ON THE BOOK

The book has 16 chapters that make up three sections. The first section contains five chapters that describe scientific results in the field of information security research in the modern information systems, and describe a new methods of the cryptography and steganography for various applications. The second section consists of five chapters that are devoted to research in the field of intelligent data processing and information security for solving various problems in industry and other spheres of human activity. The third section contains six chapters devoted to the description of research in the field of processing and recognition of images based on modern technologies, which allow to increase the efficiency of obtaining the necessary results.

Chapter 1 describes the research into the detection of a various network intrusions with a choice of traits based on entropy. Almost all types of attacks on the information systems are considered. In addition, an association rule matching algorithm for detecting attacks on the computer networks is described. The paper discusses dynamic data using the association rules mining algorithm.

Chapter 2 describes the possibilities of using cryptography and steganography to build advanced methods of the medical software. Catalan crypto keys and stego keys are used to implement the proposed methods. The software implementation of the methods is presented.

Chapter 3 examines research on the construction of pseudo-random number generators based on asynchronous cellular automata. The effect of different form of neighborhoods on the quality of the generators is described. Known graphic tests and the NIST statistical tests were used to assess of the quality of the generators. The chapter presents recommendations for choosing of a pseudo-random number generator based on the asynchronous cellular automata.

Chapter 4 addresses issues of the steganographic data protection and volume expansion based on containers represented by AVI format of audio files. The results of research in the implementation of audio data are described. The determination of the amount of embedded data for containers with different parameters, such as: color saturation, video file resolution, file size, compression quality, etc. are analyzed. The software that implements the proposed method is described.

Chapter 5 focuses on analyzing two attacks on the iris biometric recognition system. The main objective of this chapter is to provide a detailed analysis of the security issues related to iris biometric. The chapter provides the comparative analysis of existing solutions to handle each attach individually versus solutions to handle multiple attacks together. The attacks with replay and using patterns are described. The methods that combine solutions for replaying attacks for the authentication process in detail are discussed.

Chapter 6 analyzes the scientific approaches for industrial sectors related to environmental safety, the production control and health safety monitoring. The data mining algorithms that can add hidden information are discussed. Questions are described: face recognition, motion detection, video security in transport, security in railway infrastructures, security in quarry production processes, oil spill security and underground water leakage, cyber security in multimedia platform.

Chapter 7 describes intelligent data processing methods, namely event correlation methods that can be used to automatically detect asset information systems. A technique has been proposed that includes determining the types of object characteristics, the type of objects (system assets) and their hierarchy based on a statistical analysis of system events.

Chapter 8 is devoted to the analysis of an existing methods and means of processing images of the laser beam profiles, the principles of operation of systems based on similar algorithms, and the methods for determining the energy and geometric centers of images of laser beam profiles. The method of finding the optimal center of the laser spot image is described on the basis of the introduced criterion for assessing the symmetry of the contour of the laser profile image and the necessary software is developed.

Chapter 9 aims to describe one of the approaches of intellectual data processing in the banking sector using the theory of genetic algorithms. This chapter describes an attempt to identify trends and the causes that affect customers leaving the organization, and also describes a model that can predict the behavior of the bank customers based on the genetic algorithms.

Chapter 10 examines a parallel-hierarchical technology that is characterized by a high degree of parallelism, high performance and a noise immunity. Problems of a video data transmission in geographic information systems are considered. The method and mathematical apparatus of the Q-transformation of information is described, on the basis of which the quality of transmitted images in geo-information systems is improved.

Chapter 11 examines a mathematical model for restoring of the flat convex binary images. Images are recovered based on data obtained using an image processing system based on the parallel shift technology. This technology does not yet have a complete theory in terms of image recovery from the resulting function of the area of the intersection. This chapter complements the theory of the parallel shift technology to describe of the reverse processes. An algorithm for recovering images of the convex figures is described and further tasks for developing this technology are proposed.

Chapter 12 describes the methods for selecting of the skeleton of the image and the proposed method of skeletonizing images based on the cellular automata with hexagonal coating. A method for extracting of the characteristic features based on the Radon transform using the Euler zero differential is presented. The methodology for hardware implementation based on the FPGA is described. The advantages that cellular automata with hexagonal coating give are shown, which is proved in detail by the experiment described.

Chapter 13 is a continuation of the chapter 12 and displays the advantage of using cellular automata with the hexagonal coated and the Radon transform for detecting moving objects and their effective identification. The most important parameter is the speed, which due to the matrix organization of specialized computing facilities allows the detection and identification of moving objects in real time. A method for identifying of the images with a large percentage of noise is described.

Chapter 14 examines the principles of building the retina. The method of recognition of the complex images based on the structure of the retinal model of the eye using multilayer cellular automata is described. Images are described by time-pulse sequences that are formed by the cellular automata. An original structure of the asynchronous cellular automata is proposed, which specify the movement of an active signal for a single cell in a cellular automaton, which generates a pulse signal at the output at the corresponding time step.

Chapter 15 describes the method for identifying moving objects by the license plate images based on the parallel shift technology. A natural shift of the copy images is used, which is set by the moving object and forms the shape of a curve in accordance with a given speed of movement. This technology allowed the identification of the moving objects in real time. The method is effective for the freely oriented images that contain a high percentage of a noise.

Chapter 16 presents an image compression method based on the artificial neural networks like SOFM and the vector quantization. In addition, a band-pass filter is used to implement the method. Image compression is represented by three stages, which allowed forming images with a high degree of compression. The investigation evaluate approximation filters with coefficient w/8, w/4 and w/2 and evaluate of amplitude-frequency characteristic filter to release spectrum signal in range of 0 – w/8.

Stepan Bilan
State University of Infrastructure and Technology, Ukraine

Saleem Issa Al-Zoubi
Irbid National University, Jordan

Acknowledgment

The editors would like to acknowledge the help of all the people involved in this project and, more specifically, to the authors and reviewers that took part in the review process. Without their support, this book would not have become a reality. Editors thank the authors for responding to the call to send a chapter for the book. Editors know how much work the authors had to do to prepare chapters for the book. Only the joint coordinated work of editors, authors and reviewers allowed us to assemble a unique collection of chapters on research in the field of intelligent data processing and information security.

First, the editors would like to thank each one of the authors for their contributions. Our sincere gratitude goes to the chapter's authors who contributed their time and expertise to this book.

Second, the editors wish to acknowledge the valuable contributions of the reviewers regarding the improvement of quality, coherence, and content presentation of chapters. Most of the authors also served as referees; we highly appreciate their double task.

Many thanks to all the members of the IGI Global editorial board for entrusting us with the creation of this handbook!

Stepan Bilan
State University of Infrastructure and Technology, Ukraine

Saleem Issa Al-Zoubi
Irbid National University, Jordan

Section 1
Information Security

This section contains chapters devoted to research in the field of information security. The issues of analysis of attacks on information systems and on biometric identification systems are considered. Several chapters are devoted to issues of cryptography and steganography, as well as the construction of pseudorandom number generators based on cellular automata.

Chapter 1
Association Rule–Mining–Based Intrusion Detection System With Entropy–Based Feature Selection:
Intrusion Detection System

Devaraju Sellappan

(iD) https://orcid.org/0000-0003-3116-4772

Sri Krishna Arts and Science College, Coimbatore, India

Ramakrishnan Srinivasan

(iD) https://orcid.org/0000-0002-8224-4812

Dr. Mahalingam College of Engineering and Technology, Pollachi, India

ABSTRACT

Intrusion detection system (IDSs) are important to industries and organizations to solve the problems of networks, and various classifiers are used to classify the activity as malicious or normal. Today, the security has become a decisive part of any industrial and organizational information system. This chapter demonstrates an association rule-mining algorithm for detecting various network intrusions. The KDD dataset is used for experimentation. There are three input features classified as basic features, content features, and traffic features. There are several attacks are present in the dataset which are classified into Denial of Service (DoS), Probe, Remote to Local (R2L), and User to Root (U2R). The proposed method gives significant improvement in the detection rates compared with other methods. Association rule mining algorithm is proposed to evaluate the KDD dataset and dynamic data to improve the efficiency, reduce the false positive rate (FPR) and provides less time for processing.

DOI: 10.4018/978-1-7998-1290-6.ch001

INTRODUCTION

Today many people have connected with internet for their business purpose and other related purpose. So, the intrusion detection system (IDSs) is important for any industry to protect their information from intruders. Industries are using software and hardware devices to secure the information, even though many intruders were not identified. Today the information is most important role in our life. So, need to protect the data from intruders because many malicious users are using various techniques to exploit the systems vulnerabilities. While the information is sent from one system to another, there is no protection from intruders. In these aspects, need to protect the information more securely.

Intrusion Detection Systems (IDS) are typically classified into two groups: Anomaly based IDS and Signature based IDS. The anomaly-based IDS which is observed from network when it behavior deviates from the normal attacks. The signature-based IDS detects the intrusion by comparing with its existing signatures in the log files. Intrusion Detection System is classified as Host based IDS and Network based IDS. The host-based IDS is a system which monitor and analyze the computer system if there is any misbehavior. The network-based IDS is a system which detect the misbehavior whenever the system can able to communicate with each other over the network (Devaraju & Ramakrishnan, 2013).

Data mining technique is used to process the large volume of raw data easily. The various techniques are Association Rule, Clustering, Decision Trees and Neural Networks. The various authors have tried to improve the performance and reduce the false positive rate of intrusion detection system. Even though there are some misbehavior happening in IDS and could not be improve the performance and reduce the false positive rate due to the dataset contains large volume of data. The data contains many features and the authors were used all the features for processing but some features are not important.

In this paper, try to create a new set of rulesets based on the protocol features which will help us to improve the performance, reduce the false positive rate and less processing time. There are three types of protocol feature are considered such as TCP, UDP and ICMP. Mainly attacks are depending on any one of the protocol features so need to category the data based on the protocol features to reduce the feature as well. The purpose of the systems is i) to generate association rules to improve the detection rate and ii) to refine the association rules correctly to reduce the false alarm. The association rule-based systems are developed using Java Development Kit (JDK) for better performance applied to KDD dataset and dynamic data using Association Rule-Mining Algorithm.

The paper is organized as follows: In Section 2, discusses the related work, Section 3, discusses KDD Dataset Description, Section 4, discussing Entropy based Feature Selection, Section 5, describes the Methodology. Section 6 gives the results and discussion and Section 7 deals with conclusion of the research work.

RELATED WORK

There are various techniques have been proposed. They are statistical methods, neural network, data mining etc. In this section, the various techniques used for intrusion detection systems are discussed.

C-Means Clustering was applied for intrusion detection which uses minimum testing dataset and reducing the features by using reduction algorithm to improve the detection time (Minjie & Anqing, 2012). A novel twin support vector machine and SVM were used to overcome the normal traffic patterns and classification accuracy (Nie & He, 2010; Srinivas, Andrew & Ajith, 2004; Sumaiya & Aswani, 2017).

Hidden Markov Model was used to implement and determine the system call based anomaly intrusion detection system (Jiankun, Xinghuo, Qiu & Chen, 2009; Xie & Yu, 2008). Conditional Random Fields and Layered Approach were demonstrated the attack detection accuracy by KDD cup '99 dataset (Gupta & Kotagiri, 2010). The Genetic Algorithm was used to detect the intrusion which considers both temporal and spatial information of network connections during the encoding of the problem (Wei, 2004; Jiang & Junhu, 2009).

Hierarchical Gaussian Mixture Model was used to detect network-based attacks as anomalies using statistical classification techniques using KDD99 dataset. Also, it was used to reduce the missing alarm and accuracy of the attacks (Suseela, Zhu & Julie, 2005; Kabir, Jiankun, Wang & Zhuo, 2018). The various Neural Network approaches were used to improve the performance of the intrusion detection system. The KDDCup'99 dataset was used as testing data and gives the robust result (Devaraju & Ramakrishnan, 2011; Ran, Steren, Nameri, Roytman, Porgador & Yuval, 2019) (Neveen, 2009). The SVM and GA were used for classification purpose and these methods minimize the features for increase the detection rate (Iftikhar, Azween, Abdullah & Muhammad, 2011). The correlation coefficient and data mining techniques were used to improve the detection of new types of anomaly using KDD cup'99 dataset (Ning, Chen, Xiong & Hong-Wei, 2009; Anbalagan, Puttamadappa, Mohan, Jayaraman & Srinivasarao, 2008). Association rule mining algorithm was used to detect the attacks for intrusion detection system. It was considered only individual attacks to frame the rulesets applied with KDD dataset (Zhiwen, Salim & Pacheco, 2019; Devaraju & Ramakrishnan, 2015).

Recurrent Neural Network was used to improve the classification rates, especially for R2L attack. Decision trees and support vector machines were used to improve the detection accuracy and minimize the computational complexity (Mansour, Zahra & Ali, 2010; Sandhya, Ajith, Crina & Johnson, 2005; Akashdeep, Ishfaq & Neeraj, 2017; Alex, David & Aladdin, 2018). Data mining clustering technique was used for detection of intrusion and reduction algorithm was used to cancel the redundant attribute set (Nadiammai & Hemalatha, 2014; Srinivas, Andrew & Ajith, 2007; Vajiheh & Shahram, 2018). Rule-based classification, decision tree methods and novel fuzzy class association rule-mining method were used for detecting network intrusions (Anuar, Hasimi, Abdullah & Omar, 2008; Shingo, Chen, Nannan, Shimada & Hirasawa, 2011; Adnan & Cameron, 2017; Ashfaq, Wang, Huang, Abbas & Yu-Lin, 2017).

The various techniques are discussed and finding some difficulties to improve the detection rate and false positive rate. The data mining techniques is better choices to define the ruleset depends on the selected features. In order to address the limitations, in this paper, proposed a new set of association rule-mining algorithm. This proposed algorithm improves the detection rate, reduces the FPR and minimizes the processing speed. Data mining techniques are grouped into four levels, namely Mining Data Streams, Clustering, Classification and Pattern Mining. Figure 1 has shown the various techniques in data mining.

Motivation

Most of the organizations and industry are struggling with more vulnerable to threats. The intrusion detection system is used to compromise the integrity and confidentiality of the resources. In recent years, intrusion detection is the highest priorities and challenging tasks for administrators to detect the emerging threats.

Figure 1. Comparison of various data mining techniques

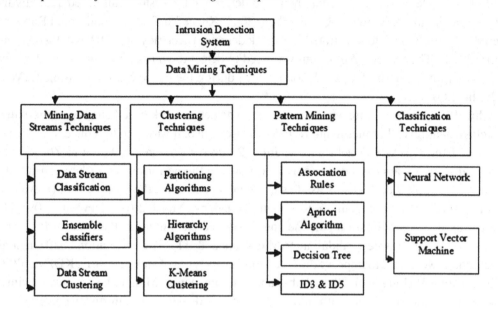

Problem Statement

In intrusion detection system, there are several methods employed like data mining techniques (Devaraju & Ramakrishnan, 2013; Minjie_& Anqing,_2012; Nadiammai & Hemalatha, 2014; Anuar, Hasimi, Abdullah & Omar, 2008; Muniyandi, Rajeswari & Rajaram, 2012), probability approach and support vector machine (Nie & He, 2010), neural network (Devaraju & Ramakrishnan, 2011), Fuzzy C-Means (Shingo, Chen, Nannan, Shimada & Hirasawa, 2011), genetic algorithm (Wei, 2004) (Jiang & Junhu, 2009), Hidden Markov Model (Jiankun, Xinghuo, Qiu & Chen, 2009; Xie & Yu, 2008), etc. The existing systems do not provide data security. The Data Mining Technique is employed to overcome the existing problem, reduce the false alarm and improve their attack detection accuracy.

KDD DATASET DESCRIPTION

The KDD dataset is the benchmarking dataset which is used to evaluate the Intrusion Detection System (Mansour, Zahra & Ali, 2010). There are categories of attacks in KDD dataset: DoS, Probe, R2L, and U2R. The dataset consists of three components which are "10% KDD Dataset", "Corrected KDD Dataset" and "Full KDD Dataset". Dataset which contains millions of records and each record contains 41 features and labeled as either normal or an attack, with exactly one specific attack type. Table 1 shows the training and testing data in KDD Dataset (Srinivas, Andrew & Ajith, 2004).

The "10% KDD Dataset" is used for training data, "corrected KDD Dataset" and "Full Dataset "is used for testing data.

KDD dataset has different types of attacks: guess_passwd, buffer_overflow, back, ftp_write, ipsweep, land, imap, multihop, loadmodule, neptune, nmap, phf, perl, pod, rootkit, portsweep, satan, smurf, spy, warezclient, teardrop, warezmaster. These attacks can be divided into following groups (Nie & He, 2010).

Table 1. Training and testing data

Dataset	Normal	DoS	Probe	R2L	U2R	Total
Training Data						
10% KDD	97278	391458	4107	1126	52	494021
Testing Data						
Corrected KDD	60593	229853	4166	16347	70	311029
Whole KDD	972781	3883370	41102	1126	52	4898431

- **Denial of Service (DoS) Attacks:** Which can deny legitimate requests to a system, example. Flood.
- **User-to-Root (U2R) Attacks:** Which is an unauthorized access to local super user (root) privileges, example. Buffer overflow attacks.
- **Remote-to-Local (R2L) Attacks:** Which is an unauthorized access from a remote machine, example. Guesses a different password.
- **Probing:** Probing is a surveillance and other probing attacks, example. Port scanning.

KDD Dataset contains 41 features that are categorized into continuous and discrete type. The features are assigned the label as c0, c1, c2, ..., c40. Table 2 shows the Description of Variable in KDD dataset.

The association rule-mining algorithm derives from the important features based on the protocol types (tcp, udp and icmp). Table 4 shows the important features that improve the performance, reduce the False Positive Rate and also reduce the evaluation time (Jiankun, Xinghuo, Qiu & Chen, 2009). The proposed system uses selected important features (Srilatha, Ajith & Johnson, 2005). The feature is selected based on the variable which is filtered if the probability of the variable is closer to minimum by the calculation of mean value.

In KDD Dataset, the normal record and snmpgetattack record of all 41 feature values are same. Due to this kind of problem the false correlation may be increased. The table 3 shows the sample records of normal and snmpgetattack.

ENTROPY BASED FEATURE SELECTION

Feature Selection

The KDD Dataset contains a millions of records and each record which contains 41 attributes. When designing a network intrusion detection system, all 41 features are not necessary. The KDD dataset may contain redundant data in which the additional features can increase the computation time and which declines the accuracy of intrusion detection system and increase the false positive rate. The feature selection is more important to improve the performance and reduce the false positive rate. Though, apply the entropy based feature selection for improving their efficiency and false positive rate. The following steps are used for feature selection:

Table 2. Description of variable in KDD dataset

Var. No.	Variable Name	Variable Type	Label Name	Var. No.	Variable Name	Variable Type	Label Name
1	duration	continuous	c0	22	is_guest_login	discrete	c21
2	protocol_type	discrete	c1	23	count	continuous	c22
3	service	discrete	c2	24	srv_count	continuous	c23
4	flag	discrete	c3	25	serror_rate	continuous	c24
5	src_bytes	continuous	c4	26	srv_serror_rate	continuous	c25
6	dst_bytes	continuous	c5	27	rerror_rate	continuous	c26
7	land	discrete	c6	28	srv_rerror_rate	continuous	c27
8	wrong_fragment	continuous	c7	29	same_srv_rate	continuous	c28
9	urgent	continuous	c8	30	diff_srv_rate	continuous	c29
10	hot	continuous	c9	31	srv_diff_host_rate	continuous	c30
11	num_failed_logins	continuous	c10	32	dst_host_count	continuous	c31
12	logged_in	discrete	c11	33	dst_host_srv_count	continuous	c32
13	num_compromised	continuous	c12	34	dst_host_same_srv_rate	continuous	c33
14	root_shell	continuous	c13	35	dst_host_di_srv_rate	continuous	c34
15	su_attempted	continuous	c14	36	dst_host_same_src_port_rate	continuous	c35
16	num_root	continuous	c15	37	dst_host_srv_diff_host_rate	continuous	c36
17	num_file_creations	continuous	c16	38	dst_host_serror_rate	continuous	c37
18	num_shells	continuous	c17	39	dst_host_srv_serror_rate	continuous	c38
19	num_access_files	continuous	c18	40	dst_host_rerror_rate	continuous	c39
20	num_outbound_cmds	continuous	c19	41	dst_host_srv_rerror_rate	continuous	c40
21	is_host_login	discrete	c20				

Table 3. Sample records of normal and snmpgetattack

Sample Records
0 udp private SF 105 146 0 0 0 0 0 0 0 0 0 0 0 0 0 0 0 2 2 0.00 0.00 0.00 0.00 1.00 0.00 0.00 255 254 1.00 0.01 0.00 0.00 0.00 0.00 0.00 0.00 normal.
0 udp private SF 105 146 0 0 0 0 0 0 0 0 0 0 0 0 0 0 0 2 2 0.00 0.00 0.00 0.00 1.00 0.00 0.00 255 254 1.00 0.01 0.00 0.00 0.00 0.00 0.00 0.00 snmpgetattack.
0 udp private SF 105 146 0 0 0 0 0 0 0 0 0 0 0 0 0 0 0 1 1 0.00 0.00 0.00 0.00 1.00 0.00 0.00 255 254 1.00 0.01 0.00 0.00 0.00 0.00 0.00 0.00 normal.
0 udp private SF 105 146 0 0 0 0 0 0 0 0 0 0 0 0 0 0 0 1 1 0.00 0.00 0.00 0.00 1.00 0.00 0.00 255 254 1.00 0.01 0.00 0.00 0.00 0.00 0.00 0.00 snmpgetattack.

Step 1: Before feature selection, normalization of data to the scale of [0,1] is done through the following formula:

$$Res_m[n] = \left(Res_m[n] - Res_{c\_min}[n] \right) \Big/ \left(Res_{c\_max}[n] - Res_{c\_min}[n] \right) \tag{1}$$

where,

$Res_m[n]$ is the value of mth data instance from n^{th} attribute.
$Res_{c\_min}[n]$ is the minimum value of attribute 'n' among the dataset Res,
$Res_{c\_max}[n]$ is the maximum value among all the data instances.

Step 2: There are four classes (DoS, Probe, R2L and U2R) used for feature selection based on the within-class entropy and between-class entropy for all the 41 features. The 10% KDD Dataset is used for training. The within-class and between-class entropy is calculated using the entropy formula for normalized data.

$$Entropy = -\sum_{i=1}^{k} P(value_i) . \log_2(P(value_i)) \tag{2}$$

where, $P(value_i)$ is the probability of getting i^{th} value.

Step 3: Using calculated value of within-class entropy and between-class entropy, grouping of the classes based on the entropy value is done (very low, low, high or very high), after computed the between-class entropy and within-class entropy for 41 features.

Step 4: After categorizing, select the features and rank the features for the following condition:

RANK 1: Between-entropy is very high and within-class entropy is very low, then the feature is selected.

RANK 2: Between-entropy is very high and within-class entropy is low, then the feature is selected.

RANK 3: Between-entropy is high and within-class entropy is very low, then the feature is selected.

Step 5: Based on the ranking, the features are ranked in Feature Rank Matrix.

Step 6: Identify number of features by considering Detection Rate and Computational Time. If Detection Rate is high and Computational Time is low, the feature is selected. Calculate the Detection Rate and Computational Time based on the selected features, which will help to select number of feature and then calculate the overall within-class entropy for only selected features.

As a result, only selected feature is used for each class. However, when performed the experiments on the selected features and compared the results, there is significant improvement in the detection rate and False Positive Rate. The feature selection is shown in table 4.

Table 4. Selected features

Class No.	Class Name	Important Features (Label Name Is Listed)		
		tcp (c1)	udp (c1)	icmp (c1)
1	DoS	c0, c2, c3, c4, c5, c6, c9, c11, c12, c22, c24, c25, c28, c29, c31, c32, c33, c37, c38, c39, c40	c0, c2, c3, c4, c5, c7	c0, c2, c3, c4, c5
2	Probe	c0, c2, c3, c4, c5, c22, c23, c24, c25,26, c27, c28, c29, c31, c32, c34, c35, c37, c38, c39, c40	c0, c2, c3, c4, c5, c23, c31, c32, c34, c35	c0, c2, c3, c4, c5, c22, c23, c28, c31, c33, c35
3	R2L	c0, c2, c3, c4, c5, c9, c10, c11, c21, c22, c23, c28, c31, c33, c35	c0, c2, c3, c4, c5, c22, c23, c28, c34	c0, c2, c3, c4, c5, c22, c23, c28, c31, c32, c34, c39
4	U2R	c0, c2, c3, c4, c5, c12, c16, c20, c21, c23, c28, c31, c32, c33, c34, c35, c36, c39, c40	-	-

Discrimination Capability of the Proposed Method

In this paper, the box plot and whisker chart are presented to exhibit the unfairness capability and represent the different distribution of data into ranges within the different classes. X-axis shows the number of classes and Y-axis shows the variation. The median of before feature selection is high when compare with the after feature selection is considered. Hence the variation is better than the box plot and whisker chart are well suited. The variables are randomly selected for finding the variations. The variation between before feature selection and after feature selection for the classes has been shown in figure 2.

In this paper, average between-class and within-class entropies are computed, before and after the feature selection method which demonstrate the effectiveness. Between-class entropy for before feature selection is low and after feature selection is high. Within-class entropy for before feature selection is high and after feature selection is low for the classes. The rulesets are applied to the Association Rule-Mining Algorithm for verifying the consistency. The selection of features and rulesets are well suitable to employ this system. Figure 3 shows the average of between-class and within-class entropy.

In this paper, a scatter plot is employed to demonstrate the discrimination capability of the proposed feature selection method which represents the relationship between the different classes. A scatter plot for the variables same_srv_rate vs diff_srv_rate is presented from the corrected dataset for the classes DoS, Probe, R2L, U2R and Normal. Six samples are selected randomly for finding the relationships. Each class in the scatter plot is shown in the figure 4. It is observed that the scatter plot for the proposed feature selection method is performing in a better way.

Figure 2. Box plot and whisker chart for the classes

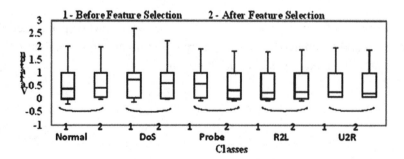

Figure 3. Average of between-class and within-class entropy

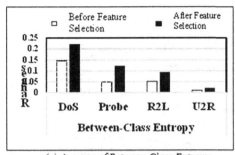 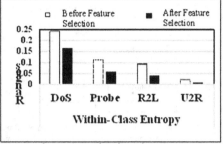

(a) Average of Between-Class Entropy   (b) Average of Within-Class Entropy

Figure 4. Scatter plot for different features

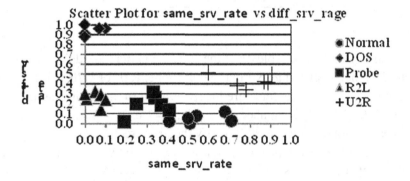

METHODOLOGY

Association Rule-Mining Algorithm

Association Rule-Mining Algorithm is utilized to create the ruleset which is different from other algorithms with larger datasets. The ruleset is performed with the help of generating rulesets step by step using support and confidence. The ruleset is generated based on the feature selection. When the numbers of samples are too big, Data Mining algorithms like decision tree and rule based can be used. It is vitally utilized to generate rulesets which consist of unordered collections of IF-THEN rules. The rulesets are generally easier to understand when compared with other algorithms. Each rule from rulesets describes a specific context associated with a class or an attribute. This approach is designed to improve the performance based on the type of classes such as Normal, DoS, Probe, R2L and U2R (Anuar, Hasimi, Abdullah & Omar, 2008) (Selvakani & Rajesh, 2011).

The data mining algorithm is modified from the apriori association rules algorithm (Hanguang & Ni Yu, 2012). Rules can be viewed simply as [If Then Else] structure (Jiang, Xindan, Wang & Zhuo, 2011). A new association rule-mining algorithm is proposed for classifying and predicting uncertain datasets. In this study, the Dataset consists of 41 features which process selected features to classify the dataset based on their protocol. The protocol may be 'tcp', 'udp' or 'icmp'. Each protocol is exemplified by

Figure 5. Architecture for association rule mining classifier

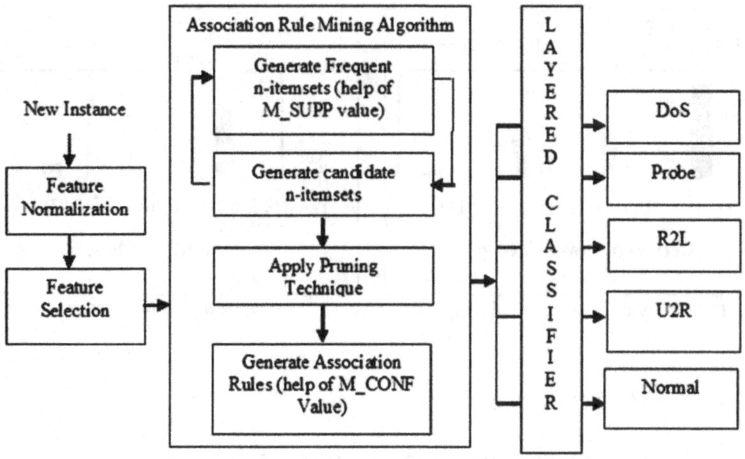

the uses of services and flags [Refer Table 4]. If the protocol is 'tcp' || 'udp' || 'icmp' then the various parameters are checked then declared as Normal, DoS, Probe, R2L or U2R (Muniyandi, Rajeswari & Rajaram, 2012). Figure 5 shows the architecture for association rule-mining classifier.

Suppose, n={N1,N2,N3,....∞} is number of records; m={ c_0, c_1, c_2, c_3, c_4 .... c_{40} } is number of features; c_j is the feature name which is used to verify the given record is normal or attack; d is the numeric value or string value of specific parameter for records. Initially, the features are compared with d and continued with number of records until the number of records turned to be empty. The Association Rule-Mining Algorithm is shown as

$$R = \sum_{i=1}^{n} \sum_{j=0}^{m} if((c_j >= d) \,||\, (c_j <= d)) \tag{3}$$

where, R is the Result variable; i,j is the initial variable; n= number of records; m=number of features used (Refer Table 4); c_j is the feature name; d is the numeric value or string value.

Calculation of χ^2 value of rule X ⇒ Y is shown as follows.

Assume support(X) = x, support(Y) = y, support(X ∪ Y) = z, and the total number of records is N. It calculates χ^2 as

$$\chi^2 = \frac{N(z - xy)^2}{xy(1 - x)(1 - y)} \tag{4}$$

If χ^2 is greater than a cutoff value, may reject the assumption that X and Y are independent.

Let A_i be an attribute in a database with value 1 or 0, and k be class labels. Then, association rule can be represented by

$$\left(A_p = 1\right) \wedge \cdots \wedge \left(A_q = 1\right) \Rightarrow \left(C = k\right) k \in \left\{0,1\right\} \tag{5}$$

as a special case of the association rule $X \Rightarrow Y$ with fixed consequent C.

In this paper, association rules satisfying the following are defined as important rules:

$$\chi^2 > \chi^2_{min} \tag{6}$$

$$support \geq sup_{min} \tag{7}$$

$$confidence \geq conf_{min} \tag{8}$$

where χ^2_{min}, sup_{min} and $conf_{min}$ are the minimum χ^2, minimum support, and minimum confidence, respectively given in advance.

Support

The rule $X \Rightarrow Y$ holds with SUPPORT if SUPPORT % of records in KDD Dataset contains $X \bigcup Y$. Minimum support (M_SUPP) is the rules that have a SUPPORT greater than a user-specified support.

$$SUPPORT = \frac{No.\,of\,Occurrences}{Total\,Records} \tag{9}$$

Confidence

The rule $X \Rightarrow Y$ holds with CONFIDENCE if CONFIDENCE % of the records in KDD Dataset that contain X and Y. The rules have a CONFIDENCE which is greater than a user-specified confidence is called as minimum confidence (M_CONF). Table 5 shown the support and confidence measures for KDD Dataset.

$$CONFIDENCE = \frac{Occurrence\left[Y\right]}{Occurrence\left[X\right]} \tag{10}$$

Table 5. Support and confidence measures for KDD dataset

Dataset	Total Records	SUPPORT	CONFIDENCE
10% KDD	494021	3.53%	88.58%
Corrected KDD	311029	3.30%	95.39%
Whole KDD	4898431	3.43%	76.57%

Summary

Intrusion Detection System is used to classify the attacks as either normal or malicious activity. Numbers of methods are available to classify the attacks. These attacks are having features with different natures. In this paper, proposed the Association Rule-Mining Algorithm to classify the attacks with the help of support and confidence. KDD dataset is used for experimentation and several attacks are grouped into Denial of Service (DoS), Probe, Remote to Local (R2L), and User to Root (U2R). The KDD dataset may contain redundant data which declines the accuracy of intrusion detection system and increase the false positive rate. The feature selection is important to improve the performance and reduce the false positive rate. In this paper, apply the entropy-based feature selection for improving their efficiency and false positive rate. Entropy based feature selection and Association rule mining algorithm are proposed to evaluate the KDD Dataset and dynamic data to improve the efficiency, reduce the False Positive Rate (FPR) and less time for processing. In future, Entropy based feature selection and Association Rule-Mining algorithm can be regenerating the rules with the help of support and confidence then apply the modified algorithm into Cloud based Intrusion Detection and Internet of Things based Intrusion Detection for improving the detection rate, reducing False Positive Rate and minimize the time.

RESULTS AND DISCUSSION

Two different metrics are used to measure the performance namely Attack Detection Rate (ADR) and False Positive Rate (FPR) by using confusion matrix (Lidio, Roberto & Mauro, 2012) (Devaraju & Ramakrishnan, 2014).

Attack Detection Rate (ADR): It is the ratio between total numbers of attacks detected by the system to the total number of attacks present in the dataset.

$$ADR = \frac{total\ detected\ attack}{total\ attacks} * 100 \qquad (11)$$

Table 6. Confusion Matrix

	Classified as Normal	Classified as Attack
Normal	TN	FP
Attack	FN	TP

TN – denotes the number of connections classified as normal while they actually were normal.

FP – denotes the number of connections classified as attack while they actually were normal.

FN – denotes the number of connections classified as normal while they actually were attack.

TP - denotes the number of connections classified as attack while they actually were attack.

False Positive Rate (FPR): It is the ratio between total numbers of misclassified instances to the total number of normal instances.

$$FPR = \frac{total\ misclassified\ instances}{total\ normal\ instances} * 100 \qquad (12)$$

The association rule-mining algorithm is used to generate the rulesets and applied with KDD dataset. The system configuration for applying the dataset is Intel(R) Core2 Duo @ 2.20GHz, 2.00GB RAM and 32-bit OS. The open source application is used to apply the dataset and improve the detection rate (Nie & He, 2010) (Lin, Ying, Lee & Zne-Jung, 2012) (Ramakrishnan & Devaraju, 2017).

The rules have been generated for each category depending on the support and confidence value. The process functions aptly by choosing minimum support and minimum confidence value. The following steps are used to generating the rules and table 6 shows the classwise rules.

Step 1: Select the frequent dataset FRQ with M_SUPP and M_CONF value.
Step 2: Generate all possible datasets of FRQ and store it in SUBSTITUTE.
Step 3: Count SUPPORT and CONFIDENCE value for each elements of SUBSTITUTE.
Step 4: If (SUPPORT>=M_SUPP && CONFIDENCE>=M_CONF) then
    Step 4.1: Choose the particular elements of SUBSTITUTE and store in RULE_GEN.
    Step 4.2: Generate various rules and store in RULE_GEN.
Step 5: Else reject the particular element of SUBSTITUTE and go to step 3.
Step 6: Return RULE_GEN.
Step 7: Terminate.

where,

FRQ – frequent dataset.
M_SUPP - user define support
M_CONF - user define confidence
RULE_GEN – rules generated from dataset

Using 10% KDD Dataset (Training Data)

Table 8 contains the Training Results for five types of classes and the efficiency is measured using open source application. Confusion Matrix and Training Results for 10% KDD Dataset when Support and Confidence are 3.53% and 88.58%

Depends on the training result, the pictorial representation is given in figure 6. Figure 6 has shown the training result for 10% KDD Dataset.

The performance of association rule-mining algorithm is applied for 10% KDD dataset. The percentage of detection rate for five classes is listed in Table 7. Here detection rate of Normal is 90.51%; detection rate of DoS attack is 99.43%; detection rate of Probe attack is 76.80%; detection rate of R2L attack is 54.44%; detection rate of U2R attack is 78.85%. The algorithm has improved the detection rate and has taken less time for processing.

Table 7. Classwise rule generation

Number	Protocol	Rule	Class
1	tcp	c1=tcp and c0 <=800 and (c2=http or c2=smtp or c2=ftp or c2=ftp_data) and c3=sf and c4 <=400 and c11=1 and c22<=30 and c23<=8 and c31<=254 and c28>=0.01 and c32>=1 and c33>=0.01and (c34>=0.01 or c35>=0.01)	Normal
2	udp	c1=udp and c0<=20750 and (c2=domain_u or c2=other or c2=private) and c3=sf and c4>=1 and c7<=3 and c11=0 and c22<=20 and c23>=2 and c28<=1.00 and c33>=0.01 and c34>=0.01	
3	icmp	c1=icmp and c0=0 and (c2=ecr_i or c2=eco_i or c2=urp_i) and c3=sf and c4>=30 and c5=0 and c7=0 and c11=0 and c22<=6 and c23<=6 and c28>=0.01 and c32>=1 and c33>=0.01 and c34>=0.01	
4	tcp	c1=tcp and c0=0 and (c2=http or c2=finger or c2=smtp) and (c3=s0 or c3=sf) and c9<=3 and c11=1 and c12<=1 and c28=1.00 and c31=255and c33>=0.50 and c40>=0.01	DoS
5	udp	c1=udp and c0=0 and c2=private and c3=sf and c4=28 and c5=0 and c7<=3	
6	icmp	c1=icmp and c0=0 and c2=ecr_i and c3=sf and (c4>=520 or c4<=1480) and c5=0	
7	tcp	c1=tcp and c0=0 and (c2=private or c2=other) and (c3=rej or c3=s0 or c3=rstr) and c4=0 and c22>=1 and c23>=0.50 and c27=1 and c29>=0.97 and c31=255 and c38=1.00 and c39>=0.50 and c40=1.00	Probe
8	udp	c1=udp and c0=0 and (c2=other or c2=domain_u or c2=private) and c3=sf and c4=1 and c5<=1 and c22>=20 and c23<=2 and c31=255 and c32<=22 and c34>=0.01 and c35>=0.01	
9	icmp	c1=icmp and c0=0 and (c2=ecr_i or c2=eco_i or c2=urp_i) and c3=sf and (c4>=37 or c4<=1032) and c5=0 and c22<=2 and c23<=50 and c28=1.00 and c31<=255 and c33>=0.01 and c35>=0.01	
10	tcp	c1=tcp and c0 <=20 and (c2=pop_3 or c2=ftp_data or c2=ftp) and (c3=sf or c3=rsto) and (c4 >=20 or c4<=28) and (c5>=90 or c5<=250) and c11=1 and c22<=8 and c28>=0.12 and c31>=1 and c33>=0.01 and c35>=0.01	R2L
11	udp	c1=udp and c0=0 and c2=other and c3=sf and (c4>=23 or c4<=516) and c5=0 and c22<=6 and c23<=6 and c28=1.00 and c34>=0.02	
12	icmp	c1=icmp and c0=0 and c2=urp_i and c3=sf and c4=552 and c5=0 and c22=1 and c23=1 and c28=1.00 and c31=255 and c32=1 and c34=0.02 and c39=0.03	
13	tcp	c1=tcp and c0=0 and (c2=ftp_data or c2=telnet or c2=ftp) and c3=sf and ((c4=0 and c5 !=0) or(c4!=0 and c5 =0)) and c23<=3 and c32<=52 and c33>=0.01 and c34>=0.01and (c36>=0.20 or c39<=0.05)	U2R

Table 8. Confusion matrix and training results for 10 percent dataset

	Normal	DoS	Probe	R2L	U2R	Detection Rate %	False Positive Rate %	Total Time Taken (seconds)
Normal	88047	374	0	2357	58	90.51	2.87	
DoS	176	389232	0	0	0	99.43	0.04	
Probe	316	1	3154	0	0	76.80	7.69	10
R2L	264	0	0	613	17	54.44	23.45	
U2R	1	0	0	2	41	78.85	1.92	

Figure 6. Detection Rate for 10% KDD Dataset

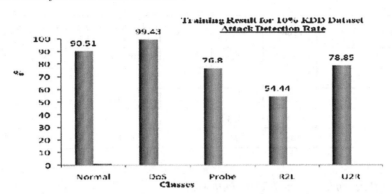

The False Positive Rate for 10% KDD dataset is also discussed. The False Positive Rate for Normal is 2.87%; False Positive Rate for DoS is 0.04%; False Positive Rate for Probe is 7.69%; False Positive Rate for R2L is 23.45% and False Positive Rate for U2R is 1.92%. The False Positive Rate for R2L is high because normal and snmpgetattack of all 41 feature values are the same (refer table 3). Figure 7 has shown the False Positive Rate for 10% KDD Dataset.

Using Corrected KDD Dataset (Testing Data)

Table 9 contains the Testing Results for five types of classes and the efficiency is measured using open source application. Confusion Matrix and Testing Results for Corrected KDD Dataset when Support and Confidence are 3.30% and 95.39%

Depends on the testing result, the pictorial representation is given in figure 8. Figure 8 has shown the testing result for Corrected KDD Dataset.

The performance of association rule-mining algorithm is applied for Corrected KDD dataset. The percentage of detection rate for five classes is listed in Table 8. Here the detection rate of Normal is 97.03%; detection rate of DoS attack is 99.33%; detection rate of Probe attack is 67.64%; detection rate of R2L attack is 33.06%; detection rate of U2R attack is 87.14%. The algorithm has improved the detection rate and has taken less time for processing (Devaraju & Ramakrishnan, 2014).

Figure 7. False Positive Rate for 10% KDD Dataset

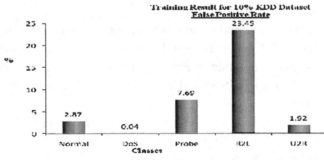

Table 9. Confusion matrix and testing results for corrected dataset

	Normal	**DoS**	**Probe**	**R2L**	**U2R**	**Detection Rate %**	**False Positive Rate %**	**Total Time Taken (seconds)**
Normal	58792	233	0	1033	28	97.03	2.14	
DoS	26	228308	0	252	0	99.33	0.01	
Probe	21	3	2818	15	0	67.64	0.50	12
R2L	3087	0	0	5404	13	33.06	18.88	
U2R	0	0	0	9	61	87.14	0.00	

Figure 8. Detection Rate for Corrected KDD Dataset

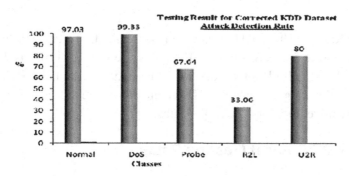

The False Positive Rate for Corrected KDD dataset is also discussed. The False Positive Rate for Normal is 2.14%; False Positive Rate for DoS is 0.01%; False Positive Rate for Probe is 0.50%; False Positive Rate for R2L is 18.88% and False Positive Rate for U2R is 0.00%. The False Positive Rate for R2L is high because normal and snmpgetattack of all 41 feature values are the same (refer table 3). Figure 9 has shown the False Positive Rate for Corrected KDD Dataset.

Using Full KDD Dataset (Testing Data)

Table 10 contains the Testing Results for five types of classes and the efficiency is measured using open source application. Confusion Matrix and Testing Results for Full KDD Dataset when Support and Confidence are 3.43% and 76.57%

Depends on the testing result, the pictorial representation is given in figure 10. Figure 10 has shown the testing result for Full KDD Dataset.

The performance of association rule-mining algorithm is applied for Full KDD dataset. The percentage of detection rate for five classes is listed in Table 9. Here detection rate of Normal is 90.41%; detection rate of DoS attack is 99.74%; detection rate of Probe attack is 76.29%; detection rate of R2L attack is 54.44%; detection rate of U2R attack is 78.85%. The algorithm has improved the detection rate and has taken less time for processing.

The False Positive Rate for Full KDD dataset is also discussed. The False Positive Rate for Normal is 3.25%; False Positive Rate for DoS is 0.03%; False Positive Rate for Probe is 9.95%; False Positive Rate for R2L is 23.45% and False Positive Rate for U2R is 1.92%. The False Positive Rate for R2L is high because normal and snmpgetattack of all 41 feature values are the same (refer table 3). Figure 11 has shown the result for Full KDD Dataset.

Figure 9. False positive rate for corrected KDD dataset

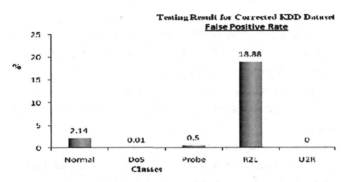

Table 10. Confusion matrix and testing results for full dataset

	Normal	DoS	Probe	R2L	U2R	Detection Rate %	False Positive Rate %	Total Time Taken (seconds)
Normal	879458	3247	0	27704	627	90.41	3.25	
DoS	1017	3873237	0	0	0	99.74	0.03	
Probe	4089	15	31356	2	1	76.29	9.95	72
R2L	264	0	0	613	17	54.44	23.45	
U2R	1	0	0	2	41	78.85	1.92	

Figure 10. Detection rate for full KDD dataset

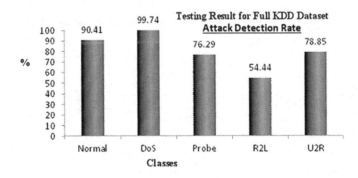

Figure 11. False positive rate for full KDD dataset

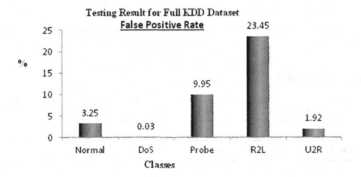

Evaluation of Dynamic Data

In this paper consider the dynamic data to be evaluated using association rule mining algorithm. The wireshark tool is used to get the dynamic data. The system is connected with local area network and internet. The wireshark tool is detected as normal as well as intruder. The Association rule mining algorithm is used to employ the dynamic data with vital use of 2500 TCP samples in which 1500 are reported to be normal and 1000 are reported to be attacks. Figure 12 shows that to trace the real-time dynamic data through wireshark.

The table 11 shows the results for dynamic data.

The detection rate of real-time data for normal is 91.53% and for attack is 92.60%. The false positive rate for normal is 5.2% and attack is 3.9%. The association rule-mining is also significantly achieving the overall performance for the dynamic data.

Figure 13 shows the ROC curves of the detection rates and false positive rates of various attack classes, namely DoS, Probe, R2L and U2R. In each ROC plots, the x-axis is the false positive rate, calculated as the percentage of normal connections classified as an intrusion and y-axis is the detection rate, calculated as the percentage of intrusions detected. In ROC plots, the inverted L represents the optimal performances. Whenever the detection rate is high and false positive rate is low, then the optimal performance is achieved. DoS class detects the detection rate which is 99.33% and false positive rate is 0.01%, and it leads the good optimal performances shown in figure 13 (a). Probe class detects the detection rate which is 67.64% and false positive rate is 0.5%, and it leads the nominal optimal performances shown in figure 13 (b). R2L class detects the detection rate which is 33.06% and false positive rate is 18.88%,

Figure 12. Generation of dynamic data using wireshark

Table 11. Results for dynamic data

Real-Time Data (TCP) With Total Records	Normal	Attacks	Detection Rate %	False Positive Rate %
Normal (1500)	1373	78	91.53	5.2
Attacks (1000)	39	926	92.60	3.9

Figure 13. ROC curves on detection rates and false positive rates

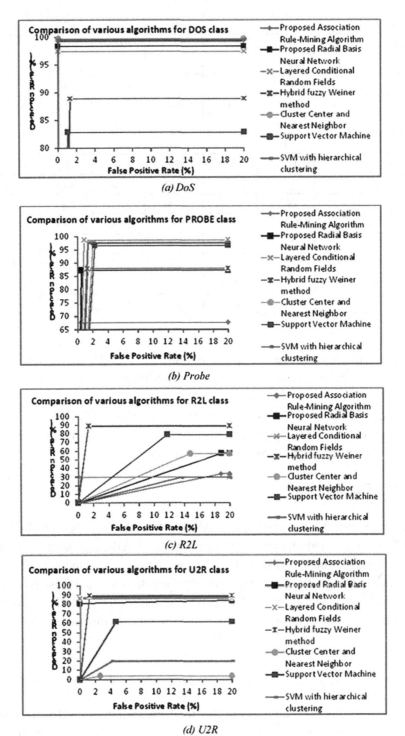

(a) DoS

(b) Probe

(c) R2L

(d) U2R

Table 12. Performance comparison of various algorithms

Algorithm		DoS	Probe	R2L	U2R	Average	CT (sec.)
Proposed Association Rule-Mining Algorithm	DR%	99.33	67.64	33.06	87.14	71.79	126
	FPR%	0.01	0.50	18.88	0.00	4.84	
Proposed Radial Basis Neural Network	DR%	98.38	87.27	57.43'	80.9	80.99	129
	FPR%	0.01	0.55	18.88	0.00	04.86	
Layered Conditional Random Fields	DR%	97.4	98.6	29.6	86.3	77.97	156
	FPR%	0.07	0.91	0.35	0.05	00.35	
Hybrid fuzzy Weiner method	DR%	88.92	87.92	89.12	89.1	88.76	343
	FPR%	1.34	1.34	1.38	1.29	01.34	
Cluster Center and Nearest Neighbor	DR%	99.68	97.61	57.02	3.85	64.54	1570
	FPR%	0.09	2.08	14.78	2.64	04.89	
Support Vector Machine	DR%	82.85	96.59	78.95	61.5	79.97	189
	FPR%	1.05	2.31	11.74	4.69	04.95	
SVM with hierarchical clustering	DR%	99.53	97.55	28.81	19.7	61.39	193
	FPR%	0.04	1.41	13.54	4.16	04.78	

and it leads the good optimal performances shown in figure 13 (c). U2R class detects the detection rate which is 80.00% and false positive rate is 0.00%, and it leads the good optimal performances shown in figure 13 (d).

However, from the ROC curves, the proposed model has the reasonable detection rate and it reduces the false positive rate when compared with other algorithms. Association rule-mining algorithm has improved the detection rate and reduces the false positive rate.

Comparison of KDD Dataset

It is considerably evident that the Association Rule-Mining Algorithm can be awfully effective in detecting the DoS and R2L attacks and minimizing the FPR and also reducing the time (Gupta & Kotagiri, 2010) (Devaraju & Ramakrishnan, 2014). In this comparison, the corrected dataset is used for testing and compared with various algorithms which improve the detection rate and False Positive Rate. The full dataset is also used for testing the dataset which improves the detection rate and False Positive Rate shown in table 9. In table 12, corrected dataset is used for comparing the performance and False Positive Rate.

CONCLUSION

The Association Rule-Mining algorithm is applied for network intrusion detection system. Feature reduction is applied to eliminate the unwanted features. The Entropy based feature selection algorithm is used to reduce the number of features and these features do not affect the overall performance of the system. The Association Rule-Mining algorithm is successfully applied in different benchmarking KDD Dataset (10%, Corrected and Full Dataset). Compared with various algorithms, the testing dataset (corrected dataset) is used to compare and the detection rate of Association Rule-Mining algorithm has improved for class DoS as 99.33% and R2L as 33.06%. It is observed that the False Positive Rate has reduced as well as the time taken for processing has become less. The dynamic data is generated using wireshark tool which is employed in this paper. The significant detection rate and false positive rate is achieved through dynamic data. The overall results for detection rate, False Positive Rate and time taken for processing are significant comparing with other algorithms. The Entropy based feature selection and Association rule-Mining algorithm are applied both known and unknown attacks to improve the detection rate, reduce the false positive rate, minimize the computational time and also improve the overall performance of the Intrusion Detection System.

For future enhancements, Association Rule-Mining algorithm can be modified or rules can be refined then apply the modified algorithm into Cloud based Intrusion Detection and Internet of Things based Intrusion Detection. Further the support and confidence will helps to identify the various attacks with regenerating the rules for improving the detection rate, reducing False Positive Rate and minimize the time.

REFERENCES

Ahmad, I., Abdullah, A., Alghamdi, A., & Hussain, M. (2013). Optimized intrusion detection mechanism using soft computing techniques. *Telecommunication Systems*, *52*(4), 2187–2195.

Akashdeep, I. M., & Kumar, N. (2017). A Feature Reduced Intrusion Detection System using ANN Classifier, Elsevier -. *Expert Systems with Applications*, *88*, 249–257. doi:10.1016/j.eswa.2017.07.005

Anuar, N. B., Sallehudin, H., Gani, A., & Zakari, O. (2008). Identifying False Alarm for Network Intrusion Detection System using Hybrid Data Mining and Decision Tree. *Malaysian Journal of Computer Science*, *21*(2), 101–115. doi:10.22452/mjcs.vol21no2.3

Chebrolu, S., Abraham, A., & Thomas, J. P. (2005). Feature deduction and ensemble design of intrusion detection systems. *Computers & Security*, *24*(4), 295–307. doi:10.1016/j.cose.2004.09.008

Chen, N., Chen, X. S., Xiong, B., & Lu, H. W. (2009, September). An anomaly detection and analysis method for network traffic based on correlation coefficient matrix. *Proceedings of the 2009 International Conference on Scalable Computing and Communications; Eighth International Conference on Embedded Computing* (pp. 238-244). IEEE.

KDD Cup 1999 Intrusion Detection Data. (2010). Retrieved from http://kdd.ics.uci.edu/databases/kddcup99/kddcup99.html

Anbalagan, E., Puttamadappa, C., Mohan, E., Jayaraman, B., & Madane, S. (2008). Datamining and Intrusion Detection Using Back-Propagation Algorithm for Intrusion Detection. *International Journal of Soft Computing*, *3*(4), 264–270.

de Campos, L. M. L., de Oliveira, R. C. L., & Roisenberg, M. (2012, September). Network intrusion detection system using data mining. *Proceedings of the International Conference on Engineering Applications of Neural Networks* (pp. 104-113). Springer. doi:10.1007/978-3-642-32909-8_11

Devaraju, S., & Ramakrishnan, S. (2011). Performance Analysis of Intrusion Detection System Using Various Neural Network Classifiers. *IEEE Proceedings of the International Conference on International Conference on Recent Trends in Information Technology (ICRTIT 2011)*, Madras Institute of Technology, Anna University, Chennai, India (pp. 1033-1038). IEEE.

Devaraju, S., & Ramakrishnan, S. (2013). Performance Comparison of Intrusion Detection System using Various Techniques – A Review. *ICTACT Journal on Communication Technology, 4*(3), 802–812. doi:10.21917/ijct.2013.0114

Devaraju, S., & Ramakrishnan, S. (2014). Performance Comparison for Intrusion Detection System using Neural Network with KDD Dataset. *ICTACT Journal on Soft Computing, 4*(3), 743–752. doi:10.21917/ijsc.2014.0106

Devaraju S. & Ramakrishnan S. (2015). Detection of Attacks for IDS using Association Rule Mining Algorithm. *IETE Journal of Research, 61*(6), 624-633.

Ghali, N. I. (2009). Feature Selection for Effective Anomaly-Based Intrusion Detection. *International Journal of Computer Science and Network Security, 9*(3), 285–289.

Gupta, K. K., Nath, B., & Kotagiri, R. (2010). Layered Approach Using Conditional Random Fields for Intrusion Detection. *IEEE Transactions on Dependable and Secure Computing, 7*(1), 35–49. doi:10.1109/TDSC.2008.20

Hajisalem, V., & Babaie, S. (2018). A hybrid intrusion detection system based on ABC-AFS algorithm for misuse and anomaly detection. *Computer Networks, 136*, 37–50. doi:10.1016/j.comnet.2018.02.028

Hanguang, L., & Yu, N. (2012). Intrusion detection technology research based on apriori algorithm. *Physics Procedia, 24*, 1615–1620.

Hu, J., Yu, X., Qiu, D., & Chen, H.-H. (2009). A simple and efficient hidden Markov model scheme for host- based anomaly intrusion detection. *Journal IEEE Network, 23*(1), 42–47. doi:10.1109/MNET.2009.4804323

Jiang, H., & Ruan, J. (2009). The Application of Genetic Neural Network in Network Intrusion Detection. *Journal of Computers, 4*(12), 1223–1230. doi:10.4304/jcp.4.12.1223-1230

Jiang, M., Gan, X., Wang, C., & Wang, Z. (2011). Research of the Intrusion Detection Model Based on Data Mining, Elsevier. *Energy Procedia, 13*, 855–863.

Kabir, E., Hu, J., Wang, H., & Zhuo, G. (2018). A novel statistical technique for intrusion detection systems, Elsevier-. *Future Generation Computer Systems, 79*, 303–318. doi:10.1016/j.future.2017.01.029

Li, W. (2004). Using Genetic Algorithm for network intrusion detection. *Proceedings of the United States Department of Energy Cyber Security Group 2004 Training Conference*. Academic Press.

Lin, S.-W., Ying, K.-C., Lee, C.-Y., & Lee, Z.-J. (2012). An intelligent algorithm with feature selection and decision rules applied to anomaly intrusion detection. *Applied Soft Computing, 12*(10), 3285–3290. doi:10.1016/j.asoc.2012.05.004

Mabu, S., Chen, C., Lu, N., Shimada, K., & Hirasawa, K. (2011). An Intrusion-Detection Model Based on Fuzzy Class-Association-Rule Mining Using Genetic Network Programming. *IEEE Transactions on Systems, Man and Cybernetics. Part C, Applications and Reviews, 41*(1), 130–139. doi:10.1109/TSMCC.2010.2050685

Mukkamala, S., Sung, A. H., & Abraham, A. (2005). Intrusion detection using an ensemble of intelligent paradigms. *Journal of Network and Computer Applications, 28*(2), 167–182.

Mukkamala, S., Sung, A. H., & Abraham, A. (2007). Hybrid multi-agent framework for detection of stealthy probes. *Applied Soft Computing, 7*(3), 631–641. doi:10.1016/j.asoc.2005.12.002

Muniyandi, A. P., Rajeswari, R., & Rajaram, R. (2012). Network Anomaly Detection by Cascasding K-Means Clustering and C4.5 Decision Tree Algorithm. *Procedia Engineering, 30*, 174-182.

Nadiammai, G. V., & Hemalatha, M. (2014). Effective Approach toward Intrusion Detection System using Data Mining Techniques. *Elsevier Egyptian Informatics Journal, 15*(1), 37–50. doi:10.1016/j.eij.2013.10.003

Nie, W., & He, D. (2010). A probability approach to anomaly detection with twin support vector machines. *Journal of Shanghai Jiaotong University (Science), 15*(4), 385–391.

Pan, Z., Hariri, S., & Pacheco, J. (2019). Context Aware Intrusion Detection of Building Automation Systems. *Computers & Security, 85*, 181–201. doi:10.1016/j.cose.2019.04.011

Peddabachigari, S., Abraham, A., Grosan, C., & Thomas, J. (2007). Modeling intrusion detection system using hybrid intelligent systems. *Journal of Network and Computer Applications, 30*(1), 114–132.

Ramakrishnan, S., & Devaraju, S. (2017). Attack's Feature Selection-Based Network Intrusion Detection System Using Fuzzy Control Language, Springer-. *International Journal of Fuzzy Systems, 19*(2), 316–328. doi:10.100740815-016-0160-6

Rana, A. R. A., Wang, X.-Z., Huang, J. Z., Abbas, H., & He, Y.-L. (2017). Fuzziness based semi-supervised learning approach for intrusion detection system. *Information Sciences, 378*, 484–497. doi:10.1016/j.ins.2016.04.019

Sarasamma, S. T., Zhu, Q. A., & Huff, J. (2005). Hierarchical Kohonenen Net for Anomaly Detection in Network Security. *IEEE Transactions on Systems, Man, and Cybernetics, 35*(2), 2, 302–312. PMID:15828658

Selvakani Kandeeban, S. & Dr. R.S. Rajesh. (2011). A Genetic Algorithm Based elucidation for improving Intrusion Detection through condensed feature set by KDD 99 data set. *Information and Knowledge Management, 1*(1), 1–9.

Shaout, A., & Smyth, C. (2017). Fuzzy zero day exploits detector system. *International Journal of Advanced Computer Research, 7*(31), 154–163. doi:10.19101/IJACR.2017.730022

Sheikhan, M., Jadidi, Z., & Farrokhi, A. (2010). Intrusion detection using reduced-size RNN based on feature grouping, Springer-Verlag London Limited. *Neural Computing & Applications, 21*(6), 1185–1190. doi:10.100700521-010-0487-0

Shenfield, A., Day, D., & Ayesh, A. (2018). Intelligent intrusion detection systems using artificial neural networks. *ICT Express*, *4*(2), 95–99. doi:10.1016/j.icte.2018.04.003

Thaseen, I. S., & Kumar, C. A. (2017). Intrusion detection model using fusion of chi-square feature selection and multi class SVM. *Journal of King Saud University-Computer and Information Sciences*, *29*(4), 462–472.

Wang, M., & Zhao, A. (2012). Investigations of Intrusion Detection Based on Data Mining. *Springer Recent Advances in Computer Science and Information Engineering Lecture Notes in Electrical Engineering*, *124*, 275–279.

Xie, Y., & Yu, S.-Z. (2008). A Large Scale Hidden Semi-Markov model for Anomaly Detection on User Browsing Behaviors. *IEEE/ACM Transactions on Networking*, *17*(1), 1–14.

Yahalom, R., Steren, A., Nameri, Y., Roytman, M., Porgador, A., & Elovici, Y. (2019). Improving the effectiveness of intrusion detection systems for hierarchical data. *Knowledge-Based Systems*, *168*, 59–69. doi:10.1016/j.knosys.2019.01.002

Chapter 2
Implementation of Encryption and Data Hiding in E-Health Application

Muzafer H Saracevic
https://orcid.org/0000-0003-2577-7927
University of Novi Pazar, Serbia.

Aybeyan Selimi
International Vision University, North Macedonia

Selver Pepić
Higher Technical Machine School of Professional Studies in Trstenik, Serbia

ABSTRACT

This chapter presents the possibilities of applying cryptography and steganography in design advanced methods of medical software. The proposed solution has two modules: medical data encryption and medical data hiding. In the first module for the encryption of patient data a Catalan crypto-key is used combined with the LatticePath combinatorial problem. In the second module for hiding patient data, the Catalan stego-key and medical image is used. The objective of the second part is to explain and investigate the existing author's method to steganography based on the Catalan numbers in the design of medical software. The proposed solution is implemented in the Java programming language. In the experimental part, cryptanalysis and steganalysis of the proposed solution were given. Cryptanalysis is based on time and storage complexity, leaking information and machine learning-based identification of the encryption method. Also, steganalysis is based on the amount of information per pixel in stego image, approximate entropy and bit distribution in stego-images.

DOI: 10.4018/978-1-7998-1290-6.ch002

INTRODUCTION

Today, the total amount of data, information, and knowledge in healthcare is extremely large. Their exponentially growth and development and is the reason which causes an "information crisis." Social development affects the scope of health care and the emergence of new standards in the medicine. These standards lead to the advancement of medicine and in introducing new medical procedures in generating an increased amount of information.

The medicine in present is characterized by the wide use of new information and communication technologies. ICT participates in resolving data processing and thus contributes to avoiding or at least alleviating the "information crisis." The increasing Internet use in medicine has allowed access to a large number of databases with bibliographic, epidemiological, image and other information. In the content digitalization process, there is space for theft and misuse of data that needs to be well protected. It is important to emphasize that besides numerous advantages, the Internet has provoked one of the basic problems of modern medicine - data protection that relates to confidentiality, integrity, authenticity and adequate data availability. All this raises new issues concerning the introduction of a multidisciplinary approach in the field of data and information protection.

In this chapter, authors show one method and software solution that allows for efficient encryption and hiding of medical data. It is precisely such areas as cryptography and steganography that give the opportunity to form a new dimension of health services and the protection of sensitive data in eHealth applications. The authors have dealt with security risks and weaknesses that affect data security. In order to protect the security of confidential data, author apply the cryptography in various types of encryption. It is important to note that encryption uses various methods of a secure connection, such as smart cards, VPNs and passwords. With cryptography, it is also desirable to provide a different type of data protection that relates to hiding information in the picture. Various steganographic methods in combination with encryption promise a lot in the field of confidential data protection in medics. In healthcare, can be found applications that provide an extremely large number of services, from simple administrative tasks to complex clinical applications. Health status assessing systems, diagnosis of diseases and clinical decision supporting systems have become available online. In addition, e-health applications offer the ability to manage over the network and the ability to distribute and collect data, archive health data, and information, use additional techniques of transmission or connect different health information systems, etc.

This chapter is organized into 6 sections. The second section investigates related works and case studies in the field of cryptography and steganography in medicine. In addition, in this section, some researches have been presented regarding the importance of combinatorial mathematics and numbers theory in the process of encryption and data hiding. In the third section, is given an analysis of the DICOM standard with aspect of data security. Some of the author's works that provide a security analysis of DICOM standards through some aspects of cryptography and steganography are listed. In the fourth section, is given an analysis of e-health application with two modules: medical data encryption and medical data hiding. The proposed solution is implemented in the Java programming language. In the fifth section, is considered the cryptanalysis and steganalysis of the proposed solution. Cryptanalysis is based on the following tests: time (speed) complexity and storage (space) complexity to find the complete Catalan-key space, leaking information and machine learning-based identification of the encryption method. Steganalysis is based on the following tests: the amount of information per pixel in stego image, approximate entropy: original vs. stego image and bit distribution in stego image. The sixth section contains concluding observations and suggestions for further works.

RELATED WORKS

Author will now consider some of the earlier research in the field of cryptography and steganography in medicine, where author will put emphasis on data security in eHealth applications. Authors in (Mahua, Koushik, Goutam et al., 2015) propose a model which use of RSA and DES algorithm consequently, with three keys for multiple level data security, for the digital patient record. The proposed methodology uses image processing techniques to build a new type of encrypted information code in image format which can be transmitted and used. In the mentioned paper a complete GUI application been developed for both encoder and decoder-receiver section.

In paper (Hamid, Rahman, et al., 2017) authors present a security model for privacy of medical data in cloud healthcare. Authors presents method to secure healthcare private data. Paper (Arslan, Rehan, 2018) proposes a new image steganography approach for securing medical data. Swapped Huffman tree coding is used to apply lossless compression and manifold encryption to the payload before embedding into the cover image. The results show that the proposed method ensures confidentiality and secrecy of patient information while maintaining imperceptibility. In paper (Tokuo, Akiko, Tsutomu, 2014) authors present a model for the secure of medical image data using steganography. Also, in paper (Tohari, Hudan, Hafidh et al., 2014), authors propose methods for protect the medical data by using steganography, specifically LSB technique. Describe the general perspective of the chapter. End by specifically stating the objectives of the chapter.

ANALYSIS OF DICOM STANDARD FROM ASPECT OF DATA SECURITY

The development and global spread of ICT caused the emergence of new areas for which two names began to be used: telemedicine and cyber medicine. Due to technological advancements, reached in this information age are changed the ability to collection, store and data management that are at disposal. For these reasons today have the introduction of new medical procedures and the emergence of new standards in medicine.

The DICOM standard (Digital Imaging and Communications in Medicine) standardization presents an important process for telemedicine systems that are oriented towards working with medical images. Besides knowledge of documentation for the adaptation of such systems, for the DICOM standard is necessary to provide: counseling and training for implementation, demonstration service, but also the development and use of the accompanying software. Within the global phenomenon that represents the information society, the need emerged for standardization in communication that supports medical information. Standardization can bring huge benefits. By promoting and applying, it would resolve the evolving challenges of the rapid development of information systems in health care facilities. The domain of medical imaging and related medical data is an important part of this development which is very demanding. The implementation of telemedicine systems for final diagnosis, which includes the domain of medical imaging requires integration of information and knowledge of doctors, information technology experts and other professionals within the standards.

The medical imaging is necessary to analyze, process, store and forward from one to another destination, which has led to issues the compatibility of devices and the appropriate application entities, and the need for a DICOM standard (Reljin & Gavrovska, 2013). Today, such a standard exists and is called the DICOM standard, which is defined as part of the documentation that has become inevitably tool for enabling and optimizing the compatibility of devices and data exchange in health care settings. DICOM standard enables the interoperability of systems for the acquisition, storage, display, processing, transmission, download, security and searches medical images (Marić, Pejnović, 2004).

In this section, authors discuss some of the earlier research in the field of security analysis of DICOM standards through the aspects of cryptography and steganography. Authors in paper (Kannammal, Subha, 2012) mainly focuses on the security in DICOM images. Their proposal includes the procedure where encrypted images are tested with common attacks and the watermarked image is encrypted using RSA algorithm (with AES). In paper (Tan, Changwei, Xu, Poh et al., 2011) authors present method for security protection of medical images (in DICOM format). The experimental results show that the method is able to ensure image integrity and authenticity. Also, in paper (Natsheh, Li, Gale, 2016), authors provided method for effective encryption multi-frame DICOM medical images.

DICOM is an object-oriented, where under the DICOM objects imply the so-called. Information Objects. In the standard, information objects are described as objects from the real world. Such objects are in the DICOM formally called the Information Object Definitions (IODs). Information objects describe real information entities using a group of related attributes. Attributes are marked and assigned to specific data values in order to an entity from reality is described independently of the way of coding. Unit information to be inserted is defined as a data element which is described as access to the data dictionary. Data Dictionary is a register of all the basic information by means of which they are assigned a unique label, the characteristics and meaning. Data Set refers to information that is exchanged, and which is described using a structured set of attributes, represented as an elementary data. The result of DICOM encoding of the data set with the use the dictionary data is called data stream (Kahn, Carrino, Flynn et al., 2007; Mustra, Delac, Grgic, 2008).

Over information objects are applied DICOM commands that represent the demands that an operation is performing during the communication in the network. Command Element represents the encoded controls parameter which carries information about the value of the parameter, while the Command Streams occurs as a result of coding of a set of command elements. UID (Unique ID, Unique Identifier), by which the real entity is fully determined. In this way medical images are completely identified within the header, even in the case of duplicates. Information Entities, which are described within the framework of DICOM, exceeds the medical image.

Information object class (IOS) or formally Service-Object Pair Class (SOP Class), represents a formal description of the information structure, its purposes and attributes that owns without specific data values. SOP class represents the basic unit of DICOM functionality, and consists of IOD, DSG and the constraints and extensions for IOD. Information Object Instance or formally Service-Object Pair Instance, describes a real entity that includes the values of an attribute of a class of information object which is associated with a specific entity (Pianykh, 2012; Kamberović, Saracevic, Koricanin, 2015).

In paper (Sampaio, Jackowski, 2013) authors present an assessment of steganographic approach in medical imaging. DICOM standard is well-established regarding storage, printing, and transmission of medical images. This paper assesses three steganographic technique: LSB (least significant bit insertion), division into blocks, mean change modified method (MCMM) – and verify their feasibility for clinical use in medical imaging. Integrating MCMM in DICOM standard would provide a breakthrough for information security in medical imaging, deterring fraud, privacy invasion, while preserving diagnostic information. In paper (Rodriguez-Colin et al., 2007) authors present a method that combines data compression, encryption and watermarking techniques. That methods applied to radiological medical images, using DICOM data as a watermark to embed in medical images. In (Mantos, Maglogiannis,

2016) authors present an algorithm developed for digital imaging in DICOM medical images. Authors emphasize that the proposed method (scheme) can be efficiently used as a steganography technique in DICOM. The experimental results prove that the original images and the stego-object (images) provide an excellent equality result. Identification of the application entity network is realized by AET (application entity title). It is necessary to establish a mutual joining or an association between two application entities for the purpose of sharing of one or more of the SOP classes that are supported by SOP classes. By the association, it means mutually establishment of the transfer syntax data that are accepted by both sides. It is an implementation model that determines the capabilities of class services, information objects and communication protocols, which are fully supported. Paper (Kobayashi, Furuie, & Barreto, 2009) presents a new method for improve the trustworthiness of medical images. This method providing a stronger link between integrity and authenticity of medical image.

IMPLEMENTATION OF ENCRYPTION AND DATA HIDING IN E-HEALTH

Cyber-medicine opens up a number of legal issues because it has become clear over time that the Internet, in addition to its advantages, has shortcomings. Those shortcomings were noticed by studying current cyber-medicine problems. Most of these problems relate to the encryption of sensitive and important data and the way they are distributed. The most significant problems related to the openness of information, but also to the rules in their structuring and communication and on their integrity protection (Mašovic, Saracevic, et al., 2010).

The modern form of cyber medicine is very closely related to the concepts of cryptography and steganography. Bearing in mind the fact that this area is very dynamic, current and very widespread, this chapter only covers some of its basic concepts, and give a small contribution in the application of cryptography and steganography in the design of an e-Health application. Steganography is a science that deals with the concealment of information in other data so that the very existence of the codes are hidden in the data carrier. The goal of each cryptographic method is to find the fastest and most convenient way to keep the downloaded information. One of the methods used today is based on the use of steganography.

The general scenario for encryption and hiding of medical data in the proposed e-Health application is presented through the following steps:

1. **First Step:** Medical data encryption
2. **Second Step:** Medical data compression
3. **Third Step:** Embedding of medical data in the image
4. **Fourth Step:** Extraction of medical data from the image

Figure 1 presents the basic phases in model of encryption and hiding of medical data. In this figure reverse procedure or extractions of medical data are also shown.

Now authors will explain in more detail why use the data compression process in combination with the encryption in the general scenario. In earlier analysis of the tested data pairs (the first pair refers to the data on patients in the open form and the second pair on the encrypted data), have established mutual information for 4 approximations which amount to 0.11 bits of information per bit. Also, testing in the second phase involved the use of Maurer's protocol and in this way, the authors managed to

Figure 1. General scenario

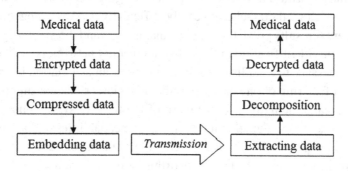

extract common bits, in average 1600 bits per pair. It was evident that there was a certain leak in the "statistical properties" of the used natural language in which patient data was entered in an open form into the system. That's why used an innovative and advanced method in order to obtain a safer method of encrypting medical data. Namely, have determined that if authors introduce compression in combination with encryption, the problem is solved. Also, the use of compression is always advisable for a number of reasons and is therefore optionally available in all protocols, however, "only optionally" due to the burden on the computer resource. In (Adamović, Šarac, Veinović et al., 2013) the authors emphasize significance of compression in cryptography. Solution implement in the JavaNetBeans environments.

Java has much functionality that supports cryptographic algorithms. Cryptographic operations are classified into classes on the basis of which Java provides cryptographic functionality through two segments:

1. **Java Cryptography Architecture (JCA):** A security framework integrated into the Java API. Classes in JCA provide work with key generation, digital signatures, and message retrieval. The JCA classes are located in the java.security.
2. **Java Cryptography Extension (JCE):** Encryption extensions. Classes in CPCs are located in the javax.crypto. JCE classes provide work for encryption and decryption.

Proposed GUI application in Java NetBeans environment has two modules: medical data encryption and medical data hiding.

Module for Medical Data Encryption

In their previous investigates, the authors have encountered the Catalan numbers in quite many places and studied their close relationships (computational geometry, combinatorial problems, steganography, cryptography). Can conclude that the Catalan numbers are ubiquitous. Authors in (Stanley 2005) present over 60 different interpretations of the Catalan numbers (some can be enumerated: the triangulation of polygons, paired brackets problem, a binary tree, steak permutations, Ballot problem, Lattice Path or the problem of motion through an integer grid, etc.). Now, will list some cases of the Catalan numbers in cryptography, for the purpose of creating a class for medical data encryption. Paper (Saracevic, Koricanin, Bisevac, 2017) examines the possibilities of applying appropriate combinatorial problems (Stack permutations, Ballot Problem and Balanced Parentheses) in data encryption. In paper (Saracevic, Selimi, Selimovic, 2018) has been presented a process of generating hidden cryptographic Catalan-keys

(Catalan numbers sequences) from selected segment of the 3D image. This procedure consists of three phases: 1) selection of one segment from the 3D image, 2) conversion in the record which represents the Catalan key and 3) Catalan-key (binary notation) is applied in encryption of a text or image. Also, paper (Saracevic, Selimi, Selimovic, 2018) analyses the properties of the Catalan numbers in data security.

In particular, for the development of the application module for the encoding of medical data, used an author's method, which was explained in detail and published in (Saracevic, Adamovic, Bisevac, 2018).

The process of encrypting information could be reduced to the following steps:

1. The medical data (open text) that is converted *(ASCII Text to Binary)* in the binary sequence is loaded. The binary sequence is divided into X segments whose length corresponds to base n, for the loaded Catalan-key C_n.
2. By applying the Catalan binary record and reading it, starting from the first bit and ending with the last bit in the key, the permutation sequence $X_1, ..., X_n$ is performed (for the details per bit permutation see the described *LatticePath* method in paper (Saracevic, Selimi, Selimovic, 2018).
3. The resulting permutations of the bits are converted *(Binary to ASCII Text)*, then the compression process is performed and in this way, a medical code is obtained.

In Figure 2, is shown a procedure for encrypting data for a patient (ID 8452) with diagnosis: *Depression / NCP: Risk for Self-Directed Violence.*

Figure 2. First and second Step: Encrypt and compress medical data

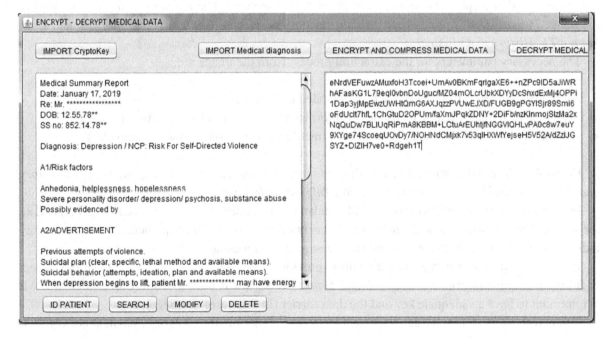

Module for Medical Data Hiding

Now, will list some examples of the Catalan numbers in steganography, for the purpose of creating a class for medical data hiding. Catalan numbers play an important role in data hiding and steganography. The purpose of paper (Saracevic, Hadzic, Koricanin, 2017) is related to investigating the possible application of the Catalan numbers in data hiding (text or image). Paper (Saracevic, Adamović, Miškovic et al., 2019) presents a new method of protect and data hiding using properties of Catalan numbers and Dyck (binary) words.

In particular, in order to create another module for the application for hiding medical data, use an author's method that was explained in detail and published in (Saracevic, Adamović, Miškovic et al., 2019). The process of hiding information could be reduced to the following steps:

1. The category of medical data want to hide is selected. The *"Clinical Data"* category was made according to the model from (Reiner, 2015).
2. Encrypted and compressed medical data or a larger amount of information from one or more categories of medical data is loaded.
3. A medical image (with Patient ID) is being loaded, which will be the carrier of encrypted information.

The procedure for installing the information in the image is presented (for more details on the method of installation based on Catalan keys, see previous papers in the field of steganography (Saracevic, Hadzic, Koricanin, 2017; Saracevic, Adamović, Miškovic et al., 2019)

Figure 3 shows the procedure for hiding the diagnosis for *Patient ID8452*. This document is firstly compressed and encrypted (as described in the previous section). The resulting code is embedded in the image *Patient ID8452.png*, where the data category is selected *Clinical Test Data / Clinical Data Source T1: History and physical*.

The necessary parameters for the extraction process from the image are:

- An adequate stego-Catalan key, which is loaded in the form of a special file.
- The medical image that is the carrier of information (PNG, JPG formats are supported).
- Selecting a category of data that want to extract from image (one or more categories).

Figure 4 illustrates the process of extracting data from the medical image for the category *Laboratory and pathology data / subsection T3: Actionable (high-priority) data*.

Figure 5 presents a case where the invalid Catalan key is loaded. The authors chose to generate data for *subtest 2* and *subtest 3*, but the message is generated in an irregular shape because the wrong key indicates the wrong bits in the image and the message is not readable.

It is important to note that proposed solution provides selective extraction of data from the image, or from obtaining data from a certain *Clinical Data* category (or if want to display all hidden data). It is important to have an adequate key and the data carrier (in this case, an image).

Figure 6 shows that from 8 categories want to produce data from the category *Pharmacology/ Laboratory and pathology data / Clinical test data*. For this combined process, a specific segment from the database will be used *"Imaging finding specific support data"*. As can be seen in Figure 6, the basis for *T5* is selected for descaling and generating hidden data related to *Differential diagnosis*.

Figure 3. Third step – embedded medical data (Category: Clinical test Data)

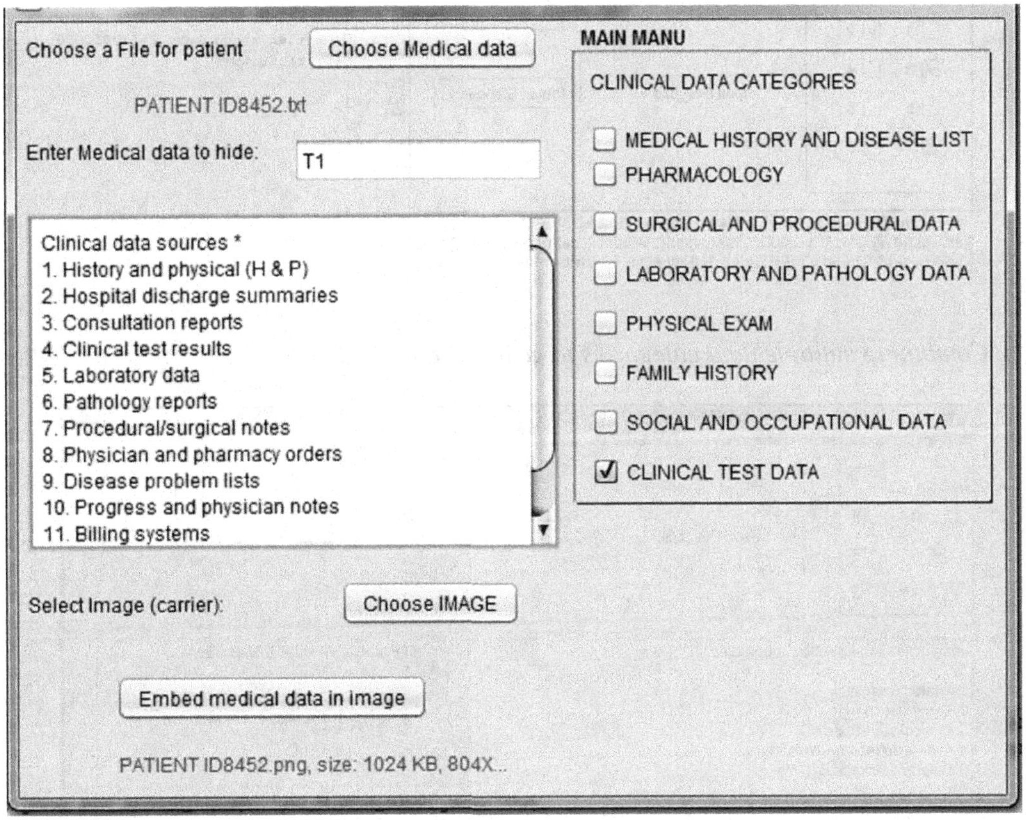

Figure 4. Four step – data extraction

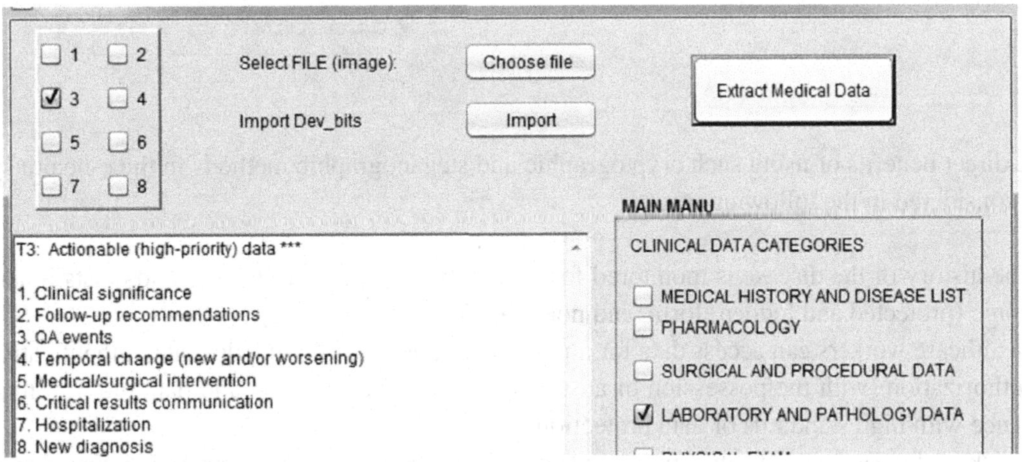

Figure 5. Loading non-valid key and wrong selection of bits in the image

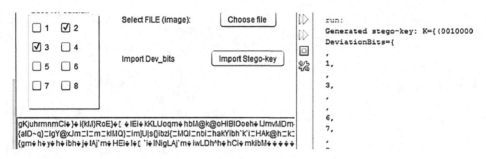

Figure 6. Combining multiple data categories to generate an output

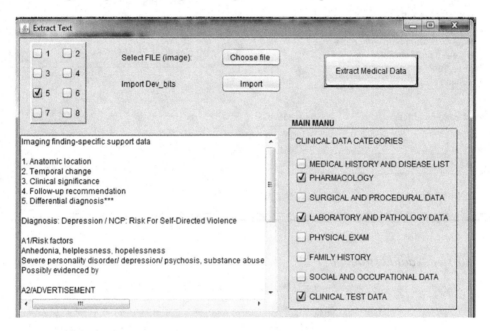

The direct benefits of using such cryptographic and steganographic methods in the e-health system can be considered in the following way:

- The history of the disease is monitored for each patient throughout his life and exists in an electronic (protected and hidden) form, and not in any open text.
- Healthcare workers can access data for a particular patient only with adequate authentication and authorization (with the possession of an adequate key for encryption and data hiding), in accordance with high standards of data protection.
- Quick and easy access to information users through services and telemedicine (for example, a steganographic approach - loading images and a specific key provide complete medical information, which combines multiple categories of medical data).

CRYPTANALYSIS AND STEGANALYSIS OF PROPOSED SOLUTION

In papers (Saracevic, Koricanin, Bisevac, 2017; Saracevic, Selimi, Selimovic, 2018; Saracevic, Adamovic, Bisevac, 2018) cryptanalysis of the application of Catalan keys in file encryption was performed. Based on the above analyses, can derive some of the basic characteristics of the generated Catalan keys that are applied in proposed solution for encrypting data:

1. The requirement for bit-balance in the Catalan-key must be fulfilled (Dyck word property), see papers (Saracevic, Adamovic, Bisevac, 2018; Saracevic, Adamović, Miškovic et al., 2019)
2. The key belonging to the base *n* has the length of *2n-bits* and based on it, the corresponding *n*-permutations can be performed.
3. Catalan numbers can serve as pseudo-random numbers generators.

From the second, it follows that if *n* is the basis for generating the keys, then C_n is the total number of different binary records that satisfy the property of the Catalan number. In proposed solution, for testing purposes, the authors used 60-bit keys for encrypting medical data, which means that the key belonging to the base *n=30*. Valid values of Catalan key for the stated base *n* can be represented by the following formula:

$$C_n = \frac{(2n)!}{(n+1)!\,n!}$$

For example, for the basis n=30 according to the formula (1) for the calculation of the Catalan number get C30 = 3 814 986 502 092 304. So, the value obtained represents the total keyspace, that is, the number of valid values that satisfy the condition to be one of the possible Catalan keys for listing of medical data.

Cryptanalysis is based on the following tests:

1. **Complexity (Time and Space):** Many authors discussed the time and memory complexity of generating Catalan numbers in different forms (*balanced parentheses, ballot problem, LatticePath or stack permutations*). In (Saba, 2018) the author analyses the time and space complexity. In this case, the asymptotic growth of C_n is estimated by the following formula:

$$C_n =\sim \frac{4^n}{n^{3/2}\sqrt{\pi}} \cdot$$

This means the algorithm uses

$$O\left(\frac{4^n}{n^{3/2}}\right) = O\left(4^n\right)$$

memory. The total number of output sequences is exactly $C_n = O(4^n)$.

2. If want to find all 60-bit Catalan numbers and if it takes *1 ms* to access each element from the C_n set, the average time of generating the total key space would be 120972/2 = 60486 years. So, this procedure is very demanding when the time is at stake. On the other hand, in an attempt to find all of these Catalan numbers and to register them in memory 28,423,864 GB or 27,757 TB, are required. So, this procedure is very demanding when the memory resources are in question. It is questionable whether, for a larger base (for example, 128-bit or 256-bit Catalan keys), a complete set of all Catalan keys can be reached at all (the complete search method). Can conclude that computing resources such as time (CPU) and memory limit the entire generation process.

3. **Leaking information** and the fulfillment of the condition that the mutual information between the code and the response message is 0. For adequate cryptanalysis, the authors made an experiment where prepared 150 pairs (open patient data - encrypted data). A complete analysis was carried out using the Shannon approximations, and in this way, certain information was obtained. In addition, the authors used Machine Learning algorithms where had two classes. One class numbered pairs Ciphertext and Plaintext, and the second class of couples obtained through TRNG where it is certain that there is no mutual information. Main goal was to determine that the classification of these two classes is not possible and in this way, confirmed the previous results obtained through Shannon.

4. **Machine Learning-Based Identification of the Encryption Method:** In their previous research the authors dealt with research of cryptography, number theory and machine learning. The authors show technics of machine learning-based identification of the encryption method directly from the cipher text. The authors have presents comparative analysis – author's method vs. DES algorithm. The obtained results favor author's method in relation to DES. More specifically, results of cryptanalysis show following - it is more difficult to recognize cipher text obtained with Catalan method than the DES.

In addition to cryptanalysis, the authors also consider some segments of the steganalysis of the proposed solution. In paper (Saracevic, Adamović, Miškovic et al., 2019), steganalysis is performed or the solution is safe enough from the aspect of easy removal of confidential information from the picture. The authors applied the most advanced methods and techniques of machine learning for classification and clustering individually above classes. In mentioned paper, the authors gave a comparative analysis where showed that the classifier works equally well or even better in relation to the existing algorithms. For details see Section 5 in (Saracevic, Adamović, Miškovic et al., 2019).

Steganalysis was based on the following tests:

1. The amount of information per pixel in stego image
2. Approximate Entropy: original vs. stego image
3. Bit distribution in stego image

The Amount of Information Per Pixel: In their previous research, the authors have determined what are the acceptable parameters of the LSB algorithm for a safe steganographic channel. Below will show the way of distributing the bits of confidential information to the R, G, and B channels in the image. Testing for the needs of steganalysis was carried out in the following way:

- Selected 200 images that represented data carriers on patients,
- Used 24 bits of images for steganalysis,
- Determined the amount of information to hide (were guided by the recommendations from previous research for steganalysis, where it was found that no tool can detect an LSB algorithm where the information is 0.005 bpp - bits per pixel).

By embedding the secret information in the image, in their application, the authors implemented additional options, and one of them is displaying additional parameters that indicate whether the process was successfully implemented and the amount of information installed per pixel.

In Figure 7, a dialog appears that appears in the "embedding data" procedure. The system user always gets feedback on whether the stego image and the appropriate stego key are successfully created, as well as details about other parameters: image size, size of secret information, and very important parameter, which is BPP bits per pixel.

Approximate Entropy: In this testing, the authors have identified another good side of proposed solution, which is that the entropy for both classes of images has remained unchanged.

In Figure 8, one testing in the Octave GUI environment is shown, where one can see the relationship of the original image with respect to the stego medical image, and this ratio is 7.2983 for the original image, while 7.2984 for the stego image.

Figure 7. Showing some parameters in the process of embedding confidential data.

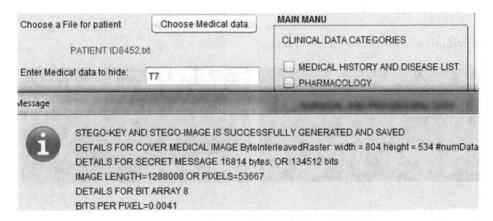

Figure 8. Comparative analysis of the entropy of the original and stego medical image

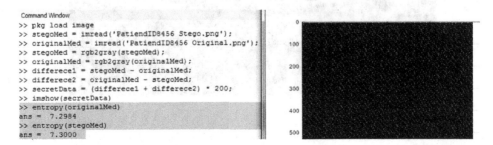

Bit Distribution: The message bit permutation is performed prior to embedding, resulting in uniform bit distribution (with CatalanStego). Popular steganography tools based on LSB differ significantly in the approach of information concealment.

Figure 9 shows the distribution of the bits for a single selected image where secret information is embedded with the LSB algorithm (left) and the distribution of the bits for a single selected image where secret information is embedded with CatalanStego method (right). In this case, only showed built-in bits for the value of 1, while the message bits are represented by the zero-omitted (Octave GUI environment). For this reason, can conclude that the proposed method gives a good distribution of the bits in the image. This certainly makes it difficult for steganalysis.

The authors will now show that the proposed method meets another condition, which is to load the three channels on the medical image (R, G, B) evenly. Figure 10 shows the distribution of bits in R, G, B channels, and it can be seen to be fairly even, which means that all channels are equally burdened (the right image is the zoomed part from the left picture). This feature in hiding medical data in the image goes hand in hand with proposed solution for encryption and hiding data in the eHealth application.

In the process of display of medical images are to be achieved the most realistic display of medical images in order to better quality of stego-image compared to the original. In thier paper (Saracevic, Masovic, et al., 2013), the authors have presented an algorithm for performing optimal triangulation on three-dimensional image data which enables a better reflection of medical images. In mentioned paper presents designed Java software solution which provides good results in terms of execution speed of extract medical data and savings of memory space. The importance of present method can be considered from two aspects: speed and effective storage.

Figure 9. Distribution of bits in the medical image

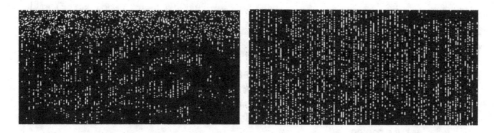

Figure 10. Uniform distribution on R, G, B channels

CONCLUSION AND FURTHER WORKS

It's visible that the specialized area of data security and cyber-medicine is becoming a very challenging area that will probably drastically change medical practice. The openness, integrity, authenticity, and availability of medical information and procedures in cyberspace is a sensitive issue of cyber medicine and medical application of the Internet in general.

Health data according to all European regulations are very sensitive data, while their processing can have a major impact on the lives of individuals. Disposing of real and protected information makes it possible to prepare reliable reports. At the same time, these reports simplify the treatment and check the information exchange with emphasis on security and reliability. The development and introduction of new communication technologies that enable global networking and the use of cryptographic and steganographic methods in the eHealth system enable the change of the health care system. They improve security in the data flow, boost healthcare system users, and reduce costs and time. Protection and security of data in the e-health system are of great importance for the development of the healthcare system of one country.

With this chapter, the authors gave several applications of encryption and the hiding of medical data. The authors create an interesting combination of cryptography and steganography in order to efficiently design an application for security, authenticity, and protection of the integrity of sensitive medical data. Their theoretical bases of research are followed by experimental testing. More specifically, the authors provide a case study which includes encryption and hiding modules and implementing in the Java programming language.

A GUI eHealth application implement that has all the necessary elements for easy and efficient encryption and hiding patient data. Cryptanalysis of the proposed solution done through the following aspects: time (speed) and storage (space) complexity to find the complete Catalan-key space, leaking information and machine learning-based identification of the encryption method.

In addition, also the authors stage steganalysis of the proposed solution in the following aspects: the amount of information per pixel in the stego image, approximate entropy - original vs. stego image and bit distribution in stego image.

Bearing in mind the fact that cryptography and steganography are very dynamic areas, that they are current and that they are very widespread, this chapter covers only some of their basic concepts and give a small contribution in the application of medical data protection. The proposed method can be further improved and adapted to more contemporary approaches in steganography and cryptography. In many scientific studies, works, and monographs, when it comes to the future of cryptography, quantum cryptography has emerged as a result of discovery in the field of quantum computing (Koscielny, Kurkowski, Srebrny, 2013). It is important to note that quantum and DNA cryptography, in the near future, will be the basis for protecting confidential documents in medics. Accordingly, the proposal for future work could relate precisely to the application of such methods based on combinatorial mathematics in quantum cryptography and the improvement of existing algorithms and methods in cryptology and steganography.

REFERENCES

Adamović, S., Šarac, M., Veinović, M., Jevremović, A., & Milosavljević, M. (2013). *An add-on for networking CrypTool 2 simulation environments.* Faculty of computing and informatics, Singidunum University, Belgrade, Serbia. (in Serbian)

Ahmad, T., Studiawan, H., Ahmad, H. S., Ijtihadie, R. M., & Wibisono, W. (2014, October). Shared secret-based steganography for protecting medical data. *Proceedings of the 2014 International Conference on Computer, Control, Informatics and Its Applications (IC3INA)* (pp. 87-92). IEEE.

Arslan, M. U., & Rehan, M. U. (2018). Using Image Steganography for Providing Enhanced Medical Data security. Proceedings of the *15*[th] *IEEE annual consumer communications & networking conference,* Las Vegas, NV. IEEE.

Hamid, H. A., Rahman, S. M. M., Hossain, M. S., & Almogren, A. (2017). A Security Model for Preserving the Privacy of Medical Big Data in a Healthcare Cloud Using a Fog Computing Facility with Pairing-Based Cryptography. *IEEE Access, 5,* 22313–22328. doi:10.1109/ACCESS.2017.2757844

Kahn, C. E. Jr, Carrino, J. A., Flynn, M. J., Peck, D. J., & Horii, S. C. (2007). DICOM and Radiology: Past, Present, and Future. *Journal of the American College of Radiology, 4*(9), 652–657. doi:10.1016/j.jacr.2007.06.004 PMID:17845973

Kamberović, H., Saracevic, M., & Koricanin, E. (2015). The standard for digital imaging and communications in medicine – DICOM. *University Journal of Information Technology and Economics, 2*(1), 1–4.

Kannammal, A., & Subha, R. S. (2012). DICOM Image Authentication and Encryption Based on RSA and AES Algorithms. In *Trends in Intelligent Robotics, Automation, and Manufacturing.* Berlin: Springer. doi:10.1007/978-3-642-35197-6_39

Kobayashi, L. O. M., Furuie, S. S., & Barreto, P. S. L. (2009). Providing Integrity and Authenticity in DICOM Images: A Novel Approach. *IEEE Transactions on Information Technology in Biomedicine, 13*(4), 582–589. doi:10.1109/TITB.2009.2014751 PMID:19244022

Kościelny, C., Kurkowski, M., & Srebrny, M. (2013). *Modern Cryptography Primer: Theoretical Foundations and Practical Applications.* Berlin, Germany: Springer. doi:10.1007/978-3-642-41386-5

Mahua, B., Koushik, P., Goutam, G., & ... . (2015). Generation of Novel Encrypted Code using Cryptography for Multiple Level Data Security for Electronic Patient Record. *Proceedings of the IEEE International Conference on Bioinformatics and Biomedicine,* Washington, DC (pp. 916-921). IEEE.

Mantos, L. K., & Maglogiannis, I. P. (2016). Sensitive Patient Data Hiding using a ROI Reversible Steganography Scheme for DICOM Images. *Journal of Medical Systems, 40*(6), 1–17. doi:10.100710916-016-0514-5 PMID:27167526

Marić, N., & Pejnović, P. (2004). Digital imaging and communication in medicine. *Proceedings of the IX Scientific Conference - Information Technology - Present and Future,* Montenegro. Academic Press.

Mašovic, S., Saracevic, M., Kamberovic, H., & Milovic, B. (2010). Information and communication technology as a tool for establishing e-health. *Proceedings of the 10th International Conference -Research and Development in Mechanical Industry RaDMI 2010* (pp. 624-632). Academic Press.

Mustra, M., Delac, K., & Grgic, M. (2008). Overview of the DICOM Standard. *Proceedings of the 50th International Symposium*, Zadar, Croatia (pp. 39–44). Academic Press.

Natsheh, Q. N., Li, A. B., & Gale, G. (2016). Security of Multi-frame DICOM Images Using XOR Encryption Approach. *Procedia Computer Science, 90*, 175–181. doi:10.1016/j.procs.2016.07.018

Pianykh, O. S. (2012). *DICOM Security: Digital Imaging and Communications in Medicine*. Berlin, Germany: Springer. doi:10.1007/978-3-642-10850-1

Reiner, B. (2015). Strategies for Medical Data Extraction and Presentation Part 2: Creating a Customizable Context and User-Specific Patient Reference Database. *Journal of Digital Imaging, 28*(3), 249–255. doi:10.100710278-015-9794-4 PMID:25833767

Reljin, I., & Gavrovska, A. (2013). Telemedicine. Belgrade, Serbia: Academic Thought. (in Serbian)

Rodriguez-Colin, R., Claudia, F., & Trinidad-Blas, G. J. (2007). Data Hiding Scheme for Medical Images. *Proceedings of the 17th International Conference on Electronics, Communications and Computers*, Cholula, Puebla (pp. 32-32). Academic Press.

Saba, S. (2018). *Generating all balanced parentheses: A deep dive into an interview question*, Retrieved from https://sahandsaba.com/interview-question-generating-all-balanced

Sampaio, R. A., & Jackowski, M. P. (2013). Assessment of Steganographic Methods in Medical Imaging. *Proceedings of the XXVI SIBGRAPI Conference on Graphics Patterns and Images*, Arequipa, Peru. Academic Press.

Saracevic, M., Adamovic, S., & Bisevac, E. (2018). Applications of Catalan numbers and Lattice Path combinatorial problem in cryptography. *Acta Polytechnica Hungarica: Journal of Applied Sciences, 15*(7), 91–110.

Saracevic, M., Adamović, S., Miškovic, V., Maček, N., & Šarac, M. (2019). A novel approach to steganography based on the properties of Catalan numbers and Dyck words. *Future Generation Computer Systems, 100*, 186 – 197.

Saracevic, M., Hadzic, M., & Koricanin, E. (2017). Generating Catalan-keys based on dynamic programming and their application in steganography. *International Journal of Industrial Engineering and Management, 8*(4), 219–227.

Saracevic, M., Koricanin, E., & Bisevac, E. (2017). Encryption based on Ballot, Stack permutations and Balanced Parentheses using Catalan-keys. *Journal of Information Technology and Applications, 7*(2), 69–77.

Saracevic, M., Masovic, S., Milosevic, D., & Kudumovic, M. (2013). Proposal for applying the optimal triangulation method in 3D medical image processing. *Balkan Journal of Health Science, 1*(1), 27–34.

Saracevic, M., Selimi, A., Selimovic, F. (2018). Generation of cryptographic keys with algorithm of polygon triangulation and Catalan numbers. *Computer Science – AGH, 19*(3), 243-256.

Stanley, R. (2005). *Catalan addendum to Enumerative Combinatorics*. Massachusetts Institute of Technology. Retrieved from http://www-math.mit.edu/~rstan/ec/catadd.pdf

Tan, C. K., Changwei, N. J., Xu, X., Poh, C. L., & ... . (2011). Security Protection of DICOM Medical Images Using Dual-Layer Reversible Watermarking with Tamper Detection Capability. *Journal of Digital Imaging, 24*(3), 528–540. doi:10.100710278-010-9295-4 PMID:20414697

Tokuo, U., Akiko, O., & Tsutomu, G. (2014). Security Model for Secure Transmission of Medical Image Data Using Steganography. In *Integrating information technology and management for quality of care*. IOS Press.

Chapter 3

Influence of Neighborhood Forms on the Quality of Pseudorandom Number Generators' Work Based on Cellular Automata

Sergii Bilan
Onseo Company, Ukraine

ABSTRACT

The chapter analyzes modern methods for constructing pseudo-random number generators based on cellular automata. Also analyzes the influence of neighborhood forms on the evolution of the functioning of cellular automata, as well as on the quality of the formation of pseudo-random bit sequences. Based on the use of various forms of the neighborhood for the XOR function, the quality of generators was analyzed using graphical tests and NIST tests. As a result of experimental studies, the optimal dimension of cellular automata and the number of heterogeneous cells were determined, which make it possible to obtain a high-quality pseudo-random bit sequence. The obtained results allowed to formulate a method for constructing high-quality pseudo-random number generators based on cellular automata, as well as to determine the necessary initial conditions for generators. The proposed generators allow to increase the length of the repetition period of a pseudo-random bit sequence.

INTRODUCTION

The world around it is built in such a way that all material objects and processes are in constant interaction with each other. As a rule, all phenomena, their occurrence and implementation in the environment cannot be foreseen. This is due to the small amount of knowledge about the laws and processes occurring around us.

DOI: 10.4018/978-1-7998-1290-6.ch003

With the growth of information volumes about phenomenon's and events, the measure of unpredictability decreases both in the form of a decrease in the time interval to the event, and in the set of characteristics of this event.

Currently, man has created a number of material objects that implement specified events according to the algorithm laid down in them. Such events a person can predict at 100%. However, for the construction of many material mechanisms, there is a need to recreate the randomness of the occurrence of certain events. One of the achievements of humankind is the creation of digital electronic calculators, which make it possible to replace each process with a numerical equivalent.

The currently existing architectures and structural solutions make it possible to describe any physical process in space and time. One of the promising solutions among the existing ones is the use and purposeful organization of cellular automata (CA), which today have no alternative for describing and modeling various physical phenomena and processes.

ACTUALITY OF RESEARCH

Today, there are a large number of pseudo-random number generators that have different quality of pseudo-random number formation and a different basis for their construction. (Schneier, 1996; Bilan, 2017; Chugunkov, 2012; Neumann, 1951; L'Ecuyer, 1998; Marsaglia, 2003; Suhinin, 2010a; Wolfram, 1986a). The implementation of generators has a various nature. A large number of developed pseudo-random number generators (PRNG) are due to their widespread use in various fields of human activity. Such areas as cryptography, protection and diagnostics of data transmission systems, game theory, simulation modeling, and many other areas have a special need for the use of PRNG. All means and processes in which PRNG are used can be divided into the use of the obtained sequence of random numbers, both in statics and in dynamics. The use of a static sequence of random numbers implies the preliminary generation of random numbers and the formation of a database. Then the resulting sequence of random numbers is effectively used.

There is also the need to generate and use random numbers in real time. However, existing requests are not always satisfied with modern generators. This is due to the difficulties of achieving the optimal values of the main parameters of the PRNG. These basic parameters include:

1. The length of the repetition period of a sequence of random numbers.
2. Low statistical properties of the generated sequence.
3. Low speed.
4. The degree of independence of consecutive values of numbers.
5. Range of numbers.

These characteristics may be acceptable for some tasks and unacceptable for others. A great importance in the construction of the PRNG is its implementation (software or hardware). Often there are such cases when the proposed generator has good statistical properties, but its implementation dramatically reduces the speed, may require additional resources and does not meet the goal.

Based on the described characteristics, it becomes clear that the need to create and develop new algorithms for generating pseudo-random sequences, combining high speed and good statistical properties of the generated initial sequence, still remains relevant.

At the moment, a lot of attention is paid by developers to the implementation of PRNG based on the CA with various architectures (Bilan, 2017; Suhinin, 2010a; Suhinin, 2010b; Temir, Siap, & Arin, 2014; Sanguinetti, Martin, Zbinden, & Gisin, 2014; Neves, Araujo, 2014; Bhattacharjee, Paul, & Das, 2016; Wolfram, 1986a). The CA properties using existing tests were studied (NIST Special Publications 800-22, 2001; NIST Special Publications 800-22, 2010; Chugunkov, 2012; Walker, 2008; Richard, 1980; Knuth, 1969; Marsaglia, 1984). The structures of the PRNG are created on the basis of synchronous CA (SCA) and asynchronous CA (ACA), as well as on the basis of hybrid CA (HCA). However, the question of the influence of the shape of the vicinity of CA cells on the quality of the formation of pseudo-random bit sequences is little studied.

PURPOSE AND TASKS OF RESEARCH

The purpose of this work is to study the influence of neighborhood forms on the quality of the formation of pseudo-random sequences in order to solve the actual scientific and technical problem of creating promising high-performance methods and software and hardware to form pseudo-random sequences of numbers based on CA. The goal is achieved on the basis of the analysis and selection of the CA and the shape of the neighborhood of the cells, which give high quality generator operation.

PRINCIPLES OF FORMATION AND PROPERTIES OF PSEUDO-RANDOM SEQUENCE OF NUMBERS

Different states are often used in different areas of human activity, which are represented as numerical sequences. Random or pseudo-random sequences of numbers are in special demand. Especially they are in demand in information cryptographic protection systems. Random sequences of numbers are determined by the fact that each number in the sequence cannot be predicted based on an analysis of the generated previous numbers in the sequence. In addition, the entire random sequence of numbers makes it impossible to determine the law of their formation.

Random sequence of numbers is represented as a set of numbers

$$Q = \left\{ q_i \right\}, \quad i = \overline{1, N},$$

where N- the amount of numbers in a sequence that can be equal $+\infty$.

In modern digital calculations, all numbers are represented by a bit code, that is, a sequence of bits is formed.

A random binary sequence is called a sequence of the form

$$B = \left\{ b_i \right\}, b \in \left\{ 0,1 \right\}, \quad i = \overline{1, N}.$$

Bit sequence is characterized by such a basic property. There is no function f with which any number b_i of sequence B could be calculated, with arguments belonging to this sequence $b_i \neq f\left(b_1, ..., b_N \right)$.

Random sequences of numbers (RSN) are formed on the basis of truly random processes that cannot be predicted by man. They can be formed with the help of special means and they transform physical quantities into a quantitative equivalent in time. Such processes include diode noise, changes in atmospheric pressure, various kinds of interference, the effects of ionizing radiation, fractional noise in a resistor, cosmic radiation and other processes. Such sequences are considered truly random.

The numerical characteristics of the random variable q_i, which takes on values of x, are the mathematical expectation, dispersion, and average square deviation.

An important characteristic of the RSN is a uniform distribution of quantities, a special case of which is the density and distribution functions.

This distribution has the same mathematical expectation and dispersion.

There are also random sequences of numbers that satisfy the basic properties of unpredictability, but are formed with the help of special tools developed by man. Such sequences of numbers are called pseudo-random (PRSN). Pseudo-random number - an element obtained by a specific algorithm of a numerical sequence, the properties of which approximation to a random. The main difference between a PRSN and an RSN is that it is always possible to recreate a PRSN, since its values depend on the initial state of the artificial means of their formation. This property can be considered as a disadvantage and advantage depending on the tasks. There are a number of tasks in which it is necessary to verify events that occurred during the formation PRSN. For this, there is a need to repeat such a sequence by establishing the specified initial states of the means of forming such a sequence.

So, PRSN must be finite, since it depends on a finite number of states of the artificial means of forming a PRSN. PRSN can be supplied by a function of three arguments.

$$B = f\left(S, T, s_0\right),$$

where

$S(s_i\}$ - the number of states of the PRSN generation tool;
T – the formation time of the PRSN, which consists of discrete time intervals;
s_0 – original state of PRSN forming tool, which is set by the user.

In modern tasks, there is a need for the formation of PRSN, which would satisfy the uniform distribution of numbers. An obligatory step in generating pseudo-random numbers is to check the periodicity and randomness of the resulting sequence and its accordance with the given distribution law.

ANALYSIS OF EXISTING MEANS OF THE FORMATION OF PSEUDO-RANDOM SEQUENCES

The means forming the sequence of numbers, which is of a random nature of their distribution in the established sequence, is called the generator of pseudo-random number sequences (PRNSG). The generator, and not just a forming device, was named because the sequence of such numbers has a limited length, after the formation of which the sequence is obtained is repeated.

PRNSG is generally presented as an algorithm (Schneier, 1996; Bilan, 2017; NIST Special Publications 800-22, 2010), based on the implementation of which a sequence of numbers is formed that are independent of each other and obey a given distribution law. PRNSG can be implemented both in software and in hardware.

All PRNSG can work in three options.

The first option is to randomly select a number from a given set of numbers. However, such a generator requires performing a function or a pre-formed RSN. Such a generator is difficult to call PRNG, because it requires an internal generator. This method is called tabular (Schneier, 1996; Bilan, 2017).

The second way of functioning PRNSG can be represented as

$$b_i = f\left(s_{i-1}, B_{i-1}\right),$$

where

s_{i-1} - the state of the generator at the (i-1)-th iteration cycle;
B_{i-1} - a sequence of numbers formed on the previous (i-1)-th generation cycles.

Such generators have a feedback that determines the dependence of the formation of the next sequence numbers on the previous numbers given by the algorithm. The essence of the operation of PRNSG is described in the following three steps.

1.   The formula or sequence of actions is installed according to which a sequence of numbers is formed.
2.   Initial data and states are set to the algorithm described in step 1.
3.   Performing of the specified algorithm presented in step 1. After performing this step, the states and data are changed, which replace the data and states.

3 step is repeated until the end of the formation of a random sequence of numbers. Depending on step 1, at a certain iteration cycle, the generator goes to states and data that coincide with step 2. From this point on, the sequence repeats. Such PRNSG are usually implemented by mathematical expressions.

The third way PRNSG functions is in its hardware implementation. That is, its circuit implementation is carried out. At the output of such a PRNSG, a number is formed, which depends on the internal state of the electronic circuit, or on the part of the circuit states. In such generators we can talk about the so-called hidden feedback. An example of a state change in such PRNSGs can be the use of a majority element (Schneier, 1996; Bilan, 2017).

To build a PRNSG, you must comply with a number of requirements. An ideal random number generator should form pseudo-random sequences of numbers that should meet the following requirements:

- Consist of quasi-evenly distributed numbers
- Contain statistically independent numbers
- Be reproducible
- Have numbers that do not repeat
- To form with the minimum cost of machine time
- Occupy the minimum amount of machine memory

The main characteristics of the pseudo-random generation algorithm: initial value and period. From the point of view of cryptology, the following requirements are put forward to PRNSG:

- The pseudo-random sequence issued by the PRNG should have the longest possible period
- The impossibility of determining the source data for the existing pseudo-random sequence
- Inability to play any member of a pseudo-random sequence in a known fragment
- High speed

The most important characteristic of the pseudo-random number generator is the information length of the period after which the numbers will either simply start to repeat, or they can be foreseen.

Quantitative indicators of all considered characteristics can be both advantages and disadvantages for each generator.

A wide interest is shown in the creation of real-time PRNSG. They are especially important for the implementation of streaming encryption systems, game theory and various training simulators. For such a PRNSG, a qualitative review was carried out (Schneier, 1996).

ANALYSIS OF EXISTING METHODS AND MODELS OF RSN GENERATION

To date, a large amount of RNG are developed (Schneier, 1996; Bilan, 2017). All of them are divided into physical and deterministic. Physical generators are based on the use of various physical phenomena and processes that occur randomly for the observer. Physical generators convert the selected parameters of any analog signals into a digital value (number). In fact, such generators act as a transforming means for the parameters of analog signals produced by various physical phenomena and processes.

A deterministic generator is a device that implements a sequence of operations (algorithm) specified by the user. As a rule, such a device can be implemented using the created mathematical or circuit models. From the point of view of the model used to implement deterministic PRNG, they are divided into:

- Mathematical
- Hardware
- Simple
- Combined
- Linear
- Non-linear
- Fibonacci generators
- Mersenne's whirlwind
- Based on shift registers
- On the basis of CA, etc.

Most often, two types of generators are used to generate a uniformly distributed pseudo-random number sequence: congruent and adaptive generators (Knuth, 1969; Schneier, 1996). Linear and nonlinear congruential generators are usually represented by a mathematical expression.

Linear and nonlinear congruential generators are usually represented by a mathematical expression

$$b_{i+1} = \left(ab_i + c\right) \bmod m$$

where

b_0 - initial value (initialization vector);
a – multiplier
c – increment
m – module

Such a generator has a maximum period of m. It is achieved, for example, by choosing Park-Miller constants (Knuth, 1969; Knut, 1998; Schneier, 1996):

$$b_{i+1} = 75b_i \bmod \left(2^{31} - 1\right).$$

The length of the period is equal to m if and only if (Knuth, 1969; Schneier, 1996):

1.   The numbers c and m are mutually simple
2. $d=a$-1 is a multiple of p for each prime p that divides m
3.   d is a multiple of 4 if m is a multiple of 4

If c = 0, then the method is called the linear multiplicative congruent method, and with c≠0 – it is called the mixed linear multiplicative congruent method.

The main disadvantages of such methods and generators, implemented on their basis: a small period, the presence of operations that require considerable time to implement them and have a consistent implementation in both software and hardware. The main statistical disadvantage of such methods is that the sequence that forms is significantly different from the random one and can be broken when used in cryptography. (Marsaglia, 1984; Marsaglia, 2003)

Nonlinear congruential generator (NCT) is implemented using quadratic, cubic and other characteristic expressions that realize the nonlinear nature of the function. Such generators have high resistance to cracking.

A quadratic congruential generator is represented by the following expression

$$X_{k+1} = \left(aX_k^2 + bX_k + c\right) \bmod m .$$

Cubic congruential generator is determined by model

$$X_{k+1} = \left(aX_k^3 + bX_k^2 + cX_k + d\right) \bmod m .$$

To increase the period using a combination of linear and nonlinear congruential generators. But they also have a significant degree of correlation and can be cracked using them for cryptographic protection of information. Compared to LKG, NCG use more complex mathematical operations that require a significant investment of time for their implementation, which limits their speed.

In previous years, adaptive PRNSGs were widely used, which are realized on the analysis of previous values obtained and the formation of a new - pseudo-random number. These methods include the Fibonacci generator (Knuth, 1969; Schneier, 1996).

The main expression that implements the Fibonacci generator is the following

$$a_t = \left(a_{t-1} + a_{t-2}\right) mod N, \quad t = 1, 2, \ldots$$

Such a classic generator has a longer period than congruent generators, and the sequence it generates has poor statistical characteristics.

Fibonacci delay generator uses the following relation

$$X_k = \begin{cases} X_{k-a} - X_{k-b}, if\, X_{k-a} \geq X_{k-b}; \\ X_{k-a} - X_{k-b} + 1, if\, X_{k-a} < X_{k-b}; \end{cases}$$

where X_k - real numbers in the range [0,1), a,b - positive integers that are called lags.

If you use integers, it is enough to use the formula

$$X_k = X_{k-a} - X_{k-b}.$$

But during the operation of such a generator, overflow may occur, and there is also a need to preliminarily determine max{a,b} for the numbers that are generated in the previous initialization steps. The period of such a generator is estimated by the formula

$$T = \left(2^{max\{a,b\}} - 1\right) \cdot 2^l,$$

where l - the number of bits in the mantissa of a essential number.

Fibonacci generators have been studied and researched for over 50 years (Schneier, 1996; Knuth, 1969; Knuth, 1998). Statistical analysis of such generators did not give positive results when applying NIST tests (NIST Special Publications 800-22, 2010). That is, the generator requires improvements in terms of improving its statistical properties. Improved statistical properties allow additional bits that are added to the low-order bits from the generator output, as well as various circuitry technical options for hardware implementation.

There are many PRNSG classifications that are presented in different ways. (Schneier, 1996; Suhinin, 2010a; Suhinin, 2010b). The presented classification describes the options for the implementation of PRNSG. In almost all classifications, PRNSG occupies a significant place on the basis of feedback shift registers (FSR) (Babitha, Thushara, & Dechakka, 2015; *Golomb, 1967;* Sahithi, MuraliKrishna, Jyothi, Purnima, Jhansi Rani, & Sudha, 2012; Schneier, 1996). Feedbacks can be either linear or non-linear.

A simple PRNSG based on FSR with linear feedback (LFSR) is presented in Figure 1.

In Figure 1, PRNG contains n memory cells and modulo-2 adders (XORi). At the outputs of memory cells (MC), the numbers a_i, are formed, which take values from the set $\{0,1\}$, and are came to the inputs of the XOR elements, if such are present at the given MC output.

If a polynomial is chosen as a primitive (for example, n = 4), then the PRNG includes four memory cells, and only the outputs of the first and fourth cells are summed modulo 2 (Figure 2).

Theoretically, the n - bit LFSR can generate a pseudo-random sequence $2^n - 1$ bit before the beginning of a new cycle. For this, the shift register must pass through all $2^n - 1$ internal states. This amount $2^n - 1$ bits in length before the start of a new cycle.

The sequence has a maximum length and is formed by the LFSR is called the M-sequence, and the corresponding LFSR is called the M-sequence generator.

PRNSG, which are implemented in shift registers with nonlinear feedback (NLFSR), use a nonlinear function, the output of which is connected to the input of the first memory cell of the register (Figure 3) (Schneier, 1996).

The initial number $a_i(t)$ is determined as a function of the state values of all the MCs at the previous time step.

Figure 1. PRNSG based on a linear feedback shift register

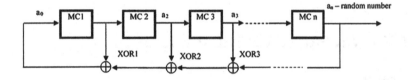

Figure 2. Functional circuit of PRNG, implemented by a primitive polynomial m=4

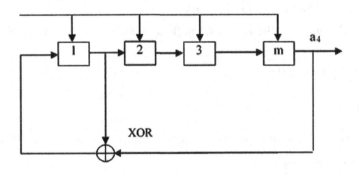

Figure 3. Shift register with nonlinear feedbacks

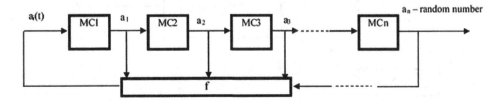

$$a_i\left(t+1\right) = f\left[a_1\left(t\right), a_2\left(t\right), ..., a_n\left(t\right)\right]$$

Such registers are easy to implement both in software and in hardware. But there are a number of works that show the weakness of such generators when using them for cryptographic transformations (Schneier, 1996; Bilan, 2017). In addition, they do not provide high statistical properties, and it is also difficult to predict the length of the period under known initial states.

An important issue is also the use of several generators that mix the generated output values. (Schneier, 1996; Bilan, 2017). The use of this approach allows you to increase the repetition period of a pseudo-random sequence and improve the stability of the generator to the calculation of its structure. The generator circuit using the union of several random sequences in Figure 4 is shown.

The outputs of all generators are connected to the inputs of the computing unit of the function g (), at the output of which a random number is generated. This function is selected in a special way to meet the requirements of reducing of a correlation relationships. The function can be both linear and non-linear (Schneier, 1996; Bilan, 2017).

PRNSG are also used, in which polynomials are switched in the process of generating a pseudo-random sequence (Alan, 2009), which significantly increases the number of pseudo-random sequences. This number can be unlimited, but requires a large number of switching and a special control device. In addition, such an organization reduces the speed and reliability of the generator.

There are also many other generators that require further research and development.

ANALYSIS OF KNOWN PRNSG ON THE BASIS OF CA

Wolfram Generator

To construct PRNSG a CA are also used. Stephen Wolfram proposed the first of the most cited generators in 1986 (Wolfram, 1986a; Wolfram, 1986b; Bhattacharjee, Paul, & Das, 2016). This generator is built on a one-dimensional CA and uses the following logical expression for the cells of the neighborhood

$$b_i\left(t+1\right) = b_{i-1}\left(t\right) \oplus \left[b_i\left(t\right) \vee b_{i+1}\left(t\right)\right] \qquad (1)$$

Figure 4. PRNSG circuit with the union of several random sequences generated by other generators

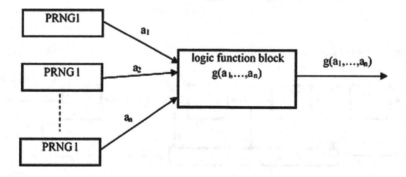

or

$$b_i\left(t+1\right) = \left[b_{i-1}\left(t\right) + b_i\left(t\right) + b_{i+1}\left(t\right) + b_i\left(t\right)b_{i+1}\left(t\right)\right] \bmod 2 \qquad (2)$$

Schematically, the following functional circuit (Figure 5) can represent this expression.

The circuit (Figure 5) and expression (1) show the transition of a single cell to a state according to a given rule. Transitions at each time step occur according to the rules presented by Stephen Wolfram and represented by the corresponding logical expressions between the cells of the neighborhood (Wolfram, 1985; Wolfram, 2002). An example of the transition of a one-dimensional CA according to rule 30 on Figure 6 is shown.

In Figure 1.6 presents the process of changing of the state cells of a CA in time for the rule, given by (1) expression. In such a generator, in each PRNSG there is a dependence of its development on the initial states of the cells. Moreover, for all zero values of the CA cell will not change its value during all time cycles.

Such CA and combinations of rules for various cells of CA give a completely random sequence of numbers. However, the invariance of their functioning and with a small total number of cells leads to the formation of repetitions of values. Moreover, if it is known that KA is used as a generator, then the rule for each cell can be calculated. Especially if such cells are little used to implement the rule. In addition, PRNSG based on CA is better implemented in hardware, since software implementation is time consuming. Also, the use of such a KA for encryption does not provide sustainable data protection and there may be a cipher disclosure with known plaintext (Bilan, 2017; David, et al., 2012; Cardell, & Fúster-Sabater, 2016; Sirakoulis, 2016; Spencer, 2015).

Figure 5. Circuit of transition of a one-dimensional Wolfram CA for one i-th cell

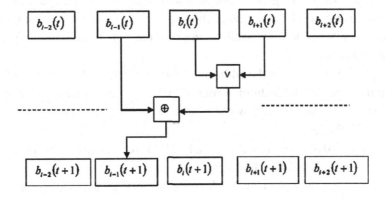

Figure 6. An example of the evolution of CA in time for Rule 30.

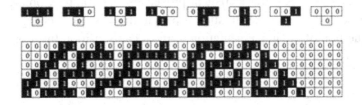

PRNSG BASED ON HYBRID SCA

It is also known the generators of pseudo-random number sequences, implemented on hybrid CA (HCA) (Rubio, & Sanchez, 2004; Cattell, & Muzio, 1996; Seredynski, Bouvry, & Zomaya, 2004; Sipper, & Tomassini, 1996; Chen, Chen, Guan, & He, 2016; Sirakoulis, 2016; Cho, at all., 2007). Combining the rules for different cells of the CA gives a pseudo-random sequence of numbers. This leads to different variants of the evolution of the CA and various pseudo-random sequences are formed. Combining the rules for different cells of the CA gives a pseudo-random sequence of numbers.

The principles of construction and the basis of the functioning of HCAs are widely described in literary sources. In such HCAs, the logical rules are different for each cell, that is, two Wolfram CA are combined (Fraile Ruboi, Hernandez Encinas, Hoya White, Martin del Rey, & Rodrigues Sancher, 2004).

To generate a pseudo-random sequence with a high degree of entropy, genetic algorithms for HCA are effectively used (Girau1, & Vlassopoulos, 2012; Sipper, & Tomassini, 1996). For this approach, the best rules were determined, which gave positive test results (Martin, & Sole, 2008).

For the analysis of HCA, a significant number of tests were used and positive results were obtained. However, such generators are difficult to implement in both software and hardware. They also require a lot of time for the formation of PRN.

PRNSG BASED ON THE CA WITH ADDITIONAL LINEAR SHIFT REGISTERS AND ADDITIONAL CA

There are PRNSG based on CA, which are implemented using an additional generator as the shift register with linear feedback (Suhinin, 2010a; Suhinin, 2010b; David, Hoe, Comer, Cerda, Martinez, & Shirvaikar, 2012).

The output sequence of the shift register is added modulo 2 with the value of one of the neighborhoods of the CA, which ensures the specified period of the sequence of internal states of the automaton. Such use of an additional generator makes it possible to improve the statistical characteristics of the PRNSG, but deprives it of its homogeneity.

The considered generator performs the addition modulo 2 of the values of the selected cell array in the KA with the initial value of the additional register. Changes are made to the cell arrays in the CA at each time step, but it is not indicated how the change occurs, and according to what law are the cell and cell array around it selected.

In the papers (Suhinin, 2010a; Suhinin, 2010b) a PRNSG study is also being conducted that is based on combinations of several CA and the shift register.

As a KA can be used as a classic, and HCA. The principle is used: the more complex the combination of generators, the better the original sequence of numbers. But in this case, the number of required initial states increases, for each component of the combined PRNSG. Such generators have better properties than basic generators, as well as better statistical properties and complex predictability of sequence elements. But also in such PRNSG little attention is paid to the process of changing arrays in both CA. The answer to the question of the implementation of the local transition function is unclear. It is only about addition modulo 2.

They also increased the neighborhood for each cell, worsening its statistical properties. For such CA, it would be logical to remove the state values from all CA cells. And with different operations inside the cell function, they will have different meanings.

This increases the number of connections for each cell of the CA, reduces the reliability. In addition, an increase in the number of cells in the analysis leads to a decrease in the performance of the generator. In addition, the use of an additional generator for mixing implemented on the shift register with feedbacks of course improves its properties. However, this increases the number of feedbacks, which also reduces the speed. The proposed generators use heterogeneity, which requires its initial hard tuning. This increases the number of initial settings. Another problem is that the use of several CA and one shift register twice complicates the implementation of the generator circuit. In this case, it is shown by what law the change of states of both CA. In fact, modulo 2 addition of three bits was performed. Two bits are determined by the functions of the array of cells that represented a part of the cells of the corresponding CA, and the third bit is the bit at the output of the generator implemented on the shift register with linear feedbacks. In fact, three separate generators are used, the output bits of which are the arguments of the resulting function.

All generators of pseudo-random numbers based on CA depend on the behavior of CA themselves and on the characteristics of their organization.

THE RELATED WORKS IN THIS AREA

PRNG Based on ACA

PRNSGs based on ACA are described in detail in the works (Bilan, Bilan, & Bilan, 2015; Bilan, Bilan, Motornyuk, Bilan, & Bilan, 2016; Bilan, 2017). The ACA construction technologies are used, as well as the theoretical methods for generating a binary number at each time step. The process of generating a binary number at each time step is described by the following model for N×M ACA size

$$B(t) = g\left[f\left(S_{i,j}^d(t)\right), S_{i,j}(t), S_{n,m}(t)\right] \qquad (3)$$

This model functions up to the time $t=N{\times}M$. In the next time step, n and m take the initial values. In model (2.8), the value of B depends on three components:

- $S_{i,j}(t)$ - state of the active cell at time t
- $f\left(S_{i,j}^d(t)\right)$ - local function of the arguments, which are the states of the neighborhood cells for the cell with (i,j) coordinates
- $S_{n,m}(t)$ - state of the CA cell on time t

The first component is determined by the state of the activ cell CA at time t. The state of this cell at the moment of time t can be foreseen and described if the initial states of the CA are known.

Initial ACA states:

- ACA dimension $N \times M$
- Initial states of ACA cells
- Coordinates of the initial active cell

With each time step, the state of a single cell that is currently active is changed. The state of the active cell depends on the selected local transitions function, which is performed only for cells in the neighborhood of the active cell.

The third component is the state value of a given individual cell, which, according to a given algorithm, is selected at a certain time step. In fact, the functions of changing the indices of the coordinates (n, m) of the additional cell are specified. These functions depend on the value of one argument t. A simple function of changing coordinates is to represent the CA as a counter with unit and position coding (Bilan, 2017). The increase in digits is carried out ahead of time from left to right and from top to bottom.

The state of such a cell at a given point in time is difficult to predict, since with each time step the state of one of the cells of the CA changes. That is, at the time of selecting an additional cell, the selected cell can change its own state several times.

Important for the operation of PRNSG is a function of local transitions of the active signal from cell to cell. This function makes it possible to determine the next cell, which goes into the active state in the next time step. That is, the function determines the process of changing the coordinates of the active cells in each time cycle.

In general, the change of coordinates is determined by the following system of functions

$$
\begin{cases}
i(t+1) = f_1 \left[S_{i(t),j(t)}^{d(t)} (t) \right] \\
j(t+1) = f_2 \left[S_{i(t),j(t)}^{d(t)} (t) \right]
\end{cases}
\tag{4}
$$

In fact, activation of the cell of the neighborhood indicated by d.

In addition, the value of t can also serve as a parameter for the local transition function. That is, the system (4) can be rewritten in the following form.

$$
\begin{cases}
i(t+1) = f_1 \left[S_{i(t),j(t)}^{d(t)} (t), t \right] \\
j(t+1) = f_2 \left[S_{i(t),j(t)}^{d(t)} (t), t \right]
\end{cases}
\tag{5}
$$

For example, odd and t even values are taken into account, or their change value with a given period, threshold value, and so on.

The generator is started and its further operation is carried out on the basis of primary installations. The removal of the generated bit at each time step is carried out according to the information output of the cell, which is active at that moment (Bilan, Bilan, & Bilan, 2015; Bilan, Bilan, Motornyuk, Bilan, & Bilan, 2016; Bilan, 2017).

Important characteristics when building a PRNSG based on a CA are the structure of the neighborhood and the local function. These characteristics should implement such an algorithm of PRNSG operation, which would give as long as possible the longest repetition period of the sequence, would require optimal costs of computing power and equipment for hardware implementation.

The structure of the neighborhood primarily depends on the shape of the mosaic of cells, is used to build the information field of the CA (Bilan, 2017). The best neighborhood option for each cell is to use the nearest neighboring cells. Such a neighborhood requires a small amount of hardware and simplifies the process of transition of the active signal from cell to cell. In addition, there is a need to increase the cells that form the neighborhood, which makes it possible to increase the degree of mixing of cell signal values, and also increases the number of options for transmitting the active signal to neighboring cells. It would be logical to increase the neighborhood of the cells, or change its shape to asymmetric (Bilan, 2014). This increases the unpredictability of the local transition. But with software and hardware implementation of a CA with such a neighborhood, such indicators as speed and reliability of operation would deteriorate, for many industries it limits the use of such PRNSG.

Significant impact on the implementation of PRNSG has a local function that implements the definition of the next cell, which the active signal is taken. The structure of the neighborhood depends on the local function. The more complex the function, the simpler the neighborhood.

The local function generates a value that indicates the cell number in the neighborhood to which the active signal is transmitted. From the point of view of hardware and computing resources, the local function should be simple to implement. The value of a local function must be a number belonging to a set of numbers.

It is theoretically rather difficult to select a local function and justify its expediency. The best choice of the local transition function is achieved by an experimental approach. The main task is to eliminate local cycles. That is, there are such cell states in which a situation may arise when at each even step a function of local transitions constantly indicates the same neighborhood cell, and at an odd step the function of local transitions indicates a cell that was active at the previous step.

In order to eliminate local cycles, there is a need to constantly change the states of cells of the CA. Such a constant change of states allows, with a certain time step, to change the state of the cells in the places of local cycles, and over time, it removes the local cycle from PRNSG. However, the existence of such cycles among the sequence numbers will allow us to calculate the law of the generator functioning.

Changes in the states of CA cells can occur through many approaches. In a well-known classical CA, all cells change their own state in one clock according to a given local function. But previous studies have shown the presence of cycles in the CA, which will lead to cycles in PRNSG.

Since finding a local function is rather difficult. An additional bit is also entered into the generator, the value of which can be predictable. This bit is read from the selected CA cell and it is an additional argument for the local function of the states of the active cell.

In the papers (Bilan, Bilan, & Bilan, 2015; Bilan, Bilan, Motornyuk, Bilan, & Bilan, 2016; Bilan, 2017) an additional bit is also proposed to form the output bit. At the same time, it is not indicated how changes in the states of the CA. In fact, PRNSG has an inhomogeneous structure, and also depends on two different complex functions.

To preserve the homogeneity of the PRNSG construction, it is proposed to form a sequence of additional bits from the bits of the cell states of the CA itself. Each bit of the additional sequence is supplied by the information output of the selected CA. In fact, the change in the information state of the active cell depends on the states of the cells in the neighborhood of that additional bit. The use of additional bits shall eliminate local cycles.

In addition, the structure of the additional sequence is constantly changing due to the constant change in the state of activation of the cells, also eliminates local cycles and increases the length of the generated random bit sequence.

This approach allows you to build a constantly changing dynamic environment that allows you to get a random sequence of numbers with good statistical properties.

PRNG BASED ON CA WITH DIFFERENT FORMS OF NEIGHBORHOOD

The structure of the CA and the principles of their operation depend on many components. One of them is the shape of the neighborhood of the cells, which affect the state of the cell, the neighborhood of which they form. The most popular neighborhoods of cells for orthogonal coverage in two-dimensional CA are the von Neumann and Moore neighborhoods. (Belan, & Belan, 2012; Bilan, 2017) (Figure 7).

The state of each active cell in the next time step is formed according to the following model

$$a\left(t+1\right) = f\left[a_1\left(t\right),...,a_n\left(t\right)\right]$$ (6)

where $a_i(t)$ – state of the i-th cell of the neighborhood at the moment of (t+1) time, $\left(i = \overline{1,n}\right)$.

For von Neumann's neighborhood $i = \overline{1,4}$ and for Moore's neighborhood $i = \overline{1,8}$.

Both neighborhoods integrate nearest adjacent cells of neighborhood cells. The nearest neighboring cells are cells that have common sides or common vertices in accordance with the chosen form of the CA coating.

Cells that have no common sides or vertices are not nearest neighbors. The smallest number of cells that are located between them determines the distance between cells in the CA.

What does the smallest number of cells mean? The smallest number of cells determines the shortest path of the signal from cell to cell. In this case, the signal may or may not be converted (changed). In synchronous CA, the smallest signal transmission path from a cell to a cell can be determined in advance, and in ACA with active cells, the shortest signal transmission path depends on the function of local transitions and on the shape of the neighborhood. Also, the shortest path in ACA with active cells depends on the initial state of all ACA cells.

Figure 7. Forms of von Neumann and Moore neighborhoods for orthogonal coverage

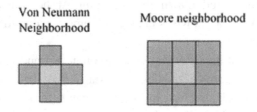

Such two approaches can be used to construct complex neighborhoods in the CA. The first approach is implemented on the basis of model (6), and the second approach is described by the following model

$$a_0\left(t+1\right) = LTF\left[a_i\left(t+1\right)\right] \tag{7}$$

The LTF operator indicates that the nearest neighbors transmit a state that is determined by a function of the states of the nearest neighboring cells of the next layer (Figure 8), which form the neighborhood. So the state of cell a_3 of the first layer is determined by the function

$$a_3 = f\left(a_{12}, a_{13}, a_{14}\right),$$

and for a_2 cell arguments two more

$$a_2 = f\left(a_9, a_{10}, a_{11}, a_{12}, a_{13}\right).$$

However, the cells of the neighborhood do not change their main state if they are not active at a given time. Forms of the neighborhood can be different, and local functions for each cell of the first layer can perform one local function of LTF_1, and cells of the second layer can perform another local function of LTF_2. Then model (7) is represented as follows

Figure 8. Multi-layer neighborhood example

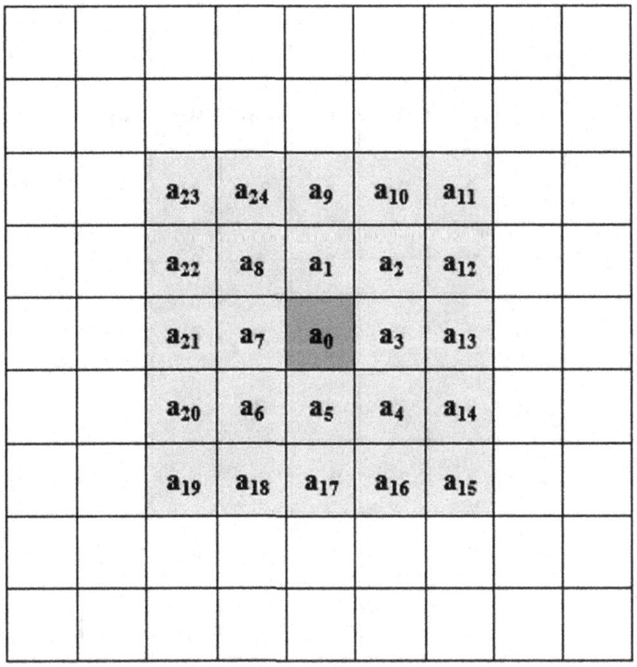

$$a_0\left(t+1\right) = LTF_0\left[a_i\left(t\right), LTF_1, LTF_2\right] \qquad (8)$$

This model does not display the geometric shape of the neighborhood. The model shows that the state of the active cell a_0 is determined by the LTF_0 function, the internal states of the cells in the neighborhood of the first layer are determined by the LTF_1 function, and the cells in the neighborhood by the LTF_2 function. If there are a large number of layers (for example, n), then an example of a model description may be as follows.

$$a_0\left(t+1\right) = LTF_0\left[a_i\left(t\right), LTF_1, LTF_i, LTF_k\right] \qquad (9)$$

Model (9) indicates that the neighborhood cells belonging to 1,2,...,i-1 layers perform the function LTF_1, and the neighborhood cells belonging to k,k+1,...,n layers perform the function LTF_k.

To specify the geometric shape of the neighborhood, we use the following cell coding (Figure 9).

According to the proposed coding, we define the following form of the neighborhood

$\{a_0,...,a_{24}, a_{27},...,a_{29},a_{33},...,a_{35}, a_{39},...,a_{41}, a_{45},...,a_{47}\}$

The form of such a neighborhood has the form shown in Figure 10.

For example, is selected LTF_0=XOR, LTF_1=OR, LTF_2=AND. An example of the operation of a synchronous CA with a given neighborhood organization on Figure 11 is presented.

Figure 9. Cell coding example

	a_{46}	a_{47}	a_{48}	a_{25}	a_{26}	a_{27}	a_{28}	
	a_{45}	a_{23}	a_{24}	a_9	a_{10}	a_{11}	a_{29}	
	a_{44}	a_{22}	a_8	a_1	a_2	a_{12}	a_{30}	
	a_{43}	a_{21}	a_7	a_0	a_3	a_{13}	a_{31}	
	a_{42}	a_{20}	a_6	a_5	a_4	a_{14}	a_{32}	
	a_{41}	a_{19}	a_{18}	a_{17}	a_{16}	a_{15}	a_{33}	
	a_{40}	a_{39}	a_{38}	a_{37}	a_{36}	a_{35}	a_{34}	

Figure 10. Geometrical shape of a neighborhood with orthogonal cover

	a_{46}	a_{47}	a_{48}	a_{25}	a_{26}	a_{27}	a_{28}	
	a_{45}	a_{23}	a_{24}	a_9	a_{10}	a_{11}	a_{29}	
	a_{44}	a_{22}	a_8	a_1	a_2	a_{12}	a_{30}	
	a_{43}	a_{21}	a_7	a_0	a_3	a_{13}	a_{31}	
	a_{42}	a_{20}	a_6	a_5	a_4	a_{14}	a_{32}	
	a_{41}	a_{19}	a_{18}	a_{17}	a_{16}	a_{15}	a_{33}	
	a_{40}	a_{39}	a_{38}	a_{37}	a_{36}	a_{35}	a_{34}	

Figure 11. An example of the operation of SCA for the neighborhood shown on Figure 10 and with local functions LTF_0=XOR, LTF_1=OR, LTF_2=AND

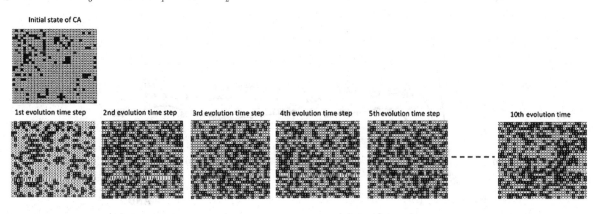

Examples of functioning of SCA for the neighborhood presented on Figure 10 and for functions LTF_0=XOR, LTF_1=OR, LTF_2=AND on Figure 12 is shown.

The figures show that CA for operations (XOR, OR, AND) and XOR with each time step have an approximately even distribution of cells that have a logical "1" state. At the same time, the number of cells in a single state is different for each group of functions (Figure 13).

The considered examples describe the evolution of synchronous CA that are homogeneous. SCAs are also homogeneous for several local functions that are involved in complex neighborhoods consisting of several layers of cells.

Figure 12. An example of the operation of SCA for the neighborhood shown on Figure 10 and with local functions $LTF_0=XOR$, $LTF_1=OR$, $LTF_2=AND$

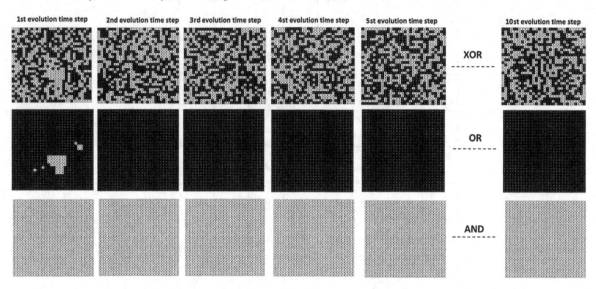

Figure 13. The distribution of single cells for the logical functions shown on Figure 11 and 12

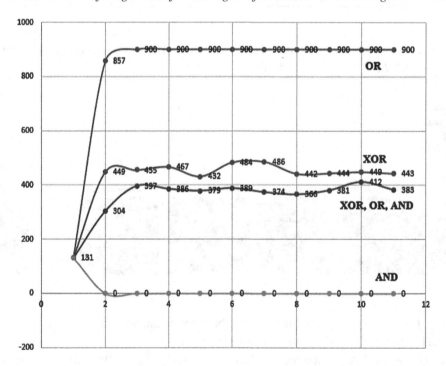

INHOMOGENEOUS SCA

In inhomogeneous SCA there can be various inhomogeneities, which are characterized by the presence of cells with different functionalities. Inhomogeneous cells - that perform another local function or have a different form of neighborhood.

Inhomogeneous cells make changes in the evolution of homogeneous CA, and can also extend the time of CA functioning before the onset of cycles or dead ends. The behavior of hybrid SCA is described in detail in (Bilan, 2017) for inhomogeneous cells that have a different local state function. However, little attention is paid to the study of CA, which contain inhomogeneous cells with different forms of neighborhoods. In such SCA, inhomogeneous cells can perform a local function of states with fewer or more arguments.

The evolution of hybrid SCA for cells that differ only in the shapes of their neighborhoods on Figure 14 is shown. All cells realize the XOR local function of states.

For all forms of neighborhoods, the same initial state of CA is used. For the first HSCA, the main cells have a neighborhood $\{a_1,a_3,a_5,a_7\}$, and inhomogeneous cells have a neighborhood $\{a_1,a_2,a_3,a_4,a_5,a_6,a_7,a_8\}$. The second HSCA is organized so that homogeneous cells have a neighborhood $\{a_1,a_3,a_5,a_7\}$, and inhomogeneous have a neighborhood $\{a_1,a_3,a_5,a_7,a_9,a_{13},a_{17},a_{21}\}$. Homogeneous cells of a third HSCA have neighborhood $\{a_1 - a_9\}$, and heterogeneous cells - $\{a_1 - a_{24}\}$.

For a quick analysis of the evolution of each HSCA, an analysis of the number of units at each time step was carried out (Figure 15). The analysis was carried out for one hundred time steps of evolution. The resulting graphs can reduce the search time for the length of the life cycle of the HSCA.

Figure 14. An example of the evolution of hybrid SCA for different forms of neighborhoods

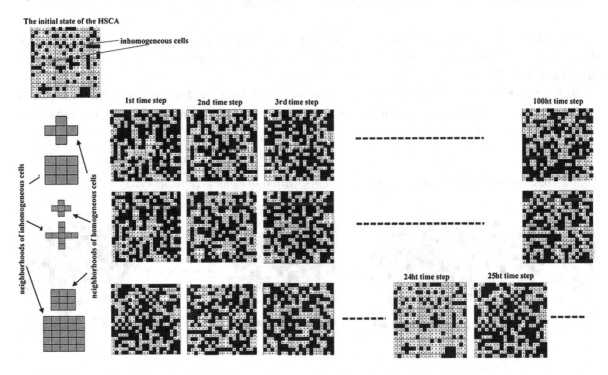

Figure 15. Graphic dependences of the change in the number of units at each time step for HSCAs presented on Figure 14

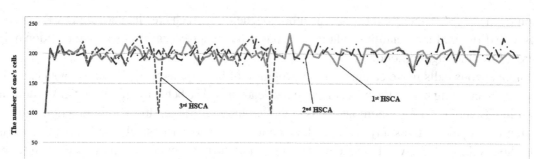

As a result of the analysis of graphs in Figure 8 shows that the third HSCA has the shortest life cycle. Already at the 24th time step, the third HSCA goes into the initial state and the process of its functioning is repeated.

In connection with the occurrence of such a situation and to increase the length of the life cycle, it becomes necessary to take into account and select the following characteristics:

- HSCA size
- Shape of the neighborhood of homogeneous and heterogeneous cells
- The amount of heterogeneous cells
- Location of heterogeneous cells
- Local state functions for homogeneous and heterogeneous cells

A good choice of these characteristics allows you to increase the life cycle of HSCA. If you change the location of heterogeneous cells for the third HSCA (Figure 16), then you can get a life cycle length of 48 time steps (Figure 17).

At the 52 time step, the HSCA state corresponds to its state at the 4th time step. The life cycle is doubled. However, studies have shown that two inhomogeneous cells do not provide the desired length of the HSCA life cycle.

Figure 16. Evolution of the third HSCA with a new location of inhomogeneous cells

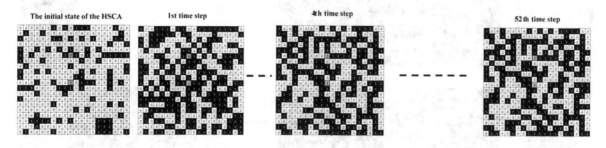

Figure 17. Graphic dependence of the number of logical "1" of the third HSCA at each time step for the variant shown on Figure 16

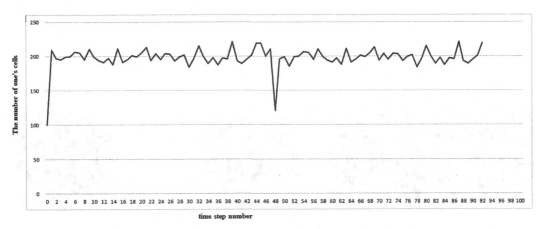

Increase the life period allows the introduction of a larger number of cells. So the work of the third HSCA with three inhomogeneous cells on Figure 18 is shown.

The evolution of the third HSCA with three inhomogeneous cells shows a longer work cycle. Thus, the more inhomogeneous cells used, the longer the life cycle of the HSCA.

In addition, inhomogeneous cells can have different forms of neighborhoods in a single HSCA. They have an impact on the work of the HSCA. In Figure 19 shows the evolution of HSCA with two inhomogeneous cells that have different forms of neighborhoods.

Figure 18. Evolution of the third HSCA with three heterogeneous cells and a graphical dependence of the number of cells with logic "1" states at each time step

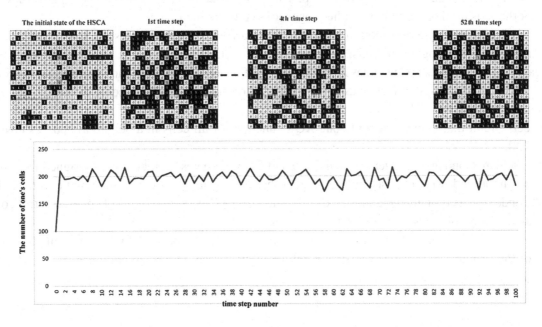

Figure 19. The evolution of HSCA with two inhomogeneous cells that have different forms of neighborhoods, and a graphical dependence of the number of cells that has logic "1" state at each evolutionary time step

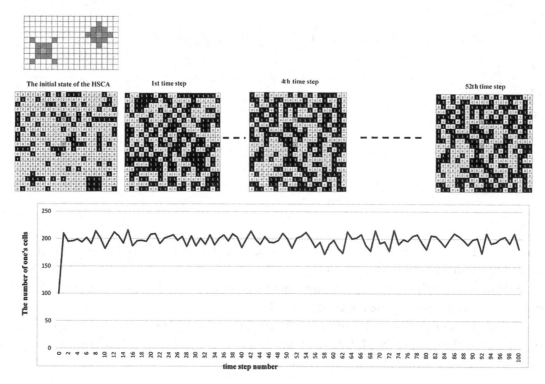

Figure 19. shows that the choice of a different form of the neighborhood for inhomogeneous cells does not have a sufficient effect on the result of functioning. Like the third HSCA (Figure 7), the repetition of the initial state begins at the 24th time step. This proves that to increase the length, a multi-layered neighborhood is used or the number of heterogeneous cells are increased.

When hardware implementation of such HSCA is carried out, complicates the implementation of the structure of inhomogeneous cells, as for multi-layered neighborhoods, the number of connections increase and the cell scheme becomes more complex. If the neighborhood of the inhomogeneous cell is multi-layered and a different LTF is used for each layer of the neighborhood cells, then each HSCA is hardware individually implemented.

A cell circuit that implements only one XOR function for all cells in a neighborhood is shown in Figure 20.

The schema contains a trigger, an XOR gate and 24 AND gates. The circuit is designed for a two-layer neighborhood, which consists of 24 neighborhood cells in the case of orthogonal coverage. The bus X sends signals from the neighborhood cells, and the bus CBUS sends control codes. Control codes indicate the shape of the neighborhood for each cell.

The advantage of this cell structure is that it is flexible and can be used for various cell configurations of the neighborhood. However, such a cell requires a large number of connections that may not always be effectively used.

Figure 20. Functional circuit of the HSCA cell that implements the XOR function for all cells in the vicinity

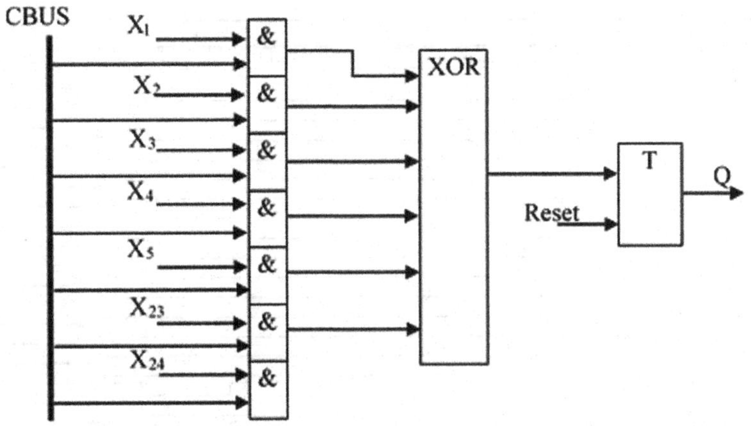

The cell circuit is modeled in CAD Active-HDL for various cell configurations of the neighborhoods (Figure 21).

Based on these cells, the HSCA scheme is implemented. It is simply modeled in modern CAD systems. Timing diagrams of HSCA size 4×4 are presented in Figure 22.

In the present HSCA, the main cells process the signals from the cells that organize by the von Neumann neighborhood, and the inhomogeneous cells have the Moore neighborhood. Large-size HSCAs can be built from completed modules, which can increase the life cycle of work.

As mentioned above, HSCA is selected as PRNG. The information output of such a PRNG is the output of one of the HSCA cells, which forms the bit sequence.

The considered HSCA-based PRNGs are characterized by the fact that all cells perform the same function, but inhomogeneous cells have a different neighborhood shape. In this case, it is possible that homogeneous and inhomogeneous cells change their homogeneity at a certain functioning cycle. For

Figure 21. Graphic representation and timing of cell work in CAD Active-HDL for neighborhoods {a_1, a_3, a_5, a_7}, {a_1, ..., a_8}, {a_1, ..., a_{24}}

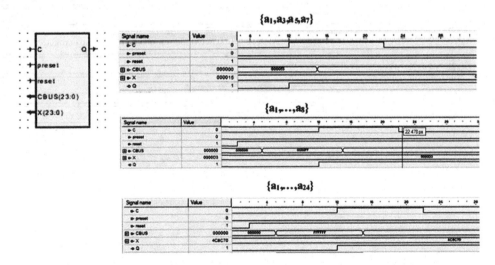

Figure 22. Timing diagrams of HSCA functioning by 4×4 size

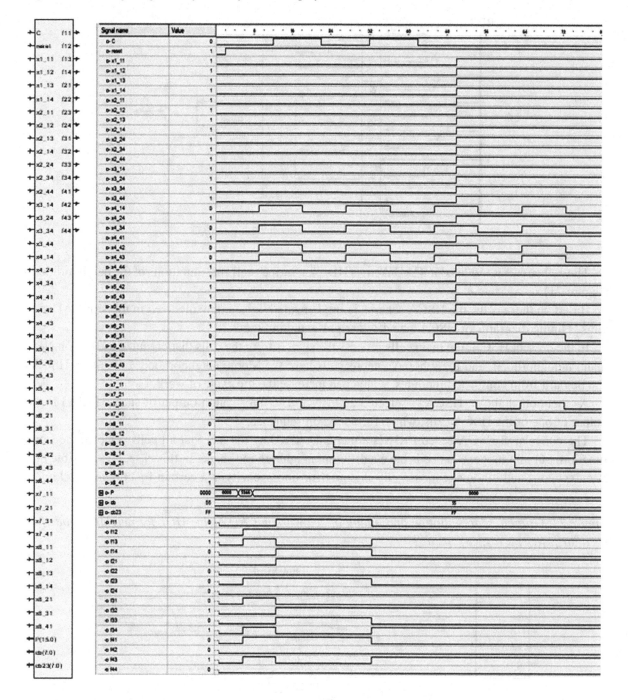

example, on every odd cycle, homogeneous cells have a von Neumann neighborhood, and inhomogeneous cells have a Moore neighborhood. On every even tact, homogeneous cells perform a function on the basis of the Mur neighborhood, while inhomogeneous cells perform a function on the basis of the von Neumann neighborhood. An example of the functioning of such a PRNG on Figure 23 is presented.

Figure 23 shows that two inhomogeneous cells do not give the desired result and organize a cycle starting with 15 time steps and ending with 62 time steps. HSCA states at 15 and 63 time steps are the same. The introduction of the third inhomogeneous cell does not cycle in the first hundred time steps.

Figure 23. The evolution of the functioning of the PRNG based on HSCA with variable variation of the forms of neighborhoods for homogeneous and inhomogeneous cells

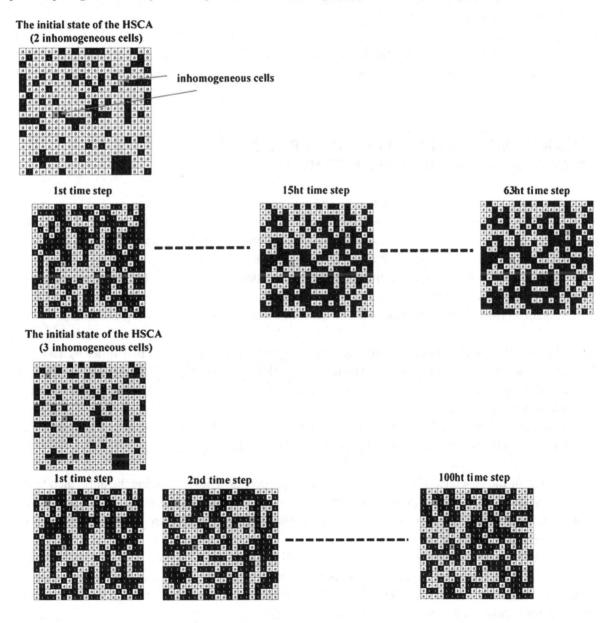

Thus, as in the case when inhomogeneous cells differ in the local function of the states, it is sufficient to use three inhomogeneous cells. The location of inhomogeneous cells, as well as the HSCA dimension, have a great influence.

To build a PRNG, the HSCA is used, which uses the following initial states.

1. HSCA size.
2. The initial state of all HSCA cells.
3. The number of inhomogeneous cells.
4. Location of inhomogeneous cells.
5. The shape of the neighborhood of homogeneous cells.
6. The shape of the neighborhood of inhomogeneous cells.
7. Local state function for each cell.

A change in at least one of these initial states leads to a change in the evolution of a two-dimensional HSCA. The length and quality of the generated pseudo-random bit sequence depends on these initial settings.

THE ANALYSIS OF A QUALITY OF THE PRNG BASED ON A CA WITH VARIABLE NEIGHBORHOOD

At present time, it is not possible to say that PRNG generates a pseudo-random sequence of high quality numbers. However, many tests have been developed that allow us to estimate the quality of a pseudo-random number sequence. (Walker, 2008; Richard, 1980; Knuth, 1998; NIST Special Publications 800-22, 2001; NIST Special Publications 800-22, 2010; Chugunkov, 2012).

If the tests give a negative result, the sequence is considered not random. If a positive result was obtained, it is considered that the sequence may be random.

To obtain a positive result, the generated bit sequence must satisfy the following conditions.

1. The number of ones and zeros in the sequence is approximately equal and may differ by 1.
2. The same sequence of bits should be distributed so that groups of logical "1" element are divided in half in the entire sequence, groups of two identical elements are divided into four equal parts in the entire sequence, etc.
3. When analyzing a match with the selected control sequence, the number of matches must be different from the number of mismatches by 1 for all bits of the sequence.

Each part of the generated bit sequence saves these properties. They determine the unpredictability of any element of the bit sequence by analyzing the previously formed elements of this sequence. The main characteristic of a random bit sequence is the inability to predict each future un-generated member of the bit sequence based on previously generated bits.

The most popular tests are graphical tests, NIST, DIEHARD, etc. (Chugunkov, 2012). It often happens that the generated bit sequence passes some tests successfully, but other tests show the presence of a defect in the generator. For example, there are bit sequences that are successful with NIST tests, and graphical tests show the presence of a defect in the PRNG.

To assess the quality of the proposed PRNG, the following initial conditions were taken into account.

1. HSCA size.
2. The local function of the states of homogeneous cells.
3. The local function of the states of inhomogeneous cells.
4. The number of cells in a state of logical "1".
5. The geometric shape of the neighborhood of homogeneous cells.
6. The geometric shape of the neighborhood of inhomogeneous cells.
7. The number of inhomogeneous cells.
8. Location of inhomogeneous cells.

Dimensions used 10×10, 15×15, 20×20, 25×25, 30×30. As a local state function for homogeneous and inhomogeneous cells, the XOR function was used.

Inhomogeneous cells were used in the work, which performed the same local function of the states as homogeneous cells. However, the number of arguments of the local function of states of inhomogeneous cells differed from the number of arguments of homogeneous cells. This is due to the fact that the number of cells that form a neighborhood for inhomogeneous cells was different from the number of cells in the neighborhood of homogeneous cells.

The use of inhomogeneous cells with the same shape of the neighborhood, but with a different local state function is described in detail in the work (Bilan, 2017). Using HSCA with these properties to build a PRNG has shown high quality. Local state functions for homogeneous and inhomogeneous cells were selected.

However, HSCA studies were not conducted for inhomogeneous cells with different neighborhood forms, but with the same local state functions. This work is aimed at conducting such research.

The number of cells with logic "1" state for HSCA of each dimension was chosen in three variants: less than 50%, more than 50%, and 50% of all HSCA cells. The number of inhomogeneous cells was selected with the same location for all HSCA.

Homogeneous and inhomogeneous cells use different forms of neighborhood. The basic form of the neighborhood was the von Neumann neighborhood. It has been used in almost all HSCAs that participated in the experiments. In addition, other combinations of neighborhoods were used. Forms of neighborhoods that were used in the experiment on Figure 24 are shown.

Each neighborhood has its own number. Single-layer and two-layer neighborhoods with orthogonal cover were used. Also, a setup with initial states of HSCA was formed. Bits of a pseudo-random sequence were formed at the output of a single cell, which had coordinates (3.3) for all HSCAs involved in the experiment. All combinations of neighborhoods that were used in the experiment in table 1 are presented.

Figure 24. Forms of neighborhoods that participated in the experiment

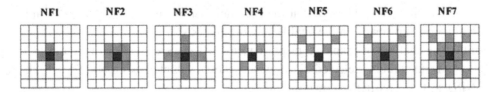

Table 1. Combinations of neighborhood forms that participated in the experiment

N° of Combination	Neighborhood of Homogeneous Cells	Neighborhood of Inhomogeneous Cells
1	• NF1	• NF2
2	• NF1	• NF3
3	• NF1	• NF4
4	• NF1	• NF5
5	• NF1	• NF6
6	• NF1	• NF7
7	• NF2	• NF1
8	• NF3	• NF1
9	• NF4	• NF1
10	• NF5	• NF1
11	• NF6	• NF1
12	• NF7	• NF1
13	• NF1	• NF4- NF7
14	• NF2	• NF1, NF4 - NF7

Based on the combinations of used neighborhoods, bit sequences of various lengths were formed. Sequences were formed in accordance with the requirements for conducting tests, as there are tests that analyze bit sequences of strictly specified length.

Initially, all sequences were analyzed using two graphical tests:

- The histogram of the distribution of the elements of the sequence (to assess the uniformity of the distribution);
- The distribution on the plane (to determine the relationship between elements).

Sequences with positive tests were selected, and PRNG were used to perform NIST tests. As a result of the used tests, a number of PRNGs showed defects. Examples of graphic tests for PRNG with defects on Figure 25 are shown.

Defects manifest themselves in a PRNG based on HSCA of a small dimension (less than 15×15) and with a small number of inhomogeneous cells (less than 3 inhomogeneous cells). Moreover, the larger the HSCA dimension, the smaller the number of used inhomogeneous cells gives positive results when passing graphic tests. Results of performance of graphic tests with use of various quantity of inhomogeneous cells on Figure 26 are presented. Every two lines in the figure are for a HSCA of a given dimension, for the length of the bit sequence, a combination of neighborhoods and the initial number of cells that have a logical "1" state.

The results of graphical tests showed that the used number of inhomogeneous cells and the HSCA dimension have a great influence on the quality of work of PRNG.

As a result of the analysis of graphical tests, sequences that were successful were selected, as well as the PRNG that formed them. Selected bit sequences were evaluated using NIST tests. The results of passing the NIST tests are partially shown in Table 2.

Figure 25. Examples of graphic tests for PRNG with defects

A successful test is indicated by a "+" sign, and an unsuccessful test is displayed by a "-" sign. All NIST tests were implemented in separate software and were applied to bit sequences of various lengths.

Also, the tests evaluated bit sequences that were formed by PRNG based on HSCA with inhomogeneous cells that have different forms of neighborhoods. For such bit sequences used tests showed a positive result.

CONCLUSION

The analysis of HSCA, which uses inhomogeneous cells with different forms of neighborhoods, allowed us to determine the influence of neighborhood forms on the evolution of such two-dimensional HSCA. The results of the analysis allow us to construct PRNGs that can compete with existing PRNGs based

Figure 26. Examples of graphical tests for PRNG based on HSCA with the same initial settings and different numbers of inhomogeneous cells

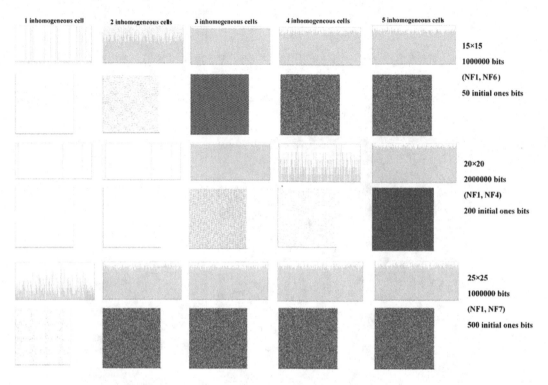

Table 2. NIST test results

N° of Test	HSCA Size	The Initial Number of Cells With a Logical State of "1"	The Number of Inhomogeneous Cells	The Length of the Bit Sequence	Forms of Neighborhoods		Test Result
					For Homogeneous Cells	For Inhomogeneous Cells	
1	25×25	100, 315	7	1000000	NF1	NF2	+
	30×30	190	5	1000000	NF1	NF5	+
	30×30	770	3	1000000	NF6	NF1	+
2	25×25	100, 315	7	10000	NF1	NF2	+
	30×30	190	5	1000	NF1	NF5	+
	30×30	770	3	10000	NF6	NF1	+
3	25×25	100, 315	7	10000	NF1	NF2	+
	30×30	190	5	1000	NF1	NF5	+
	30×30	770	3	100000	NF6	NF1	+
4	25×25	100, 315	7	6272	NF1	NF2	+
	30×30	190	5	6272	NF1	NF5	+
	30×30	770	3	6272	NF6	NF1	+

continues on following page

Table 2. Continued

Nº of Test	HSCA Size	The Initial Number of Cells With a Logical State of "1"	The Number of Inhomogeneous Cells	The Length of the Bit Sequence	Forms of Neighborhoods		Test Result
					For Homogeneous Cells	For Inhomogeneous Cells	
5	25×25	100, 315	7	1000	NF1	NF2	+
	30×30	190	5	1000	NF1	NF5	+
	30×30	770	3	1000, 2000	NF6	NF1	+
6	25×25	100, 315	7	10000	NF1	NF2	+
	30×30	190	5	10000	NF1	NF5	+
	30×30	770	3	100000	NF6	NF1	+
7	25×25	100, 315	7	10000	NF1	NF2	+
	30×30	190	5	100000	NF1	NF5	+
	30×30	770	3	10000, 100000	NF6	NF1	+
8	25×25	100, 315	7	10000	NF1	NF2	+
	30×30	190	5	10000	NF1	NF5	+
	30×30	770	3	10000	NF6	NF1	+
9	25×25	100, 315	7	387840	NF1	NF2	+
	30×30	190	5	387840	NF1	NF5	+
	30×30	770	3	387840	NF6	NF1	+
10	25×25	100, 315	7	10000	NF1	NF2	+
	30×30	190	5	100000	NF1	NF5	+
	30×30	770	3	1000000	NF6	NF1	+
11	25×25	100, 315	7	1200000	NF1	NF2	+
	30×30	190	5	1000000	NF1	NF5	+
	30×30	770	3	1000000	NF6	NF1	+
12	25×25	100, 315	7	10000	NF1	NF2	+
	30×30	190	5	100000	NF1	NF5	+
	30×30	770	3	10000	NF6	NF1	+
13	25×25	100, 315	7	10000	NF1	NF2	+
	30×30	190	5	10000	NF1	NF5	+
	30×30	770	3	10000	NF6	NF1	+
14	25×25	100, 315	7	10000	NF1	NF2	+
	30×30	190	5	1000	NF1	NF5	+
	30×30	770	3	10000	NF6	NF1	+
15	25×25	100, 315	7	1000000	NF1	NF2	+
	30×30	190	5	1000000	NF1	NF5	+
	30×30	770	3	1000000	NF6	NF1	+
16	25×25	100, 315	7	1000000	NF1	NF2	+
	30×30	190	5	1000000	NF1	NF5	+
	30×30	770	3	1000000	NF6	NF1	+

on CA. Using only other forms of neighborhoods to define inhomogeneous cells simplifies the structure of the HSCA cell, which allows any HSCA cell to choose as inhomogeneous. In this case, it is possible to implement a change in the location of inhomogeneous cells during the entire period of PRNG operation, which significantly lengthens the repetition period of the generated bit sequence. The use of tests for assessing the quality of PRNG based on HSCA with various forms of neighborhoods made it possible to formulate recommendations for choosing: forms of neighborhoods, HSCA dimensions and number of inhomogeneous cells for XOR function. In addition, studies have shown how the number of cells, which initially have a logical "1" state for the HSCA dimensions under study, effects the quality of PRNG. The research results make it possible to initially select the necessary PRNG structure based on the HSCA and set a favorable initial initialization vector.

REFERENCES

Babitha, P. K., Thushara, T., & Dechakka, M. (2015). P. FPGA Based N - bit LFSR to generate random sequence number. *International Journal of Engineering Research and General Science, 3*(3), 60–10.

Belan, S., & Belan, N. (2012). Use of Cellular Automata to Create an Artificial System of Image Classification and Recognition, *ACRI2012* [), Springer-Verlag Berlin Heidelberg.]. *LNCS, 7495*, 483–493.

Bhattacharjee, K., Paul, D., & Das, S. (2016). Pseudorandom Pattern Generation Using 3-State Cellular Automata. In S. El Yacoubi, J. Wąs, & S. Bandini (Eds.), Lecture Notes in Computer Science: Vol. 9863. *Cellular Automata. ACRI 2016* (pp. 3–13). doi:10.1007/978-3-319-44365-2_1

Bilan, S. (2017). *Formation Methods, Models, and Hardware Implementation of Pseudorandom Number Generators: Emerging Research and Opportunities*. IGI Global.

Bilan, S., Bilan, M., & Bilan, S. (2015). Novel pseudorandom sequence of numbers generator based cellular automata. *Information Technology and Seqcurity, 3*(1), 38–50.

Bilan, S., Bilan, M., Motornyuk, R., Bilan, A., & Bilan, S. (2016). Research and Analysis of the Pseudorandom Number Generators Implemented on Cellular Automata. *WSEAS TRANSACTIONS on SYSTEMS, 15*, 275–281.

Cardell, S. D., & Fúster-Sabater, A. (2016). Linear Models for the Self-Shrinking Generator Based on CA. *JCA, 11*(2-3), 195–211.

Cattell, K., & Muzio, J.C. (1996). Syntesis one-dimensional linear hybrid cellular automata. IEEE Trans. *On Computer – aided desing of integrated circuits and systems, 15(3)*, 325 – 335.

Chen, B., Chen, F., Guan, J., & He, Q. (2016). Glider Collisions in Hybrid Cellular Automata Rule 168 and 133. *JCA, 11*(2-3), 167–194.

Cho, S.J., Choi, U. S., Kim, H.D., Hwang, Y.H., Kim, J.G., & Heo, S.H. (2007). "New syntheesis of one-dimensional 90/150 liner hybrid group CA". *IEEE Transactions on comput-aided design of integrated circuits and systems*, 25(9). pp. 1720-1724

Chugunkov, E.V. (2012). *Methods and tools to evaluate the quality of pseudo-random sequence generators, focused on solving problems of information security: Textbook*/M.: NEYAU MIFI, 236.

David, H. K., Hoe, J. Comer, M., Cerda, J. C., Martinez, C. D., & Shirvaikar, M. V. (2012). Cellular Automata-Based Parallel Random Number Generators Using FPGAs. *International Journal of Reconfigurable Computing Volume 2012*, 1-13, Article ID 219028.

Fraile Ruboi, C., Hernandez Encinas, L., Hoya White, S., & Martin del Rey, A., & Rodrigues Sancher. (2004). The use of Linear Hybrid Cellular Automata as Pseudorandom bit Generators in Cryptography. *Neural Parallel & Scientific Comp.*, *12*(2), 175–192.

Giraul, B. & Vlassopoulos, N. (2012). Evolution of 2-Dimensional Cellular Automata as Pseudo-random Number Generators./ *Springer-Verlag Berlin Heidelberg, ACRI 2012*, LNCS 7495, 611–622

Golomb, S. W. (1967). *Shift register sequences*. Holden-Day.

Knuth, D. E. (1969). The Art of Computer Programming: Vol. 2. *Seminumerical Algorithms*. Reading, MA: Addison-Wesley.

Knuth, D. E. (1998). The art of computer programming: Vol. 2. *Seminumerical algorithms* (3rd ed.). Reading, MA: Addison-Wesley.

Konheim, A. G. (2009). *Computer Security and Cryptography*. John Wiley & Sons.

Marsaglia, G. (1984). *The Marsaglia Random Number CDROM including the Diehard Battery of Tests of Randomness*. Department of statistics and supercomputer computations and research institute, from http://www.stat.fsu.edu/pub/diehard

Marsaglia, G. (2003). Random number generators. *Journal of Modern Applied Statistical Methods; JMASM*, *2*(1), 2–13. doi:10.22237/jmasm/1051747320

Martin, B., & Sole, P. (2008). Pseudorandom Sequences Generations, Prders and Graphs, *Interactions with Computer Science*, Mahdia Tunisia, Nouha editions, 401 - 410.

Neumann, J. (1951). The general and logical theory of automata. In L.A. Jefferess, ed., Cerobral Mechanisms in Behavior, *The Hixon Symposium* (pp. 1-31), John Wiley & Sons, New Yirk.

Neves, S., & Araujo, F. (2014). Lecture Notes in Computer Science: Vol. 8384. *Engineering Nonlinear Pseudorandom Number Generators. Parallel Processing and Applied Mathematics. PPAM 2013* (pp. 96–105).

Richard, W. (1980). *Hamming. Coding and Information Teory/Englewood Cliffs N.1. 07632.* Prentice-Hall.

Rubio, C. F., & Sanchez, L. H. (2004). The use of Linea Hybrid Cellular Automata as Pseudorandom Bit Generator in Cryptography, *Neural Parallel, Sciens. Comput*, *12*(2), 175–192.

Sahithi, M., MuraliKrishna, B., Jyothi, M., Purnima, K., Jhansi Rani, A., & Sudha, N.N. (2012). Implementation of Random Number Generator Using LFSR for High Secured Multi Purpose Applications. *International Journal of Computer Science and Information Technologies*, *3*(1), 3287–3290.

Sanguinetti, B., Martin, A., Zbinden, H., & Gisin, N. (2014). Quantum Random Number Generation on a Mobile Phone. *Physical Review X*, *4*(031056), 1–6.

Schneier, B. (1996). Applied Cryptography, Second Edition: Protocols, Algorthms, and Source Code in C, Wiley Computer Publishing, John Wiley & Sons, Inc, 784.

Seredynski, F., Bouvry, P., & Zomaya, Y. (2004). Cellular automata computtions and secret rey cryptography. *Parallel Computing*, *30*(5-6), 753–766. doi:10.1016/j.parco.2003.12.014

Sipper, M., & Tomassini, M. (1996). *Co evolving parallel random number generators. In parallel Problem Solving from Nature – PPSN IV* (pp. 950–959). Berlin: Springer Verlag. doi:10.1007/3-540-61723-X_1058

Sirakoulis, G. Ch. (2016). Parallel Application of Hybrid DNA Cellular Automata for Pseudorandom Number Generation. *JCA*, *11*(1), 63–89.

NIST Special Publications 800-22. (2001). A statistical test suite for random and pseudorandom number generators for cryptographic applications.

Special Publications, N. I. S. T. 800-22. (2010). A statistical test suite for random and pseudorandom number generators for cryptographic applications. Revision 1. NIST.- *National institute of standarts and technology. Computer security division. Computer security resource center*. - Download Documentation and Software, from http://csrc.nist.gov/groups/ST/toolkit/rng/documentation_software.html

Suhinin, B. M. (2010a). High generators of pseudorandom sequences based on cellular automata, *Applied discrete mathematics, N° 2*, 34 – 41.

Suhinin, B. M. (2010b). Development of generators of pseudorandom binary sequences based on cellular automata. *Science and education*, (9): 1–21.

Temir, F., Siap, I., & Arin, H. (2014). On Pseudo Random Bit Generators via Two-Dimentional Hybrid Cellular Automata. *Acta Physica Polonica A*, *125*(2), 534–537. doi:10.12693/APhysPolA.125.534

Walker, J. (2008). *ENT. A Pseudorandom Number Sequence Test Program*. January 28th, from http://www.fourmilab.ch/random

Wolfram, S. (1986a). Random Sequence Generation by Cellular Automata. *Advances in Applied Mathematics*, *7*(2), 429–432. doi:10.1016/0196-8858(86)90028-X

Wolfram, S. (1986b). Cryptography with Cellular Automata. *Lecture Notes in Computer Science*, *218*, 429–432. doi:10.1007/3-540-39799-X_32

Wolfram, S. (2002). *A new kind of science*. Wolfram Media.

Chapter 4
Research of Methods of Steganographic Protection of Audio Information Based on Video Containers

Mykola Bilan

The Municipal Educational Institution Mayakskaya Secondary School, Moldova

Andrii Bilan

The Municipal Educational Institution Mayakskaya Secondary School, Moldova

ABSTRACT

The chapter describes investigations of steganographic methods of information protection, which use containers represented by files in AVI format. MP3 audio files are selected as data that is embedded in the used container. For the introduction of audio data, the video container was divided into control and information parts. Secret data were embedded in the information part of the video file, which did not lead to distortions when the container file is played. Studies have been conducted to find repetitive blocks in the structure of a video container. The chapter analyzed the determination of the amount of embedded data for containers with different parameters: color saturation, video file resolution, video file length, compression quality, and frames per second. An algorithm has been developed for the introduction and extraction of information represented by sound formats.

INTRODUCTION

XXI century marked the rapid development of information technology. The concept of the information society has appeared. Digital technologies, either willy-nilly or not, are being introduced into all spheres of life of an ordinary person, from network communication and electronic payments to "smart" houses, navigators and "cloud" technologies. Total digitalization of the economy has led to the massive use of digital technology in the workplace.

DOI: 10.4018/978-1-7998-1290-6.ch004

Naturally, in these conditions, the factor of information protection from unauthorized access is of great importance. Back in the 19th century, the founder of the British branch of the Rothschilds, Nathan Rothschild, said the famous phrase "Who owns the information, owns the world".

Currently, in connection with the frequent cases of theft of confidential information and its use for unseemly purposes, there is an acute problem of protecting information from access by unauthorized persons.

There are many ways to protect information. To protect information from intruders from outside the firewalls are installed. To encrypt information a cryptography methods are used. Currently, the so-called steganography methods are becoming increasingly popular, which allow you to embed the necessary information into the "body" of open information.

All methods for protecting information for communication networks use methods of cryptography and steganography (Hedieh, 2012; Yahya, 2019; Schneier, 1996; Abawajy, Mukherjea, Thampi, & Ruiz-Martínez, 2015). At the present time, steganography is gaining in popularity, because it combines cryptographic methods that are implemented together with a message in the stegocontainer. In this regard, steganography is more resistant to breaking the attacker (Hegarty, & Keane, 2018; Kumar, 2019; Blokdyk, 2019).

The classic task of steganography is to organize the transmission of a secret message so that not only the content of the message, but the very fact of its transmission were hidden from all except the intended ("legitimate") recipient. This task is usually solved by embedding a secret message in some other message, called a container, the contents and the fact of transmission which can not cause any suspicion.

STEGANOGRAPHIC PROTECTION OF INFORMATION ON THE BASIS OF CONTAINERS OF VARIOUS FORMATS

Currently, there are many methods of steganography. The earliest example of protection using steganography methods is reading the text from a pattern, when a secret pattern (key) with cutouts for individual letters is superimposed on a plain text sheet and cut-down text is readable.

With the development of the information society, the steganography methods have spread by leaps and bounds into the digital realm. The variety of methods of digital steganography is determined by the variety of types of information presentation and ways to embed information in a digital container. In addition to this, the following fundamental condition must be observed: the information being introduced must not violate the integrity of the data in the initial container.

The following container variants are available:

- The container is generated by the stegosystem itself. An example is a program in which a Mandelbrot fractal is generated as a container for embedding a message (Sprott, 2019; Shehab, 2012; Dewangan, Sharma, & Bera, 2015). Such an approach can be called constructive steganography.
- The container is selected from a set of containers. In this case, a large number of alternative containers is generated to then select the most suitable for hiding of the message. This approach can be called selective steganography. In this case, when selecting the optimal container from the set of generated, the most important requirement is the nature of the container. The only problem remains that even an optimally organized container allows to hide a small amount of data at a very large volume of the container itself.

- The container comes from the outside of system. In this case, there is no possibility to select a container and to hide the message, the first container that is caught is not always appropriate to the embedded message. Such steganography is called non-alternative.

Such containers are of limited size. However, a stream container can be selected which is a continuously generated bit sequence.

The message is embedded in it in real time, so it's not known in advance in the encoder whether the container's size will be enough to transmit the entire message. In one large container can be embedded and several messages. The intervals between the embedded bits are determined by a pseudorandom sequence generator with a uniform distribution of intervals between the reference values.

The main difficulty is the implementation of synchronization, determining the beginning and end of the sequence. If these containers have bits of synchronization, packet headers, etc., then the concealed information can go immediately after them. The complexity of providing synchronization turns into an advantage in terms of ensuring the secrecy of the transmission. In addition, the stream container is of great practical importance, for example, a stego prefix to the usual phone. Under the cover of the usual insignificant telephone conversation, it would be possible to transfer another conversation, data, etc., and without knowing the secret key, it would be possible not only to know the content of the latent transmission, but also the very fact of its existence. It is not by chance that works devoted to the development of stegosystems with the flow container practically do not occur.

In a fixed container, sizes and characteristics are known in advance. This allows to attach data optimally in some way. In this paper, we will consider mainly fixed containers (hereinafter - containers).

Embedding a message in a container can be made using a key, one or more. The key is a pseudorandom sequence (PRS) of bits generated by a generator that meets certain requirements (a cryptographic safe generator).

For example, a linear recursive register can be used as a base generator (Bilan, 2017; Schneier. 1996). The recipient can then be informed of the initial filling of this register. The numbers generated by the PRS generator can determine the positions of counting points that the modifying, in the case of a fixed container, or the intervals between them in the case of a stream container. It should be noted that the method of random selection of the value of the interval between embedded bits is not particularly pleasant. There are two reasons for this. First, the hidden data must be distributed throughout the image. Therefore, the uniform distribution of the lengths of the intervals (from the smallest to the largest) can be achieved only approximately, because we must be sure that the message is embedded, that is, "fit" into the container. Second, the lengths of the intervals between the noise samples are not distributed uniformly, but according to the exponential law. The generator of PRS with exponentially distributed intervals is complex in realization.

STEGANOGRAPHIC HIDING OF A MESSAGE ON THE BASIS OF CONTAINERS PRESENTED BY A GRAPHIC FORMAT FILE

The introduction of a message in a container represented by a graphic file is to replace the selected bits in the bytes of the graphic file. Moreover, such a replacement should not lead to visual distortions of the images represented by the graphic format. If, as a result of hiding information, there is a distortion of the image or sound, etc., then such an algorithm is unacceptable for steganographic protection of messages.

Consider the effect of an embedded message in a container represented by a graphic file. For this purpose, an algorithm is used, a real implementation of the procedure for passing a home file to a graphic file into bits, which are chosen by the algorithm developer in an arbitrary order.

The procedure for introducing a message is as follows.

The selected graphic file for writing is opened (Figure 1). Each cell in the image displays the byte. Inside the cell, the number of bytes in the file is recorded. Bytes from the first to 311st remain unchanged. They have the service information for the file and the beginning of the picture.

From the 312th to the 314th position in the file are written characters («`», «+», «m»), indicating that the picture contains an encrypted message. The specified characters can be changed during the development stage of the program.

Beginning from the 317th position records the number of characters in the message. Under the number of characters, 4 bytes are selected from 317 to 320. Theoretically, if the file size allows, then you can write messages of 9999 characters. Maximum file size must be at least 339+9999*5*8+5=400304 bytes.

Sequentially lines of text of the message are read. Each bit of each byte of the message is written in every 2nd bit of each 5th byte of the graphic file, starting from 339th byte, with the back of the front. The numbering of bits in a byte is considered from right to left and starts from scratch. For example, the letter "a" consists of the following bits 11100000. The eighth bit is 1 and they will be replaced by the second bit of the 339th byte, the seventh bit equal to 1, and they will be replaced by the second bit of the 344th byte, the sixth bit is equal to 1, and they will be replaced by the second bit of the 349th byte, the fifth bit is 0 and they will be replaced by the second bit of the 354th byte, the fourth bit is 0 and they will be replaced by the second bit of the 359th byte, etc.

From the 321-byte password is written with an interval of 5 positions each character. So the password can be written in 321, 326, 331, etc. In Figure 1, "y" is the first character of the password, "y_1" is the second character of the password, etc.

The 316th byte records the number of characters in the password (in Figure 1, "x" is the number of characters in the password). The file is closed.

The procedure for extracting messages from a graphic container file is as follows.

The selected graphic file to read is opened.

Of the 312th byte of the file, the characters are read that indicate that the image contains an encrypted message. If they are present, then the procedure continues, otherwise the graphic file is closed and a message is displayed that this picture does not contain a message of the appropriate format.

Figure 1. Byte structure of the graphic file

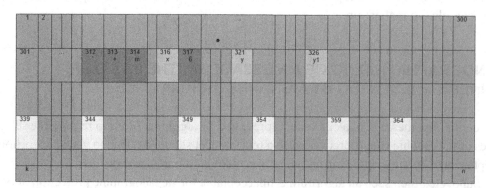

From 321 byte, a password is read at intervals of 5 positions each character. If the password coincides, then the procedure continues, otherwise the graphic file closes and a message is displayed that the password is incorrect.

From the 317th byte the number of characters in the message is read.

Starting from the 339th position of the graphical file, are read bytes from the interval into five positions that can be seen as the 2nd bit. From these bits, the characters of the original message are sequentially formed. In this case, due to the encoding format, the rows are inverted, since they are written from end to end. Message is automatically displayed.

This algorithm uses the embedding of information bits in strictly selected positions of the structure of a graphic file. An example of the operation of such an algorithm in Fig. 2 is presented.

Obviously, no significant visual distortion has occurred. This is due to the fact that the container has a large size and resolution. If a small container is used, visual distortion is significant (Fig. 3).

Analysis of the figure suggests that it is necessary to search for new methods that would allow an increase in the volume of a text message with insignificant container volumes.

ACTUALITY OF THE PROBLEM

The simplest method of steganography is the method of replacing the least significant bit in the codes of individual elements of the container, i.e. LSB method (Albdour, 2018). The LSB method allows to

Figure 2. An example of embedding a text message in a graphic file using the specified algorithm

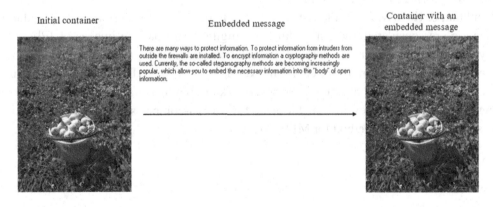

Figure 3. An example of embedding a text message in small containers

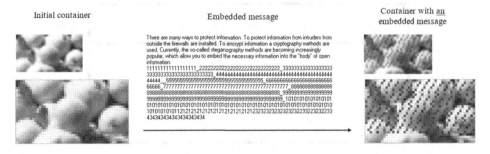

embed a message without visual distortion of the image itself. However, the dimension of the container limits the volume of the injected message. To increase the volume of the embedded message, you need to increase the size of the container. Also, with the total replacement of the low-order bit, the integrity of the image files of containers is violated, which include such types of graphic formats as: jpeg, mp3, avi, etc. The solution in this situation is to replace the low-order bit in the information part of the container. The service part is left unchanged. An illustration of the method in Fig. 4 is shown.

However, this method is only acceptable for graphic type containers and audio. For video files, this method presents certain difficulties due to the large number of video codecs and, therefore, a large number of video container formats, in which there is no clear boundary between service and information blocks.

In addition, it is impossible to embed large amounts of information in a graphic or audio container due to their relatively small size.

For example, a large container is required to embed audio information. Such a container can be a video file (for example, a movie) encoded using a specific codec. It would seem easier to embed the necessary information in an uncompressed video file, i.e., created without the use of codecs. However, storing large amounts of uncompressed video information leads to certain thoughts. Therefore, the task of introducing sound information into a compressed video file is quite relevant today.

REVIEW OF EXISTING DECISIONS ON THE USE OF CONTAINERS PRESENTED BY VIDEO FILES

There are a large number of video file formats. Despite this, in practice, MPEG-2 and MPEG-4 formats are used to hide information (Modenova, 2010).

In (Shelukhin, & Kanaev, 2017) the issues of introducing a digital watermark using scalar and vector quantization are considered, the embedding of a digital watermark in images of JPEG and JPEG 2000 lossy compression formats is analyzed. Correlation methods for embedding watermarks in the MPEG coefficients are considered, as well as embedding by modifying DC coefficients, evaluating the effectiveness of the embedding algorithm for watermarks in the bit domain is analyzed. A method of embedding information at the level of the bit plane for MPEG-compressed data is also proposed. This method is similar to the LSB method for MPEG formats.

Figure 4. The structure of the container, represented by a file of graphic format

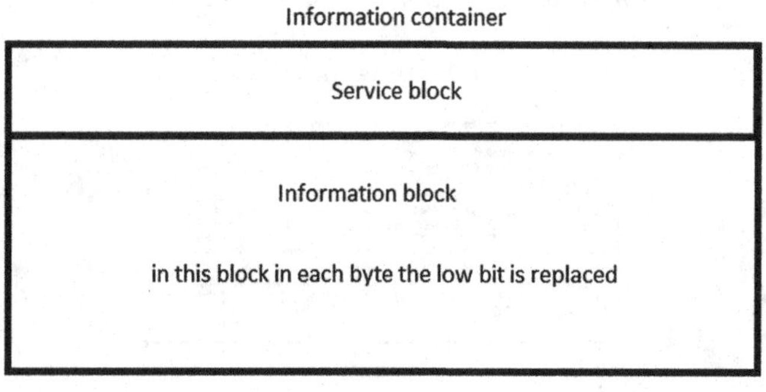

Information container

Service block
Information block in this block in each byte the low bit is replaced

In paper (Gribunin, Okov, & Turiptsev, 2002) describes three ways to embed information in MPEG-2 files: embedding at the level of coefficients, at the level of the bit plane and due to the energy difference between the coefficients.

FORMULATION OF THE PROBLEM

Currently, the objective is to conceal the transfer of large amounts of information using steganographic methods. In modern digital transmission systems, files of various formats are mainly transmitted. At the same time, graphic and audio files have large volumes. In order to hide a large file, a container file is also used, which should be larger than the file being injected. Therefore, the most appropriate file as a container can be an AVI file. Therefore, the task is to embed a sound file with the ability to extract a specific file format. The video file after the audio file is inserted into it must be played in the video player as well as before embedding. When embedded, the sound file can be encrypted using the key or without it.

THE METHOD OF STEGANOGRAPHIC PROTECTION OF AUDIO DATA USING THE VIDEO CONTAINER

The paper proposes a method for embedding data into a container, which is represented by an "AVI" file. This format is used to display changes over time. This format displays movement over time. The hidden data are audio data, represented by files of graphic formats. There may be data represented by files of other formats. There are no fundamental differences for the representation of the method, the hidden data does not have to, since the data being introduced was represented as a sequence of bits. The method was developed on the basis of a large amount of experimental research of file of video formats that are used to represent video.

For research of method, the following initial data are used.

1. Sound file of any format. The size of this file is limited by the ability to encrypt it into a video file.
2. "Avi" format video file created (encoded) using the MicrosoftVideo codec by Camtasia Studio 9. This program is very popular for creating videos.

To study the structure was created several files with the extension "avi". The first video was recorded in the size of 200 × 124 of white color with a duration of 8 seconds. Then, byte-by-by-by-one viewing of the specified video file through the text editor Notepad ++, repeated blocks with the same beginning and several variants of endings were identified. An example of a block of the first type in Fig. 5 is shown.

The SOH symbol is displayed as # 1, the NULL symbol is displayed as # 0. The JUNKк#1#0#0 segment is the beginning, the 01wb symbol is the end of the block. The content of this type of blocks is 490 bytes.

Then an attempt was made to write random symbols inside these blocks and after that it was noticed that the video itself (image and sound) did not affect the recording of symbols in these blocks.

Then, having walked around the entire video file in a text editor, blocks were found, whose beginnings differ only in the character between JUNK and #1#0#0, as well as 4 types of endings: 00dc, 01wb,

Figure 5. Example of the first type block

```
JUNKkSOHNULNULᴚᴚᴚᴚᴚᴚᴚᴚᴚᴚᴚᴚᴚᴚᴚᴚᴚᴚᴚᴚᴚᴚᴚᴚᴚᴚᴚᴚᴚᴚᴚᴚᴚᴚᴚᴚᴚᴚᴚᴚᴚᴚᴚᴚᴚᴚᴚᴚᴚᴚᴚᴚᴚᴚᴚᴚᴚᴚᴚᴚᴚᴚᴚᴚᴚ
ᴚᴚᴚᴚᴚᴚᴚᴚᴚᴚᴚᴚᴚᴚᴚᴚᴚᴚᴚᴚᴚᴚᴚᴚᴚᴚᴚᴚᴚᴚᴚᴚᴚᴚᴚᴚᴚᴚᴚᴚᴚᴚᴚᴚᴚᴚᴚᴚᴚᴚᴚᴚᴚᴚᴚᴚᴚᴚᴚᴚᴚᴚᴚᴚᴚᴚᴚᴚᴚᴚᴚᴚᴚᴚᴚ
ᴚᴚᴚᴚᴚᴚᴚᴚᴚᴚᴚᴚᴚᴚᴚᴚᴚᴚᴚᴚᴚᴚᴚᴚᴚᴚᴚᴚᴚᴚᴚᴚᴚᴚᴚᴚᴚᴚᴚᴚᴚᴚᴚᴚᴚᴚᴚᴚᴚᴚᴚᴚᴚᴚᴚᴚᴚᴚᴚᴚᴚᴚᴚᴚᴚᴚᴚᴚᴚᴚᴚᴚᴚᴚᴚ
ᴚᴚᴚᴚᴚᴚᴚᴚᴚᴚᴚᴚᴚᴚᴚᴚᴚᴚᴚᴚᴚᴚᴚᴚᴚᴚᴚᴚᴚᴚᴚᴚᴚᴚᴚᴚᴚᴚᴚᴚᴚᴚᴚᴚᴚᴚᴚᴚᴚᴚᴚᴚᴚᴚᴚᴚᴚᴚᴚᴚᴚᴚᴚᴚᴚᴚᴚᴚᴚᴚᴚᴚᴚᴚᴚ
ᴚᴚᴚᴚᴚᴚᴚᴚᴚᴚᴚᴚᴚᴚᴚᴚᴚᴚᴚᴚᴚᴚᴚᴚᴚᴚᴚᴚᴚᴚᴚᴚᴚᴚᴚᴚᴚᴚᴚᴚᴚᴚᴚᴚᴚᴚᴚᴚᴚᴚᴚᴚᴚᴚᴚᴚᴚᴚᴚᴚᴚᴚᴚᴚᴚᴚᴚᴚᴚᴚᴚᴚᴚᴚᴚ
ᴚᴚᴚᴚᴚᴚᴚᴚᴚᴚᴚᴚᴚᴚᴚᴚᴚᴚᴚᴚᴚᴚᴚᴚᴚᴚᴚᴚᴚᴚᴚᴚᴚᴚᴚᴚᴚᴚᴚᴚᴚᴚᴚᴚᴚᴚᴚᴚᴚᴚᴚᴚᴚᴚᴚᴚᴚᴚᴚᴚᴚᴚᴚᴚᴚᴚᴚᴚᴚᴚᴚᴚᴚᴚ01wb
```

Figure 6. Example of a fragment of additional blocks of the second type

```
JUNK2NULNULNULNULNULNULNULNULNULNULNULNULNULNULNULNULNULNULNULNULNULNULNULNULNULNULNUL
NULNULNULNULNULNULNULNULNULNULNULNULNULNULNULNULNULNULNULNULNULNULNULNULNULNUL00dc
```

00db, idx1. An experiment was conducted to replace the contents of all blocks with random characters. The beginning was taken on a pattern JUNKɷ#1#0#0 (ɷ – any character), ending - the closest one found 00dc, 01wb, 00db, idx1. The result of the experiment was positive, i.e. the introduction of arbitrary characters into these blocks did not affect the playback of the video file.

In the process of further research, as well as with the additional search for the combination of JUNK symbols, another type of repeating blocks having the beginning of JUNK2 and the endings 00dc, 01wb, 00db.

An example of a fragment of additional blocks of the second type in Fig. 6 is shown.

JUNK2 segment is the beginning, 00dc segment - the end of the block.

The content of the blocks is 53 bytes. An attempt was made to write random symbols inside these blocks and after that it was noticed that the recording of symbols in these blocks did not affect the video itself (image and sound).

The calculation of the content of all the found blocks of this video produced the result: 134623 bytes, which means the ability to record information in 134623 bytes.

From the above, conclusions were drawn:

- Any characters can replace the contents of the blocks (containers) without affecting the image and sound of the video.
- Blocks of the first type have approximately eight times more capacity than blocks of the second type (490 bytes and 53 bytes).
- Blocks of the second type are more common than blocks of the first type.

Further studies were devoted to the influence of the following video file parameters on the video container capacity, i.e. the amount of information that can be embedded in the video container:

- Color saturation;
- Video file resolution;
- Video file duration;
- Compression quality;

- Amount of frames per second.

To study the effect of color saturation on the video container capacity, video files were taken with a white frame and a color frame with a resolution of 640x480 pixels, 5 and 15 seconds long, the number of frames per second equal to 30, compression quality 75. The research results are summarized in table 1.

Analysis of the data in Table 1 allows to conclude that the color saturation of the frames significantly affects the capacity of the video container. The more colors in the frame, the less information it is possible to embed in this video container.

To study the effect of the duration of the video container and the resolution of capacity, video files with a resolution of 320x240, 640x480 and 1024x768 pixels, a duration of 5, 10, 15 and 20 seconds, frames per second equal to 30, compression quality of 50% and 75% were used. The research results are summarized in table 2.

According to Table 2, were constructed graphs of the dependence of the capacity of the video container on the duration at different resolutions. Graph of embedding capacity versus video container duration for compression quality of 50% at resolutions of 320x240, 640x480 and 1024x768 pixels in fig. 7 is shown.

A plot of embedding capacity versus video container duration for a compression quality of 75% at resolutions of 320x240, 640x480 and 1024x768 pixels in fig. 8 is shown.

Analyzing the data of table 2 and graphs fig. 7 and fig. 8 we can draw the following conclusions:

- As the duration of the video file increases, the embedding capacity of the video container varies slightly in percentage terms and fluctuates around a certain value, and for a resolution of 1024x768 it is almost constant;
- With increasing video file resolution, the embedding capacity of the video container decreases in percentage terms. The plot of container embedding capacity versus video file resolution for compression quality of 50% in fig. 9 is shown. The plot of container embedding capacity versus video file resolution for compression quality of 75% in fig. 10 is shown.
- Increasing the quality of compression significantly reduces the embedding capacity of the video container (see Fig. 7, 8 and Fig. 9,10).

The effect of the number of frames per second on the embedding capacity of the video container was examined on video files with a resolution of 320x240, 640x480 and 1024x768, with a duration of 5 and 20 seconds and the number of frames per second equal to 30 and 15. The results of this effect are summarized in table 3.

Table 1. Table of the effect of the color saturation of the video container on capacity

Chromaticity	Duration, seconds	Amount Frames per Second	Compression Quality, %	Volume of Video Container, Kb	Capacity, bytes	Capacity, %
white	5	30	75	469	75788	16,1
color	5	30	75	8091	57685	0,7
white	15	30	75	1070	232843	21,7
color	15	30	75	30342	130197	0,4

Table 2. Table of dependence of video container capacity on duration

Resolution, pixels	Duration, seconds	Amount Frames per Second	Compression Quality, %	Capacity, bytes	Embedding Capacity, bytes	Embedding Capacity, %
• 320x240	• 5	• 30	• 50	• 473088	• 71540	• 15,1
• 320x240	• 5	• 30	• 75	• 3856896	• 24669	• 0,6
• 320x240	• 10	• 30	• 50	• 996864	• 148991	• 14,9
• 320x240	• 10	• 30	• 75	• 8508928	• 52960	• 0,6
• 320x240	• 15	• 30	• 50	• 1591808	• 224710	• 14,1
• 320x240	• 15	• 30	• 75	• 12689408	• 63815	• 0,5
• 320x240	• 20	• 30	• 50	• 1993216	• 302849	• 15,2
• 320x240	• 20	• 30	• 75	• 15200768	• 98084	• 0,6
• 640x480	• 5	• 30	• 50	• 698368	• 52991	• 7,6
• 640x480	• 5	• 30	• 75	• 8285184	• 57685	• 0,7
• 640x480	• 10	• 30	• 50	• 2589184	• 56444	• 2,2
• 640x480	• 10	• 30	• 75	• 20551168	• 92236	• 0,4
• 640x480	• 15	• 30	• 50	• 4535296	• 91791	• 2,0
• 640x480	• 15	• 30	• 75	• 31070720	• 130197	• 0,4
• 640x480	• 20	• 30	• 50	• 5797888	• 151625	• 2,6
• 640x480	• 20	• 30	• 75	• 37263360	• 179237	• 0,5
• 1024x768	• 5	• 30	• 50	• 4173824	• 61090	• 1,5
• 1024x768	• 5	• 30	• 75	• 20135936	• 48134	• 0,2
• 1024x768	• 10	• 30	• 50	• 7370752	• 122710	• 1,7
• 1024x768	• 10	• 30	• 75	• 39453696	• 88823	• 0,2
• 1024x768	• 15	• 30	• 50	• 9732608	• 181802	• 1,9
• 1024x768	• 15	• 30	• 75	• 57396224	• 126231	• 0,2
• 1024x768	• 20	• 30	• 50	• 12184576	• 241418	• 2,0
• 1024x768	• 20	• 30	• 75	• 69048320	• 142973	• 0,2

Figure 7. A plot of embedding capacity versus video container duration for compression quality of 50% at resolutions of 320x240, 640x480 and 1024x768 pixels

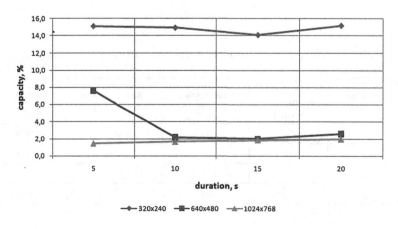

Figure 8. A plot of embedding capacity versus video container duration for a compression quality of 75% at resolutions of 320x240, 640x480 and 1024x768 pixels

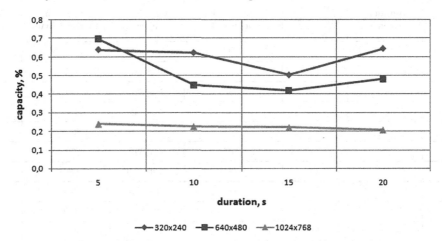

Figure 9. A plot of container embedding capacity versus video file resolution for a compression quality of 50%

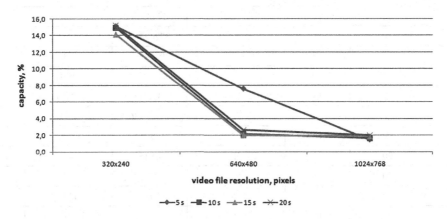

Figure 10. Graph of container embedding capacity versus video file resolution for compression quality of 75%

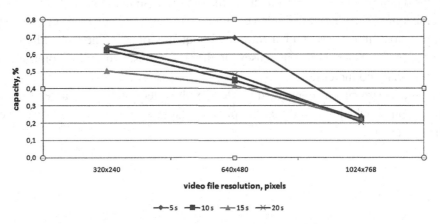

Table 3. Table of dependence of video container embedding capacity on the number of frames per second

Resolution, pixels	Duration, seconds	Amount Frames per Second	Compression Quality, %	Capacity, bytes	Embedding Capacity, bytes	Embedding Capacity, %
320x240	5	30	50	473088	71540	15,1
320x240	5	15	50	435200	38243	8,8
320x240	5	30	75	3856896	24669	0,6
320x240	5	15	75	2139648	13625	0,6
320x240	20	30	50	1993216	302849	15,2
320x240	20	15	50	1848320	159743	8,6
320x240	20	30	75	15200768	98084	0,6
320x240	20	15	75	8157696	76692	0,9
640x480	5	30	50	698368	52991	7,6
640x480	5	15	50	572928	29478	5,1
640x480	5	30	75	8285184	57685	0,7
640x480	5	15	75	4318720	31760	0,7
640x480	20	30	50	5797888	151625	2,6
640x480	20	15	50	5433344	98993	1,8
640x480	20	30	75	37263360	179237	0,5
640x480	20	15	75	20226560	105349	0,5
1024x768	5	30	50	4173824	61090	1,5
1024x768	5	15	50	3458560	33597	1,0
1024x768	5	30	75	20135936	48134	0,2
1024x768	5	15	75	11142144	17571	0,2
1024x768	20	30	50	12184576	241418	2,0
1024x768	20	15	50	10756608	129963	1,2
1024x768	20	30	75	69048320	142973	0,2
1024x768	20	15	75	37903872	79447	0,2

Analyzing the data of table 3, we can conclude that an increase in the number of frames per second increases the embedding capacity of the video container. However, this increase greatly depends on the quality of compression. In this case, with a compression quality of 50%, the embedding capacity of the video container in terms of percentage increases by almost 2 times, and with a compression quality of 75%, there is practically no increase.

In addition, an experiment was conducted to identify the effect on the container embedding capacity of a key frame pitch, which showed that the pitch of the key frame does not affect the embedding capacity of the container.

ALGORITHM FOR EMBEDDE AND EXTRACT OF AUDIO FILE IN A CONTAINER PRESENTED BY AN "AVI" VIDEO FILE

The algorithm for embedding and extracting an audio file (secret information) is in the following steps.

1. The search for the total number of blocks of the first and second type, in which it is possible to record information.
2. The total number of bytes to recording is counted.
3. The capacity of the audio file in this container is estimated, i.e. the size of the audio file and the area to record is compared. It should be noted here that the embedding capacity depends on the write algorithm. For example, if the implementation is conducted only by replacing the zero (low) bit, then one bit of the container accounts for one bit of the source file. Consequently, the capacity decreases eight times. If the introduction is carried out in two low bits, then the embedding capacity is reduced four times. If embedded in all bits (which significantly reduces the security of information), then the embedding capacity is equal to the original.
4. The first four bytes are recorded in the length of the encrypted audio file in the binary number system.
5. The audio file is recorded in the video file according to the selected algorithm. A fragment of a container with selected blocks and an indication of the first four bytes, in which the length of the audio file is written in binary form, in Fig. 11 is shown.
6. When decrypting, the first block is searched.
7. In the first four bytes, the size of the embedded sound file is read.
8. Information is read from the container in accordance with the selected implementation algorithm and stored in the appropriate audio format.

Figure 11. A fragment of a container with selected blocks and an indication of the first four bytes, in which the length of the audio file is embedded in binary form

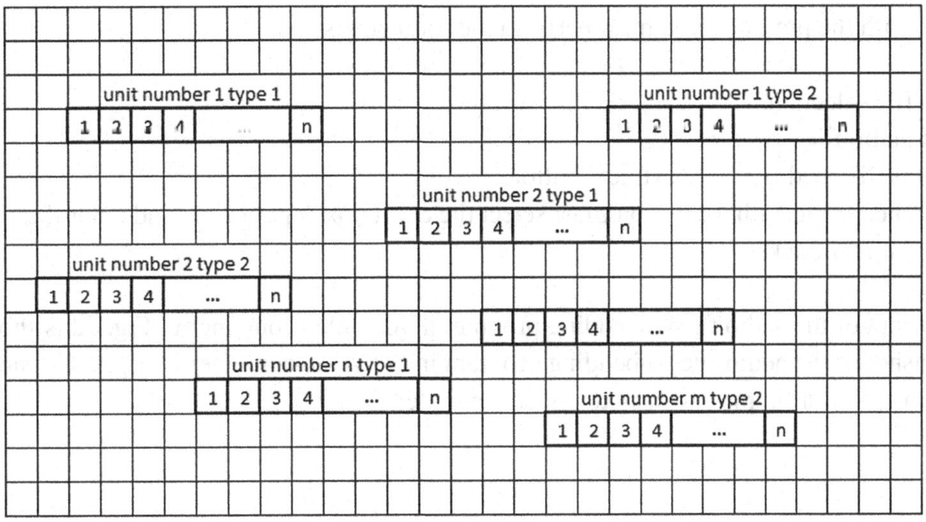

ENCRYPTION AND DECRYPTION WITH KEY

When embedding an audio file into a video container, it is possible to encrypt the embedded information using the key. Encryption is performed by bitwise overlaying the initial information on a random sequence generated by a pseudo-random number generator based on a cellular automaton with the implementation of the local XOR state function (Bilan, Bilan, Motornyuk, Bilan, & Bilan, 2016; Bilan, 2017).

The key is the generator initial data. In the specified generator the initial data are:

1. Blank, which is a text file with a field from 3x3 to 20x20 characters, consisting of zeros and ones;
2. The x and y coordinates of the output cell, i.e. cells from which the next generated bit will be read. The coordinate values start counting from zero and do not exceed the size of the field minus one;
3. The neighborhood of the output cell, which is a text file containing the characters 0 and 1 defining the neighborhood of the main cell (Bilan, 2017);
4. Majority cell count;
5. X and Y coordinates of majority cells in a format similar to the coordinates of the main cell;
6. Neighborhoods of majority cells in a format similar to the neighborhood of the main cell;

The initial data specified in paragraphs 1) and 2) are mandatory for encryption with a key, the rest are optional and are set in options.

Encryption is performed according to the following algorithm: a bit from the generator is superimposed on each bit of the audio file using the XOR operation. The result is recorded in the video file. When decrypting, the initial data of the generator is set, and the generated bits are repeated by the XOR operation superimposed on the bits read from the video container.

PROGRAM IMPLEMENTATION OF THE METHOD

To implement the method, a program was developed that was used to carry out basic research on using the "AVI" format file as a container.

To work with the program, you must perform the following steps.

1. Video file selection.
2. Select audio file.
3. Press the "Embed file" or "Extract" button.
4. When encrypting with a key, you must select the checkbox "apply key" and enter the appropriate initial data for the key.

A screenshot of the audio file embedding program in the video container in Fig. 12 is shown.
A screenshot of the audio file embedding program in the video container in Fig. 13 is shown.
The program has a simple and easy to understand interface.

Figure 12. Screenshot of the audio file embedding program

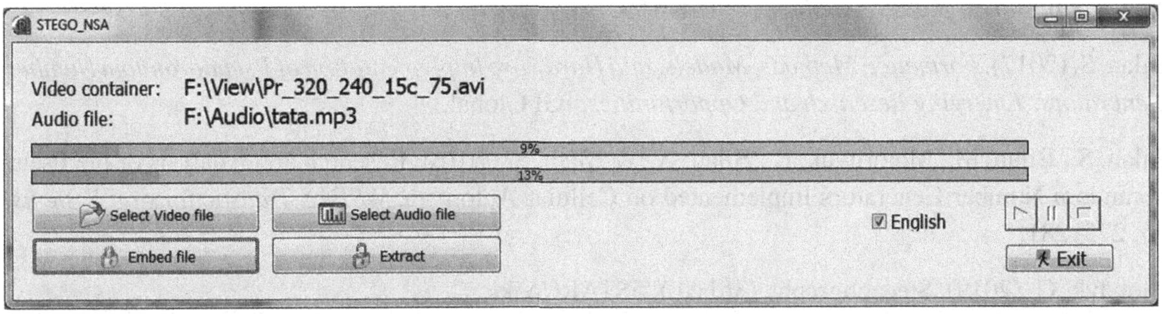

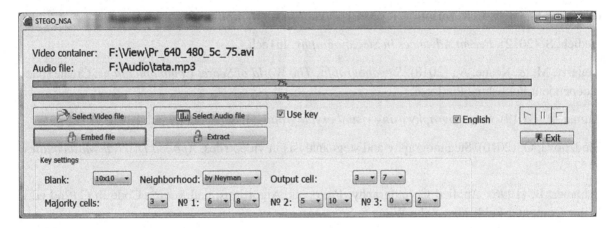

Figure 13. Screenshot of the audio file embedding program in the video container

CONCLUSION

As a result of the work done, the following conclusions can be drawn:

1. In the video container, you can embed an audio file without compromising the integrity of the video file and image quality, as well as without changing the parameters of the video codec.
2. The capacity of the video container in percentage terms depends significantly on the video file parameters, such as color saturation, resolution, compression quality and number of frames per second, and insignificantly on the duration.
3. Only one type of "avi" video file and one type of codec are considered. In the future, we plan to study other types of video containers using other types of codecs.

REFERENCES

Abawajy, J. H., Mukherjea, S., Thampi, S. M., & Ruiz-Martínez, A. (2015). Security in Computing and Communications. *Third International Symposium, SSCC 2015*, Kochi, India.

Albdour, N. (2018). Selection Image Points Method for Steganography Protection of Information. *WSEAS Transactions on Signal Processing*, *14*, 151–159.

Bilan, S. (2017). *Formation Methods, Models, and Hardware Implementation of Pseudorandom Number Generators: Emerging Research and Opportunities*. IGI Global.

Bilan, S., Bilan, M., Motornyuk, R., Bilan, A., & Bilan, S. (2016). Research and Analysis of the Pseudorandom Number Generators Implemented on Cellular Automata. *WSEAS Transactions on Systems*, *15*, 275–281.

Blokdyk, G. (2019). Steganography (3rd ed.). 5STARCooks.

Dewangan, U., Sharma, M., & Bera, S. (2015). *Devlopment and Analysis of Stego Images Using Wavelet Transform*. Lap Lambert Academic Publishing.

Gribunin, V., Okov, I., & Turiptsev, I. (2002). *Digital steganography*. SOLON-Press.

Hedieh, S. (2012). *Recent Advances in Steganography*. InTech.

Hegarty, M., & Keane, A., (2018). *Steganography, The World of Secret Communications*. CreateSpace Independent Publishing Platform.

Kumar, P., (2019). *Steganography using visual cryptography*. Independently published.

Modenova, O. (2010). Steganography and stegoanalysis in video files. *Applied Discrete Mathematics*, *3*, 37–39.

Schneier, B. (1996). Applied Cryptography: Protocols, Algorthms, and Source Code in C (2nd ed.). Wiley Computer Publishing, John Wiley & Sons, Inc.

Shehab, N. (2012). *Toward a New Steganographic Algorithm for Information Hiding: With our algorithm, Wendy should not be able to distinguish in any way between cover-image and stego-image*. LAP LAMBERT Academic Publishing.

Shelukhin, O., & Kanaev, S. (2017). Steganography. Algorithms and software implementation. RiS.

Sprott, J. (2019). Elegant Fractals: Automated Generation of Computer Art: Fractals and Dynamics in Mathematics, Science, and the Arts: Theory and Applications. World Scientific Publishing Company.

Yahya, A. (2019). *Steganography Techniques for Digital Images*. Springer. doi:10.1007/978-3-319-78597-4

Chapter 5
A Secure Iris Biometric Recognition System:
Recent Trends and Solutions

Richa Gupta
University of Delhi, India

Priti Sehgal
University of Delhi, India

ABSTRACT

Security-related issues are creeping in almost every authentication problem. Even the secured systems may be exposed to unknown attacks. While addressing one aspect of security, one tends to forget how vulnerable our system is to other attacks. Therefore, it is necessary to understand the impact of these attacks completely and also to get a vision of the hazard they may put when combined together. In this chapter, the authors focus on two such attacks on iris biometric: replay attack and template attack. They provide a detailed analysis of current research work on each of it individually. The comparative study of solutions to these individual attacks is done with the techniques that aim at combining these two attacks. The authors clearly bring out the advantages of the latter approach, which is the driving force in need for a shift to more innovative ideas.

INTRODUCTION

The rising rate of population is one of the biggest concerns throughout the world. It is not only creating more and more human data, but also paving path to unemployment, poverty, frustration, drug addiction etc., leading to an increase in crime rate. With so many cases of sexual harassment, murders, rapes, scams being reported each day, another challenge that comes along with it, is the concern to correctly authenticate the person. To be able to clearly segregate criminals, intruders from the "good" citizens, the now outdated methods of issuing a unique identification cards like social security number (SSN) in America, social insurance number (SIN) in Canada to individuals are just not enough. The manual verification of these cards/numbers involves human involvement which is easily prone to errors. There can be fake generation of these cards and these are also prone to thefts.

DOI: 10.4018/978-1-7998-1290-6.ch005

Biometric came as a savior by eradicating the necessity of maintaining these cards, yet allowing unique individual identification. Biometric is derived from Greek word which literally means "to measure life". It is not bounded by any sort of physical boundaries and allows inter-disciplinary verification at multiple platforms. Its widespread usage and popularity began surfacing in early 2000's with the inception of generic systems to identify several different biometrics – finger, hand geometry, iris, face, vein etc.

In the past decade, iris biometric has emerged as a powerful and a stable biometric. It is an internal part to the eye, which is formed at the seventh month of gestation and remains stable throughout the life span of an individual. The non-intrusive ways of capturing this biometric over others like fingerprint, palm, makes it easily acceptable. It has been recently deployed in one of the biggest projects of Aadhaar Card in India. Some other applications include its successful deployment in Apple iPhone, for border security in UAE since 2001, Canada's Restricted Area Identity Card (RAIC) for airport staff to get access to restricted area, by Google to control access to their data centers.

So, does it mean that the problem of uniquely identifying the user is solved? The answer is NO. Hackers and impostors always find a way around to crack and fool any system. So is the case with biometrics, hackers hired by Chinese government in 2014 were able to break through the Office of Personnel Management and carried off with fingerprints data of 5.6 million Americans. Researchers have been able to build a 3D model of person's head using photographs. This was able to fool some of the facial recognition tools they tested. Researchers have been able to identify several possible attack points on a biometric system. These attack points can identify various attacks as spoofing attack, replay attack, overriding system, tampering with the feature representation, corrupting the matcher, database attack, channel attack and tampering with final decision. Out of these, most potential attacks on a system are – spoofing and template attack. Replay attack though less explored, has been found to pose a great challenge to the security.

The main objective of this chapter is to provide a detailed analysis of the security issues related to iris biometric. With the focus on addressing one attack, one tends to overlook the threat of other attack at that time. The pitfalls of handling each attack in isolation are explored. The chapter further provides the comparative analysis of existing solutions to handle each attach individually versus solutions to handle multiple attacks together. The chapter is organized as, first the security related issues in case of biometrics are discussed, and then replay attack and template attack is discussed in detail. This is followed by overview of modules of the techniques discussed here for the authentication process of iris biometric. Then the techniques combining solution to replay attack and template attack are reviewed in detail along with the importance they play in the authentication process. Lastly, the accuracy of each combined approach in comparison to other techniques has been presented.

BACKGROUND

Security Issues with Respect to Iris Biometric

Although, biometric is used to ensure correct user authentication, there remain a number of open issues and challenges. Authors discuss these attacks and focus on two of these attacks here. These identified attacks are presented in Figure 1. Ratha et al. (Ratha, Connell, & Bolle, 2001) were first to identify and channelize these attacks on a biometric system

Figure 1. Attack points on a biometric system

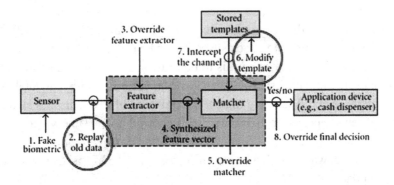

- **Spoofing Attack:** With many advanced devices and technology, it is getting easier to create a dummy of the biometric and use it for authentication. For example, use of artificial eye, textured contact lens, printed head and wax hand. This allows illegal access to the system. Spoofing is the presentation of a fake copy of biometric which has been imitated and made to look real to any biometric system. It is a method by which impostor is able to fool the system and pretend as someone else in an attempt to get access to the system by presenting fake biometric data.
- **Replay Attack:** With open exposure of communication network between sensor and the system, it is very cheap to tap and exploit the biometric data. The impostor can easily overhear the channel and record the data for a correct authentication. Replay attack is playing back of this intercepted data back to the system to gain illegal access.
- **Overriding System:** In this attack, the software of the system can be hacked and overridden with a desired version. This attack is performed by hacking the system, example by using Trojan horse, and producing a feature set which is pre-determined as per the desired specifications.
- **Tampering with Feature Representation:** This attack is possible under the assumption that the matcher and the feature extraction modules are separate. The system is attacked and the feature set of the template is replaced by a fraudulent one.
- **Corrupting the Matcher:** The matching module is attacked and is corrupted to produce desired match results.
- **Database Attack:** Also known as template attack, means getting access to the stored biometric templates from the database. The impostor may steal the template or even replace the template with a spoofed one in order to get access to the system. It has an adverse impact as it compromises the privacy of the user, can be used to generate fake biometrics from it.
- **Channel Attack:** The channel between the database and the matcher is intercepted to change the templates being transferred.
- **Tampering with Final Decision:** The final outcome of the authentication system is hacked to produce desired results. This attack renders the whole authentication system useless as it is capable of producing spoofed results which nullifies the purpose of the authentication system itself.

But, does all these attacks hold equally important? Or, is the probability of some attacks more likely as compared to others. Out of the above eight such attack points identified, spoofing attack, template attack and replay attack are most explored till date.

There have been several attempts of spoofing like, researchers at Germany had been able to spoof hand-vein biometric reader by using a hand made out of wax, 3D printed head had been able to fool facial recognition system at fur of the Android devices - LG G7 ThinQ, a Samsung S9, a Samsung Note 8, and a OnePlus 6. The biggest template attack suspected to be is the theft of user data of Aadhaar card holders in India. Though, UIDAI is claiming this to be refuted, questions are arising at the security of users at such a large scale. In another case, Canadian government is warning that database attack to their fingerprint and face database could severely impact the traveling of residents and also bar the innocent travelers to Canada. A news reported in February 2017, showed a YouTube video of replay attack on biometrics and in the same month, UIDAI filed case against an employee of Suvidhaa Infoserve alleging the use of Axis Bank gateway to UIDAI's server to conduct illegal transactions on 397 biometrics using stored fingerprint data.

Wasn't that scary enough? In an attempt to make the human authentication more accurate, we are paving path to a "new" variety of security-based attacks. These may even be fatal to the privacy of the person. But, that's the truth behind every new development. It takes time for it to reach a maturity level where most of the aspects could be covered to lay a foundation to a well-established and secured system. Funds are been widely released and research is being diligently carried out to find solutions to these attacks. Solutions to spoofing attack and database attack are already available in market and being incorporated into biometric systems. Techniques pertaining to replay attack are few but upcoming in the market. A complete background of replay attack and template attack is provided further.

ATTACKS

Attacks to the biometric system has already been discussed above. This chapter mainly focusses on replay attack and template attack.

Replay Attack

It is defined as the play back of an illegally intercepted data from the interface between the sensor and the system, refer to figure 1. The replay data could be a modified version of the captured template or in its original form. It is usually achieved by substituting the IP packets at the lower layers.

Real World Susceptibility

1. The wide use cloud-based environment requires a diversified use of interfaces. The authentication on such a system can easily fall prey to this attack ("BIOMETRY-MobiComBiom," n.d.)
2. The remote-less key of car for authentication can access the cars from the distance. The data if intercepted could be replay back easily.
3. Online transaction systems are at the threat of this attack. The user detail etc. can be tapped and replayed back to make transactions, example in banking system.

Existing Solutions

Czajka and Pacut (Czajka & Pacut, 2008) proposed the use of randomized iris sectors as a technique to prevent this attack. The aim was to generate a "new" template for each access. To achieve this, they first identify occlusions in iris image. The two iris sectors that are free are selected and converted to strips using Zak-Gabor transform. The coefficients from Zak-Gabor transform are ignored to get the non-reversible iris codes. The iriscodes obtained are further divided into striplets, which are permuted within each stripe to form a new iris template. The advantage of this approach is that, to get original template from the "new" template, permutation key (used for permuting striplets) along with the original template is required. The approach was tested on BIOSBASE and BATH DB1600. Hammerle-Uhl et al. (Hämmerle-Uhl, Raab, & Uhl, 2011) proposed the use of watermarking to allay this attack. Watermarking aims at hiding some identification in biometric template to ascertain the originality and authenticity of the template. They embed the watermark at the sensor side before transmitting the biometric image over the network. In case this data is intercepted, the presence of watermark can be detected and the data be ignored. The major drawback with this approach is that, there is no way to know the time of this transaction, which can lead to replay and accept of watermarked data itself. Shelton et al. (Shelton, Roy, O'Connor, & Dozier, 2014) proposed a genetic algorithm based technique to extract the features from biometric sample. They divide the iris image into variable sized patches, and use LBP to obtain the feature vectors for these patches. They present a non-deterministic approach where a different feature vector is used on each authentication. The results on Casia-Iris-Interval v3 DB reported the accuracy of 98.6%. Smith et al. (Smith, Wiliem, & Lovell, 2015) proposed use of challenge response system on handheld devices to mitigate this attack. They watermark the face video based on the sequence of dynamic reflections from the screen. The verification was done by extracting the features from the reflected region and determining if the reflection matches with the sequence of images used for watermarking. Richa and Priti (Gupta & Sehgal, 2016) tried to overcome the limitation of Hammerele-Uhl (Hämmerle-Uhl et al., 2011) approach by watermarking the iris image with timestamp of transaction along with the sensor ID. They proposed use of reversible watermarking to avoid the decline in accuracy due to watermark. This approach had a limitation that it is not robust against image processing attacks. Richa and Priti (Gupta & Sehgal, 2018b) in another approach proposed concept of robust iris regions in an attempt to mitigate this attack. They proved that not all of the regions are important and contribute effectively to authentication. A selective and carefully chosen subset of these regions is sufficient enough to authenticate the user. They propose a non-deterministic approach using these regions to mitigate this attack. The accuracy on Casia-Iris-Interval v3 is reported to be of 98.14%.

Template Attack

It is defined as an illegal access to the biometric database to get the biometric templates of the potential users, marked in figure 1. The impostor can copy or even replace the templates. This attack compromises the user's privacy and can even generate spoofed biometrics for use in same or different locations.

Real World Susceptibility

1. With wide database for storing the templates, they could be vulnerable at revealing important information like clinical condition of population of a country.
2. The stolen templates can be used to create spoof biometrics to be presented at the system.

Existing Solutions

The template attack has been mainly addressed in three ways – watermarking, biometric cryptosystem and cancelable biometrics. Watermarking as a technique to handle template attack was proposed in early days Biometric Cryptosystem (BC) emerged as a variation over cryptosystem which uses biometric data to generate the key or bind the template with a key (Davida, George I., Frankel, & Matt, 1998; Wu, Qi, Wang, & Zhang, 2008a, 2008b). The former method of BC is known as key-generation method while the latter is termed as key-binding method. The regular or freely available information about the biometric data is stored as part of "helper data". Key-generation scheme works by generating the biometric key using biometric template and helper data. Key-binding scheme involves binding a key to the biometric data and generating a biometric template or "helper-data" from it. Cancelable Biometrics (CB) is quite an effective technique while handling template attack. It works by distorting or transforming the original biometric template. The transforms must be non-reversible and the authentication is carried out in this transform domain itself. The transformed template must be irreversible to ensure the security of the database.

Biometric Cryptosystem (BC)

Zhang et al. (Zhang, Sun, Tan, & Hu, 2009) proposed a "robust key extraction" approach to encode keys into iris. The burst errors in iriscodes are reduced with the help of bit masking. The Reed-Solomon codes along with convolution code was used to extract long keys from iriscodes. The system achieved FRR of 0.52% with key length of 938 bits on undisclosed iris database. Rathgeb and Uhl (C. Rathgeb & Uhl, 2009a) presented a technique of generating cryptographic keys from biometric data using Interval-Mapping techniques. The experiments on Casia-Iris-Interval v3 DB attained an FAR of 0% with FRR of 35.21%. In other approach (Christian Rathgeb & Uhl, 2009), they proposed biometric cryptosystem technique using fuzzy commitment method. They used Hadamard codes and Reed Solomon codes for error correction at bit and block level respectively. The approach was tested on Casia-Iris-Interval v3 DB with FRR of 4.64% at FAR 0%. In yet another approach (C. Rathgeb & Uhl, 2010) they presented a method of bit shuffling in iriscodes as a means to an efficient error correction in Fuzzy Commitment Scheme. They identify the most stable bits in iriscodes and rearrange them to perform error correction decoding. The efficiency was recorded as FRR of 4.92% at FAR of 0% on Casia-Iris-Interval v3 DB. Chauhan and Sharma (Chauhan & Sharma, 2019) presented a fuzzy commitment scheme based on more than one key. The extra key bars the intruder to access the information about biometric. They conduct experiments on left eye images of 70 users from Casia-Iris-Thousand database.

Cancelable Biometrics (CB)

Hammerle-Uhl (Hämmerle-Uhl, Pschernig, & Uhl, 2009) proposed a cancelable biometric generation technique using block re-mapping and texture warping. The experiments on Casia-Iris-Interval v3 DB presented EER of 1.2%. Rathgeb and Uhl (Christian Rathgeb & Uhl, 2010) utilized the variations in local intensity of iris textures to develop iris recognition technique. The revocable biometric template is generated by applying row permutations to the iriscodes. The experiments were conducted on Casia-Iris-Interval v3 DB attaining FRR of 1.978% at FAR 0%. Ouda et al. (Ouda, Tsumura, & Nakaguchi, 2010a) proposed one-factor cancelable biometric method. They extract the non-invertible consistent bits from iriscodes and encode it into a protected BioCode using a random seed. The experiments on Casia-Iris-Interval v3 DB yield FRR of 6.96% at FAR of 0%. Hammerle-Uhl et al. (Hammerle-Uhl, Pschernig, & Uhl, 2013) applied two variants of wavelet transform – parameterized filters and wavelets packets to get the cancelable biometrics. The combination of these two approaches is used at feature extraction phase. The EER of 1.07% was obtained at Casia-Iris-Interval v3 DB. Lee et al. (Sang Hwa & Cho, 2018) proposed cancelable biometric method to template security combining non-invertible transform with biometric salting method. They also define coherent and non-coherent matching regions, and prove that embedding noise in non-coherent regions leads to minimal performance degradation while achieving the non-invertibility of template. The experiments were conducted on ND-iris-0405 database attaining almost 0.0% EER. Randa et al. (Soliman, Banby, et al., 2018)proposed an optical double random phase encoding algorithm for generating the "new" template from the original one. The experiments were conducted on face and iris biometric. The images from the left and right iris of each user were combined from Casia-Iris-Interval v3 database and used for experimentation achieving the best EER of 0.63% and accuracy of 99.75%. In another approach, they (Soliman, Ramadan, et al., 2018b)proposed use of convolution kernels with chaotic maps for generating Gabor features from iris image. The generated features are sensitive to original template and key, but they are robust due to a large key space. The experiments were conducted on Casia-Iris-Interval v3 DB attaining EER of 1.17% and accuracy of 99.08%.

AIM OF CHAPTER

The question is that "is it sufficient enough to handle these attacks in isolation"? Doesn't the future needs to collaborate solutions to multiple attacks under a single roof and get a complete end to end solution.

Issues, Controversies, Problems

With so many solutions available to handle spoofing, it is possible to detect fake iris being presented to the system, but still the system would be prone to database attack. Similarly, a system secured of database attack is not fool proof against replay attack or spoofing. A solution capable of handling these attacks separately, does not always fit together to work collectively For example, a solution to template attack may be using a variation on gabor transforms as a measure to handle this attack, whereas, the solution to handle replay attacks may be working on Local Binary Patterns. In such a scenario, a mutual consent on the iris representation is not achieved, which makes it difficult to collate these two solutions together to get a complete solution.

The complexity, in terms of time, may be very high for combining two solutions. It would require transforming iris from one domain to other thereby putting an extra burden on the system. Hence, rise in the computational cost.

The transformation of information from one representation to another can also lead to a loss in precision, hence a compromise to the accuracy of the system. Summarizing the issues below are-

1.   The solutions might not be compatible
2.   The cost of combining these solutions is far too expensive
3.   There might be a compromise to system accuracy on combining two solutions.

Innovative methods to collectedly handle these attacks is the need for future.

The liveness detection as a measure to detect the spoofing attack is proving to be quite effective. It tracks and checks for some movements in the biometric and bifurcates it from the spoofed one. In other scenario, emphasis is now being laid on "not" storing biometric data at one central device, in an attempt to handle database attacks. Different forms of cryptographic techniques are also being proposed as a solution to database attack.

OVERVIEW OF THE SYSTEM FOR AUTHENTICATING IRIS BIOMETRIC

This section discusses in detail the modules involved in the identification process of iris biometric system. It discusses the method used for representing features of iris biometric and its extraction. This is followed by the module used for feature matching, module that determines the robust iris regions from the iris image and the tools used for measuring the performance of the system.

Feature Representation

The first and most important question as a precursor to any image processing technique is – how to represent the image. It is indeed an important step as the correct representation itself is capable of solving half of the problem. Several techniques like 2D Gabor Wavelets (Daugman, 2009), Gray level co-occurrence matrix (Chen, Huang, & Hsieh, 2009; Patil & Patilkulkarni, 2010), Local Binary Patterns (He, Feng, Hou, Li, & Micheli-Tzanakou, 2011; Sun, Tan, & Qiu, 2006) etc. are used which transform the iris image into some useful data. Further details provide the feature representation technique (Local Binary patterns (LBP)) employed in techniques explored in this chapter.

Local Binary Pattern (LBP)

Motivation to LBP Codes

The motivation behind using LBP codes is that they are – 1) rotation invariant – they do not change with the change in orientation of the eye. This allows to skip the alignment step before extracting features from the eye unlike other approaches like 2D gabor wavelets. 2) Resistant to illumination changes – they are resistant to illumination changes and required no special hardware to capture the images. 3) computational inexpensive – they are faster than other approaches like 2D gabor wavelets and require less of computational time

Average Local Binary Pattern (ALBP) Codes

The texture of an iris image is very rich. It contains a huge lot of data which needs to be tamed properly to get some useful information out of it. Local binary patterns are good at extracting the useful information from an image. Ojala et al. (Ojala, Pietikainen, & Maenpaa, 2002) were first to propose this as a tool for feature extraction. This was later modified by Li et al. (Li, Zhou, & Yuan, 2015) who proposed the concept of averaging the intensity values of the image pixels. This was done so as to normalize the variations in intensity levels of the image. The image is first averaged around the center pixel as given by the equation (1)

$$g_c^{'} = c_{x,y} = \sum_{u=x-1}^{x+1} c_{u,y} + \sum_{v=y-1}^{y+1} c_{x,v} - c_{x,y} \tag{1}$$

where,

$g_c^{'}$ and $c_{x,y}$ is the intensity of center pixel

$c_{u,y}$, $c_{x,v}$ are the intensities of its neighboring pixels

The normalized iris image is divided into 64 non-overlapping, equal sized regions of size 16x32 pixels (Gupta & Sehgal, 2018b) and ALBP thresholding is applied to each with radius $R=4$ and $P=16$ neighbors, given as follows by equation (2):

$$ALBP_{P,R}^{u2} = \sum_{p=0}^{P-1} s\left(g_p - g_c^{'}\right) 2^p, s\left(x\right) = \begin{cases} 1, x \geq 0 \\ 0, x < 0 \end{cases} \tag{2}$$

where, $g_c^{'}$ is as defined by equation (1). g_p is the gray value of neighboring pixels whose co-ordinates are given by

$$\left(x_c + R\cos\frac{2\Pi p}{P}, y_c - R\sin\frac{2\Pi p}{P}\right).$$

This texture information extracted from ALBP thresholding can be generated in two ways for different applications and purposes. The information can be produced such as 1) To get the ALBP threshold itself with no mapping and 2) To get the histograms of the uniform ALBP patterns.

Rep 1: ALBP Thresholding

ALBP thresholding has different parameters while extracting data from the image – no mapping (i), uniform LBP patterns (u2), rotation-invariant LBP (ri), uniform rotation-invariant LBP (riu2). Mapping as 'i' is selected when LBP thresholding is simply required with no filtering of output based on the mappings. 'u2' generates the uniform LBP patterns or codes, which satisfy the uniformity condition of atmost two transitions in a code example 11100001, 00011100. 'riu2' generates the normalized code from uniform patterns by circularly rotating the code to its minimum value. For example, the code 11100011, 11111000, 10001111 corresponds to same LBP code but from different rotations. This is normalized to its minimum value as 00011111. The technique explored in this chapter uses 'i' that is, no mapping variant of ALBP thresholding. The data from this technique is processed to extract useful information out of it.

Rep 2: Histograms of Uniform Patterns

The histogram for the uniform LBP patterns is formed as follows in equation (3) and used further. The histogram contains a bin for each uniform pattern and a separate bin for all non-uniform patterns together.

$$H_n = Hist\left(n\right) = \sum_{i,j} f\left(ALBP_{P,R}^{u2}\left(i,j\right), n\right), n \in \left[0, k\right]$$

$$f\left(x, y\right) = \begin{cases} 1, & x = y \\ 0, & otherwise \end{cases} \tag{3}$$

where, $ALBP_{P,R}^{u2}\left(i,j\right)$ gives LBP code for center pixel at index (i,j).

The feature vector or feature template is formed by concatenating the features of 64 blocks, extracted using any of the above method. This method required a Chi-Square distance matching module for determining robust regions which is discussed in detail in following sub-sections.

Chi-Square Distance: Histogram based Matching

Chi-Square distance χ^2 is a metric popularly known to be used to measure the distance between two histograms. Its name is derived from Pearson's chi-square test statistic which is used for comparing discrete probability distributions for example histograms. The chi-square distance χ^2 between two feature templates that is, histograms is defined as

$$\chi^2\left(FV_a^i, FV_b^j\right) = \sum_{k=1}^{n} \frac{\left(FV_{a,k}^i - FV_{b,k}^j\right)^2}{2 * \left(FV_{a,k}^i + FV_{b,k}^j\right)}, n = 243 \tag{4}$$

where,

FV_a^i and FV_b^j represents feature vector of ith region of iris sample 'a' and j[th] region of iris sample 'b' respectively

n is the total number of histogram bins

Robust Region Determination

The robust regions are identified with the reasoning that not all of the regions are required to authenticate the user. Some of these regions may contain data that do not contribute effectively to iris recognition. These regions can be discarded with an aim to reduce the size of feature set and also to get the randomness in the template. This randomness allows to play with the regions and help mitigate attacks over the system. It allows to randomize the sequence of the regions and achieve non-determinism rather than using a deterministic template for authentication always. As compared to deterministic approach that uses the same set of features for authentication at each access, the non-deterministic approach uses a "new" set of features on each access.

Steps for Identifying Robust Regions

Step 1: Get three images randomly chosen as training images for each user.
Step 2: Compare the histogram generated using Rep 2, of each region of an image with every other region from other images in the training set, using Chi-Square distance.
Step 3: The regions which have minimum chi-square distance with the corresponding counterparts are marked as candidate regions. The score is calculated as follows:

$$Score\left(u^i\right) = \sum_{a=1}^{3} \sum_{b=a+1}^{3} f\left(i\right) \tag{5}$$

where,

$$f\left(i\right) = \begin{cases} 1, & if \ i = j \ and \min\left[\chi^2\left(FV_a^i, FV_b^j\right)\right] where, j = \left[1, 64\right] \\ 0, & otherwise \end{cases}$$

Step 4: The candidate regions attaining a minimum score of 40% of the total comparisons amongst the training set is marked as stable and fit for authentication. This threshold has been experimentally chosen, as if we are stricter, and select 60% as threshold, the experiments showed drastic decrease in number of stable regions was observed whereas no improvement was seen in the performance.

Performance Measures

The performance of the biometric system is measured in terms of False Accept Rate (FAR) and False Reject Rate (FRR). FAR accounts the users that are falsely accepted when actually they don't belong to the system. FRR measures the users that are falsely rejected when actually they belong to the system. The values of these metrics should be close to zero as much as possible. These two are calculated using the values from confusion matrix as follows:

$$FAR = \frac{FP}{FP + TN} \tag{6}$$

$$FRR = \frac{FN}{FN + TP} \tag{7}$$

where, FP is the number of false positives, FN is the number of false negatives, TP is the number of true positives and TN is the number of true negatives.

The crossover point between FAR and FRR is known as Equal Error Rate (EER). This point is important in measuring the performance of the system, as it considers the occurrence of false accepts and false rejects equal, that is, it gives equal weightage to the occurrence of them.

The accuracy of the system defines its efficiency. It is measured in terms FAR and FRR as follows:

$$Accuracy = 100 - \frac{FAR\left(\%\right) + FRR\left(\%\right)}{2} \tag{8}$$

COMBINED SOLUTION TO MITIGATE FUSION OF REPLAY ATTACK AND DATABASE ATTACK

Till recent research, focus had been mainly on tackling the issue related to attacks solely. Efforts in the direction of combining the attacks and presenting a single solution has not been made. Richa and Priti (Gupta & Sehgal, 2018a, 2019) were first to present a solution catering to more than a single attack. A solution of this type, is capable of not only tackling attacks but also providing a multi-facet direction to the future research in this direction.

Advantages

1.   The system is capable of handling more than one attack simultaneously.
2.   Compatibility of different approaches is of no concern as the solution caters to these attacks providing a single solution.
3.   The system accuracy is preserved while getting the solution to multiple attacks.

Referring to figure 1 again, replay attack relates to the interception of interface between the sensor and the system. The database or template attack is the hacking of database containing the biometric templates. The database attack can be mitigated using two approaches – biometric cryptosystem and cancelable biometrics. The section discusses how these two approaches can be used further to mitigate replay attack and database attack simultaneously.

Replay Attack + Biometric Cryptosystem (ReBC)

Biometric cryptosystem (Davida, George I. et al., 1998; Jain, Nandakumar, & Nagar, 2008) is a technique which works by encrypting the biometric data to some unrecognizable form. This has been indeed very popular technique which has been extended to be used for biometric authentication. Biometric templates contain information regarding the biometric identity of the users. Any attack can seriously deteriorate the performance of the system, rather cripple it completely. This can be further subdivided into two techniques – key binding and key generation (Ouda, Tsumura, & Nakaguchi, 2010b). The authors discuss here the mechanism to combine key generation method, which is the solution to alleviate template attack with solution to diminish replay attack. It is an attempt to make the system secure.

Key generation (Davida, George I. et al., 1998; Wu et al., 2008a) is a technique to generate a biometric key from the templates. This key is saved in the database which is `used for user authentication. Richa & Priti (Gupta & Sehgal, 2019) developed a system pertaining to this. The working as presented in figure 2 and summarized here in steps.

- The iris image is pre-processed and features are extracted using ALBP.
- The histograms of extracted features are used to identify the robust iris regions.
- Out of these, 40 regions are randomly identified and selected for each user. This set is used to generate the biometric key which is saved in the database.
- The mean value of each identified region is calculated from the ALBP image using Rep1.
- This mean is normalized to lie in the range [0,7], which is further encoded using Reed-Solomon (RS) codes.
- The generated check bits along with the location of identified 40 best regions in encrypted form is saved in the database as the helper data. This helper data is used at the time of authenticating the user, which is used to handle the variance in biometric data, and assist in key generation.

The non-deterministic approach of authenticating user based on a random selection of identified robust regions assists in mitigating replay attack. On the other hand, the absence of need to save the biometric template directly and rather save key and check bits, helps in mitigating the database attack. The experimental results show acceptable performance, which is marginally less but at the cost of proofing against replay attack and database attack. The generated key achieves an entropy of 57 bits which is good with respect to the length of the key as detailed in (Gupta & Sehgal, 2019).

Figure 2. Working of ReBC based system

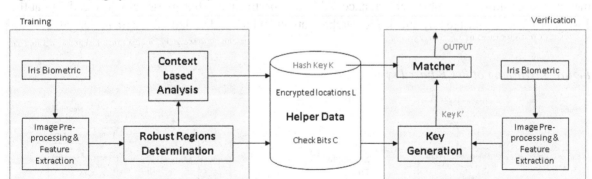

Replay Attack + Cancelable Biometrics (ReCB)

Cancelable biometrics (Gomez-Barrero, Rathgeb, Galbally, Busch, & Fierrez, 2016; Christian Rathgeb, Breitinger, & Busch, 2013; Rudresh, Dey, Singh, & Prasad, 2017) is a technique to generate templates that resemble original template in term of properties but are actually different. This is another popular way to protect the user's identity from being permanently revealed. This does not exactly protect the system against database attack, but in case the database is attacked, a new template can be issued to the user. This new template allows the user to still access the system without any problem. The absence of this technique reveals the original template, which makes it nearly impossible for the user to use that biometric for further authentication. This is further divided into two categories – biometric salting and non-invertible transform. The authors in (Gupta & Sehgal, 2018a) presented the use of non-invertible transform based approach in combination with robust iris regions method to mitigate database attack and replay attack simultaneously.

Non-invertible transform (Lang, 2012) is a method to apply non-linear transformations over the original template, such that it satisfies three important properties – irreversibility, renewability and unlinkability, yet is different from the original template. Richa and Priti (Gupta & Sehgal, 2018a) presented such a system. The working of this system is depicted in figure 3 and summarized here in steps:

- The iris image is pre-processed and features are extracted using ALBP.
- The histograms of extracted features are used to identify the robust iris regions.
- Then, a seed is generated using an application specific key and User ID. This seed is used to generate a random subset of 40 robust regions.
- The histograms of these identified regions are combined to form a feature template (X).
- This template is then transformed using a non-invertible transform as given by equation 9.

$$I\left(X\right) = round\left(\sqrt[k]{X} + X\right) \tag{9}$$

The non-deterministic approach of authenticating user based a random selection of identified robust regions assists in mitigating replay attack. On the other hand, the absence of need to save the biometric template directly and rather save a transformed form, helps in mitigating the database attack. The experimental results show acceptable performance. Although performance has marginally lowered, but at the cost of proofing against replay attack and database attack, which is detailed in (Gupta & Sehgal, 2018a).

Figure 3. Working of ReCB based system

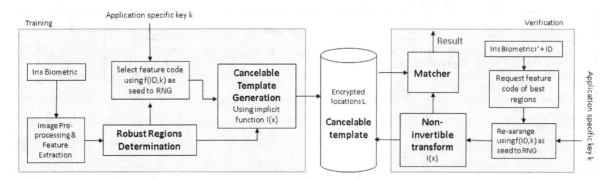

EXPERIMENTAL RESULTS AND DISCUSSIONS

Experimental Setup

The system is tested on two popular and publicly available databases CASIA-Iris-Interval v4 and IIT Delhi. CASIA-Iris-Interval v4 DB, is developed by Chinese Academy of Sciences. It is same as CASIA-Iris-Interval v3, just with the name changed. It is rich in iris texture and widely used for experimentation in researches. The database has been captured using their proprietary close-up iris camera. It is designed using circular NIR LED array, which is capable of capturing very clear iris images. The database has 249 subjects with 2639 images of resolution 3208280 pixels. Since, each eye is considered to be unique, this database can be considered to have 395 subjects with 2639 images. IIT Delhi database is database containing iris images of Indian users, and is developed by Biometrics Research Laboratory at IIT Delhi. The database has been captured using JIRIS, JPC1000 digital CMOS camera. The database contains 2240 images from 224 different users comprising of 176 males and 48 females. Since, each eye is considered to be unique, the database is considered to have 435 subjects with 2240 images.

This database is further pre-processed using OSIRIS v4.1. It is a freeware to support iris recognition. We used this freeware to segment and normalize the iris image. The normalized iris image of 320*480 pixels is obtained and then passed through the proposed approaches. The obtained images are scrutinized for inconsistency and the database is pruned to contain correctly segmented images only. After this step, the CASIA-Iris-Interval DB is said to have 373 subjects with 2376 images, while IIT Delhi DB required no such support and has 435 subjects with 2240 images. These datasets are chosen for experimentation as they are considered to be rich in iris texture. The implementation is carried on system with INTEL core i5-7200U processor with 2.5GHz speed. Matlab 2018a is used as a tool for developing software further.

Comparing System Based on ReBC and ReCB

The results of the system (Gupta & Sehgal, 2019) based on ReBC are compared with the system (Gupta & Sehgal, 2018a) on ReCB. As discussed above, former combines method to mitigate replay attack with biometric key generation method to mitigate template attack while the latter combines the same with cancelable template approach. The results present the ReBC method on different length of messages used for generating the key, while ReCB method presents the results of using different application key being used as a seed for the system. Figure 4 shows the results on CASIA-Iris-Interval DB v4, that ReCB system achieves lower FAR and FRR compared to ReBC system. This graph presents the system performance by clustering the accuracy of ReBC and ReCB and comparing them. The line in red demarcates the two cluster of information. Entire data of ReCB is seen clustered towards lower left side, which corresponds to low FAR and FRR, while for ReBC the data is clustered towards right top which means higher FAR and FRR Similarly, figure 5 presents results on IIT Delhi DB, which marks the similar observation. The lower FAR and FRR values implies that system is performing better with lower acceptance for impostors and lower rejection rate of genuine users which is important to maintain the system equilibrium.

Table 1 and Table 2 presents the FRR and accuracy of the system on CASIA and IITD DB respectively. For comparison the best performing message length and key length data is collected and presented here. The message length for the ReBC system is 82, while the key length of ReCB system is 12. The data is presented at low FAR of 0.1%, which is important to ensure the acceptable working of the system. From the tables, it can be observed that ReCB achieves higher accuracy for both the databases.

Figure 4. Results of Casia-Iris-Interval v4 DB on ReBC and ReCB system

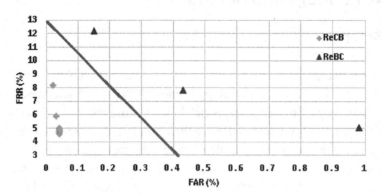

Figure 5. Results of IITD DB on ReBC and ReCB system

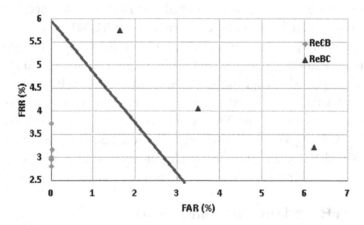

Table 1. System accuracy on Casia-Iris-Interval v4 DB

	FRR (%)	Accuracy (%)
ReBC	12.22	93.81
ReCB	3.14	98.33

Table 2. System accuracy on IITD DB

	FRR (%)	Accuracy (%)
ReBC	5.75	96.3
ReCB	2.96	98.5

Security Aspect

Another important criterion to measure the accuracy of Cancelable Biometrics based system is to ensure that generated "new" template is – irreversible, unlinkable and renewable. Irreversibility – it should not be possible to recover the original template back from the generated "new" template. Unlinkability – the templates from different applications should not be linked up, that is, there should be no cross-matching amongst them. Renewability – it should be possible to generate another "new" template from the original template, in case of any compromises to the system.

Applying the same definition to key on biometric cryptosystem, ReBC system's generated key achieves all three as well. Redefining these definitions pertaining to BC, irreversibility – it should not be possible to get the original template from the generated key. Unlinkability – the two keys generated from different applications should not be linked up, that is, no cross matching should be there. Renewability – it should be possible to generate another "new" key from the original template, in case the earlier one is compromised.

Irreversibility analysis – With respect to ReCB, this is achieved by the use of 1) histograms, which are themselves irreversible in nature, and 2) by use of randomization which further complicates it. With respect to ReBC, this is achieved by use of 1) mean values of each regions, which is non-reversible and 2) by use of randomization to the ordering of these regions which further complicate it.

Unlinkability analysis – With respect to ReCB, this is achieved by the use of 1) application specific key to randomize and select the regions and 2) the same key to transform these templates. The key is different for each application, which ensures that two templates are not linkable. With respect to ReBC, this is achieved by the use of 1) randomization of regions which means a different key which doesn't allow any cross matching.

Renewability analysis – with respect to ReCB, this is achieved by use of different application key (k) to select the order of robust regions and hence a new template. With respect to ReCB, this is again achieved by using a different randomized set of robust regions, and hence a new key.

Comparison with State-of-Art Results

The system based on ReBC and ReCB, based on combining the solution to replay attack and template attack, is compared with the system focusing on only one point of attack. Table 3 and table 4 presents the performance comparison of state-of-art techniques on Casia-Iris-Interval v4 DB and IITD DB respectively. The results reveal not the best performance of the proposed system, but shows comparable results, slight variation but at the cost of increased security.

CONCLUSION

The importance of combining replay attack and database attack has been clearly presented in this chapter. The limitations of individually tackling these attacks show clearly the need to change and present a futuristic solution. The comparative study of the presented approaches has been compared with state-of-art techniques which shows comparable results.

Table 3. Performance comparison with state-of-art techniques for Casia-Iris-Interval v4 DB

Approach	FAR (%)	FRR (%)	Accuracy (%)	EER (%)	Attack Support	Methodology
Shelton et al. (Shelton et al., 2014)	-	-	96.42	-	Replay Attack	Genetic Algorithm
Richa and Priti (Gupta & Sehgal, 2018b)	0.1	2.61	98.63	1.24	Replay Attack	Non-deterministic approach with robust regions
Rathgeb et al. (C. Rathgeb & Uhl, 2009b)	0.07	36.5	-	-	Database Attack	Interval Mapping
Rathgeb et al. (Christian Rathgeb & Uhl, 2009)	0	4.64	-	-	Database Attack	Fuzzy Commitment Scheme
Rathgeb et al. (C. Rathgeb & Uhl, 2010)	0	4.92	-	-	Database Attack	Fuzzy Commitment scheme with bit shuffling
Hammerle-Uhl (Hämmerle-Uhl et al., 2009)	-	-	-	1.2	Database Attack	Block remapping and texture warping
Rathgeb et al. (Christian Rathgeb & Uhl, 2010)	0	1.978	-	1.016	Database Attack	Row permutation
Ouda et al. (Ouda et al., 2010b)	0	6.96	2.3	-	Database Attack	Encoding by use of non-invertible consistent bits
Hammerle et al. (Hammerle-Uhl et al., 2013)-	-	-	-	1.07	Database Attack	Wavelet transform
Rathgeb et al. (Christian Rathgeb et al., 2013)	0	4.64	-	-	Database Attack	Cancelable biometrics using bloom filters
Randa et al. (Soliman, Banby, et al., 2018)	0.5	0	99.75	0.63	Database Attack	Optical double random phase encoding
Randa et al. (Soliman, Ramadan, et al., 2018a)	1.33	0.5	99.08	1.17	Database Attack	Convolution kernels with chaotic map
ReBC	0.9	5.07	97.01	-	Replay + Database Attack	Biometric cryptosystem using RS code
ReCB	0.01	4.95	97.5	1.75	Replay + Database Attack	Cancelable biometrics with non-invertible transform

Table 4. Performance comparison with state-of-art techniques for IITD DB

Approach	FAR (%)	FRR (%)	Accuracy (%)	EER (%)	Attack Support	Methodology
Richa and Priti (Gupta & Sehgal, 2018b)	0.01	3.74	98.12	1.26	Replay Attack	Non-deterministic approach with robust regions
ReBC	1.6	5.75	96.3	-	Replay + Database Attack	Biometric cryptosystem using RS code
ReCB	0.01	2.99	98.5	1.32	Replay + Database Attack	Cancelable biometrics with non-invertible transform

REFERENCES

BIOMETRY-MobiComBiom. (n.d.). Retrieved December 5, 2019, from http://biometry.com/media/downloads/files/BIOMETRY White Paper.pdf

Chauhan, S., & Sharma, A. (2019). Improved fuzzy commitment scheme. *International Journal of Information Technology*.

Chen, W.-S., & Huang, R.-H., & Hsieh, L. (2009). Iris recognition using 3D co-occurrence matrix. In *International Conference on Biometrics* (pp. 1122–1131). Springer.

Czajka, A., & Pacut, A. (2008). Replay attack prevention for iris biometrics. *Proceedings - International Carnahan Conference on Security Technology*, 247–253. 10.1109/CCST.2008.4751309

Daugman, J. (2009). How iris recognition works. In The Essential Guide to Image Processing. Academic Press.

Davida, G. I., Frankel, Y., & Matt, B. J. (1998). On enabling secure applications through off-line biometric identification. In *Proceedings. 1998 IEEE Symposium on Security and Privacy (Cat. No. 98CB36186)* (pp. 148–157). IEEE.

Gomez-Barrero, M., Rathgeb, C., Galbally, J., Busch, C., & Fierrez, J. (2016). Unlinkable and irreversible biometric template protection based on bloom filters. *Information Sciences*, *370*, 18–32. doi:10.1016/j.ins.2016.06.046

Gupta, R., & Sehgal, P. (2016). Mitigating Iris based Replay Attack using Cuckoo Optimized Reversible Watermarking. *Seventh International Conference on Advances in Computing, Control, and Telecommunication Technologies*.

Gupta, R., & Sehgal, P. (2018a). A Non-deterministic Approach to Mitigate Replay Attack and Database Attack Simultaneously on Iris Recognition System. In *International Conference on Intelligent Human Computer Interaction* (pp. 239–250). Springer. 10.1007/978-3-030-04021-5_22

Gupta, R., & Sehgal, P. (2018b). Non-deterministic approach to allay replay attack on iris biometric. *Pattern Analysis & Applications*, 1–13.

Gupta, R., & Sehgal, P. (2019). A Complete End-to-End System for Iris Recognition to Mitigate Replay and Template Attack. In *Soft Computing and Signal Processing* (pp. 571–582). Singapore: Springer. doi:10.1007/978-981-13-3600-3_54

Hämmerle-Uhl, J., Pschernig, E., & Uhl, A. (2009). Cancelable iris biometrics using block re-mapping and image warping. *Information Security. Springer Berlin Heidelberg*, 135–142. doi:10.1007/978-3-642-04474-8_11

Hammerle-Uhl, J., Pschernig, E., & Uhl, A. (2013). Cancelable iris-templates using key-dependent wavelet transforms. In *2013 International Conference on Biometrics (ICB)* (pp. 1–8). IEEE. 10.1109/ICB.2013.6612960

Hämmerle-Uhl, J., Raab, K., & Uhl, A. (2011). Robust watermarking in iris recognition: Application scenarios and impact on recognition performance. *Applied Computing Review*, *11*(3), 6–18. doi:10.1145/2034594.2034595

He, Y., Feng, G., Hou, Y., Li, L., & Micheli-Tzanakou, E. (2011). Iris feature extraction method based on LBP and chunked encoding. In *2011 Seventh International Conference on Natural Computation*, (pp. 1663–1667). IEEE. 10.1109/ICNC.2011.6022302

Hwa, S., L., & Cho, N. I. (2018). Cancelable biometrics using noise embedding. *24th International Conference on Pattern Recognition (ICPR)*. 10.1109/ICPR.2018.8545121

Jain, A. K., Nandakumar, K., & Nagar, A. (2008). Biometric Template Security. *EURASIP Journal on Advances in Signal Processing*, *579416*(1), 579416. doi:10.1155/2008/579416

Lang, S. (2012). *Introduction to Linear Algebra*. Springer Science & Business Media.

Li, C., Zhou, W., & Yuan, S. (2015). Iris recognition based on a novel variation of local binary pattern. *The Visual Computer, Springer*, *31*(10), 1419–1429. doi:10.100700371-014-1023-5

Ojala, T., Pietikainen, M., & Maenpaa, T. (2002). Multiresolution gray-scale and rotation invariant texture classification with local binary patterns. *IEEE Transactions on Pattern Analysis and Machine Intelligence*, *24*(7), 971–987. doi:10.1109/TPAMI.2002.1017623

Ouda, O., Tsumura, N., & Nakaguchi, T. (2010a). Tokenless cancelable biometrics scheme for protecting iriscodes. *Proceedings - International Conference on Pattern Recognition*, (1), 882–885. 10.1109/ICPR.2010.222

Ouda, O., Tsumura, N., & Nakaguchi, T. (2010b). Tokenless cancelable biometrics scheme for protecting iriscodes. *Proceedings - 20th International Conference on Pattern Recognition (ICPR). IEEE*, 882–885. 10.1109/ICPR.2010.222

Patil, C. M., & Patilkulkarni, S. (2010). A comparative study of feature extraction approaches for an efficient iris recognition system. In *International Conference on Business Administration and Information Processing* (pp. 411–416). Springer. 10.1007/978-3-642-12214-9_68

Ratha, N. K., Connell, J. H., & Bolle, R. M. (2001). Enhancing security and privacy in biometrics-based authentication systems. *IBM Systems Journal*, *40*(3), 614–634. doi:10.1147j.403.0614

Rathgeb, C., & Uhl, A. (2009a). An iris-based Interval-Mapping scheme for Biometric Key generation. *2009 Proceedings of 6th International Symposium on Image and Signal Processing and Analysis*, 511–516.

Rathgeb, C., Breitinger, F., & Busch, C. (2013). Alignment free cancelable iris biometric templates based on adaptive bloom filters. In *Biometrics (ICB), 2013 International Conference on* (pp. 1–8). IEEE. 10.1109/ICB.2013.6612976

Rathgeb, C., & Uhl, A. (2009). Systematic construction of iris-based fuzzy commitment schemes. *Advances in Biometrics*, 940–949. doi:10.1007/978-3-642-01793-3_95

Rathgeb, C., & Uhl, A. (2009b). An iris-based Interval-Mapping scheme for Biometric Key generation. *2009 Proceedings of 6th International Symposium on Image and Signal Processing and Analysis*, 511–516.

Rathgeb, C., & Uhl, A. (2010). Adaptive fuzzy commitment scheme based on iris-code error analysis. In *2010 2nd European Workshop on Visual Information Processing (EUVIP)* (pp. 41–44). IEEE. 10.1109/EUVIP.2010.5699103

Rathgeb, C., & Uhl, A. (2010). Secure iris recognition based on local intensity variations. *Image Analysis and Recognition*, 266–275. doi:10.1007/978-3-642-13775-4_27

Rudresh, D., Dey, S., Singh, R., & Prasad, A. (2017). A privacy-preserving cancelable iris template generation scheme using decimal encoding and look-up table mapping. *Computers & Security*, *65*, 373–386. doi:10.1016/j.cose.2016.10.004

Shelton, J., Roy, K., O'Connor, B., & Dozier, G. V. (2014). Mitigating Iris-Based Replay Attacks. *International Journal of Machine Learning and Computing*, *4*(3), 204–209. doi:10.7763/IJMLC.2014.V4.413

Smith, D. F., Wiliem, A., & Lovell, B. C. (2015). Face Recognition on consumer devices: Reflections on replay attack. *IEEE Transactions on Information Forensics and Security*, *10*(4), 736–745. doi:10.1109/TIFS.2015.2398819

Soliman, R. F., El Banby, G. M., Algarni, A. D., Elsheikh, M., Soliman, N. F., Amin, M., & El-Samie, F. E. A. (2018). Double random phase encoding for cancelable face and iris recognition. *Applied Optics*, *57*(35), 10305–10316. doi:10.1364/AO.57.010305 PMID:30645240

Soliman, R. F., Ramadan, N., Amin, M., Ahmed, H. H., El-Khamy, S., & El-Samie, F. E. A. (2018a). Efficient Cancelable Iris Recognition Scheme Based on Modified Logistic Map. In *Proceedings of the National Academy of Sciences, India Section A: Physical Sciences* (pp. 1–7). Academic Press.

Soliman, R. F., Ramadan, N., Amin, M., Ahmed, H. H., El-Khamy, S., & El-Samie, F. E. A. (2018b). Efficient Cancelable Iris Recognition Scheme Based on Modified Logistic Map. In *Proceedings of the National Academy of Sciences, India Section A: Physical Sciences* (pp. 1–7). Academic Press. 10.100740010-018-0555-x

Sun, Z., Tan, T., & Qiu, X. (2006). Graph matching iris image blocks with local binary pattern. In *International Conference on Biometrics* (pp. 366–372). Springer.

Wu, X., Qi, N., Wang, K., & Zhang, D. (2008a). A novel cryptosystem based on iris key generation. *Proceedings - 4th International Conference on Natural Computation*, *4*, 53–56. 10.1109/ICNC.2008.808

Wu, X., Qi, N., Wang, K., & Zhang, D. (2008b). An iris cryptosystem for information security. *Proceedings - 2008 4th International Conference on Intelligent Information Hiding and Multimedia Signal Processing*, 1533–1536. 10.1109/IIH-MSP.2008.83

Zhang, L., Sun, Z., Tan, T., & Hu, S. (2009). Robust biometric key extraction based on iris cryptosystem. *Advances in Biometrics*, 1060–1069. doi:10.1007/978-3-642-01793-3_107

Section 2
Intellectual Data Processing and Information Security in Various Aspects of Human Activity

The chapters that describe research in the field of specific practical applications of modern methods of intelligent data processing and information security in industry and in various specific areas of human activity (banks, space, geographic information systems, ecology, medicine, transport, oil production, etc.) are collected.

Chapter 6

Image Processing and Post-Data Mining Processing for Security in Industrial Applications:
Security in Industry

Alessandro Massaro
https://orcid.org/0000-0003-1744-783X
Dyrecta Lab srl, Italy

Angelo Galiano
Dyrecta Lab srl, Italy

ABSTRACT

The chapter analyzes scientific approaches suitable for industrial security involving environment health monitoring and safety production control. In particular, it discusses data mining algorithms able to add hidden information important for security improvement. In particular k-means and artificial intelligence algorithms are applied in different cases of study by discussing the procedures useful to set the model including image processing and post clustering processing facilities. The chapter is focused on the discussion of information provided by data mining results. The proposed model is matched with different architectures involving different industrial applications such as biometric classification and transport security, railway inspections, video surveillance image processing, and quarry risk evaluation. These architectures refer to specific industry projects. As advanced applications, a clustering analysis approach applied on thermal radiometric images and a dynamic contour extraction process suitable for oil spill monitoring are proposed.

DOI: 10.4018/978-1-7998-1290-6.ch006

. INTRODUCTION: RESEARCH TOPICS AND APPLICATIONS

Image and data processing in security systems are important research topics in different application fields. In order to improve security detection it is important to preliminary study the best requirements referring to a specific case of study. According to this, in this chapter are discussed some cases of industry research projects, by highlighting the data processing algorithms and security procedures. In this framework is analysed the state of the art suggesting the research topics of the proposed projects. Specifically, some works in literature analyses face recognition systems (Massaro et al. 2016) by creating a training dataset by means of synthetic data generated by original ones thus increasing the efficiency of the face recognition algorithm. Face recognition can be applied in different security applications involving different hardware and technologies, including mobile devices (Galiano et al. 2017). Another interesting research topic is the video surveillance processing and optimization, where a critical aspect is the edge detection of a body in motion which can be affected by different aspects such as hardware sensitivity and environment noise (Massaro, Vitti et al. 2018). In transport sector security and monitoring can be improved by (i) predictive maintenance, (ii) by data mining algorithms supporting fleet management (Siddharth et al. 2013), by the prediction of faults (Fan et al. 2015), and (iii) by efficient video surveillance systems (Xu et al. 2011). Concerning railway infrastructure, reliability, availability, maintainability and Safety –RAMS- algorithm could provide security efforts (Park 2013) by means of implementation of defined procedures (Simões 2008). In this last case, also the adoption of technologies such as Ground Penetrating Radar –GPR- monitoring ballast (Zhang 2015), and laser scanner controlling rail surface defects (Xiong 2017) can optimize inspections thus improving monitoring procedures. In this direction data mining could play an important function in the optimization of maintenance procedures (Bastos et al. 2014). In particular Artificial Neural Network –ANN- can be useful to model repairable systems (Rajpal et al. 2006) thus contributing to the intelligent scheduling of maintenances operations. Concerning quarry monitoring systems, Unmanned Aerial Vehicle -UAVs- technologies, combined with reconstruction of topography techniques (Rossi et al. 2017), represent an important way to control the quarry work evolution and consecutively the unsafe areas. By means of the UAVs it is possible the engineering of the risk assessment and of management procedures (Salvini et al. 2017). In all production line processes, image vision techniques can support the risk analysis by automating and integrating a wide range of processes and representations used for defect vision perception (Tushar et al. 2013). The image vision is suitable also for crack detection (Qiao et al. 2013) in quarry conveyor belt. Technology upgrading, RAMS and data mining algorithms can be adopted together for inspections and monitoring applications including quarry machine monitoring.

Other image processing techniques as active contour snake approach, can be applied for data post processing risk verification for oil spill detection (Massaro et al. 2012) and for underground water leakage. Thermography is another technique useful for non-destructive testing of components (Ciampa et al. 2018), thus achieving accurate analysis of thermal risks. In order to find hidden information or to highlight defects and anomalies can be applied the data mining k- Means algorithm (Massaro, Galiano et al. 2018). Also cyber security systems (Nagesh 2013) are very important for industrial applications involving data network. In this direction data mining could help to understand the impact of cyber security in different application fields (Ansari at al. 2007). Finally, the risk management of human health can be optimized by analyzing the specific requirements of the case of study as for transport systems. According with the state of the art, the goal of the proposed chapter is to provide an overview of topics of preliminary industry research projects oriented on risk management. In particular, in this chapter are proposed different preliminary architectures oriented on service innovation in security systems and on production process innovation. In this direction, technology innovation, data mining and image processing techniques provide a knowledge gain (Frascati, 2015) which can be achieved for each specific cases of study. The topics cited before can be merged into a specific research industry case of study, by creating new concepts or ideas that improve existing knowledge (Frascati, 2015). For this purpose the proposed models and architectures are based on the formulation of new concepts to solve and optimize industry problems involving automated security systems.

The requirements preliminary of projects proposed in this chapter are related to:

- Face recognition;
- Motion detection in video surveillance systems;
- Video security in transports;
- Security in railway infrastructures;
- Security in quarry production processes;
- Oil spill security and underground water leakage;
- Cyber security in multimedia platform;

For each project will be discussed the basic architectures and discussed the aspects concerning security improvements for the knowledge gain. The shown architectures represent a part of the requirements (prototype demonstrators).

SECURITY SYSTEMS BASED ON FACE RECOGNITION

In this section are shown some applications about face recognition. Facial recognition is the subject of study in various scientific works (Aghajanian et al. 2009) based on the concepts of "training" and "testing" data processing. An example of sequence diagram involving training and testing in face recognition application is illustrated Figure 1. Concerning critical aspects, some researchers have analyzed the procedures for recognizing human faces in uncontrolled environments (Nefian et al. 1997), (Fu, 2015) from cameras which can be placed in front of a personal computer –PC- or laptop. Other researchers have described in detail algorithms able to identify a person by exploiting images from a database, and analyzing different facial poses and light conditions (Tan et al. 2006), thus highlighting the difficulty to recognize correctly biometric data. These critical aspects represent the main topics of a research project.

Face Recognition Project 1

An example of face recognition application applied for an industry project architecture is illustrated in Figure 2 (architecture of the project titled: "Analysis of Facial recognition analysis from PC using a software application based on recognizing criteria of stored matrix data of images"): the facial features are extracted, normalized, and stored into a database enabling face recognition response.

The subject of the project is of considerable importance, as also demonstrated by the tendency to transfer facial recognition procedures from a technological point of view. In this context the project is based on extraction of features such as the recognition of the somatic characters of a face that has already been inserted in a reference database as training dataset. In this way it will be possible to identify and

Figure 1. Unified modeling language –UML- sequence diagram of the face recognition phases

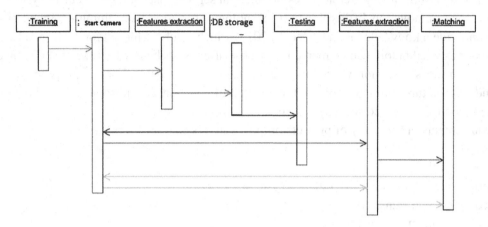

Figure 2. Face recognition phases for local PC data processing

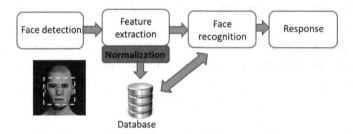

recognize a person sitting in front of a PC, whose image is acquired automatically by a webcam. The recognition of biometric distances will be carried out by the implementation of a java script code (developed by means of Eclipse platform) able to identify the characteristic distances of points characterizing eyes, nose, mouth and ear: some of biometric distances are indicated in Figure 3 as distances related to points of the rectangular boxes enclosing eyes, nose and mouth.

Figure 3. Feature extraction: calculation of distances

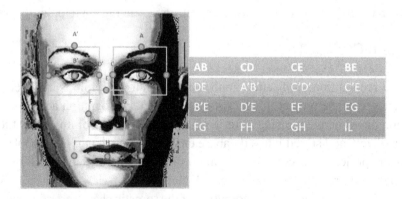

AB	CD	CE	BE
DE	A'B'	C'D'	C'E
B'E	D'E	EF	EG
FG	FH	GH	IL

The adopted algorithm covers the following functions:

- Automatic configuration of webcam image acquisition;
- Tracking and identification of boxes embedding face, nose, eyes and mouth;
- Identification of somatic characters from the processing of the image acquired by webcam;
- The procedures performed for recognition are defined by the following steps:
- Database training and training procedures;
- Definition of distances of the data contained in vectors associated with the somatic traits, for the comparison of similar images (identikit type, matching algorithm);
- Identification test.

The face recognition algorithm is structured in the following steps illustrated by the sequence diagram of Figure 1:

1. Image pre-processing;
2. Face detection;
3. Feature extraction;
4. Normalization;
5. Face recognition.

All the phases are summarized by the following example: (i) an user is detected for the first time by a smart camera (user registration) extracting face features which will be stored into a database (the first images constitute the training dataset of the face recognition mode); (ii) in a second period the user is recognized by the camera (testing processes) by matching the new detected features with the training ones.

The image pre-processing is performed by setting the input image size (for example 800 x 600), and by applying the histogram equalization able to control luminosity noise. The face detection is performed by OpenCV libraries able to detect and track eyes, nose and mouth. The feature extraction is executed by evaluating the distances between the reference points illustrated in Figure 3: the points are on the rectangular perimeters and inside the boxes enclosing eyes, nose and mouth by defining segments reported in the table of Figure 3. The data normalization is then applied for the Euclidean distance expressed by:

$$d(P,Q) = d(Q,P) - \sqrt{\left(q_1 - p_1\right)^2 + \ldots + \left(q_{14} - p_{14}\right)^2} = \sqrt{\sum_{i=1}^{14}(q_i - p_i)^2} \tag{1}$$

A possible normalization is represented by the following formula: Nd(P,Q)=d(P,Q)/(*fbh*), being *fbh* the height of the box tracking dynamically the face (see yellow dashed line of Figure 2).

The features are extracted and stored into a database, and then classified by a data mining classificatory (Naïve Bayes). The system is trained by initial photos constituting the training dataset. The executed tests provide the response of the recognized face expressed as probability to check correctly the biometric distances.

Face Recognition Project 2

Concerning Android mobile application, the face recognition algorithm can be executed by means of web service data processing system. In Figure 4 is illustrated an architecture implementing the web service (architecture of the project titled: "Mobile software tool for face recognition by means of identification algorithms for points corresponding to the somatic relevant features"). The webservice allows to transfer normalized biometric data of segments to an external database containing training and testing datasets.

Improvements, General Observations and Case Uses

The two proposed face recognition architectures represent two different research topics because are related to different hardware technologies which can influence the recognition. In fact, the factors which can contribute for the final face recognition are:

- Environment (lighting);
- Camera motion conditions (mobile application);
- Web service access (see a performed test reported in Figure 5);
- Face perspective;
- Other factors (long beard, etc.) .

Figure 5 analyzes the behavior of the Web Service, with respect to a face recognition mobile application with a number of 30 connected user (use of BlazeMeter tool) indicating a good load and response time conditions.

In order to create a god training dataset it is important to fix the technology and the environment conditions. It is also preferable to maintain the same conditions for the testing process.

In both the face recognition cases, the adopted algorithms for face recognition is based on Weka Naïve Bayes data mining classifier. In data mining, Naïve Bayes classifiers are a family of simple "probabilistic classifiers" based on applying Bayes' theorem which is characterized by a strong (naive) independence assumptions between the features.

Figure 4. Mobile application: face recognition by means of web service call

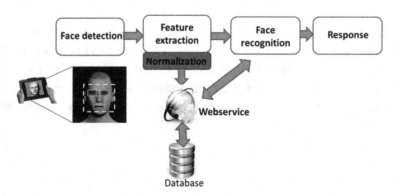

Figure 5. Mobile face recognition: web service test (web service performance monitoring)

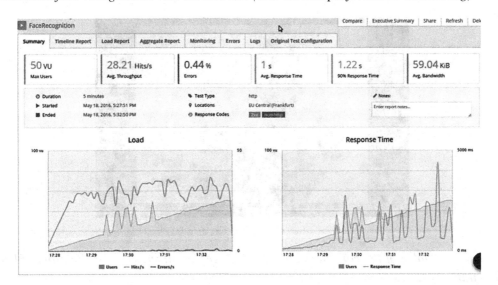

In Figure 6 is illustrated a test performed by changing face perspective: the face position of the user change during the test processing by rotating slowing the face and by changing the user position respect to the camera center . Below is reported the example of the script calling the classifier:

```
}
// Create a naïve bayes classifier
//Classifier cModel = (Classifier) new NaiveBayes();
//cModel.buildClassifier(isTrainingSet);
// Create a 5-NN Classifier
Classifier cModel = new IBk(5);
cModel.buildClassifier(isTrainingSet);
//SMO cModel = new SMO();
//cModel.buildClassifier(isTrainingSet);
return cModel;
}
```

A parameter used for testing, and useful to estimate the correct recognition is the correlation index. Figure 7 shows the correlation indexes between the occurrences and the probabilities of belonging to a class of each individual with the device in variable position. The correlation index allows to correct the probability of belonging to a wrong class, as in the case of recognition of user 'Ottavio' and user 'Alessandro' for the analyzed example. The table of Figure 7 shows that the diagonal values (true positive) are always greater than the other values representing false positive.

Figure 6. Testing process performed during the project development

Figure 7. Summary table of the correlation indexes between occurrence and probability of belonging by individual in a variable position

	Letizia	Mattia	Ottavio	Donato	Alessandro
Letizia	25.9168	0	0	1.1968	0
Mattia	6.7797	33.5013	0	0	4.188
Ottavio	1.7944	0	9.57	2.3936	8.3736
Donato	0	0	0	18.543	0.5984
Alessandro	0	1.396	0	5.7816	14.3565

Improvements and Use Cases

The proposed applications can be furthermore optimized in a security system by:

- Increasing the biometric points;
- Increasing the computing power (external calculus engine, parallel computing, etc.);
- Using massive data (big data system useful for multiple images acquired without knowledge of the person);
- Recognizing of more faces in the same area;
- Using simultaneously more classifiers (the comparison of more data mining algorithms could optimize the calculus of the probability error).

The face recognition can be adopted:

- Over a door (enabling an automatic open system);
- In front of a telematic training station (recognition of the user enabled for a specific course);
- In airports or railway stations;
- In outdoor place (squares, streets, etc.);
- Inside a public office.

In the table 1 are reported the working conditions of the real scenario testing (main use cases)

Table 1. Main use cases of the face recognition projects

Use Case	Short Description
System training phase	An user decides to follow a course (or an user is enabled to visualize a multimedia content) and his face is detected by the face recognition system which acquires different photos enabling training model.
User begins a course or requires a content visualization	An user is recognized by a webcam or by a mobile phone (the face recognition algorithm execute the testing dataset for a secure recognition).
Model testing of the security system	The algorithm test the model providing a recognition result. The visualization starts when the probability error of the recognition is under a fixed threshold.
Improvement of the training dataset	The testing photos are used in order to optimize the training dataset in order to decrease the error in future recognitions.

SECURITY AND VIDEOSURVEILLANCE SYSTEMS

Video surveillance systems represent the first level of security systems. Actually, a part of the research, is oriented on the optimization of image processing approaches based on motion detection. In fact, the goal of different studied is to furthermore improve the motion detection technology by optimizing the detection in function of the hardware (resolution, optics, etc.), and of the background (edge resolution, noise, etc.). The video surveillance system, due to its functional characteristics, is designed in the proposed project specifically for indoors environments such as home and office. In fact it is structured to carry out a selection of images that can be of interest by registering only in the presence of movement thus optimizing the computational cost. The goal of the project is to create a video surveillance system that, through a webcam as a sensor layer, automatically recognizes in real time the movement of objects, people or animals in a monitored indoor area. Specifically it is structured to capture the images and to save them into a GIF file only when the sensor detects a relevant movement. This last aspect is also important for standalone surveillance system where is required a low battery consumption (as for photovoltaic self-powered systems). The system distinguishes better what moves from what is fixed in the background, and is characterized by a sensor layer level constituted by a camera or webcam detecting images. The quality of the images are due mainly to sensor technology. The amount of captured images is regulated by a recording algorithm. Usually the video data flows are large. In order to reduce the amount of frames that are not of interest and to use as little memory and energy consumption as possible, is implemented a "selective" algorithm reducing the acquisition ratio: this algorithm, in fact, requires that the system registers only the images in which an effective movement has been detected (significant movement means a significant variation in percentage of points of a body with respect to those detected in the background). The image processing layer collects data by the image processing system (IPS) module able to segment the detected object. The IPS is composed by a subtraction background algorithm and by dynamic background refreshing. As the authors in (Sahasri et al. 2017) specify, background subtraction is a suitable technique for segmenting movement in static images. This algorithm detects moving regions by subtracting the current pixel-by-pixel image from a reference background image that is created by calculating the average of the images over time in an initialization period. The basic idea of the background subtraction method is to initialize a background first, and then subtracting the current frame in which the moving object is present. This method is simple and easy to implement, and accurately extracts the characteristics of the target data, but it is sensitive to changes in the external environment (important aspect for the system testing). Background subtraction methods operate directly on pixels. One of these methods (Seki at al.2006) is based on the concept that the neighboring pixels of the background models must remain constant or show similar variations over time. This theory is valid as long as the neighboring pixels belong to a single background object. For different background objects, it is especially difficult to apply for pixels distributed at the edges. All pixels are divided into groups before N × N blocks and each block is processed as an NxN vector. The Principal Component Analysis (PCA) model is calculated for each block by collecting some samples over time (Oliver et al. 2000). The pixels are then classified by the threshold difference between the current image and the backspace projection of its PCA coefficients as background or foreground. The Independent Component Analysis (ICA) model is similar to the above approach (Tsai al. 2008): this method uses a demixing vector and compares it with a new image to separate the foreground from the background image taken as a reference. Both the methods PCA and ICA can be applied for edge extraction.

The adopted phases for video surveillance process based on motion detection are:

- Camera opening;
- Camera closing;
- Slider management (controller);
- Motion retrieval;
- JPGs saving;
- Gif saving (optimization of the memory storage volume).

In Figure 8 is illustrated a block diagram of the video surveillance approach based on background subtraction: the background substraction is performed before the image segmentation extracting moving edges thus optimizing the image processing and the computational cost . In Figure 9 is illustrated a testing image proving the correct functionality of the implemented algorithm: in the image test of Figure 9 is illustrated the edge extraction of a person walking quickly into an office.

Improvements and Use Cases

The proposed applications can be furthermore optimized in security systems having the following characteristics:

- Detecting outdoor motion by distinguishing object moved by the wind from edges to detect;
- Low computational time (smart camera having a good computing power);
- Possibility to distinguish edge of different objects moving in the same monitored environment;
- Possibility to adapt automatically the background subtraction function to different lighting conditions (outdoor and indoor applications).

Figure 8. Phases of the motion detection video surveillance (project: "CEPIM Surveillance Security")

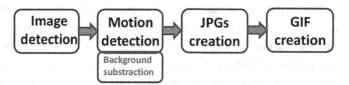

Figure 9. Edge extraction of a person walking into an office

Table 2. Main use cases of the project: 'CEPIM surveillance security'

Use Case	Short Description
Camera allocation into an indoor environment	A webcam or a camera is placed into an indoor environment.
Camera connection	The camera is connected to a laptop or transmit video to an external processor unit enabling data processing.
Camera setting	The camera is calibrated in function of the environment (back ground lighting, angle of view according with the used lens, distance, ecc.).
Surveillance system activation	The camera and the processor are active and enabled to recognize movements.
Alerting condition	When a movement is detected the system entries in an alerting status (the send an alert signal to the mobile of the user).

In the table 2 are reported the working conditions of the real scenario testing (main use cases).

SECURITY IN TRANSPORTS

The proposed research project concerns the design and development of a tailored system oriented on the acquisition of data from a bus fleet and on the management of their predictive maintenance. The project also includes the monitoring of the activity of each individual bus using a Global Positioning System –GPS- system and the integration of image vision security systems. Specifically, the main project requirements are:

- The use of data acquisition interfaces (electronic interfaces) from the control unit based on CAN (Controller Area Network)/OBD-II (On Board Diagnostics) communication standards (the data are extracted from the control units by means of cadenced procedures and after the deposit of the vehicles);
- The use of a central database (MySQL) to collect data from the control units (data that will be processed by data mining/artificial intelligence algorithms allowing to formulate an efficient predictive fleet maintenance plan by processing data such as number of stops, refueling, fuel consumed, inconsistencies between loaded values and volumes actually consumed, etc.);

- The creation of graphical dashboards (graphical reporting) indicating the security levels of each monitored bus, the predictive scheduling (scheduler) of the maintenance plan based on the outputs of the artificial intelligence algorithms, and the workflows for displaying all the data stored in the central database;
- A video monitoring module consisting of two night vision cameras to be mounted on each vehicle (front side and back side) using Network Video Recorder –NVR- technology suitable for streaming video transmission and video recording (the cameras, in addition to a visual verification of the GPS, will also be used to check the driving style of the driver, and for the analysis of the road status which could influence in a long time the breakage of specified parts of the vehicle recording intense traffic conditions, roads with holes, etc.).
- A GPS monitoring module allowing to track all the movements and activities of each vehicle, and to monitor any inefficiencies (for example excessive consumption due to an inappropriate driving style, risky driving styles due to an uncontrolled speed limits, etc.); the GPS data will also be processed by the data mining engine to define the drivers reliability indexes (the analyses combined with the driver driving style profiling will formulate the Key Performance Indicators-KPI- of drivers), to map the activities of each vehicle, and to formulate correctly the maintenance procedures (GPS signals provides important information to match with the road typology). The interruption status of GPS signals will be stored into the database in order to reconstruct the bus pattern by means of data post-processing.

The project involves the definition of process workflows indicating the best procedures to achieve optimal maintenance. The workflows can be designed using Business Process Modeling (BPM) application tools. The BPM will map both the current "AS IS" processes and the new engineered projects ("TO BE"), simulating at the same time the new operational scenarios.

Among the processes to be re-engineered by workflows are the planning of monitoring activities related to the introduction of the new GPS and Camera Monitoring technologies. The processes to re-engineer are:

- Operating procedures for the activation of registrations and for real time visualizations of critical transport conditions (snow, ice, accident, traffic, etc.)
- Interpretation procedures from the GPS data about the bus movement (stationary vehicle, refueling, planned parking, etc.),
- Procedures for assessing bus consumption;
- Procedures for the assessment of average trafficking speed (for verifying speed limits or precautionary trends in the presence of critical conditions);
- Information extraction procedures related to the driver's driving style.

The prediction activity is related to:

- Bus security based on data processing of the control unit;
- Driver safety (through the definition of security indicators integrating information on driving style);
- Prediction of specific controls for finding "hidden anomalies" of the vehicle (predictive maintenance by using artificial neural network –ANN-);

- Dynamic rescheduling of the bus maintenance by updating the processed data (dynamic scheduling of the vehicle revision activity);
- Replenishment of spare parts by the prediction of certain breaking parts (optimal management of the spare parts warehouse);
- Prediction of lists of vehicles at risk for long journeys;
- Prediction of the number of users (customers) based on the reference period (optimal scheduling of the trips based on the number of users);
- Trip prediction based on customer analysis (segmentation, geolocation, labor market analysis, attitudes, etc.)

In Figure 10 is illustrated the main architecture of the research project integrating the requirements above described: (i) bus fleet is equipped by electronic prototype systems able to transmit vehicles data an external database; (ii) transmitted data are processed by a data mining engine providing different efficiency indicators such as vehicle reliability, drivers reliability, consumption efficiency, secure patterns etc..

The security transport platform can be improved by:

- Clustering analysis of reliable drivers;
- Clustering of travel routes based on driving difficulties;
- Processing of images associated with the GPS signal in order to define a risk level for travel routes;
- Installing different sensor controlling the guidance style and reliability of the driver (accelerometers, alcohol sensor, etc.).
- Installing other sensors facilitating the night vision (as thermal cameras).

Figure 10. Architecture of bus security platform (project: "bus predictive maintenance")

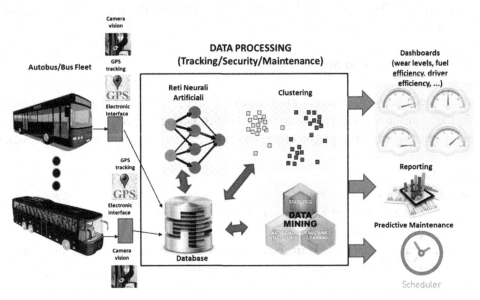

Table 3. Main use cases of the project: 'CEPIM Surveillance Security'

Use Case	Short Description
Bus traceability	The GPS system traces the travels and the pattern of each bus.
Monitoring	Cameras send images of anomalous conditions (traffic, snow, ice, car crash, ecc.)
Bus and driver security checking	The CAN /OBD-II unit provides information about bus and drivers style. The data mining algorithms provide the predictive maintenance plan of the bus and the KPI drivers.
Dashboard visualization	All the information are stored into a database and are analyzed simultaneously in order to provide graphically the security indicators about buses and drivers.

Improvements and Use Cases

In the table 3 are reported the working conditions of the real scenario testing (main use cases).

RAILWAY INSPECTIONS: SECURITY IN RAILWAY INFRASTRUCTURES

In this section is discussed the main platform of a research project involving railway infrastructure monitoring and security. Specifically, the project includes the development of the following specifications and tasks.

1.   Infrastructure Topography Monitoring Using a Georeferenced Laser Scanner.

A mobile rail system will be designed to stabilize a laser scanner able to detect cloud points of the railway infrastructure and possible anomalies (proximity of obstacles, structural defects of bridges and tunnels, etc.). A prototype laser scanner system is suitable for topographic survey which can be optimized by image processing techniques and by detection procedures (acquisition methodology, data alignment, definition of reference points, pre-processing, cleaning points, fitting pints, interpolation of measurement points). The georeferencing will allow to simplify the inspections traceability of the railway network to control.

2.   Georeferenced Underground Monitoring.

The georeferenced underground monitoring is carried out by using georadar (GPR technology). The procedures for the acquisition of radargrams combined with topographic acquisition represent the solution to adopt for underground monitoring. The image processing of radargrams allows the classification of:

a.   underground cavities;
b.   different stratifications of the subsoil;
c.   different layers stratification of ballast / sub-ballast / subgrade layers;
d.   presence of water layers / accumulations;
e.   other types of ground defects, substructures, crankcase breakage, structural failure, etc.

The georadar images can be also combined with endoscopic photos thus facilitating the reading, the analysis, and the formulation of risk levels of the infrastructure. The raw images and the data processed are stored into a database containing other data and information of the railway infrastructure (historic data, temperature data, etc.) useful to predict risks.

3. Implementation of Real Time Temperature Monitoring Modules Setting Alert Thresholds.

A wireless prototype temperature sensors are designed to be installed on critical points of the railway network. The design and development take into account the International Protection – IP- degrees for atmospheric agents of the package, and the definition of alerting thresholds (under-temperature and over-temperature threshold limits). The threshold limit values can be set by programming a microcontroller coupled with the temperature sensor. This module communicates the real time temperature of the rail to the data acquisition platform (control room), showing the geolocation map of the installed sensors. The data are stored into a database and are processed by data mining and artificial intelligence algorithms in order to predict risk conditions (cross data-processing with weather data, georadar images and laser scanners data). The prediction allows to formulate risk maps of the railway network.

4. Definition of Combined Laser Scanner/Georadar/Temperature Analysis Procedures for the Definition of Risk Maps.

The inspection processes are engineered by the design and the development of process workflows. The new designed operational processes are integrated into the current inspection processes. The outputs of the inspection procedures and processes allow to define risk conditions and risk probabilities of the infrastructure. These risk conditions are reported into a risk map.

5. Predictive Risk Analysis of Network Anomalies by Analysing Acquired Data.

Data mining algorithms process historical data of laser scanner, georadar and temperature sensors thus creating an efficient predictive analysis model.

6. Integration of the Latest Generation Endoscopic Probes into the Inspection Process of Georadar System.

Endoscopic images improve the georadar inspection process. The procedures describing the use of the endoscopic probes are standardized and classified based on the type of inspection to be performed.

7. Predictive Maintenance.

The predictive maintenance of the railway network infrastructure and of the machines follows the functional logic of the RAMS algorithms. The operational workflow of the RAMS algorithm is integrated with the outputs of the data mining algorithms. The infrastructure data and the vehicles data are processed by formulating a predictive maintenance plan.

The description of the research relevant to the predictive maintenance of the machines is based on a scenario defined by the following phase of activities:

a. **Activity 1:** Classification and preparation of a database and machine monitoring protocol.
b. **Activity 2:** Data analysis with a view to preventive maintenance of all vehicles with identification of possible solutions to existing problems that generate downtime.
c. **Activity 3:** Identification of the parameters to be monitored during operation with the aim of determining the type of predictive maintenance about most critical machines.
d. **Activity 4:** Implementation of an Information Technology – IT- system for maintenance management.

Below are indicated some activity details:

a. Classification and preparation of data collection and machine monitoring protocols; the activity aims to analyse and classify the maintenance history of each individual machine in order to frame the current situation; the critical parameters of each machine are evaluated; a database collects data useful for the checking of the maintenance parameters;
b. Data analysis (the activity aims to critically analyse and engineer what is classified during the first activity in order to define an efficient maintenance plan; this activity is carried out by privileging the most critical fleet of vehicles, for which the downtime is more expensive; during this phase are evaluated possible solutions to existing problems by providing technical improvements and evaluating the cause of failures);
c. Identification of the parameters to be monitored during operation with the aim of determining the type of predictive maintenance on the most critical machines (for the most critical machines, based on the needs of the client, are evaluated the main operating parameters in order to determine a predictive maintenance plan oriented on a minimization of machine downtime);
d. Implementation of an IT system for maintenance management (the activity aims to implement an IT system that allows the management, control and analysis of machine maintenance).

The main specifications are summarized in the architecture of Figure 11: the proposed architecture takes into account the different phases of the prototype platform such as the design of the inspection processes by prototype devices such as laser scanner, georadar and endoscopy sensors (the assembly of the sensors into a system able to move on the train tracks represents the prototype systems), the data acquisition system, the data processing by innovative algorithms, the data reporting (outputs of the algorithms).

Improvements and Use Cases

The railway security can be furthermore improved by:

- Matching historical data and measurements with current ones in order to predict defect evolution (underground anomalies, rail defects, etc.);
- Considering the output of the RAMS algorithms as inputs of the data mining algorithms enabling predictive maintenance;
- Optimizing the training dataset of a neural network predicting the risk for a specific geolocalized point;

- Applying different image processing and data mining algorithms in order to optimize the risk evaluation;
- Automatizing the inspection procedures and processes by means of alerts generated by the proto-type platform.

In the table 4 are reported the working conditions of the real scenario testing (main use cases).

Figure 11. Monitoring risk railway infrastructure and predictive maintenance –MRRIPM- platform layout

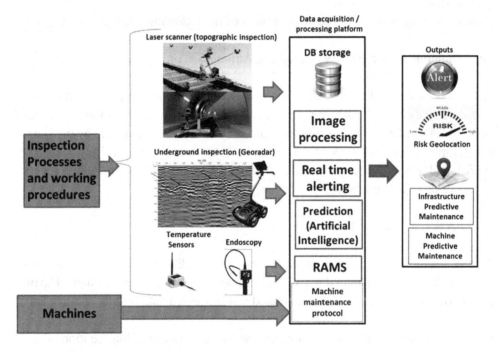

Table 4. Main use cases of the project: 'MRRIPM'

Use Case	Short Description
Assignment of the inspection procedures	The inspection procedures are assigned to the worker after a preliminary plan based on the definition of the high risk parts of the railway infrastructure.
Device assignment	The inspection devices (georadar, laser scanner, endoscopes, temperature sensors) are assigned in function of the inspection procedure to follow.
Real time monitoring	A control room receives in real time the data of the devices (remote access). In particular alert signals are send in the case of anomalous detection (rail crack or deformation, too high or too low rail temperature, etc.).
Data processing	Different algorithms (data mining algorithms and image processing ones) process data and provide more information about hidden risks, railway predictive maintenance, and predicted risks.
Dashboards visualization	Graphical dashboards provides the risk map of the whole railway network.

SECURITY IN QUARRY PRODUCTION PROCESSES

Security in quarry activities is the topic of an industry project discussed in this section. The project idea is based on the following points matching with the actual industry needs exposed and the scenario shown in the state of the art. The functional architecture of the research project is shown in Figure 12. This architecture integrates data of different modules into a software level thus creating a single data management tool and visualization platform (control room): the data entry process is the core of the platform allowing the information digitalization processes able to predict risks and the maintenance of critical parts of the production lines such as vertical rotators, conveyor belt, and risks correlated with the quarry evolution.

Specifically, the project involves the development of the following main specifications.

1. Process Mapping and Data Entry (Recording Automation of Production Data).

The data entry is used for the new mapping and digitization of the quarry production processes. In a first phase, are carried out some interviews in order to re-analyze the roles of the workers and to define the control points of the data entry process. The data are added into the platform by using a tablet and an user friendly Graphical User Interface - GUI- suitable for the use of workers. The data entry is designed to facilitate risk and predictive analysis: artificial intelligence and RAMS algorithm process data of the production layout providing predictive maintenance procedures.

2. Data Collection in a Single Database.

Is performed a migration of the current data contained in traditional ACCESS tables into a single database collecting data and containing the new ones provided by the data entry system. The operator from the external control room accesses to all the entered and processed data (predictive data and risk maps).

3. Predictive Algorithms for Planning of Maintenance and Operating Interventions.

The input data of the predictive algorithms (artificial intelligence –AI- algorithms) are pre-processed (normalization, filtering, attribute selection, roles identification, cleaning operation, etc.), to then be processed by the calculation engine. Clustering algorithms, artificial neural networks and other data mining algorithms are executed by the control room user having the possibility to analyze the outputs through graphical dashboards. The analytical advanced algorithms provide important indications also about the logistic efficiency, the breackage risks of quarry machines, the predictive maintenance plan (predictive maintenance scheduling), the production forecasting, and the risk maps of plant breakdown and safety of workers. These algorithms are applied following the RAMS logic. Some tools useful for the predictive maintenance are: Orange Canvas, Rapid Miner, Weka, KNIME Studio, Keras, TensorFlow, Theano (Ahmad et al. 2014), (Gulli, 2017), (Wimmer et al. 2015), (Kovalev et al. 2016).

4. Graphical Dashboards.

Using dashboards, the data of the installed sensors (such as accelerometers and image vision sensors) are displayed remotely. The dashboards also allow to plot graphically (i) the risk levels of breakage, (ii) the risk maps associated with dangerous areas for workers, and (iii) the scheduler of the maintenance plan.

5.   UAV drone for the Topographic Survey of the Quarry (Photogrammetry).

The UAV includes accessories for the specific application (flight terminator, power supply, compact full-frame camera with remote video capability, software for generating high resolution georeferenced orthophotos, detailed Digital Elevation Models –DEMs-, etc.). Before UAV testing, are carried out studies on the use methods, including the analysis of trajectories and of reference points.

6.   Installation of Sensors on Vertical Rotors.

Accelerometers are designed and installed to monitor any "internal" anomalies of vertical gyrators by predicting the breakage. Several accelerometers should be tested in order choose those most suitable for the frequencies and amplitudes characterizing typical oscillation of vertical gyrators (signal processing). The analysis of the vibration signals is useful both to verify the imminent mechanical breakdown, and to predict malfunctions (by analyzing the oscillations that are considered "anomalous" on the basis of a determined thresholds value and on the basis of the artificial intelligence algorithm outputs).

7.   Image vision for Remote Display of Cracks on the Conveyor Belt.

A prototype image vision system is designed and developed in order to detect automatically the cracks and lacerations of conveyor belts. This system includes the image processing tool characterizing the conveyor belt features by classifying the cracks. The predictive artificial intelligence algorithms will estimate the crack evolution. To facilitate the processing, the images are acquired without load on the conveyor belt and controlled by the control room (remote viewing). Based on the analysis results, suggestions it is possible to analyze layout variations by re-analyzing the load distribution on the whole conveyor belt system.

Figure 12. Layout architecture of the project 'QuarryTechnologies'

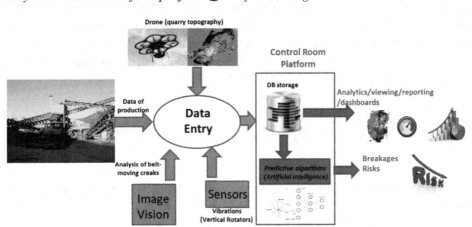

Table 5. Main use cases of the project: 'QuarryTechnologies'.

Use Case	Short Description
Data entry	Workers by means of mobile devices insert data of the production activities (different control points of the production layout).
Quarry morphology mapping	A drone is activated to detect during the time the quarry evolution mapping.
Sensor detection	Image vision and vertical rotors monitoring (accelerometers).
Data processing	Artificial Intelligence is applied for the predictive maintenance of the production line.
Dashboard visualization	Graphical dashboards indicate breakage risks of the monitored machines.

Improvements and Use Cases

The quarry production security can be furthermore improved by:

- Predicting risks due to creation of dangerous areas due to incorrect works of the quarry;
- Installing different image vision modules for each conveyor belt;
- predicting breakages of vertical gyrators by processing historical data of accelerometers;
- Creating a high performance training dataset of cracks an defects classification (conveyor belt application);
- Creating a high performance training dataset of vibration signal (vertical gyrator application);
- Reconfiguring automatically the quarry machine layout by considering the progress of the works and by analyzing during the time the risk maps.

In the table 5 are reported the working conditions of the real scenario testing (main use cases).

OIL SPILL SECURITY AND UNDERGROUND WATER LEAKAGE: IMAGE PROCESSING AND RADIOMETRIC UNDERGROUND WATER LEAKAGE DATA CLASSIFICATION

Oil spill is a topic of interest about risk management. In this direction image segmentation techniques by means of active contour snake approach (Massaro et al. 2012) represent a good solution for leakage detection also for underground liquid leakages. This image processing technique is dynamic: snakes are active contour models converging in different time steps on edges having a minimum energy. Parametrically the snake contour is $v(t) = (x(t), y(t))$. The functional energy associated with the snake is defined as (Kass et al. 1987):

$$E_{snake} = \int_0^t E_{snake}\left(v(t)\right)dt = \int_0^t \left[E_{\text{int}}\left(v(t)\right) + E_{image}\left(v(t)\right) + E_{con}\left(v(t)\right)\right]dt \qquad (2)$$

Being E_{int} the internal energy of the spline due to the bending, E_{image} the image forces, and E_{con} the constraint forces.

Another technique useful for detecting oily contaminants on surface waters is the thermography (Ekuakille et al. 2019). In this direction the security detection systems could be furthermore improved by means of data mining post processing algorithms such as K- Means (Raval et al. 2016). Below is reported the K- Means pseudo-algorithm which has been applied to the image post processing:

1. Initialize cluster centroids μ_1, μ_2, μ_2, μ_3,...,μ_k $\in \Re^n$ randomly;
2. Repeat until convergence for every i and j set as follows:

$$c^{(i)} := \arg \min_j \left\| x^{(i)} - \mu_j \right\|^2$$
$$\mu_j := \frac{\sum_{i=1}^{m} 1\left\{ c^{(i)} = j \right\} x^{(i)}}{\sum_{i=1}^{m} 1\left\{ c^{(i)} = j \right\}}$$

(3)

where $x^{(i)}$ represent a value of the training dataset (in the image case it is a group of pixel radiometric intensities). In Figure 13 is shown an example of k-Means image post-processing (k=4) of an area characterized by underground water leakage: the thermogram of Figure 13 (a) illustrates an area of a possible underground leackage which is better enhanced by the k-Means image of 13 (b). The k-Means processing helps to highlight the clusters of pixels characterized by similar temperature values. The cluster having different temperatures classified into different ranges will define hot and cold areas. We observe that, in Figure 13, the area related to the asphalted road on the left is characterized by two main clusters (one white and the other one black, where the black indicates the underground water leakage), beside the surrounding field is clustered by all the four cluster (the gray color indicates the underground water leakage in the field): this explain how the material response to the temperature gradient is different passing from a material to another one.

By applying snake contour algorithm to the same thermographic image is possible to highlight the exact point of the underground water leakage. In Figure 14 is illustrated this last post processing case: dynamically the red contour encloses step by step the area characterized by the minimum energy (final convergence of the snake contour).

Figure 13. Experimention of the ThermRadLeack project: (a) Thermographic image of a region characterized by an underground water leakage. (b) K-Means algorithm applied to the radiometric image (k=4)

Figure 14. Active contour snake algorithm highlighting the exact point of the underground leakage

Figure 15. (a) 3D Surface Plot and (b) height levels represented by isolines

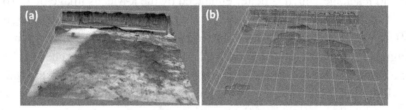

Other image post-processing technique could be adopted to highlight the evolution. By applying for example the '3D Surface Plot' function of ImageJ tool (Cicala et al. 2014), it is possible to observe also how the leakage plume trend changes during the observation time. In Figure 15 are shown two examples '3D Surface Plot' post processing indicating the plume evolution: Figure 15 (a) is the 3D reconstruction of the leackage area where the higher levels represent the areas corresponding the underground leackage; Figure 15 (b) is the same reconstruction by adopting isolines where each colored line indicates a gradient intensity level.

Improvements and Use Cases

Security level about leakage detection can be furthermore improved by:

- Applying the post processing algorithms to different radiometric images acquired in different time steps;
- Classifying different material responses according with the thermal properties (asphalt, field, brick, etc.);
- Applying other data mining algorithms such as ANN to the clusters K-means data in order to predict the leakage extension (important aspect for large leakage areas);
- Using classification results in order to know the nature of the dispersed liquid.

Table 6. Main use cases of the project: 'ThermRadLeack'

Use Case	Short Description
Thermogram acqusition	An IR camera detect radiometric information about a possible area of possible underground liquid leakage.
Real time leakage monitoring	The thermograms are processed in real time by setting alerting thresholds.
Data post- processing	Radiometric data are processed by data mining algorithm (K-Means algorithm or by applying other image processing tools) in order to extract hidden information highlighting leakage evolution.
Data storage	Thermograms are stored into a database. The thermograms acquired during the time provide information about leakage evolution.

In the table 6 are reported the working conditions of the real scenario testing (main use cases).

RESEARCH IN CYBER SECURITY PLATFORM ABOUT MULTIMEDIA ONLINE MANAGEMENENT: PRELIMINARY RESEARCH STEPS

Cyber security and multimedia content management are important research topics because the web communication today is extended to gaming (Zhao 2018) and other interactive applications such as Augmented Reality –AR-. The Virtual Private Network –VPN- can be attacked during the multimedia communication process. In this direction an important issue is the design technologies to support secure architectures innovative if compared with the state of the art.

The preliminary requirements of a research project oriented on secure multimedia online management, cover the following main themes.

1. **Architecture validation of a multimedia platform** (prototype system) with strong cyber security and cyber defense features by using of ICT and IT networking functions and services (Multimedia Cross Platform), able to provide numerous services such as publishing, content management, demand content, live content, mailing, chat, phonebook, file sharing, grouping, etc.. Specifically, the attention is focused on the aspects of modularity useful for the engineering of different functions and for the scalability: the architecture must be able to manage a growing number of users, and must be able to develop and deliver an ever-increasing number of services and benefits. The architecture must also be composed of several subsystems and modules capable of interacting with each other in a harmonious way and as a single entity (management of different VPN channels). Some performance indexes can provide a scenario about network and security efficiency. The beta testing is indicated for the evaluation of all the functionalities of the architecture by identifying some bugs, hardware and software incompatibilities, and system conflicts. The engineering of the multimedia platform concerns:

   a. Web interface with VPN access;
   b. The simultaneous comparison of data with reading keys to guarantee the security system;
   c. The classification of characteristics inherent to different levels of flexibility of the prototype system (consumer oriented, enterprise oriented, enterprise security architecture, firewall Implementation, etc.).

    d.   Adaptability to a multi-channel systems.

2.   **Technological upgrade of the engineered platform.** The prototype system is 'upgraded' by big data and data mining technologies.

Below are indicated some tasks of the an industry project useful for the implementation of a secure multimedia platform:

a.   Technology watching of the state of the art about functional architectures compatible with the prototype system and of scientific interest;

b.   Technology watching at the scientific level of big data technologies and data mining oriented to the functionality of the platform prototype;

c.   Deepening of design of big data architectures and of development environments suitable for mobile applications oriented on the management of multimedia contents, and on the storage in general of multimedia data archives;

d.   Economic analysis of the potential of new services deriving from the new analysed models;

e.   Analysis of new procedures related to internet data encryption (symmetric, asymmetric, quantum cryptography) able to obscure data communication in transit between client and server and in big data systems (SSH, SSL / TSL protocols, HTTPS, IPsec, etc.);

f.   Analysis of new procedures and technologies related to steganography and cryptography applicable to the prototype system;

g.   Analysis of use cases related to the new services deriving from the use of the technological upgrade models the functional schemes (design by Unified Modeling Language –UML-);

h.   Analysis of the models of level security SSH (Secure SHell), about security in transport levels on authentication, about channel management, and about security systems for accessing data in big data systems interfaceable with mobile applications;

i.   Use of data mining models for the purposes of service innovation related to the use of multimedia files in VPN channels;

j.   Study of data mining methodologies concerning the prediction of network attacks, system failures, and network blocking by using the prototype architecture as testing network;

k.   Classification of different security levels by systemic analysis of use cases;

l.   Definition and simulation of critical issues related to the functioning of the prototype system based on the identification of some failure system conditions (the simulation allows to optimize the design of a flowchart suitable for the management of blocking and interruption conditions of the transmission of multimedia data packets in packet-switched systems);

m.   Study and resolution of possible conflicts between hardware and software.

In Figure 16 we report a functional scheme of the proposed research project where are distinguished both the tasks above described: (i) the first step is the engineering of a prototype network enabling bi-directional multimedia data transmission; (ii) the second step is the design of a network upgrading the engineered network including innovations such as data mining and big data analytics able to improve data security and cybersecutity.

Figure 16. Functional scheme improving scientific research in a multimedia secure platform (project "advanced multimedia cyber platform")

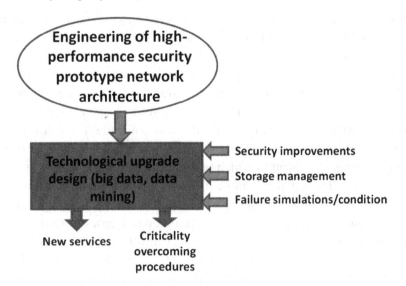

Improvements and Use Cases

The security of the multimedia platform can be improved by:

- Mapping automatically the new attacks (learning of a data mining system able to block different typologies of attacks);
- Predicting new attacks based on the analysis of historical attacks about a specific multimedia communication;
- Correlating different attacks in order to optimize their dynamic classification (by means of data mining algorithms).

In the table 7 are reported the working conditions of the real scenario testing (main use cases).

Table 7. Main use cases of the project: 'advanced multimedia CYBER platform'

Use Case	Short Description
Testing of a prototype network	Basic hardware of a prototype is tested for multimedia transmission and security
Design of an innovative architecture	The prototype is integrated with big data systems and data mining algorithms in order to improve security of multimedia content transmission.
Basic test	Basic test about Big Data connection and data mining recognizing attacks are performed before to integrate the tools in the network prototype.

CONCLUSION

The goal of the proposed chapter is to show how image processing and data mining can improve research topics in industry applications focused on security and on risk detection. Different architectures have been discussed by highlighting how data processing can gain the knowledge base about security systems following "Frascati" guidelines. The analysed examples helps to understand where research topics are allocated into a main project, by describing the critical aspects and risks about results reliability such as a correct recognition or a reliable prediction. Research outputs are originated mainly by data mining or by image processing algorithms applied for the specific cases of study. The chapter, showing different applications, highlights how the safety of the individual's health can be observed from several points of view: depending on the environment in which one works, the types of safety level and of the risks connected to the health of the individual can be different. Specifically have been analysed the risks associated with a correct biometric recognition, intrusion, transport, pollution, a correct inspection of the work environment, and online network systems. The proposed cases of study represent guidelines about the preliminary design approach of research projects involving security and risks as topics. The proposed overview of project requirements helps the reader to formulate a research project following similar guidelines. The significance of the proposed chapter is to show an overview proving how design a research industry project starting to true needs of a company. The proposed architectures are useful for the reader in order to set up a security project by analyzing the different implementation steps. The proposed procedures can be applied to similar applications improving technological and scientific innovations necessary to write a research project. The proposed architectures refer to recent projects which are under investigation or in testing phase. The implementations results will be published in other works.

ACKNOWLEDGMENT

The work has been carried out during the development of the following different industry projects: *"Analisi di riconoscimento facciale da PC di una persona mediante applicativo software basato su criteri di riconoscimento di dati matriciali memorizzati da rilievo di imagine"* [Analysis of Facial recognition analysis from PC using a software application based on recognizing criteria of stored matrix data of images]; *"Applicativo software mobile per il riconoscimento di persona mediante algoritmi identificativi di punti corrispondenti a tratti somatici rilevanti"* [Mobile software tool for face recognition by means of identification algorithms for points corresponding to the somatic relevant features]; "Studio applicazione e sperimentazione di soluzioni innovative per sistemi di videosorveglianza integrata e sicurezza in remoto con riconoscimento e archiviazione dati: 'CEPIM SURVEILLANCE SECURITY' [Study application and experimentation of innovative solutions for video surveillance integrated systems and remote security with recognition and data archiving: "CEPIM SURVEILLANCE SECURITY"]"; "Gestione Predittiva della Manutenzione della flotta Autobus/Bus mediante Acquisizione Dati da Centralina e Sistemi Integrati di Monitoring Camera/GPS: 'Bus Predictive Maintenance'"[Predictive Management of the maintenance of the Bus / Bus fleet through Data Acquisition from the ECU and Integrated Monitoring Camera / GPS Systems: 'Bus Predictive Maintenance']; *"Tecnologie di monitoraggio laser scanner/georadar integrate a sensoristica endoscopica e di temperatura per la definizione di mappe di rischio dell' infrastruttura ferroviaria e manutenzione predittiva del sistema rete/macchine: MonitoringRiskRailwayInfrastructure and Predictive Maintenance -MRRIPM-"* [Laser scanner / georadar monitoring technologies integrated with endoscopic and temperature sensors for defining risk maps of the railway infrastructure and predictive maintenance of the network / machine system: MonitoringRiskRailwayInfrastructure and Predictive Maintenance -*MRRIPM*-]; "*Digitalizzazione dei processi legati alla produzione in cava ed integrazione delle tecnologie a supporto del monitoraggio basate sulla predizione di rischi di rottura degli impianti e sul monitoraggio topografico con drone 'QuarryTechnologies'* " [Processes digitization for quarry production and integration of monitoring technologies based on the prediction of plant breakage risks and topographic monitoring with drone "*QuarryTechnologies*"]; "*Sistema tecnologico non invasivo per il rilevamento e la localizzazione intelligente delle perdite idriche mediante immagini termiche automatizzate, sistema di monitoraggio/alerting, image processing e sistema decisionale di gestione interventi con tecnologie alternative 'ThermRadLeack'* " [Non-invasive technological system for the intelligent detection and localization of water leackage by means of automated thermal images, monitoring / alerting system, image processing, and decision-making systems for managing interventions with alternative technologies 'ThermRadLeack']; Piattaforma ingegnerizzata per il management avanzato ad alte performance di dati multimediali con implementazione di nuove tecniche di cybersecurity: 'ADVANCED MULTIMEDIA CYBER PLATFORM' "[Engineered platform for advanced management of high performance multimedia data implementing new cybersecurity techniques: 'ADVANCED MULTIMEDIA CYBER PLATFORM'].

REFERENCES

Aghajanian, J., & Prince, S. J. D. (2009). Face pose estimation in uncontrolled environments. *Proceeding of British Machine Vision Conference, 1*, 1-11.

Ahmad Al-Khoder, A., & Harmouch, H. (2014). Evaluating four of the most popular Open Source and Free Data Mining Tools. *IJASR International Journal of Academic Scientific Research, 3*(1), 13–23.

Ansari, A. Q., Patki, T., Patki, A. B., & Kumar, V. (2007). Integrating fuzzy logic and data mining: impact on cyber security. *Proceeding of Fourth International Conference on Fuzzy Systems and Knowledge Discovery*. 10.1109/FSKD.2007.365

Antonio Gulli, A., & Pal, S. (2017). Deep learning with Keras- implement neural networks with Keras on Theano and TensorFlow. Mumbai: Packt Book.

Bastos, P., Lopes, I., & Pires, L. (2014). Application of data mining in a maintenance system for failure prediction. In Safety, Reliability and Risk Analysis: Beyond the Horizon. Taylor & Francis Group.

Ciampa, F., Mahomoodi, P., Pinto, F., & Meo, M. (2018). Recent analysis in active infrared thermography for non-destructive testing of aerospace components. *Sensors (Basel), 18*(609), 1–37. PMID:29462953

Cicala, G., Massaro, A., Velardi, L., Senesi, G. S., & Valentini, A. (2014). Self-assembled pillar-like structures in nanodiamond layers by pulsed spray technique. *ACS Applied Materials & Interfaces, 6*(23), 21101–21109. doi:10.1021/am505974d PMID:25402729

Ekuakille, A.-L., Durikovic, I., Lanzolla A., Morello, R., De Capua, C., Girao, P. S., … Van Biesen, L. (2019). Effluents, surface and subterranean waters monitoring: Review and advances. *Measurements, 137*(1), 567-579.

Fan, Y., Nowaczyk, S., & Rögnvaldsson, T. (2015). Incorporating expert knowledge into a self-organized approach for predicting compressor faults in a city bus fleet. *Frontiers in Artificial Intelligence and Applications, 278*(1), 58–67.

Frascati Manual. (2015). *The Measurement of Scientific, Technological and Innovation Activities- Guidelines for Collecting and Reporting Data on Research and Experimental Development.* OECD.

Fu, Y. (2015). *Face recognition in uncontrolled environments* (PhD thesis). University College London.

Galiano, A., Massaro, A., Barbuzzi, D., Legrottaglie, M., Vitti, V., Pellicani, L., & Birardi, V. (2016). Face recognition system on mobile device based on web service approach. *International Journal of Computer Science and Information Technologies, 7*(4), 2130–2135.

Kass, M., Witkin, A., & Terzopoulos, D. (1987). Snakes: Active contour models. *International Journal of Computer Vision, 1*(4), 321–331. doi:10.1007/BF00133570

Kovalev, V., Kalinovsky, A., & Kovalev, S. (2016). Deep learning with Theano, Torch, Caffe, TensorFlow, and deeplearning4j: which one is the best in speed and accuracy? *XIII Int. Conf. on Pattern Recognition and Information Processing*, 99-103.

Massaro, A., Barbuzzi, D., Galiano, A., Vitti, V., & Pellicani, V. (2017). Simplified and efficient face recognition system on real image set and synthesised data. *International Journal of Biometrics, 9*(2), 143–162. doi:10.1504/IJBM.2017.085678

Massaro, A., Ekuakille, A. L., Caratelli, D., Palamara, I., & Morabito, F. C. (2012). Optical performance evaluation of oil spill detection methods: Thickness and extent. *IEEE Transactions on Instrumentation and Measurement, 61*(12), 3332–3339. doi:10.1109/TIM.2012.2210336

Massaro, A., Galiano, A., Meuli, G., & Massari, S. F. (2018). Overview and application of enabling technologies oriented on energy routing monitoring, on network installation and on predictive maintenance. *International Journal of Artificial Intelligence and Applications, 9*(2), 1–20. doi:10.5121/ijaia.2018.9201

Massaro, A., Vitti, V., Maurantonio, G., & Galiano, A. (2018). Sensitivity of a video surveillance system based on motion detection. *Signal and Image Processing: an International Journal, 9*(3), 1–21. doi:10.5121ipij.2018.9301

Nagesh, S. (2013). Role of data mining in cyber security. *Journal of Exclusive Management Science, 2*(5), 2277–5684.

Nefian, A. V., Khosravi, M., & Hayes, M. H. (1997). Real-time detection of human faces in uncontrolled environments. *SPIE Proceeding of Visual Communications and Image Processing, 3024*(1), 211-219.

Oliver, N., Rosario, M. B., & Pentland, A. P. (2000). A Bayesian computer vision system for modeling human interactions. *IEEE Transactions on Pattern Analysis and Machine Intelligence, 22*(8), 831–843. doi:10.1109/34.868684

Park, M. G. (2013). *RAMS management of railway systems integration of RAMS management into railway systems engineering* (Thesis). School of Civil Engineering College of Engineering and Physical Sciences, University of Birmingham.

Qiao, T., Tang, Y., & Ma, F. (2013). Real-time detection technology based on dynamic line-edge for conveyor belt longitudinal tear. *Journal of Computers, 8*(4), 1065–1071. doi:10.4304/jcp.8.4.1065-1071

Rajpal, P. S., Shishodia, K. S., & Sekhon, G. S. (2006). An artificial neural network for modeling reliability, availability and maintainability of a repairable system. *Reliability Engineering & System Safety, 91*(7), 809–819. doi:10.1016/j.ress.2005.08.004

Raval, U. R. & Jani, C. (2016). Implementing & improvisation of K-means clustering algorithm. *International Journal of Computer Science and Mobile Computing, 5*(5), 191-203.

Rossi, P., Mancini, F., Dubbini, M., Mazzone, F., & Capra, A. (2017). Combining nadir and oblique UAV imagery to reconstruct quarry topography: Methodology and feasibility analysis. *European Journal of Remote Sensing, 50*(1), 211–221. doi:10.1080/22797254.2017.1313097

Sahasri, M., & Gireesh C. (2017). Object motion detection and tracking for video surveillance. *International Journal of Engineering Trends and Technology*, (1), 161-164.

Salvini, R., Mastrorocco, G., Seddaiu, M., Rossi, D., & Vanneschi, C. (2017). The use of an unmanned aerial vehicle for fracture mapping within a marble quarry (Carrara, Italy): Photogrammetry and discrete fracture network modeling. *Geomatics, Natural Hazards & Risk, 8*(1), 34–52. doi:10.1080/19475705.2016.1199053

Seki, M., Wada, T., Fujiware, H., & Sumi, K. (2003). Background subtraction based on occurence of image variations. *Proceeding of IEEE International Conference on Computer vision and Pattern Recognition, 2*(72), 1-8.

Siddharth, A., Parneet, K., & Prachi, A. (2013). Economical maintenance and replacement decision making in fleet management using data mining. *The SIJ Transactions on Computer Science Engineering & its Applications, 1*(2), 37-48.

Simões, G. M. P. (2008). *RAMS analysis of railway track infrastructure (Reliability, Availability, Maintainability, Safety)* (Thesis). Instituto Siperior Tecnico.

Tan, X., Chen, S., Zhou, Z.-H., & Zhang, F. (2006). Face recognition from a single image per person: A survey. *Pattern Recognition, 39*(9), 1725–1745. doi:10.1016/j.patcog.2006.03.013

Tsai, D. M., & Lai, S. C. (2008). Independent component analysis-based background subtraction for indoor surveillance. *IEEE Transactions on Image Processing, 18*(1), 158–167. doi:10.1109/TIP.2008.2007558 PMID:19095527

Tushar, J. & Meenu. (2013). Automation and integration of industries through computer vision systems. *International Journal of Information and Computation Technology, 3*(9), 963–970.

Wimmer, H., & Powell, L. M. (2015). A comparison of open source tools for data science. *Proceedings of the Conference on Information Systems Applied Research, 8*(3651), 1-9.

Xiong, Z., Li, Q., Mao, Q., & Zou, Q. (2017). A 3D laser profiling system for rail surface defect detection. *Sensors (Basel), 17*(8), 1–19. doi:10.339017081791 PMID:28777323

Xu, L., Xuegang, Y., & Ke, H. (2011). Towards effective bus lane monitoring using camera sensors. *Wireless Sensor Network*, *3*(5), 174–182. doi:10.4236/wsn.2011.35020

Zhang, Y., Venkatachalam, A. S., & Xia, T. (2015). Ground-penetrating radar railroad ballast inspection with an unsupervised algorithm to boost the region of interest detection efficiency. *Journal of Applied Remote Sensing*, *9*(1), 095058. doi:10.1117/1.JRS.9.095058

Zhao, C. (2018). Cyber security issues in online games. *AIP Conference Proceedings*, *1955*(040015), 1–5.

KEY TERMS AND DEFINITIONS

Artificial Neural Network (ANN): The artificial neural network is a data mining framework able to work together and process complex data inputs. Such systems "learn" to perform tasks by considering examples, generally without being programmed with any task-specific rules.

Biometric Recognition: Is the technical approach for body measurements and calculations (it refers to metrics related to human characteristics).

Cyber Security: Computer security sub-class that depends only on technology.

Data Mining: Data mining is the process of discovering patterns in defined data sets involving methods at the intersection of machine learning, statistics, analytics and database systems.

Image Segmentation: Is the process of partitioning a digital image into multiple segments (sets of pixels, also known as super-pixels).

Infrared Termography: The use of radiometric thermograms to study heat distribution in structures or regions.

Reliability, Availability, Maintainability, and Safety (RAMS): Reliability is a system's ability to perform a specific function and may be given as design reliability or operational reliability; availability is the capability of a system to be considered in a functioning state; maintainability is determined by the simplicity of a system to be repaired or maintained; safety is the requirement not to harm people, the environment, or any other assets during a system's life cycle.

Risk Management: Identification, evaluation, and prioritization of followed by application of resources able to minimize, monitor, and control the probability or impact of unfortunate events and health accidents.

Chapter 7
Towards Intelligent Data Processing for Automated Determination of Information System Assets

Andrey Fedorchenko

iD https://orcid.org/0000-0002-5727-653X

St. Petersburg Institute for Informatics and Automation of the Russian Academy of Sciences (SPIIRAS), Russia

Elena Doynikova

iD https://orcid.org/0000-0001-6707-9153

St. Petersburg Institute for Informatics and Automation of the Russian Academy of Sciences (SPIIRAS), Russia

Igor Kotenko

iD https://orcid.org/0000-0001-6859-7120

St. Petersburg Institute for Informatics and Automation of the Russian Academy of Sciences (SPIIRAS), Russia

ABSTRACT

The chapter discusses how the intelligent data processing techniques, namely, the event correlation, can be used for automated discovery of information system assets. The authors believe that solving of this task will allow more accurate and detailed construction of the risk model for cyber security assessment. This task is complicated by the features of configuration and operation of modern information systems. The chapter describes different types of event analysis, including statistical, structural, dynamic, applied to this task. The authors propose a technique that incorporates determining the types of object characteristics, the types of objects (system assets), and their hierarchy based on the statistical analysis of system events. Significant attention is given to the stage of source data pre-processing. In addition, the developed technique has the broad application prospects to discover the inappropriate, dubious, and harmful information. The case studies and experiments that demonstrate an application of the developed technique are provided and analyzed.

DOI: 10.4018/978-1-7998-1290-6.ch007

INTRODUCTION

Well-known challenge of the modern information world is related to the analysis of huge amounts of data. It affects almost all research areas. In the chapter the authors consider this challenge on the example of tasks related to discovering of various data objects, or assets, including an inappropriate, dubious and harmful information, and the tasks of security assessment. Security assessment is directly connected with discovering of various objects. Assessment quality significantly depends on the accuracy of identifying the objects of various nature including the components of the analyzed system, vulnerabilities, attacks, attackers, etc.

The chapter focuses on the determination of information system assets. For any organization it is important to discover as primary assets as well as secondary assets that support viability of primary assets. While the assets should be specified on the design stage, this does not always happen. The features of the modern information systems complicate this task. In modern organizations the assets are connected by various data channels and semantic relations, and they can be strongly distributed. In such conditions if the architecture of the target information infrastructure is sufficiently large-scale then the expert inventory of assets requires significant time costs and human resources. Besides, in process of the system operation its infrastructure may change as a result of installing new software and hardware, system updates, countermeasure implementation, etc.

The authors believe that an automation of assets discovery and determination of hierarchy of relationships between them will allow more accurate and detailed construction of the risk model for cyber security assessment. This task is rather challenging. Currently network scanners can detect various network objects, such as services, the ports they use, the hosts on which they are deployed, and communication nodes. However, these tools do not allow automated determination of different types of static and dynamic objects (for example, processes, sessions, users, privileges, operation systems, etc.) and of their hierarchy. This prevents obtaining an actual dynamical model of the information system, which is initially uncertain.

In the chapter the authors propose a technique that incorporates determining the types of object characteristics, the types of objects (or system assets), and their hierarchy based on the statistical analysis of system events.

The proposed technique is based on the methods of correlation of events accumulated in security logs. The authors believe that dynamic analysis of system events and calculation of static and dynamic indexes, including frequency characteristics of event types, variability of event property values, pair utilization rates of event properties, and total utilization rates of the properties will allow one to determine the main event sources (objects) and the hierarchy of object types. Namely, the authors use calculated pair utilization rates for event properties, variability of values of object properties, and the total utilization rates of the properties. It allows determining the object types and their hierarchical interconnections from the point of view of a target infrastructure operation. This process can be realized from root object type "infrastructure" to leaf atomic object types, e.g. process id, taking into account subordination relations. The chapter describes different types of event analysis (statistical, structural, dynamic, etc.) that allows one to do it with maximum accuracy that is limited only by the source data on the assets in the event logs.

Though the approach is limited by the information stored in the event logs, the authors believe that further integration of dynamic models of infrastructure objects with the static data on the software and hardware will eliminate this limitation. Consideration of the conditionally static types of security data (vulnerabilities, weaknesses, attack patterns, etc.) will make possible proactive monitoring of organization security state for the preventive deployment of countermeasures. The developed approach has the broad application prospects to discover the inappropriate, dubious and harmful information.

Thus, the main objective of this chapter is to demonstrate how intelligent data processing can help to make an adequate representation of the initially uncertain infrastructure and its processes on the basis of the variety of heterogeneous information about events in the system.

The chapter includes analysis of the related research in the area of automated discovery of system configuration and events correlation, description of the proposed technique of assets discovery using intelligent data analysis (namely, event correlation), consideration of a case study and conducted experiments with the system security logs and their results, as well as conclusion and discussion of possible future research directions.

BACKGROUND

As soon as the task of automated discovery of system assets is chosen as the main problem, this section reviews the research in this area first. The various classes of data analysis methods are used in this area, namely signature analysis methods and intelligent data analysis, including statistical data analysis.

The signature analysis methods (that implies comparison with rules, patters, etc.) are the most stable when working with known types of objects and their actions. But these methods are complicated from the set up and implementation point of view. Besides, they do not allow decision making for the uncertain, corrupted and unreliable data.

Statistical data analysis (used for statistical data and based on mathematical statistics and probability) are widely used to analyze behavior of the target infrastructure and of its objects. But these methods react unpredictably to possible anomalies in the analyzed system. Besides, they cannot take into account the semantics of input data.

Intelligent data analysis (that is used to extract new knowledge from data) is powerful tool for processing high-dimensional data, as well as inconsistent and incomplete data in the tasks of asset classification and ranking, and forecasting their behavior. Main disadvantages of such methods and approaches are rigid binding of the trained model to the target infrastructure (i.e. strong dependence of the model operation from training data sets), as well as not always predictable accuracy rates.

The authors propose to use statistical analysis together with structural and dynamic ones to turn to the intelligent data analysis.

More specific examples of applying the methods of different classes are provided below.

One of the main tools to automatically specify the network infrastructure are network scanners (signature methods) such as Nmap ("NMap reference guide," n.d.), Nessus ("Nessus vulnerability scanner," n.d.), and Wireshark ("Wireshark vulnerability scanner," n.d.). Currently network scanners can detect various network objects, such as services, the ports they use, the hosts on which they are deployed, and communication nodes. However, these tools do not allow automated determination of different types of static and dynamic objects (for example, processes, sessions, users, privileges, operation systems, etc.) and of their hierarchy. This prevents obtaining an actual dynamical model of the initially uncertain information system.

There are techniques for automated detection of service dependencies They include the following methods and techniques (Agarwal, Gupta, Kar, Neogi, & Sailer, 2004): get knowledge on dependencies from system files or specially designed configuration store; use code to determine dependencies (Ensel, 2001); passive identification methods based on analysis of interaction of objects (Tuchs & Jobmann, 2001); methods based on neural networks (Hellerstein, Ma, & Perng, 2002); and data mining methods.

Detection of service dependencies allows automated generation of service dependencies graphs that are used to determinate cyber attack impact propagations. The described studies mainly take into account the objects of one type (services).

The proposed in this chapter approach is based on the correlation methods. These methods can use both intelligent data analysis and other types of analysis. Data correlation can be used to solve various security tasks. They include determination of interconnections between heterogeneous security information, grouping of low-level events into high-level meta events, aggregation of network events into security incidents and subsequent detection of attacks, discovery of the types of information system objects and relationships between them.

Existing methods for correlation of events and security information can be nominally divided into signature-based and heuristic (behavior analysis) ones that relate to statistical and intelligent data analysis. They are based on similarity analysis, statistical analysis, machine learning, etc. At present, the self-learning approaches to correlation such as Bayesian networks, immune networks, artificial neural networks are the most promising. The advantage of these approaches is the possibility of an unconditional event correlation with minimization of manual settings. However, building of learning models requires a preliminary data analysis and it is difficult to automate it. In addition, the application of intelligent approaches imposes the requirements for assessing the adequacy and quality of the models, and the original training data should be complete. Although these methods are used for attack detection, the authors argue that the data correlation approach is also applicable for automated discovery of information system assets.

There is also a small amount of research works related to intelligent correlation methods, including the ones for objects discovery. There are works using data mining (Motahari-Nezhad, Saint-Paul, Casati, & Benatallah, 2011; Sadoddin & Ghorbani, 2006). In (Sadoddin & Ghorbani, 2006) the event correlation and generation of event correlation rules based on the empirical evidence is proposed. In (Motahari-Nezhad et al., 2011) the authors use only frequency characteristics of event types to discover the objects, while other characteristics of the source data, such as the utilization rate and variability of properties and their values, can improve correlation accuracy. It allows the more accurate determination of objects. In (Müller, 2009) the authors analyze event sequences to detect incidents. Analysis of the hierarchy of objects and their types first, and subsequent transition to the analysis of event sequences of separate objects can results in the more accurate comparison of event sequences, division of the events by relation to the objects, and determination of connections between the objects.

Finally, while correlating events one of the key challenges is variety of event formats in different sources. Therefore, event log normalization and correlation is an important task.

In (Sapegin et al., 2014) new log format is proposed as superstructure for the existing formats. The common idea consist in the analysis of existing formats and extraction of minimum number of required identical fields. This approach can be also used for event log normalization.

In (US7308689, 2002) the "method, apparatus, and program for associating related heterogeneous events in an event handler" were patented. The events are represented as a vector of attributes and then normalized via renaming, deriving new attributes from existing, converting the attribute value ranges. Then the associations are defined between the vectors of different events. The advantage of this approach compared to the previous one is that it can be used for attributes with different names.

In (US20090276843, 2009) the approach to security event data normalization was patented. It includes adding tag to each event, depending on the nature of the source, and further transformation them to the common format for all sources. The disadvantage of this approach is the need for such a format.

The patent (US7376969B1, 2008) proposes the approach to the event normalization that consists in event transformation to the common format and rule-based correlation.

Thus, there are different methods for event correlation, but the task of automated determination of the uncertain architecture is not resolved to date. At the same time the intelligent data analysis methods for correlation of the collected data are being actively developing. The authors believe that dynamic analysis of system events and calculation of the static and dynamic indexes, including frequency characteristics of event types, variability of event property values, pair utilization rates of event properties, and total utilization rates of the properties will allow one to determine the main event sources (objects) and the hierarchy of object types

INTELLIGENT DATA ANALYSIS FOR DETERMINATION OF SYSTEM ASSETS

Currently to solve the tasks of analyzing the heterogeneous and unmarked data from complex dynamically generated infrastructures, the various methods of machine learning are used. Thus, the separate but close to the considered in this chapter task is recognition of the Internet of things devices on the base of observed network traffic. In these tasks the intelligent data analysis methods with learning are used. Such approach implies existence of the related device traffic sample. The other area of application of the intelligent data analysis is to discover the network protocols and their belonging to known sources of their generation in the network traffic.

This chapter considers the problem of automated classification (clustering) of types of action sources registered in event logs of the analyzed infrastructure. It is supposed that initially there is no any information both on a number of sources types and on difference in data they generate. In this case, the initial markup is based on the structural analysis of event records with their further probabilistic interpretation.

Before the determination of system assets in scope of the approach based on data analysis the data should be gathered and pre-processed. The event data can be collected from system logs and should be normalized for further analysis.

Input Data Gathering and Processing

The proposed approach implies that there is no any input data on the analyzed infrastructure (namely, system assets, where asset is any object of the analyzed system including physical and logical objects) except system logs. Thus, input data for the analysis is a set of security events E from a system log L: $E^L = \{e_1, e_2, ..., e_n\}$, where event e describes an action and is a result of an action attempt (e.g. an event of denying access to a OS file system resource), a fact of the action start (e.g. an event of process launching in OS) or a fact or result of the action completion (e.g. an event of modification of OS security policy). In its turn, each event is described by the set of properties related to the assets (objects) involved in the action. Each event e consists of a set of pairs: $e=(p_i, v_i)$, where p_i – an event property, v_i – an event property value. At any time moment the sets of event properties and their values are finite and not empty, but their cardinality can vary.

The event properties and their values should be normalized on the initial stage because there are empty properties that do not contain any values or contain only zero value. Besides, the values of properties of different types can match by zero and empty values, and vice versa the values of properties of the same type can differ because of encoding and description format (e.g., heximal and decimal representation). This can significantly decrease the quality of determination of property types and object types. The authors accomplished the task of normalization manually on the basis of expert evaluation. Automation of this stage is promising direction for the future research.

After the preprocessing the data can be analyzed to discover types of system assets and their hierarchy.

Determination of Asset Types, Their Hierarchy and Roles

The intelligent data analysis of the collected data can help to determine types of properties (these properties describe assets and appear in the events related to the appropriate assets), types of assets of the target infrastructure, their hierarchy and roles. To solve this task the chapter proposes an approach based on the structural and statistical analysis of raw data that allows extracting new data on the analyzed infrastructure. In this study the authors use correlation methods to determine assets (i.e. information and physical objects of target infrastructure) and their characteristics.

Application of the proposed event correlation approach to determine system assets and their hierarchy based on statistical analysis allows specifying a model of analyzed infrastructure. To achieve this goal a model of the uncertain infrastructure and its relation to the input data should be introduced first.

The Model of the Uncertain Infrastructure

At each point in time, an uncertain infrastructure I consists of a set of information objects (assets) O:

$$O = \left\{ o_1, o_2, \ldots, o_s \right\},$$

where s – a total number of objects. Their state is described by one or more characteristics x and their values v:

$$o = \left(x_i, v_i \right),$$

$$x_i \in X, X = \left\{ x_1, x_2, \ldots, x_r \right\}, \left| X \right| \geq 1,$$

where

r – a total number of possible characteristics;
$v_i \in V^{x_i}$; V^{x_i} – a set of possible x_i values, $V^{x_i} = \left\{ v_1, v_2, \ldots, v_k \right\}$,
k – a number of possible values of characteristic x_i, $V^{x_i} \subset V$;
V – a set of all object characteristic values, $V = \left\{ V^{x_1}, V^{x_2}, \ldots, V^{x_k} \right\}$.

Information objects are obligatorily connected to each other by the possession relations. That is, each object is a part of a higher-level object and (or) contains low-level objects (for example host and processes). The relation between objects is determined by their direct interaction. It allows constructing an object hierarchy. The set of characteristics X_o that describe an information object o, uniquely identifies its type ot, i.e. each characteristic x from the set X belongs to only one type of object ot. Examples of object types are "process", "file", "session", "sensor", "host", and others.

The last element of the model of the uncertain infrastructure I is a set of relations R between objects O. But determination of this set is out of this research. It will be considered in the future work for refinement of assets discovery.

Thus, model M of an uncertain infrastructure I consists of a set of information objects O, a set of their types OT and a set of object relations R: $M = \langle O, OT, R \rangle$.

The Proposed Technique

Based on the above, the technique should transform the input data of the correlation process into the set of objects and their types of the uncertain infrastructure model: $\{E, P, V\}^f_{\rightarrow} \{O, OT\}$, where E – a set of events to analyze, P – a set of object's properties observed in the event records, V – a set of properties' values observed in the event records.

The correlation method based on the dynamic events analysis is used to determine data types (semantic). The stage of determination of object types and their hierarchy for the developed technique includes the following steps:

1. Determination of types of event properties based on the analysis of their possible values;
2. Determination of object types based on the property types;
3. Determination of hierarchy of object types.

The *first step* that consists in the determination of event properties' types is required:

(1) to specify the set of possible types of properties $PT = \{pt_1, pt_2, ..., pt_n\}$, where n – a total number of types, and

(2) to determine the type of the observed property value for further allocation of object types.

For this goal it is necessary to analyze the set of event properties $P = \{p_1, p_2, ..., p_m\}$, where m – a total number of properties of all events, that can take a set of values $V = \{V^{p_1}, V^{p_2}, ..., V^{p_m}\}$. As a result each property type pt is mapped to the set of properties p. To determine the properties of the same type it is proposed to analyze the variability of their values compared to other properties (to find properties that take the same values). The Jaccard index which specifies the belongingness of properties to one data type is used:

$$\mu_{pt} = \frac{\left| V^{p_i} \cap V^{p_j} \right|}{\left| V^{p_i} \cup V^{p_j} \right|}, \tag{1}$$

where V – a set of property values. One can say that properties p_i and p_j belong to one type if their values are equivalent.

At the same time, it should be noticed that the nature of properties is different. While some properties remain their values almost unchanged (the authors call them static properties, an example of static property is process name), other properties vary rather often (the authors call them dynamic properties, an example of dynamic property is process id). This should be considered while relate the properties to the same type on the basis of the Jaccard index value. Thus, to calculate the index of similarity (that specifies the belongingness to one data type) for dynamic properties the lifetime intervals of objects specified with these properties should be previously found.

On the *second step*, the pair utilization rate for the event properties is calculated to outline specific groups. These groups indicate the presence of objects of specific types. The pair utilization rate for properties p_i and p_j is also based on the Jaccard index. It represents relation of number of properties' joint utilization in events to the total number of events where these properties were observed:

$$\mu_{ot} = \frac{\left| E^{p_i} \cap E^{p_j} \right|}{\left| E^{p_i} \cup E^{p_j} \right|}. \tag{2}$$

The authors propose to outline properties of one type inside the groups for further specification of object types and/or roles. In this case, the role is a purpose of the infrastructure object in action that is described using the event (for example, Subject, Object, Source, Target, etc.). At the same time, interpreting the role of object automatically is not possible. But one can divide different roles of objects of the same type. To outline the role of object type in the events the following condition should be satisfied: properties of the same type and unequal properties that form the semantic type of infrastructure objects must meet at least twice in the property groups outlined by pair utilization.

On the *third step* the hierarchy of object types is determined. It is based on the total utilization rate of their properties (the higher the utilization rate, the higher the object in the hierarchy). The total utilization rate of the property is the ratio of the property utilization number in the events to the total number of events. The relations between object types depend on the appropriate event types. The authors outline two main types of events: (1) changing of the object state and (2) interaction between objects. Interaction between objects determines an existence of connection between object types.

The technique for the assets inventory can be used in scope of the security management systems. The main users of the technique are security administrators of the large-scale heterogeneous distributed information systems.

IMPLEMENTATION AND EXPERIMENTS

This section describes a case study and experiments that demonstrate the application of the developed technique. Significant attention is given to the stage of source data pre-processing. At present, this task is implemented on the basis of expert evaluation. In the experiments the authors use introduced indexes to determine property types (the pair variability of property values), object types (the pair utilization rate of properties) and their hierarchy (the total utilization rate of properties).

To conduct the experiment the developed technique was implemented using Python 3.5 language, libraries numpy, scipy and pandas, GraphViz and matplotlib, pyplot and seaborn modules for visualization. The experiments were conducted on computing platform with one 6-core processor Intel(R) Xeon(R) CPU E5-2603 v3 @ 1.60GHz and 64 GB RAM.

In the conditions of an uncertain target infrastructure the set of events E, the set of properties P and the set of their values V are initially empty. The sets P and V should be initially specified using historical records of event logs, or accumulating information in real time. At the moment the authors conducted experiments in scope of one host. In the future it is planned to expand experiments on various information systems.

Source data for the case study and experiments are events of security log of the host running OS Windows 8. The logging subsystem of the operation system was set to gather maximum number of security events types.

The log for experiments has the following features: (1) events number: ~ 6700000; (2) original event types number: ~40 (from more than 250 stated by the security log developers ("Windows Security Log Events," n.d.)); (3) events properties number: ~100; (4) number of possible values of properties (without merging of the same values between different properties): ~240000; (5) total number of possible values (all properties): ~210000; (6) log disk space: 7GB in the XML format, ~1 GB in the CSV format; (7) duration of log: ~30 days; (8) time reference accuracy: 0.1 microseconds.

The stage of source data pre-processing assumes normalization of event properties and their values for correct further analysis. The normalization results are as follows.

Event types 5156 "The Windows Filtering Platform has allowed a connection" and 5157 "The Windows Filtering Platform has blocked a connection" contain property "ProcessID", which name differs from other process ID properties "ProcessId". This can significantly reduce both the quality of determination of property types and the quality of determination of object types. Besides, significant deviation in structures of event types describing information objects can lead to inaccurate results of analysis of the pair utilization rate in spite of an unambiguous comparison of the indicated names for these types of properties. A possible solution of this problem is converting the property names to one case. The further analysis should consider the possible gaps in the source data in case of unmatched structures for properties of event types. In the described case we converted the property name "ProcessID" to "ProcessId". In the process of analysis the authors found out that for 6 event properties a single semantically zero value was observed: '-'. Such properties were excluded from the further analysis. Besides, the indicated value was observed for 23 properties having other possible values. In this case the authors excluded '-' from the list of possible values. Such an omission in the source data can indicate an incorrect structure of types of events that use these properties. For a number of properties only zero values were observed represented in various formats, for example: "S-1-0-0" and "{00000000-0000-0000-0000-000000000000}". However, these values have a certain semantic load, so we used properties with such values in the further analysis.

In the case study and experiments the authors used the indexes introduced in previous section to determine property types (the pair variability of property values, Eq.1), object types (the pair utilization rate of properties, Eq.2) and their hierarchy (the total utilization rate of properties).

Fig. 1, Fig. 2 and Fig. 3 represent the results of processing of OS Windows 8 security events log.

The key elements of these figures are names of event properties (SourceAddress, ProcessName, etc.). These properties are grouped (in rectangular elements) via utilization rate (pair utilization). Thus, the obtained property groups are observed in the event log only jointly. The task of determination of event property types is required to generate a list of characteristics of information objects. The set of

Figure 1. The scheme of properties' groups specifying the object type NetworkResource

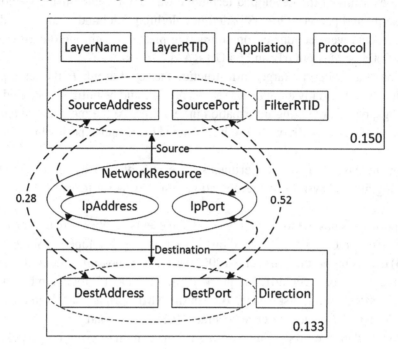

Figure 2. The scheme of properties' groups specifying the object type Process

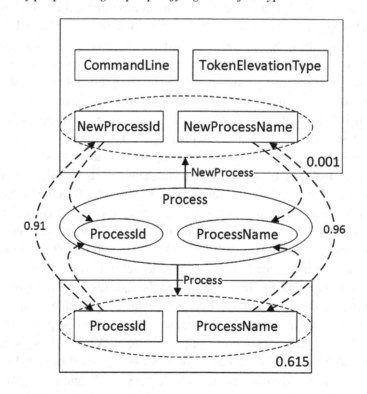

Figure 3. The scheme of properties' groups specifying the object type SystemResource

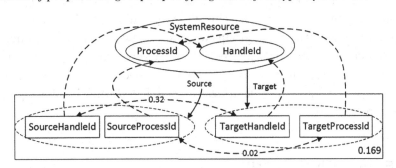

these characteristics specifies the type of described object on the next step. The pair utilization rate is represented for each group in the bottom right corner. The dotted bidirectional arrows in these figures denote the relation between the properties considering their observed values. These arrows are noted with appropriate values. It can be seen that an intersection of values for all linked properties are rather strong except properties SourceProcessId and TargetProcessId (pair variability is equal 0.02). This fact is explained by the nature of these properties. As soon as the set of source processes rarely intersects with the set of target processes. Besides, the incorrect determination of type can be a result of type I and type II errors. Type I error consists in excluding property from the type to which it actually belongs. The possible reasons for such errors are the following: (1) high total variability; (2) an insufficient total variability of one of the properties. Type II error consists in merging of two types of properties. For example, it can be explained by the similarity of description formats of properties of different types.

As soon as variability is the indicator of property dynamics, overcoming of the described errors is possible in case of analysis of the pair variability in dynamics. This operation assumes comparison of the possible property values on the short time interval. The hypothesis is that while observing the specific property value at the current time moment the object described by this value is "alive" in the vicinity of this moment. Thus, dynamics of values of event properties is defined by the lifetime of such objects. The pair comparison of property values with reference to the time scale allows more accurate calculation of properties variability and minimizing of the described errors.

The dotted directed arrows denote belongingness of the property events' instances to their semantic types. Determination of object types using the pair utilization rate of the properties is based on the hypothesis that the same utilization of the event properties indicates their belongingness to one or more object types of the same level. The semantic types are represented in the single (not grouped) oval elements with solid border.

The authors grouped these items by semantic description of object types. The schemes of properties' groups of OS Windows specifying object types NetworkResource, Process and SystemResource and their roles are depicted in Fig. 1, Fig. 2 and Fig. 3, accordingly.

The oval group elements with dotted border denote the groups of properties describing one object type. Thus, the condition of allocation of object types is both the index of pair utilization rate and the index of pair variability of their values.

The directed solid rows denote the roles in which the allocated object types are used in event logs. The roles are noted in arrows' labels, but their semantic is determined manually. An illustrative example is depicted in Fig. 3, where one object type is used in two roles simultaneously.

More detailed determination of object types, for example, based on calculating correlation coefficients, will allow avoiding these inaccuracies. This direction will be considered in the future research.

As the result of experiment 60 property groups were determined. It should be noticed that properties of one group are used in event types only jointly. The properties were grouped semantically correctly. The total utilization rates of properties relative to the total number of events show that separate groups of properties are equal or very close in value utilization rate. It confirms that the approach is applicable for the assets determination tasks.

FUTURE RESEARCH DIRECTIONS

In the future work the authors plan to enhance the proposed approach and technique applying interval analysis of the events characteristics, to expand it for determining different types of relations between objects, and to connect it with a security assessment technique. It is planned to connect the developed approach and technique with criticality and security assessment tasks. Besides, it is planned to connect an analysis of dynamic data from event logs with static data from security databases for detection of the malicious objects

CONCLUSION

Intelligent data analysis has a great prospective in the various research areas. The chapter reviewed intelligent data analysis methods in application to the assets determination task.

The authors proposed the technique to discover information system assets based on the event correlation methods. The chapter described the technique and its key components including input data, used models and indexes, with special attention to the used data analysis methods, including statistical, structural, and dynamic analysis.

Source data pre-processing was described. The case study and the obtained results of the experiments were provided and confirmed the possibility to apply the suggested approach and technique for the assets determination tasks.

ACKNOWLEDGMENT

The work is performed by the grant of Russian Science Foundation (#18-11-00302) in SPIIRAS.

REFERENCES

Agarwal, M. K., Gupta, M., Kar, G., Neogi, A., & Sailer, A. (2004). Mining Activity Data for Dynamic Dependency Discovery in e-Business Systems. *IEEE eTransactions on Network and Service Management, 1*(2), 49–58. doi:10.1109/TNSM.2004.4798290

Black, S., Debar, H., Michael, J., & Wespi, G. A. (2002). US7308689. US Patent Office.

Ensel, C. (2001). A scalable approach to automated service dependency modeling in heterogeneous environments. *Enterprise Distributed Object Computing Conference, 2001. EDOC '01. Proceedings. Fifth IEEE International*. 10.1109/EDOC.2001.950429

Hellerstein, J. L., Ma, S., & Perng, C.-S. (2002). Discovering actionable patterns in event data. *IBM Systems Journal*, *41*(3), 475–493. doi:10.1147j.413.0475

Motahari-Nezhad, H. R., Saint-Paul, R., Casati, F., & Benatallah, B. (2011). *Event correlation for process discovery from web service interaction logs*. VLDB. doi:10.100700778-010-0203-9

Müller, A. (2009). *Event Correlation Engine*. ETH. doi:10.1109/45.954656

Nessus Vulnerability Scanner. (n.d.). Retrieved July 2, 2018, from http://www.tenable.com/products/nessus-vulnerability-scanner

Njemanze, H. S., & Kothari, P. S. (2008). *US7376969B1*. US Patent Office.

NMap Reference Guide. (n.d.). Retrieved July 2, 2018, from http://nmap.org/book/man.html

Patel, R. (2009). US20090276843. US Patent Office.

Sadoddin, R., & Ghorbani, A. (2006). Alert Correlation Survey: Framework and Techniques. *Proceedings of the International Conference on Privacy, Security and Trust: Bridge the Gap Between PST Technologies and Business Services*.

Sapegin, A., Jaeger, D., Azodi, A., Gawron, M., Cheng, F., & Meinel, C. (2014). Normalisation of Log Messages for Intrusion Detection. *Journal of Information Assurance and Security*, *9*, 167–176.

Tuchs, K. D., & Jobmann, K. (2001). Intelligent search for correlated alarm events in databases. *2001 7th IEEE/IFIP International Symposium on Integrated Network Management Proceedings: Integrated Management Strategies for the New Millennium*. 10.1109/INM.2001.918040

Windows Security Log Events. (n.d.). Retrieved January 22, 2018, from https://www.ultimatewindowssecurity.com/securitylog/encyclopedia/Default.aspx

Wireshark Vulnerability Scanner. (n.d.). Retrieved July 2, 2018, from https://www.wireshark.org

KEY TERMS AND DEFINITIONS

Event: The result of some action(s) (or attempt) added to the log of observed information system.

Event Property: An atomic part of event record that characterizes the separate aspect of object of observed infrastructure. This object participates in the recorded action(s).

Information Object (Asset): The holistic element of infrastructure that have properties, state, and a certain functional load.

Information Object Type: The set of characteristics (structure) that describes semantically distinct group of objects of information infrastructure (for example, the process, the network resource).

Properties' Pair Utilization Index: Numerical characteristic in [0,1] range based on the Jaccard index and calculated using the observed sets of two properties in the events.

Semantic Type of Event Property: Characteristic of the action described in the event or characteristic of the information object that identifies it among the other objects or defines its state.

Similarity Index: Numerical characteristic in [0,1] range based on the Jaccard index and calculated using the set of observed values of two event properties.

Chapter 8
Modified Methods for Image Processing of Laser Beam Profiles

Sergii Bilan
Onseo Company, Ukraine

ABSTRACT

The chapter is devoted to the analysis of the object of the study and highlighted its features as a means of information processing. The review of the existing methods of processing images of the profiles of laser beams, the principles of the operation of systems on the basis of similar algorithms, an analysis of the accuracy of the determination of the energy and geometric centers of the beam of laser beam, its diameter, and the differences of laser radiation are carred out. On the basis of the introduced criterion for estimating the symmetry of the contour of an image of a laser profile, a method for finding the optimal center for such an image is proposed. A comparative software model of effective methods for analysis of laser radiation parameters, namely, the search for laser image contour centers and the determination of the diameter of a laser beam, was constructed.

DESCRIPTION AND SUBJECTS OF THE RESEARCH OBJECT

Indisputable factor in the development of our society is the introduction of laser technologies into all areas of human activity. Such an implementation, according to all existing indicators, is first of all implemented in systems where there is a problem of accuracy and speed of transmission and processing of information (Fig. 1) (Goodman, 2017; Shack, & Platt, 1971; Pennington, 1993; Welsh, Roggemann, Ellerbroek, & Pennington, 1995; Vasiliev, Sumerin, Chervonkin,. et al., 2002; Chervonkin, Nabokin, & Hyppenen, 2006; GOST 26086–84, 1984). The introduction of laser and optoelectronic devices can eliminate a number of shortcomings that are present in purely electronic systems (Goodman, 2017; Shack, & Platt, 1971; Pennington, 1993; Welsh, Roggemann, Ellerbroek, & Pennington, 1995; Vasiliev, Sumerin, Chervonkin,. et al., 2002; Chervonkin, Nabokin, & Hyppenen, 2006; GOST 26086–84, 1984; Dakin, & Brown, 2017; Piprek, 2017; Dutta, & Zhang, 2018).

DOI: 10.4018/978-1-7998-1290-6.ch008

Figure 1. Classification of tasks that arise when processing images of laser profiles

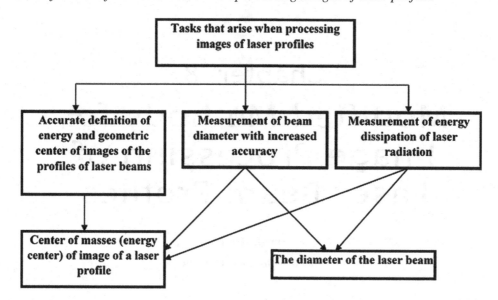

But the use of laser devices to improve the accuracy of the operation of laser location systems, aiming systems, open optical communication systems, etc. imposes tight requirements for both the laser as well as the optical-mechanical means that form and direct the laser beam in the required manner.

From this point of view, the laser becomes the base node of the entire system. Therefore, when they are manufactured, strict control of all its parameters is carried out, which is carried out by different methods and technologies.

One of the approaches to controlling the parameters of lasers, when they are aligned, is a technique based on the evaluation of the characteristics of the image of the profile of the laser beam (GOST 26086–84). According to such technology, accurate estimation of the energy and geometric centers, forms (perimeter values, diameters, shape distortions, etc.) of a laser beam, energy dissipation, etc. is achieved.

But the methods and means currently in use, which use such technologies, as a rule do not give the desired result (Goodman, 2017; Shack, & Platt, 1971; Pennington, 1993; Welsh, Roggemann, Ellerbroek, & Pennington, 1995; Vasiliev, Sumerin, Chervonkin,. et al., 2002; Chervonkin, Nabokin, & Hyppenen, 2006; GOST 26086–84, 1984; Dakin, & Brown, 2017; Piprek, 2017; Dutta, & Zhang, 2018). First, they use sophisticated algorithms (GOST 26086–84; Kovzel, Timchenko, Kutaev, et. Al. 2006) and hardware that worsen precision, since they do not always take into account "deep" distortion of the shape of the spots, reducing the number of suitable images in the track (package of cuts of the beam). Also, existing methods use system training (GOST 26086–84; Kovzel, Timchenko, Kutaev, et. Al. 2006; Timchenko, Kokriatskaia, Yarovyy, & Denysova, 2013; Yarovyy, Timchenko, & Kokriatskaia, 2012) to further process images. Such algorithms need to be improved. So the problem is not removed.

In aiming systems and laser locations, the task of precision aiming also stands. It depends on the deviation of the laser beam from the base axis, which leads to the deterioration of adjustments of the channel of the direction of optical direction finding (Vasiliev, Sumerin, Chervonkin,. et al., 2002; Chervonkin, Nabokin, & Hyppenen, 2006; GOST 26086–84, 1984; Dakin, & Brown, 2017; Piprek, 2017; Dutta, & Zhang, 2018). In such systems, there is a need for a continuous analysis of the marker radiation source, which is projected onto a matrix photodetector. The time taken for the reaction of the system depends on the processing speed and the analysis performed. That is, in such systems, the speed and accuracy of the interrelated characteristics, and the methods that they increase need to be improved.

Thus, in order to improve the operation of systems using laser technology, the task of high-precision image processing of laser beam profiles requires the search for efficient algorithms based on a combination of software and hardware that reduces the time spent on its solution.

TASKS AND REQUIREMENTS FOR EVALUATION OF LASER SYSTEM PARAMETERS

The need to control and analyze the images of the profiles of laser beams is related to the following tasks:

- Alignment of laser emitters (GOST 26086–84);
- The restoration of the shape of distorted partially reflective surfaces and the analysis of phase heterogeneities in transparent media by non-contact sensors operating on the Shaka-Hartmann method (Goodman, 2017; Shack, & Platt, 1971; Pennington, 1993);
- The accuracy and reliability of the operation of optical location systems (Vasiliev, Sumerin, Chervonkin,. et al., 2002; Chervonkin, Nabokin, & Hyppenen, 2006; GOST 26086–84, 1984; Dakin, & Brown, 2017; Piprek, 2017; Dutta, & Zhang, 2018).

The first task is put in the manufacture of laser emitters, as well as in laser communication systems. The question of the solution of such problems is put in literary sources (Vasiliev, Sumerin, Chervonkin,. et al., 2002; Chervonkin, Nabokin, & Hyppenen, 2006; GOST 26086–84, 1984; Dakin, & Brown, 2017; Piprek, 2017; GOST 26086–84).

The question of the exact location of the energy centers of the laser beam profiles is placed at the second task of processing the Hartmanograms to restore the shape of the curved partially reflective surfaces and to analyze the heterogeneities in the transparent media by non-contact sensors working on the Shaka-Hartmann method (Goodman, 2017; Shack, & Platt, 1971; Pennington, 1993).

The key element of the Shaka-Hurtman sensor is a square or hexagonal lens raster. Each lens usually has a size of 1 mm or less. The sensor lens divides the investigated wave front into subaperticles, forming in the focal plane of the raster an array of focal spots. There's a CCD camera that registers the image to be received - a gartmanogram. When applied to the input beam with a plane wave front (it is obtained using a high-quality gauge mirror), the outline is formed by a pattern consisting of spots regularly arranged on the optical axes of the lenses. This picture is taken as the template. When the input to the sensor of the beam with a distorted wave front, each spot shifts relative to the axis of the lens. The displacement of the "center of mass" of each spot is proportional to the local tilt of the wave front within the boundaries of this subaperture.

Also, the restoration of the shape of the wave front of the probe beam allows not only to analyze the relief of the reflecting surface, but also to measure the "illumination" of various phase heterogeneities in transparent objects associated with variations in the thickness of the object or its refractive index.

To determine the position of the spots, we search for areas above the noise cutoff level and determine their "centers of mass". However, at a large depth of modulation of the analyzed wave front, the shape of focal spots is strongly distorted and the traditionally used algorithm of mass centers gives inaccurate results. Therefore, the creation of more precise algorithms for searching centers of masses of laser spots is an actual problem in the described area (Goodman, 2017; Shack, & Platt, 1971; Pennington, 1993).

An effective solution to the third task is achieved by determining the parameters of the alignment of the optical path of the detection channel (Vasiliev, Sumerin, Chervonkin,. et al., 2002; Chervonkin, Nabokin, & Hyppenen, 2006; GOST 26086–84, 1984; Dakin, & Brown, 2017; Piprek, 2017; Dutta, & Zhang, 2018). In such systems, a marker radiation source is analyzed, which is projected onto all receivers and points to a single basic optical direction. In them the basic optical axis of the system is connected with the marker source of radiation.

Optical - mechanical path of similar optical location systems (OLS) can be submitted as typical directional nodes.

The marker source of radiation is projected onto all photodetectors and indicates a single basic optical direction. The base optical axis of the system is associated with a marker source of radiation.

If in the course of operation the optical axis of the directional channel changed its direction, then, thanks to the built-in system of the reference source of radiation, it is possible to determine how far the channel has been displaced in relation to its previous position or how far the channels of the directional links have been diverted relative to each other and, on the basis of this information, the emerging discrepancies are corrected.

The position of the energy center of radiation of a marker source on a photodetector matrix by methods of mathematical processing of an image can be determined with an accuracy several times better than the angular size of the matrix resolution element. For this, the angular beam size of the beam should exceed the angular pixel size several times (Chervonkin, Nabokin, & Hyppenen, 2006).

In the general case, previously unknown parameters of the distribution spot, for example, change during operation. Thus, it is necessary to define a law that describes the position of the energy center of the spot of radiation on a photodetector matrix with the precision of the pixel's pixel, based solely on the assumption of the symmetry of the energy distribution in the spot relative to the axial direction.

The formula for determining the center of the radiation spike on information about the energy value on each of the elements of the matrix can be represented as follows:

$$\Delta X = \frac{\sum_{i=1}^{N} A_i \cdot W_i}{\sum_{i=1}^{N} W_i} - 0.5, \tag{1}$$

were ΔX – spot center position relative to the start of the bitmap coordinate system; A_i – weight coefficients of elements in a raster coordinate system; W_i – pixel signal level; N – linear size of the tracking window.

REVIEW OF METHODS FOR LASER BEAM ANALYSIS

Classification of methods used to analyze the parameters of laser beams on Fig. 2 are shown.

Figure 2 shows the methods for measuring the basic characteristics of laser beams in accordance with existing tasks.

Figure 2. Existing methods for measuring the basic characteristics of laser beams

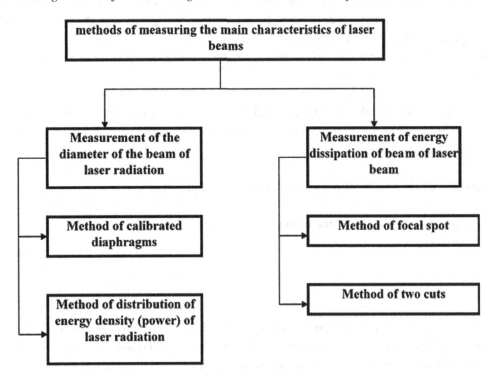

There are standardized methods for measuring the parameters of laser beams, which extends to lasers of continuous and pulsed modes of operation, and establish methods for measuring the diameter of a beam of radiation by the following methods:

- Method of calibrated diaphragms;
- Method of distribution of energy density (power) of laser radiation.

As well as methods for measuring the energy dissipation of laser radiation:

- Method of focal spot;
- Method of two profile.

Measurement using the calibrated diaphragm method is based on determining the diameter of the diaphragm, through which the given fraction of the energy (power) of laser radiation passes.
The measurements are as follows.

1. The measuring instruments and auxiliary devices and prepare them for operation in accordance with the operational documentation on them are Installed.
2. The laser are turned and warmed up during the readiness time set in the standard for a laser of a particular type.

3. Alignment are performed, achieving a beam of laser radiation into the central part of the diaphragm, receiving areas of the dimming device, the coupler, the optical system and the means of measuring the energy (power) of the laser radiation.
4. The diameter of the diaphragm D1, in which the total energy z_1 (power) of the radiation passes through the diaphragm, are set.
5. The energy (power) of laser radiation z_1 and z'_1 are measured.
6. Reducing the diameter of the diaphragm z_i and z'_i ($i=2, 3 ... n$) are determined. Measurement is carried out on at least five different diaphragm diameters, unless otherwise specified in the standards for lasers of specific types.

The processing of measurement results is carried out as follows.

1. For each i-th diameter value Di the ratio are calculated

$$\gamma_i = \alpha \frac{z_i}{z'_i},$$

(2)

2. Where α — coefficient determined according to the tables (GOST 26086–84); $i= 1, 2, ... n$.
3. The obtained data are approximated by the dependence $\gamma=F(D)$ and determine the diaphragm diameter corresponding to the level of energy γ_H, specified in the standards for lasers of specific types.

The diameter of the diaphragm found is taken as the beam diameter of the laser radiation. The processing of results is also possible with the use of computer technology.

The method for distributing the density of energy (power) of laser radiation is based on the determination of the diameter of the circle, which contains a given fraction of the energy (power) of laser radiation. The center of this circle must correspond to the point of intersection of the beam of laser radiation, which coincides with the energy center of the relative distribution of the energy density (power) (RDED (P)). Under the energy center of the RDED is understood to be the point in the plane of the intersection of the beam of laser radiation, which is the center of gravity of the distribution of the density of energy (power) in the corresponding section.

The resulting image of the laser spot is treated as follows.

1. A matrix of values of the relative density of energy (power) β_{kl} is constructed at different points of the intersection of the laser beam (where k, l - are the coordinates of the point of intersection).
2. The total energy (power) of laser radiation z_1 is calculated by the formula

$$z_1 = \Delta_x \Delta_y \sum_{k=1}^{M} \sum_{l=1}^{N} \beta_{kl},$$

(3)

were Δ_x, Δ_y – it is a uniform step between adjacent points of the RDED (P), in which β_{kl} is defined on the corresponding axes of coordinates; M, N - the number of points in the intersection of the beam on the row and the column of the matrix of values, respectively.

3.   The coordinates of the energy center O (x_0, y_0) RDED (P) are calculated by the formulas:

$$x_0 = \Delta_x \frac{\sum_{k=1}^{M}\sum_{l=1}^{N}(k\beta_{kl})}{\sum_{k=1}^{M}\sum_{l=1}^{N}\beta_{kl}}, \tag{4}$$

$$y_0 = \Delta_y \frac{\sum_{k=1}^{M}\sum_{l=1}^{N}(l\beta_{kl})}{\sum_{k=1}^{M}\sum_{l=1}^{N}\beta_{kl}}. \tag{5}$$

4.   Diameter D1 of the circle, in which the matrix of values β_{kl}, fully encloses, are calculated by the formula

$$D_1 = \sqrt[2]{(k_0\Delta_x - x_0)^2 + (l_0\Delta_y - y_0)^2}, \tag{6}$$

were $k_0\Delta_x$ and $l_0\Delta_y$ — the coordinates of the most remote from the energy center of the matrix element.

5.   The diameter D_i (where i = 1, 2, 3 ...) are reduced so that the circle with the center at the point O (x_0, y_0) covers at least one measured point less than a circle diameter D_{i-1}.
6.   The energy (power) z of the laser radiation, which is in a circle of diameter D determined.
7.   For each i-th D_i value, the relation γ_i is calculated by the formula:

$$\gamma_i = \frac{z_i}{z_1}. \tag{7}$$

8.   The obtained data are approximated by the dependence $\gamma=F(D)$ and determine the diaphragm diameter corresponding to the level of energy γ_H, specified in the standards for lasers of specific types.

The diameter of the diaphragm found is taken as the beam diameter of the laser radiation. It is also advisable to process the results with the use of computer equipment.
The method of focal spot utilizes one of the above methods for measuring the diameter of a laser beam. The measurements are as follows.

1. Measuring instruments and auxiliary devices are installed and are prepare them for work. In this case, the optical axis of measuring instruments and auxiliary devices should coincide with the direction of the propagation of laser radiation.
2. The diameter of the radiation beam d_F in the focal plane of the optical system are measured using one of the aforementioned methods for measuring the diameter of the laser beam.
3. The energy difference of the laser radiation $\Theta_{W(P)}$ in radians are calculated by the formula:

$$\Theta_{W(p)} = \frac{d_F}{F},$$ (8)

The two-cuts method can be used to measure the difference between a beam of laser radiation at a distance from the source window of the laser to the 1st cross-section larger than d^2/λ (were d – the diameter of the beam of laser radiation, specified in the standards for lasers of specific types, λ - wavelength of laser radiation). The distance from the laser's initial window to the first intersection must correspond to the specific lasers set in the standards. Measurements are carried out as follows.

1. Using one of the above methods, the diameters of a beam of laser radiation in two sections, which are at a distance l, which are chosen to be the largest for the conditions of a concrete measurement, are measured.
2. The distance between the intersections are measure. Error measuring distance must be within range ± 3%.
3. Energy dissipation of laser radiation is calculated in radians by the formula:

$$\Theta_{W(P)} = \frac{d_2 - d_1}{l},$$ (9)

were d_1 i d_2 — the diameters of the beam of laser radiation in the first and second sections, respectively (GOST 26086–84).

ANALYSIS OF ALGORITHMS FOR PROCESSING IMAGES OF PROFILES OF LASER BEAMS FOR ESTIMATING ENERGY CHARACTERISTICS AND BEAM SPATIALS

In (Kovzel, Timchenko, Kutaev, et. Al. 2006; Timchenko, Kokriatskaia, Yarovyy, & Denysova, 2013; Yarovyy, Timchenko, & Kokriatskaia, 2012), the method for determining the coordinates of images of laser beam stains is based on the approximation of boundary lines. The method determines the output vector of the $Y(t)$ signal and analyzes the deformed vector $Y'(t)=X(g(t))$, which is conditioned by the following factors:

- Refraction of the beams of laser beams;
- Absorption of energy of a laser beam by atmospheric gases; scattering of energy of a laser beam by particles of aerosols on fluctuations of air density, etc.;
- Fluctuations in the parameters of laser beams due to atmospheric turbulence.

Each of the above-mentioned groups of phenomena of interaction of laser radiation with the atmosphere can be found in the regions of both linear and nonlinear optics. At the same time, each of these groups has clear specific features that should be taken into account in relevant theoretical and experimental studies (Zuev, 1971).

For the analysis according to this method, by means of which it is possible to restore the vector $Y'(t)$ it is necessary to geometrically characterize the signal. The key idea is the following: 1) for an unmodified deformed vector there are optimal nonlinear weights of all components; 2) for a displaced deformed vector is its shift with the correlation of the approximation coefficients; 3) errors from sampling and statistical parameters are eliminated. This paper shows that there are a number of correlations between the deformation function $g(t)$ and the approximation factors, as well as the distribution of the geometric characteristics of the signal, which is limited by various thresholds.

In the experiments carried out, the reliability of the restoration of the geometric characteristics of the signal exceeds other methods based on traditional means of approximation (Bronshteyn, & Semendayev, 1986). This work consists of a description of the method of determining the point of attachment, the algorithm that teaches, and experimental results. The formalization of the determination of bunching points is possible with the help of the multilevel hierarchical network proposed in (Kohonen, 2000).

In (Sugimura, & Takashima, 1999) it was shown that for the natural images, when approximating the boundary lines, we can use the ratio of square and cubic approximation coefficients. In this case, monotone components have a close relationship, and it has been shown that the various components (phases) of a monotonous image have a small but understandable divergence.

In this work, for the choice of groups of images with near-substituted signals, the least squares approximation was used (Kohonen, 2000). It was observed that close-substituted images may have a close relationship between square and cubic coefficients. Additionally, the seventh-degree coefficient was used for detecting small displacements and for the criterion of the accuracy of the comparison of coefficients.

The method uses the learning algorithm in parallel – hierarchical (PH) network and the tunneling algorithm (Timchenko, Kutaev, Gertsiy, & Baybak, 2000; Timchenko, Kutaev, Zhukov, Gertsiy, & Shveyki, 2000; Ta-Hsin, & Gibson, 1997).

This is achieved with the help of boundary line approximation coefficients such as c_2, c_3 (Sugimura, & Takashima, 1999*)* and c_7, as well as the use of several systems of equations in training calculations and the presence of an ordinary power center in other calculations. The results give the maximum error of the definition of the reference point of 1.5 pixels, which is significantly less than that of conventional approximation methods (Kohonen, 2000), under the same conditions.

Also known is the teaching method of a parallel-hierarchical network based on the formation of a normalizing equation.

By analogy with RBF networks (Liu, 2013), the task of teaching the proposed PH network (Timchenko, Kokriatskaia, Yarovyy, & Denysova, 2013) is practically reduced to the idea of controlled learning (Werbos, 1974; Taylor, & Koning, 2017; Aggarwal, 2018) elements of the output layer of the network. Using the general idea of the structural organization of artificial neural networks according to the scheme - the input layer→ hidden layer→ source layer, it is possible to synthesize the learning PH network, which uses the 1st layer of the network as the input layer, use the levels as- $2 \div k$, and as a source - traditionally used in artificial neural networks, the source layer.

From the laser paths, you can remove "bad" images and process them in a similar way. Comparative analysis shows that the proposed methods allow to measure the coordinates of the center of laser images on the basis of equilibrium operations and approximation of boundary lines with the accuracy of determining the point of attachment not more than 1.5 pixels.

The experiments carried out show that for the images of the stains of laser beams, as a result of the action of various destabilizing factors, it is impossible to accurately measure the coordinates of their energy centers.

Therefore, a method for measuring coordinates was proposed based on the analysis of the relative positioning of two adjacent laser images. The result of the analysis of such a mutual arrangement of two neighboring images was the adjusted value of the coordinates of the power center of the current image, which can be measured as it is done in the works (Kormanovsky, Shvejki, & Timchenko, 2001; Kozhemyako, Tymchenko, Kutaev, & Yaroviy, 2002). Such a principle of measuring the coordinates of a power center makes it possible to exclude the use of inaccurate procedures based on various approximating operators (Kormanovsky, Shvejki, & Timchenko, 2001; Kozhemyako, Tymchenko, Kutaev, & Yaroviy, 2002; Yarovyy, Timchenko, & Kokriatskaia, 2012; Timchenko, Kokriatskaia, Yarovyy, & Denysova, 2013).

Physical modeling of such a method for determining the coordinates of images of extended laser paths using a signal processor type TMS320C5510 with a clock frequency of 200 MHz shows that for the processing of one image requires ~10,65 ms.

There are also modified algorithms for determining the coordinates of images of laser beams, which are in the following (Timchenko, Kutaev, Gertsiy, & Baybak, 2000).

The algorithm for determining the brightest points analyzes the image of the laser beam and creates an array of appearances of brightness points. Selected from this array a certain number of brightest, "no noise" points. The point was considered "noise" if its presence in the image was less than 0.05% of the total number of points in the contours.

Since each image has 150-160 boundary contours, points with transient brightness were formed at or sometimes between sections of some images. The number of points with such brightness is not sufficient (1-7) in order to outline the boundary contour, so the points with the occurrence less than 0.05% (less than 5 - 7 points) were ignored, because in the vast majority contributed to a sharp shift of the desired energy center thereby worsening overall result. Also, the points that were in the extreme positions of the image and other points corresponding to their brightness were not considered, since it is impossible to completely delineate the boundary contour, and accordingly, to find the right center.

The contours with the above values of brightness are outlined.

The coordinates of the centers of the boundary contours determine the general energy center (x, y), which is expressed in the following form:

$$x = \frac{1}{K}\sum_{m=0}^{M-1}\sum_{n=0}^{N-1}\big(f(x_n, m)\big), \quad y = \frac{1}{K}\sum_{m=0}^{M-1}\sum_{n=0}^{N-1}\big(f(y_n, m)\big), \tag{10}$$

K – total number of points in the boundary contours;
N – the number of points in the boundary contour;
M – number of boundary contours;
$f(x_n, m)$ and $f(y_n, m)$ – the corresponding displacements of points relative to O(0,0).

The second algorithm is almost analogous to the first algorithm.

The difference lies only in the brightness of the points forming the boundary contours. These points are no longer the brightest, and their brightness is as close as possible to J, which is determined by the formula:

$$J = \frac{j_{\min} + j_{\max}}{4} + \frac{1}{2M} \sum_{n=1}^{H} f(n) ; \tag{11}$$

j_{min} — the smallest value of brightness $\forall$ a point belonging to the general boundary contour;

j_{max} — maximum brightness value $\forall$ point of the overall boundary contour;

H — total number of points in the array of brightness;

M — number of boundary contours;

$f(n)$ — the value of the brightness of the point with the serial number n.

The third algorithm is as follows.

From a given array of appearances of brightness of points, they find an average value, which uses only points that are within the contours. In an array of brightnesses are find a predetermined number of closest in value, to the calculated value above, brightness (points). The extreme points of each of the ranges form the boundary lines. As a result, the M edge lines are obtained.

Boundary lines are outlined. Into each contour, circle are inserted, with the maximum possible radius and are described with a minimum radius. As a result of averaging centers of two circles the center of the boundary contour is obtained. The overall energy center in accordance with the first algorithm is founded.

All provided images have power centers using 1st or 2nd algorithms are determined. Their values are averaged, with the help of which the reference value of the energy center is obtained.

The image is considered "good" if the displacement of its energy center relative to the reference is not greater than Ψ ($\Psi = 2.5\%$), otherwise it is "bad" (in principle, Ψ can be varied within 1-10% depending on the required accuracy of selection or number of images provided for selection).

Sorting images (using 3rd algorithm).

The number of images for learning are specified. Using the 3rd algorithm, the values of the reference center are finded. Other images are selected in the same way as using the 1st and 2nd algorithms.

After analyzing 3 tracks with ~ 2000 images, using this program, it turned out that the results of the 2nd and 3rd algorithms are similar (centers of power beams), while the first one is slightly different and are biased. This is a consequence of the uneven density distribution of points within the contours relative to the energy center.

Another approach to the processing of laser paths is the time algorithm for linear processing of laser paths to measure the speed and location coordinates.

The method is based on the processing of groups of spatial images of laser beams. A group can contain from hundreds to thousands of images that determine the sequence of a frame number. Each image is received at the appropriate time countdown and its shape determines the velocity, as well as the change of coordinates in time.

The essence of the algorithm is to determine the following parameters:

- Spot area;
- Spot center coordinates;
- Area of the bounding window;
- The ratio of the area of the spot to the area of the window.

The shape of the bounding window is chosen according to the specified bounding boundaries, which depend on the given number of covering points along the edges of the spot. From this, the speed of determination also depends. The algorithm makes it possible to perform batch processing of a group of images (laser path), which results in the results of the deviations of the center of the spot on each coordinate, and also determines the images whose geometric centers coincide and which determine the change in speed and coordinates.

Suitable images are chosen to accurately determine the coordinates of the object and its speed. The ratio of the number of selected images to the total number of images is also determined. Suitability is estimated by the deviation of their geometric centers from the average value of all trailing spot images. Image processing includes image analysis at different brightness thresholds and determines the coefficient of the ratio of the number of eligible images to the total number. The magnitude of such a coefficient does not change practically at brightness of 20 and above units. When changing a scanning window, no significant changes occur in the value of the coefficient, and its value varies slightly to values of 0.2-0.6.

Let's assume that the laser path contains a plurality of spotted images belonging to their own time frame.

$$L = \left\{ l\left(t_i\right) \right\}, i = \overline{1, N} ,$$

were N – number of laser paths (frame number).

Assume that suitable images in the track is $l^1(t_i)$. Adjacent suitable images and average personnel time are determined t_{aver}^j .

$$t_{aver}^j = \frac{t_p^j - t_q^{j-1}}{p - q}$$

were p,q – the number of closest frames with suitable images; t^j – the time the images appear in the corresponding frame.

The total time of the change in the track is determined as

$$T_{aver} = \sum_{j-1}^{k} t_{aver}^j$$

were k – number of eligible images.

The obtained expressions allow to determine the time of the deviation of the laser beam between the processed images, which makes it possible to determine the speed of the motion of the track (locomotive) on which the laser equipment is installed. On the received deviations of the center of coordinate of a laser beam there is an opportunity of high-precision measurement of deviation of coordinates of movement of object by a monitoring body.

The proposed approach allows us to accurately estimate the deviations of the centers for each image and for each coordinate. Compared to other methods aimed at solving similar problems, this method allows to increase the number of received images and to experimentally select the most effective threshold of brightness, as well as the boundary form of the scan.

In the methods (Fig. 3), where cell processing is used, each image is processed using a captive window, the area of which may vary, depending on the specified boundaries of the images. The borders of the window are specified by the number of cells belonging to the image of the spot on each of the four sides. The area of the windows and stains, as well as the coordinates of their geometric centers for both initial and transformed images, are calculated. In addition, the program tracks the tracks at a given threshold (Timchenko, Kutaev, Gertsiy, & Baybak, 2000).

Based on the results of the processing, a table is constructed in which all the parameters of the images of the spots are entered and their suitability for further processing is determined. The coordinates of the spot center, which is calculated by default, are determined. Such changes are presented by the deviation graphs for each coordinate presented in a different color (Figure 4). The match (suitability) is given by a large white dot on the zero line. Also, the coordinates of the spot center with boundary constraints are presented.

In order to increase the informativeness of the received results of processing of laser tracks, the coefficient of suitability of laser tracks was introduced K_{suit}.

$$K_{suit} = \frac{N_{suit}}{N_{\pounds}}, \quad M = \langle O, OT, R \rangle \tag{12}$$

were N_{suit} – number of eligible images in the track; N_{Σ} - total number of images in the track.

Figure 3. Interface of the program of processing and research of laser tracks

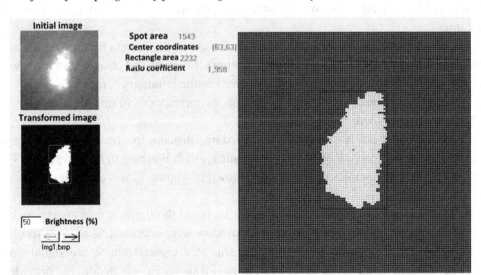

Figure 4. An example of the deviation graphs according to the coordinates of the center for each trace image

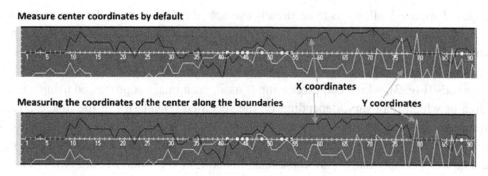

K_{suit} expresses the ratio of suitable and not suitable images in the route, and also expresses its suitability according to the given parameters. The program allows to calculate K_{suit} at different values of the brightness border, as well as at given limits of the cover window.

The largest value of K_{suit} is observed within the brightness value from 0 to 15%. With a brightness of more than 20% and less than 70%, the value of the K_{suit} is practically unchanged. Changes are within 0.05 of the value K_{suit}.

$$K_{suit} \approx \begin{cases} 1, & if\ 0 < L < 15\% \\ K_{const}, & if\ 20\% < L < 70\% \\ K_0 \left\langle K_{const}, if\ L \right\rangle 75\% \end{cases} \tag{13}$$

were L – the value of the brightness of the cell as a percentage; K_{const} – average value K_{suit}, which is the most and practically unchanged; K_0 – average value K_{suit} when L>75%.

The value of the K_{suit} does not change significantly when the boundaries of the capture window are larger than the intersection of 20 pixels at each boundary.

The developed program allows to make a sample of suitable images according to the coordinates of geometric centers.

This approach allows to accurately evaluate the deviations of the centers for each image and for each coordinate. The method also allows to increase the number of received images and to experimentally select the most effective threshold of brightness, as well as the boundary form of the scan.

Error in the determination of the centers of the images corresponds to one discrete field (one pixel) to which the image is projected.

The study of spot images of laser beams is provided by Spiricon, Inc. on its own Internet site and in publications (Ta-Hsin, & Gibson, 1997; Taylor, & Koning, 2017; Werbos, 1974; Kovzel, M. Timchenko, L., Kutaev, et. Al., 2006). Samples of images are shown in Figure 5, and examples of their software processing - in Fig. 6.

A number of parameters were determined, which included the definition of energy and geometric centers. At the same time various forms of the cover window were selected and an analysis of the choice of a digital camera was conducted. Much attention was paid to determining the signal / noise ratio. Centers were determined by the width of the most powerful spot area, which does not provide sufficient

Figure 5. Profiles of laser beams supplied by Spiricon, Inc.

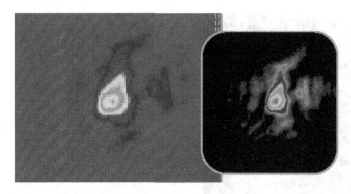

accuracy of the determination of the coordinates. In addition, not every human image passed computer processing, which leads to loss of information.

The approach proposed in the work makes it possible to repeatedly process the image of the spots in each frame and increases the accuracy of the determination of the centers to one discrete processing medium.

From the same series, a method is considered in which from the selected center a scan of the image carried out across all its boundary lines (Fig. 7) and a specific values of distances l_i^j (where i is the scan step, j is the edge number number) are found. The smaller i, the higher the accuracy of the reproduction of the scan.

There is a set of curves that allow to determine the average value for each image (Figure 8), shifted at a certain moment of time.

For each step of the scan, the average distance is determined l_i^{mean}. Then the fixed mean lengths are determined respectively for the fixed point of the boundary line. That is, the step of scanning is determined by the direction of the determined boundary line of the image of the laser profile.

The comparative analysis shows that the proposed methods allow to measure the coordinates of the center of laser images based on the averaging of boundary lines with the accuracy of the determination of the point of attachment not more than 1.5 pixels, which accuracy exceeds the known, for example, by determining the center of gravity by means of momentary features, on average 1.5 times. In the experiments carried out, 15 laser tracks with the number of images were used - 1000 in each track. The experiments carried out show that for the images of the stains of laser beams, as a result of the action of various destabilizing factors, it is impossible to accurately measure the coordinates of their energy centers. Therefore, the method of measuring coordinates on the basis of analysis of the mutual arrangement of two neighboring laser images is proposed. The result of the analysis of such a mutual arrangement of two adjacent images was the corrected value of the coordinates of the power center of the current image that can be measured. Such a principle of measuring the coordinates of a power center makes it possible to exclude the use of inaccurate procedures based on various approximating operators.

Figure 6. Examples of the LBA-500PC-D4 Demo program

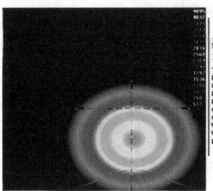

	Deviation	Minimum	Maximum	Units
Statistics				
Samples	272	272	272	
Quantitative—90/10 Knife Edge				
Total	21,508,702	19,767,330	123,314,822	
% in Aperture	1	86.50	86.55	%
Peak	2.679e+02	3.201e+03	4.080e+03	
Min	0.000e+00	0.000e+00	0.000e+00	
Peak Loc X	7.356e+01	1.280e+02	3.830e+02	PX
Peak Loc Y	6.747e+01	1.230e+02	3.590e+02	PX
Centroid X	7.367e+01	1.280e+02	3.830e+02	PX
Centroid Y	6.732e+01	1.230e+02	3.590e+02	PX
Width X	4.965e+01	1.188e+02	2.967e+02	PX
Width Y	5.011e+01	1.132e+02	2.798e+02	PX
Diameter	3.491e+01	1.231e+02	2.792e+02	PX

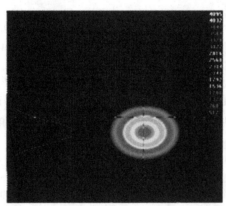

	Deviation	Minimum	Maximum	Units
Statistics				
Samples	282	282	282	
Quantitative—90/10 Knife Edge				
Total	21,504,172	19,767,330	123,314,822	
% in Aperture	1	86.50	86.55	%
Peak	2.657e+02	3.201e+03	4.080e+03	
Min	0.000e+00	0.000e+00	0.000e+00	
Peak Loc X	7.405e+01	1.280e+02	3.830e+02	PX
Peak Loc Y	6.763e+01	1.230e+02	3.590e+02	PX
Centroid X	7.415e+01	1.280e+02	3.830e+02	PX
Centroid Y	6.749e+01	1.230e+02	3.590e+02	PX
Width X	5.009e+01	1.188e+02	2.967e+02	PX
Width Y	5.013e+01	1.132e+02	2.798e+02	PX
Diameter	3.501e+01	1.231e+02	2.792e+02	PX

	Current	Mean	Deviation	Units
Statistics				
Samples	282	282	282	
Quantitative—90/10 Knife Edge				
Total	24,678,350	59,261,336	21,504,172	
% in Aperture	86.50	86.52	1	%
Peak	3.928e+03	3.672e+03	2.657e+02	
Min	0.000e+00	0.000e+00	0.000e+00	
Peak Loc X	3.270e+02	2.534e+02	7.405e+01	PX
Peak Loc Y	3.000e+02	2.410e+02	6.763e+01	PX
Centroid X	3.270e+02	2.538e+02	7.415e+01	PX
Centroid Y	3.000e+02	2.417e+02	6.749e+01	PX
Width X	1.414e+02	2.082e+02	5.009e+01	PX
Width Y	1.132e+02	1.965e+02	5.013e+01	PX
Diameter	1.273e+02	2.024e+02	3.501e+01	PX

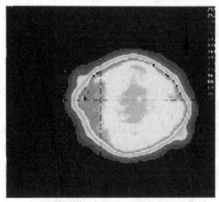

	Deviation	Minimum	Maximum	Units
Statistics				
Samples	54	54	54	
Quantitative—90/10 Knife Edge				
Total	1,247,156	1,141,502	6,408,292	
% Above Clip	5	86.50	86.73	%
Peak	2.767e+02	3.214e+03	4.080e+03	
Min	0.000e+00	0.000e+00	0.000e+00	
Peak Loc X	1.701e+03	3.300e+03	9.500e+03	um
Peak Loc Y	1.932e+03	3.300e+03	9.400e+03	um
Centroid X	1.702e+03	3.300e+03	9.500e+03	um
Centroid Y	1.937e+03	3.300e+03	9.400e+03	um
Width X	1.243e+03	2.833e+03	7.069e+03	um
Width Y	1.317e+03	2.833e+03	7.050e+03	um
Diameter	8.033e+02	2.833e+03	6.657e+03	um

Figure 7. Edge lines of the template image

Figure 8. An example of constructing a curve scan for boundary lines

THEORETICAL FOUNDATIONS OF METHODS FOR DETERMINING THE ENERGY CENTER OF A BEAM OF LASER RADIATION AND ITS DIAMETER

Determination of the diameter of the laser beam by the methods of calibrated diaphragms and the distribution of radiation power can be performed using computer technology. In this case, you can use the algorithm given in the work (GOST 26086–84).

When entering the initial data and in calculations, it must be taken into account that the structure of the matrix can be rectangular or radial.

The type of structure of the matrix are specified. Below are the formulas for a rectangular structure. In the case of a radial structure, all the given formulas should be transformed into polar coordinates (r_k, φ_1).

The value of the values by formulas (3), (4), (5) are calculate. The coordinates of the energy center (EC) are calculated in relative units:

$$\xi_x = r_0 / \Lambda_x , \tag{14}$$

$$\xi_y = y_0 / \Delta_y . \tag{15}$$

The minimum diameter of a circle with a center at point O and which covers the area of the matrix, are found:

$$D_1 = \sqrt{(k_0 - \alpha_x)^2 + (l_0 - \alpha_y)^2} , \tag{16}$$

were k_0 and l_0 — the coordinates of the most remote from the EC element of the matrix.

177

Then in the cycle are carried out an array of values γ_i for different D_i.

On the basis of the obtained values of γ_i, with the help of approximation, the diameter D_γ is estimated at a given level γ.

When processing the results of measuring the diameter of the beam by the method of calibrated diaphragms is used the same algorithm. The calculations of γ_i are carried out in a loop. Further $D\gamma$ are evaluated.

All standard methods (except for the calibrated diaphragm method) are tied to finding the coordinates of the laser center energy center. Consequently, the use in this case of improved methods for finding energy centers for laser spots will improve the performance of the above standard methods, including the accuracy of measurements.

The proposed method uses recursive coordinate search for the center of the segments formed between the extreme points of the image of the laser dot. The method works as follows.

1. The input image is pre-processing to determine the array of the brightest points of the image (Figure 9).

2. After the image pre-processing, it need to find an array of points in the edge of the image. This is achieved by scanning the matrix of the image with the further separation and recording of the coordinates of the required boundary points.

3. The next step is to choose the first diameter - between the initial and middle points of the found array. If the array has the form R[A0, A1, ..., An], then the first diameter is chosen between the points A0 and An/2 (Fig. 10).

4. The found extreme points of the circuit are used as the ends of the segments crossing the contour. The ends of each next segment will be points adjacent to the points - the ends of the first segment, selected in opposite directions. For example, if an array of points in the boundary contour R[A0, A1, A2, ..., An] is found, while the A0Aj, is taken for the first segment, then the segment should be selected as follows A1Aj+1 or AnAj-1.

5. For each next segment there are coordinates of its center. To do this, use the following formula:

$$x_c = \frac{x_1 + x_2}{2}; \quad y_c = \frac{y_1 + y_2}{2}; \tag{17}$$

were (x_1, y_1) and (x_2, y_2) – the coordinates of the points of the boundary contour, which are also the ends of the segment; (x_c, y_c) – coordinates of the center of the segment (Figure 11).

6. The found centers for each segment form a new boundary contour when connecting each two neighboring points found by straight lines. In this case, binding to the discrete environment of the matrix of the image may be missing, which increases the accuracy of the next recursive iteration of items 3-6.

7. The center of the image of the laser spot is considered to be found when reaching a given threshold of accuracy, or if the coordinates of all the found centers of the segments (possibly, for example, for an ideal round spot).

Graph - scheme of the search center algorithm on Fig. 12 is shown.

Figure 9. An example of a preprocessing process

Figure 10. An example of finding the extreme points of a profile image of a laser beam

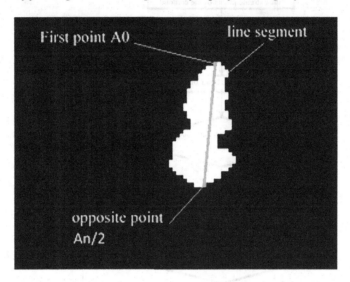

Figure 11. An example of determining the center of a segment of two extreme points

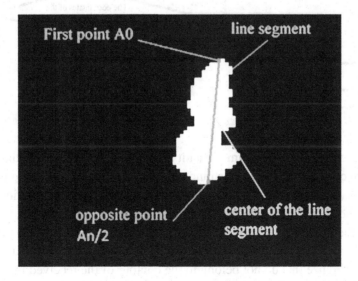

Figure 12. The algorithm for the mid - diametric determination of the energy center of the images of the profiles of laser beams

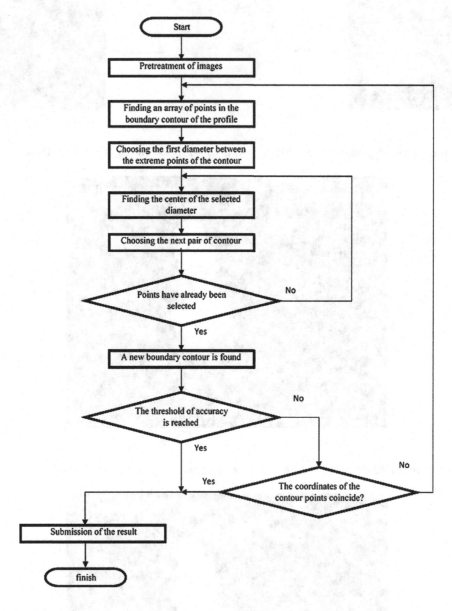

The specialty of the proposed algorithm is that it takes into account the peculiarities of the shape of the laser spots, which can change in real time randomly in real time, in contrast to the standard method, the work of which is based on the assumption about the symmetry of the distribution of radiation energy in a spot relative to the axial direction of the laser path. This is achieved by the fact that the length of the images between the extreme points of the image of the spots of the segments is affected by any of its distortions. From this follows another feature of the proposed method - the absence of the need to search for points of reference that do not belong to the contour of the received image of the laser spot.

OPTIONAL IMAGE CENTER SEARCH METHOD FOR LASER PROFILE PROFILE

It is known that when propagating the wave front in the atmosphere, it falls under the influence of its nonlinear properties, which leads to its distortions. It is also known that the wave front, reflected from a certain surface, changes its shape to the shape of this surface.

Fluctuations in the distribution of radiation energy in the profile of a laser beam when it passes through an inhomogeneous medium, or when reflected from a certain surface, are manifested through the curvature of the boundary path of an image of a laser dot - profile of a laser beam. This, in turn, affects the position of the center of the current profile of the laser path, the exact definition of which is relevant for the tasks given in the work.

Since the distorted profile contour of the distorted laser spot is not symmetric with respect to one point, the question arises about finding an optimal geometric center-the point most equidistant from the boundary points of the contour of the image of the profile of the laser spot and introducing the corresponding criterion for evaluating the contour relative to one point. Existing methods, including those proposed, do not test the result for matching to its geometric center of the contour of the image of the laser profile. Therefore, when working with the contours of laser profiles finding it's optimal, most equidistant from contour points, the center will increase the accuracy of obtaining the result.

Let the contour of the image of the laser profile represented by an array of points $A[A_1, A_2, ..., A_j, ..., A_n]$. Coordinates of some contour point $A_j (x_j, y_j)$. Circuit scaneer having a circle shape and symmetric with respect to one point $C(x_c, y_c)$, on Fig. 13 is shown.

Figure 13. Contour scan of an image of a laser profile, symmetric with respect to one point

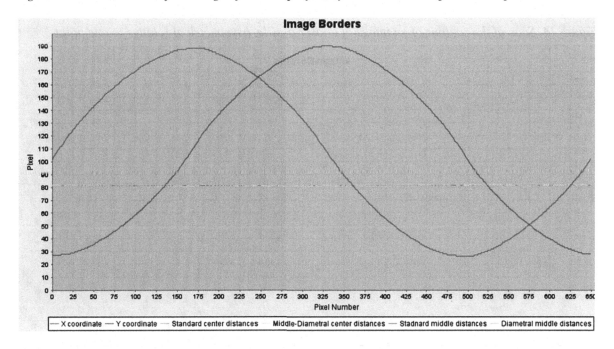

The contour is symmetric relative to some point $(x_c; y_c)$, if all points of the contour are set at the same distances l_j from it (Figure 13), while the mean distance L_c from the point of symmetry (center of the contour) is equal to the distances from each point of the contour to the point of symmetry – $L_c = l_j$.

$$l_j = \sqrt{(x_j - x_c)^2 + (y_j - y_c)^2}; \quad L_c = \frac{l_1 + l_2 + ... + l_n}{n}. \tag{18}$$

were $(x_j; y_j)$ – coordinates of the contour point; n – number of contour points.

If the contour of the image of the laser profile is not symmetric with respect to one point (Figure 14), then the point most consistent with its geometric center is one that is most evenly spaced from all points of such a contour. The quantitative representation of such a feature allows us to apply the proposed criterion for evaluating the symmetry of the laser profile image contour relative to one point.

The criterion for evaluating the symmetry of the contour of the image of the laser profile F_c is the mean value of the deviations F_j of the distances from the contour points to the predicted point of symmetry l_j from the mean value of the distance L_c between the points of the contour and the predicted point of symmetry.

$$F_j = \left| l_j - L_c \right|; \quad F_c = \frac{F_1 + F_2 + ... + F_n}{n} \tag{19}$$

were n – number of contour points.

Figure 14. Scan of the contour of an image of a laser profile, asymmetrical relative to one point

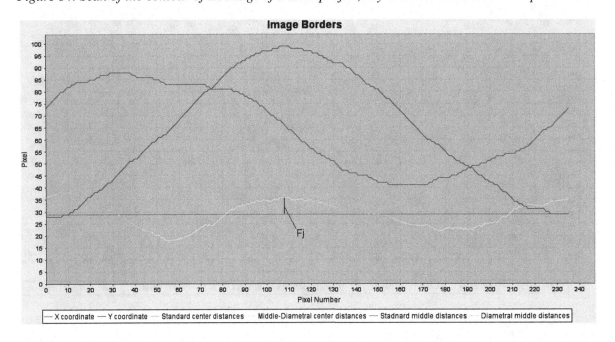

Given this, the optimal geometric center of the image of the boundary circuit is the point for which the average deviation of the distances from the points of the contour to the given point from the mean of these distances will be the smallest.

Since the methods considered and proposed in the operation find points that are close in their arrangement to the optimal centers of the contours of laser profiles or coincide with them, then it is advisable to search for optimal centers of the contours of laser profiles in the neighborhoods is found by the methods examined in the points.

Graphic diagram of the algorithm for finding the optimal center of the contour of the image of the laser profile on Fig. 15 is shown.

Finding the optimal center of the contour of the image of the laser profile is as follows.

The input data of the algorithm are the coordinates of the point in the neighborhood of which the search for the optimal center of the contour $(x_0; y_0)$, the maximum radius of the vicinity of R and the sampling steps of the radius of the circle r_j and the angle of rotation φ_j. The steps of discretization the radius of a neighborhood and the angle of rotation determine the accuracy of calculation the optimal center of the contour of the laser profile and are calculated depending on the desired number of iteration steps in the radius of an angle and the angle of rotation according to the following formulas.

$$r_j = \frac{R}{n}; \quad \phi_j = \frac{2\pi}{m}; \tag{20}$$

were n – the number of iterations in the radius of the neighborhood; m – the number of iterations in a corner of the turn.

Figure 15. Algorithm for finding the optimal center of the image contour of the laser profile

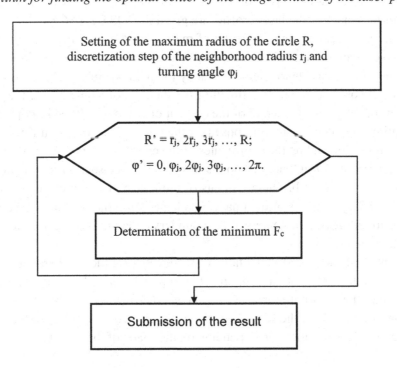

During each iteration of the algorithm, the F_C value is calculated for the criterion for evaluating the symmetry of the laser profile circuit at the point defined by the current values of the steps of the radius of the circle and the angle of rotation. Coordinates of points are calculated by the formula of the parametric representation of the circle.

$$x = x_0 + r \cos \phi; \quad y = y_0 + r \sin \phi; \quad 0 < \phi < 2\pi. \tag{21}$$

were

$(x_0; y_0)$ – coordinates of the circle center;
$(x; y)$ – coordinates of the point of the circle;
r – circle radius;
φ – turning angle.

After passing all the iterations of the cycle of determining the values of F_C at the points of the given neighborhood, the search for the point of the point with the smallest value of F_C is performed, and the search also takes into account the value of F_C at the starting point $(x_0; y_0)$ in the vicinity of which the search for the optimal contour center.

The result of the proposed algorithm is the coordinates of the point in which the Fc value of the criterion for assessing the symmetry of the contour of the laser profile will be the smallest.

COMPARISON OF EFFECTIVE METHODS FOR LASER RADIATION ANALYSIS

Almost all considered methods of analysis of parameters of laser radiation, in particular, methods requiring the location of the center of the laser profile, are given in GOST 26086-84, and also considered in this paper, the formula for calculating the center of mass is used to find the energy center of the laser profile. Since the accuracy of determining the coordinates of the power center directly affects the accuracy of the result, it is advisable to compare exactly the methods of searching for energy centers of laser profiles. The proposed criterion for estimating symmetry allows quantifying the accuracy of finding the coordinates of the geometric center of the contour of the image of the laser profile. The method of finding the optimal geometric center proposed on the basis of this criterion finds its application in the modified algorithms for finding the coordinates of the energy centers of laser profiles based on the analysis of the occurrence of brightness of points of profile. Since such methods allow us to proceed from the analysis of the array of brightness points of the image of the laser profile to the analysis of the forms of the boundary contours of the image, and hence from the search of the common center of mass to the search for the geometric centers of the boundary contours. The main characteristics of these methods are summarized in Table 1.

Studies of the methods discussed in the table of methods using the comparative software model of the search methods for the centers of the contours of laser profiles have shown that the modified method using the middle-diameter algorithm for searching the geometric center of the contour of the laser profile gives a greater accuracy than the formula of the center of mass (GOST 26086-84) 50% of the images of the studied laser paths. However, depending on the shape of the laser profile and the method of

Table 1. Main characteristics of the considered methods

Method	Characteristics	
	Relative Accuracy	Relative Speed
Formula of the center of masses (GOST 26086-84)	1	1
Modified method (search of mass centers)	1÷1,1	~5
Modified method (Medium-diameter algorithm)	0,88÷1,12	~17
Modified method (search of the optimal center)	1÷1,3	~44

edge detection, the proposed mid-diametric algorithm can give even less accuracy than the formula for searching the center of mass. The proposed algorithm should be used together with others, for example, the standard formula of the center of mass (GOST 26086-84), while the results of the work are selected data of the algorithm, which turned out to be more precise.

The modified method of searching the power centers of laser profiles using the algorithm for finding optimal geometric contour centers based on the proposed symmetry evaluation criterion gives a 3 times greater increment of accuracy than a modified algorithm using the formula for searching the center of mass. At the same time, the zero increment of accuracy is observed only when processing symmetric laser profiles, when the results of using the formula for searching the center of mass and the algorithm for finding the optimal geometric center coincide.

Also, the table shows the speed of modified methods relative to the formula for searching the center of mass. As can be seen from the table, the proposed mid-diametric method and the search method for an optimal geometric center of the contour have a lower rate of performance with respect to the method using the formula for searching the center of mass. At the same time, data on speed was also obtained using a comparative software model, but it should be noted that the speed of the methods depends on the method of their implementation. Since the purpose of creating a comparative software model was a study of the accuracy of the methods, and not the speed, therefore optimization of the software code and program implementation of the proposed methods will significantly increase their speed.

MODIFIED WAVEFORM RECOVERY METHOD BASED ON SHAKA-HARTMANN'S CONTACTLESS SENSORS

The exact calculation of the angle of incidence of laser radiation on the processing medium is relevant to the problems of restoring the shape of the optical fronts in the contactless waveguide sensors of Shaka-Hartmann.

The method of searching for optimal geometric centers of images of laser profiles makes it possible to propose an algorithm for finding the angle of inclination of a local wave front with increased precision.

In general, the non-contact waveguide sensor of Shak-Hartmann consists of a lens raster and a CCD-matrix located in the focal plane of the lens raster.

The contactless sensor works in general as follows. When the wave front enters the lens, it is flat, then all the images on the matrix formed by its passage through the subapertura of the lens of the raster are arranged in the correct grid, which is determined by the geometry of the matrix of lenses. When the wave front is distorted, the images on the matrix are shifted from their nominal positions. The displacement of the energy centers (centroids) of the spots of images in two orthogonal directions is proportional to the average inclination of the wave front in these directions along subaperatures. Thus, the contactless wavefront sensor of Shaka-Hartmann measures the inclination of the wave front. The wave front itself is reconstructed (restored) from an array of measured slopes up to a constant that does not play a role for the image. An additon, the following ratio is used:

$$\frac{\partial W(x,y)}{\partial x} = \frac{\Delta x}{f}, \quad \frac{\partial W(x,y)}{\partial y} = \frac{\Delta y}{f}, \tag{22}$$

were f – focal length of the lenses included in the lens raster; Δx, Δy – displacement of energy centers of images of spots in the subapertures of a lenticular raster with corresponding axes of coordinates.

Obviously, a more precise determination of the coordinates of the energy centers will increase the accuracy of the measurements of the inclination of the wave fronts in the contactless waveguide sensors of the Shaka-Hartmann as it increases the accuracy of the measurement of the deviations of the centroid images of the spots on the subaperatures. Figure 16 shows a block diagram of a modified algorithm for determining the inclination of a wave front with increased precision.

The algorithm works as follows. The image obtained gartmangraph on the CCD matrix is decomposed into an array of stains images for each sub-parter. For example, if a lens raster contains n lenses, then the decomposition of the gartmanogram forms an array $A[a_1, a_2, a_3, \ldots, a_i, \ldots, a_n]$ (were a_i image of spots in sub aperture lens raster).

The next step is to process all the stains from the resulting array in a loop. The purpose of spot processing in a substrate of a lens raster is determination its energy center. For this, in the image different ranges of brightness select the edge contours. The image may have an average of 150-160 boundary contours, of which an array of contours is formed:

$$K[k_1(x_1, y_1), k_2(x_2, y_2), k_3(x_3, y_3), \ldots k_i(x_i, y_i), \ldots, k_m(x_m, y_m)].$$

Further, the processing of the formed array of boundary contours of the image in a cycle of the image is performed, during which the calculation of the optimal geometric center is made using the proposed algorithm for finding the optimal geometric center of the laser profile. The edge image contour represents an array of image points corresponding to the border of one of the ranges of brightness of the image points. The preliminary calculation of the coordinates of the center of the current boundary contour of the image is carried out according to the following formula:

$$x_c = \frac{\sum_{i=1}^{m} x_i}{m}, \quad y_c = \frac{\sum_{i=1}^{m} y_i}{m}, \tag{23}$$

were

x_c, y_c – the coordinates of the pre-calculated geometric center of the edge contour of the image;
x_i, y_i – coordinates of the point of the boundary contour;
m – the number of points in the boundary contour.

Figure 16. Block diagram of the modified algorithm for determining the inclination of the wave front with increased precision in the contactless Shaka-Hartmann vendors

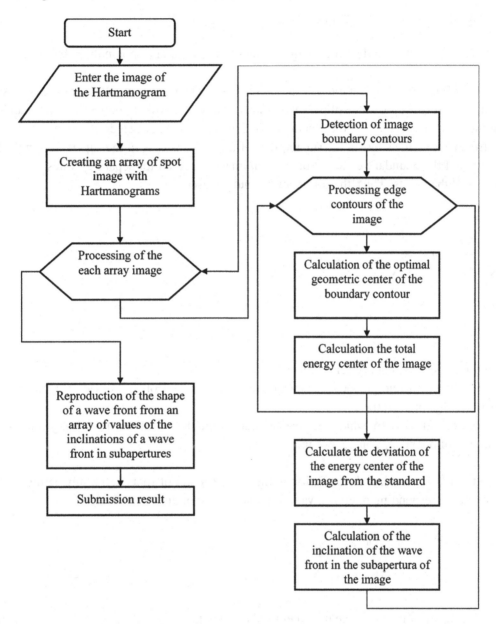

The next step is to calculate the coordinates of the optimal geometric center of the edge contour of the image. In this case, formula (18) is used to calculate the distance between the contour point to the point-center of the contour and the mean value of such distances, as well as formula (19), by which the distances between the points of the contour and the point-center of the contour is calculated, as well as the criterion value symmetry of the contour relative to the selected center. Proceeding from the specificity of the proposed criterion, the point with its smallest value is chosen for the optimal geometric center of the contour of the processed image.

The geometric centers of the boundary contours form an array:

$G[g_1(x_{C1}, y_{C1}), g_2(x_{C2}, y_{C2}), g_3(x_{C3}, y_{C3}), ..., g_j(x_{Cj}, y_{Cj}), ..., g_n(x_{Cn}, y_{Cn})].$

This array is used when finding the energy center of the image of a spot in the subaperture of a laser raster.

Since each of the boundary contours of the image in the subaperture of the laser raster of a sensor is selected in its corresponding value of the range of brightness, it allows to move from the search for the values of the geometric centers of the contours to calculate the energy center of the image. The energy center of the image of the spots in the subaperture of the lens raster is in the superposition of the geometric centers of the boundary contours of such an image, selected for separate values from the range of brightness of the points. Thus, the following formula is used:

$$x_e = \frac{\sum\limits_{j=1}^{n} x_{Cj} I_j}{\sum\limits_{j=1}^{n} I_j}, \quad y_e = \frac{\sum\limits_{j=1}^{n} y_{Cj} I_j}{\sum\limits_{j=1}^{n} I_j}, \tag{24}$$

were

x_e, y_e – coordinates of the energy center image spots;
x_{Cj}, y_{Cj} – coordinates of the geometric center of the edge contour of the image of a spot taken for a separate range of brightness;
I_j – the value of brightness, by which the corresponding boundary contour of the image, was selected;
n – the number of boundary contours of image spots.

The next step is to calculate the deviation of the energy center of spots in the subaperture of the lens raster from the corresponding reference values by the corresponding coordinates:

$$\Delta x = x_e - x_0, \quad \Delta y = y_e - y_0 \tag{25}$$

were

Δx, Δy – displacement of energy centers (centroids) of spots images in subaperture of a lens raster at corresponding coordinates;
x_e, y_e – the coordinates of the energy center of the image of the spots in the subaperture of the lens raster;
x_0, y_0 – reference coordinates of the energy center of the image of the spots in the subaperture of the lens raster, obtained for the plane wave front.

Further, on the basis of the obtained values of deviations for each substrate of a lenticular raster, using the formula (22), the inclination of the local wave front for each substrate of the lens raster is calculated. Obtained values of the slopes are used to restore the shape of the wave front.

188

The proposed modified algorithm for determining the wavefront inclination in the Schak-Hartmann contactless sensors provides increased accuracy of the resulting result due to the increased accuracy of the determination of the energy centers of the spots images in the subapertures of the lens render of the sensor.

MODIFIED METHOD FOR CALCULATING THE DIAMETER AND ENERGY DISSIPATION OF A LASER BEAM

The method of focal spot is the most common method of measuring the divergence. For measurements in the distant zone, that is, in the region of Fraunhofer diffraction, it is usually necessary to have significant distances from the source of radiation. The conditions of the Fraunhofer diffraction can be obtained in the focal plane of the perfect not aberration positive lens (Fig. 17).

To move to the angular distribution, it is necessary to divide the linear distribution in the focal plane by the focal length of the lens, that is, the angle of laser divergence is determined by the formula:

$$\Theta \approx \frac{a}{f'}, \tag{26}$$

were a — radius of spot on the focal plane.

In this method, to exclude the influence of diffraction on the edges of the lens, long-focus lenses with a large aperture are used that exceeds approximately 2 times the diameter of the incident laser beam, and the focal length of the lens must satisfy the following condition:

$$f' = \frac{2,44\lambda}{\Theta_{W,p}^{e}}, \tag{27}$$

were λ — wavelength of laser radiation; $\Theta_{W,P}$ — energy dissipation of laser radiation, set in standards for lasers of specific types.

The error of measurement of this method is mainly due to inaccuracy in determining the size of the spot and does not exceed 27%. In automated systems, for determining the diameter of a beam of radiation, the method of distribution of energy density (power) of laser radiation is mainly used (GOST 26086-84).

Figure 17. Principle diagram of measurement of energy divergence of a laser beam on the basis of a method of a focal spot

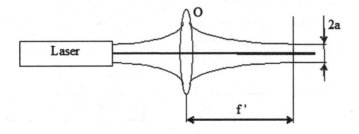

To improve the accuracy of this method, it is expedient to use the proposed method of searching for optimal geometric centers of laser radiation.

The block diagram of the modified algorithm for the search for energy discrepancy on Fig. 18 is shown.

The algorithm works as follows. The coordinates of the energy center of the received image of the focal spot are calculated using the proposed method of searching the optimal geometric centers of the boundary contours of the image. For this, in the image different ranges of brightness detect the edge contours. The image may have an average of 150-160 boundary contours, of which an array of contours is formed.

Further, the processing of the formed array of boundary contours of the image in a cycle of the image is performed, during which the calculation of the optimal geometric center is made using the proposed algorithm for finding the optimal geometric center of the laser profile. The edge image contour represents an array of image points corresponding to the border of the spot on one of the ranges of brightness of the image points. The preliminary calculation of the coordinates of the center of the current boundary contour of the image is carried out by the formula (23).

The next step is the coordinates calculate of the optimal geometric center of the edge contour of the image, using the formula (18) to calculate the distance between the point of the contour to the point-center of the contour and the mean value of such distances. Also, with the aid of (19), deviations of distances between points of the contour and the point-center of the contour, as well as the value of the criterion

Figure 18. Block diagram of a modified algorithm for energy dissipation

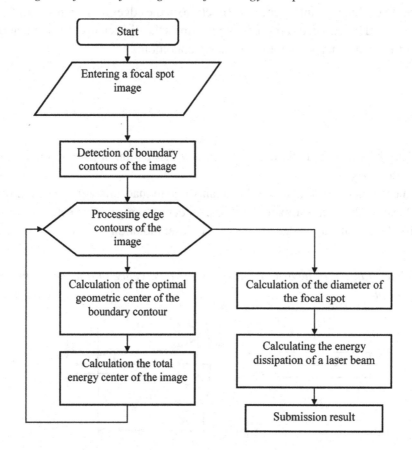

of the symmetry of the contour relative to the selected center, are calculated. Taking into account the specificity of the proposed criterion, the point with its smallest value is chosen as the optimal geometric center of the contour of the processed image.

The obtained array of points-centers of boundary contours is used when finding the energy center of the image of the focal spot.

Since each of the boundary contours of the focal spot image is selected in the corresponding value of the brightness range, it allows to move from searching for the values of the geometric contour centers to calculating the energy center of the image. The energy center of the image of the spots in the subaperture of the lens raster is in the superposition of the geometric centers of the boundary contours of such an image, selected for separate values from the range of brightness of the points. The coordinates of the energy center of the focal spot are calculated by the formula (24).

The next step is calculation of the diameter of the focal spot on the based on the coordinates of its energy center. For this purpose, is searched the point of the contour of the image of the focal spot, the most distant from the point of its energy center, using formula (6).

The final step of the modified algorithm is calculation of the energy divergence of a laser beam based on formula (26) using the calculated value of the diameter of the focal spot.

The proposed modified method for determining the energy divergence of a laser beam has increased accuracy compared with the known using the proposed method of searching the optimal geometric centers of the boundary contours of images of laser profiles on the basis of the proposed criterion of contour symmetry relative to one point.

COMPARATIVE SOFT MODEL OF EFFECTIVE METHODS FOR ANALYSIS OF LASER RADIATION PARAMETERS

The Structure of the Comparative Software Model

The comparative software model of effective methods for analyzing laser radiation parameters has a modular structure, shown in Fig. 19.

Figure 19. Modular structure of comparative software model of effective methods for analysis of laser radiation parameters

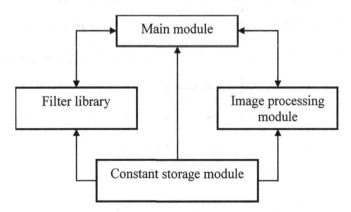

The main module of the model contains the entry point in the program, and also performs the basic logic of the work of the software model. The filter library is used to preprocess the images by providing the corresponding functionality for the main module. Analysis of parameters of laser radiation on the basis of images of the profiles of laser beams implemented directly in the module of image processing. Constant storage module contains all the necessary constants for the program model to work.

A comparative software model of effective methods for analyzing laser radiation parameters is created using the Java programming language and has the following object-oriented structure (Figure 20).

In the main package of classes com.analyzer software model contains the main class of the product ImageAnalyzer, which contains the point of entry in the program and the main logic of work, and corresponds to the main module software model. Also, the core package contains the IConstants interface, which contains all the constants necessary for the operation of the system and corresponds to the modulus for storing the model constants.

The com.analyzer.GUI class package contains the MainScreen class, which is responsible for the user interface of the software model and the logic of its operation. The class refers to the main module of the software model.

The com.analyzer.objects classes package contains service classes that are responsible for storing and displaying data within the software process model. The DoubleDimension class is used to store the coordinates of the image point, whose values have both whole and fractional parts. In this case, this class contains methods for returning the coordinates of a point in the form of integers. The ImageDisplay class is used to download images from external files, to store image data and display it in the software user interface. The ImageEdgeData class is used to store the results of comparable search methods for image centers of laser beam profiles, as well as other data needed to perform computations by comparable methods. The ImageListItem class is used to display the list of images uploaded to the model and contains a link to the file of the corresponding image. The PreparedPixelArray class is used to store the array of coordinate points of the image when performing computations by comparable methods. This class packet corresponds to the software model image processing module.

Figure 20. Object-oriented structure of the comparative software model

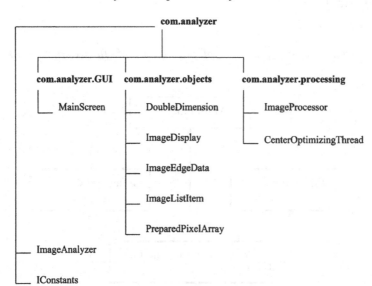

The com.analyzer.processing class package contains classes that are used directly when processing laser image. The ImageProcessor class contains functionality for pre-processing images, as well as performing computations by comparable methods. The CenterOptimizingThread class contains functionality to perform the search for the optimal center of the image of a profile of a laser beam in a separate stream. This class packet corresponds to the software model image processing module.

Also, the software model uses a freely distributed image filter library from a third-party manufacturer. It corresponds to the module of the library of filtering software model.

The Algorithm of the Work of the Comparative Software Model

The comparative software model of effective methods for laser radiation analysis works according to the following algorithm (Fig. 21).

Input data of the software model are image files of the profiles of laser beams, as well as the values required for the operation of comparable algorithms.

Preliminary processing of the entered image is carried out in order to improve the quality of the image being processed. It includes clearing images from specks and median noise filtering. Next, binaryization of the image is performed at the selected brightness threshold, which simplifies the execution of the next image operation - selecting the path of the laser spot at the selected brightness threshold.

For further work with images, it is necessary to determine the contour of the image of the laser profile, binarized with the chosen threshold of brightness, which will have a thickness of 1 pixel. To accomplish this task, a combination of the Roberts filter and the beetle method is used. First, the selection of the contours of the image of the laser profile is carried out using the Roberts operator. The result of this operation is the contour of the image of the laser profile, the individual sections of which have a thickness greater than 1 pixel. To select a contour with a thickness of 1 pixel by the method of "beetle", a choice of a continuous sequence of points of the image is made, which will form the path necessary for further work.

The next operation is to determine the center of the received contour of the image of the laser profile. In this case, the program model compares two methods of determining the centers - the standard formula of the center of masses, the use of which is considered in this paper, and the proposed algorithm for the mid-diametric definition of the center of the contour. The results of this operation are the coordinates of the contour centers of the image of the laser profile, obtained by comparable methods.

On the basis of the obtained results obtained by comparison methods, an optimal center of the contour of a laser profile is searched for by the proposed criterion for evaluating the contour symmetry relative to one point. For the results of each of the comparable methods, finding the coordinates of the optimal center is carried out in a separate program flow.

The next step is to show the results of comparable methods of searching the centers of the contours of images of laser profiles and found on their basis of optimal centers. The results of the program model work are the values of the coordinates of the centers found on the comparable methods, the significance of the symmetric criteria for the found centers, and also for the optimal centers, which gives the user the opportunity to compare the accuracy of the investigated methods according to the proposed criterion for assessing the symmetry of the contour relative to one point. The user interface of the software model contains three main components (Figure 22).

The selected files are downloaded to the software model, and they are added to the list of open files. When is selected a file from this list, it automatically starts processing it.

Figure 21. The algorithm of the work of the comparative software model

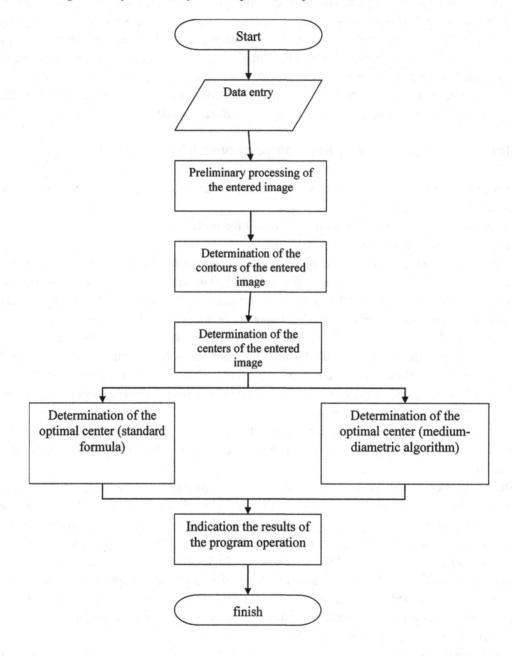

The processed image container contains an image of the current processed image of the laser profile, which shows its contour.

The results container contains two tabs - Image Borders and Image Processing Parameters (Fig. 23). The "Image Borders" tab contains a graph of the scan of the contour of the laser profile and the distances from its points to the found centers. The user has the ability to save the generated schedule to a restore file, as well as to customize the look of the graph.

Figure 22. User interface of the comparative software model

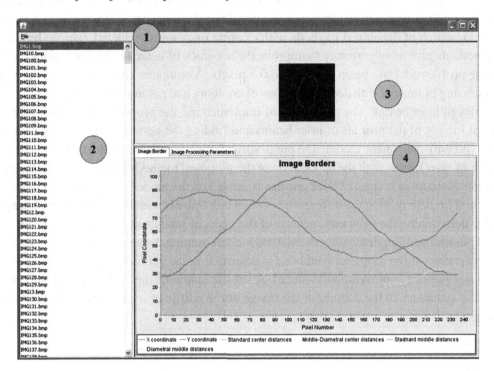

Figure 23. Tab «Image Processing Parameters»

Image Border	Image Processing Parameters	
Parameter	**Value**	
Standard method center coordinate	31.536; 43.692	
Middle-Diametral method center coordinate	32.0234375; 44.1796875	
Standard method middle fluctuation	4.68482236889938	
Middle-Diametral method middle fluctuation	4.630710130118261	
Optimized standard method middle fluctuation	4.5312489420148685	
Optimized middle-diametral method middle fluctuation	4.531229833588296	

The "Image Processing Parameters" tab contains a table of the results of processing the image of the laser profile, which gives the user the opportunity to get not only numerical values of coordinates of the geometric centers of the boundary contours of images of laser profiles, but also quantitative assessment of the accuracy obtained using the investigated methods of results.

CONCLUSION

The criterion for evaluating the symmetry of the laser profile image contour relative to a certain point is proposed, which provides an opportunity to evaluate the accuracy of the methods for determining the centers of images of the profiles of laser beams.

Based on the deviation of distances from the found center to the points of the contour, the method of finding the optimal center of the image of the profile of the laser beam is proposed. A comparative analysis and research of developed methods with existing ones was conducted, which showed that the proposed methods give an opportunity to improve the accuracy of determining the energy center of the image of the profile of a laser beam from 0.1 to 0.3 pixels. A computer model has been developed that allows processing of images with deep distortions of contours and parameters of the intensity of images of the profiles of laser beams. The possibility of implementing the proposed methods for determining the center of images of the profiles of laser beams and finding the optimal center of the contour of the laser profile is confirmed on the model. The possibility of implementation of the method for determining the diameter of laser beams with the application of the proposed methods for determining the geometric centers of the contours of images of laser profiles is proved on the model. The possibility of implementing the method for determining the difference between laser beams with the application of the proposed methods for determining the geometric centers of the paths of images of laser profiles is proved on the model. The possibility of implementing the method for determining the angle of incidence of laser beams with the application of the proposed methods for determining the geometric centers of the contours of images of laser profiles is proved on the model. A substantiation of the application of the criterion for evaluating the symmetry of the contour of the image of the profile of a laser beam relative to one point is carried out.

REFERENCES

Aggarwal, C. (2018). Neural Networks and Deep Learning: A Textbook. Springer. doi:10.1007/978-3-319-94463-0

Bronshteyn, I., & Semendayev, K. (1986). *Mathematics: Moscow, Science*. Academic Press. (in Russian)

Chervonkin, A., Nabokin, P., & Hyppenen, A. (2006). Compact two-coordinate beam guidance device for atmospheric optical communication lines between moving objects. *Optical Journal, 5*.

Dakin, J., & Brown, R. (2017). Handbook of Optoelectronics (2nd ed.). CRC Press. doi:10.1201/9781315157009

Dutta, N., & Zhang, X. (2018). *Optoelectronic Devices*. World Scientific Publishing Company. doi:10.1142/10894

Goodman, J. (2017). *Introduction to Fourier Optics* (4th ed.). W. H. Freeman.

GOST 26086–84. (1985). *Lasers. Methods for measuring the beam diameter and the energy divergence of laser radiation*. IPK Publishing House of Standards.

Kohonen, T. (2000). *Self-organized Maps* (3rd ed.). Springer.

Kormanovsky, S., Shvejki, N., & Timchenko, L. (2001). Approach to determining the center of image connectivity. *Bulletin of the FPI*, (4), 71-73.

Kovzel, M., Timchenko, L., Kutaev, Y., Svechnikov, S., Kozhemyako, V., Stasyuk, O., ... Zohoruiko, L. (2006). Parallel - hierarchical transformation and Q-processing of information for real-time systems. Kyiv: KUETT.

Kozhemyako, V., Tymchenko, L., Kutaev, Y., & Yaroviy, A. (2002). Approach for real-time image recognition. *Opto-Electronic Information Technologies*, (1), 110-124.

Liu, J. (2013). *Radial Basis Function (RBF) Neural Network Control for Mechanical Systems: Design, Analysis and Matlab Simulation*. Springer.

Pennington, T. (1993). *Performance Comparison of Shearing Interferometer and Hartmann Wave Front Sensors*. PN.

Piprek, J. (2017). Handbook of Optoelectronic Device Modeling and Simulation: Lasers, Modulators, Photodetectors, Solar Cells, and Numerical Methods (vol. 2). CRC Press.

Shack, R. V., & Platt, B. C. (1971). Production and use of a lenticular Hartmann screen. *Journal of the Optical Society of America*, *61*, 656.

Sugimura, H., & Takashima, K. (1999). On a fractal approach to actual plant images. *Proc. of Int. Conf. Pattern Recognition and Image Processing'99*, 130-133.

Ta-Hsin, L., & Gibson, J. (1997). Time corellation analysis of a class of nonstationarysignals with an application to radar imaging. *IEEE Intl. Conf. Acoust., Speech and Signal Proc. (ICASSP97)*, *5*, 3765-3769.

Taylor, M., & Koning, M. (2017). *Blue Windmill Media. The Math of Neural Networks*. Academic Press.

Timchenko, L., Kutaev, Y., Zhukov, K., Gertsiy, A., & Shveyki, N. (2000). Coordinate Reference System Of Nonstationary Signals. *Proc. Machine Vision and Three-Dimensional Imaging Systems for Inspection and Metrology SPIE Symposium*, 4189, 211-217.

Timchenko, L., Kokriatskaia, N., Yarovyy, A., & Denysova, A. (2013). Application of multi-level parallel-hierarchic systems based on gpu in laser beam shaping problems. *Journal of Theoretical and Applied Information Technology.*, *54*(3), 525–534.

Timchenko, L., Kutaev, Y., Gertsiy, A., & Baybak, J. (2000). Coordinate Reference System Of Nonstationary Signals. *Proc. Xth Conference on Laser Optics (LO'2000)*.

Vasiliev, V. P., Sumerin, V. V., & Chervonkin, A. P. (2002). The equipment for the optical communication line increased secrecy. *Wuxiandian Gongcheng*, 12.

Welsh, B. M., Roggemann, M. C., Ellerbroek, B. L., & Pennington, T. L. (1995). Fundamental performance comparison of a Hartmann and a shearing interferometer wave-front sensor. *Applied Optics*, *34*(21), 4186. doi:10.1364/AO.34.004186 PMID:21052244

Werbos, P. (1974). *Beyond Regression: New Tools for Prediction and Analysis in the Behavioral Sciences* (Ph.D. Thesis). Applied Mathematics, Harvard University.

Yarovyy, A., Timchenko, L., & Kokriatskaia, N. (2012). Parallel-Hierarchical Computing System for Multi-Level Transformation of Masked Digital Signals. *Advances in Electrical and Computer Engineering, 12*(3), 13–20. doi:10.4316/aece.2012.03002

Zuev, B. (n.d.). *Laser navigation devices*. Academic Press.

Zuev, V. (1971). *Lazernye navigacionnye ustrojstva*. Academic Press.

Chapter 9
A Secured Predictive Analytics Using Genetic Algorithm and Evolution Strategies

Addepalli V. N. Krishna
Christ University, India

Shriansh Pandey
Christ University, India

Raghav Sarda
Christ University, India

ABSTRACT

In the banking sector, the major challenge will be retaining customers. Different banks will be offering various schemes to attract new customers and retain existing customers. The details about the customers will be provided by various features like account number, credit score, balance, credit card usage, salary deposited, and so on. Thus, in this work an attempt is made to identify the churning rate of the possible customers leaving the organization by using genetic algorithm. The outcome of the work may be used by the banks to take measures to reduce churning rates of the possible customers in leaving the respective bank. Modern cyber security attacks have surely played with the effects of the users. Cryptography is one such technique to create certainty, authentication, integrity, availability, confidentiality, and identification of user data can be maintained and security and privacy of data can be provided to the user. The detailed study on identity-based encryption removes the need for certificates.

INTRODUCTION

In today's new age world it is seen that almost everyone now has a bank account with him or her. It is the banks that a provides with the safety of the individuals and their various business assets and they also support with productive human endeavor and economic process by expeditiously and effectively allocating funds, and that they bridge the divergent maturity desires of short-run depositors and long borrowers.

DOI: 10.4018/978-1-7998-1290-6.ch009

In the last few years it has been seen that in any type of market regaining back the customers are now the major areas of concern. Especially now for the banks due to the increase in the competition in the market due to the entry of new banks that are offering the competing services. It is also a proven fact that a banking client becomes profitable to a bank solely in the second year of his association with the bank and any client that would leave before the period of two years would be a loss making client to the company. If the bank does not offer the customers a powerful reason to remain with them, then the competition can offer them a powerful reason to leave them.

The work is based on paper Genetic Algorithms for feature selection by Kevin R.Coombes where the class prediction package selects a subset of features and combines them to a fully specified Model that can predict the result of newly derived samples. Predictive Models for Bank churning rates were attempted Using Machine learning algorithms like Decision Tree, Gradient Boosting Algorithm, Random Forest and Artificial Neural Networks which have their own Advantages and Limitations. In this work an attempt is made to apply Genetic algorithm and see for its increased performance in its predictions.

Problem Identification

While looking for a suitable topic, we stumbled upon the idea of creating a predictive analysis model, we had decided upon an ideal way of going about it by using the genetic algorithm. We also decided to use 'R' as it provided an efficient to provide us with the outcomes. Since Security is an underlying requirement for any data Model we thought of applying attribute based cryptography (IBE) for security purpose.

Problem Formulation

As mentioned earlier the increasing churn rate is the new age problems for the banks in the current market system. So it is the work of the bank to keep a close eye on the banking customers and should also fulfill their needs on the customers who are more probable to leave the bank. The factors that would determine is by watching out for the following factors like customer name, credit score, tenure, age, balance, number of products has a card or not. The aforementioned factors can be used to find out the number of customers or the banking clients who are going to stay with the bank using the data-set available to us.

The work requires us to use these data-sets in order to find out the banking clients which are going to stay with the bank. Since it is a new way of predictive analysis it is expected to get good results and getting more accuracy than the existing system.

The reason for using the genetic algorithm was as, we have seen that GA totally works on the basis of feature selection means it will select those features (attributes) from the dataset which are the most important for the churning rates of customer and because of that the results will be more precise and accurate. Side by side we have used our own model (logic) that how to make a table of data set, so that GA gets optimized and can produce more good results.

The work is appended with IBE based Security as the top layer, which forms an integral part with any data based Model in increasing its performance.

Problem Statement and Objectives

In the banking industry regaining of customers is the most important thing for a bank so as to gain benefits due to the engagement of the baking clients. In order to know about the problem we have taken a bank data set which has been collected by a bank after doing certain sort of surveys. The bank has been seen the unusual churn rates. They found out that the customers are leaving the bank at very high and unusual rates, so the bank wants to understand that what the particular problem is behind the high churning rates. In order to provide security to the data, attributes to be identified for which we tried with Identity based encryption.

RESEARCH METHODOLOGY

While looking for a suitable topic, we stumbled upon the idea of creating a predictive analysis model after consulting with our guide, we had decided upon an ideal way of going about it by using the genetic algorithm in figure 1. We also decided to use 'R' as it provided an efficient to provide us with the outcomes.

Figure 1. Genetic Algorithm Architecture (GAA)

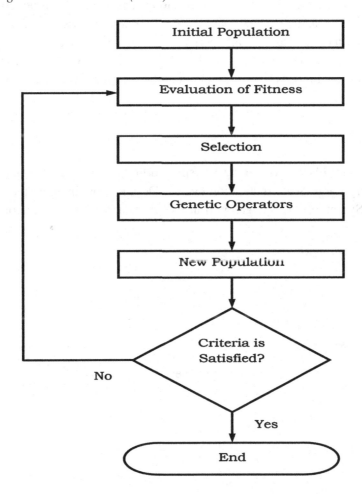

Genetic algorithm is the search based optimization technique which is based on the postulates of Genetics and Natural Selection methods form the biology and Genome study. It is constantly used to find optimal or near-optimal solutions to difficult problems which otherwise would take a lifetime to solve. The major areas where Genetic algorithm plays a vital role and the branch of computer science is Machine Learning, research methods, model building, in order to perform the predictive analysis, solving the optimization problems in research and etc. It can also be defined as the search Heuristic that is persuaded from the Charles Darwin's theory of natural selection where the fittest individuals are selected for the reproduction in order to fabricate the offspring of next generation.

Optimization is the process of making some existing thing more sustainable and better. Lets us say in general for an instance, any process always have a set of inputs and the set of outputs as shown in the figure 2.

So, optimization refers to finding the values of inputs in such a way that we can harness the best output values. The preciseness of best values varies from problem to prob lem. In terms of arithmetic it refers to the maximizing or minimizing one or additional objective functions, by varied the input parameters.

Failure of Gradient Based Methods

Traditional calculus based techniques work by beginning at an arbitrary point and by moving toward the gradient, till we achieve the highest point of the slope. This method is productive and works great for single-crested target capacities like the cost capacity in linear regression. Be that as it may, in most true circumstances, we have an exceptionally perplexing issue called as landscapes, which are made of numerous pinnacles and numerous valleys, which makes such techniques bomb, as they experience the ill effects of an inalienable propensity of stalling out at the nearby optima as appeared in the accompanying figure 3.

GA as a Solution

Some troublesome issues like the Travelling Salesperson Problem (TSP), have appli cations like finding the path and Very Large-Scale Integration (VLSI) Design. Now imagine that you are using your Global Positioning System (GPS) Navigation frame work, and it takes a couple of minutes (or even a

Figure 2. Optimization process

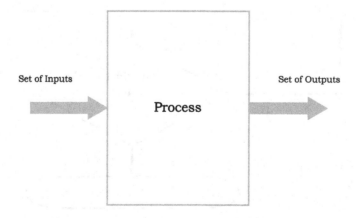

Figure 3. Failure of gradient based method

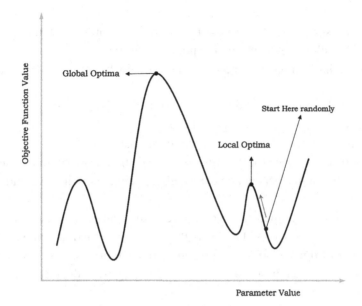

couple of hours) to compute the "optimal" path from the source to goal. Delay in such applications is not acceptable and therefore a "good-enough" solution, which is delivered "quickly" is required. Now let's discuss Predictive analysis using GA, Numerous regular utilizations of predictive analytics, from client division to medicinal analysis, emerge from complex associations between highlights (likewise called factors or attributes).

Feature selection is the way toward finding the most applicable factors for a predictive model. These methods can be utilized to distinguish and evacuate unneeded, superfluous and excess features that don't contribute or diminish the precision of the predictive model.

Numerically, feature selection is formulated as a combinatorial optimization problem. Here the function to enhance is the generalization performance of the predictive model, represented by the error on a selected data set. The design variables are the inclusion (1) or the exclusion (0) of the features. An exhaustive selection of features would evaluate lots of different combinations (2N, where N is the number of features). This process requires lots of computational work and, if the number of features is very large, then it becomes impracticable. Therefore, we need intelligent techniques that allow us to perform feature selection in practice. One of the most advanced algorithms for feature selection is the genetic algorithm. A stochastic technique for function optimization is dependent on the mechanic of natural genetics and biological evolution.

Genetic Algorithm: Fundamentals

This section acquaints the fundamental phrasing required to comprehend GAs. Like wise, a nonexclusive structure of GAs is displayed in both pseudocode and graphical structures.

Basic Terminology

- **Population**: It is a subset of all the possible (encoded) solutions to the given prob- lem. The populace for a GA is closely resembling the populace for people with the exception of that instead of the populace we have different candidate solution which represents the populace as shown in figure 4.
- **Chromosomes:** A chromosomes is one such result to the given issue.
- **Gene:** A gene is one element position of a chromosome.
- **Allele:** It is the value a gene takes for a specific chromosome.
- **Genotype:** Genotype is defined the populace in the calculation space. In the calculation space, the arrangements are shown in a way which can be effectively comprehended and controlled utilizing a computing system.
- **Phenotype:** Phenotype is defined as the populace in the actual real world solution space in which the result to the problem is depicted in a way they are represented in real world situations.
- **Decoding and Encoding:** Decoding is a procedure of changing the result from the genotype to the phenotype space, while encoding is a process of changing from the phenotype to genotype space as shown in figure 5.
- **Fitness Function:** A fitness function is characterized as a function which takes the solution as input and produces the appropriateness of the solution as the output. In some cases, the fitness function and the objective function may be the same, while in others it might be dependent on the problem.
- **Genetic Operators:** These alter the genetic composition of the offspring. These in clude cross-over, mutation, selection, etc.

We start with a fundamental populace (which may be made unpredictably or seeded by various heuristics), select parents from this populace for mating. Apply hybrid and change administrators on the guardians to make new off-springs. Ultimately, these off springs supersede the present individuals in the people and the methodology goes over. Along these lines, hereditary calculations truly try to emulate human improve ment somewhat. Hereditary calculations work on a populace of people to create better and better approximations. At every age, another populace is made by the way toward choosing people

Figure 4. Basic terminology

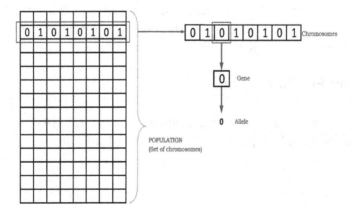

Figure 5. Decoding & Encoding

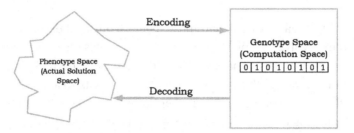

as indicated by their dimension of wellness in the issue area and recom bining them together utilizing administrators acquired from normal hereditary qualities. The posterity may likewise experience change. This procedure prompts the develop ment of populaces of people that are more qualified to their condition than the people that they were made from, similarly as in regular adjustment as shown in figure 6.

Genotype Representation

The champion is among the populace who makes the best decision while completing a genetic algorithm is picking the depiction that we will use to address our answers. It has been seen that less than ideal depiction can provoke poor execution of the GA. Accordingly, picking a suitable portrayal, having a significant meaning of the mappings between the phenotype and genotype spaces is fundamental for the achievement of a GA.

Figure 6. Basic structure

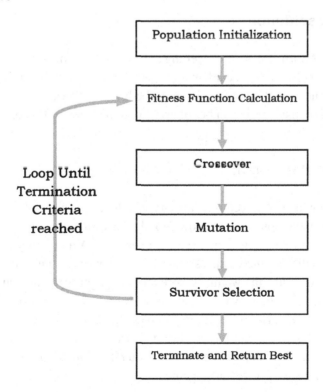

Binary Representation

This is the standout amongst least difficult and most generally utilized depictions in GAs. In this kind of portrayal, the genotype involves the bit strings. For certain issues when the arrangement space comprises of Boolean choice factors, yes or no, the two fold portrayal is normal. Take for instance the 0/1 Knapsack Problem. In the event that there are n things, we can speak to an answer by a paired string of n components, where the xth component tells whether thing x is picked (1) or not (0). For different issues, explicitly those managing numbers, we can speak to the numbers with their parallel portrayal. The issue with this kind of encoding is that distinctive bits have diverse essentialness and hence mutation and crossover operators can have undesired results. This can be set out to some degree by utilizing Gray Coding, as an adjustment in one piece does not massively affect the arrangement.

Real Valued Representation

For issues where we need to characterize the qualities utilizing nonstop as opposed to discrete factors, the genuine esteemed portrayal is the most characteristic. The accuracy of these genuine esteemed or skimming point numbers is anyway constrained to the computer.

Integer Representation

For discrete regarded characteristics, we can't by and large control the game plan space to parallel 'yes' or 'no'. For example, if we have to encode the four partitions, North, South, East, and West, we can encode them as 0,1,2,3. In such cases, the entire number of depiction is charming.

Permutation Representation

An exemplary case of this portrayal is the Travelling Salesman Problem (TSP). In this the sales rep needs to take a voyage through every one of the urban areas, visiting every city precisely once and return to the beginning city. The all out separation of the visit must be limited. The answer for this TSP is normally a requesting or stage of the considerable number of urban communities and accordingly utilizing a change portrayal bodes well for this issue.

Genetic Algorithm: Population

The fitness work basically characterized is a capacity which takes a hopeful answer for the issue as information and creates as yield how "fit" our how "good" the arrangement is as for the issue in thought.

Computation of wellness esteem is done over and over in a GA and thusly it ought to be adequately quick. A moderate calculation of the wellness esteem can unfavorably influence a GA and make it extraordinarily moderate. As a rule, the wellness work and the target work are equivalent to the goal is to either expand or limit the given target work. In any case, for progressively complex issues with various targets and imperatives, an Algorithm Designer may have an alternate wellness work.

The fitness function should contain the following characteristics:1. The fitness function should be sufficiently fast to compute. 2. It should quantitatively quantify how fit a given arrangement is or how fit people can be created from the given arrangement

At times, figuring the fitness work straightforwardly probably won't be conceivable because of the inherent complexities of the current issue. In such cases, we do fitness estimation to suit our requirements.

Genetic Algorithm: Parent Selection

Parent Selection is the way toward choosing parents which mate and recombine to make off-springs for the people to come. Parent selection is exceptionally vital to the conver gence rate of the GA as great parents drive people to better and fitter arrangements. In any case, care ought to be taken to keep one very fit arrangement from assuming control over the whole population in a couple of ages, as this prompts the arrangements being near each other in the arrangement space in this way prompting lost decent variety.

Fitness Proportionate Selection

Fitness Proportionate Selection is a standout amongst the most famous methods for parent selection. In this each individual can turn into a parent with a probability which is corresponding to its fitness. In this way, fitter people have a higher shot of mating and proliferating their highlights to the people to come. In this way, such a selection technique applies a selection weight to the more fit people in the populace, advancing better people after some time.

Think about a round wheel. The wheel is separated into n pies, where n is the quantity of people in the populace. Every individual gets a bit of the circle which is relative to its fitness esteem.

There are two ways for performing the fitness proportionate selection:

1. **Roulette Wheel Selection-** In a roulette wheel selection, the round wheel is parti tioned as por-trayed previously. A fixed point is picked on the wheel circuit as appeared and the wheel is turned. The locale of the wheel which comes before the fixed point is picked as the parent. For the second parent, a similar procedure is rehashed.

Plainly a fitter individual has a more prominent pie on the wheel and in this manner a more note-worthy possibility of arriving before the fixed moment that the wheel is turned. Thusly, the likelihood of picking an individual depends specifically on its well ness as shown in figure 7.

Figure 7. Roulette wheel selection

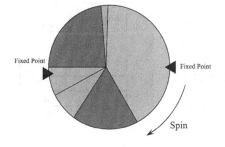

Chromosome	Fitness Value
A	8.2
B	3.2
C	1.4
D	1.2
E	4.2
F	0.3

■ A ■ B ■ C ■ D ■ E ■ F

The steps which have been used during implementation are:

a. Calculate S = the sum of a finesses. 2. Generate a random number between 0 and S.
b. Starting from the top of the population, keep adding the fitness to partial sum P, till P < S.
c. The individual for which P exceeds S is the chosen individual.

Thus the expression will be

```
Define Fitness S
Do P= P+ r where r is 0<=r<=S
Calculate P.
```

2. **Stochastic Universal Sampling (SUS):** Stochastic Universal Sampling is very like Roulette wheel selection, notwithstanding, rather than having only one fixed point, we have numerous fixed focuses as appeared in the accompanying picture. In this way, every one of the guardians are picked in only one turn of the wheel. Likewise, such a setup empowers the exceedingly fit people to be picked at any rate once as shown in figure 8.

Tournament Selection

In K-Way tournament selection, we have to select K individuals from the populace aimlessly and select the best out of these to end up a parent. A similar procedure is rehashed for choosing the following parent. It is likewise very prevalent in writing as it can even work with negative fitness values.

Rank Selection

Rank Selection moreover works with negative fitness values and is, for the most part, utilized when the people in the populace have extremely close fitness values (this hap pens as a rule toward the finish of the run). This prompts every individual having a practically equivalent offer of the pie (like in the event of fitness proportionate selection) as appeared in the accompanying picture and subsequently every

Figure 8. Stochastic universal sampling

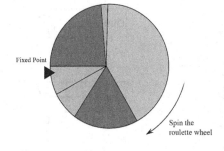

Chromosome	Fitness Value
A	8.2
B	3.2
C	1.4
D	1.2
E	4.2
F	0.3

▪ A ▪ B ▪ C ▪ D ▪ E ▪ F

individual regardless of how fit in respect to one another has an around same likelihood of getting close as a parent. Thus it prompts a misfortune in the selection pressure towards fitter people, making the GA make poor parent choices in such circumstances.

In this, we evacuate the idea of fitness esteem while choosing a parent. Be that as it may, each person in the population is positioned by their fitness. The choice of the guardians relies upon the position of every person and not fitness. The higher positioned people are favored more than the lower positioned ones.

Random Selection

In this system, we haphazardly select guardians from the current population. There is no determination weight towards fitter people and along these lines this technique is normally dodged.

GENETIC ALGORITHMS: CROSSOVER

Introduction to Crossover

The crossover operator is undifferentiated from multiplication and biological crossover. In this, more than one parent is chosen and at least one off springs are created utilizing the genetic material of the guardians. Crossover is ordinarily associated in a GA with a high probability "pc".

Crossover Operators

It is to be noticed that these crossover operators are extremely nonexclusive and the GA Designer may actualize an issue explicit crossover operators too. The most popularly used crossover operators are:

1. **One Point Crossover:** In this one-point crossover, an random crossover point is chosen and the tails of its two guardians are swapped to get new off springs.
2. **Multi Point Crossover:** Multi point crossover is a generalization of the one-point crossover where in substituting sections are swapped to get new off spring.
3. **Uniform Crossover:** In a uniform crossover, we don't partition the chromosome into parts, rather we treat each quality independently. In this, we basically flip a coin for every chromosome to choose whether or not it'll be incorporated into the posterity. We can similarly incline the coin to one parent, to have increasingly genetic material in the youngster from that parent.
4. **Davis' Order Crossover (OX1):** OX1 is utilized for change based crossovers with the goal of sending data about relative requesting to the off springs.

Steps

1. Make two arbitrary crossover focuses in the parent and duplicate the portion between them from the principal parent to the primary offspring.
2. Now, beginning from the second crossover point in the second parent, duplicate the staying unused numbers from the second parent to the main youngster, folding over the rundown.
3. Repeat for the second child with the parent's job reversed.

Genetic Algorithms: Mutation

In easy terms, mutation could also be outlined as atiny low random tweak within the body, to induce a brand new answer. it's wont to maintain and introduce diversity within the genetic population and is sometimes applied with an occasional likelihood, "pm". If the likelihood is extremely high, the GA gets reduced to a random search.

Mutation is a part of the GA that is expounded to the "exploration" of the search area. it's been discovered that mutation is important to the convergence of the GA whereas crossover isn't.

Mutation Operators

In this area of research, we tend to describe a number of the foremost usually used mutation operators. Just like the crossover operators, this can be not a thorough going list and also the GA designer would possibly realize a blend of those methodologies or a problem-specific mutation operator a lot of helpful.

1. **Bit Flip Mutation:** In this bit flip mutation, we select one or more random bits and flip them. This is utilized for binary encoded GAs.
2. **Random Resetting:** Random Resetting is an extension of the bit flip for the number illustration. In this, a random price from the set of permissible values is assigned to a arbitrarily chosen sequence.
3. **Swap Mutation:** In swap mutation, we select two points on the chromosome at ran dom, and interchange the values. This is a regular method performed in permutation based encodings.
4. **Scramble Mutation:** Scramble mutation is additionally fashionable permutation rep resentations. In this, from the whole body, a set of genes is chosen and their values are disorganized or shuffled arbitrarily.
5. **Inversion Mutation:** In inversion mutation, we tend to choose a set of genes like in scramble mutation, however rather than shuffling the set, we tend to just invert the complete string within the set.

Genetic Algorithms: Selection

1. **Survivor Selection:** The Survivor choice Policy determines that people area unit to be kicked out and that area unit to be unbroken within the next generation. it's crucial because it ought to make sure that the fitter people aren't kicked out of the population, whereas at identical time diversity ought to be maintained within the population.

Some GAs use political orientation. In easy terms, it means that this fittest member of the population is often propagated to consecutive generation. Therefore, underneath no circumstance will the fittest member of this population get replaced.

The easiest policy is to kick random members out of the population, however such Associate in Nursing approach often has convergence problems, thus the subsequent ways area unit wide used.

2. **Age Based Selection:** In Age-Based choice, we have a tendency to not have a notion of fitness. It is supported on the premise that every individual is allowed within the population for a finite generation wherever it is allowed to breed, after that it is kicked out of the population in spite of however smart its fitness is.

For example, the age is that the range of generations that the individual has been in side the populace. The oldest members of the population that is P4 and P7 are kicked out of the population and further more the ages of the remainder of the members are incremented by one as shown in figure 9.

3. **Fitness Based Selection:** In this fitness based choice, the youngsters tend to switch the smallest amount match people within the population. The choice of the smallest amount match people is also done employing a variation of any of the choice policies delineated before – tournament selection, fitness proportionate choice, etc.

For example, within the following image, the youngsters replace the smallest amount match people P1 and P10 of the population. it's to be noted that since P1 and P9 have identical fitness price, the choice to get rid of that individual from the population is bigoted as shown in figure 10.

Genetic Algorithms: Termination Condition

The end state of a Genetic algorithmic principle is vital in determinative once a GA run can finish. it's been discovered that originally, the GA progresses in no time with higher solutions coming back in each few iterations, however this tends to saturate within the later stages wherever the enhancements area unit terribly tiny. we tend to sometimes desire a termination condition such our resolution is near to the optimum, at the top of the run.

Usually, we tend to keep one in all the subsequent termination conditions:-

1. When there has been no improvement within the population for X iterations.
2. When we reach associate absolute variety of generations.
3. When the target operate price has reached a precise pre-defined price.

Figure 9. Age based selection

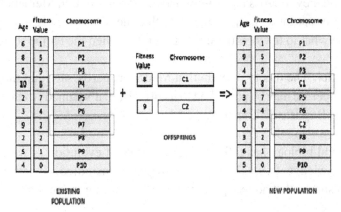

Figure 10. Fitness based selection

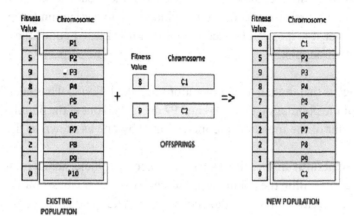

For example, during a genetic algorithmic rule, we tend to keep a counter that keeps track of the generations that there has been no improvement within the population. Initially, we tend to set this counter to zero. Every time we tend to don't generate off springs that area unit higher than the people within the population, we tend to increment the counter.

However, if the fitness any of the off-springs is healthier, then we tend to reset the counter to zero. The algorithmic rule terminates once the counter reaches a planned price.

Like alternative parameters of a GA, the termination condition is additionally extremely drawback specific and therefore the GA designer ought to try numerous choices to en- vision what suits his explicit drawback the most effective.

Models of Lifetime Adaptation

In nature, exclusively the learning contained within the individual's genotype may be transmitted to consequent generation.

However, alternative models of life adaptation – theory of organic evolution model and baldwinian model conjointly do exist. It is to be noted that whichever model is that the best, is open for discussion and also the outcomes acquired by analysts demonstrate that the selection of life adaptation is very drawback explicit.

Often, we have a tendency to cross a GA with native search – like in Memetic Algo rithms. In such cases, one would possibly opt for do keep company with either theory of organic evolution or Baldwinian Model to determine what to try to with people generated when the native search.

1. **Lamarckian Model:** The theory of evolution Model primarily says that the traits that a personal acquires in his/her period may be passed on to its offspring. it's named when French man of science Jean-Baptiste Jean Baptiste de Lamarck.

Even although, natural biology has fully forgotten theory of evolution as we have a tendency to all grasp that solely the knowledge within the genotype may be transmitted. However, from a computation read purpose, it's been shown that adopting the theory of evolution model provides sensible results for a few of the issues.

In the theory of evolution model, a neighborhood search operator examines the neigh borhood (acquiring new traits), and if a higher body is found, it becomes the offspring.

2. **Baldwinian Model:** The Baldwinian model is associate intermediate plan named when James Mark Baldwin (1896). within the Baldwin model, the chromosomes will code an inclination of learning useful behaviors. This means, that not like the Lamarck ian model, we have a tendency to don't transmit the non-heritable traits to consequent generation, and neither will we fully ignore the non-heritable traits like within the Dar winian Model.

The Baldwin Model is inside the center those 2 boundaries, whereby the tendency of a private to accumulate sure attributes is encoded instead of the attributes themselves.

In this Baldwinian Model, a neighborhood search administrator examines the neighbor hood (acquiring new traits), and if a improved body is discovered, it solely assigns the improved fitness to the body and doesn't modify the body itself. The alteration in fitness signifies the chromosomes capability to "acquire the trait", although it's not passed on to the longer term ages.

Genetic Algorithms: Application Areas

1. **Optimization:** Genetic Algorithms ar most commonly utilized in optimisation issues whereby we've got to maximise or minimize a given goal perform price beneath a given set of constraints.
2. **Economics:** GAs also are accustomed characterize varied economic models just like the cobweb model, scientific theory equilibrium resolution, quality rating, etc.
3. **Neural Networks:** GAs also are accustomed train neural networks, notably repeated neural networks.
4. **Parallelization:** GAs even have excellent parallel capabilities and persuade be ter ribly effective suggests that in determination sure issues, and conjointly offer a decent space for analysis.
5. **Image process:** GAs ar utilized for varied digital image process (DIP) undertakings additionally as dense segment matching.
6. **Vehicle Routing Issues:** With many different soft time windows, numerous spots, and a heterogeneous fleet.
7. **Scheduling Applications:** GAs are accustomed solve varied programming issues additionally, notably the timetabling downside.
8. **Machine Learning:** As already mentioned, genetics-based machine learning (GBML) could be a niche space in machine learning.

LITERATURE SURVEY AND REVIEW

The thought of about of pursuing our work as predictive analysis using genetic algo rithm is came after referring many research papers. We will be discussing some of them one by one in brief. So according to work (Arun, Garg & Kaur, 2016), with the sweetening within the banking sector legion individuals are applying for bank loans however the bank has its restricted assets that it's to grant to restricted individuals solely, thus sorting out to whom the loan is granted may be able to be a safer choice for the bank is a typical method. Thus during this paper we tend to try and scale back this risk issue behind choosing the safe person thus on save legion bank efforts and assets. This can be done by mining the large knowledge of the previous records of the individuals to whom the loan was granted before and on the idea of those records/experiences the machine was trained victimization the machine learning model that offer the foremost correct result. The objective of this paper is to predict whether or not distribution of the loan to a specific person is safe or not. The authors of the paper deemed this method to be quite accurate and the application is properly functioning. However, we had only used the knowledge of predictive analysis in our work.

From the work of authors (Fariborz, Saber & Keyhan, 2012) we can say that in this analysis, the bankruptcy of corporations has been surveyed through the genetic rule. To try and do this and so as to style its connected genetic model, the monetary ratios are used and a genetic model has been conferred so as to predict bankruptcy of the accepted corporations in Tehran exchange Market. Formulating the connected model has been done through the relevant knowledge of 2 teams of the businesses accepted as those in Tehran exchange Market. The primary cluster consists of forty non bankrupt corporations, and also the second just like the initial cluster includes forty corporations however they were bankrupt ones. The model is delineating by mistreatment twenty four monetary ratios consisting of four teams of liquidation, profit, activity, and lever age ratios (Capital Structure).The purpose of this essay is that not like the opposite previous ways that simply gift the genetic algorithms to resolve the matter of predicting bankruptcy, here during this article additionally to specializing in the answer for the matter, the conferred model has used the connected rule so as to be told and converge on the acceptable answer. The check results of the prediction capability of the model indicate the actual fact that the conferred model will predict the companies' bankruptcy and non-bankruptcy accurately and with the smallest amount error some years before they extremely occur, and bypassing the time of bankruptcy, its prediction ability de- creases since its prediction indexes become weak step by step. The results of this study gift the economical functions of this methodology employed by completely different researches. In this paper the authors have tried to develop a genetic rule. The model has been developed so as to predict the bankruptcy of the accepted corporations in the Teheran exchange Market. This paper had helped us to analyze and decide of how to prepare a model with respect to our work and which algorithm we are interested in to work with and research on.

In their work he authors (Ganesh & Rasheed, 1953) have tried to develop a model for the future stock price prediction for the users using genetic algorithm and evolution strategies. By using genetic algorithm they try to find out the connection weight for each attribute and the input for each attribute is given to a sigmoid function. After it is amplified based on its connection weights the approach of using the genetic algorithm was compared to be better than the evolution strategy as it had yielded a better stock predicting percentage for the future. As in each case the results found to obtain was higher than 70% . The result will hence give us a better idea of whether the previously recorded data or the historical data are good enough to predict the results. If the historical data does not give the expected results then we should find other factors which will affect the prices and there will a high chance that there will be an increase in the accuracy. Thus this work implement the use of genetic algorithm and evolution strategy. The model used by them was to compare the results of the genetic algorithm method or the evolution strategy. The model was also used to check of whether the outcomes are recorded better in the historical data or on the real time data with more number of parameters involved. The research paper helped us to give a proper understanding of the working of genetic algorithm and evolution strategy.

From the work of authors (Alisa, 2016) states that the case study of usage of one of the data mining ways, neural network, in data discovery from databases within the industry. Methoding is automatic process of analyzing, organization or grouping an outsize set of knowledge from totally different views and summarizing it into helpful information exploitation special algorithms. Data processing will facilitate to resolve banking issues by finding some regularity, relation and correlation to business data that aren't visible initially sight as a result of their hidden in massive amounts of information. During this paper, we have a tendency to use one amongst the few mining ways, neural network. It used Alyuda Neuro-Inteligence package to predict client churn in bank. The main target on client churn is to determinate who are at the verge of leaving the bank and making an analysis of whether is it worth retaining those banking clients. Neural network is applied math learning model galvanized by biological neural and its accustomed estimate or approximate functions which will depend upon an outsize range of inputs that are typically unknown. Though the tactic itself is difficult, there are tools that change the employment of neural networks while not abandoning the previous data of how they operate. The results show that the banking clients use a lot of bank services (products) square measure a lot of loyal, therefore bank ought to specialize to those customers and supply them with the product as per their desires. Similar results were obtained for various network topologies. Thus this work states the case of using different mining ways, neural net in discovering the data from the databases of the companies. It uses Alyuda NeuroInteligence package to predict client churn in bank. The main target on client churn is to determinate who are at the verge of leaving the bank and making an analysis of whether is it worth retaining those banking clients. We however do not use this method as well but it gives a us a clear idea of what can be applied.

With the work of authors (Shriansh, Stuti & Addepalli, 2018), it is observed that Artificial neural networks are often employed in several applications like analysis, manipulation, predictions on the given applied mathematics information. Neural net is the method that is employed to coach the multi-layered perceptron once mentioned the multivariate analysis, i.e to maximize the practical relationship between predictors (input variables) and the response variables (output). Therefore neural networks are often used as associate degree extension of generalized linear models (supervised learning). This paper deals with a quick introduction concerning multi-layered perceptron and therefore the validation of resilient back-propagation and the ancient back propagation algorithms. A period of time bank dataset is taken into account and predictions are being done on the Churning rates of shoppers by the above mentioned two algorithms. It is ascertained that resilient back propagation algorithmic rule offers additional correct and precise results in comparison with ancient back-propagation algorithmic rule by the quantity of steps taken by each the algorithms in a very convergence of the total neural network and therefore the error rate of each the algorithms. In this work the authors have tried to generate a model which employs to coach the multi-layered perceptron. The results help us in with the comparison of resilient back-propagation and the ancient back-propagation algorithms. The results show that the resilient back-propagation algorithmic rule offers additional correct and precise results in comparison with ancient back-propagation algorithmic rule by the quantity of steps taken. This paper shows us with the accuracy of the results in both the algorithms.

The research provided by author (John, 2005), Genetic algorithms (GAs) is a heuristic search and optimization technique galvanized by natural evolution. They need been with success applied to a large vary of real-world issues of serious complexness. This paper is meant as Associate in Nursing introduction to GAs aimed toward immunologists and mathematicians inquisitive about medical specialty. We have a tendency to describe the way to construct a GA and also the main strands of GA theory before with speculation distinctive potential applications of GAs to the study of medical specialty. Associate in Nursing illustrative example of employing a GA for a medical best management draw- back is provided. The paper conjointly includes a quick account of the connected space of artificial immune systems.

The authors (Jitcha & Sridhar, 2018), have tried to develop a model to predict the different weather conditions across the sub-continent using the machine learning techniques. The parameters used for the model are like the temperature across the various regions of the sub-continent and many other parameters like the maximum and the minimum temperature, mean humidity and the average humidity. The proposed model had used the concept of linear regression which had predicted the high and low temperatures as a combination of all features. Another algorithm which is the functional regression had looked for the historical patterns and then predicts the future weather conditions on the available data. To check the validation of the model both the systems had been compared to check the fitness of the application. Thus this work has tried to develop a model to predict the different weather conditions across the sub-continent using the machine learning techniques. It uses the concept of functional regression and linear regression in predicting the temperatures.

The analysis and comparison of all the methods gave us a clear understanding of which method to be used and would be relevant for our implementation. Also some papers gave us the understanding of the various other machine learning techniques and their study has helped us to understand which method to choose for our work.

'Attribute based encryption implies identity based encryption' proposed by author (Javier, 2016) points about attribute-based encryption schemes which is difficult to design compare to identity based-encryption. The attribute based encryption uses hash function which is collision-resistant to obtain identity based encryption.

In the paper, 'Identity Based Encryption from the Diffie Hellman Assumption', the authors (Nico & Sanjom, 2017) puts forward chameleon encryption to identity-based encryption and hierarchical identity-based encryption based on Factoring or Diffie Hellman problem without the use of pairings groups. The proposed creation accomplishes a standard identity-based encryption mentioned by Boneh and Franklin. The impossibility results are avoided by using garbled circuits without use of the underlying cryptographic primitive details.

In the work (McCarthy, 2017), 'A Practical Implementation of Identity-Based Encryption over NTRU Lattices', an identity-based encryption allows key distribution in a multi-user system which are commonly useful in environment with constraint resources. The paper discusses IBE scheme which use of lattice in small devices. The C implementation of the DLP-IBE scheme gives different software optimizations to improve performance and find further improvement in variety targeted devices. The paper discussed method as a benchmark for improvement in constrained devices using client-side optimizations. The main bottleneck of the scheme was Gaussian sampler. The scheme is also evaluated using extended Euclidean algorithms and hash functions. The memory-heavy Gram-Schmidt orthogonalization is used to find other variants of sampler on demand by increase the rate NTRU basis structure properties. The parameter selection is also the important feature for the scheme.

Methodology for the Study

When it comes to predictive analysis, Genetic algorithm has played a very major and vital role in this area. There are a lot of works which has been performed using genetic algorithm and are discussed in detail in the literature survey section. Here, we are going to discus about how we have genetic algorithm in order to perform the predictive analysis on churning rates of customers in the banking environment. Where we can predict that what all are the best customers which are going to stay with the bank, the top customers. So that for rest of the customers bank can take several measures and can provide best services to them so that they can prevent their loss. This is the real time model, that every needy bank with similar kind of problem can implement this model.

As mentioned earlier the increasing churn rate is the new age problems for the banks in the current market system. So it is the work of the bank to keep a close eye on the banking customers and should also fulfill their needs on the customers who are more probable to leave the bank. The factors that would determine is by watching out for the following factors like customer name, credit score, tenure, age, balance, number of products, has credit card or not. The aforementioned factors can be used to find out the number of customers or the banking clients who are going to stay with the bank using the data set available to us.

As we discus about the dataset it has several attributes like Customer name, credit score, tenure, age, geography, balance, number of products, has credit card or not, estimated salary of customer, is active member of not and Exited. We will be discussing about each and every attribute/ parameter one by one.

1. **Customer Name:** As the word itself suggest that it is the name of the customer.
2. **Credit Score:** It is the score of the customer's bank account, which basically tells that how good the account is, means to say that how active that account is. If the number of transactions is more in the particular account then that account will automatically have good credit score. And if the transaction frequency is less then it has low credit score.
3. **Tenure:** The time period of a customer that is associated with the bank.
4. **Age:** As the name suggest, the age of the customer.
5. **Balance:** The balance in the particular bank account.
6. **Number of Products:** The number of products and services which are being availed by the customers.
7. **Has Credit Card:** It tells you about that whether that customer has the credit card or not.
8. **Estimated Salary:** The expected salary of the customer.
9. **Is Active Member:** Gives the details about whether the customer is regularly using his/her account or not.
10. **Exited:** Tells that which customer has left the bank or not.

Showcasing of how genetic algorithm is being mapped or used for this particular predictive analysis.

Prediction Methods

The various prediction methods involve the most important two parts:

1. **Feature Selection:** The deciding concept which decide that which are all the poten tial predictors that can be included in the model.
2. **Model Optimization:** The main work of the model optimization is that it selects the parameters to combine the selected features in a model to make predictions. Here in this problem the genetic algorithm will select the features or we can say that the predictors from the dataset which are more important in order to perform the predictive analysis and do model optimization for the same.
3. **Security Features Adopted for the Proposed Model:** An identity based encryption may be used for the problem as security can provided based based on attributes of the Customers.
    4.Modeling, Analysis and Design

Modeling

In our work, we have proposed to models of the dataset and then we have performed the genetic algorithm on those models. The models are divided in to 2 parts:-

1. **Random Miscellaneous Model:** In this model, we have taken two independent at tributes and in 3rd attribute which is known as miscellaneous attributes, in that we have randomly assigned the values to each row by referring the Fundamentals of Financial statistics by Ali Omar. After giving the values to miscellaneous section we implemented genetic algorithm on it with crossover probability as 0.001and mutation probability as 0.75. Motivation for taking these particular probabilities came after referring the paper [Genetic Algorithm for feature selection – Kevin R Coombes]. There's no hard and fast rule that only these two values are supposed to be chosen but the literature states that with these values of probabilities the results were promising and accurate. We tired with several other values as well but as we mentioned earlier we did not get valid and good results. After Implementation of random miscellaneous Model we got the result of top 5 customers out of 25 entries from the dataset. The validity of this random miscellaneous model result will be discussed later on this work.

2. **Logic Based Miscellaneous Model 1:** In this model of the dataset, we have created a new table of dataset based on our proposed logic that how the values should be as signed to the miscellaneous attribute of the dataset. As per our logic, which states that the Credit Score of the customer and the balance has been taken as two separate inde pendent parameters or predictors and in order to generate the miscellaneous attribute we have taken three main attributes, The Age of the customer, the Estimated Salary of the customer and whether that customer is having the credit card or not. Now, let us say that if a customer is having an age of greater than 40 with the estimated salary greater than 1,00,000 and that customer is holding the bank's credit card then the miscellaneous value provided to that customer is 1000. Similarly, if customer is having the credit card and age greater than 40 but with estimated salary of 50,000 then the miscellaneous value will be 800. If customer has credit card and is in between the age group of 35-40 with the estimated salary of 55,000 then the miscellaneous value will be from 800-600, depending upon the different ages and salaries and etc. The miscellaneous values are ranging from 1000-100, where 1000 being the highest and 100 being the lowest. We have also mentioned about some exceptional cases in the dataset which states that if the age of a person is varying between the age group of 20-30 and they are holding the credit card service and also they have the salary which is greater than 1,00,000 then the miscellaneous values which are assigned to them is the mean of the whole range of miscellaneous values, 500.

After analyzing the dataset we have also seen and analyzed that if there's a customer whose age is greater than 40 and he/she is having the credit card with the salary greater than 1,00,000 then the probability of that customer staying with the bank is higher. Whereas the customer with the age group of 20-30 and salary more than 1,00,000 have less probability of staying with the bank. After implementing the proposed dataset model on the genetic algorithm with the crossover probability of 0.001 and the mutation probability of 0.75, we got the top 5 customers from the dataset of 25 customers entry.

3. **Logic Based Miscellaneous Model 2:** In this model of dataset, we have tried to analyze the predictive results by keeping Bank balance of the customer and Estimated Salary as two different independent attributes and we have tried to generate the miscel laneous values by keeping credit score as one parameter, age being 2nd and the credit card being 3rd. However, this model did not give us the promising and accurate results. The results of this model will be discus during the later part of this section.

Identity Based Encryption

The type of public key encryption represents the mechanism where the public key of a user is some unique information about the identity of the user. It is developed by Adi Shamir in 1984 but the schemes were not fully used or created until 2001. The sender has access to the public parameters of the system can encrypt message using key such as text value of the receiver's name or email address. The receiver obtains its decryption key from a central authority, which needs to be trusted as it generates secret keys for every user as shown in figure 11. A central authority usually trusted third party maintains private key and sends the private to receiver for decryption. This proposed encryption was later improved by Boneh and Franklin using bilinear pairings which was the first approach. The second approach was proposed by Clifford Cocks based quadratic residues assumption. The third approach was by using lattices.

PKG will generate the public key and private key corresponding to an ID which is a "Domain Name" using RSA. How RSA is used to generate public key and private key for a "Domain Name" is shown below. In this method we find a number which is relatively prime to phi by continuously verifying

```
publickeytemp = gcd(publickeytemp, phi)
where gcd(publickeytemp, phi) = 1, and select it as public key.
```

Figure 11. IBE process

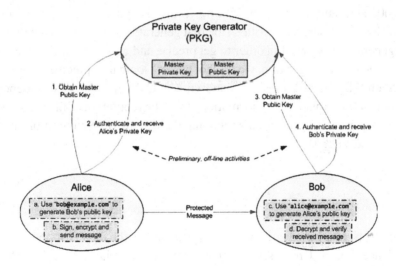

In Client side, we take ID of Bank Representative (sender), ID of the customer (receiver) and MESSAGE which is to be sent. Then Bank representative will receive the public key corresponding to the ID of receiver and 'n' which is p*q from PKG. Using this data Bank representative can encrypt the message using the public key of Customer using RSA algorithm. Then store the encrypted message along with USER ID in a file named "EncryptedMessage.txt".

In Server side, customer (Receiver) will consider private key corresponding to his ID from PKG and Encrypted message along with sender ID from the file "EncryptedMessage.txt". Thus by considering Bank representative ID and Private Key of self received from PKG decryption process can be done.

Analysis

1. **Random Miscellaneous Model** After implementation of genetic algorithm with crossover probability of 0.001 and mutation probability of 0.75 also keeping the gener ation evolution up to 10 generations. However, there's no written rule that generations should only be up to 10, We can give as many as generations we want in order to get precise and good results. In this model we got top 5 customers who are going to stay with the bank and after comparing those results with the original dataset we got only 2 predictions correct out of those top 5 customers. So, If we analyze that result in terms of accuracy and precision, this model has only 2/5 correct results which means roughly around 40% of accuracy as shown in figures 12, 13 & 14.

2. **Logical Miscellaneous Model 1:** After implementation of genetic algorithm with crossover probability of 0.001 and mutation probability of 0.75 also keeping the gener ation evolution up to 10 generations. However, there's no written rule that generations should only be up to 10, We can give as many as generations we want in order to get precise and good results. In this model we got top 5 customers who are going to stay with the bank and after comparing those results with the original dataset we got only 3 predictions correct out of those top 5 customers. So, if we analyze that result in terms of accuracy and precision, this model has only 3/5 correct results which mean roughly around 60% of accuracy as shown in figure 15 & 16.

3. **Logic Miscellaneous Model 2:** After implementation of genetic algorithm with crossover probability of 0.001 and mutation probability of 0.75 also keeping the gener ation evolution up to 10 generations. However, there's no written rule that generations should only be up to 10, We can give as many as generations we want in order to get precise and good results. In this model when we try to implement the genetic algorithm, we did not get any logical or precise results. Hence, we found that credit Score plays a very important and vital role when it comes to independent parameter. Because Credit Score explains the information about the reputation of the customer's bank account and it plays a major and important on explaining the leaving or staying information with the bank as shown in figure 17 & 18.

Design

Security Analysis:

In the proposed work IBE based encryption is considered as the data is supported with features like Customer ID, Balance, Salary, Credit score which forms confidential part of data. As RSA based IBE is used it supports security features like Confidentiality and Authentication of Customers.

Figure 12. Bank Data Set

RowNumber	CustomerId	Surname	CreditScore	Geography	Gender	Age	Tenure	Balance	NumOfProducts	HasCrCard	IsActiveMember	EstimatedSalary	Exited
1	15634602	Hargrave	619	France	Female	42	2	0	1	1	1	101348.9	1
2	15647311	Hill	608	Spain	Female	41	1	83807.86	1	0	1	112542.6	0
3	15619304	Onio	502	France	Female	42	8	159660.8	3	1	0	113931.6	1
4	15701354	Boni	699	France	Female	39	1	0	2	0	0	93826.63	0
5	15737888	Mitchell	850	Spain	Female	43	2	125510.8	1	1	1	79084.1	0
6	15574012	Chu	645	Spain	Male	44	8	113755.8	2	1	0	149756.7	1
7	15592531	Bartlett	822	France	Male	50	7	0	2	1	1	10062.8	0
8	15656148	Obinna	376	Germany	Female	29	4	115046.7	4	1	0	119346.9	1
9	15792365	He	501	France	Male	44	4	142051.1	2	0	1	74940.5	0
10	15592389	H?	684	France	Male	27	2	134603.9	1	1	1	71725.73	0
11	15767821	Bearce	528	France	Male	31	6	102016.7	2	0	0	80181.12	0
12	15737173	Andrews	497	Spain	Male	24	3	0	2	1	0	76390.01	0
13	15632264	Kay	476	France	Female	34	10	0	2	1	0	26260.98	0
14	15691483	Chin	549	France	Female	25	5	0	2	0	0	190857.8	0
15	15600882	Scott	635	Spain	Female	35	7	0	2	1	1	65951.65	0
16	15643966	Goforth	616	Germany	Male	45	3	143129.4	2	0	1	64327.26	0
17	15737452	Romeo	653	Germany	Male	58	1	132602.9	1	1	0	5097.67	1
18	15788218	Henderso	549	Spain	Female	24	9	0	2	1	1	14406.41	0
19	15661507	Muldrow	587	Spain	Male	45	6	0	1	0	0	158684.8	0
20	15568982	Hao	726	France	Female	24	6	0	2	1	1	54724.03	0
21	15577657	McDonald	732	France	Male	41	8	0	2	1	1	170886.2	0
22	15597945	Dellucci	636	Spain	Female	32	8	0	2	1	0	138555.5	0
23	15699309	Gerasimo	510	Spain	Female	38	4	0	1	1	0	118913.5	1
24	15725737	Mosman	669	France	Male	46	3	0	2	0	1	8487.75	0

Figure 13. Random Model Data Set

Surname	CreditScore	Balance	Misce	Total
Hargrave	619	0	1,000	1000
Hill	608	83807.86	500	84307.86
Onio	502	159660.8	1,000	159760.8
Boni	699	0	400	400
Mitchell	850	125510.8	500	126010.8
Chu	645	113755.8	1,000	113855.8
Bartlett	822	0	300	300
Obinna	376	115046.7	800	115846.7
He	501	142051.1	600	142651.1
H?	684	134603.9	600	135203.9
Bearce	528	102016.7	700	102716.7
Andrews	497	0	500	500
Kay	476	0	200	200
Chin	549	0	700	700
Scott	635	0	400	400
Goforth	616	143129.4	300	143429.4
Romeo	653	132602.9	500	133102.9
Henderso	549	0	600	600
Muldrow	587	0	1,000	1000
Hao	726	0	300	300
McDonald	732	0	1,000	1000
Dellucci	636	0	500	500
Gerasimo	510	0	900	900
Mosman	669	0	700	700

Figure 14. Top 5 Customers from Random Model

	Surname	CreditScore	Balance	Misce	Total
3	Onio	502	159660.80	1,000	159760.80
16	Goforth	616	143129.41	300	143429.40
5	Mitchell	850	125510.82	500	126010.80
8	Obinna	376	115046.74	800	115846.70
2	Hill	608	83807.86	500	84307.86

Figure 15. Logic Based Model

	A	B	C	D	E
1	Surname	CreditScor	Balance	Misce 2	Total
2	Hargrave	619	0	1000	1000
3	Hill	608	83807.86	900	84707.86
4	Onio	502	159660.8	1000	160660.8
5	Boni	699	0	800	800
6	Mitchell	850	125510.8	800	126310.8
7	Chu	645	113755.8	1000	114755.8
8	Bartlett	822	0	100	100
9	Obinna	376	115046.7	500	115546.7
10	He	501	142051.1	900	142951.1
11	H?	684	134603.9	400	135003.9
12	Bearce	528	102016.7	600	102616.7
13	Andrews	497	0	400	400
14	Kay	476	0	300	200
15	Chin	549	0	500	700
16	Scott	635	0	600	600
17	Goforth	616	143129.4	800	143929.4
18	Romeo	653	132602.9	800	133402.9
19	Henderso	549	0	200	200
20	Muldrow	587	0	1000	1000
21	Hao	726	0	500	500
22	McDonald	732	0	900	900
23	Dellucci	636	0	800	800
24	Gerasimo'	510	0	1000	1000
25	Mosman	669	0	300	300

Figure 16. Top 5 customers from logic model 1

	Surname	CreditScore	Balance	Misce 2	Total
1	Onio	502	159660.8	1000	160660.8
2	He	501	142051.1	900	142951.1
3	H?	684	134603.9	400	135003.9
4	Romeo	653	132602.9	800	133402.9
5	Obinna	376	115046.7	500	115546.7

Figure 17. The Logical Miscellaneous Model 2

	A	B	C	D	E	F
1	RowNumb	Surname	Balance	Estimated	misce 3	total
2	1	Hargrave	0	101348.9	800	102148.9
3	2	Hill	83807.86	112542.6	750	113296.6
4	3	Onio	159660.8	113931.6	600	114531.6
5	4	Boni	0	93826.63	650	94476.63
6	5	Mitchell	125510.8	79084.1	1000	80084.1
7	6	Chu	113755.8	149756.7	850	150606.7
8	7	Bartlett	0	10062.8	950	11012.8
9	8	Obinna	115046.7	119346.9	450	119796.9
10	9	He	142051.1	74940.5	500	75440.5
11	10	H?	134603.9	71725.73	480	72205.73
12	11	Bearce	102016.7	80181.12	550	80731.12
13	12	Andrews	0	76390.01	450	76840.01
14	13	Kay	0	26260.98	450	26710.98
15	14	Chin	0	190857.8	550	191407.8
16	15	Scott	0	65951.65	600	66551.65
17	16	Goforth	143129.4	64327.26	700	65027.26
18	17	Romeo	132602.9	5097.67	800	5897.67
19	18	Henderso	0	14406.41	480	15186.41
20	19	Muldrow	0	158684.8	700	159384.8
21	20	Hao	0	54724.03	550	55274.03
22	21	McDonald	0	170886.2	850	171736.2
23	22	Dellucci	0	138555.5	600	139155.5
24	23	Gerasimo'	0	118913.5	500	119413.5
25	24	Mosman	0	8487.75	750	9237.75
26	25	Yen	0	187616.2	1000	188616.2

Figure 18. Model with No Precise Results

```
> summary(my.ga)
An object representing generation 1 in a genetic algorithm.
Population size: 25
Mutation probability: 0.001
Crossover probability: 0.75
Fitness distribution:
   Min. 1st Qu.  Median    Mean 3rd Qu.    Max.
      0       0       0       0       0       0
```

Figure 19. GA Model Flowchart

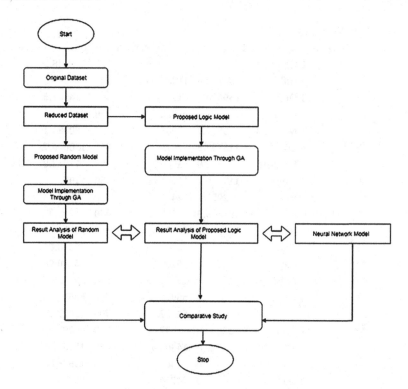

RESULTS, DISCUSSIONS AND CONCLUSIONS

Comparative Study

In this work the comparative study has been made on the churning rate of the customers using genetic algorithm and neural networks. First being the Genetic algorithm which is further divided in to 2 proposed models, the random miscellaneous model and Logic based miscellaneous model. The second concept on which the comparative study is being performed is the artificial neural network. While performing the comparative study we found out that results of Random model gives the 40% accuracy and precision when validate with original dataset with only 2 correct predictions out of 5 customers from the dataset of 25 entries. Whereas, if talk about the results of logical model which gave the accuracy and precision and of 60% when the results are validated with the actual dataset, it has been found out that it shows the 3 correct predictions out of 5 customers from 25 entries of dataset. Now, with the concept of predictive analysis using Artificial Neural Network, as in our previous work of study we have performed the predictive analysis using artificial neural networks on the same real time problem that is the churning rates of customer in the bank. While performing the predictive analysis using neural network we have found out that this concept predict the percentage of each customer for staying with the bank for example a customer whose has the credit score of 608 and his age is 41 with bank balance of 83807.86 will have the probability for staying with the bank is 36.07% similarly a person with credit score of 699 and his age is 39 with the balance of 0 in the bank will have the probability of 19.45% staying with the bank.

Hence, with this comparison we can state that random model is not accurate and precise in comparison with logical model which has the accuracy and precession of 60%. We can also say that since this logical model was only implemented for only 25 entries of the dataset so if this can be implemented over a larger dataset, it will give the more good and precise results. When it comes to comparison between Genetic algorithm and neural networks we can say that both are useful and helpful models and can be used on the similar kind of dataset and problem, depending on the organization's need and requirements.

Discussions

The resultant model can be used by the employers in the bank who have the access to the required dataset attributes as it will help the bank in knowing about the possible customers who have the high chance of leaving the bank. There could be a chance of getting better results with more number of inputs in the dataset rather restricting it just twenty five values. Any data base needs to be supported with security aspects without which the results may be tampered which may hurt the organization beyond repairable levels. As the data base is supported with attributes like Credit card score, Balance, Salary details as parameters to in taking a decision on their churning rate, security provided on these features adds value to the Model. Thus IBE based encryption is proposed to make a Model more precise and efficient.

CONCLUSION AND FUTURE WORK

The work presents the usage of predictive analysis using genetic algorithm and evolu tion strategies in order to find out the Churning rate of the possible customers leaving the organization. The model being used and its implementation have also been discussed. Using genetic algorithm with the help of feature selection, optimal attributes for the three models have been identified. The results shows that logical model has given an accuracy and precision of 60% as there were three correct predictions out of five from the 25 entries of the dataset.

For providing security to the selected features IBE based encryption is proposed which not only supports Security features like Confidentiality and Integrity but also provides authentication of Users.

It may also be tried to improve the results in respect to the accuracy and the precision if this can be implemented over a larger dataset. The IBE Model discussed is based on RSA based Model. Any newer Versions of IBE may be used for better performance of the proposed work.

REFERENCES

Ahmadi, Amjadian, & Pardegi. (2012). New Approach to Bankruptcy Prediction using Genetic Algorithm. *International Journal of Computer Applications, 44*(4).

Arun, Ishan, & Sanmeet. (2016). Loan Approval Prediction based on Machine Learning Approach. *IOSR Journal of Computer Engineering, 18*(3).

Bonde, G., & Khaled, R. (1953). *Stock price prediction using genetic algo- rithms and evolution strategies*. New York: McGraw Hill.

Carthy, S. M. (2017). A Practical Implementation of Identity Based Encryption over NTRU Lattices. *Cryptography and Coding, 16th IMA International Conference*, 227-246.

Dottling, N., & Garg, S. (2017). *IDE from Deffie Hellman Assumption*. Retrieved from https://eprint.iacr.org/2017/543.pdf

Herranz, J. (2016). Attribute-based encryption implies identity based encryption. *IET Information Security Journal, 11*(6), 2016.

Jitcha Shivang, S. S. (2018). Weather prediction for Indian location using Machine learning. *International Journal of Pure and Applied Mathematics, 118*(22).

McCall, J. (2005). Genetic algorithms for modeling and optimization. *Journal of Computational and Applied Mathematics, 184*(1), 205–222. doi:10.1016/j.cam.2004.07.034

Pandey, Bajpa, & Krishna. (2018). Predictive analysis using resilient and traditional back propagation algorithm. *IACSIT International Journal of Engineering and Technology, 7*(4).

Zoric´, A. B. (2016). Predicting customer churn in banking industry using Neural Networks. *Interdisciplinary Description of Complex Systems, 14*(2), 116–124. doi:10.7906/indecs.14.2.1

Chapter 10
Protection of Information From the Influence of Noise on the Transmission of Video Data in a Geoinformation System

Olga Galan
State University of Infrastructure and Technologies, Ukraine

ABSTRACT

The chapter describes parallel-hierarchical technologies that are characterized by a high degree of parallelism, high performance, noise immunity, parallel-hierarchical mode of transmission and processing of information. The peculiarities of the design of automated geoinformation and energy systems on the basis of parallel-hierarchical technologies and modified confidential method of Q-transformation of information are presented. Experimental analysis showed the advantages of the proposed methods of image processing and extraction of characteristic features.

INTRODUCTION

Actuality of Theme

The scientific and technological progress of recent decades has led to the creation and widespread use of personal computers, as well as the emergence and rapid development of computer science and their revolutionary influence on virtually all human activities. With the emergence and development of the geoinformation systems in the early 90's, experts from many industries quickly appreciated the broad possibilities for geospatial modeling and spatial decision making. This period is marked by the emergence in the periodical geoinformation publications of a large number of educational and educational publications on remote sensing, coordinate systems, satellite positioning, as well as the development of geoinformation terminology and the formation of a new scientific direction - geoinformatics.

DOI: 10.4018/978-1-7998-1290-6.ch010

Today, with the growing needs of society in energy resources, there is a need for a widespread information environment that would ensure high-quality, high-speed and noise-free information exchange. In the work as a data processing environment, parallel-hierarchical technologies are proposed, which, in contrast to existing ones, are characterized by high degree of parallelism, high performance, noise immunity, parallel-hierarchical method of transmission and processing of information. In the process of development of this direction there is a new opportunity for the user to provide information and new opportunities for its use and supply, related, including, with Internet technologies.

In the framework of the decision of the tasks of territorial management and energy provision, it is important to create an automated geoinformation and energy system at the level of the city, region, region, country, etc., which will allow, on the basis of the information-energy component, to introduce, in addition to well-known geoinformation systems of environmental monitoring, also systems of management of industrial enterprises and transport, medical, scientific-educational, law-enforcement, communal, financial, land and other branches and one's a system for video surveillance and video processing. The geoinformation and energy system is a global means of accelerating scientific and technological progress due to its widespread, public availability and high quality indicators of the transmission and processing of information, which is achieved by integrating into a widely distributed electric power transmission system of a specialized conductor that constructively combines information dissemination environments and energy, namely, the fiber-optic communication line covered by a metal conductor of electricity.

Researchings in the creation of AGIES are based on the development of systems that perform not only calculations, but also simulate imaginative perception of the world and decision-making and focus on performing functional modeling of human intellectual activities related to the main areas of scientific and technological development. Such ideas are based on the development of domestic computer science in recent decades. Therefore, the task is to create an automated geoinformation system based on the principles of opto-electronic parallel-hierarchical technologies, and to study the transmission and processing of information in it, which makes it possible to apply new principles and methods of parallel processing and high-quality information transmission.

THE ANALYSIS OF MODERN TECHNOLOGIES OF THE DEVELOPMENT OF AUTOMATED GEO-INFORMATION SYSTEMS

The information revolution that took place in the twentieth century greatly raises the intellect of man due to the rapid development and accumulation of the knowledge base of mankind. Over time, the volume of knowledge and information grows in a geometric progression, which requires more and more improvement of its knowledge, which in turn improves the technologies developed by them to provide a comfortable and productive life. For some time, humanity subjectively separated the concept of energy and information. But objective development involves knowledge of the universe as a whole, where everything is interdependent and interrelated. Such an understanding of the universe brings humanity into a new plane of intelligence, which generates new tasks and opens up new perspectives.

At the present stage of human development, the natural process is the combination of such substances as information and energy. The reason for this is the fact that humanity is increasingly deepening into the knowledge of the universe, where the concepts of energy and information are not separate (Kozemyako, Bilan & Kozemyako, 2004).

In this case, the law of the dialectics of the transition of the quantity of knowledge to a new quality of the law acts. In addition, there is a biological axiom that argues that the evolution and functioning of living organisms are impossible without the time factor and the information-energy content, the bearer of which is light. That is, this axiom is based on the assumption that the light is self-sufficient for reproduction and realization under certain conditions with a relatively zero time mark of the program of reproduction (realization) of all natural information about everything with which light interacts. That is why it is possible to assume, as with photosynthesis, that the additional carrier of such information-energy substance is light, which obviously serves as a catalyst and carrier of information-energy and logical-temporal (software) development of any living substance (Kovzel, Kutaev & Tymchenko, 2006).

On the way of development, humanity transmitted information separately from the transmission of energy. With the growth of energy needs and the full transition to electricity, as the main type of energy consumption, energy networks were created that today represent the Unified Energy Network, which combines all power plants within each continent (except Antarctica). Energy processes of nature are the foundation upon which all human achievements are kept. At the same time, technological progress leads to a significant increase in the volume of information, which is especially noticeable since the creation of computers. This allowed for the storage and exchange of a large amount of data, and as a result of rapid progress led to the creation of the largest in the history of the global Internet information network. The top of the development of information systems today is the creation of a geoinformation system that plays a key role in the development of mankind.

That is, there is a situation where the quantitative separation of information and energy networks leads to their unification (Genov & Cauwenberghs, 2002), which implies the development of these systems and humanity as a whole to a qualitatively new level. Such a system should be formed on the combination of energy and information processes in nature and will create a Geoinformation and energy system (GIES).

Realizing the environment of simultaneous distribution and transfer of information and energy flows, global GIES becomes for humanity a means of optimizing the ways of its further development, harmoniously solving problems of optimal energy redistribution and a whole range of other global problems. As previously industrial and information revolutions have greatly increased the energy and intellectual capacity of a person, the introduction of the GIES in the near future will be able to raise humanity to a fundamentally new level of information and power facilities (Coronel & Morris, 2014).

In order to construct an effective GIES, as well as any other system of society, one must also take into account the knowledge base of all other anthropological systems (AUs). The term AU absorbs all the systems created by mankind. The common feature of all systems is "the definition of goal functions". GIES, as a means of defining the functions of the global goals of human civilization, if built, will become the largest and most complicated AU of mankind (Tyagur, 2017).

The current condition of geinformation support is characterized by the following:

1. Lack of theoretical developments. There are incomplete discussions on terminology, research object, etc. Methods of spatial objects and spatial analysis are developed. There are separate methods of spatial solutions (Gusev & Evans D, 1994).
2. A good geoinformation software that mainly meets the modern needs of the development and operation of the geographic information system (GIS) at the stages of geoinformation gathering, the transformation of projections and coordinate systems, the modeling of spatial objects, spatial analysis (Zacerkovnyi, 2015).

3.   GIS are generated mainly for the solution of specific sectoral tasks. There are successful examples of creating separate municipal GIS. But GIS for state authorities is still in a position of projects and proposals. The development of territorial inter-sectoral GIS is hampered by inter-departmental multilingualism and the lack of a theoretical framework guaranteeing a significant life expectancy and system development (Mitchell, 1999).

4.   Distinction of information and energy component in geographic information networks. There are successful examples of a combination of the transfer of information and energy components, but such examples are partial (single) and do not create a single information and energy space.

FEATURES OF DESIGN AND CLASSIFICATION OF AUTOMATED GEOINFORMATION AND ENERGY SYSTEMS (AGIES)

Developments in the creation of AGIES are based on the development of systems that perform not only calculations, but also simulate imaginative perception of the world, figurative decision-making and focused on the implementation of functional modeling of human intellectual activity, which are the main areas of scientific and technological development. The developers of the AGIES architectures face the problems associated with ambiguity in the choice of possible options for constructing many functional blocks that can be implemented by hardware, software or hardware-software tools (Kozemyako, Tymchenko, Kutaev & Ivasyuk, 1994). The right choice of specific means of implementing architectures is particularly important for achieving the required technical and economic indicators.

An expedient and important step in the creation of the AGIES is the integration of the latest and advanced developments, one of which recognizes parallel-hierarchical (PI) Q-transformation of information for efficient data transfer in the system and their parallel-hierarchical processing (Kupchenko, 2003).

However, not always, even when trying to apply hierarchical structures, the most important feature of hierarchy was taken into account as regular, which consists in the fact that the law of integrity manifests itself at each level of the hierarchy. Due to this, at each level there are new properties that cannot be given as the sum of the properties of the elements. It is important that not only the combination of elements in each node leads to the emergence of new properties that they did not have, and the loss of some properties of elements, but also that each subordinate member of the hierarchy acquires a new property that is missing from it in an isolated condition.

Let's analyze those coding methods, the algorithms of transformation which are connected with the mechanism of vision. Using the sensitivity of the neurons in the visual system to the parallel-hierarchical analysis of the orientation of the stimulus in conjunction with the separation (by fragment) pyramidal parallel-hierarchical processing leads to the creation of a new class of methods of coding. This class of methods, that can be attributed to neural-like methods, is the subject of research.

Such coding techniques include pyramidal coding (Musman, Pirsch, & Grallert, 1985), anisotropic nonstationary predictive encoding (Musman, Pirsch, & Grallert, 1985), field-based encoding (Verhagen, Debir, et al. 1985) and coding based on decomposition in directions (Musman, Pirsch, & Grallert, 1985), the best of which are able to provide a compression ratio up to 70.

If the algorithms for submitting video data do not depend on their content and are predetermined, then there is a possibility of their rapid parallel input into the system simultaneously with obtaining a generalized description. Obtaining such a generalization does not require the allocation of the semantic structure of the IP, that is, obviates the long analytical path of perception. It is this approach, which is related to the invariance of the algorithm of representation of IP in its composition, is the most perspective.

Through these positions a fundamentally new approach to parallel-hierarchical representation and transformation of data (video data) of a pyramidal type for which the algorithm is universal is not dependent on the structure of the data content and is determined at the design stage.

Let's look through the basic ideas that underlie the proposed approach (Gealow & Sodini,1999). The parallel-hierarchical representation of the pyramidal type implies the same law of transition from one level to another in the middle and outside of each hierarchical level, and this law is formulated in relation to the group of sets of data elements (images) of the lower level and the intermediate group of sets of elements of the transformed data of all subsequent levels.

Thus, for the construction of a pyramidal parallel-hierarchical structure at the algorithmic and structural levels, only the rule of transforming the group of sets of data elements is set, which then extends "horizontally" to the remaining elements, and "vertically" to elements of other levels. This rule describes both the schema of converting output data and the resulting data structure and its processing algorithm. The filling of this structure takes place at the task of a specific set of data as input information. The natural way of describing the parallel-hierarchical (PI) structure of the interconnections of elements is recursion: for constructing a PI of transformation it is enough to indicate the dimension of sets, the law of the distribution of probabilities of its elements, Q-transformations, and the F-criteria (Hertz, Krogh & Palmer, 1991). In other words, only a certain "information gene" (information about Q-transformations and F-criteria) and the law of the development of the structure of the PI of the transformation itself are stored for the construction of the transformation structure, the successive application of which allows the step-by-step expansion of the original description by degree of detail. Such an approach to the description of information processes was first formulated in (Mitchell, 1999). Structurally, AGIES can be submitted as follows (Figure 1). The Global AGIES consists of the lowest level local networks, which include their management, monitoring and coordination centers, which include the information storage server, document processing server, information processing server and video information (Figure 2), to which the relevant structures and institutions are connected, located in this limited area and power station (or power line). The local level monitoring, monitoring and coordination center performs monitoring and management at the local level, provides storage and distribution of information, decision-making, and also provides communication and information exchange with the centers of management of the higher levels of the AGIEC hierarchy.

It should be noted that on the basis of one technical implementation of the local level network implement themselves a number of systems specialized, industry-specific, as shown in Figure 1. Such systems do not interfere with each other in terms of the technical aspect and functionality, but rather complement each other, thereby creating a global information and energy system. Links in such a local level network are set up in accordance with the flow of information. All nodes of the system have a direct connection with the local control, monitoring and coordination unit. In line with this, with the constant need for information exchange between certain nodes of the AGIES of the local level, it is necessary to establish a corresponding direct link between them. Thus, the number of connections at the local level of the system will be:

$$P=E\lambda +E=E(\lambda +1), \tag{1}$$

where E - the number of nodes of the system of the local level; λ - the coefficient of the need for communications between the nodes of the local system.

Consequently, the total number of connections in the AGIES can be defined as follows:

$$N=nE(\lambda +1)+m(k+1), \tag{2}$$

where n - the number of local systems of the lowest level in the AGIES; k - coefficient of connections between local systems in all AGIES hierarchies.

Let's consider the orientation stages of the passage and processing of information presented on the structural model of data processing in the automated optical-electronic GIES (Figure 3)

Information in geoinformation and energy systems is transmitted through communication lines (CL). In the case of the creation of automated GIES we use fiber-optic communication lines with a binary conductor, which provides high-speed and high-quality transmission of large volumes of data and power supply of electrical components of automated GIES.

The information received from the CL is sent to the block of obtaining information (BOI) from external devices or from the devices of GIES. At the next stage, the filtering, pre-processing and decoding of information in the block of the BFPD takes place.

The delineation of the information in the directions and determination of the channels in which the processing should take place is carried out at the next stage in the transmission direction block (TDB).

Further information comes directly to the information processing unit (IPU), which is built on the principles of the above-mentioned eye-processor, and structurally consists of a number of computing devices and devices, interconnections and interactions between them.

Figure 1. Structural organization of opto-electronic AGIES

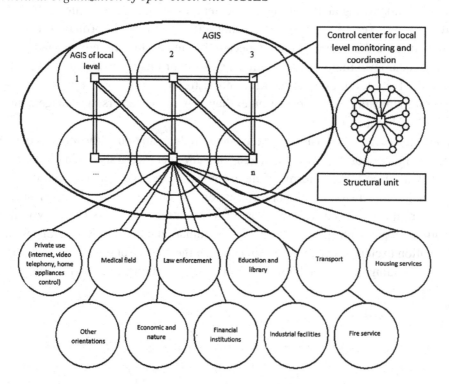

Figure 2. Center for the management, monitoring and coordination of the local level

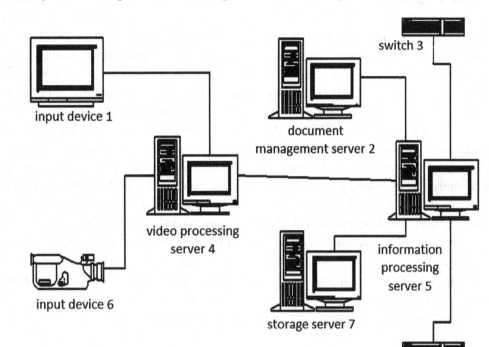

Figure 3. Structural model of the process of transmission and processing of information in optical-electronic AGIES

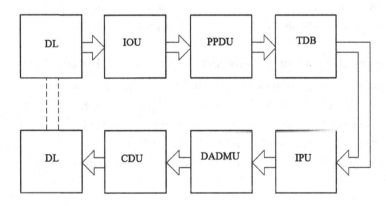

Functionally, IPU consists of many blocks and sub-blocks of different purposes, including an operation unit containing a block of logical operations, a block of arithmetic operations, etc., an image processing unit including an image shift unit, an image scaling unit, an image rotation block at a predetermined angle (Balashov, 1985), an image center definition unit, a block of selection of contours of image of a given thickness, a bit logic execution unit, and others.

Further information comes to the block of analysis of the resulting data and decision making (BARD), in which the formation of the corresponding response to the request and the block of encoding and sending of the source information (BE) for subsequent processing to the user optical channels of drugs.

It's functioning is based on the developed noise immunity algorithms of parallel-hierarchical Q-transformation, while their program realization and simulation of the channel of information transmission with the definition of the noise immunity of the method of parallel-hierarchical Q-transformation of information are executed. Creating a parallel vector-matrix multiplier that is used in such a block of stages of information passing in the GIES as IPU, allows to significantly expand the range of presentation of input data due to the organization of matrix computation in a floating-point form, as well as developed parallel structures on their basis allow for an order of magnitude performance of information processing.

Consequently, an automated geoinformation and energy system is a global information and energy network, which will ensure the functioning of virtually all sections of human activity, and will carry out continuous monitoring of their functionality. Such a system expands the capabilities and functionalities of an automated geographic information system. In addition, an automated geographic information system can be considered as a separate case of an automated geoinformation and energy system. As already mentioned, the AGIES includes a network of medical structures, educational, educational and libraries, law enforcement agencies, road transport institutions, communal infrastructures, industrial facilities, fire brigades, financial institutions, government bodies, private use, and others.

MODIFIED CONFIDENTIAL METHOD OF Q-TRANSFORMATION OF INFORMATION

Solving the problems of parallel processing of information entirely depends on the development of high-speed and fully parallel intellectual-computational processes. The ever-increasing requirements for processing signals in real time and for increasing the speed of the hardware lead to the need to create computing structures with a new architecture capable of processing huge amounts of data with a very high speed.

For effective use in solving a number of problems of adaptive signal processing $G\left(r\right) = \left\{g_r\right\}, r \in \Omega_g$, in particular images, it is of interest to use the parallel-hierarchical (PI) network on the basis of g -order (Kovzel, Kutaev, Tymchenko, et. all 2006; Kozemyako, Tymchenko, Kutaev & Ivasyuk 1994). In this case, it is advisable to represent the local amplitude of the signal or the primary local characteristic of the signal through its secondary secondary local characteristics.

We will consider the local amplitude as the primary local characteristic g_{Fr_0} of the signal

$$G_F\left(r\right) = \left\{g_{Fr}\right\}, \ r \in \Omega_{gF}, \ \Omega_{gF} \in \Omega_r,$$

which is obtained as a result of the implementation of a transformation over a plurality of local amplitudes $\left\{g_r\right\}, \ r \in \Omega_{gFr_0}$ coordinates of which are determined relative to the reference coordinate r_0 in the area Ω_{gFr0}:

$$F : \left\{ g_r \right\} \xrightarrow{\quad F \quad} g_{Fr_0} \; .$$

(3)

Under the repeated local characteristic of the signal we consider the local amplitude $\Delta_{r_0}^{(j)}$, which receives in *j*- th cycle of recursion using transformation Φ_{*j}:

$$\Delta_{r_0}^{(j)} = \Phi_{*j}\left(\Delta_{r_0}^{(j-1)}, \left\{\Delta_r^{(j-1)}\right\}_r\right).$$

We construct *CQ* and *AQ*-sequences of secondary local characteristics, formed by generalized recursive treatment by the pyramidal method [63], "differences from the general" and "general in differences" respectively, and we obtain the primary local characteristic:

CQ - the sequence can be represented as follows:

$$g_{Fr_0} \leftarrow \Delta_{r_0}^{(1)}, \Delta_{r_0}^{(2)}, ..., \Delta_{r_0}^{(i)}, ...$$

$$\Delta_{r_0}^{(j)} = \Phi_{*j}\left(\Delta_{r_0}^{(j-1)}, \left\{\Delta_{r_0}^{(j-1)}\right\}_r\right) = \overset{i}{\underset{j=1}{\Theta}} \Phi_{*j}\left(\Delta_{r_0}^{(0)}, \left\{\Delta_{r_0}^{(0)}\right\}_r\right) = \Phi_{*j}^i\left(\Delta_{r_0}^{(0)}, \left\{\Delta_{r_0}^{(0)}\right\}_r\right),$$
$$j = 1, 2, ..., i = \overline{1, i},$$

$$\Delta_{r_0}^{(0)} = g_{Fr_0},$$

where operator Φ_{*j} is a composition (generalized convolution) of a binary difference operator Φ_{lj}, averaging operator Φ_{cj}, operator *k*- comparison [5, 16, 63] Φ_{kj}, switching operator Φ_c and of the operator of local transformation Φ_{lj}, which is simplified in the following form:

$$\Phi_{*j} = \Phi_{lj} \times \Phi_{Oj} \times \Phi_{kj} \times \Phi_c \times \Phi_{lj},$$

In this case the operator Φ_{lj} includes a subtraction operator Φ_d, and operator Φ_{Oj} - the operator of the summation Φ_s.

The definition of local transformation Φ_{lj} similar to the definition (3) of the local transformation *F*, with:

$$\Phi_{lj}\left(\Delta_{r_0}^{(j-1)}, \left\{\Delta_r^{(j-1)}\right\}\right) = \left(\Delta_{\Phi l, r_0}^{(j)}, \left\{\Delta_{\Phi_l, r}^{(j)}\right\}\right).$$

The conversion that averages results in the next result:

$$\Phi_{Oj}\left(\left\{\Delta_{\Phi_l, r_0}^{z(j)}\right\}_z, \left\{\left\{\Delta_{\Phi_l, r}^{z(j)}\right\}_z\right\}_r\right) = \left(\left\{\Delta_{\Phi_l, r_0}^{z(j)}\right\}_z, \left\{\Delta_{\Phi_l}^{\overline{z(j)}}\right\}_z\right)$$

$$\Delta_{\Phi_l}^{\overline{z(j)}} = \begin{cases} \dfrac{1}{n_j^z} \sum_{r_z} \Delta_{\Phi_l,r}^{z(j)} & \text{with } n_j^z \neq 0 \\ 0, & \text{with } n_j^z = 0, \end{cases}$$

$$n_j^z = \sum_{r_z} c_{j,r_z}^z, c_{j,r_z}^z = 1.$$

Coordinates r_z match the coordinates r, for each of are: $c_{j,r_z}^z = 1$.

AQ - the sequence appears in the form:

$$g_{Fr_0} \leftarrow \sigma_{r_0}^{(1)}, \sigma_{r_0}^{(2)}, \ldots, \sigma_{r_0}^{(j)}, \ldots,$$

$$\sigma_{r_0}^{(j)} = \sum_z c_{j,r_0}^z * \Delta_{\Phi_l}^{\overline{z(j)}} \qquad (4)$$

$$\sigma_{r_0}^{(0)} = 0.$$

Expression (4) is not only the relation of the members of the equation CQ and AQ- sequences, and also demonstrate that CQ- sequences is a producing, but AQ- sequences – sequence which is made.

In the absence of a local transformation $\Phi_{lj}, \Phi_{lj} = \Phi_1$, where Φ_1 - single operator and $\Phi_{ij} = \Phi_d$.

Let's make a pawn CQ i AQ - sequences:

$$\begin{aligned} CQ: \quad &{}_+\Delta_{r_0}^{(1)}, \Delta_{r_0}^{(2)}, \ldots, \Delta_{r_0}^{(j)}, \ldots \\ AQ: \quad &\sigma_{r_0}^{(1)}, \sigma_{r_0}^{(2)}, \ldots, \sigma_{r_0}^{(j)}, \ldots \\ \hline &\Delta_{r_0}^{(0)}, \Delta_{r_0}^{(1)}, \ldots, \Delta_{r_0}^{(j-1)}, \ldots \end{aligned}$$

where $\Delta_{r_0}^{(0)} = g_{Fr_0}$,

Let's $S_c^{(i)}$ i $S_a^{(i)}$ - are sums i parts CQ and AQ- sequences in accordance:

$$S_c^{(i)} = \sum_{j=1}^{i} \Delta_{r_0}^{(j)}, S_a^{(i)} = \sum_{j=1}^{i} \sigma_{r_0}^{(j)} \qquad (5)$$

Then from the expressions (2.3) formed:

$$S_c^{(i)} + S_a^{(i)} = \Delta_{r_0}^{(0)} + S_c^{(i)} + \Delta_{r_0}^{(i)},$$

where

$$g_{Fr_0} = \sum_{j=1}^{1} \sigma_{r_0}^{(j)} - \Delta_{r_0}^{(j)}. \tag{6}$$

Going to the limit on the right side of the expression, it is formed

$$g_{Fr_0} = \lim_{i \to \infty} \sum_{j=1}^{1} \sigma_{r_0}^{(j)} = \lim_{i \to \infty} \sum_{j=1}^{1} \sum_{z} C_{j,r_0}^{z} \cdot \Delta^{\overline{z(j-1)}}, \tag{7}$$

subject to fulfillment

$$\lim_{i \to \infty} \Delta_{r_0}^{(j)} \to 0, \tag{8}$$

where C_{j,r_0}^{z} - operator coefficients Φ_{kj}^{z}, which as shown in (Kovzel, Kutaev & Tymchenko, 2006) leads to significantly different results of the pyramid Q- transformation.

So, CQ and AQ- rows are called the following rows:

AQ-row $\sum_{j=1}^{\infty} \Delta_{r_0}^{(j)}$.

CQ-row $\sum_{j=1}^{\infty} \sigma_{r_0}^{(j)}$.

From (6)-(8) leads, that AQ-row converges in the fulfillment of the necessary sign in the expression (8) of convergence CQ-row.

For CQ-row, received from Q transformation using operator k- comparison, the fulfillment of the condition of convergence follows from the fact

$$\left| \Delta_{r_0}^{(j)} \right| \leq \left(\max \left\{ \Delta_r^{(j)} \right\} + \left| \min \left\{ \Delta_r^{(j)} \right\} \right| \right) = h^{(j)},$$

and sequence $\{h^{(j)}\}$ is strictly declining:

$$h^{(0)} > h^{(1)} > h^{(j)} > ... \geq 0. \tag{9}$$

Examples (6), (7) show, that $\lim_{i \to \infty} \Delta_{r_0}^{(j)} = 0$.

Consequently, we obtain an expression of the fulfillment of the condition of convergence:

$$\left| \Delta_{r_0}^{(j)} \right| \leq p = h^{(j)}.$$

The fundamental difference is the pyramid Q-transformation from decomposition into such well-known series, for example, as a Taylor series or Fourier series, consists in the fact that in the first case decomposition is a power series with coefficients calculated only by local characteristics (derivatives) of the signal, whereas for the second the case of members of the Fourier series is a generalized signal characteristic, but of another physical nature (amplitude of spectral frequencies) than the signal itself.

For unambiguous restoration of the initial signal is used Q-code. Generation by the operator Φ_{kj} for each j three coefficients $\left\{C^z_{j,r_0}\right\}_z$, $z \in \{<, 0, >\}$, allows, subject to convergence of the Q-row, consider the entire set of generated coefficients triples as a code $N^{(i)}_{GFr_0}$ (Q-code) local characteristics g_{Fr_0}:

$$N^{(i)}_{GFr_0} = \left\{N_{j,r_0}\right\}_j, j = \overline{1, i}.$$

$$N_{j,r_0} = \left\{C^z_{j,r_0}\right\}_z, C^z_{j,r_0} \in \{0, 1\}.$$

Note that discrete Q-transformation of the signal carried out by a digital computing structure in the form of an integer, with an error of rounding δ_b ($2\delta_b \leq b_0$, b_0 - weight of the unit of the junior digit of the integer code), representation of local characteristics.

$$\Delta^{(j)}_r \rightarrow ENT\left(\Delta^{z_1(j)}_r + \delta_{\blacklozenge}\right) = \left|\Delta^{(j)}_r\right[$$

where $ENT(\bullet)$-the hole part $(\bullet)$, $]\bullet[$ - rounding to the nearest whole number, $z_1 \in \{+, -\}$.

In the case of equality of the local threshold $q^{z_2(k)}_\Lambda = 0$, $q^{z_2(k)}_k = 0$, $z_2 \in \{<, >\}$, for $j=k$ when determining the operator k- comparison, as is shown in (Balashov, 1985) discrete Q-row includes (k-1) non-zero members, and the number of members of this series does not exceed (k-1).

The largest number of members of discrete Q-row will be in the case when the value of local characteristics $\left|\Delta^{z_2(k-1)}_r\right[$ form an arithmetic progression with a step

$$2\delta^{z_1}_b \left(z_1 \in \{+, -\}, z_2 \in \{<, >\}\right),$$

the amount of which equals $n^{z_2}_{k-1} - \delta_b$ with the maximum number of members exceeding the absolute value of the threshold $q^{z_2(k)}_n$.

It is easy to show that in the most unfavorable case it is discrete Q-row will include no more than (k-1+c) parts, where

$$c = \left[\frac{-1 + \sqrt{8n^{z_2}_{k-1} - 7}}{4}\right] < \infty.$$

Marking Q-transformation through $Q\left(\Delta_{r_0}^{(j)}\right)$, the mathematical model of PI conversion based on Q- decomposition can be shown as:

$$\Phi^{p-1}\left[T\left(Q\left(\Delta_{r_0}^{(j-1)}\right)\right)=\bigcup_{t=2}^{p}\left(\Delta_{r_{0t}}^{(1,1)},\sigma_{r_{0t}}^{(1,1)}\right),\right.$$

where $p=\overline{2,k}$, p - number of hierarchical levels, $\Delta_{r_{0t}}^{(1,1)}$ - the tail elements of a networked network based on Q-row.

To reduce the time costs that go directly to Q-transformation enter the threshold of accuracy P, which represents the optimal average of the elements of the network and is calculated by the formula:

$$P=round(\,\Delta_{r_{0t}}^{(1,1)}\,,n), \tag{10}$$

where $round(x,n)$- operator of mathematical rounding of the expression x to n characters after a comma.

If the expression (10) is applied to the entire processing information sequence, we will receive a significant improvement in the timing characteristics of the processing of information, and as a result - less hardware load. In order to increase the noise immunity of the Q-transform method, we introduce the notion of a dynamic threshold, which can be described by expression:

$$P_{\Pi}=\begin{cases}round(\Delta_{r_{0t}}^{(1,1)},n_1)\\round(\Delta_{r_{0t}}^{(1,1)},n_2)\\....\\round(\Delta_{r_{0t}}^{(1,1)},n_m)\end{cases}, \tag{11}$$

where n_1, n_2, ..., n_m – parameter for dynamically changing mathematical rounding operator; m – the number of changes to the parameter m.

In this case, in direct Q-transformation, at each stage of data processing, threshold values are determined, in which the inverse transformation will occur without distortion. In this case, when calculating the threshold, account is taken of the value of the tail elements of the adjacent Q-rows.

Consider the filtering properties of the PI transformation on the basis of the Q-row in relation to the additive normal white noise.

The useful and noise signals $M(r)=\{\mu_r\}$ of the registered mixture can be represented as

$$G_M\left(r\right)=G\left(r\right)+M\left(r\right)=\left\{g_{\mu_r}\right\},$$

$$g_{\mu_r}=g_r+\mu_r,r\in\Omega_g.$$

Than j- part CQ and AQ- sequences represent this way:

$$\Delta_r^{(j)} = \Delta_{gr}^{(j)} + \Delta_{\mu r}^{(j)},$$

$$\Delta^{\overline{z(j)}} = \Delta_g^{\overline{z(j)}} + \Delta_\mu^{\overline{z(j)}},$$

Parallel-hierarchical Q-transformation through initial S sets Of the local amplitudes $\{g_r\}$ can be written also as:

$$\overset{p}{\underset{t=2}{\Phi}}\left[T\left(Q\left(\overset{S}{\underset{S=1}{U}}\left(\overset{n_S}{\underset{r=r_0}{U}}\right)\right)\right)\right] = \overset{p}{\underset{t=2}{U}}\left(\Delta_{r_{0t}}^{(1,1)}, \sigma_{r_{0t}}^{(1,1)}\right).$$

Conditionally denoting PI Q- transformation through $\Phi^{p-1}\left\{g_r\right\}_s$ and putting it in order to simplify the consideration in the expression (1) $F=\Phi_1$; $\Phi_{lj}=\Phi_1$; $\Phi_{ij} = \Phi_d$ i $\Phi_{oj} = \Phi_{oaj}$ (the operator of the arithmetic mean averaging) we obtain:

$$\Phi_{*j} = \Phi_d \bullet \Phi_{oaj} \bullet \Phi_{kj},$$

$$\Phi^{p-1}\left(\Delta_r^{(j,s)}\right) = \Phi^{p-1}\left(\Delta_{g_r}^{(j,s)}\right) + \Phi^{p-1}\left(\Delta_{\mu_r}^{(j,s)}\right), \tag{12}$$

$$\Phi^{p-1}\left(\Delta^{\overline{z(j,s)}}\right) = \Phi^{p-1}\left(\Delta_g^{\overline{z(j,s)}}\right) + \Phi^{p-1}\left(\Delta_\mu^{\overline{z(j,s)}}\right), \tag{13}$$

$$\begin{cases} \Delta^{\overline{z(j,s)}} = \dfrac{1}{n_{j,s}^z}\underset{r_z}{\sum}\Delta_r^{z(j,s)} \\[2ex] \Delta_g^{\overline{z(j,s)}} = \dfrac{1}{n_{j,s}^z}\underset{r_z}{\sum}\Delta_{g_r}^{z(j,s)}, \\[2ex] \Delta^{z(j,s)} = \dfrac{1}{n_{j,s}^z}\underset{r_z}{\sum}\Delta_{\mu_r}^{z(j,s)} \end{cases}$$

where $\Delta_{g_r}^{z(j,s)}$ and $\Delta_{\mu_r}^{z(j,s)}$ - local characteristics for the s silent signal and s noise, $n_{j,s}^z$ - area of masonic function for z- the drug.

The presence of noise leads to deformation both PI parts CQ, and PI AQ- sequences:

$$\Phi^{p-1}\left(\Delta_r^{(j,s)}\right) \neq \Phi^{p-1}\left(\Delta_{g_r}^{(j,s)}\right), \quad \Phi^{p-1}\left(\Delta^{\overline{z(j,s)}}\right) \neq \Phi^{p-1}\left(\Delta_g^{\overline{z(j,s)}}\right).$$

These deformations can be practically neglected, that is

$$\Phi^{p-1}\left(\Delta^{\overline{z(j,s)}}\right) \approx \Phi^{p-1}\left(\Delta_g^{z(j,s)}\right) \tag{14}$$

under the following conditions:

$$\left|\Phi^{p-1}\left(\Delta_{\mu_r}^{(j,s)}\right)\right| << \left|\Phi^{p-1}\left(\Delta_{g_r}^{(j,s)}\right)\right|, \quad \left|\Phi^{p-1}\left(\Delta_\mu^{\overline{z(j,s)}}\right)\right| << \left|\Phi^{p-1}\left(\Delta_g^{\overline{z(j,s)}}\right)\right|.$$

Considering the small influence of local characteristics $\Delta_{g_r}^{z(j,s)}$ in the ranges of their values $\left[g_\Lambda^{z(j,s)} - k_\delta \delta^{(j,s)}, g_\Lambda^{z(j,s)} + k_\sigma \sigma^{(j,s)}\right]$, easy to get

$$\left|\lim_{n_{j,s}^z \to \infty} \Delta_\mu^{\overline{z(j,s)}}\right| = \lim_{n_{l,s}^z \to \infty} \frac{\sigma^{(j,s)}}{\sqrt{n_{j,s}^z}} = 0\,8 \tag{15}$$

$$\left|\Delta_\mu^{\overline{z(j,s)}}\right| << h_\mu^{(j,s)} = k_\sigma \sigma^{(j,s)},$$

where $\sigma^{(j,s)}$ mean square deviation (SD) of the local noise characteristics $\Delta_{\mu_r}^{(j,s)}$, k_σ - the coefficient, which defines the confidence interval and the confidence probability corresponding to it.

According to expression (15), the half-range of probable values of the constant components of the local noise characteristics is much less than the half-range of probable values of the amplitude of these characteristics.

Taking into account the relations (14) i (15)

$$\Delta^{(j,s)} = \Delta^{z(j-1,s)} - \Delta^{\overline{z(j-1,s)}} = \Delta_{g_r}^{z(j-1,s)} - \Delta_g^{z(j-1,s)} + \Delta_{\mu_r}^{z(j-1,s)}$$

$$-\Delta_\mu^{z(j-1,s)} \approx \Delta_{g_r}^{z(j,s)} + \Delta_{\mu_r}^{z(j-1,s)} \approx \Delta_{g_r}^{z(j,s)} + \mu_r^{z(j,s)}, \quad \sigma^{(j,s)} = \sigma,$$

$$\Phi^{p-1}\left(\Delta^{(j,s)}\right) = \Phi^{p-1}\left(\Delta_{g_r}^{z(j,s)}\right) + \Phi^{p-1}\left(\mu_r^{z(j,s)}\right).$$

It can be shown that the effect of noise on the members *AQ*- sequences (Gealow & Sodini,1999) is manifested primarily in the interval $(g_\Lambda^{<(j,s)}, g_\Lambda^{>(j,s)})$ of the values of local characteristics $\Delta^{\diamond(j,s)}$, where for neglecting this influence, it is necessary to perform the following relations:

$$\left|\Delta^{\overline{\diamond(j,s)}}\right| \geq m_a k_\sigma \frac{\sigma^{(j,s)}}{\sqrt{n_{j,s}^\diamond}},$$

$$\left|\Phi^{p-1}(\Delta^{\overline{\circ(j,s)}})\right| > m_a k_\sigma \frac{\sigma^{(j,s)}}{\sqrt{n_{j,s}^\Diamond}}, \tag{16}$$

$$m_a \gg 1, \quad \left|\Phi^{p-1}(\Delta_r^{(j,s)})\right| > m_a k_\sigma \sigma^{(j,s)} \left(1 + \frac{1}{\sqrt{n_{j-1,s}^z}}\right). \tag{17}$$

With equal left parts of the inequalities (16) i (17)

$$m_a = m_c \frac{\sqrt{n_{j,s}^\Diamond}}{1 + \dfrac{1}{\sqrt{n_{j-1,s}^z}}},$$

and

$$m_a \begin{cases} < m_c \Pi P I \sqrt{n_{j,s}^\Diamond} = 1 \\ \ll m_c \Pi P I \sqrt{n_{j,s}^\Diamond} \gg 1 \end{cases},$$

what shows that the deformation of the parts PI *AQ*- sequence is substantially smaller than the size of the members of the PI *AQ*- sequence.

Therefore, we can conclude that there are good filtration properties of PI *Q*-transformation in comparison with such known decompositions of uncomplicated local characteristics as the Taylor series, etc.

Basic on the *Q*-row let's show the forming of the PI network at the level of the functional model. Initial signals M_s on the first hierarchical level form $CQ^{(s)}$ I $AQ^{(s)}$ sequences:

$$CQ^{(1)} : \Delta_{r_{01}}^{(1,1)}, \Delta_{r_{01}}^{(2,1)}, ..., \Delta_{r_{01}}^{(j_1,1)}.$$
$$AQ^{(1)} : \sigma_{r_{01}}^{(1,1)}, \sigma_{r_{01}}^{(2,1)}, ..., \sigma_{r_{01}}^{(j_1,1)}.$$
$$... \quad ... \quad ... \quad ... \quad ... \quad ... \quad ...$$
$$CQ^{(s-1)} : \Delta_{r_{01}}^{(1,s-1)}, \Delta_{r_{01}}^{(2,s-1)}, ..., \Delta_{r_{01}}^{(j_{s-1},s-1)}.$$
$$AQ^{(s-1)} : \sigma_{r_{01}}^{(1,s-1)}, \sigma_{r_{01}}^{(2,s-1)}, ..., \sigma_{r_{01}}^{(j_{s-1},s-1)}.$$
$$CQ^{(s)} : \Delta_{r_{01}}^{(1,s)}, \Delta_{r_{01}}^{(2,s)}, ..., \Delta_{r_{01}}^{(j_s,s)}.$$
$$AQ^{(s)} : \sigma_{r_{01}}^{(1,s)}, \sigma_{r_{01}}^{(2,s)}, ..., \sigma_{r_{01}}^{(j_s,s)}.$$

At the second hierarchical level, transformation forms $CQ^{(s)}$ i $AQ^{(s)}$ sequences:

$$CQ^{(1)} : \Delta^{(1,1)}_{r_{02}}, \Delta^{(1,2)}_{r_{02}}, ..., \Delta^{(1,s)}_{r_{02}}.$$
$$AQ^{(1)} : \sigma^{(1,1)}_{r_{02}}, \sigma^{(1,2)}_{r_{02}}, ..., \sigma^{(1,s)}_{r_{02}}.$$
$$CQ^{(2)} : \Delta^{(2,1)}_{r_{02}}, ..., \Delta^{(2,s-1)}_{r_{02}}, \Delta^{(2,s)}_{r_{02}}.$$
$$AQ^{(2)} : \sigma^{(2,1)}_{r_{02}}, ..., \sigma^{(2,s-1)}_{r_{02}}, \sigma^{(2,s)}_{r_{02}}.$$

$$... \quad ... \quad ... \quad ... \quad ... \quad ... \quad ...$$

$$CQ^{(s)} : \Delta^{(j_1,1)}_{r_{02}} ...$$
$$AQ^{(s)} : \sigma^{(j_1,1)}_{r_{02}} ...$$

At the third level, PI form the transformation of the $CQ^{(s)}$ i $AQ^{(s)}$ sequences:

$$CQ^{(1)} : \Delta^{(1,1)}_{r_{03}}, \Delta^{(1,2)}_{r_{03}}.$$
$$AQ^{(1)} : \sigma^{(1,1)}_{r_{03}}, \sigma^{(1,2)}_{r_{03}}.$$

$$... \quad ... \quad ... \quad ... \quad ...$$

$$CQ^{(s)} : \Delta^{(1,s-1)}_{r_{03}}, \Delta^{(1,s)}_{r_{03}} ...$$
$$AQ^{(s)} : \sigma^{(1,s-1)}_{r_{03}}, \sigma^{(1,s)}_{r_{03}} ...$$

Similarly, while continuing the specified conversion, you can obtain the desired CQ and AQ - sequences of the PI network.

PI CQ: $\Delta^{(1,1)}_{r_{02}}, \Delta^{(1,1)}_{r_{03}}, ..., \Delta^{(1,1)}_{r_{0p}}.$

PI AQ: $\sigma^{(1,1)}_{r_{02}}, \sigma^{(1,1)}_{r_{03}}, ..., \sigma^{(1,1)}_{r_{0p}}.$

To implement the PI of the Q-transformation, as for Q-rows it is necessary to determine the convolution of operators $\Phi_c^{(p-1)}$ i $\Phi_{kj}^{(p-1)}$, that is

$$\Phi_c^{(p,l)} * \Phi_{kj}^{(p,l)} = \Phi_{kcj}^{(p,l)}.$$

$$\Phi_{kcj}^{(p,l)} \left(\Delta^{(j)(pl)}_{\Phi_l,r_0}, \left\{ \Delta^{(j)(pl)}_{\Phi_l,r} \right\}_r \right) = \left(\left\{ \Delta^{(j)(pl)}_{\Phi_l,r_0} \right\}_r, \left\{ \left\{ \Delta^{(j)(pl)}_{\Phi_l,r} \right\}_z \right\}_r \right),$$

$$z \in \left\{ <, \Diamond, > \right\}, \nu \in \left\{ r_0, r \right\},$$

$$\Delta^{z(j)(p,l)}_{\Phi_l,\nu} = C^{z(p,l)} * \Delta^{(j)(p,l)}_{\Phi_l,\nu},$$

$$C_{j,\nu}^{z(p,l)} = \Phi_{kj}^{z(p,l)}\left(\Delta_{\Phi_l,\nu}^{(j)(p,l)}\right),$$

$$\Phi_{kj}^{z(p,l)} = \left\{\Phi_{kj}^{z}\right\}_{z}^{(p,l)},$$

where (p,l) - is the hierarchical number and the number of its branch. Possible set of variants of definition of operators $\Phi_{kj}^{z(p,l)}$ through coefficients $C_{j,\nu}^{z(p,l)}$, which lead to significantly different PI results of the Q-transformation.

1. $\quad C_{i,v}^{<(p,l)} = \begin{cases} 1 & as & \Delta_{\bullet_{l,v}}^{(j)(p,l)} > g_{\wedge}^{<(j)(p,l)} \\ 0 & as & \Delta_{\bullet_{l,v}}^{(j)(p,l)} \leq g_{\wedge}^{<(j)(p,l)} \end{cases},$

$C_{i,v}^{<>(p,l)} = \begin{cases} 1 & as & g_{\wedge}^{>(j)(p,l)} \leq \Delta_{\bullet_{l,v}}^{(j)(p,l)} \leq g_{\wedge}^{<(j)(p,l)} \\ 0 & as & in\ other\ case \end{cases},$

$C_{i,v}^{>(p,l)} = \begin{cases} 1 & as & \Delta_{\bullet_{l,v}}^{(j)(p,l)} < g_{\wedge}^{>(j)(p,l)} \\ 0 & as & \Delta_{\bullet_{l,v}}^{(j)(p,l)} \geq g_{\wedge}^{>(j)(p,l)} \end{cases},$

2. $\quad C_{i,v}^{<(p,l)} = \begin{cases} 1 & as & \Delta_{\bullet_{l,v}}^{(j)(p,l)} \geq g_{\wedge}^{<(j)(p,l)} \\ 0 & as & \Delta_{\bullet_{l,v}}^{(j)(p,l)} < g_{\wedge}^{<(j)(p,l)} \end{cases},$

$C_{i,v}^{<>(p,l)} = \begin{cases} 1 & as & g_{\wedge}^{>(j)(p,l)} \leq \Delta_{\bullet_{l,v}}^{(j)(p,l)} \leq g_{\wedge}^{<(j)(p,l)} \\ 0 & & in\ other\ case \end{cases},$

$C_{i,v}^{>(p,l)} = \begin{cases} 1 & as & \Delta_{\bullet_{l,v}}^{(j)(p,l)} \leq g_{\wedge}^{>(j)(p,l)} \\ 0 & as & \Delta_{\bullet_{l,v}}^{(j)(p,l)} > g_{\wedge}^{>(j)(p,l)} \end{cases},$

where $g_{\wedge}^{<(j)(p,l)}$ 8 $g_{\wedge}^{>(j)(p,l)}$ - top and bottom local thresholds in j cycles of recursion of the p level of the l-branch. The operator $\Phi_{*j}^{(p,l)}$ will be written as:

$$\Phi_{xj}^{(p,l)} = \Phi_{Ij}^{(p,l)} * \Phi_{oj}^{(p,l)} * \Phi_{c}^{(p,l)} * \Phi_{kj}^{(p,l)} * \Phi_{lj}^{(p,l)}. \tag{18}$$

These operators act on p level of the l branch and coincide with the above definition of operators. Let's name the PI CQ and the PI as AQ-rows as next rows:

PI CQ-row: $\sum_{p=2}^{\infty} \Delta_{r_{op}}^{(1,1)}$.

PI AQ-row: $\sum_{p=2}^{\infty} \sigma_{r_{op}}^{(1,1)}$.

The generation by the operator $\Phi_{kj}^{(p,l)}$ for each p, l and j of the three coefficients

$$\left\{ C_{j,r_o}^z \right\}_z^{(p,l)}, z \in \left\{ <, \Diamond, > \right\}, p = 2, 3, ...; l = 1, ..., s$$

allows, subject to convergence PI of the Q-row, consider the entire set of generated coefficients triples as a code of $N_{GFr_0}^{(p,l)(i)}$ (PI Q-row) of the set of local characteristics $\left\{ g_{Fr_0} \right\}$:

$$N_{GFr_0}^{(p,l)(i)} = \left\{ N_{j,r_0}^{p,l} \right\}_j^{p,l}, j = \overline{1, i}.$$

$$N_{j,r_0}^{p,l} = \left\{ \overset{z\ p,l}{C_{j,r_0}} \right\}_z^{p,l}, \overset{z\ p,l}{C_{j,r_0}} \in \left\{ 1, 0 \right\}.$$

For continuous functions in previously obtained expressions for calculating PI members of the Q-sequences it is necessary to replace the summation sign on the discrete set of coordinates of the levels with the integral sign in the coordinate field of the levels, and instead of the numbers $n_j^{2^{p,l}}$ when calculating the averaged characteristics it is necessary to apply the area of the corresponding mask function.

According to such given information, let's note the benefits of the proposed PI network based on the Q transformation (Kozemyako, Tymchenko, Kutaev & Ivasyuk,1994).

1. The parallelism and hierarchy of the transformation algorithm and its orientation on the systolic transformation architecture;
2. The good noise reduction characteristics due to operator's use of the Φ_0 global averaging at all hierarchical levels of the PI network;
3. Independence from the angle of rotation of a two-dimensional image in the plane of observation with a large number of readings or integral form of decomposition;
4. Qualitative restorative properties, application in various signal processing devices (filtering devices, recognition, archivists etc.).
5. The versatility of application for solving applied problems.

In AGIPP is the use of parallel-hierarchical noise-preventing Q-transformation of information (Steven & Riedl,1986). The growing amount of data and computations needed to handle large amounts of information in AGIES, such as video surveillance images, needs more and more productivity for the systems used. Since the density of "packing" elements in integrated circuits is determined by physical constraints, the speed of the result is limited to the finite rate of propagation of electromagnetic oscillations from one element to another. To overcome this physical barrier is possible only by parallelization of computational processes in the system, which, in turn, leads to the complication of its architecture. Intelligent processing of information requires consideration of each element in a certain context of its connections, and this is possible only in a computing system that has a topographic structure with a three-dimensional arrangement of processor elements (PE).

A high-performance information processing system can only be obtained by adapting the architecture to the corresponding data structure. However, the data structure in the process of pyramidal processing varies from a large fixed array at the lower level to a small flexible structure on the upper one. The most interesting are the homogeneous undistributed computing structures that correspond to the class of SIMD systems, in which several levels of identical PEs operate in SIMD mode. Each level contains a large number of simple PEs. In a more complex case of homogeneous distributed pyramidal computing structures, several powerful identical processor blocks are combined into a hierarchical pyramidal structure. Each processor unit corresponds to a portion of the processed data. Such a pyramid system can function in both SIMD and MIMD modes.

The principle of constructing a parallel-hierarchical data structure can be defined as a sequence of data arrays of the same information field at different levels of resolution:

$$P = (A0, A1, A2,...,AL),$$

where A_i - information field, i - number of level of permission, $i = \overline{0,l}$.

Such an order of informational fields forms a computing structure that permits the realization of methods of intellectual sensory perception. In particular, this structure allows you to control the level of permission of the processed data, as well as the size of the analysis area. The dimensions of the analyzed "window" of data can be constant, but moving from one level of placement to another, one can process the same element of the information field with varying degrees of detail. In this case, the decision on the need for further processing can be taken at the upper processing level after analysis of the information field with a low resolution, each element of which contains integral estimates of the corresponding fragments of the output field at the lowest level, which leads to an increase in their processing speed. The essence of the parallel-hierarchical approach is the simultaneous use in analyzing the sequence of data arrays at various levels of the hierarchy. This allows you to implement a strategy from "general to partial", which makes it possible to implement the concept of neural-like processing. Each element of a parallel-hierarchical information field is characterized by three coordinates (i,j,k), where i - the row, j - the column, k - the level.

The principle of constructing a parallel-hierarchical data structure (Gealow & Sodini,1999) can be defined as the sequence of operations over sets of data arrays that form the set of information fields of various levels of the hierarchy, the interaction between which is carried out by a pyramidal parallel-hierarchical structure and implemented on the basis of network architecture. The network structure allows to simulate the principle of the distributed parallel-hierarchical network and at the expense of spatial division in time, forms a deterministic parallel-hierarchical network (Figure 4, a). A network based on a parallel-hierarchical transformation consists of a set of subnets (Figure 4, b), the formation of signs about the states of the PFMS, the structure of which is homogeneous and consists of a series of interrelated hierarchical levels.

The algorithm of the network is universal and consists in parallel-hierarchical formation of sets of general and various computing structures about the states of the spatial-frequency signal (PSF) (Balashov, 1985). The generalization of all kinds of sensory information occurs at the very final stage of the transformation beyond the hierarchical processing of each type of sensory information.

Consequently, the process of generalization between various types of sensory information begins only when the construction of a defined set of signs is over.

"Intelligent" level of the parallel-hierarchical network is determined by the degree of generalization of sensory information in its branches. The greater the degree of generalization of sensory information, when it passes through the branches of the network, the higher its "intellectual" level. The network method investigated in the work combines the two described rewrite signals - detector and spatial-frequency - and describes the image by expanding it to an adaptive system of basic functions, the formation of which depends on the structure of the image itself.

The essence of the parallel hierarchical approach is the simultaneous use of a sequence of sets of data arrays that form sets of information fields at different levels of the hierarchy, recursive formation of new sequences of information flows at various levels of the hierarchy, which allows implementing the strategy of multilevel interaction from "general to partial". Each element of the parallel-hierarchical system is characterized by four coordinates (i,j,k_1,k_2), where k_1 - level pyramid of the first level, k_2 - level parallel to the hierarchical pyramid of other levels.

The pyramidal computing structure based on the PI of the transformation forms the network in the form of a parallel-hierarchical pyramid. Here for each pyramid, its PE is used, and the number of PE is determined by the total number of branches of the network's IP. In a general form, the methodology for the formation of network interconnection can be presented in a formalized form, based on the following provisions. Let there be multiple streams of input data. The following problem occurs. In what way can a parallel computing process be organized in real time in order to obtain a strictly distributed time and hierarchy computing network? The answer to this question can be given by the principle of constructing the next computing network.

Consider the methodological peculiarities of the multilevel IP network organization (Kozemyako, Tymchenko, Kutaev & Ivasyuk,1994), given in Figure 5, for which it is necessary to obtain a functional description of the basic network. Here the processing is subject to a plurality of input data streams on a variety of (k) hierarchical levels. Each level represents a set of the PE, which function in strictly fixed moments of time (r_j).

In the research of parallel-hierarchical Q-transformation of information for AGIES in order to identify and improve the noise-resistant characteristics of the method, algorithms of direct and inverse parallel-hierarchical Q-transformation of information were developed (Figures 6 and 8).

Direct parallel-hierarchical Q-conversion begins with reading and defining the file type. When implementing a direct and a reverse transformation in one program, determining the type of file makes sense to select further actions. Before the start of the conversion, it is necessary to specify the accuracy of the calculations, that is, to determine the threshold of the accuracy of the calculation of tail elements (block 3, see Figure 6). There is the possibility of choosing a fixed value for the entire sequence of calculations, as well as selecting the dynamic threshold value (11). Dynamic threshold allows increasing the noise immunity of the method, while practically not losing on hardware-time costs.

Figure 4. Network structure based on parallel-hierarchical transformation

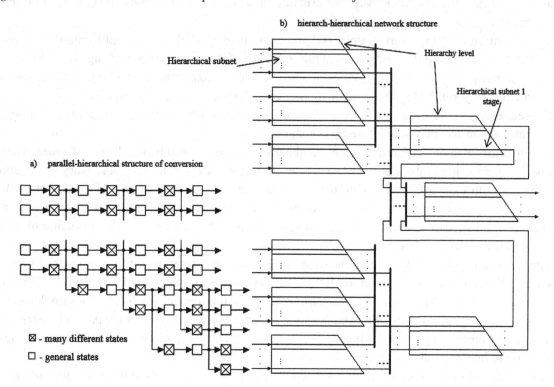

After determining the accuracy threshold of the calculations, the cyclic process of processing the file begins (blocks 4-10, see Figure 6). At the same time, the values of the tail elements, the value of the characters of the elements of a row are determined in parallel, and the preservation of these values is maintained until the next portion of the data is processed. The next step is to create an output file (block 9, see Figure 6). In this case, the file contains encoded data, and information about the file type (what it is encoded)

When using as a precision dynamic threshold calculations for direct Q-transformation, block 6 (see Figure 6) can be represented as follows (Figure 7).

As can be seen from the above block diagram, the definition of the threshold is carried out in several stages: first we determine the weight values of the coefficients for the current series, analyze, and compare them with the values of the coefficients of the adjacent rows, then adjust the value. If the calculations are carried out in the optimal way, processing of the next portion of data begins.

When reversing the information in the first stage, the type of file is determined (block 3, see Figure 8), that is, the file is encoded. Next, directly reading the information from a file that occurs cyclically with blocks corresponding to the size and number of parallel processors (blocks 3-6, see Figure 8) begins directly. At this stage, the formation of a series occurs with the help of tail elements, after which the preparation of the array to the next series is carried out. This process is cyclic and occurs before the complete conversion of the input file.

The inverse Q-transformation ends with the formation of an output file, in which, unlike the encoded file, only decoded information is recorded (without superfluous information for transmission and decoding), since the file should generally be identical to the file that came for direct Q-transformation.

Figure 5. Structural diagram of the interaction of information flows in the parallel hierarchical computing structure

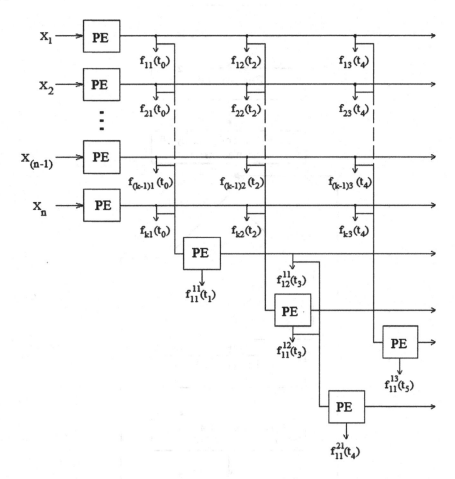

Experimental Researches of the Obtained Indicators of Practical Realization of Q-Transformation in the Automated Geoinformation-Energy System

In order to assess the impedance of the communication system, the average probability of an error in the information bit Pb, or the sequence of bits (code block) of the PB, with a certain relation of signal-to-noise in the communication channel, is often used. Error data probabilities can be determined by exact or approximate formulas, as well as obtained by statistical simulation of the communication system on a PC.

To estimate the probabilities of the error in the bit Pb and the block RB of the linear block code of length n, which is decoded using the decoder of maximum probability (that is, a decoder that selects from all possible codewords the one that is at a minimum distance from the received sequence from the channel) can be used additive estimate (Tyagur, 2017), characterized by sufficient precision with a large signal-to-noise ratio.

$$P_B \leq \sum_{j=1}^{n} N_j P_c(j);$$

Figure 6. A disturbing method of direct parallel-hierarchical Q-transformation of information for AGES

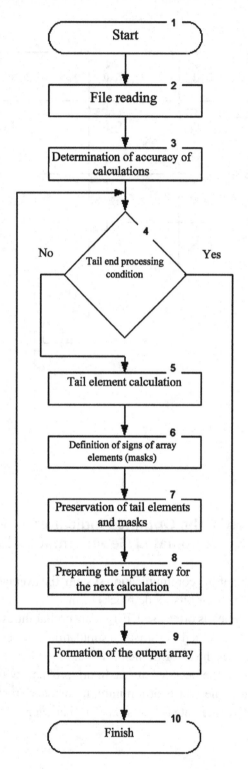

Figure 7. Fragment of the block diagram of the noise-proof method of direct parallel-hierarchical Q-transformation of information with a dynamic threshold.

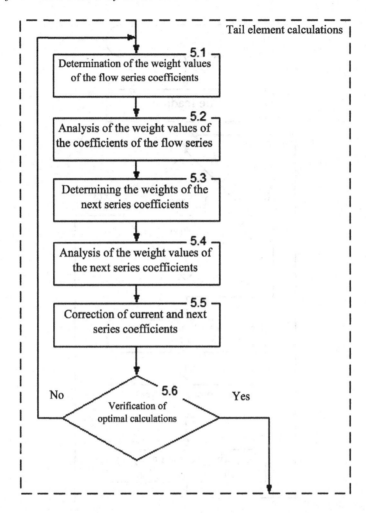

$$P_b \le \sum_{j=1}^{n} \frac{j}{k} N_j P_c(j);$$

where k – the number of information symbols of the code; N_j - the number of codewords meaningful j;

$$P_c(j) = \begin{cases} \sum_{i=(j+1)/2}^{j} C_j^i p^i (1-p)^{j-i} & - \ with \ an \ odd \ j; \\ \frac{1}{2} C_j^{j/2} p^{j/2} (1-p)^{j/2} + \sum_{i=(j/2)+1}^{j} C_j^i p^i (1-p)^{j-i} & - \ with \ an \ even \ j; \\ Q(\sqrt{2jE_S / N_0}) & - \ for \ a \ channel \ with \ additive \ white \ Gaussian \ noise \end{cases}$$

Figure 8. Impedance-proof method of reverse parallel-hierarchical Q-transformation of information for AGIES.

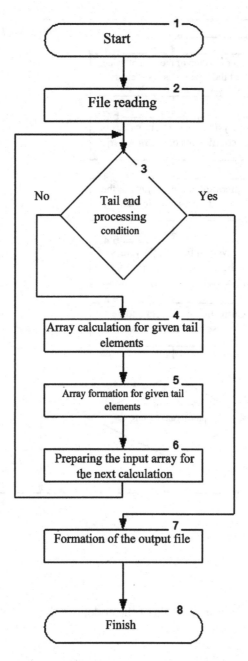

where p – the probability of a bit error at the decoder input (i.e., in the channel); ES / N0 - signal-to-noise ratio in the channel; Q (x) is a function of Q-preparation.

On the basis of the above material, an estimation of various methods of encoding information was made and the following numerical dependences of the probability of error occurrence on the signal / noise value, which are presented in the form of graphs in Figure 9. As can be seen from the dependence curves, with different ratios of signal / noise in communication channels, there is a different probability of occurrence of the error, and with the increase of the signal / noise ratio the probability decreases. Thus, for example, in graph 9 a) at a signal / noise level of 7 dB, the probability of an error is 10-3-10-4, while with a value of 3 dB, the probability of error is 10-1,5-10-1,7 in Depending on the index m, that is, the length of the codeword.

In this case, the entropy and bandwidth of the communication channel, depending on the signal-to-noise ratio, will have the following form (Figure10):

By analyzing the above relationships and comparing various noise immunity methods and codes with the proposed method of noise immunity parallel-hierarchical Q-transformation, it can be noted that the self-orthogonal code is closest to the characteristics and dependencies of the probability of the error from the signal-to-noise value. It has a signal / noise level, for example, -3 dB, the probability of an error is 5.65x10-6, and in the case of a modified parallel-hierarchical

Q-transformation with the same level of noises - 5,03x10-6. Determine the coefficient of improvement of the probability value of the error in the method of noise immunity parallel-hierarchical Q-transformation:

$$k_n = 100\% - (5{,}65*10^{-6}*100\%/5.03*10^{-6}) = 11\%.$$

Consequently, the coefficient of improvement of the value of probability of error k_n in the method of noise immunity parallel-hierarchical Q-transformation is 11%.

MODELING OF APPARATUS-SOFTWARE Q-CONVERTING PART OF AUTOMATED GEOINFORMATION SYSTEM

On the basis of developed parallel methods of Q-transformation of information for AGIES hardware-software modeling was carried out and the data transmission channel was engineered in the environment of the automated geoinformation and energy system. A software package was developed that allowed to simulate the transmission of data in the channel of communication with interruptions of various types of forms (Gaussian and uniform noise), as well as conduct a series of experiments to determine the level of impedance of using Q-transformation of information in automated geographic information systems. The main software developed in this task is the direct program realization of the method of Q-transformation of information (Figure 11). Assistive software means:

- specially designed software implementation of the process of imposing noise on the encoded file, which allows you to apply noise over the encoded (transmitted) data packet of different intensities and different distributions (Gaussian and uniform noise) (Figure 12);
- use of standard resources such as Photoshop, MSExel, etc.

Using the above-mentioned specially developed and standard software tools, experiments were conducted to decode the noise-free information in a different way with different noise levels and different noise distributions (Figure 12). For comparison, a typical equivalent overlay of a noise load of a similar level and distribution is shown. It should be noted that during the experiment, noise was superimposed on numerical units. This limits the experiment to a certain extent, since this does not take into account the length of the file being processed, which, in the case of a file of encoded information, depends on

Figure 9. Dependence of probability of occurrence of error on signal/noise ratio.

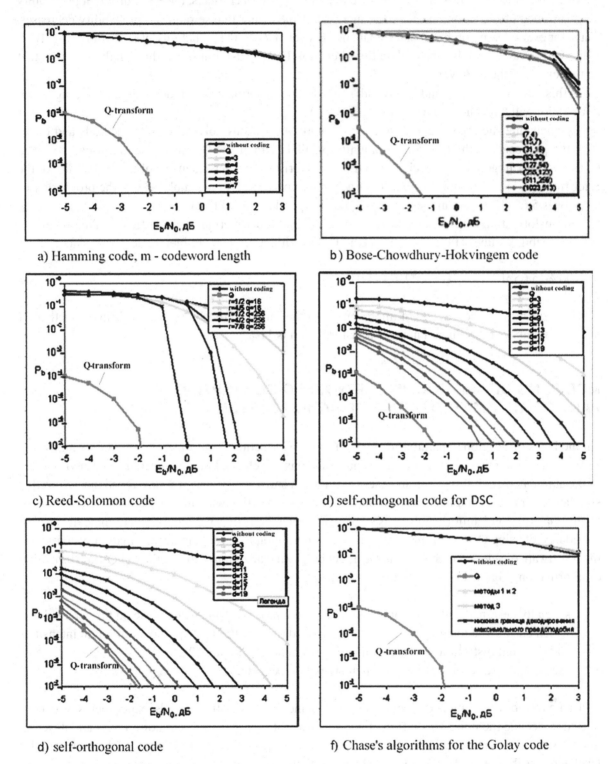

a) Hamming code, m - codeword length

b) Bose-Chowdhury-Hokvingem code

c) Reed-Solomon code

d) self-orthogonal code for DSC

d) self-orthogonal code

f) Chase's algorithms for the Golay code

Figure 10. Dependence of bandwidth and entropy of the communication channel in the signal-to-noise ratio

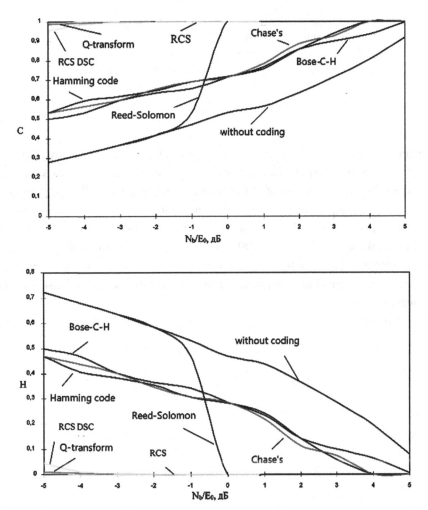

Figure 11. Software realization of Q-transformation of information method.

20	15	6	100	7	3	20.25	0
-0,25	-5,25	-14,25	79,75	-13,25	-17,25	79,75	-11,3928
11,14285	6,142857	-2,85714	0	-1,85714	-5,85714	6,142857	-4,60714
5	0	1,75	0	2,75	-1,25	3,16666	-3,16666
1,833333	0	-1,41666	0	-0,41666	1,916668	1,875	-0,9375
-0,04166	0	-0,47916	0	0,520833	0,041668	0,472222	-0,47222
0,430555	0	-0,00694	0	0,048611	-0,43055	0,287037	-0,28703
0,143518	0	0,280092	0	-0,23842	-0,14351	0,172839	-0,17283
-0,02932	0	0,107253	0	-0,06558	0,029320	0,057613	-0,05761
0,028292	0	0,049639	0	-0,00797	-0,02829	0,038966	-0,01948
-0,01067	0	0,010673	0	0,011509	-0,00880	0,011091	-0,00554
-0,00512	0	-0,00041	0	0,000417	-0,00326	0,002938	-0,00293
-0,00219	0	0,002518	0	-0,00251	-0,00032	0,001678	-0,00167
-0,00051	0	0,000839	0	-0,00083	0,001352	0,000762	-0,00076

Figure 12. Software implementation of the process of imposing noise on the encoded file.

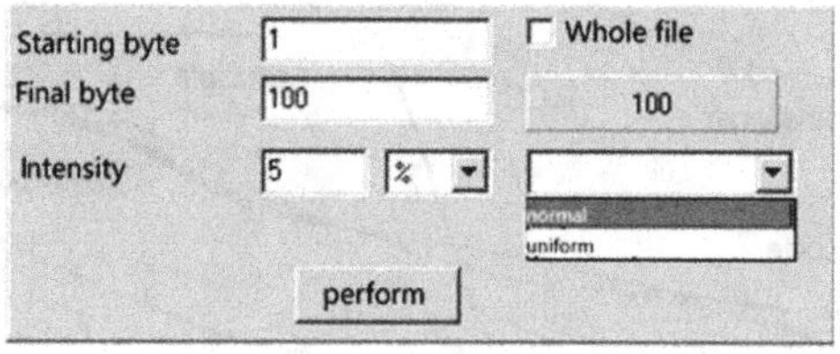

the accuracy selected. Therefore, taking into account such a feature, an accuracy of 0.1 was chosen for the objectivity of the obtained experiments, while the size of the studied files varies insignificantly, which does not affect the overall picture of the experiment. In the course of experiments, the developed system was tested on a publicly accessible manchester database of facial expressions [manch intern]. This database was created at the University of Manchester and used for various experiments, for example, for facial recognition (Lanitis et al., 1995). For the analysis of the stability of the method to the influence of noise, two basic distributions of the noise that most often meet in the tasks of processing and transmission of images: the Gaussian (normal) and the uniform density of distributions of the probability of noise were selected.

Gaussian distribution:

$$p(x) = \frac{1}{\sqrt{2\pi\sigma}} e^{-\frac{(x-a)^2}{2\sigma^2}}, \ 45 \ \sigma > 0, -\infty < a < \infty.$$

Equal distribution:

$$p(x) = \begin{cases} \dfrac{1}{b-a}, x \in [a,b] \\ 0, x \notin [a,b] \end{cases}.$$

The original image was selected as the agj-01.pcx file from the face image gallery. Parameters of the initial image are presented in Table 1.

Examples of noisy images using uniform and Gaussian noises with different degrees of noises are given in Figure 13.

In the course of the experiment, the comparison of the coefficients of correlation was also compared. As a reference, the image agj-01.pcx was used. A correlation comparison of the chosen reference image with a noisy image and a decoded image after noises was performed. The comparison was made by two types of noise: Gaussian and uniform. The results of the correlation comparison are shown in Figure 14. From the results of the correlation comparison (see Figure 14) it is seen that the image decoded after the noise is closer to the reference image (level 1) than the noise-free image with the same noise level. Moreover, in the case of Gaussian noise, the percentage of improvement will be:

$\Delta k = k_{\kappa} - k_{H} = 0.91 - 0.57 = 0.33$, is 33%,

Table 1. Parameters of the initial IMAGE

Image Type	Half Tone 8 Bit
Size	62515 byte
Width	250 pix.
Height	250 pix.
Resolution	300 dpi
File format	Zsoft PCX
Type of encoding	RLE

where k_{κ} – image correlation factor for decoding after noise with Gaussian distribution with reference, $k_{_H}$ – correlation coefficient of a noisy image with a reference.

In the case of a uniform noise, the corresponding factor will be:

$$\Delta k = k_{_H} - k_{\kappa} = 0.84 - 0.42 = 0.42, \text{ is } 42\%,$$

where k_{κ} – the correlation coefficient of an image when decoded after zeroing with a uniform distribution with the reference, $k_{_H}$ – correlation coefficient of a noisy image with a reference.

The decoded average after the noisy image is closer to the standard shutter than the noisy image with the same noise level at the maximum noise level at:

$$(33\% + 42\%)/2 = 37,5\%.$$

In the process of analyzing existing research papers (Riedl, 1986) devoted to Q-transformation, as well as in the process of realizing the method of direct and inverse Q-transformation, attention was paid to the unclosed questions of the k-comparison operator before. As it turned out, the choice of the optimum threshold for the accuracy of p leads to significant savings in machine resources. However, on the other hand, choosing the optimal threshold for the criteria for saving resources leads to some differences between the incoming and the processed files. The results of investigations of correlation coefficients of input images and images after direct / reverse Q-transformation are presented in the following graph (Figure 15).

As can be seen from the graph, starting with the value threshold of accuracy 2, as well as using the dynamic threshold, we obtain the correlation coefficient that goes to one, that is, 100%.

The following diagram (Figure 16) shows the dependence of the cost of machine resources (in steps) on the choice of a threshold value, where it can be noted that increasing the value of the threshold increases the value and spent machine resources for encoding-decoding by the Q-transform. That is, with an increase in the accuracy of the method, the amount of machine resources spent on processing files is significantly increased and, accordingly, the processing time of the information. When using a dynamic threshold, without losing accuracy in calculations (see Figure 16), hardware resources are also significantly reduced when processing data.

It is also important to note that using the dynamic threshold in the Q-transform method significantly reduces the size of the encoded file that needs to be transmitted over the communication lines. And since the main disadvantage of noise-proof encoding is its redundancy, then using a dynamic threshold is possible, without reducing the accuracy of the method, to achieve and acceptable sizes of the encoded file. In Figure 17 shows how the threshold value affects the ratio of the size of the input and the encoded files.

Figure 13. Images using uniform and Gaussian noises with different degrees of noisiness.

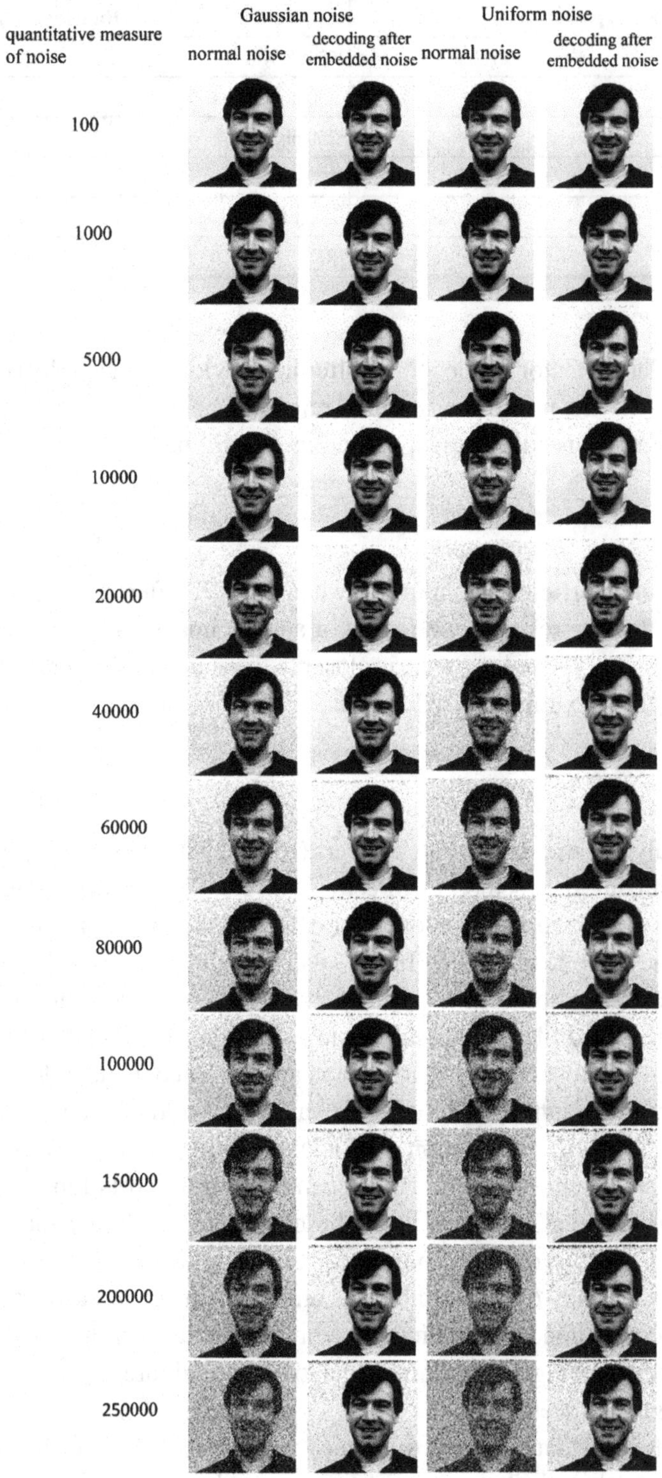

Figure 14. Images with reference.

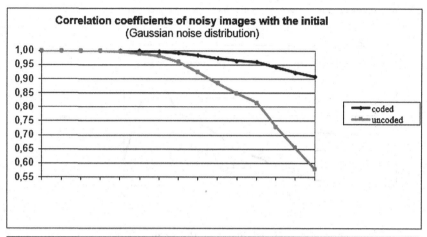

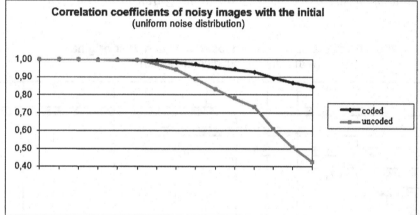

Figure 15. Coefficients of correlation of input images and images after direct / reverse Q-transformation at different thresholds of rounding and at dynamic threshold.

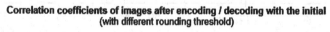

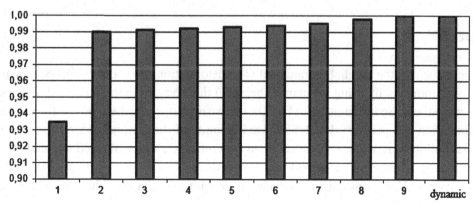

Figure 16. Hardware costs for Q-transformation with different threshold of accuracy.

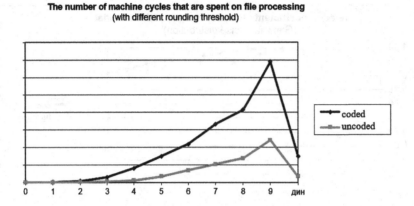

Figure 17. The ratio of the size of the encoded file to the Q-transform using a different threshold and its source file.

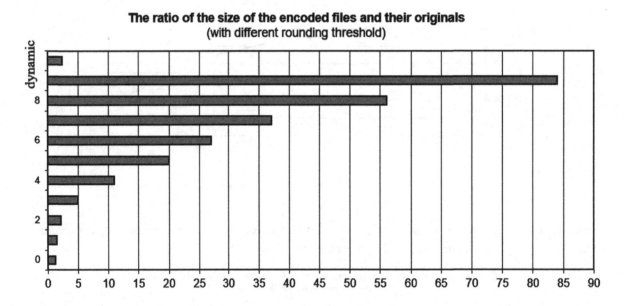

CONCLUSION

Further development of the parallel-hierarchical Q-transformation method for AGIES, which provides increased noise immunity by using a dynamic threshold that changes in the process of data processing and can increase the noise immunity by 11%. On the basis of the modified Q-transformation method, software simulation was performed and the noise immunity of the method under noise disturbance of different distributions was analyzed. The obtained concrete data, which allowed to clearly describe all stages of the process of direct and reverse Q-transformation. It is established that the image decoded after the noise is closer to the reference than the noisy image with a similar noise level of 37.5% on average.

REFERENCES

Balashov, E. (1985). Evolutionary synthesis of systems. Radio & Communication, 1(1), 328.

Coronel, C., & Morris, S. (2014). Database Systems: Design, Implementation, and Management. Academic Press.

Gealow, C., & Sodini, G. (1999). A pixel-parallel image processor usinglogic pitch-matched to dynamic memory. Academic Press.

Genov R., & Cauwenberghs G. (2001). *Charge-Mode Parallel Architecture for Vector–Matrix Multiplication.* Academic Press.

Genov, R., & Cauwenberghs, G. (2002). Stochastic mixed-signal VLSI architecture for high-dimensional kernel machines. *Advances in Neural Information Processing Systems, 14.*

Gusev, M., & Evans, D. (1994). A new matrix vector product systolic array. Parallel and Distribute Computing, 22(2), 346-349. doi:10.1006/jpdc.1994.1094

Hertz, J., Krogh, A., & Palmer, R. (1991). *Introduction to the Theory of Neural Computation.* Academic Press.

Karpyk, A. (2004). Methodological and technological bases of geoinformation support of territories. Academic Press.

Kohonen, T. (1989). Self Organization and Associative Memory (3rd ed.). Academic Press. doi:10.1007/978-3-642-88163-3

Kovzel, M., Kutaev, I., & Tymchenko, Y. (2006). Parallel-hierarchical transformation and Q-processing of information for real-time systems. Academic Press.

Kozemyako, V. (1997). A look at the nature of artificial intelligence. Herald of VPI, 1, 26-30.

Kozemyako, V., Bilan, O., & Kozemyako, A. (2004) Optical-electronic geoinformation and energy system as a global means of harmonious solving of problems of development of civilization. Optoelectronic Information and Energy Technologies, 2(8), 5-10.

Kozemyako, V., Tymchenko, Y., Kutaev, I., & Ivasyuk, I. (1994). Introduction to the algorithmic theory of the hierarchy and parallelism of neural-like computing environments and its application to the transformation of images. Fundamentals of the Theory of Pyramid-Network Image Transformation, 2.

Kupchenko, Y. (2003). Home networks on electric wires - time has come? Computer Review, 18-19(387), 24-38.

Mitchell, A. (1999). *ESRI Guide to GIS Analysis.* Retrieved from www.nanonewsnet.ru

Riedl, S. E. (1986). An Electronic Support System for Optical Matrix-Vector Processors. Academic Press.

Tyagur, V. (2017). Optical-electronic system. Academic Press.

Ubardulaev, R. (1989). Fiber optic networks. Engineering Encyclopedia, Electronic Communications Technologies, 1(1), 184.

Zacerkovnyi, V. (2015). Geoinformation system. Academic Press.

Section 3
Image Processing and Recognition

This section contains chapters that describe new research in image processing and recognition. For this purpose, the parallel shift technology, cellular automata and retinal simulation tools are used.

Chapter 11

Reproduction of Images of Convex Figures by a Set of Stored Reference Surfaces

Sergey Yuzhakov

Haisyn Department of the SFS General Directorate in Vinnytsia Region, Ukraine

ABSTRACT

Image processing is one of the important tasks of creating artificial intelligence. The methods for digital images processing are widely used by developers at this time. The parallel shift technology makes it possible to create alternative ways of describing and processing images. It involves the transformation of images not into a set of pixels, but into a set of functions that are organized in a certain way. The completeness of the system is determined by the ability to perform some basic tasks. Image processing includes image pre-processing, video data storage, various image manipulations, images restoration. This chapter discusses a mathematical model for the recovery of flat convex binary images. Images are restored on the basis of data generated by an image processing system based on parallel shift technology. Two methods are provided for determining the imaging area.

INTRODUCION

The task of images restoration is one of the most important tasks of image processing. Recovery is the transformation of an image, which is represented by a set of functions, into its original form. When digitally processing images, images are described by a set of pixels (Gonzalez et al. 2004). Each of them has attributes (location, color, brightness). The restoration of the original image of the image in this case consists in placing each element in the appropriate place.

Image processing based on parallel shift technology (PST) (Belan et al. 2018) implies the description of images not by a set of pixels, but by a set of functions of the area of intersection (FAI). Characteristic features of images are determined by its transformation (Belan 2012, Belan et al. 2013a). FAI is the dependence of the area of intersection of the original figure and its copy, which is shifted in a given direction, from the shift distance. It is necessary to create a set of functions of the area of intersection for

DOI: 10.4018/978-1-7998-1290-6.ch011

the directions from 0 to π to description the image. This set forms a certain reference surface. The functions of the area of intersection for directions from π to 2π do not need to be formed, since the reference surface has the property of central symmetry. The greater the number of FAIs describes the image, the more accurate the shape of the reference surface.

When using the PST, the recovery process will be quite complicated, because the initial information is minimized into two-dimensional functions. This will lead to the need to iterate over a large number of options when restoring images.

The main parameters of each FAI are the area of the original figure (S_0) and the distance of the maximum shift in a given direction (X_{max}) (Belan et al. 2013b). The maximum shift is the longest shift distance of an images copy at which the area of intersection will have a non-zero area.

This chapter describes methods for recovering convex binary images based on data that are generated by an image processing and recognition system based on parallel shift technology (Bilan et al. 2013c, Chen at al. 1995).

GENERAL SCHEME OF THE IMAGES RECOVERY PROCESS

At the initial stage, the image recovery system (IRS) receives a set of functions of the area of intersection for a range of shift directions from 0 to π. The shift direction with an angle of 0 is chosen arbitrarily. The most convenient way to use one of the orthogonal directions. In this chapter, the zero direction is considered the vertical direction (up).

If the system has a memory that contains sets of reference images, then a recognition process takes place, which is described in detail in works on image processing based on parallel shift technology (Belan et al. 2013b, Belan et al. 2013c, Bilan et al. 2018). If the IRS has no memory, or if there is no match for the source information among the etalons, then it becomes necessary to form an intermediate image. An intermediate image (InIm) is an image that may be equivalent to the original one. This work is devoted to the description of possible mechanisms for the formation of intermediate images.

To verify the identity of the original and intermediate images, a comparison is made of the sets of their functions of the area of intersection with a given accuracy. If no match is found, then it is necessary to conduct a learning process to put this object in the array of etalons. Training can take place both with the teacher and on the basis of the classification of existing etalons. If no match is found for all possible InIm options, and the image recovery system has no memory, then the image cannot be restored.

In general, the image recovery process will be a sequence of actions, which is shown in Figure 1.

This chapter will focus on the process of reconstructing convex binary images. Any image in the process of segmentation can be represented by a set of convex figures.

A necessary condition for the convexity of the figures in terms of using the parallel shift technology is the following. Each subsequent value of each FAI, which form the reference surface, must be less than the previous one.

$$FAI(i+1) < FAI(i) \tag{1}$$

The first check of the set of functions of the area of intersection, which describes the original figure, should be a check for convexity.

Figure 1. Sequence of actions at the process of image restoration

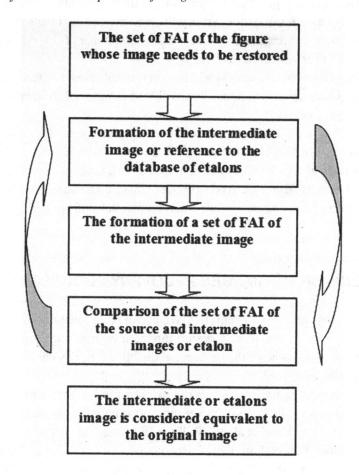

FORMATION OF INTERMIDIATE IMAGES

The process of forming intermediate convex binary images can be organized in two ways. One way is to fill a convex contour (Belan 2011, Kozhemyako at al. 2001) with unit elements. In this case, it is necessary to organize the formation of this contour, using the data of the set of FAI of the original image. The second method is based on the selection of a subset of elements that make up the original shape from the set of all elements of the visual area. In both cases, it is necessary to limit the search area for the location of the elements of the original figure. Such a restriction may be a rectangle that circumscribes the image.

Since the description of images on the basis of PST is invariant relative to the location in the area of the receptor field, the presence of parameters of the circumscribe rectangle (A and B) will reduce the area of manipulation with the elements of the figure during restoration. A and B are the lengths of the sides of the circumscribe rectangle (CR). This area will have the size A×B, where $A \geq X_{max}$, $B \geq Y_{max}$. If X_{max} is the maximum shift in the α direction, then Y_{max} is the maximum shift in the $\alpha + 90°$ direction.

To obtain the parameters of the circumscribe rectangle from the data of the FAIs set, we will use a simple property, which is shown in Figure 2 and in formula 2. Hereinafter, we will call a similar original figure a test figure.

Figure 2. The property of equality of areas of figure and its copies

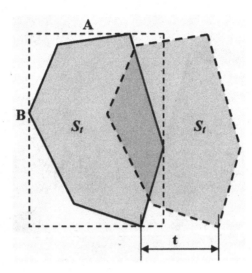

$$S_t = S_0 - FAI(t) \tag{2}$$

When a copy of an image is shifted, the areas of the original figure and its copies that are not included in the area of their intersection are equal. The size of this area is related to the function of the area of intersection. Imagine the area parameter as the sum of the set of elements with a unit area. Then these areas correspond to the sum of the elements of the original image that were not included in the set consisting of the intersection of the figure and its copy at a certain moment of shift.

The contour of a convex figure can be considered formed by a pair of limiting functions. If the shift direction changes, we get a new pair of limiting functions. The original figure is bounded by the functions $f_1(x)$ and $f_2(x)$ for the direction of the vertical shift. An example of the image of these functions is presented in Figure 3.

Restrictive functions can be associated with specific parts of the image. Use the property equal areas at shift to do this. This property when shifted vertically is shown in Figure 4.

When shifts horizontally figure bounded by the functions $f_4(y)$ and $f_5(y)$. An example of the image of these functions is presented in Figure 5.

Figure 3. Example of Bounding Functions for Vertical Shift

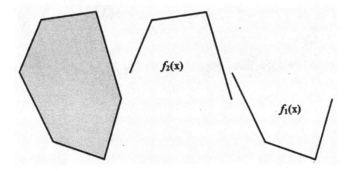

Figure 4. Equal areas for vertical shift

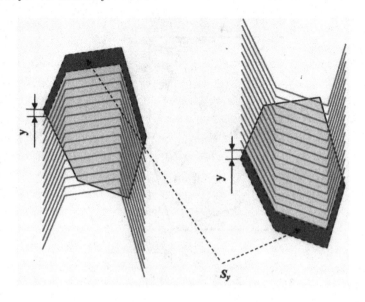

Figure 5. Example of Bounding Functions for horizontal Shift

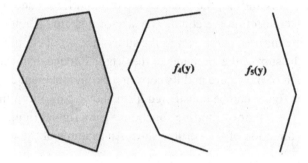

Figure 6. Equal areas for horizontal shift

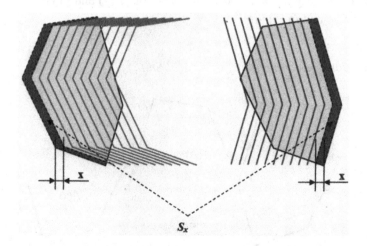

The property of areas equality when shifting vertically is shown in Figure 6.

The smaller the shift distance in a given direction, the more accurately the limiting functions of those parts of the image that are not included in the intersection area reflect the bounding functions. The thickness of the area is determined by the size of some single element. It depends on the properties of the image processing system during the shift process. This property is typical for non-raster graphics.

For raster graphics, the shift distance cannot be less than a sampling unit. Then limiting function displays the figure contour thickness of one pixel.

Formulas 3 and 4 display the circumscribed rectangle parameters for the selected direction.

When shifting vertically:

$$A = S_0 - FAI(y), \tag{3}$$

where $y=1$.

When shifting horizontally:

$$B = S_0 - FAI(x), \tag{4}$$

where $x=1$.

Here is an example to confirm these findings (Figure 7). Suppose we have orthogonally disposed rectangle of size 3×4.

$$S_0 = 12 \; FAI(y) = 9 \; FAI(x) = 8$$

Then $A = 12 - 9 = 3$, $B = 12 - 8 = 4$.

Thus, it was determined that using the data obtained from the functions of the area of intersection, it is possible to calculate the parameters of the circumscribed rectangles. The lengths of their sides can be used in the process of restoring images. The parameters of the circumscribed rectangles can be defined for all directions, which are represented by the functions of the area of intersection of the input figure.

Figure 7. Example of defining circumscribed rectangle parameters

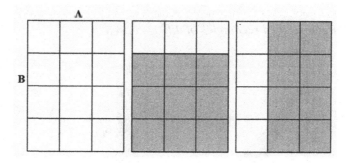

AREA OF CONSTRUCTION OF THE CONTOUR OF THE INTERMIDIATE IMAGE

A convex binary image can be restored by filling the contour with unit elements. To do this, we need to define the contour of the intermediate image. The contour of the *InIm* is located inside the circumscribed rectangles. Moreover, the contour can either touch the sides of each of them at one point, or coincide with some part of the side of the CR. For each side of the circumscribed rectangle, such a section can be only one. Otherwise, the figure described is not convex.

The length of the intersection depending on the side of the circumscribed rectangle will be from 1 to A_i (B_i). The unit of measurement for the digital image will be a value dependent on the discretization. For a non-raster image, this value is selected in accordance with the parameters of the image processing system.

The search for points of intersection must be made on the sides of the circumscribed rectangle. The size of the circumscribed rectangle should be the minimum to minimize the number of options for the location of these points.

$$S_{\min} = \min(A_0 B_0, ..., A_i B_i, ..., A_{n-1} B_{n-1}),$$ (5)

where n is the total number of circumscribed rectangles.

In this case $A_i B_i > A_j B_j$.

The circumscribed rectangle with the minimum area will be considered orthogonal. In accordance with this, all the angles of rotation (Belan at al. 2013) α_i are recalculated. So, if the area of the circumscribed rectangle number 3 (the rotation angle α_3) is minimal, then all the CR numbers and rotation angles are reduced by 3. $CR_i \equiv A_i B_i$ becomes $CR_{i-3} \equiv A_{i-3} B_{i-3}$, and α_i becomes α_{i-3}. Due to cyclicity of the set of FAIs, the CR_i with numbers less than indicated (3) pass to the end of the list of rectangles. For example, $A_2 B_2$ becomes $A_{n-2} B_{n-2}$, and α_2 becomes α_{n-2}. Thus, the contour points location area should be located inside the circumscribed rectangle with the minimum area value.

There are other criteria limiting contour points location area. We can use the property of equality of areas, shown in Fig.2. Let's imagine in the form of a histogram the parts of the image that are not included in the area of intersection of the image and its copy during the shift. Such histograms for the horizontal direction of the shift are shown in Figure 9.

Figure 8. Example of circumscribed rectangles of different area

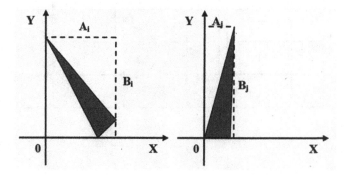

Figure 9. Transformation of the image parts into histograms

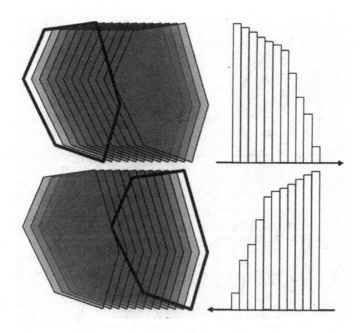

In this case, a shift of the copy of the image is shown both to the right and to the left. Parts of the image of the same brightness are transformed into sections of the histogram with the same area. The shift step Δx is chosen large enough to better demonstrate the transformation process. The values of the height of the sections of the histogram (h_i) are taken from formula 6.

$$h_i = FAI(x_i) - FAI(x_{i+1}) \tag{6}$$

where $x_{i+1} - x_i = \Delta x$.

If the value $\Delta x \rightarrow 0$, then the histograms are transformed into some functions. The histogram of horizontal shift to the right in Figure 9 in Figure 10 corresponds to the function $y=f_8(x)$. Its values (7) for each i-th point of the argument are equal to the value h_i from formula 6.

$$f_8(x) = FAI(x) - FAI(x+1) \tag{7}$$

The corresponding function for a vertical shift is called $f_7(y)$.

$$f_7(y) = FAI(y) - FAI(y+1) \tag{8}$$

The function $f_8(x)$ is obtained from the function $f_6(y)$ by aligning the bottom edge of the image bounded by the function $f_6(y)$ and the axis 0Y. The function $f_7(y)$ is obtained from the function $f_3(x)$ by aligning the left edge of the image bounded by the function $f_3(x)$ and the axis 0X. The area of images that are limited to the functions $f_7(y)$ and $f_8(x)$ is equal to the area of the original image.

Figure 10. Formation of the resulting functions

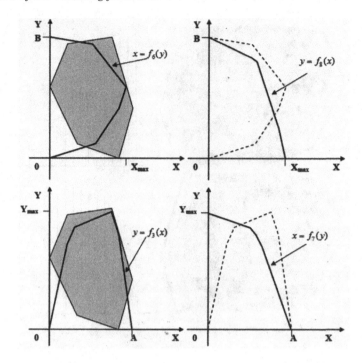

In turn, the functions $f_6(y)$ and $f_3(x)$ depend on the functions forming the contour (Fig. 3, Fig. 5).

$$f_3(x) = f_2(x) - f_1(x) \tag{9}$$

$$f_6(y) = f_5(y) - f_4(y) \tag{10}$$

The functions $f_7(y)$ and $f_8(x)$ are called the resulting functions (RF).Images that limit by these functions and coordinate axes are called resulting images (RI). The relationship between the values of the FAIs of the resulting functions, and functions that are based on the elements of the contour of the figure is shown in formulas 11 and 12.

$$FAI(x) = \int\limits_{x}^{X_{max}} f_8(x)dx = \int\limits_{y_1}^{y_2} f_6(y)dy - x \cdot (y_2 - y_1), \tag{11}$$

where $\begin{cases} x = f_6(y_1) \\ x = f_6(y_2) \end{cases}$ and $f_8(x) = y_2 - y_1$

$$FAI(y) = \int\limits_{y}^{Y_{max}} f_7(y)dy = \int\limits_{x_1}^{x_2} f_3(x)dx - y \cdot (x_2 - x_1), \tag{12}$$

where $\begin{cases} y = f_3(x_1) \\ y = f_3(x_2) \end{cases}$ and $f_7(y) = x_2 - x_1$

The value of the area of the initial figure, expressed through these functions, is shown in formula 13.

$$S_0 = \int_0^B f_6(y)dy = \int_0^A f_3(x)dx = \int_0^{X_{max}} f_8(x)dx = \int_0^{Y_{max}} f_7(y)dy \tag{13}$$

In the course of a series of parallel shifts, we obtain two sequences of three images. The first one is the original image. Denote its index as 1. The second in each sequence is an image that is shifted once horizontally or vertically. It is bounded by the function $f_6(y)$ and the axis 0Y or the function $f_3(x)$ and the axis 0X. In the first case, we denote its index as 2h. In the second case, we denote its index as 2v. The indexes of the corresponding resulting images are called 3v and 3h. Image 3v is bounded by the function $f_8(x)$. Image 3h is bounded by the function $f_7(y)$. All indexes consist of the image number in the sequence and the first letter of the name of the last direction of the shift during alignment. Let's consider the equality of the FAIs of figures where the elements are located equally in the direction of the shift. Then the relationship between the FAIs of all figures is shown in the system of equations 14.

$$\begin{cases} FAI_{3v}(x) = FAI_{2h}(x) = FAI_1(x) \\ FAI_{3v}(y) = FAI_{2h}(y) \\ FAI_{3h}(y) = FAI_{2v}(y) = FAI_1(y) \\ FAI_{3h}(x) = FAI_{2v}(x) \end{cases} \tag{14}$$

The coordinates of the centers mass of the resulting images (x_{cm3h} and y_{cm3h}, x_{cm3v} and y_{cm3v}) are determined from the system of equations 15.

$$\begin{cases} \dfrac{S_0}{2} = FAI_{3v}(x) = \displaystyle\int_0^{x_{cm3v}} f_8(x)dx = \int_{x_{cm3v}}^{X_{max}} f_8(x)dx \\[2mm] \dfrac{S_0}{2} = FAI_{3v}(y) = \displaystyle\int_0^{y_{cm3v}} f_8^T(y)dy = \int_{y_{cm3v}}^{B} f_8^T(y)dy \\[2mm] \dfrac{S_0}{2} = FAI_{3h}(x) = \displaystyle\int_0^{x_{cm3h}} f_7^T(x)dx = \int_{x_{cm3h}}^{A} f_7^T(x)dx \\[2mm] \dfrac{S_0}{2} = FAI_{3h}(y) = \displaystyle\int_0^{y_{cm3h}} f_7(y)dy = \int_{y_{cm3h}}^{Y_{max}} f_7(y)dy \end{cases} \tag{15}$$

The function $f_7^T(x)$ is the transposed function $f_7(y)$. The function $f_8^T(y)$ is the transposed function $f_8(x)$. All parameters of these equations can be determined from the set of the FAIs of the original figure.

The coordinates of the centers of mass of the images after the first alignment (x_{cm2h} and y_{cm2h}, x_{cm2v} and y_{cm2v}) are as follows.

$$x_{cm2h} = x_{cm3v} \tag{16}$$

$$\begin{cases} y_{cm2h} = y_{cm3v} + f_1(x_{cm3v}) \\ \dfrac{S_0}{2} = \displaystyle\int_0^{y_{cm2h}} f_6(y)dy = \int_{y_{cm2h}}^{B} f_6(y)dy \end{cases} \tag{17}$$

$$\begin{cases} x_{cm2v} = x_{cm3h} + f_4(y_{cm3h}) \\ \dfrac{S_0}{2} = \displaystyle\int_0^{x_{cm2v}} f_3(x)dx = \int_{x_{cm2v}}^{A} f_3(x)dx \end{cases} \tag{18}$$

$$y_{cm2v} = y_{cm3h} \tag{19}$$

The coordinates of the center of mass of the initial image (x_{cm} and y_{cm}) are obtained from the following formulas.

$$x_{cm} = x_{cm2v} = x_{cm2h} + f_4(y_{cm2h}) = x_{cm3v} + f_4(y_{cm2h}) = x_{cm3h} + f_4(y_{cm3h}) \tag{20}$$

$$y_{cm} = y_{cm2h} = y_{cm2v} + f_1(x_{cm2v}) = y_{cm3h} + f_1(x_{cm2v}) = y_{cm3v} + f_1(x_{cm3v}) \tag{21}$$

The function $f_4(y)$ at a point $y = y_{cm}$ can take values from zero to $A - x_{cm3h}$.
The function $f_1(x)$ at a point $x = x_{cm}$ can take values from zero to $B - y_{cm3v}$.
We don't know the exact meaning of these functions.

The center of mass is the unchanged point if no affine transformations occur to the image. Further, the chapter will describe the use the center of mass of the image for superposition the circumscribed rectangles. The ability to analytically determine the center of mass of the image is necessary when restoring images. When creating a FAIs set, we should use another method of its search, which is described in previous works (Belan at al. 2013c, Bilan at al. 2018). However, its analytical calculation is possible only for convex images.

In the example above, the resulting functions are obtained by shifting the elements of the original image "left then down" ($f_8(x)$) and "down then left" ($f_7(y)$). Alignment of elements can be made by the CR boundaries. If we change the order and direction of the shift in the area that is limited by the circumscribed rectangle, then we can get three more figures similar to the resulting images. An example of four such figures for shifts "left then down", "right then down", "left then up", "right then up" is shown in Figure 11. We denote them MX1, MX2, MX3, MX4.

Four similar result images for the first shift in the vertical direction are obtained similarly. We denote them MY1, MY2, MY3, MY4.

Elements of all eight resulting images are elements of the original figure. These elements are subjected to several parallel shifts. The common area of intersection of these sets is called the mutual set (MS).

$$MS_0 = MX1 \cap MX2 \cap MX3 \cap MX4 \cap MY1 \cap MY2 \cap MY3 \cap MY4 \tag{22}$$

Figure 11. Similar resulting images

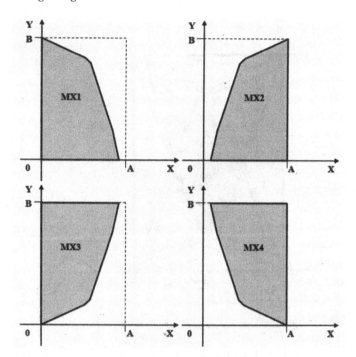

The construction of a mutual set for a test figure with $\alpha = 0°$ is shown in Figure 12.

Elements of a mutual set are located inside the original image. MS is a subset of the elements that make up the initial figure. The points that are included in the MS area belong to the original image. The contour consists of elements located on the edge of the figure. Therefore, the figures contour points may coincide with the contour of the mutual set. The presence of MS_i set, the area of construction of the contour of the intermediate image is decreases.

For this example, this area is shown in Fig. 13. It corresponds to the gray area.

The mutual set MS_i can be calculated for all directions α for which there exist sets of the FAIs of the initial figure. Then the area of construction of the contour of the intermediate figure will decrease by some area MS.

$$MS = \sum_{i=0}^{n-1} MS_i , \qquad (23)$$

where n is a half of the set of the FAIs of the initial figure.

Extreme variants of the formation of a mutual set exist for the following source images. For triangles all $MS_i = \varnothing$. For an orthogonally located rectangle $MS_i = A_iB_i$. However, these figures will be classified as simple at the recognition stage (Chen at al. 1995, Belan at al. 2013c, Bilan et al. 2018). Their parameters will be determined analytically. Therefore, to restore such images by methods that are considered in this chapter will not be necessary.

Figure 12. Constructing a common MS_0 set for a test figure with $\alpha = 0°$

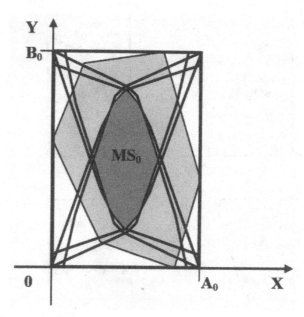

Figure 13. The area of construction of the image contour points considering MS_0

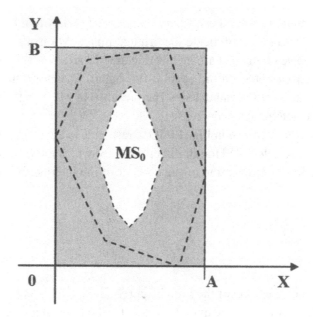

Analogically, when searching the coordinates of the center of mass of the original figure to consider the presence of similar resulting image. Four variants of the resulting image with the last vertical shift (MX1, MX2, MX3, MX4) produce two options for the y_{cm} coordinate:

$$y_{cm3v} + f_1(x_{cm3v}) \text{ and } B - (y_{cm3v} + f_1(x_{cm3v})).$$

Four variants of the resulting image with the last horizontal shift (MY1, MY2, MY3, MY4) produce two options for the x_{cm} coordinate:

$$x_{cm3h} + f_4(y_{cm3h}) \text{ and } A - (x_{cm3h} + f_4(y_{cm3h})).$$

The values of the functions $f_1(x)$ and $f_4(y)$ are not known. Let's consider them equal to zero. In this case, the area of possible location of the center of mass of the original figure is maximal and bounded by a rectangle. Its sides lie on such straight lines.

$$\begin{cases} x = x_{cm3h} \\ x = A - x_{cm3h} \\ y = y_{cm3v} \\ y = B - y_{cm3v} \end{cases} \tag{24}$$

The area of the possible location of the center of mass of the initial figure for the i-th circumscribed rectangle (S_{cmi}) is determined from the following formula.

$$S_{cmi} = (A_i - 2x_{cm3hi})(B_i - 2y_{cm3vi}) \tag{25}$$

The area of construction of the contour of the intermediate image can also be reduced by defining the area of intersection of all possible circumscribed rectangles. Methods of their correct placement will be discussed later. They are the basis for restoring convex images by the method of circumscribed rectangles.

FORMATION OF THE CONTOUR OF THE INTERMIDIATE IMAGE

When constructing the contour of the intermediate image, the starting point is searched. This point is selected on one of the sides of the circumscribed rectangle.

At the points of contact of the contour and the circumscribed rectangle, the values of $f_3(x)$ and $f_6(y)$ are as follows.

Figure 14. The points of contact of the circumscribed rectangle with the contour of the image

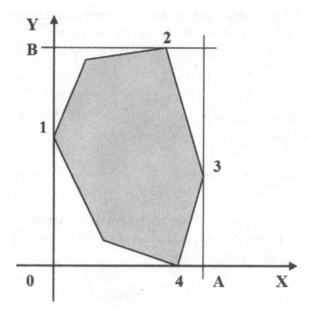

$$
\begin{cases}
x_1 = f_4(y_1) = 0 \\
y_1 = f_1(x_1) = f_2(x_1) \\
f_3(x_1) = 0 \\
f_6(y_1) = f_5(y_1) \\
x_2 = f_4(y_2) = f_5(y_2) \\
y_2 = f_2(x_2) = B \\
f_3(x_2) = B - f_1(x_2) \\
f_6(y_2) = 0 \\
x_3 = f_5(y_3) = A \\
y_3 = f_1(x_3) = f_2(x_3) \\
f_3(x_3) = 0 \\
f_6(y_3) = A - f_4(y_3) \\
x_4 = f_4(y_4) = f_5(y_4) \\
y_4 = f_1(x_4) = 0 \\
f_3(x_4) = f_2(x_4) \\
f_6(y_4) = 0
\end{cases}
\tag{26}
$$

It should be noted that for a convex image, the horizontal size of the figure for at least one of the points of contact with the coordinates (x_1, y_1) or (x_3, y_3) will be equal to X_{max}. And for the vertical direction at least for one of the points of contact with the coordinates (x_2, y_2) or (x_4, y_4) it will be equal to Y_{max}. The area of possible location of points of contact coincides with the contour of the circumscribed rectangle. To minimize this area the circumscribed rectangle with the smallest area (5) should be considered as orthogonally located. The points of contact also belong to the contour of the original image. Therefore, the area of their location can be minimized due to the correct location of a set of circumscribed rectangles.

Formation of the contour of the intermediate image is carried out by search all of possible options for the location of its elements. The search is performed in an area that is limited to the common area of intersection of all the circumscribed rectangles and does not include the set of MS elements.

FORMATION OF THE INTERMIDIATE IMAGES BY THE METOD OF CIRCUMSCRIBED RECTANGLES

The possible dimensions of the intersection area for each possible pair of the circumscribed rectangles have the following property.

$$A_i B_i \cap A_j B_j = S_{ij} \geq S_0 \tag{27}$$

Figure 15 shows the intersection of three circumscribed rectangles for rotation angles relative to the vertical $\alpha = 0°$, $\alpha = 15°$ and $\alpha = 45°$.

The greatest possible number of circumscribed rectangles should be used for the most accurate figures shape recovery.

Figure 15. The intersection of three circumscribed rectangles

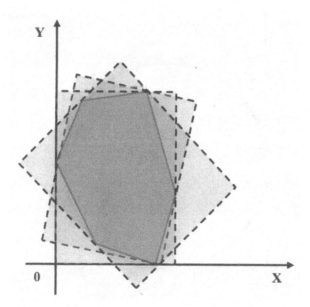

Let the intermediate image be denoted In Image, and the i-th circumscribed rectangle be denoted CR_i, then image is formed as follows.

$$Inimage = CR_0 \cap CR_1 \cap ... \cap CR_i \cap ... \cap CR_{n-1}, \tag{28}$$

where n is number of circumscribed rectangles.

The main problem with the location of the circumscribed rectangles in the visual area is to properly place the intersection points of the diagonals of each of them. These points coincide with the centers of mass of the corresponding circumscribed rectangles. The location of the intersection points of the diagonals of the circumscribed rectangles is the same for figures that have the property of central symmetry. For example, for a circle, the intersection of three CR_i is shown in Figure 16.

C_i is the intersection point of the diagonals of the i-th circumscribed rectangle. C_0 is the center of mass of the CR_0 with orthogonally located sides.

For images without central symmetry, the centers of mass of the circumscribed rectangles and the center of mass of the original figure do not coincide. The main task for this method of image restoration is to accurately select their location. Further studies are directed at minimizing the area of possible location of the intersection points of the diagonals of the circumscribed rectangles.

Depending on the shape of the figure, the circumscribed rectangles can be located inside a certain area called the outer rectangle (OR). The outer rectangle is indicated by a dash-dotted line, and the circumscribed rectangles are indicated by dashed lines in Figure 17. The sides of the i-th outer rectangle pass through the corners of the circumscribed rectangle CR_0 and are parallel to the sides of CR_i. The intersection point of the diagonals of CR_0 and the centers of mass of all OR_i coincide. This point is marked with C in Figure 17. The intersection point of the diagonals of the circumscribed rectangle C_i, depending on the shape of the original figure, can be at any point of the rectangle which bounded by lines of the central range.

Figure 16. An example of the intersection of three CR_i for a circle

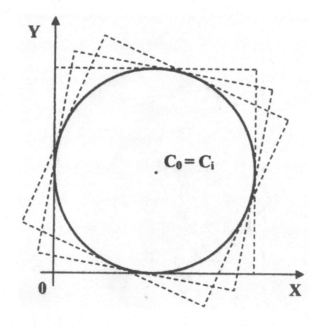

Figure 17. Forming the area of possible location of the intersection point of the diagonals of the circumscribed rectangle CR$_i$

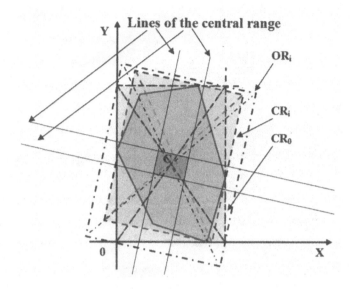

The outer rectangle for the direction of shift $\alpha = 45°$ for any shapes will be a square, the diagonals of which are orthogonal (Figure 18).

Formulas 29 and 30 show the interrelation of the parameters of the outer rectangle (A_{ORi}, B_{ORi}), the parameters of the circumscribed rectangles (A_0, B_0, A_i, B_i), the parameters of the rectangle, which is bounded by lines of the central range (A_{Ci}, B_{Ci}).

$$A_{ORi} = Ac_i + A_i = A_0 \cos\alpha + B_0 \sin\alpha \qquad (29)$$

$$B_{ORi} = Bc_i + B_i = B_0 \cos\alpha + A_0 \sin\alpha \qquad (30)$$

The initial figure is inside the area defined by the circumscribed rectangles (CR$_i$). In turn, the circumscribed rectangles are located inside the corresponding outer rectangles.

The dimensions of the rectangle, which is bounded by the lines of the central range, depend on the angle of rotation of the i-th circumscribed rectangle relative to the orthogonal OR$_0$. They increase from zero at the angle of rotation $\alpha = 0°$, become maximum at $\alpha = 45°$, and again decrease to zero at $\alpha = 90°$. It is necessary that the sizes of the rectangles, which are bounded by the lines of the central range, be minimal to minimize the number of calculations. For this, the base rotation angle α (equal to zero) should be associated with a circumscribed rectangle with the smallest area (5). On the basis of its parameters all the other calculations are made.

There is one more circumstance that minimizes the size of the possible localization area of the centers of the circumscribed rectangles. Each of the sides of these rectangles intersects with the sides of the other CR at several points. Intersection options are two: at one point or two points.

Figure 18. The outer rectangle for the direction of shift α = 45°

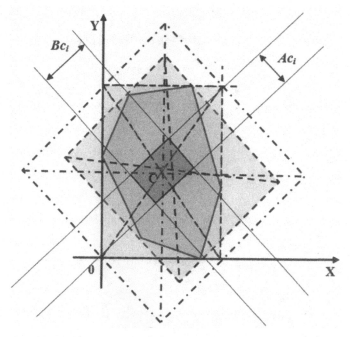

For next calculations, it is necessary to determine the possible location of the intersection centers of the diagonals of the circumscribed rectangles relative to CR_0. Consider an example of the possible location of the i-th circumscribed rectangle for a rotation angle α = 15° for a test figure.

Here the lower right corner of the rectangle, which is bounded by the lines of the central range, coincides with the intersection point of the diagonals of the circumscribed rectangle. However, the point of contact between this circumscribed rectangle and the top side of the CR_0 is missing.

Sometimes there is such location of the i-th circumscribed rectangle inside the outer rectangle that the intersection of some sides of CR_i and CR_0 is absent (Figure 19). Then an adjustment is needed.

$$\Delta B_i = \begin{cases} \dfrac{B_i}{\cos \alpha_i} - B_0, & if \left(\dfrac{B_i}{\cos \alpha_i} - B_0 \right) > 0 \\[3mm] 0, & if \left(\dfrac{B_i}{\cos \alpha_i} - B_0 \right) \leq 0 \end{cases} \tag{31}$$

$$\Delta A_i = \begin{cases} \dfrac{A_i}{\cos \alpha_i} - A_0, & if \left(\dfrac{A_i}{\cos \alpha_i} - A_0 \right) > 0 \\[3mm] 0, & if \left(\dfrac{A_i}{\cos \alpha_i} - A_0 \right) \leq 0 \end{cases} \tag{32}$$

Figure 19. An example of the possible location of the i-th circumscribed rectangle for a rotation angle α = 15° for a test figure

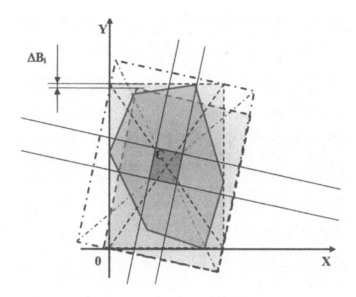

Adjusting the area of possible location of the intersection point of the diagonals CR_i is carried out in the following way. The upper and lower corners of the area bounded by the lines of the central range are shifting on ΔB_i down and up respectively. The left and right corners of the area bounded by the lines of the central range are shifting on ΔA_i to the right and left respectively.

The result of the correction will be a certain area in the form of a parallelogram (CP_i), which may contain the center of the i-th circumscribed rectangle. An example of such area for a test image with α = 45° is shown in Figure 20. In this case $\Delta A_i = 0$.

The area (Scp_i) of each CP_i will be next.

$$Scp_i = Ac_i Bc_i - 2(Bc_i \Delta B_i \sin\alpha + Ac_i \Delta A_i \cos\alpha - 2\Delta A_i \Delta B_i \sin(2\alpha)) \tag{33}$$

The mutual location of the circumscribed rectangles is defined in two ways. The first is the search for the center of mass of the original figure. The second is the search for the coordinates of the intersection points of the diagonals for all CR_i. In both cases it is necessary to choose too much of the options. All calculations must be made in the coordinate system of the circumscribed rectangle with orthogonally located sides.

Let, depending on the discretization, Ncmi of the points of the nodes of the coordinate grid be into the area of the center of mass for the i-th circumscribed rectangle. Its area is Scm_i (25). Then the number of options for mutual location of the centers of mass of all the circumscribed rectangles (Ncm) will be as follows.

$$Ncm = \prod_{i=0}^{n-1} Ncm_i \tag{34}$$

Figure 20. The area of possible location of the center of the circumscribed rectangle

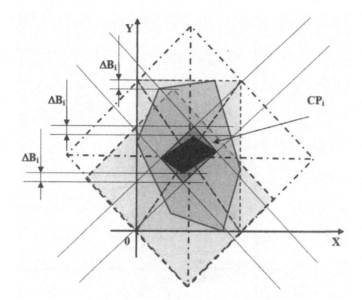

$$Scm = \prod_{i=0}^{n-1} Scm_i \qquad (35)$$

where n is the number of the circumscribed rectangles. If the step of rotation angle for the circumscribed rectangles is 5°, then n = 18.

When searching for the coordinates of the points of intersection of the diagonals of the circumscribed rectangles, depending on the discretization, the Ncpi of the points of the coordinate grid be into the CP_i construction area. Its area is Scp_i (33). Then the number of options for mutual location of the intersection points of the diagonals of all the circumscribed rectangles (Ncp) will be as follows.

$$Ncp = \prod_{i=1}^{n-1} Ncp_i \qquad (36)$$

$$Scp = \prod_{i=1}^{n-1} Scp_i \qquad (37)$$

where n is the number of the circumscribed rectangles. The coordinates of the intersection point of the diagonals for orthogonally located CR_0 are known.

To minimize the number of choices should be compared the values of Ncm and Ncp values for raster images. For non-raster images, compare the Scm and Scp values. The minimum of these parameters will indicate how to determine the mutual location of the CR. For each of the variants necessary to build an intermediate image and define a set of functions of the area of intersection. It is necessary to perform a large number of operations in both cases.

THE COMBINATION OF THE CENTERS OF MASS OF INTERMIDIATE IMAGES

The above methods for determining the relative position of the circumscribed rectangles should be used if the reference surface of a figure without additional data (Bilan et al. 2014) is at the system input. We can determine the initial area (S_0), the maximum shift (X_{max}) and the shape of the FAI for each direction directly from the data of the reference surface. It is necessary to add the parameter cmr (center mass ratio) to this information.

$$cmr = \frac{x_{cm}}{X_{max}},$$ (38)

where x_{cm} is the coordinate of the center of mass for a corresponding direction α.

Then for each circumscribed rectangle you can determine the coordinates of the center of mass depending on the actual size of the initial figure.

$$x_{cmi} = cmr_i X_{max\,i}$$ (39)

The y_{cmi} coordinate is determined from the data for the $\alpha + 90°$ direction. If the step of angle of rotation for the FAIs, which make up the reference surface, is 5°, then their number is 36. Due to the possession of the property of central symmetry, the data set of this functions is defined for the directions α from zero to π.

$$y_{cmi} = cmr_{i+18} X_{max\,i+18}$$ (40)

The obtained coordinates for each i-th circumscribed rectangle are calculated relative to the coordinate system of this rectangle. The point zero for each of them coincides with the lower left corner of this rectangle. To combine the centers of mass (cm_i) of all CRi, it is necessary to recalculate their coordinates relative to the CR_0. Its sides are orthogonal. An example of combining the centers of mass of the CR_0 and some i-th circumscribed rectangle is shown in Figure 21.

If we know the coordinates of the centers of mass of all the circumscribed rectangles (x_{cmi} and y_{cmi}), then we can combine all these rectangles in one coordinate system.

For convex figures, the intersection area of all the circumscribed rectangles with a given accuracy must correspond to the shape of the original figure. For non-convex images, the intersection of all CR_i is the area within which the original figure is located.

IMAGE RECOVERY ALGORITHM

Thus, the image recovery algorithm by a set of FAIs will be as follows.

1. Get a set of FAIs of image that needs to be restored.
2. Carry out the process of image recognition using the available reference surfaces.

Figure 21. An example of combining the centers of mass of the circumscribed rectangles

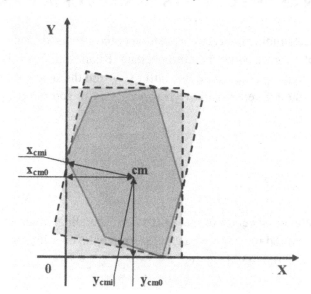

3. If the image is not found among the standards, then calculate the sides of the circumscribed rectangles for all directions of the angles of rotation of the CR (A_i, B_i).

4. Determine the coordinates of the centers of mass of each of them (x_{cmi} and y_{cmi}).

5. Combine the circumscribed rectangles, assuming that their diagonals intersect at one point.

6. Build an intermediate image and calculate its area.

7. Compare the area of the intermediate image with S_0 with a given accuracy. If there is no match, then the found intermediate image does not possess the property of central symmetry and is not equal to the original figure. Then go to step 15 of the algorithm. If there is a match, then go to step 8 of the algorithm.

8. Build the functions of the area of intersection of the intermediate image for all directions.

9. Compare these sets of FAIs with the obtained set of FAIs of the original figure with a given accuracy.

10. If the FAIs set of the initial figure for all directions coincide with a given accuracy with the obtained functions, then the initial image is considered equivalent to this intermediate figure.

11. Otherwise, using the methods of combining the circumscribed rectangles or the coordinates of the centers of mass, construct an intermediate image and calculate its area.

12. Compare the area of the intermediate image with S_0 with a given accuracy. If there is no match, then the found intermediate image is not equal to the original figure. Then go to step 15 of the algorithm. If there is a match, then go to step 13 of the algorithm.

13. Build the functions of the area of intersection of the intermediate image for all directions.

14. Compare these sets of FAIs with the obtained set of FAIs of the original figure with a given accuracy.

15. If the functions of the FAIs set of the original figure for all directions coincide with a given accuracy with the obtained functions, then the image is considered equivalent to this intermediate figure. Otherwise, it is necessary to change the accuracy of the function comparison or image discretization and repeat steps 11÷14 of the algorithm.

16. If the image could not be restored, then it is necessary to form a new reference surface from the set of initial FAIs and perform the learning process.

Figure 22. Example of a non-convex image and its construction area

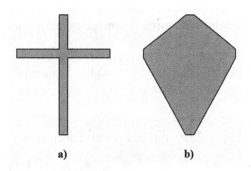

a)   b)

The possibility of comparing the areas of the intermediate image and the original figure (S_0) will in many cases avoid the formation of a set of FAIs and their further processing. This will reduce the number of performed operations.

Restoration of a convex binary image is possible using this algorithm. The method of circumscribed rectangles will only determine the image contour search area for non-convex images. For example, this method for the image from Figure 22a will determine the area bounded by Figure 22b.

Non-convex images can be restored in several ways. The original image can be segmented to form a set of convex shapes. After the restoration of these images, they should be combined into one using structural recognition methods (Fu 1982).

We can use the fact that at a certain stage of the shift the intersection area of a non-convex figure and its copies can be a convex figure. Then its FAI in the given direction of shift (α), from the current distance of shift (x) and to the point of maximum shift (X_{max}) will coincide with the FAI of the source image.

For the method of filling the contour with single elements, it is necessary to make for many selections of variants of contour construction. Points of contact with an orthogonally located circumscribed rectangle should be sought at the intersection of the contour of this rectangle and the area determined by the method of circumscribed rectangles. This method can also be used to restore non-convex figures.

The principles of information processing will be similar in the case of data recovery of volumetric images. A component of the third dimension will appear in all formulas. We need to carry out a shift in three directions to obtain the resulting volumetric images.

This chapter discusses the possibility of recovering convex binary images using parallel shift technology. Restoration of convex figures is the basis for the restoration of images of any type.

CONCLUSION

Each self-sufficient information processing system should include tools for performing certain tasks. The parallel shift technology in image processing should have mechanisms for the recovery of objects. This chapter describes how to restore convex images. Of course, there are more advanced methods for image restoration. However, for TPS it is the first steps in this direction. Most of the issues raised need to be improved. Further work on the research of parallel shear technology will be aimed to this.

REFERENCES

Belan, S. (2011). Specialized cellular structures for image contour analysis. *Cybernetics and Systems Analysis, 47*(5), 695-704.

Belan, S., & Belan, N. (2012). Use of Cellular Automata to Create an Artificial System of Image Classification and Recognition. *LNCS, 7495*, 483-493.

Belan, S., & Belan, N. (2013). *Temporal-Impulse Description of Complex Image Based on Cellular Automata. In PaCT2013, LNCS* (Vol. 7979, pp. 291–295). Springer-Verlag Berlin Heidelberg.

Belan, S., & Yuzhakov, S. (2013b). A Homogenous Parameter Set for Image Recognition Based on Area. Computer and Information Science, 6(2), 93-102.

Belan, S., & Yuzhakov, S. (2013c). Machine Vision System Based on the Parallel Shift Technology and Multiple Image Analysis. Computer and Information Science, 6(4), 115-124.

Belan, S. N., & Motornyuk, R. L. (2013a). Extraction of characteristic features of images with the help of the radon transform and its hardware implementation in terms of cellular automata. Cybernetics and Systems Analysis, 49(1), 7-14.

Bilan, S., & Yuzhakov, S. (2018). *Image Processing and Pattern Recognition Based on Parallel Shift Technology*. Boca Raton, FL: CRC Press.

Bilan, S., Yuzhakov, S., & Bilan, S. (2014). Saving of Etalons in Image Processing Systems Based on the Parallel Shift Technology. Advances in Image and Video Processing, 2(6), 36-41.

Chen, C. H., Rau, L. F., & Wang, P. S. P. (1995). *Handbook of pattern recognition and computer vision*. Singapore: World Scientific Publishing Co. Pte. Ltd.

Fu, K. S. (1982). *Syntactic pattern recognition and applications*. Prentice-Hall.

Gonzalez, R. C., Woods, R. E., & Eddins, S. L. (2004). *Digital Image Processing using MATLAB*. Pearson Prentice Hall.

Kozhemyako, V., Bilan, S., & Savaliuk, I. (2001). Optoelectronic self-regulation neural system for treatment of vision information. *SPIE Proceedings, 3055*, 120–126.

Chapter 12
Methods for Extracting the Skeleton of an Image Based on Cellular Automata With a Hexagonal Coating Form and Radon Transform

Ruslan Leonidovich Motornyuk
PU "Kiev Department" Branch of the Main Information and Computing Center of the JSC "Ukrzaliznytsya", Ukraine

Stepan Bilan
iD https://orcid.org/0000-0002-2978-5556
State University of Infrastructure and Technology, Ukraine

ABSTRACT

The chapter describes a brief history of the emergence of the theory of cellular automata, their main properties, and methods for constructing. The image skeletonization methods based on the Euler zero differential are described. The advantages of using hexagonal coverage for detecting moving objects in the image are shown. The software and hardware implementation of the developed methods are presented. Based on the obtained results, a hexagonal-coated cellular automata was developed to identify images of objects based on the Radon transform. The method and mathematical model of the selection of characteristic features for the selection of the skeleton and implementation on cellular automata with a hexagonal coating are described. The Radon transform allowed to effectively extract the characteristic features of images with a large percentage of noise. An experiment for different images with different noises was conducted. Experimental analysis showed the advantages of the proposed methods of image processing and extraction of characteristic features.

DOI: 10.4018/978-1-7998-1290-6.ch012

THE HISTORICAL DEVELOPMENT OF THE PARALLEL COMPUTING PARADIGM OF CA

Due to the fact that the CA were repeatedly invented under different names, in many countries by people working in different fields of science, the terms "iterative arrays", "computing spaces," "homogeneous structures" and "cellular automata" are practically synonymous. At the same time, under one term ("cellular automaton"), there were different concepts. In pure mathematics, they can be found as one of the sections of topological dynamics, in electrical engineering they are sometimes called iterative arrays.

It is generally accepted that the concept of "cellular automata" (CA) was introduced in the late 40s of the last century by John von Neumann from Stanislaw Ulam works as formal models of the self-reproduction of organisms.

When Stanislaw Ulam began his research (Ulam, 1952), he could hardly imagine that, based on his ideas, an outstanding American scientist John von Neumann would introduce the concept of "cellular automaton".

Despite the fact that von Neumann was a mathematician and a physicist, the idea came to him when constructing an explanation of certain objects of biology. He used cellular automata that to create the more plausible models of spatially extended systems. Indeed, the mechanisms of self-reproduction structures on the cellular automaton that were proposed by them strongly resemble the regularities discovered in the next decade in biological systems are observed. The results of von Neumann's research are given, in particular, in the fundamental work (Neumann, 1951, Neumann, 1966). Its first edition appeared in 1966, while the author died in 1957. His student Arthur Burks, who became a famous specialist in the field of cellular automata, completed the book.

However, much earlier, at the end of the Second World War, while von Neumann was creating one of the first electronic computers, German engineer Konrad Zuse proposed a number of ideas that would make him one of the founders of the theory of parallel computing. His ideas at once became widely known.

Among other things, Zuse came up with "computational spaces" - CA (Zuse, 1969). His special interest was caused by the application of these systems to problems of numerical modeling in mechanics. Unfortunately, the situation in the world prevented the work of the scientist from obtaining propagation, while the work of von Neumann was watched by the entire scientific world.

Mathematicians came to cellular automata, considering iterative transformations of spatially-distributed structures with a discrete set of states (Hedlung, 1969). So there were appear "iterative arrays".

Immediately began to arise solutions to important theoretical problems in this area, for example, issues of reversibility, computability, attainability, etc.

In the group of computer logic at the University of Michigan, John Holland first used cellular automata to solve problems of adaptation and optimization (Holland, 1966).

Unfortunately, lack of discussions and of the common terminology led to a significant duplication of works. So the important characteristics of cellular automata, proved by Richardson [6] on twenty pages in the continuum substitution in the topology of Cantor sets, could be written in two lines as a consequence of the previous work of Hedlund (Hedlung, 1969).

The concept of "homogeneous structures" (Wolfram, 1986; Adamatzky, 1994; Adamatzky, 2010; Twelfth International Conference on Cellular Automata for Research and Industry, [ACRI 2016]) is extremely close to "cellular automata" in its origin and designates their hardware implementation, in which the key property of these systems is their homogeneity.

The effect of the exploded bomb was produced by the article of the leading of rubric of mathematical games and puzzles of the magazine "Scientific American" by Martin Gardner (Gardner, M. (1970). He published a description of the cellular automaton John Horton Conway called "Life". The game "Life" has become cult and has made the concept of "cellular automaton" an integral part of the everyday jargon of people with technical education.

Cellular automata form a general paradigm of parallel computations, just as Turing machines form the paradigm of sequential computations. As a result, they can be used to implement parallel algorithms, as models that have natural parallelism (Wolfram, 1986; Adamatzky, 1994; Adamatzky, 2010; 11th International Conference on Cellular Automata for Research and Industry [ACRI 2014]; Twelfth International Conference on Cellular Automata for Research and Industry, [ACRI 2016]).

It is unnecessary to mention that in our time the range of application of cellular automata is extremely wide (Adamatzky, 2010; 11th International Conference on Cellular Automata for Research and Industry [ACRI 2014]; Twelfth International Conference on Cellular Automata for Research and Industry, [ACRI 2016]; Bilan, 2017; Hadeler, & Müller, 2017; Steeb, 2014).

Stephen Wolfram made a major contribution to the development of the theory of CA. In his works he described the elementary cellular automata. On the basis of elementary cellular automata theory, Stephen Wolfram developed a theory of true randomness (Wolfram, 1986; Wolfram, 1986a; Wolfram, 1986b; Wolfram, 2002).Wolfram describes a set of rules that each the CA cell performs. He argues that all processes can be described using a set of rules on a cellular automaton. Stephen Wolfram examines the rules and indicates that rule 110 can be universal. Matthew Cook proved this assertion in the 1990 year (Cook, 2004; Cook, 2008).

In 1987, Brian Silverman proposed a Turing complete cellular automaton cakkecakedwerld (Dewdney, 1990).

Widely popular work by Stephen Wolfram under the name "A New Kind of Science". In this paper, he investigates one-dimensional, two-dimensional and three-dimensional cellular automata. Wolfram argues that the world is discrete and that it can be studied using a CA. Thanks to the theory of Wolfram, CA became very popular. The simple rules that Wolfram has proposed to this day are used to solve many problems.

Alonso-Sanz offered a CA with memory and conducted a wide analysis of their behavior and use (Alonso-Sanz, 2006; Alonso-Sanz, 2009; Alonso-Sanz, 2013).

Based on the obtained results, Gutowitz developed a statistical analysis for the classification of elementary cell automata of Wolfram (Gutowitz, Victor, & Knight, 1987). The same attempts were made by Li and Packard (Li, & Packard, 1990), Aizawa and Nishikawa (Aizawa, & Nishikawa, 1986) and Sutner (Sutner, 2009).

A. Adamatzky paid a lot of attention to the research of CA (Adamatzky, 1994). In his further works, he actively relies on the theory of CA. At present, CA are used in various fields of human activity. With their help, various dynamic processes are studied. They have special popularity in the image processing systems.

MODELS AND BASIC PROPERTIES OF CA

We call a space over a discrete set elements as a discrete. An instance of a space of this class will be called a lattice of CA, and each of its elements is called a cell. Each cell is characterized by a specific value from a certain set. About a cell is said that it contain an appropriate value, or is in a state encoded by this value.

The CA is a discrete dynamic system whose behavior is completely determined in terms of local dependencies. The set of states of all lattice cells is called a lattice state, which varies according to a certain law, called the CA rules. Each change in the lattice state is called as iteration.

The set of cells that influence its meaning, except for itself, is called the cell neighborhood. The cell neighborhood will be more convenient to choose if we introduce the metric of the lattices, so for convenience we will speak of lattices as a discrete metric space.

We denote the basic properties of the classical model of the CA.

1. Locality of rules. Only the elements of neighborhood can effect on the new state of cells and, perhaps, the cell itself.
2. Homogeneity of the system. No area of the lattice can not be indistinguishable from the other by any features of the landscape, rules, etc. However, in practice, the lattice is a finite set of cells (it is impossible to single out an unlimited amount of data). As a result, edge effects may occur, the cells at the boundary of the lattice will have a different number of neighbors. To avoid this, we can introduce boundary conditions; wrap the lattice in a torus.
3. The set of possible states of a cell is a finite quantity. This condition is necessary to obtain a finite number of operations in order to obtain a new state of the cell. Let's note that this does not prevent the use of cells for storing floating-point numbers in solving applied problems.
4. The value in all cells changes simultaneously, at the end of the iteration, and not as the calculation. Otherwise, the order of selection of the lattice cells, during the iteration, would have a significant effect on the result.

One of the main differences of the cellular system from other computing systems is that in all others there are two fundamentally different parts: architectural (control), which is fixed and active (i.e., performs some operations) and data that are variable and passive (i.e., they can not do anything by themselves).

In cellular automata, both these components are assembled from fundamentally isomorphic, indistinguishable from each other elements. Thus, the computing system can operate with its material part, to modify, to expand itself and to build its own kind. Although John von Neumann invented the systems of this class, this parallel architecture was called "non-von Neumann", as he created the von Neumann architecture earlier.

This statement may seem controversial. It would seem that it is more logical to attribute to the architectural part, for example, the lattice and rules of an automaton. However, this is more a hardware part. Here we mean that, for example, when considering an automaton implementing the "Life" game, the lattice and rules are used. Only the state of cells changes. Then you can implement a universal computing system that allows you to perform any calculations. In terms of expressive abilities, such a model will be equivalent to arbitrary Turing machines and cellular automata. In this case, the cells describing the architecture of the simulated computing system will be indistinguishable from cells representing data.

A cellular automaton, called the Banks computer, also has the computational universality property. Use it is extremely inefficient, but from a theoretical point of view the fact of its existence is an important result.

Definition of a cellular automaton.

Formally, the A cellular automaton is a four-objects {G, Z, N, f}, where:

- G – discrete metric space, automaton lattice, set of its cells. The presence of the metric allows us to provide a finite distance from the selected cell for all cells. This is achieved because for no metric any two points of a discrete metric space can not be infinitely distant from each other. In addition, the concept of the metric and the coordinates of the cell is extremely useful in determining the set of cells of the neighborhood N, described below. As a rule, the space G is one-, two-, or three-dimensional. However, it can have a larger dimension.
- Z – a finite set of possible cell states. Thus, the state of the entire lattice is an element of the set $Z^{|G|}$.
- N – a finite set defining the neighborhood of a cell – those | N | cells that affect the new state of the given cell. It can be set, for example, as the set of relative displacements from the cell needed to reach neighboring cells. The elements of this set will be called "neighbors" of 1 cell.
- f – the transition function or the automaton rules. Computable function acting $Z \times Z^{|N|} \rightarrow Z$ for automate with cells with memory and $Z^{|N|} \rightarrow Z$ for automata with cells without memory. The difference lies in the fact that in the transition function of cellular automaton with cells with memory the current state of the cell is also transmitted as a parameter.

Cellular automata in the general case are characterized by the following fundamental properties:

1. The lattice is homogeneous - no two areas can be distinguished from one another in the landscape. This is ensured by the semantics of the space G, as well as by the uniqueness of the definition of the neighborhood of N, the set of values of Z and the transition function f.
2. Interactions are local. The states of neighborhoods cells only affect the state of a given cell, which is ensured by the semantics of the function f.
3. Updating of the values of states of all lattice cells occurs simultaneously after the calculation of the new state of each of them.

It should be noted that in solving some problems, it becomes necessary to refuse to perform these properties of "classical" cellular automata.

Automata, for which the third of them is not performed, are called the asynchronous cellular automata.

THE BASIC FEATURES SELECTION BASED ON THE RADON TRANSFORM

The Fourier transform is successfully used in image recognition (Holland, 1966) and is one of the spectral transformations. The selection of a characteristic features (CF) on its basis refers to the first type - the method of choice in transformed spaces (Gardner, 1970). However, identification based on the resource-intensive in terms of calculations of the Fourier transform is rather slow and suitable for the analysis of static images, and is unacceptable for systems functioning in real time. The appearance of the Fast Fourier Transform (FFT) algorithm stimulated interest in other types of spectral transformations. In the tasks of filtering, compressing, and extracting informative features, the most widely used are the transformations Hadamard, Hough, Haar, Hartley, Radon (Pratt, 2016; Solomon, & Breckon, 2011; Nixon, & Aguardo, 2002; Gonzalez, & Woods, 2008; Belan, & Motornyuk, 2013; Minichino, & Howse, 2015; Jain, 1989; Deans, & Roderick, 1983; Ell, Bihan, & Sangwine, 2014; Ryan, 2019). Despite the difference in the types of functions, it turned out that most of the fast conversion algorithms have a similar structure and differ by no more than the values of the coefficients of the base operations (Richard, Duda, & Hart, 1972), and therefore have the same drawbacks in the form of resource-intensive calculations.

The summary data on the basic discrete transformations and the possibilities of their realization in CA are listed in Table 1.

Despite the fact that the Radon transform (RT), compared with other transformations, is not so widely used in image processing. However, thanks to the physical meaning (integral along the straight line), it has a better predisposition for realization in the CA (Table 1). In addition, there is a close relationship between the Radon-Haff transformations-the direct conversion for them is almost equivalent (Jain, 1989; Fernandes, & Oliveira, 2008), Radon and Hartley (Bracewell, 1986; Li, Robles-Kelly, & You, 2017), Radon and Fourier (we will discuss in detail later). Thus, theoretically, having an implementation of the RT on the CA, if necessary, it will be possible to quickly proceed to another type of transformation at the cost of small additional computations. In addition, the projection transformation (Belan, & Motornyuk. 2013) based on the Radon transform, is well suited for extracting the characteristic features of the image as well as it is resistant to noisy and distorted input data. It is invariant to rotation and scaling, and it is concluded that it can be used to identify objects. Consider the RT more.

Radon Transformation

In 1917, the mathematician I. Radon (Deans, & Roderick, 1983; Helgason, 2014;, 2015) proposed a method for reconstructing multidimensional functions with their integral characteristics, that is, a method for solving the inverse problem of integral geometry.

The RT principle is the basis of many information processing tools, the most famous of which are: tomography in medicine, image processing, seismological studies.

This method in computed tomography is widely used (Natterer, 2001). When light passes through the object, the intensity of the beam at the output is equal to the integral of the distribution function of the matter density along the ray trajectory. Thus, the radiation is recorded (Radon image or projection), calculated at different angles, allows using the RT to reproduce the images of the cross section.

Table 1. The main types of discrete transformations and the possibility of their realization in the CA

Type of Discrete Transformation	Features	Disadvantages	Potential Possibility of Realization in CA
Fourier	CF extraction based on the energy spectrum	resource-intensive, sensitive to noisiness, only for static data is used	unknown
Hadamard	decrease in the space of features by 2/3 without significantly worsening the results [55]	resource intensive	complicatedly
Haara	edge detection on weakly contrasting images	resource intensive	complicatedly
Hafa	parametric lines selection (straight lines, ellipses, circles, etc.)	resource-intensive, noise-sensitive	complicatedly
Hartley	calculation of geometric moment functions	resource intensive, a big mistake with fast conversion	complicatedly
Radon	CF extraction, the possibility of image reconstruction	resource intensive	easy - based on the physical meaning of the transformation

Another wide area of application of the RT and its various modifications is the digital processing of images, namely the determination of the parameters of various curves and their identification, whether it is a simple straight line, a handwritten font or a photograph of a person's face (Natterer, 2001; Natterer, F. & Wubbeling, 2001; Belan, & Motornyuk. 2013; Toft,1996).

The RT is most convenient to start with a simple case of a function of two variables, in addition, it is this case that is most practically important.

Let f (x, y) be a function defined on some interval D (Kobasyar, & Rusin, 2001). Consider the line L on the xy-plane that intersects the domain D (Figure 1). Then, integrating the function f (x, y) along the line L, we obtain the projection or linear integral of the function f. Integration along all possible lines L allows us to determine the RT for the function f(x,y):

$$\check{f} = Rf = \int_L f(x,y)ds, \tag{1}$$

where ds is the length increment along the line L.

The RT can be represented by the normal equation of the straight line L:

$$p = x\cos\phi + y\sin\phi, \tag{2}$$

where p is the distance from the coordinate start to the line (Figure 1); φ – the angle between p and x.

Using formulas: $x=p\cos\phi - s\sin\phi$, $y=p\sin\phi + s\cos\phi$, can be written:

$$\check{f}(p,\phi) = Rf = \int_{-\infty}^{\infty} f(p\cos\phi - s\sin\phi, p\sin\phi + s\cos\phi)ds. \tag{3}$$

Figure 1. The determination of the Radon transform

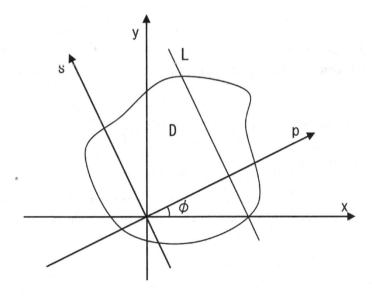

Having resorted to the vector notation of a line in the plane, (2) can be written in the form:

$$p(x,\xi) = x\cos\phi + y\sin\phi, \tag{4}$$

where

$\xi=(\cos\phi,\sin\phi)$- unit vector along the p axis;
(x,ξ) - scalar multiplication of two vectors.

Then the RT can be represented using the δ-function for the line $p=(x,\xi)$:

$$\breve{f}(p,\xi) = \int \int\limits_{-\infty}^{\infty} f(x)\delta(p - (\xi,x))dx, \tag{5}$$

and taking into account (4):

$$\breve{f}(p,\phi) = \int \int\limits_{-\infty}^{\infty} f(x,y)\delta(p - x\cos\phi - y\sin\phi)dxdy, \tag{6}$$

With a fixed angle φ, the $f(p,\phi)$ projection varies with respect to ρ in the direction defined by the vector ξ. In cases where the $\breve{f}(p,\phi)$ function is known only for certain values of p,ϕ, one can speak of a sample from the RT.

The main properties of RT, which are of particular importance for working with images:

1.   The $\breve{f}(p,\xi)$ transformation is a homogeneous function with a degree of homogeneity of 1, that is:

$$\breve{f}(\alpha p,\alpha\xi) = |\alpha|^{-1} \breve{f}(\alpha p,\alpha\xi), \tag{7}$$

for α≠0. For α = -1 we have: $\breve{f}(-p,-\xi) = \breve{f}(p,\xi)$.
It follows from (1.7) that with fixed p, changing the ξ value, we can completely determine the RT function f (x).

2.   The RT is linear for any functions f_1, f_2 and constants a_1, a_2:

$$R[a_1f_1 + a_2f_2] = a_1R[f_1] + a_2R[f_2]. \tag{8}$$

The linearity property can be formulated as follows: The Radon transform of a weighted sum of functions is equal to the weighted sum of the transformations of each function (8).

3.　　The displacement of the function in the spatial domain leads to a displacement of the projections along p, and its value depends on the angle φ:

$$R[f(x - a)] = \breve{f}(p - (\xi, a)).$$ (9)

One of the most important properties of an RT is its connection with the Fourier transform. It is known (Kobasyar, & Rusin, 2001) the formula of the n-dimensional Fourier transform of the function $f(x) = f(x_1, x_2, \dots x_n)$:

$$F(\omega) = F_n^{+1}\left[f(x)\right] = \int f(x)e^{-i2\pi(\omega, x)}dx,$$ (10)

where

$\omega = (\omega_1, \omega_2, ..., \omega_n)$ - coordinates in the frequency plane;
$F_n^{+1}\left[f(x)\right]$ - operator of the n-dimensional Fourier transform.

Inverse Fourier transform:

$$f(x) = F_n^{-1}\left[F\right] = \int F(\omega)e^{i2\pi(\omega, x)}d\omega$$

To find the connection between the Radon and Fourier transforms, we write (10) in the following form:

$$F(\omega) = \int\limits_{-\infty}^{\infty} dt \int dx f(x)e^{-i2\pi t}\delta(t - (\omega, x)),$$

where t – real variable.
Then, taking (5) into account, we have:

$$F(\alpha\xi) = \int\limits_{-\infty}^{\infty} \breve{f}(p, \xi)e^{-i2\pi\alpha p}dp,$$ (11)

where αp = t – real variable, ω=(αξ) (ξ - unit vector).

The fundamental connection between the n-dimensional Fourier transform and the Radon transform emerges from the last formula (11): in order to perform the n-dimensional Fourier transform of the function, it is necessary first to perform its Radon transform, then to perform the one-dimensional Fourier transform of the projection from its radial variable.

In the operator form this can be written down:

$$F = F_1^{+1}\left[\breve{f}\right] = F_1^{+1}R\left[f\right],$$

and taking into account the linearity, this transformation can be represented in the form: $R[f] = F_1^{-1} F_n^{+1}[f]$. That is, to calculate the Radon transform of a function, one can define its n-dimensional Fourier transform and take the inverse one-dimensional Fourier transform with respect to one coordinate (Kobasyar, & Rusin, 2001).

METHOD AND MATHEMATICAL MODEL OF CF EXTRACTION BASED ON THE RADON TRANSFORM FOR IMPLEMENTATION ON HCCA

Hexagonal coverage is almost an ideal choice in terms of the physical implementation of the allocation of CF on the basis of the previously considered RT on the CA.

The scientific literature describes studies on the comparison of hexagonal and orthogonal rasters from the point of view of their effectiveness in image processing operations (Dudgeon, & Mersereau, 1984; Mersereau, 1979; Golay, 1969; Staunton, 1989; Belan, & Motornyuk, 2013; Bilan, Motornyuk, & Bilan, 2014; Nicoladie, 2014; Basurto, Leon, Martinez, & Seck-Tuoh-Mora, 2013).

Based on the analysis of these works, the main advantages of hexagonal coverage are formulated:

- Requires 13.4% fewer points to represent the same signal (Mersereau, 1979; Dudgeon, & Mersereau, 1984; Woodward, & Muir, 1984; Nicoladie, 2014);
- Simple and unambiguous determination of connections and neighborhoods (Golay, 1969);
- Local and global computations are more efficient (Staunton, 1989; Mersereau, 1979);
- Simplicity of operator development (Staunton, 1989);

The disadvantages include the historically established situation in which almost all the algorithms and operators are designed for execution on an orthogonal raster, their adaptation to the hexagonal raster is possible, but requires some time and effort from the developers.

But the overriding advantage is the fact that in the case of hexagonal discretization, for reconstructing the initial image from its Radon transforms, a sufficient minimum number of projections is equal to three: in the directions 0°, 60° and 120° (Levin, & Vishnyakov, 1989), which exactly coincide with the main directions of the hexagonal coating: x0-x4, x0-x2, x0-x1 (Figure 2). Moreover, this not only guarantees the simplicity of the hardware implementation, but also proves that a set of even three projections of RT can act as a full-fledged CF that provides image identification.

It is clear from the detailed description of the RT that it is necessary to integrate the original image in the right direction in order to build the projection of this transformation. To illustrate this operation on a CA, consider the simplest case of a binary image on an orthogonal raster. In this case, the physical meaning of the RT is to find the sum of the pixels that form this image along a straight line along the main directions 0° and 90°. The result of the operation will be two arrays of values: {1,4,3,4} and {3,4,3,2} (Figure 3).

To CF extraction, a minimum of three projections are required. However, CA with orthogonal cover have only two directions for building projections, which is not enough.

The hexagonal coverage is not enough to ensure the construction of projections along the main directions (Figure 2), it also allows, without additional costs, to realize three more projections along additional directions 30°, 90° and 150° (Figure 4).

Figure 2. Encoding of neighbors and main directions of hexagonal coverage

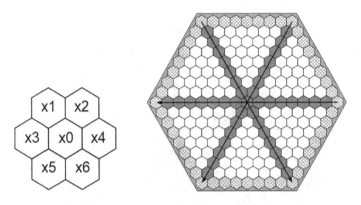

Figure 3. RT projections on orthogonal cover for corners 0° and 90°

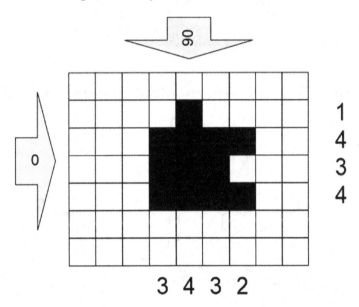

Additional directions of the hexagonal coverage (Figure 2,) are determined by the location of the vertices of the central cell (and not its faces, as for the main directions):

1. x2-x4 ⇒ x3-x5 (upper right direction - lower left top) - corresponds to the corner 30°;
2. x1-x2 ⇒ x5-x6 (direction upper - lower peak) - corresponds to the corner 90°;
3. x1-x3 ⇒ x4-x6 (left upper direction - lower right top) – corresponds to the corner 150°,

where x2-x4 – the verge between adjacent cells x2 and x4, defines the right upper vertex of the cell x0 (similarly for other designations xY-xZ) (Figure 4).

The lines thus constructed have the form of lines with an alternate displacement of 1/2 pixel thickness relative to the axis (Figure 4).

Figure 4. Additional directions of hexagonal coverage, corresponding to the corners 30°, 90° and 150°

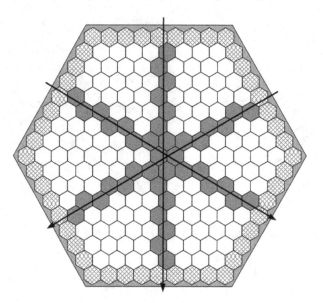

Figure 5. The RT directions of hexagonal coverage based on the geometric features of the cellular structure

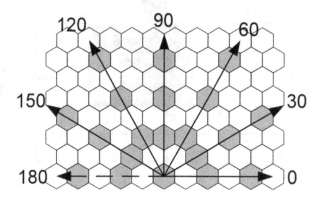

Thus, the total number of RT projections, hardware implemented on one HCCA is six. In Figure 5 arrows indicate the directions corresponding to the corners 0°, 30°, 60°, 90°, 120° and 150°. The dotted line indicates the direction of 180°, which is "mirror" to 0°.

For CA with hexagonal coating (HCCA), having a hexagonal shape (Figure 2, 4) and, depending on the size, consisting of different numbers of cells, we define the maximum and minimum number of pixels in the rows of main and additional directions.

If the length of one edge side in pixels of such HCCA is taken as n, then we get:

maximum number of pixels of a row in the main direction of HCCA:

$$Z_{max} = 2 \cdot n - 1, \tag{12}$$

minimum number of pixels of a row in the main direction of HCCA:

$$Z_{min} = n, \tag{13}$$

maximum number of pixels in a row in the additional direction of HCCA:

$$Z'_{max} = Z_{max} = 2 \cdot n - 1, \tag{14}$$

minimum number of pixels in a row in the additional direction of HCCA:

$$Z'_{min} = 1, \tag{15}$$

where n – the number of pixels that make up the HCCA one edge.

Let Q is the set of HCCA directions (main and additional, Figure 5): Q = {0°, 30°, 60°, 90°, 120°, 150°}. If each i-th direction line q is represented as a set of pixels L_{qi}, and $i = \{1, 2, ..., k\}$, such that $L_{qi} = \{x_1, ..., x_k\}$, hen we can write the formula for the sum of the brightness values of all pixels of a given line:

$$S_{qi} = \sum_{j=1}^{Z_i} x_j, \tag{16}$$

where Z_i – the maximum number of pixels in the i-th line lies within the limits defined by the formulas (12) – (15).

Then the projection of the Radon transform for the direction q can be represented as an ordered set R_q, consisting of all sums S_{qi} of a given direction:

$$R_q = \{S_{q1}, S_{q2}, ..., S_{qk}\} . \tag{17}$$

Taking into account the specific values of the angles of the main and additional directions of the HCCA, namely 0°, 30°, 60°, 90°, 120° and 150°, based on the expression (3), we can write formulas for special cases of constructing the RT projections.

The RT projection ($R_0 f$) for direction 0°:

$$\breve{f}_0(p, 0) = R_0 f = \int_{-\infty}^{\infty} f(p, s) ds . \tag{18}$$

The RT projection ($R_{30} f$) for direction 30°:

$$\breve{f}_{30}(p, 30) = R_{30} f = \int_{-\infty}^{\infty} f\left(\frac{\sqrt{3}}{2} p - \frac{1}{2} s, \frac{1}{2} p + \frac{\sqrt{3}}{2} s\right) ds . \tag{19}$$

The RT projection ($R_{60}f$) for direction 60°:

$$\breve{f}_{60}(p,60) = R_{60}f = \int\limits_{-\infty}^{\infty} f\left(\frac{1}{2}p - \frac{\sqrt{3}}{2}s, \frac{\sqrt{3}}{2}p + \frac{1}{2}s\right)ds \,. \tag{20}$$

The RT projection ($R_{90}f$) for direction 90°:

$$\breve{f}_{90}(p,90) = R_{90}f = \int\limits_{-\infty}^{\infty} f(s,p)ds \,. \tag{21}$$

The RT projection ($R_{120}f$) for direction 120°:

$$\breve{f}_{120}(p,120) = R_{120}f = \int\limits_{-\infty}^{\infty} f\left(-\frac{1}{2}p - \frac{\sqrt{3}}{2}s, \frac{\sqrt{3}}{2}p - \frac{1}{2}s\right)ds \,. \tag{22}$$

The RT projection ($R_{150}f$) for direction 150°:

$$\breve{f}_{150}(p,150) = R_{150}f = \int\limits_{-\infty}^{\infty} f\left(-\frac{\sqrt{3}}{2}p - \frac{1}{2}s, \frac{1}{2}p - \frac{\sqrt{3}}{2}s\right)ds \,, \tag{23}$$

where in the formulas (18) – (23)

ds – length increment along a straight line L,
p – distance from the start to the straight line (Figure 6).

If it is necessary to ensure the hardware construction of a larger number of RT projections, 2 or more HCCAs can be used, with each subsequent rotate along an axis perpendicular to its plane by an angle β:

$$\angle\beta = 30/n, \tag{24}$$

where n – the number of HCCA implementing RT in 6 directions.

For the case of two HCCA $\angle\beta = 15°$, get 12 directions in increments of 15° (Figure 7). In Figure 7 the solid arrows indicate the direction of the first, the dotted - the second HCCA.

Formulas for constructing the RT projections (16), (17) indicate the need to calculate the amounts in the lines of the processor element (PE) in six directions HCCA. The simplest hardware implementation of this operation on this architecture is possible in two ways:

1. the summation starts from the extreme PE in the line corresponding to the required direction of construction of the RT projection. Each PE takes the value of the accumulated amount from the neighboring PE, adds its own brightness value to it and transfers it to the next PE in a series;

Figure 6. Radon transformation definition

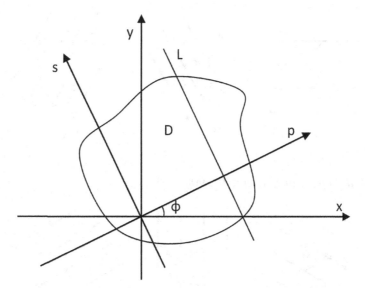

Figure 7. Directions of the two HCCA, implementing the construction of RT

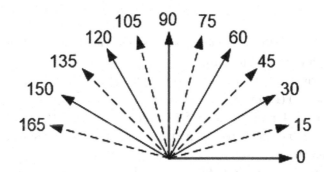

2. HCCA shifts the entire image in the direction coinciding with the specified direction of the RT projection. The accumulation of the sum of the PE brightness is not formed in the cells themselves, but in special accumulative adders located along the perimeter of the HCCA.

Although the first method seems to be simpler, in fact, its implementation requires much higher hardware costs for building adders in each PE, and adders must have a bit capacity sufficient to save the sum of the brightness of all pixels in a line.

The second method is somewhat more difficult to implement, but incomparably cheaper in terms of hardware costs, so our choice fell on it.

Construction of the projections of RT on HCCA for angles of 0°, 60°, 120° - is quite simple to implement and consists in shifting the image along the main directions.

RT for angle 0° - the left shift is performed, that is, each PE (x0) takes the value of its right neighbor (x4) (Figure 8, a).

Figure 8. Image shift direction for corners 0°, 60°, 120°

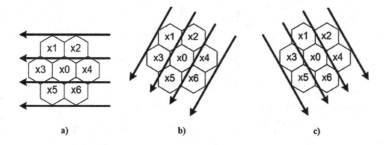

Figure 9. Image shift direction for corners 30°, 90°, 150°

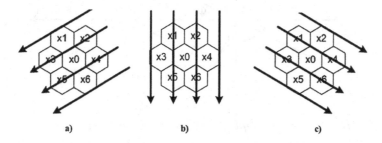

RT for angle 60° - the shift to the left is down (60°) is performed, that is, each PE (x0) takes the value of its right upper neighbor (x2) (Figure 8, b).

RT for angle 120° - a right downward shift is performed (120°), that is, each PE (x0) takes the value of its left upper neighbor (x1) (Figure 8, c).

The construction of the RT projections on HCCA for angles of 30°, 90°, 150° is somewhat more complicated than similar operations in the main directions and consist in shifting the image in the corresponding additional directions.

The difficulty lies in the impossibility of a direct shift, as is done for the main directions. As can be seen from Figure 4 - straight lines with tilt angles of 30°, 90° and 150° have some form of zigzags. That is, we need to combine alternately shift in the neighboring main directions. Consider this operation in more detail.

RT for angle 30° - the shift to the left is down is performed (30°), that is, each PE (x0) takes in turn the values of its right upper (x2) and right neighbor (x4) (Figure 9, a).

RT for angle 90° - a downward shift (90°), is performed, that is, each PE (x0) takes in turn the values of its right upper (x2) and left upper neighbor (x1) (Figure 9, b).

RT for angle 150° - a right downward shift is performed (150°), that is, each PE (x0) takes in turn the values of its left (x3) and left upper neighbor (x1) (Figure 9, c).

The specificity of the developed method of searching for integral values by shifting the image brings certain conditions to the size of incoming images, based on the size of HCCA.

The homogeneous cellular environment consists of PE and the appearance repeats the shape of a single pixel of the hexagonal coating, that is, a regular hexagon (Figure 10). All six directions for shifts are given in two cases:

1. Shift along the additional direction of the HCCA perpendicular to the face of projection;
2. Shift along the main direction of the HCCA at an angle of 30° to the face of projection.

The first case is typical for RT building 30°, 90° and 150°. In this case, the shift itself is more complicated (alternately in two adjacent main directions), as a result of which a restriction is imposed on the size of the image, the projection of which must fully located on the edge (Figure 10).

The second case is typical for the construction of the RT projections 0°, 60° and 120°. In this case, the shift is performed easier, but the plane of the projection construction is located at an angle of 30° to the direction of the shift (Figure 11).

Taking into account the restrictions imposed by the first case of shifts (Figure 10), we obtain the active area of HCCA for recording the processed image (Figure 12).

In view of the foregoing, it is sufficient to arrange cumulative counters not around the entire HCCA perimeter, but only on the planes of building projections in all six directions. In Figure 13, the area for the image is marked in gray, and the outermost ones are dark, the outputs of which are connected to the counter inputs.

We derive a formula for finding the total amount of PE in HCCA, based on the size of its projection face. Let n be the length of the HCCA face, expressed by the number of PEs in it (in Figure 14 n = 4). All PEs that are part of the HCCA, conventionally represented in the form of six segments, triangles (Figure 14). The number of PEs in a triangle is expressed by rows of natural numbers from 1 to (n–1). Using the formula to find the sum of the first n – 1 natural numbers, we have:

$$t = \frac{(n-1) \cdot n}{2},$$ (25)

wheret – the number of PE in the triangular segment,n – HCCA length of projection face.

Figure 10. Shift in additional direction, the image should be between the dotted lines

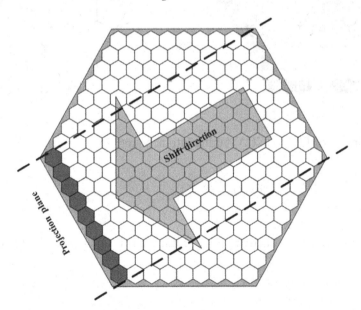

Figure 11. The shift the main direction and the plane of the construction of projections

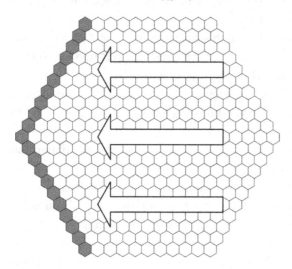

Figure 12. HCCA area for image capture

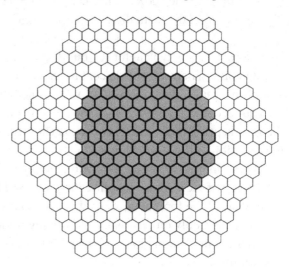

Figure 13. Scheme of the extreme PE, connected to the counters

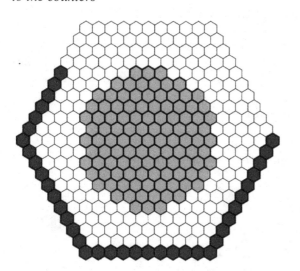

Figure 14. HCCA fragmentation into six triangular segments

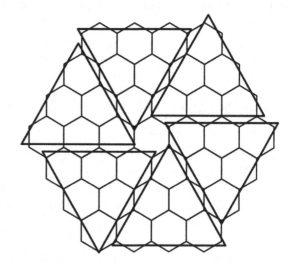

Then the total number of PE in HCCA, taking into account (25):

$$p = 6 \cdot t + 1 = 6 \cdot \frac{n \cdot (n-1)}{2} + 1 = 3n \cdot (n-1) + 1 \,. \tag{26}$$

The amount of PE in the HCCA active region (Figure 13) is determined by the empirically derived formula:

$$a = n \cdot (n - 1) + b, \tag{27}$$

where b – coefficient depending on the residual of the division n/3: b=-with a residual of 2, in all other cases b = 1.

Thus, the developed for HCCA mathematical model for constructing the RT projections (17), which implements the formulas of RT (18) - (23) within the framework of a single cellular environment, allows the hardware selection of CF on the basis of the Radon transform.

METHOD AND MATHEMATICAL MODEL OF THE CF EXTRACTION TO SELECTION OF THE SKELETON AND IMPLEMENTATION ON HCCA

The hardware implementation of the image skeleton selection will provide speed sufficient for the real-time identification system to function. The selected skeleton will be the CF used to implement the image identification method.

First, the input image is input to the system. It selects the area containing a moving object, which is transmitted for further processing to the HCCA, which, through certain iterative transformations, provides a description of the input image as a skeleton of the original image. As result of the HCCA functioning output will be a formed 1-pixel-shaped skeleton, which can be represented by a code sequence of a set of geometric elements in the form of straight lines, arcs, circles, forks, etc.

A review of the literature has shown that most of the existing methods for selecting an image skeleton are based on complex data analysis and are designed without taking into account the possibility of parallel execution on CA architectures (Kwok, 1988; Ahmed, & Ward, 2002; Patil, Suralkar, & Sheikh, 2005; Wu, at all. 2019; Lu, Chen, Yeung, Deng, & Chen, 2018). Some of these algorithms are based on the concepts of Voronoi diagrams and Delaunay triangulation of images (Guibas, & Stolfi, 1985; Fortune, 1987; Floriani, Falcidieno, Nagy, & Pienovi, 1991), being in themselves rather complicated from an algorithmic point of view, implementations on a CA. Therefore, a direct transfer of such decisions on the selection of the skeleton to the developed HCCA will both be too complicated and require significant modification, or it may turn out to be unrealistic or impractical for a given architecture.

At the same time, there is a small amount of work in which the operation to extract the skeleton image is considered from the point of view of parallel execution in the CA (Rosin, 2005; Lam, & Suen, 1995). However, in the aforementioned papers, the rules of operation were developed for CA with orthogonal coverage, which are known to have ambiguities in the definition of neighboring cells, and this is an essential parameter for determining the continuity of the skeleton and its resulting pixel thickness of 1 pixel.

Based on this, it seems quite appropriate to develop your own method that satisfies the following requirements:

1. Algorithm orientation to parallel execution in HCCA;
2. Work with a binary image (with the possibility of easy extension of functionality for working with color images);
3. The selected skeleton must be a set of points equidistant from the contours of the input image;
4. The thickness of all lines of the selected skeleton must be equal to one pixel;
5. Inseparable image segments must be represented by uninterrupted skeleton lines.

THE EULER NUMBER AS A MEASURE OF SPATIAL INTEGRITY IN THE ALLOCATION OF THE SKELETON OF A BINARY IMAGE

The following ensure achieving the stated requirements in the process of extracting the image skeleton on HCCA.

The original image is captured as input data to the HCCA. This data includes a part of the original image of the visual scene in which the movement of the object was recorded. Almost all the considered methods for extracting the skeleton work with binary images, since this type of images does not contain redundant data for the skeleton construction operation. We will assume that the binary image will be fed to the input of the developed HCCA, and to ensure the simplicity of the formulation of the modification rules, all further actions will be carried out on the basis that each pixel (PE) in the "0" state encodes a background or a hole on the object, and the pixels (PE) in the state "1" encode the image of the object:

$$\begin{cases} F = \{x_i \mid x_i = 1\} \\ B = \{x_i \mid x_i = 0\}, \\ B \cap F = \varnothing \end{cases} \tag{28}$$

where

F – the set of all pixels that form the image of the object,
B – the set of all pixels of the background area,
x_i – i-th pixel of the image.

In cases when the input data is a color image, it is necessary to execute its binarization, and then process it in accordance with the developed rules as a binary. In this case, binarization can be carried out using HCCA means, and the binarization threshold can be determined either as a constant or dynamically depending on the established rules.

If the value of each image element is determined as the result of a local operation on the corresponding element of the original image and the resulting binary image can be used again in the next cycle of calculations - this process is called iterative modification (Horn, 1986; Second International Workshop, Robot Vision, [RobVis 2008]).

The implementation of equidistance of the selected skeleton from the contour boundaries of the object is provided by iterative modification of the input image, which consists in the simultaneous refinement of the image of the object by one pixel for one iteration. That is, the original image of the object can be considered as a sequence of strictly decreasing sets:

$F_0, F_1, F_2, ..., F_n$, such that:

$$F_n \subset F_{n-1} \subset ... \subset F_1 \subset F_0, \tag{29}$$

where

$F_0 = F$ – many pixels of the initial image of the object,

$F_1, F_2, ..., F_{n-1}$ – the set of pixels of the refined images of the object, obtained respectively after the 1st, 2nd, ..., (n-1) -th iterations,

F_n – set of pixels after the last iteration - corresponds to the selected skeleton of the initial image.

From the last formula it follows that at each iteration step the set of pixels of the background area is increased by the difference of the object pixel sets between the corresponding iteration steps:

$$B_{k+1} = B_k \cup (F_k \setminus F_{k+1}), \tag{30}$$

where

B_k, B_{k+1} – the set of pixels of the background area at the current (k) and next (k + 1) iteration steps,

F_k, F_{k+1} – the set of pixels of the image of the object, respectively, at the current (k) and next (k + 1) iteration steps.

Iterative refinement of the original image to the final thickness of all lines of 1 pixel and will signal the end of calculations and the readiness of the formed skeleton.

Thus, the main task for further solution is to find local rules for the HCCA PE, which will determine the set of limit points to be zeroed at each iteration step: $(F_k \setminus F_{k+1})$. The main criterion for the selection of rules should be the condition of the integrity of the skeleton.

To preserve the continuity of the skeleton when it is allocated to HCCA, a certain control is needed at each iteration step, which would ensure that the spatial integrity of the resulting image remains unchanged until the final extraction of the skeleton. The known and most common measure of spatial integrity is the Euler number (E) (Horn, 1986; DeMers, 2008; Berry, 1993), which is defined as the difference between the number of connected objects (C) and the number of holes (H) in the binary image (Rosenfeld, & Kak, 1982):

$$E = C - H, \tag{31}$$

For example, the Euler number of a capital letter "B" E = 1, since this letter consists of one object and two holes; Euler's number of letters "i" E = 2 etc. (Figure 15).

Figure 15. Binary images of letters "B" and "i"

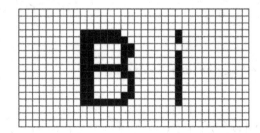

Based on the definition of the Euler number, it is necessary to operate with the concepts of the image of objects and holes, and with gradual thinning the thickness of the lines will approach 1 pixel, which, when using an orthogonal coating, will necessarily lead to ambiguity in determining connectivity, and to cases similar to the illustration of Jordan theorem. So for this task, the use of hexagonal coverage is more justified.

We investigate the change in the Euler number with a change in the value of one element on the hexagonal coating. As is known, the Euler number has the property of additivity, so its change depends only on the neighbors of a particular element. If we replace the zero value of a pixel with zero neighbors by one, then independently of other elements, the Euler number will increase by one (Figure 16).

Similarly, if all neighbors (except for one) are zeros or ones, then the Euler number will remain unchanged when the value in the central element is inverted. In this case, the object simply expands or the opening narrows (Figure 17).

Since each element of the image has six neighbors and each of them can take the value "1" or "0" (subject to the binary image), there are 26 = 64 possible environments. For each of the options, you can calculate the Euler differential (E *), that is, the change in the Euler number when zero is replaced by one in the central element (0 => 1). In the case of the opposite replacement (1 => 0), the Euler number will change to Э *. Of particular interest are cases in which E * = 0, so you can arbitrarily modify the image without changing the Euler number, and, consequently, its spatial integrity.

For hexagonal coverage, there are five fundamentally different cases of the location of the environment (Figure 18).

1. E * = 1, if all neighboring points are zeros, a new object arises and thus the Euler number is increased by 1;
2. E * = 1, if all adjacent points are 1- the hole is filled;
3. E * = 0, if six neighbors, which are considered as a cyclic sequence, can be divided into one consecutive group of zeros and one consecutive group of ones — the hole or object is narrowed;
4. E * = 1, if there are two groups of units that alternate with two groups of zeros - the hole intersects or two objects combine;
5. E * = 2, if three ones alternate with three zeros - the hole is divided into three or three objects are combined.

Figure 16. Replacing "0" with "1"

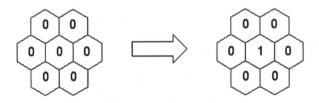

Figure 17. Cases for which the Euler number is constant

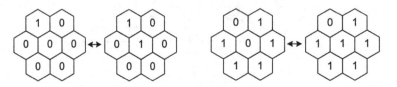

Figure 18. Cases that differ in the values of the Euler differential

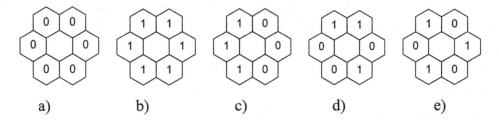

a) b) c) d) e)

The case of E* = 0 is taken as the initial version of the desired zeroing rule. Moreover, if at each iteration cycle, each point of the image, the neighborhood of which corresponds to any kind of case c) (Figure 18, c) and has a single value, will be zeroed out. Moreover, if at each iteration cycle, each point of the image, the environment of which corresponds to any kind of case b) (Figure 18, c) and has a single value, will be zeroed out, then we obtain an image that is the same as the original Euler number, but one pixel thick (Figure 19).

Since in the future it will be necessary to operate with a variant of the location of neighboring PEs depending on their values, in order to build a mathematical model, it is necessary to distinguish these cases. To do this, we introduce the concept of a linearly ordered set of all neighboring elements of the current element x0. Taking into account the adopted coding of neighbors (Figure 2), if we move clockwise starting from x1, we have:

$$S = \{x1, x2, x4, x6, x5, x3\},$$ (32)

where S - an ordered set of six neighboring PEs, and the linear ordering is cyclical, that is, the elements of the set x1 and x3 are also considered to be adjacent:

$$x1 \prec x2 \prec x4 \prec x6 \prec x5 \prec x3 \prec x1 \prec ....$$ (33)

Figure 19. The result of the allocation of the skeleton by the method of zero Euler differential

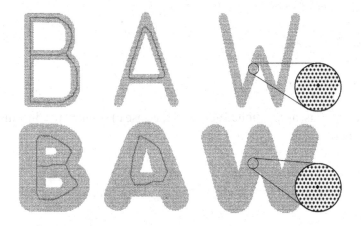

Let S_k be a linearly ordered subset of the set S (32) and correspond to an indissoluble ordered segment $[x_{first}; x_{last}]$, such that all its elements belong to a certain set Y, and for the last elements there are neighboring elements according to (33) $x_{first-1}$ x_{first} and x_{last+1} x_{last}, do not belong to the set Y:

$$\begin{cases} S_k \subset S = \{x \in S_k = [x_{first}; x_{last}] \mid (\forall x \in Y) \Leftrightarrow (S_k \subset Y)\} \\ ((x_{first-1} \prec x_{first}) \Leftrightarrow (x_{first-1}; x_{first}) = \varnothing) \wedge (x_{first-1} \notin Y) \\ ((x_{last} \succ x_{last+1}) \Leftrightarrow (x_{last}; x_{last+1}) = \varnothing) \wedge (x_{last+1} \notin Y) \end{cases} , \tag{34}$$

where

x_{first} and x_{last} - respectively, the first and last elements of a linearly ordered set S_k,
$x_{first-1}$ and x_{last+1} - elements of the set S, respectively, the previous element x_{first} and the next element x_{last}
$\quad$ $(x_{first-1}$ x_{first}, x_{last+1} $xl_{ast})$,
Y - set, is a criterion in determining the set S_k.

For completeness, it should be noted that in the case when $S_k = S$, all neighboring PEs have the same value and the extreme elements of the segment (x_{first} and x_{last}) are absent, then the whole set $S \subset Y$. For example, in Figure 18, a) there is only one segment, which consists of 6 elements, and $Y \subset B$, that is, all neighboring PEs belong to the background. Similarly in Figure 18, b) is also only one segment, which consists of 6 elements, moreover $Y \subset F$, that is, all neighboring PEs belong to the image.

Denote by S_B - the segment belongs to the background area, and by S_F - the segment belongs to the image of the object.

Formula (34) introduces the concept of a segment (S_k set) of neighboring PEs.

Given that the set S (32) consists of 6 elements ($|S| = 6$), then we can write the minimum ($|S_k|_{min}$) and maximum ($|S_k|_{max}$) number of elements in one segment of the HCCA neighbors:

$$|S_k|_{min} = 1, \tag{35}$$

$$|S_k|_{max} = 6 . \tag{36}$$

Denoting by S_s the set of S_k, on the basis of (35), (36) we write down the minimum ($|S_s|_{min}$) and maximum ($|S_s|_{max}$) number of segments for HCCA:

$$|S_s|_{min} = 1, \text{ if } |S_k| = |S_k|_{max}, \tag{37}$$

$$|S_s|_{max} = 6, \text{ if } \forall |S_k| = |S_k|_{min} . \tag{38}$$

The most interesting for us, as mentioned above, is the case c) (Figure 18), in which $E* = 0$. Consider the introduced concept of a segment for this case:

$|S_s| = 2$ - as the number of segments = 2;
$S_F = \{x5, x3, x1\}$ - image segment for which: $Y \subset F$, $x_{first} = x5 \in F$, $x_{last} = x1 \in F$, $x_{first-1} = x6 \notin F$, x_{last+1}
$\quad = x2 \notin F$;

$S_B = \{x2, x4, x6\}$ - background segment for which: $Y \subset B$, $x_{first} = x2 \in B$, $x_{last} = x6 \in B$, $x_{first-1}=x1 \notin B$, $x_{last+1} = x5 \notin B$.

Thus, to unambiguously determine the location of neighboring PEs, it suffices to specify the sequence of segments and their power, which, taking turns into account, will give many of all possible options. For this case, we write down all possible variants of two segments (S_B, S_F) of different powers in the form of a system of equations:

$$\begin{cases} S_S = \{S_B, S_F\} \Leftrightarrow |S_S| = 2 \\ S_B \subset S = \{x_b \in S_B \mid \forall x_b \in B\} \\ S_F \subset S = \{x_f \in S_F \mid \forall x_f \in F\} \\ |S_F| = \{1,2,3,4,5\} \Leftrightarrow |S_B| = 6 - |S_F| \end{cases} \tag{39}$$

Then, taking into account (39), we can write a formula for determining the PE, which are to be zeroing at the next step of the iteration, depending on the current state of the neighboring PE:

$$x_i(t+1) = 0, if\, x_i(t) \in E0 = S_B + S_F, \tag{40}$$

where

E0 - the set of all possible combinations of values of neighboring PE, corresponding to all cases with a zero Euler differential (Figure 18, c),

S_B and S_F - image and background segments defined by the formula (39).

As can be seen from Figure 19, the application of an iterative modification in which at every step $E* = 0$ (40) is saved leads to the destruction of all the processes of the selected skeleton. There is no contradiction here, because the Euler number remained unchanged: two holes and one object of the letter "B" (E = 1) remained in the selected skeleton, one hole of the letter "A" (E = 0) also remained, but from the letter "W" left one point (E = 1). Therefore, the use of iterative modification of the input binary image to extract the skeleton using the zero differential Euler criterion in its pure form (40) does not give the desired results and requires further refinement and adaptation under HCCA.

THE METHOD OF EXTRACTING THE IMAGE SKELETON BASED ON THE EULER ZERO DIFFERENTIAL AND HCCA

Any process of the skeleton has a unit thickness and ends with a central pixel (Figure 20).

Moreover, the figure shows one of six possible cases, which are one of the possible combinations for $E* = 0$ (Figure 18, c), which is determined by the segments $|S_F| = 1$ and $|S_B| = 5$. Let rewrite formula (39), eliminating this set of segments (Figure 20):

Figure 20. The end of the process of the skeleton

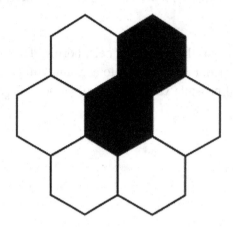

$$\begin{cases} S_S = \{S_B, S_F\} \Leftrightarrow |S_S| = 2 \\ S_B \subset S = \{x_b \in S_B \mid \forall x_b \in B\} \\ S_F \subset S = \{x_f \in S_F \mid \forall x_f \in F\} \\ |S_F| = \{2, 3, 4, 5\} \Leftrightarrow |S_B| = 6 - |S_F| \end{cases} \qquad (41)$$

Then, taking into account (41), we can write a new formula for determining PE to be reset in the next iteration step, depending on the current state of neighboring PE:

$$x_i(t+1) = 0, \text{ if } x_i(t) \in E0' = S_B + S_F, \qquad (42)$$

where E0` - modification of the set E0, the set of all possible combinations of the values of neighboring PE, defined by the segments S_B and S_F by the formula (41).

Simulation of a HCCA performing an iterative image modification using formula (42) gave the result shown in Figure 21.

Figure 21. Skeleton gaps

Figure 22. Combinations leading to rupture of the skeleton

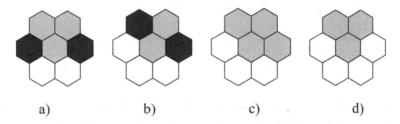

a)	b)	c)	d)

The changes made it possible to preserve the processes, but also revealed a negative effect in the form of loss of the integrity of the core (Figure 21). Further analysis of the method revealed three possible combinations leading to ruptures of the skeleton. All of them are presented in Figure 22, where white color indicates background pixels (S_B segment), black — image pixels (S_F segment), gray — pixels to be zeroed by the formula (41) (S_{E0} ` segment).

1. Case a) (Figure 22) most often occurs in those places of the skeleton where three processes converge into one point;
2. Case b) (Figure 22) most often occurs in those places where the skeleton thickness alternately has a thickness of 1, 2, 1, etc. pixel;
3. Case c) (Figure 22) most often occurs in those places where the skeleton has not yet fully formed (extracted), and its thickness is 2 pixels, or in narrow spaces with the same thickness;
4. Case d) (Figure 22) is characteristic of the penultimate iteration step, when only three pixels remain.

Combinations a), b) (Figure 22) have the same set of segments, but differ in their power, so these two cases can be written by the formula:

$$\begin{cases} S_S = \{S_B, S_{F1}, S_{E0}, S_{F2}\} \Leftrightarrow | S_S | = 4 \\ S_B \subset S = \{x_b \in S_B \mid \forall x_b \in B\} \\ S_{F1} \subset S = \{x_{f1} \in S_{F1} \mid (\forall x_{f1} \in F) \wedge (| S_{F1} | = 1)\} \\ S_{F2} \subset S = \{x_{f2} \in S_{F2} \mid (\forall x_{f2} \in F) \wedge (| S_{F2} | = 1)\} \\ S_{E0} \subset S = \{x_{e0} \in S_{E0} \mid \forall x_{e0} \in E0'\} \\ | S_B | = \{1,2\} \Leftrightarrow | S_{E0} | = 4 - | S_B | \end{cases} \quad (43)$$

where S_{E0} - the set of neighboring PEs, for which the relation (42) is true within local rules.

Denote by D1 the set of cases (Figure 22, a, b) defined by the formula (43):

$$x \in D1 = S_B + S_{F1} + S_{E0} + S_{F2}, \quad (44)$$

where sets S_B, S_{F1}, S_{E0}, S_{F2} - segments defined by (43).

Similarly, combinations c), d) (Figure 22) also differ only in the power of the segments; therefore, we will describe them with the formula:

$$\begin{cases} S_S = \{S_B, S_{E0}\} \Leftrightarrow | S_S | = 2 \\ S_B \subset S = \{x_b \in S_B \mid \forall x_b \in B\} \\ S_{E0} \subset S = \{x_{e0} \in S_{E0} \mid \forall x_{e0} \in E0'\} \\ | S_B | = \{3,4\} \Leftrightarrow | S_{E0} | = 6 - | S_B | \end{cases} \tag{45}$$

where S_{E0} - the set of neighboring PEs, for which, within local rules, the correct relation is (42).

Denote by $D2$ the set of cases (Figure 22, c, d) defined by the formula (45):

$$x \in D2 = S_B + S_{E0}, \tag{46}$$

where the sets S_B, S_{E0} are the segments defined by formula (45).

Subtracting from the set E0' the union of the sets D1 and D2, we obtain a new formula for determining the PE to be zeroed in the next iteration step depending on the current state of the neighboring PE:

$$x_i(t+1) = 0, \text{ if } x_i(t) \in (E0' \setminus (D1 \cup D2)). \tag{47}$$

Modeling a HCCA performing an iterative image modification using formula (47) gave the result shown in Figure 23.

As can be seen from Figure 23, the skeleton out almost perfectly is extracted, but in some places its thickness is two pixels. In order to get rid of the extra points on the last iteration step, you need to do a thinning, using the formula to find PE that have E* = 0 (40). However, in order to avoid gaps in places with double thickness, we divide the pixels into three areas - as shown in Figure 24.

Let the area denoted by the number "1" (Figure 24) correspond to the set P1, in a similar way we define the sets P2 and P3. With this breakdown, no PE has a neighbor that belongs to the same set:

$$\begin{cases} P1 = \{x_{p1} \in P1 \mid S \cap P1 = \varnothing\} \\ P2 = \{x_{p2} \in P2 \mid S \cap P2 = \varnothing\}, \\ P3 = \{x_{p3} \in P3 \mid S \cap P3 = \varnothing\} \end{cases} \tag{48}$$

where S - many neighboring PEs within local rules for each individual PE (x_{sp1}, x_{sp2}, x_{sp3}).

Figure 23. Skeleton without pseudo-processes and gaps

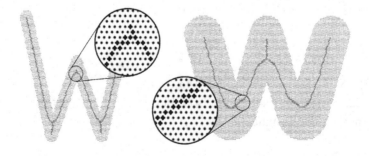

Figure 24. Splitting pixels into three areas

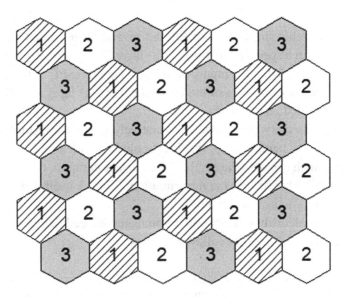

Now if all the PEs belonging to the P1 set, then those belonging to the P2 set and, finally, all the PEs belonging to P3, work consistently in time using the formula (40), then the skeleton thickness will be equal to one pixel everywhere (Figure 25). Thus, the selected skeleton fully complies with the previously put forward requirements.

Thus, the mathematical model for constructing a skeleton based on the zero Euler differential (47), developed for implementation on HCCA, allows hardware to select CF as an integral skeleton with a thickness of 1 pixel. Computer identification of the image of a moving object based on the selected skeleton is performed by comparing this CF with the template. Since in order to achieve the highest possible performance, the most voluminous in terms of calculations, the operations of finding a moving object and extracting its CF as a skeleton are performed by hardware on HCCA, the implementation of a simple comparison operation with template values can be performed using any of the known methods programmatically on a computer or FPGA.

Figure 25. The skeleton, selected according to the developed method

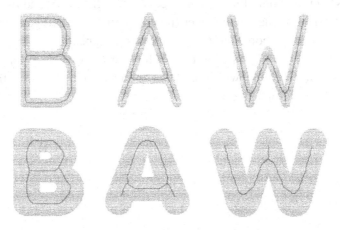

Multilayer HCCA

Cell media can consist of both a single layer of PE and several layers. In addition, each layer is built from certain PEs that perform a specific function of this layer. The layers are connected as follows: the PE outputs of the first layer are fed to the inputs of the corresponding PE of the second layer, the input function of which is the outgoing function of the PE of the previous layer, etc. Thus, the layers consistently perform one task, divided into subtasks.

Based on the fact that the image will be processed iteratively, that is, the result of the previous step will be fed to the input of each new iteration step, the CA should be divided into several layers. Thus, from the outputs of the layer, which captures the result of the current iteration, the image will be transferred to the inputs of the layer, which will start the next iteration. The CA itself is asynchronous, but for the iteration divide it is necessary to use a clock pulse.

Based on the developed algorithm, we obtain a homogeneous cellular environment (HCE), which will be multi-layered and consisting of the following layers:

- **Input Image Filter:** The first layer of HCE, which finds and corrects one-time errors;
- **Input Image Filter:** One first time of HCE, which finds and corrects one-time errors;
- **Image Thinner:** The third layer of HCE, which determines candidates for zeroing, that is, shrinks the image formed by the previous layer;
- **Fuse of Breaks:** The fourth layer of the HCE, which detects situations leading to gap of the skeleton, and prevents their occurrence;
- **Thinner:** The last fifth layer of the HCE, which performs the final reduction of all lines of the resulting skeleton to a thickness of one pixel.

The structure of a multilayer HCE for iterative image modification and interconnection of layers on Figure 26 is shown.

The principle of operation of this HCE is as follows: the original image is fed to the input of the first layer, which filters out all single errors and transfers the cleaned image to the second layer. The second layer forms an image at the end of each iteration and transfers it to the third layer, which begins the next iteration. The third layer identifies candidates for zeroing, and transmits information about them to the fourth layer. The fourth layer excludes those candidates, the zeroing of which will lead to the gap of the skeleton and transmits this information to the second layer, which forms the image at the end of the iteration. This process continues until there is a change between the initial and final image of each iteration. All changes are tracked by the second layer (new imaging unit) and generates the corresponding signal. After the signal about the completion of the iterations appears, the image from the other layer is tramsmit to the last fifth layer, the function of which consists in the final formation of the skeleton (bringing the thickness of the skeleton, which has been obtained so far and has a thickness of 2-3 pixels in some places to a thickness of one pixel).

Figure 26. Block diagram of multilayer HCE

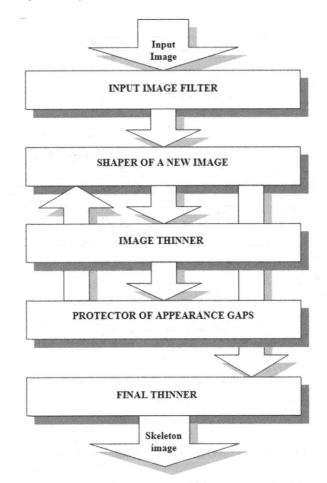

HARDWARE IMPLEMENTATION OF THE SKELETON EXTRACTION METHOD BASED ON HCCA

In the previous papes (Belan, & Motornyuk, 2013; Bilan, Motornyuk, & Bilan, (2014), a hardware and software simulation of the HCCA on the Radon transform was carried out, which allows to extract CF of images of the object.

To model of the processor elements in the Active-HDL environment, the standard library of logical elements ORCA was used. Functional diagrams were built using Block Diagram Editor. The corresponding signals were formed at the input of each circuit and time diagrams were plotted. The models of PE of the filtering layer, of thinner layer of the image, of the layer of the former image shaper and of the fuse layer of the appearance of breaks were obtained.

Timing diagrams of the PE of fuse layer and of occurrence of breaks consists of four different discontinuous combinations, which were identified and warned (Figure 27).

The decoding of the signals presented at the inputs (Figure 27) on Figure 28 is presented.

Figure 27. Timing diagrams of the breaks fuse layer PE

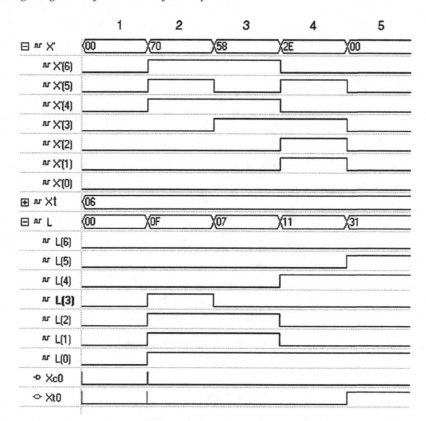

Figure 28. Interpretation of timing diagrams of the PE of layer to prevent breaks

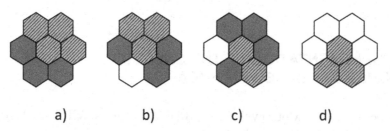

Figure *28*, a) - corresponds to the time point "2" on the time diagram (Figure 27), Figure 28, b - the moment of time "3" on the time diagram (Figure *27*), Figure 28, c - time point "4" on the time diagram (Figure 27), Figure 28, d - time points "5" on the time diagram (Figure 27).

Based on the PE models of each layer, the corresponding HCA is constructed. For modeling, 100 PE (10 × 10 pixels) were used.

To build a single layer, it is sufficient to combine processor elements in 10 lines, each with 10 elements. All inputs and outputs of each PE must be connected to the input / output ports. As a result, five layers of HCA were obtained.

To build a fully completed device, layers are combined according to the structural scheme of a multilayer HCA (Figure 26). The signals from the outputs of the control unit are transmitted to the corresponding inputs of the final thinning layer.

For the convenience of loading the HCA model with test binary images, the input 100-bit bus is divided into ten 10-bit buses, each of which enters the data into the corresponding row of the matrix of processor elements. This makes it quite easy to interpret the simulation results presented in the form of time diagrams.

To verify the correct functioning of the HCCA, two experiments were conducted, during each of which three images were loaded for processing.

Experiment Nº1: Timing diagrams of HCCA operation during experiment No.1 on Figure 29 are presented.

Figure 29. Timing diagrams of the HCCA functioning during the experiment Nº1

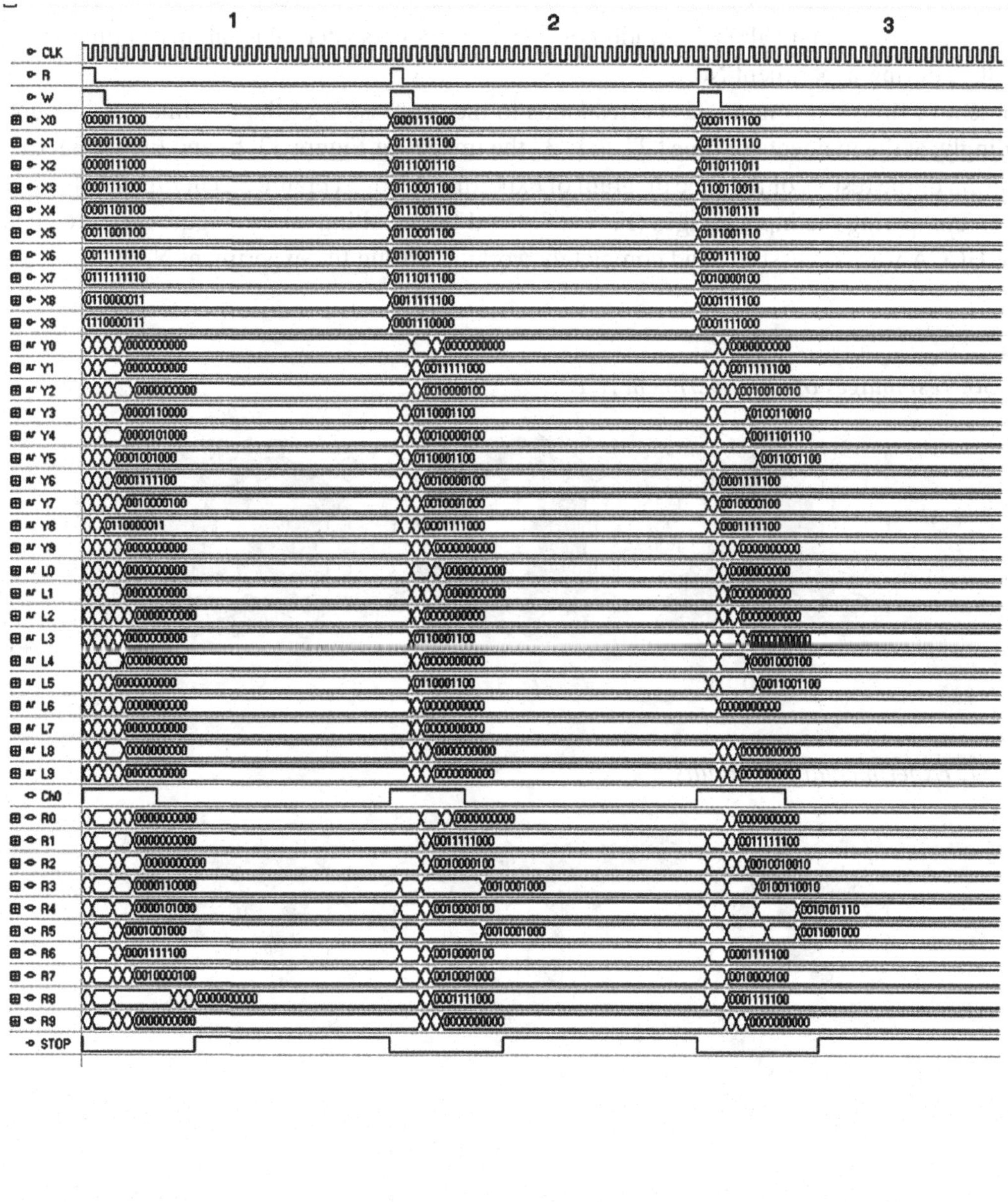

In the time diagrams of the experiments (Figure 29), X0-X9 are the input buses, Y0-Y9 are the internal communication buses between the imaging layer and the image thinner layer, L0-L9 are the internal communication buses between the image thinner layer and the discontinuity fuse layer, R0 -R9 - output tires of the final thinning layer, on which the result is formed in the form of codes of the selected image frame.

In Figure 30 is presents a graphical interpretation of image codes, wich sequentially in time were transmitted at the inputs of the cellular environment during the experiment N°1.

Time "1" (Figure 29) corresponds to the processing of the test image of Figure 30, a). Accordingly, at the moments of time "2" and "3" the images of Figure 30, b) and Figure 30, c). The results according to the time diagram of experiment No. 1 (Figure 29) in Figure 31 are presented.

When comparing the input images (Figure 30) and the resulting skeleton (Figure 31), it can conclude that the HCCA was successfully and correctly operating during the experiment N°1.

Experiment N°2: Timing diagrams of the HCCA operation during experiment No. 2 on Figure 32 are presented.

In Figure 33 is a graphical interpretation of image codes presented sequentially in time to the inputs of the HCA during experiment No. 2.

Moment of time "1" (Figure 32) corresponds to the processing of the test image of Figure 33, a). Accordingly, at the moments of time "2" and "3" the images of Figure 33, b) and Figure 33, c). The interpretation of the results of the time diagram of experiment No. 2 (Figure 32) in Figure 34 is presented.

When comparing the input images (Figure 33) and the resulting cores (Figure 34), it can conclude that the HCCA was successfully and completely working during the experiment N°2.

Figure 30. Test images of the experiment N°1

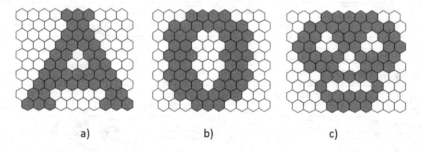

a)   b)   c)

Figure 31. Experimental N°1 results

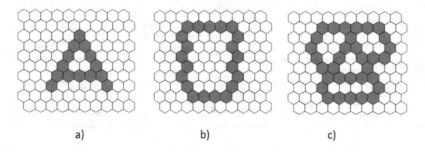

a)   b)   c)

Figure 32. Timing diagrams of the HCCA operation during experiment N°2

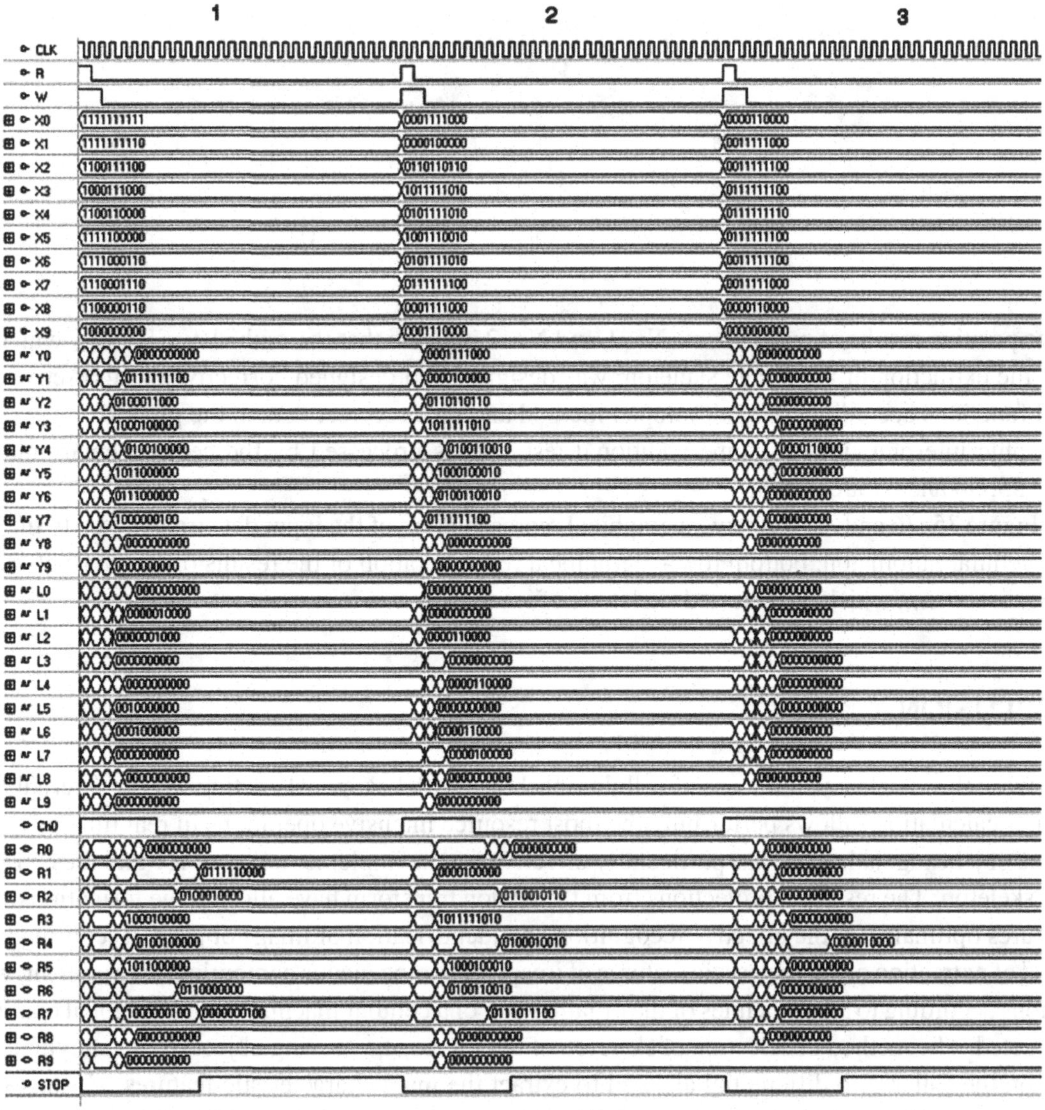

Figure 33. Test images of the experiment N°2

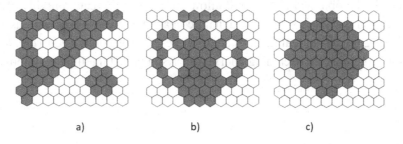

a) b) c)

Figure 34. Experimental Nº2 results

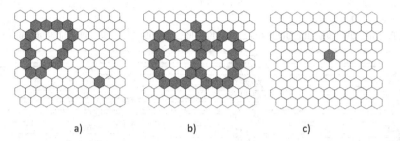

a)   b)   c)

The positive results of experiments No. 1 and No. 2 indicate that the multi-layer HCCA, which performs the extraction of the image skeleton, was designed and designed correctly, and its Active-HDL model functions according to the developed method and gives correct data in the process.

Graphic interpretations of some additional test images processed by the cellular environment in Figure 35, 36 and 37 are shown.

In Figure 35, 36 and 37: top row - a graphical representation of the input data transmitted to the input of the cellular automaton; bottom row - a graphical representation of the results of the work of the cellular environment, which are selected skeletons of images.

CONCLUSION

In the work the efficiency of the use of cellular machines with hexagonal coating, whose internal parallelism of calculations allows performing the most resource intensive operations in real time, is proved. The use of a hexagonal raster was particularly effective for the implementation of RT and the extraction of the skeleton. The resulting projections from the Radon transform have allowed the formation of a set of features optimally for the effective recognition and identification of image objects. According to this method of extraction of characteristic features of images a homogeneous computing environment, which functions according to the principles of the organization of a cellular machine with hexagonal coating, is constructed. The method of selecting of skeleton of the image of a moving object from a moving object based on the Euler zero differential allowed to extract the main characteristic features of images with high efficiency. The results of software modeling showed a high performance of the developed methods, which coincides with the results of hardware simulation in the environment of Active-HDL computing devices based on cellular hexagonal coated machines.

In future research, the obtained results will allow specialists to create a highly efficient system of biometric identification based on static and dynamic characteristics of a person, as well as a system for identifying moving objects in real time. In addition, research is conducted to create pseudo-random number generation structures for streaming encryption systems and intelligent systems modeling.

Figure 35. Test image number 3 and the results of the HCA

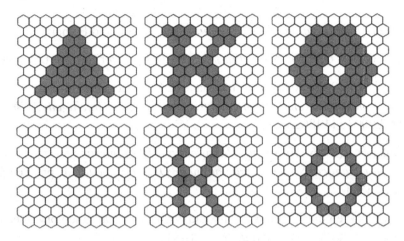

Figure 36. Test image number 4 and the results of the HCA

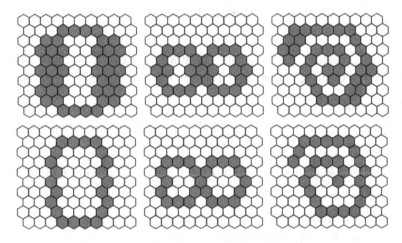

Figure 37. Test image number 5 and the results of the HCA

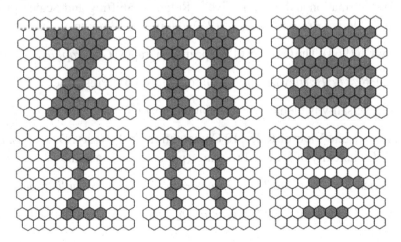

REFERENCES

Adamatzky, A. (1994). *Identification of Cellular Automata*. Taylor and Francis.

Adamatzky, A. (Ed.). (2010). *Game of Life. Cellular Automata*. Springer. doi:10.1007/978-1-84996-217-9

Ahmed, M., & Ward, R. (2002). A Rotation Invariant Rule-Based Thinning Algorithm for Character Recognition. *IEEE Transactions on Pattern Analysis and Machine Intelligence*, *24*(12), 1672–1678. doi:10.1109/TPAMI.2002.1114862

Aizawa, Y., & Nishikawa, I. (1986). *Toward the classification of the patterns generated by one-dimensional cellular automata. In Dinamical Systems and Nonlinear Oscillators* (Vol. 1, pp. 210–222). Advanced Series in Dinamical Systems.

Alonso-Sanz, R. (2006). Elementary cellular automata wiyh elementary memory rules in cell: The case of linear rules. *Journal of Cellular Automata*, *1*(1), 71–87.

Alonso-Sanz, R. (2009). *Cellular Automata with Memory*. Old Sity Publishing.

Alonso-Sanz, R. (2013). Cellular Automata with Memory and the Density Classification Task. *JCA*, *8*(3-4), 283–297.

Basurto, R., Leon, P. A., Martinez, G. J., & Seck-Tuoh-Mora, J. C. (2013). Logic Gates and Complex Dynamics in a Hexagonal Cellular Automaton: The Spiral Rule. *JCA*, *8*(1-2), 53–71.

Belan, S. N., & Motornyuk, R. L. (2013). Extraction of characteristic features of images with the help of the radon transform and its hardware implementation in terms of cellular automata. *Cybernetics and Systems Analysis*, *49*(1), 7–14. doi:10.100710559-013-9479-2

Berry, J. K. (1993). *Beyond Mapping: Concepts, Algorithms, and Issues in CIS*. Fort Collins, CO: GIS World.

Bilan, S. (2017). *Formation Methods, Models, and Hardware Implementation of Pseudorandom Number Generators: Emerging Research and Opportunities*. IGI Global.

Bilan, S., Motornyuk, R., & Bilan, S. (2014). Method of Hardware Selection of Characteristic Features Based on Radon Transformation and not Sensitive to Rotation, Shifting and Scale of the Input Images. *Advances in Image and Video Processing*, *2*(4), 12–23. doi:10.14738/aivp.24.392

Boyce, R. R., & Wav, C. (1964). The Concept of Shape in Geography. *Geographical Review*, *54*, 561–572.

Bracewell, R. N. (1986). *The Hartley transform*. Oxford University Press, Inc.

Cook, M. (2004). Universality in elementary cellular automata. *Complex Systems*, *15*(1), 1–40.

Cook, M. (2008). A Concrete View of Rule 110 Computation. In T. Neary, D. Woods, A.K. Seda, & N. Murphy (Eds.), The Complexity of Simple Programs (pp. 31-55). Academic Press.

Deans, S. R., & Roderick, S. (1983). *The Radon Transform and Some of its Applications*. New York: Wiley.

DeMers, M. N. (2008). *Fundamentals of Geographic Information Systems* (4th ed.). Wiley.

Dewdney, A. K. (1990). Computer recreations. The cellular automata programs that create Wireworld, Rugworld and the diversions. *Scientific American*.

Dudgeon, D. E., & Mersereau, R. M. (1984). *Multidimensional Digital Signal Processing*. Englewood Cliffs, NJ: Printice-Hall, Inc.

Ell, T. A., Bihan, N. L., & Sangwine, S. J. (2014). *Quaternion Fourier Transforms for Signal and Image Processing (Focus Series)* (1st ed.). Wiley-ISTE.

Fernandes, L. A. F., & Oliveira, M. M. (2008). Real-time line detection through an improved Hough transform voting scheme. *Pattern Recognition*, *41*(1), 299–314. doi:10.1016/j.patcog.2007.04.003

Floriani, L., Falcidieno, B., Nagy, G., & Pienovi, C. (1991). On sorting triangles in a Delaynay tessellation. *Algorithmica*, *6*(6), 522–535. doi:10.1007/BF01759057

Fortune, S. (1987). A sweepline algorithm for Voronoi diagrams. *Algorithmica*, *2*(2), 153–174. doi:10.1007/BF01840357

Gardner, M. (1970). The Fantastic Combinations of John Conway's New Solitaire Game "Life". *Scientific American*, (223): 120–123. doi:10.1038cientificamerican1070-120

Golay, M. J. E. (1969). Hexagonal parallel pattern transformations. *IEEE Transactions on Computers*, *C-18*(8), 733–740. doi:10.1109/T-C.1969.222756

Gonzalez, R. C., & Woods, R. E. (2008). *Digital Image Processing* (3rd ed.). Prentice Hall.

Guibas, L., & Stolfi, J. (1985). Primitives for the manipulation of general subdivisions and the computation of Voronoi diagrams. *ACM Transactions on Graphics*, *4*(2), 74–123. doi:10.1145/282918.282923

Gutowitz, H. A., Victor, J. D., & Knight, B. W. (1987). Local structure theory for cellular automata. *Physica D. Nonlinear Phenomena*, *28*(1-2), 18–48. doi:10.1016/0167-2789(87)90120-5

Hadeler, K. P., & Müller, J. (2017). *Cellular Automata: Analysis and Applications (Springer Monographs in Mathematics)* (1st ed.). Springer. doi:10.1007/978-3-319-53043-7

Hedlung, G. A. (1969). Endomorphism and Automorphism of the Shift Dynamic System. *Mathematical Systems Theory*, (3): 51–59.

Iclgason, S. (2014). *Integral Geometry and Radon Transforms*. Springer.

Holland, J. (1966). *Universal Spaces: A Basis for Studies in Adaptation. In Automata Theory* (pp. 218–230). Academic Press.

Horn, B. K. P. (1986). *Robot Vision*. MIT Press.

Jain, A. (1989). *Fundamentals of Digital Image Processing*. Prentice-Hall.

Kobasyar, M.I. & Rusin, B.P. (2001). Detection of curves from binary images by Radon transformation. *Bulletin of the National University "Lviv Polytechnic" "Radioelektronika i telekomunikatsiia"*, (428), 6-9.

Kwok, P. A. (1988). thinning algorithm by contour generation. *Univ. of Calgary*, *31*(11), 1314–1324.

Lam, L., & Suen, C. Y. (1995). An evaluation of parallel thinning algorithms for characterrecognition. *IEEE Trans. PAMI, 17*(9), 914–919. doi:10.1109/34.406659

Li, J., Robles-Kelly, A., & You, S. (2017). A Frequency Domain Neural Network for Fast Image Super-resolution. *International Joint Conference on Neural Networks*.

Li, W., & Packard, N. (1990). The Structure of the Elementary Cellular Automata Rule Spase. *Complex Systems, 4*(3), 281–297.

Lu, X., Chen, H., Yeung, S. K., Deng, Z., & Chen, W. (2018). *Unsupervised Articulated Skeleton Extraction from Point Set Sequences Captured by a Single Depth Camera*. Association for the Advancement of Artificial Intelligence.

Mersereau, R. M. (1979). The Processing of Hexagonally Sampled Two-Dimensional Signals. *Proceedings of the IEEE, 67*(6), 930–949. doi:10.1109/PROC.1979.11356

Minichino, J., & Howse, J. (2015). *Computer Vision with Python*. Packt Publishing.

Natterer, F. (2001). *The Mathematics of Computerized Tomography (Classics in Applied Mathematics, 32)*. Philadelphia, PA: Society for Industrial and Applied Mathematics. doi:10.1137/1.9780898719284

Natterer, F., & Wubbeling, F. (2001). *Mathematical Methods in Image Reconstruction*. Philadelphia, PA: Society for Industrial and Applied Mathematics. doi:10.1137/1.9780898718324

Neumann, J. (1951). The general and logical theory of automata. In *Cerobral Mechanisms in Behavior, The Hixon Symposium* (pp. 1-31). John Wiley & Sons.

Neumann, J. (1966). *Theory of Self-Reproducing Automata*. University of Illinois Press.

Nicoladie, D. T. (2014). Hexagonal pixel-array for efficient spatial computation for motion-detection pre-processing of visual scenes. *Advances in Image and Video Processing, 2*(2), 26 – 36.

Nixon, M. S., & Aguardo, A. S. (2002). *Feature Extraction and Image Processing*. Newnes.

Patil, P. M., Suralkar, S. R., & Sheikh, F. B. (2005). Rotation invariant thinning algorithm to detect ridge bifurcations for fingerprint identification. *17th IEEE International Conference on Tools with Artificial Intelligence (ICTAI'05)*, 634-641. 10.1109/ICTAI.2005.112

Pratt, W. K. (2016). *Digital Images Processing* (3rd ed.). Wiley.

Richard, O., Duda, P., & Hart, E. (1972). Use of the hough transformation to detect lines and curves in pictures. *Comm. ACM, 15*(1), 11-15.

Rosenfeld, A., & Kak, A. (1982). *Digital Picture Processing* (2nd ed.). New York: Academic Press.

Rosin, P. L. (2005). Training Cellular Automata for Image Processing. *LNCS, 3540*, 195–204.

Rubin, B. (2015). *Introduction to Radon Transforms: With Elements of Fractional Calculus and Harmonic Analysis (Encyclopedia of Mathematics and its Applications)* (1st ed.). Cambridge University Press.

Ryan, Ø. (2019). *Linear Algebra, Signal Processing, and Wavelets - A Unified Approach: Python Version (Springer Undergraduate Texts in Mathematics and Technology)* (1st ed.). Springer.

Solomon, C., & Breckon, T. (2011). *Fundamental of Digital Image Processing. A Practical Approach with Examples in Matlab*. Wiley – Blackwell.

Staunton, R. C. (1989). Hexagonal image sampling, a practical proposition. *Proceedings of the Society for Photo-Instrumentation Engineers, 1008*, 23–27. doi:10.1117/12.949123

Steeb, W. H. (2014). *The Nonlinear Workbook: Chaos, Fractals, Cellular Automata, Genetic Algorithms, Gene Expression Programming, Support Vector Machine, Wavelets, Hidden ... Java And Symbolicc++ Programs (6th ed.)*. Wspc. doi:10.1142/9084

Sutner, K. (2009). *Classification of cellular Automata*. In R. A. Meyers (Ed.), *Encyclopedia of Complexty and Systems Science* (pp. 755–768). New York: Springer –Verlag.

Toft, P. (1996). *The Radon Transform: Theory and Implementation* (PhD thesis). Dept. of Math. Modelling Section for Digital Signal Processing, Technical Univ. of Denmark.

Ulam, S. (1952) Random Processes and Transformations. *Procedings Int. Congr. Mathem.,* (2), 264-275.

Wolfram, S. (1986). *Appendix of Theory and Applicat ions of Cellular A utomata*. World Scientific.

Wolfram, S. (1986a). Random Sequence Generation by Cellular Automata. *Advances in Applied Mathematics, 7*(2), 429–432. doi:10.1016/0196-8858(86)90028-X

Wolfram, S. (1986b). Cryptography with Cellular Automata. *Lecture Notes in Computer Science, 218*, 429–432. doi:10.1007/3-540-39799-X_32

Wolfram, S. (2002). *A new kind of science*. Wolfram Media.

Woodward, M., & Muir, F. (1984). Hexagonal Sampling. *Stanford Exploration Project, SEP-38*, 183–194.

Wu, S., Wen, W., Xiao, B., Guo, X., Du, J., Wang, C., & Wang, Y. (2019). An Accurate Skeleton Extraction Approach From 3D Point Clouds of Maize Plants. *Frontiers in Plant Science, 10*, 1–14. doi:10.3389/fpls.2019.00248 PMID:30899271

Zuse, K. (1969). *Rechnender Raum*. Braunschweig: Vieweg. doi:10.1007/978-3-663-02723-2

Chapter 13
The Moving Object Detection and Research Effects of Noise on Images Based on Cellular Automata With a Hexagonal Coating Form and Radon Transform

Ruslan Leonidovich Motornyuk

PU "Kiev Department" Branch of the Main Information and Computing Center of the JSC "Ukrzaliznytsya", Ukraine

Stepan Bilan

ⓘ https://orcid.org/0000-0002-2978-5556

State University of Infrastructure and Technology, Ukraine

ABSTRACT

Methods for image identification based on the Radon transform using hexagonal-coated cellular automata in the chapter are considered. A method and a mathematical model for the detection of moving objects based on hexagonal-coated cellular automata are described. The advantages of using hexagonal coverage for detecting moving objects in the image are shown. The technique of forming Radon projections for moving regions in the image, which is designed for a hexagonal-coated cellular automata, is described. The software and hardware implementation of the developed methods are presented. Based on the obtained results, a hexagonal-coated cellular automata was developed to identify images of objects based on the Radon transform. The Radon transform allowed to effectively extract the characteristic features of images with a large percentage of noise. Experimental analysis showed the advantages of the proposed methods of image processing and identification of moving objects.

DOI: 10.4018/978-1-7998-1290-6.ch013

INTRODUCTION

Today, the creation of specialized computing tools for automation and intelligent solving of various tasks in transport is gaining more and more importance. One of these tasks is image processing and analysis, which is associated with the recognition and identification of visual images in real time. This task is inseverable related with the organization of protection of objects in real time. Currently, such problems are solved with the help of authoring methods and technologies (Tamanaha, Murphy, Onorato, & Tafralian, 2019; Land, McConnell, & McMahon, 2006). However, such technologies use complex identification algorithms and are implemented mainly on a software platform, which limits the speed of the motion detection system and the identification of moving objects in real time. Therefore, the chapter does not pay attention to authoring technologies due to their limitations in hardware implementation and the complex organization of the full automation of the identification process. It is possible to give examples in which there are moving objects and the movement of which must be controlled in a certain way: track movements, record their presence, keep records of them, calculate movement characteristics (direction, speed), calculate physical dimensions, etc. This, for example, may be freight railcars; cars; objects that cross special checkpoints (at airports, seaports, etc.) of a video surveillance system for certain objects or for monitoring a certain terrain; parts and spare parts on conveyor lines, etc. The starting point for performing all these operations is the identification of an object that moves.

Radio frequency and optoelectronic identification systems are very popular in many areas of human activity. They have certain advantages and disadvantages. Optoelectronic identification tools are the most attractive. They are the cheapest and use various methods for converting optical signals, as well as methods for processing images represented by an array of electrical signals. Also, in order to identify images of objects in real time, cellular automata (CA) are used, which, due to the matrix organization, make it possible to organize parallel computing (Belan, & Motornyuk. 2013; Bilan, 2017; Hadeler, & Müller, 2017).

RELEVANCE OF RESEARCH

Identification of complex objects and phenomena requires the creation of special recognition systems - complex dynamic systems consisting generally of a team of trained specialists and a set of technical means of obtaining and processing information that are designed to solve, on the basis of specially developed algorithms, the problems of identifying the corresponding images (objects, phenomena).

Currently, there are many operating automated systems that, to varying degrees, solve identification problems (assigning an object to one particular class from a set of previously defined classes of objects) moving objects. Each identification system is highly specialized; therefore, it is adapted to recognize only one type of image (for example, a system that recognizes car license plates cannot recognize a person's face, etc.). This is due to the complexity of the identification task itself, which in itself is a rather complicated and time-consuming task and depends on the type of object and the conditions for monitoring it.

For computer image identification systems, input information comes in via a visual information channel, for example, video cameras that work with images. The identification process is based on the decision to classify an image (image of an object) based on a comparison of its characteristic features (CF) with previously known CF reference images. To obtain a CF object from a graphic image, it is necessary to pre-process this image in order to eliminate redundant information and extract CFs or classifiers (image edges, segment borders, image frame).

FORMULATION OF THE PROBLEM

The paper sets the task of efficiently extracting CF and moving parts of the image to improve the accuracy of real-time identification of moving objects using the Radon transform (RT) and cellular automata with hexagonal coating (HCCA).

The Method and Model of the Detection of Moving Parts of the Image Based on Cellular Automata with Hexagonal Coating

The hardware implementation of the image skeleton allocation provides speed sufficient for the operation of the identification system in real time. The selected skeleton will be the CF used to implement the image identification method.

The method of extracting the skeleton of the image based on the HCCA and the Radon transform is considered in the papers (Belan, & Motornyuk. 2013; Bilan, Motornyuk, & Bilan, 2014). The efficiency of using HCCA with the use of the Radon transform is shown. Radon transformation on the basis of a hexagonal-coated spacecraft allows us to construct six Radon projections, which increases the accuracy of identification by increasing the CF.

First, the input image is enter to the system. It selects the area containing a moving object, which is transmitted for further processing to the HCCA, which, through certain iterative transformations, provides a description of the input image as a skeleton of the original image. The result of the HCCA working at the output will be a 1-pixel-shaped skeleton, which can be represented by a code sequence of a set of geometric elements in the form of straight lines, arcs, circles, forks, etc.

The simplest method of searching for moving objects in an image is the frame difference method (Orten, & Alalan, 2005), which consists in pixel-by-pixel comparison of two consecutive frames: pixels that have changed their color code, taking into account a certain sensitivity threshold, are considered to be pixels in which movement is detected; all others are recognized as belonging to the background area. This method is the simplest to implement and is suitable for the case of a fixed camera, that is just our case. To use it on HCCA, some refinement is needed to extend the functionality and eliminate some of the shortcomings, namely:

1. "Moving" pixels obtained by this method in most cases will not fully correspond to the entire area of a moving object (Alavi, 2012; Niitsiima, & Maruyama, 2004; Talukder, & Maithies, 2004; Yuan, & Mallot, 2010; Orten, & Alalan, 2005; Dkhil, Wali, & Alimi, 2016; Gariepy, Tonolini, Henderson, Leach, & Faccio, 2016), and a small part of them belong to the background area. In terms of set theory (Hausdorff, 1962), this can be written:

$$\begin{cases} F \cap M \neq F \\ F \cap M \neq M, \\ B \cap M \neq \varnothing \end{cases} \tag{1}$$

where

M – the set of pixels of the image that recorded the movement,

F – the set of pixels of the image of a moving object,

B – the set of pixels of background area.

Thus, it is necessary not only to identify the pixels that have changed their state, but also to select, if possible, the entire area occupied by the moving object. It is proposed to fix the area of a moving object by building projections of PE, defined as "moving", to the extreme PE of HCCA;

2. Based on the geometric dimensions of the selected area, it is possible to calculate certain parameters defining certain characteristics of a moving object, for example, its size, average and instantaneous speed, distance traveled, etc.

ADAPTING MOTION SEARCH BY FRAME DIFFERENCE FOR HCCA

Denoting by M as the set of image points where motion is recorded, S - the set of neighboring pixels (S = {x1, x2, x3, x4, x5, x6}), $x_i(t-1)$ and $x_i(t)$ - respectively, the pixel codes in the previous and current frames (points in time), a - the threshold of sensitivity, you can write a mathematical expression for determining whether a pixel belongs to a moving region:

$$x_i(t) \in \begin{cases} M, if \left| x_i(t-1) - x_i(t) \right| > a \\ \bar{M}, if \left| x_i(t-1) - x_i(t) \right| \le a \end{cases}. \tag{2}$$

Now is considered the features of using this method on HCCA and for simplicity is started with the most primitive case - the binary image.

A typical (classic) PE of a cell environment is one-bit, that is, each PE represents one pixel of a binary image. In the logical "1" state, it encodes a black pixel, in the "0" state - a white pixel. This is the simplest type of image and to work with it requires a correspondingly simple one in terms of its circuit implementation of PE. To detect motion in this case, it is necessary to compare the current state at the input of the PE with its previous state. If these states are the same («0» = «0», «1» = «1»), then there was no movement in this pixel, and at the output of motion detection, is set a logical «0». If there was a change («0» → «1» or «1» → «0»), then the movement was and at the output of the motion, detection is set «1». This rule can be written as a sum modulo 2 of PE values at the previous and current point in time:

$$x_i(t) \in \begin{cases} M, if\, x_i(t-1)x_i(t) = 1 \\ \bar{M}, if \left| x_i(t-1)x_i(t) \right| = 0 \end{cases} \tag{3}$$

In Figure 1, a) an example of two consecutive frames of a binary image with a moving rectangle and a circle is shows, and the result of the simulation of the cellular environment (right), where the binary image of the current frame is shown in black and the PE in which the change of state was recorded, i.e. there was a movement.

But such simplified conditions, where the background of the image has one (white) color, and moving objects are clearly different from the background and therefore have a different (black) color, are not very similar to the actual conditions of use of such systems. In practice, a moving object will not always have sufficient contrast with the background so that during binarization they do not "merge".

In Figure 1, b) an example of a complex color image with low-contrast moving objects is shown. In this case, the binarization "destroyed" two objects with low contrast in the left part of the frame, while the high-contrast objects in the right side remained and the movement was correctly recorded.

Above it was considered purely theoretical types of images that are almost never met in real conditions. In Figure 2 an example of the work of the cellular environment in detecting movement on real images with a contrasting and low contrast background / object a) and b) respectively is shown.

As can be seen from Figure 2, binarization gives satisfactory results when working with contrast and is generally unacceptable when working with low-contrast real images. The only way out is to use not single-bit, but multi-bit PE, which will be able to encode and compare not only binary, but also multi-gradation images. Since the main functional orientation of HCCA is motion search, and in the overwhelming majority of cases, it is successfully fixed even on a sequence of images represented by shades of gray, the developed HCCA will be adapted to work with a single color channel, which will

Figure 1. Motion detection, a) - on a binary image, b) - on a complex low-contrast image after its binarization

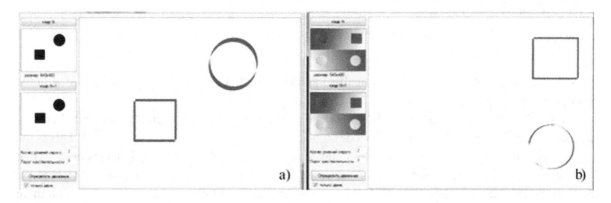

Figure 2. Motion detection on real images after their binarization, a) - contrast, b) - low contrast

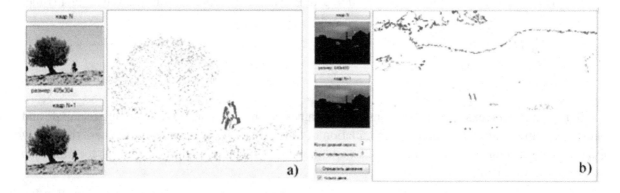

reduce hardware costs by about three times with three channel color coding (RGB). If it is necessary to use color coding, it will suffice to supplement each PE with two more similar channels and accordingly increase the capacity of hardware (data buses, registers), where necessary.

To encode an image, which is represented by a different number of shades (gradations) of gray, a correspondingly different depth of PE is also required. For example, if the image has 256 shades of gray, then digital PE should have $\log_2(256) = 8$ bits. For 128 gradations, the number of digits $\log_2(128) = 7$, etc.

When working with images that have a large number of gradations, the image itself is transmitted most accurately in terms of details and is closest to its appearance in a real (non-digitized) state. However, a serious drawback is the large hardware costs for the implementation of calculators due to the increase in the bit depth of all circuit components of the CA. Therefore, it is necessary to find such a minimum value of bit depth, at which the key details of the image are not lost and at which it is still possible to track changes in the visual scene.

In Figure 3 is illustrated the processing of 256-, 32, 16- and 8-gradation images a) an example of 8-bit PE working with 256 shades (gradations) of gray b) 5-bit PE (32 shades) c) 4-bit PE (16 shades) 3-bit PE (8 shades). For this particular case, a decrease in the number of colors to 8 (d) leads to the results that were manifested when processing this image on binary PEs (Figure 1,b), namely: there is a fusion (partial) of the object with the background. However, already at 16 shades (Figure 3, c) the object is clearly separated from the background.

As you can see, reducing the bit gives a gain in hardware costs, but too little bit has a negative effect on the quality of the selection of moving objects. The less gradations, the less hardware costs for building PE. At the same time, the more details of the image will be lost and there is a high probability that if the contrast between the moving object and the background is insignificant, the object and the background will merge, as a result of which the movement will not be fixed at all, or not the entire moving object will be extracted. When developing HCCA we will focus on working with images represented by 16 shades, that is, we will have 4-bit PE. If you need to work with a large number of shades (or less) - it just increases (or decreases) and the bit-depth of PE.

Using a different sensitivity threshold for the same visual scene, different results can be achieved depending on the problem statement. In general, the determination of the sensitivity level is individual for each application of the system and can be adjusted to the desired result. Therefore, it is possible to formulate certain rules, the use of which will make it possible to build a special control system for the cellular environment that will be able to automatically set the required sensitivity threshold itself.

One of these rules may be the percentage of the number of PEs that recorded movement from the total number of all PE of CA on which images were submitted (for cases when a moving object has a certain predetermined maximum size, projection area):

$$
a(t+1) = \begin{cases} a(t) + \Delta a, & \text{if } \dfrac{|M|}{|F \cup B|} > m_{\max} \\[2ex] a(t) - \Delta a, & \text{if } \dfrac{|M|}{|F \cup B|} < m_{\min} \\[2ex] a(t), & \text{if } \dfrac{|M|}{|F \cup B|} > m_{\min} \end{cases} \tag{4}
$$

Figure 3. Motion detection on complex low-contrast real images represented by different numbers of grayscale

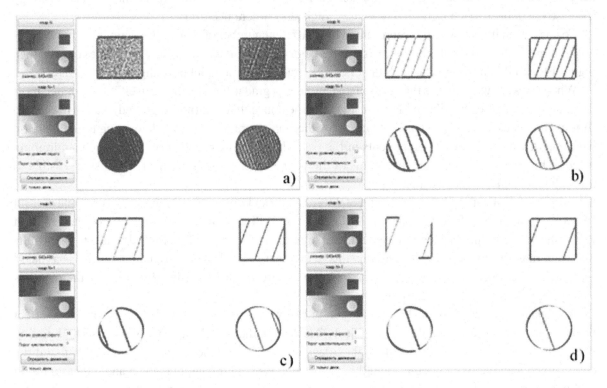

where

a(t+1) – the value of the sensitivity level for the next point in time,

a(t) – the value of the sensitivity level at the current time,

Δa – amount of change in sensitivity level,

M – set of pixels of motion-captured image,

F – set of pixels of the image of a moving object,

B – set of pixels of background area,

m_{min}, m_{max} – respectively, the minimum and maximum allowable levels of the ratio of the number of PEs with a fixed movement to the total number of PEs of the image of the current visual scene.

Another variant of the defining rule is the presence of spatial variation on the image plane of PE with fixed motion. A moving object usually occupies a well-defined localized space on this plane.

$$a(t+1) = \begin{cases} a(t) + \Delta a, if \dfrac{|P|}{|h|} > m_{max} \\ a(t) - \Delta a, if \dfrac{|P|}{|h|} < m_{min} \\ a(t), if\ m_{max} > \dfrac{|P|}{|h|} > m_{min} \end{cases}, \tag{5}$$

where

a(t+1) – the value of the sensitivity level for the next point in time,

a(t) – sensitivity value for current time,

Δa – sensitivity change amount,

P – set of lines with fixed motion (in fact, the projection of the moving region on one of the coordinate axes),

h – the size of the corresponding coordinate axis in pixels,

m_{min}, m_{max} – respectively, the minimum and maximum allowable levels of the ratio of the projections of the moving area to the size of the image along the corresponding axis of coordinates for this visual scene.

The level selection begins with small sensitivity levels with its gradual increase until a satisfactorily localized cluster of "moving" pixels is obtained. In Figure 4 is illustrated the result of the last rule.

The sensitivity level varied from 0 to 140. Depending on the parameters set, the sensitivity control system could choose options c) or d) as the most informative in terms of the result. There is no longer a chaotic scatter of "moving" pixels across the entire image plane, and the moving area is quite clearly localized.

Figure 4. Different levels of sensitivity for one 16-gradation image: a – 0, b – 20, c – 40, d – 65, e – 100, f – 140

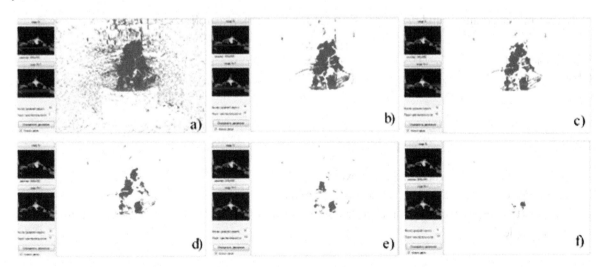

SEPARATION OF SINGLE ERRORS AND CONSTRUCTION OF PROJECTIONS OF THE MOVING REGION ON HCCA

In practice, when digital photography and video recording, as a result of digitizing the signal, its initial noise or interference, single errors can occur: individual pixels whose color code has changed more than the threshold value (i.e., motion is detected), but in fact there was no movement at this point. A feature of such cases is that no movement was recorded in any of the neighboring PEs. To filter out such single interference, it is necessary:

1. All PE, whose code has changed more than the threshold value, designate as candidates for the definition of motion;

$$x_i(t) \in \begin{cases} K, if \left| x_i(t-1) - x_i(t) \right| > a \\ \bar{K}, if \left| x_i(t-1) - x_i(t) \right| \le a \end{cases}, \tag{6}$$

where K – set of pixels of motion detection candidates.

2. For such PEs it necessary check the status of all neighbors, if there are any candidates among them, and if not, consider this pixel to be wrong, otherwise, fix movement in this PE:

$$x_i(t) \in \begin{cases} M, \ if \ S \cap K \ne \varnothing \\ \bar{M}, \ if \ S \cap K = \varnothing \end{cases}, \tag{7}$$

where

K – set of pixels of motion detection candidates,
M – set of pixels, in which recorded the movement,
S – set of adjacent pixels (S = {x1, x2, x3, x4, x5, x6}).

Taking into account (6) and (7), expression (2) can be written as follows:

$$x_i(t) \in \begin{cases} M, if \left(\left| x_i(t-1) - x_i(t) \right| > a \right) \wedge \left(S \cap M \ne \varnothing \right) \\ \bar{M}, if \left| x_i(t-1) - x_i(t) \right| \le a \end{cases}, \tag{8}$$

where

M – set of pixels, in which recorded the movement,
S – set of adjacent pixels (S = {x1, x2, x3, x4, x5, x6}),
$x_i(t-1)$ and $x_i(t)$ – respectively, the pixel codes in the previous and current frames (points in time),
a – sensitivity level.

For the possibility of a mathematical description of the construction of projections, let us introduce the concept of main (main) directions on HCCA. In Figure 2. PE is depicted surrounded by six neighbors: x1, x2, x3, x4, x5, x6. The hexagonal coating has three main directions (passing through the edges of the central PE), which can be conventionally denoted by a transition from one neighboring PE to another (Figure 5):

1. x4 ⇒ x3 (from the right side to the left) - corresponds to the corner 0°;
2. x2 ⇒ x5 (from the top right edge to the bottom left) - corresponds to the corner 60°;
3. x1 ⇒ x6 (from the upper left side to the lower right) - corresponds to the corner 120°.

If the number of PE in HCCA, constituting one face, denoted by n (in Figure 5 n = 9), then in each of the three main directions of HCCA has k lines:

$$k = 2 \cdot n - 1. \tag{9}$$

If each i-th line is represented as a set of points L_i, and P - the set of lines of the corresponding direction, forming the projection of points with fixed motion, then:

$$x_i \in L_i \subset P, \text{ if } x_i \in M. \tag{10}$$

Using (10) and representing the set P for each of the three main directions as P1, P2, P3, we will be able to construct projections in the corresponding directions (Figure 6).

Figure 5. The main directions of hexagonal coverage by 0°, 60° and 120°

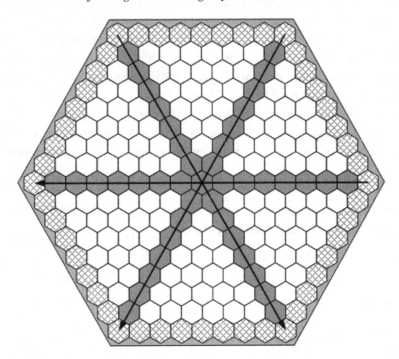

Figure 6. The principle of forming the projections of the moving area

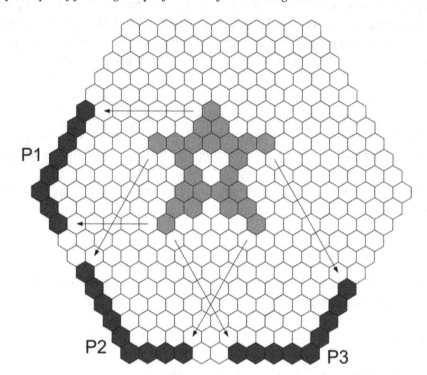

DETERMINING CHARACTERISTICS OF THE MOTION OBJECT

Further additional analysis of the obtained projections will provide information about some geometrical features of the moving object, its location and orientation in the field of the visual scene. If you also know such an important parameter as the distance to a moving object, then, knowing the viewing angle of the video camera as the source of the image, you can additionally calculate such characteristics of the object as its physical dimensions, movement speed (instantaneous in the current frame and average), acceleration, its trajectory, the distance he walked and others.

In Figure 6 moving area is marked in gray, constructed projections of the moving area marked on the extreme PE dark gray. Further calculations are more convenient to carry out in an orthogonal coordinate system. Knowing the ratio of the distances between the centers of neighboring pixels vertically and horizontally for hexagonal coverage, namely $= \dfrac{2}{\sqrt{3}}$ (Levin, & Vishnyakov, 1989; Woodward, & Muir, 1984), we write the transition expressions from the powers of the sets P1, P2, P3 to the size of the moving region in pixels in the (x, y) coordinates, respectively x_{pix}, y_{pix}:

$$x_{pix} = (\mid P2 \mid + \mid P3 \mid) \cdot \frac{1}{2} \cdot \frac{2}{\sqrt{3}} = \frac{\mid P2 \mid + \mid P3 \mid}{\sqrt{3}}, \tag{11}$$

$$y_{pix} = \mid P1 \mid. \tag{12}$$

The coordinates of the geometric center of the moving region (x_c, y_c):

$$x_c = x_1 + \frac{x_{pix}}{2},$$

(13)

$$y_c = y_1 + \frac{y_{pix}}{2},$$

(14)

where (x_1, y_1) – coordinates of the upper left corner of the moving area.

To go from the size in pixels on the image to the actual size in meters, it is necessary to determine the physical size m, represented by one pixel of the image of the object:

$$m = \frac{l \cdot \left(\sin\left(\frac{\alpha}{2}\right) + tg\left(\frac{\alpha}{2}\right) \right)}{N_x},$$

(15)

where

l – distance to the object (м),
α - camera viewing angle (x axis),
N_x – the number of pixels (dimension) of the video image horizontally.

Height (H) of the moving area in meters:

$$H = m \cdot y_{pix},$$

(16)

where y_{pix} – the size of the moving area in pixels vertically.
Width (W) of the moving area in meters:

$$W = m \cdot x_{pix},$$

(17)

where x_{pix} – horizontal size of the moving area in pixels.
The displacement of the object in the image plane for 1 frame:

$$S_i = m \cdot \sqrt{\Delta x_c^2 + \Delta y_c^2},$$

(18)

where Δx_c and Δy_c – changing the coordinates of the geometric center of the moving region between frames:

$\Delta x_c = |x_c(t-1) - x_c(t)|$, $\Delta y_c = |y_c(t-1) - y_c(t)|$.

Moving an object in 1 frame:

$$P_i = \sqrt{S_i^2 + \Delta l^2} \,, \tag{19}$$

where $\Delta l = |l\,(t-1) - l\,(t)|$ – change the distance to the object between frames.

General object movement:

$$P = \sum_{i=1}^{n} P_i \,, \tag{20}$$

where n – number of processed frames.

Object speed per frame (м/с):

$$V_i = P_i \cdot f \,, \tag{21}$$

where f – video frame frequency per second.

Average object speed:

$$V = \frac{\sum_{i=1}^{n} V_i}{n} \,, \tag{22}$$

where n – number of frames processed.

Thus, using the above formulas (11) - (22), it is possible to determine the important characteristics of the movement of an object, based on the parameters of its image, the distance to the object and the parameters of the camera.

HARDWARE IMPLEMENTATION OF THE METHOD OF IDENTIFICATION OF IMAGES OF OBJECTS BASED ON THE RADON TRANSFORM

The Algorithm of PE of HCCA To Find and Select the Moving Parts of the Image

On the basis of the developed method and the mathematical model of HCCA to find and select the moving parts of the image, the algorithm for the functioning of the PE cell environment is following. In this case, the coding of neighboring PEs will be taken according to the previously stipulated:

1. According to the Write signal, in the cellular environment of the cellular environment, the grayscale codes of the corresponding pixels (x) of the video frame are entered. The code is written to the register to save the current pixel value. At the same time, the code stored in this register prior to this action is written to the register to save the previous pixel value.

2. The code comparison procedure starts immediately after the Write signal changes from a logical "1" to "0", that is, the inverted Write () signal is the comparison signal.

3. Find the difference between the values stored in the register for the current code and the register for the preliminary pixel code.

4. Compare the difference modulus obtained in step 3 with the threshold value (accuracy). If the modulus of the difference is above the threshold of sensitivity, go to step 6; otherwise, go to step 5.

5. At the *mov* output of PE, set the value of the logical "0", that is, assume that the pixel does not change its state between the previous and current frames, taking into account the sensitivity threshold accuracy. Go to step 7.

6. At the *mov* output of PE, set the logical value "1", that is, consider the given pixel to change its state between the previous and current frames, taking into account the sensitivity threshold accuracy, therefore, there is movement in this pixel.

7. Analyze the input signals from the *mov* outputs neighboring PE (mov1, mov2, mov3, mov4, mov5, mov6). If among them there is at least one with the signal "1" - go to step 9.

8. The motion in this pixel is fixed, but motion in any of the neighboring PEs is not fixed, most likely this is an erroneous response to noise or interference. Therefore, on the *mov* output of PE, set the value of the logical "0" - movement in pixels not found.

9. Analyze the signals at the inputs P1, P2, P4, received from the corresponding outputs (xP1, xP2, xP4) of neighboring PEs (x1, x2, x4). At the PE xP1 output, set the "1" signal if the output of the given PE is *mov* = "1" or at the input P1 = "1". Similarly for xP2 and xP4 outputs.

10. End of algorithm.

Figure 7. Graphic image of PE to detect moving parts of the image

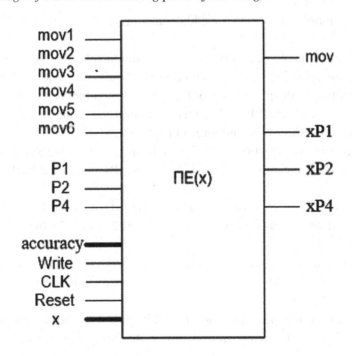

Based on the presented algorithm, the PE should have the following inputs and outputs (Figure 7)

In Figure 7 mov1, mov2, mov3, mov4, mov5, mov6 - the inputs from the output signals of neighboring PEs, which determine the belonging of a given pixel of the image of the moving region; P1, P2, P4 - PE inputs, on which information is coming about the projection of the moving area from neighboring PEs; «X» - the input bus for entering in the PE of a code gradations (shades) of the gray image represented by the corresponding pixel; accuracy - input bus of the threshold value of sensitivity (accuracy) of determining the change in the pixel code from the previous to the current frame; Write - control signal by which the image is recorded in PE; CLK - sync pulse; Reset - initial state signal; mov - the output signal of PE determines the belonging of the given pixel of the image of the moving region; xP1, xP2, xP4 - PE exits on which the projection of the mobile area is formed in three main directions of the hexagonal coating.

As a result of this algorithm, at the outputs of *mov*, the bit mask of those image pixels in which the state has changed, taking into account the sensitivity threshold, will be encoded. The signals at the xP1, xP2, xP4 outputs of extreme PEs, which determine the projection of the moving region (taking into account the sensitivity threshold), will help localize this part of the image.

ANALYTICAL SYNTHESIS OF THE MAIN FUNCTIONAL UNITS PE OF HCCA FOR THE IMPLEMENTATION OF THE DEVELOPED ALGORITHM

It was decided that an image with 16 shades of gray would be fed to the CA, that is, the PE itself should be 4-bit. In the case of increasing (decreasing) the number of shades of the input image, the bitness of the PE varies accordingly (scaled) by simply increasing (decreasing) the bitness of all its components (registers, adders, tires).

The method of detection of moving parts of an image is based on the comparison of binary numbers encoding the brightness of each pixel in the current and previous frame. Therefore, the comparator should be the main node of the developed PE.

To build the PE, it is more expedient to use additional numbers codes, which will simplify the circuit implementation.

The obtained difference should be compared with a given threshold of sensitivity, for which it (the difference) should be presented in the form of an inverse or additional code.

To realize the extraction of the projections of the area in which movement was recorded (according to step 9 of the algorithm), PE must be supplemented with three more inputs P1, P2, P4 from three neighboring PE x1, x2, x4 respectively, and three outputs xP1, xP2, xP4.

To form a projection in the direction of 0° it is sufficient to take the value of P4 from the right neighboring PE (x4) and set the value of *mov + P4* to the xP4 output for further transfer to the left neighboring PE (x3).

To form a projection in the direction of 60° it is sufficient to take the value of P2 from the upper right neighboring PE (x2) and set the value of mov + P2 to the xP2 output for further transfer to the lower left neighboring PE (x5).

Similarly, to form a projection in the 120° direction, it is sufficient to take the value of P1 from the left upper neighboring PE (x1) and set the value xP1 to the value *mov + P1* for further transfer to the right lower neighboring PE (x6).

Constructed according to this principle, the PE will be able to receive, form and transmit in three main areas of the CA. To the extreme PE, information about the existence of at least one PE in a given line, which has registered movement, can be transmitted, which will be a projection of a moving object. Thus, the resulting projections on each clock cycle of the CA will be formed at the corresponding outlets of the outermost PE (Figure 6).

In Figure 31 the moving area is shown in gray, the constructed projections of the moving area - on the extreme PE in dark gray. Moreover, the projection in the direction of 0° will be formed at the xP4 outputs, the projection of 60° - at the outputs of xP2, the projection of 120° - at the outputs of xP1 extreme PE.

Further additional analysis of the projection data will provide information about some of the geometric features of a moving object, its location and orientation in the field of the visual scene according to the formulas (11) - (22).

HCCA FOR THE IMPLEMENTATION OF THE METHOD OF IDENTIFYING IMAGES OF OBJECTS BASED ON THE RADON TRANSFORM

On the basis of the developed method and the mathematical model of the HCCA, the characteristic features of the image of a moving object based on the six projections of the Radon transform are effectively extracted. To control the computer environment (CE), it is necessary to synthesize the control unit. HCCA contains register arrays for storing results. Based on the developed method, PE was synthesized (Figure 8).

Figure 9 shows a block diagram of the connections of the control unit (CU) with HCCA: SX1 ... SX4, WR0 ... WR150 - control signals; Rad_0 ... Rad_150 - the arrays of registers for storing results; Write - external signal to record the image in the CA.

ALGORITHM OF ITERATIVE IMAGE MODIFICATION FOR EXTRACTING A SKELETON BASED ON ZERO EULER DIFFERENTIAL

Given the specificity of homogeneous cellular media, an algorithm that will be executed in parallel when processing all points of the image was created. The requirement of parallelism follows from the parallel nature of cellular media (Zuse, 1969; Neumann, 1966; Ulam, 1952; Wolfram, 2002).

The developed algorithm should be executed sequentially in time, but in parallel for all cells of the medium. Based on this, the following algorithm is proposed for the operation of the processor element (PE) of the environment:

1. The image to the cellular environment is recorded;
2. Identification of candidates for zeroing. PE, which belong to the area of the object (in the state "1"), are subject to zeroing. For this you need to analyze the signals that came from neighboring PE. If neighboring PEs form two connected areas - the background (are in the "0" state) and the object (are in the "1" state). Moreover, at least 2 neighboring PEs belong to the object, then this PE is considered to be a candidate for zeroing;
3. If this PE is a candidate for zeroing, check the neighbors for possible discontinuous combinations corresponding to the skeleton extraction and if this is so, then this PE is not a candidate for zeroing;
4. Determination of the possibility of destruction of the skeleton. If a given PE is a candidate for zeroing and has two regions among its neighbors, one of which is the background (of four PEs)

Figure 8. Functional diagram of PE of HCCA for the extraction of characteristic features based on the Radon transform

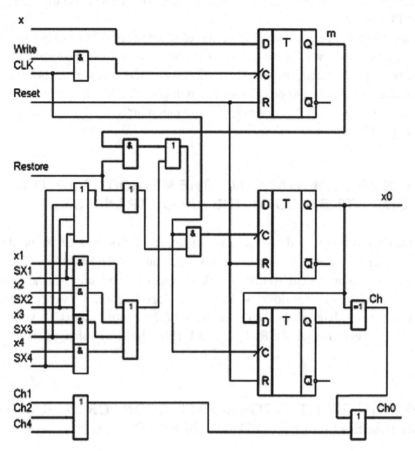

Figure 9. Block diagram of the control unit and HCCA

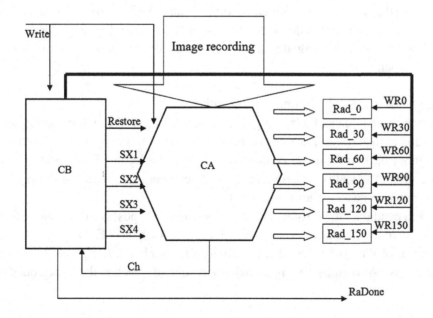

and the other is candidates for zeroing (of two PEs), the output, signaling the possibility of the destruction of the skeleton, is necessary set in "1" state;

5. Warning of the possibility of destruction of the skeleton. If the output of the alarm about the possibility of rupture of this PE is present "1" and similar outputs of two neighbors also received "1", then this PE is not a candidate for zeroing;

6. PE reset. If this PE is still a candidate for zeroing, set it to "0" (i.e. zeroing);

7. If at least one PE is reset, go to the next iteration step - point 2;

8. Holding the final thinning. If this PE is in the state "1" and the Euler differential for it is zero ($E^* = 0$), then in the presence of an enabling signal to transfer the reset of this PE;

9. Read the image frame from the cellular environment. Those PE, which remained in the state "1" and will determine the pixels of the skeleton;

10. End.

Based on the developed method and algorithm for extracting the image skeleton based on the Euler zero differential, the device for extracting the image skeleton of the object will consist of the following structural units:

- Control unit;
- Homogeneous cell environment.

Experimental Analysis and Computer Simulation of Methods for Identifying Images of Moving Objects Based on HCCA

For verification of the developed HCCA, software modeling of both the algorithm as a whole and the HCA in particular was cerried out, as well as VHDL modeling of the single processor element of HCA.

For computer modeling, the Microsoft Visual Studio 2008 development environment was used in the Microsoft Visual C # programming language using the .NET Framework 2.0 libraries.

The written program allows to download a sequence of images that are in the same directory and represent the cutting of frames of the video stream.

The following parameters were configured to calculate certain motion characteristics:

- **"Distance to the Object"**: The distance to the moving object (may vary from frame to frame)
- **"Camera Viewing Angle"**: Is configured before the start of calculations;
- **"Threshold of Sensitivity"**: The threshold of sensitivity for the difference of the pixel codes between frames, in exceeding which the pixel is considered to have changed its state;
- **"Grayscale"**: The number of shades (gradations) of gray color, to which the input image is given for processing it in this HCA;
- **"Frame Rate"**: The frame rate of the incoming video stream.

Calculations of the characteristics of the movement of the object in real time were performed in accordance with formulas (11) - (22).

The simulated HCA is fully consistent with the proposed method.

An example of modeling a method for complex images on Figure 10 is presented. In general, the simulation results fully confirmed the efficiency of the developed method and the HCCA built on its basis.

Figure 10. Examples of finding and a moving object detection

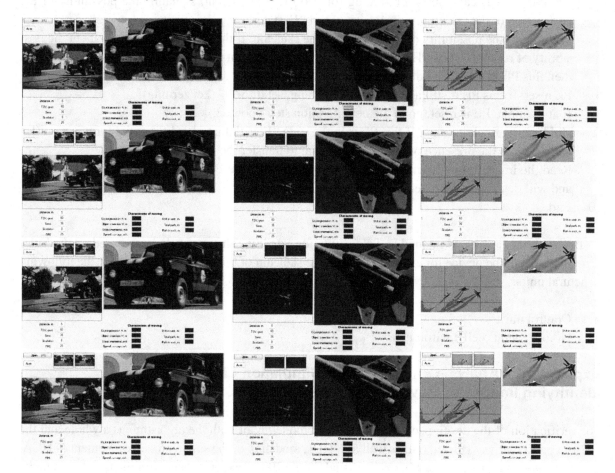

CAD - MODELING HCCA FOR DETECTING MOVING PARTS OF THE IMAGE

To verify the correctness of the synthesis of the main elements of HCCA, Active-HDL was used. The simulation was carried out according to the hierarchical principle, starting from PE. A model of CS with additional counters and registers was obtained (Figure 11)

CAD - model of a hardware RT represented by six 52-bit output buses, each of which corresponds to a RT in a certain direction.

To simplify the analysis of the data that will be obtained in the process of modeling of this device operation, the output tires are divided into separate four-digit numbers (Figure 12).

At the output of such a device, six arrays of 4-digit numbers are formed, according to the six projections of the Radon transforms for the angles 0°, 30°, 60°, 90°, 120°, 150°.

Test images were used to verify the model. The results were compared with the results of processing similar images obtained by computer simulation.

The results of the operation of the device Active-HDL model - it is 6 arrays of numbers. For a better perception and clarity, they are presented in graphical form, in conjunction with the results of software modeling of the work of this HCCA (Figure 13).

Figure 11. General view of the HCA with counters and registers

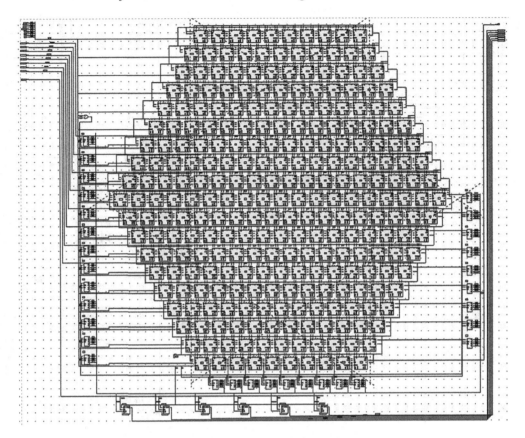

HCCA SOFTWARE MODELING FOR THE EXTRACTION OF CHARACTERISTIC FEATURES BASED ON THE RADON TRANSFORM

In order to further verify the results of the HCCA hardware simulation, a special program was written that performs simulation of the HCA operation that performs the Radon transform in six directions of the hexagonal coverage.

Programming was carried out in the environment and with the use of libraries, described in detail earlier.

The written program allows to perform Radon transformation in six directions of hexagonal coverage for an image loaded from a graphic file *.jpg or *.bmp. The input image is binarized, and the binarization threshold can be adjusted both before the image is loaded and during operation. The number of PEs that are in a logical "1" state at the given binarization threshold is indicated in the lower part of the window below the image of the HCCA itself. The results of the work - the characteristic features in the form of a graphical representation of the Radon transformations in six directions are displayed in the right-hand part of the window.

In Figure 14 are shown the results of the program for the extraction of the characteristic features of the main geometric shapes. Each of them has its own characteristic projection of the RT, but the figures similar in some parameters have similarities in the characteristic features.

Figure 12. Active-HDL model of device of the hardware Radon transform

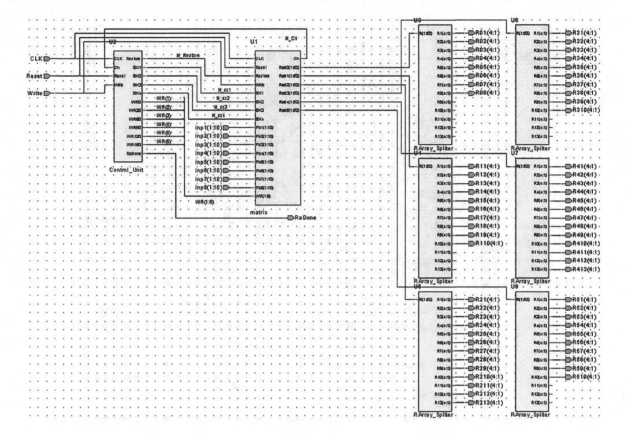

In Figure 15 shows the Radon transform for the image of a triangle 0°, 180°, 90°, 270°, respectively. Similarly, for a hexagon rotated by 30° on Figure 15 is shown.

The results show that when the shape is rotates by 30°, its RT for 0° before the turn will be equal to the RT for 30° after the turn. That is, when the figure is rotated by an angle that is a multiple of the difference between the directions of the hexagonal coating (30°), the extracted RT will be repeated in directions equal to the multiplicity step.

In Figure 16 the result of the program for the extraction of the characteristic features of the letter "A", which have a different image is shown. The greater the differences in the contours of the letters, the more distinguished in detail are the extracted RTs, but their main configuration is clearly visible and is characteristic of this letter.

Based on the definition of the signal-to-noise ratio as the ratio between the signal power (relevant information) and the background noise power (unwanted signal) (Russ, 2007; Stathaki, 2008; Bilan, & Yuzhakov, 2018; Gonzalez, & Woods, 2017; Russ, & Neal, 2015), for each of the images is calculated (Figure 17). Another area of application for the Radon transform is a search for straight lines in an image, and the input image may have a significant degree of noise and distortion. In Figure 24, an example of a search for straight lines for the last four images is given. On the input image, there are 6 straight lines with tilt angles 0°, 30°, 60°, 90°, 120° and 150°. Moreover, from left to right there are 4 images with varying degrees of noise.

Figure 13. Test images that were used in the experiment

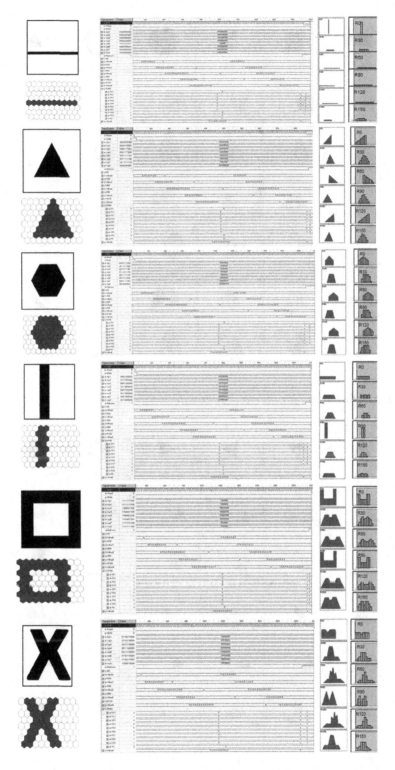

Figure 14. RT projections for basic geometric shapes

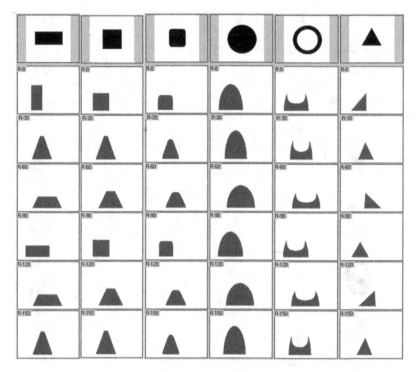

Figure 15. Radon transformation for image shapes with rotation variations

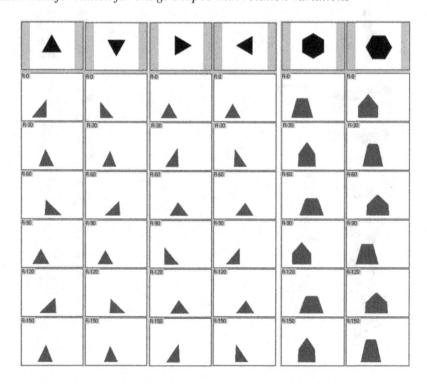

Figure 16. RT for different images of the letter "A"

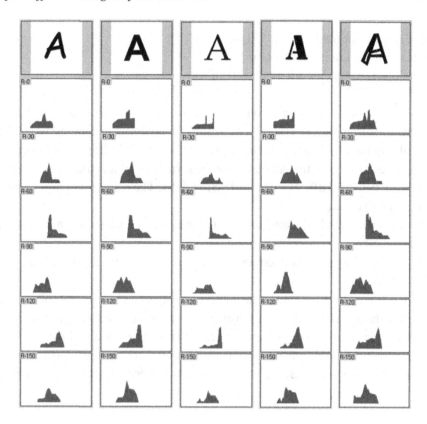

In Figure 17, the effect of noise on the RT for the image of the letter "A" is shown. To get the result in decibels, the formula is used:

$$SNR_{dB} = 10 \log_{10} \left(\frac{P_{signal}}{P_{noise}} \right) = P_{signal,dB} - P_{noise,dB},$$ (23)

where:

P_{signal} - signal power,
P_{noise} - noise power.

In this case, a binary image is used, and the number of significant points forming the image can be considered the equivalent of power for a given formula: since the total signal power of the image will be equal to the sum of the powers of all its points, then based on (71) the formula is used:

$$SNR_{dB} = 10 \cdot \log_{10} \left(\frac{N_{signal} \cdot P_{pix}}{N_{noise} \cdot P_{pix}} \right) = 10 \cdot \log_{10} \left(\frac{N_{signal}}{N_{noise}} \right)$$ (24)

where

N_{signal} - number of significant image points («1»),
N_{noise} - number of significant noise points («1»),
P_{pix} - power of one pixel, which has a logical state of «1».

Since the Radon transform is most effective when the straight lines are extracted, consider two cases that are more interesting. In Figure 18 is shown the results for an image consisting of 18 lines with angles of inclination similar to those in Figure 17, that is, three lines of each direction at once.

For Figure 18 signal-to-noise ratio calculated by the formula (24) has the following meanings (from left to right): no noise; 9 dB; 2,2 dB; -0,2 dB; -1,9 dB; -2,5 dB. The result is slightly worse than a similar input image with 6 lines (Figure 17).

Now let will consider the work of the method on the image consisting of a single line with a tilt angle of 0° (Figure 19).

According to formula (24), was obtained the signal-to-noise ratio for Figure 19: no noise; -7 dB; -10 dB; -14 dB; -15,4 dB.

Such a difference in sensitivity to interference when finding straight lines is explained by the fact that each additional line in the input image can act as a disturbance for the rest. Consequently, the more straight lines contains the incoming image, the greater their mutual interference and the worse the sensitivity (Figure 18). Then, quite predictably, the best result was demonstrated just by working in a single straight line and made up impressive -15,4 dB, which corresponds to approximately 35-fold predominance of noise power over the signal (Figure 19)!

Figure 17. The research of the influence of noise on the images of symbols and straight lines

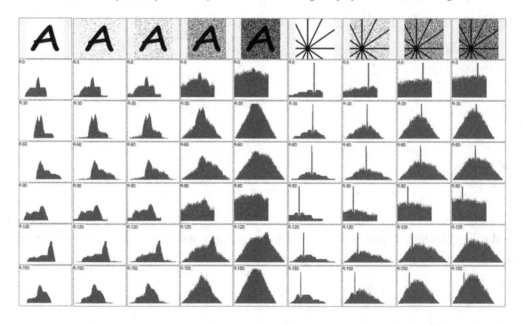

Figure 18. Investigation of images multiple straight lines with the noise

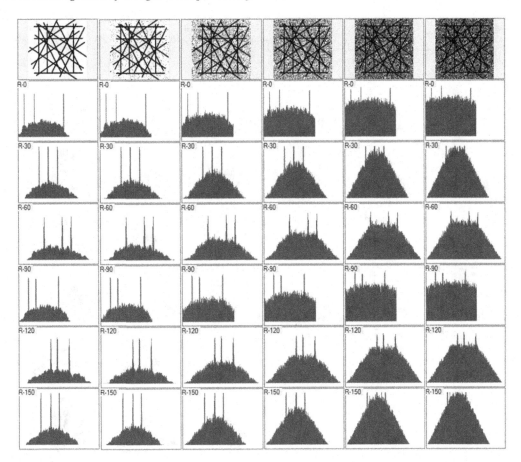

The sensitivity of the method when working with noisy characters does not have such a scatter as the processing of multiple straight lines. In general, this corresponds to the conclusion to Figure 17 on the possibility of extracting the necessary characteristic features with positive signal-to-noise ratios according to (24), which is shown in Figure 20 and Figure 21.

Signal-to-noise ratio for Figure 20: no noise; 5,7 dB; 3,2 dB; -0,01 dB; -2,7 dB; -5,4 dB.

Signal-to-noise ratio for Figure 21: no noise; 6,8 dB; 4,3 dB; 1,1 dB; -1,5 dB; -4,3 dB.

Using the formula (24) and knowing the number of pixels in all the images (Figure 17), we will enter the results of the signal-to-noise calculation in table 2.

As can be seen from the table. 2 and Figure 17-21, with positive values (in decibels), the signal-to-noise ratio RT still retains its original contours and most likely it will be possible to use CF to further identify the image of the symbol.

Similarly to the above calculations, was calculated the signal-to-noise ratio for images of straight lines (Figure 17-21), which can occur when solving the problem of finding straight lines using the RT.

The results of the calculations are listed in Table 3.

As can be seen from the table 3 and Figure 17-21, when detecting straight lines on noisy images, even at a -5 dB signal-to-noise ratio, the Radon transform still allows for the selection of characteristic peaks indicating the found straight line.

Figure 20. The research of the noisiness of the image of the symbol «F»

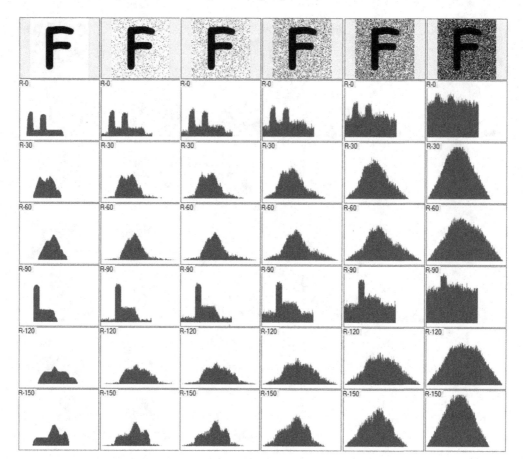

Figure 19. Research of noise in the image of a single straight line

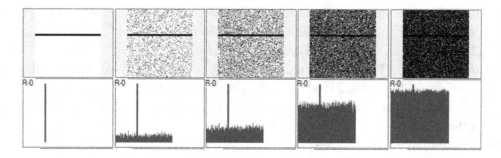

In Figure 17-21 each Radon transform "found" its "own" straight line with the angle of inclination corresponding to this particular direction of transform. Minor and average noise of the input image (two images in the center) had little effect on the result. Even with considerable noise (right), you can point to straight lines and their angle of inclination using characteristic maxima.

So, positive results with the use of RT as a means for extracting CF can be obtained even with the noise of the image of characters reaching 0 dB, and when detecting straight lines - up to -5 dB.

Figure 21. The research of the noisiness of the image of the symbol «Z»

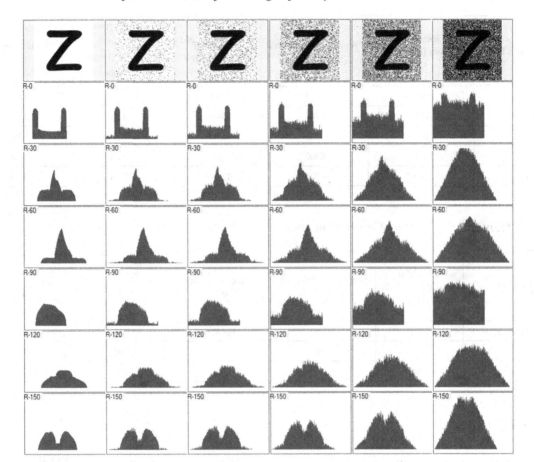

CONCLUSION

This paper presents methods and algorithms for computer identification of moving objects based on cellular automata with a hexagonal coating, as well as using the Radon transform. The most important parameter is the speed, which due to the matrix organization of specialized computing facilities allows the detection and identification of moving objects in real time. The developed hexagonal-coated cellular automaton allows the identification of characteristic features for the detection of moving objects in real time. Using the Radon transform improves the accuracy of identification of images of objects invariant to rotation, shift and scaling. Also, the Radon transform gives positive results when extracting the characteristic features on the images of lines in which the noise level corresponds to - 5 dB.

These studies are aimed at improving the accuracy of detection of moving objects, their identification as well as studying the behavior of biological organisms. In the first place, the results obtained will make it possible in the future to create a biometric identification system based on individual dynamic characteristics, such as gait, lip movement, arm movement, etc. In addition, the simplicity of the hardware implementation will allow to create low-cost tracking systems for moving objects in real time.

Table 2. Signal / noise ratio for image letters «A»

Figure 17	The Total Number of Pixels in the State «1»	Number of Pixels in a Letter «A»	Number of Noise Pixels	Signal / Noise $\dfrac{N_{signal}}{N_{noise}}$	Signal / Noise, dB
1 column	7580	6705	875	7,66	**8,84**
2 column	8746	6705	2041	3,29	**5,17**
3 column	10951	6705	4246	1,58	**1,98**
4 column	14662	6705	7957	0,84	**-0,74**
5 column	21902	6705	15197	0,44	**-3,55**

Table 3. Signal-to-noise ratio of straight line images

Figure 17	The Total Number of Pixels in the State «1»	Number of Pixels in a Letter «A»	Number of Noise Pixels	Signal / Noise $\dfrac{N_{signal}}{N_{noise}}$	Signal / Noise, dB
7 column	7802	6138	1664	3,69	5,67
8 column	13341	6138	7203	0,85	-0,69
9 column	25443	6138	19305	0,32	-4,98

REFERENCES

Alavi, S. (2012). Comparison of Some Motion Detection Methods in cases of Single and Multiple Moving Objects. *International Journal of Image Processing, 6*(5), 389–396.

Belan, S. N., & Motornyuk, R. L. (2013). Extraction of characteristic features of images with the help of the radon transform and its hardware implementation in terms of cellular automata. *Cybernetics and Systems Analysis, 49*(1), 7–14. doi:10.100710559-013-9479-2

Bilan, S. (2017). *Formation Methods, Models, and Hardware Implementation of Pseudorandom Number Generators: Emerging Research and Opportunities*. IGI Global.

Bilan, S., Motornyuk, R., & Bilan, S. (2014). Method of Hardware Selection of Characteristic Features Based on Radon Transformation and not Sensitive to Rotation, Shifting and Scale of the Input Images. *Advances in Image and Video Processing, 2*(4), 12–23. doi:10.14738/aivp.24.392

Dkhil, M. B., Wali, A. & Alimi, A. M. (2016). Towards a Real Time Road Moving Object Detection and Tracking System. *Journal of Information Assurance and Security, 11*, 39-47.

Gariepy, G., Tonolini, F., Henderson, R., Leach, J., & Faccio, D. (2016). Detection and tracking of moving objects hidden from view. *Nature Photonics, 10*(1), 23–27. doi:10.1038/nphoton.2015.234

Hadeler, K. P., & Müller, J. (2017). *Cellular Automata: Analysis and Applications (Springer Monographs in Mathematics)* (1st ed.). Springer. doi:10.1007/978-3-319-53043-7

Hausdorff, F. (1962). *Set theory*. Chelsea Pub. Co.

Land, M., McConnell, P., & McMahon, M. (2006). US 7,155,676 B2. US Patent Office.

Neumann, J. (1966). *Theory of Self-Reproducing Automata: Edited and completed by A. Burks*. University of Illinois Press.

Niitsiima, H., & Maruyama, T. (2004). Real-Time Detection of Moving Objects. *LNCS, 3203*, 1155–1157.

Orten, B., & Alalan, A. (2005). *Moving Object Identification and Event Recognition in Video Surveillance Systems* (Ms. Thesis). Electric and Electronic Department. METU.

Talukder, T., & Maithies, L. (2004). Real-time Detection of Moving Objects from Moving Vehicles using Dense Stereo and Optical Flow. *Intelligent Robots and Systems, 4*, 3718–3725.

Tamanaha, E., Murphy, M., Onorato, M., & Tafralian, J. (2019). US20190088025. US Patent Office.

Ulam, S. (1952) Random Processes and Transformations. *Procedings Int. Congr. Mathem.*, (2), 264-275.

Wolfram, S. (2002). *A new kind of science*. Wolfram Media.

Yuan, C., & Mallot, H. A. (2010). Real-Time Detection of Moving Obstacles from Mobile Platforms. *Workshop on Robotics and Intelligent Transportation System*, 109-113.

Zuse, K. (1969). *Rechnender Raum*. Braunschweig: Vieweg. doi:10.1007/978-3-663-02723-2

Chapter 14

Image Processing and Pattern Recognition Based on Artificial Models of the Structure and Function of the Retina

Mykola Bilan

The Municipal Educational Institution Mayakskaya Secondary School, Moldova

ABSTRACT

The chapter considers principles of construction of retina of the eye. It proposed a system recognition of complex images that models the structure of the retina and the signals at its output. The system is capable of recognizing images and creating new classes. The time impulse description method of images using cellular automata is considered. Images are described by pulse sequences that are created with the help of specially organized cellular automata. The system allows the authors to recognize images of complex shape, which can have an arbitrary location in the field of the visual scene and can have a different scale.

INTRODUCTION

At the present stage of development of information technologies and artificial intelligence systems, experts pay much attention to the parallel processing of large data sets. Particularly noteworthy development of data processing and pattern recognition. These systems, by their functional activities occupy an important place in the creation of artificial intelligence.

All existing elaboration depends on the individual classes of images. It is an objective characteristic of the current level of data processing and pattern recognition. Each existing system is aimed at processing a particular class of images. These systems are not interchangeable. Modern analysis showed that all existing systems perform preprocessing of images for the purpose of description. A feature is assigned to a single number (a set of numbers) to each individual feature.

However, the problem is that the all features for each system and method are set subjectively. Feature selection depends on the skills of developers. In these systems there is no intelligence. In addition, there

DOI: 10.4018/978-1-7998-1290-6.ch014

are no methods of formation of characteristic features to describe the image. Therefore now we do not have the scientific grain, which will give an impetus to the proper development of such systems and methods. Also important is the ability of the system to identify and efficiently describe the unfamiliar images and create new classes.

Today, the systems is already created and been developed methods to efficiently process and recognize images of individual objects (Pratt, 2016; Xingui Shaohua, 2010; Mohamad, 1995; Mertoguno and Boubakis, 2003, Bishop, 2006, Jain and Duin, 2000, Belan and Yuzhakov, 2013, Belan, 2011; Lavee, Rivlin and Rudzsky, 2009; Minicino, & Howse, 2015; Li, Robles-Kelly, & You, 2017; Ryan, 2019; Bilan, & Yuzhakov, 2018). However, they are not able to recognize the images of complex objects, which are composed of an ordered set of simple objects. The search for more effective methods and means is a solution to this problem. One such approach is the use of cellular automata (CA). They allow you to create tools that efficiently describe complex images at the input (Belan, 2011, Bandini & Bonomi, 2012; Ioannidis, & Andreadis, 2012; Belan & Belan, 2012; Bilan, 2017; Bilan, Motornyuk, & Bilan, 2014).

In this chapter we solve the problem in the application CA to build recognition system of complex objects automatically.

BIOLOGICAL PECULIARITIES OF THE IMAGE DESCRIPTION

The retina in the adult has a size of about 22 mm (Roska, & Molnar, 2006; Gladilin, & Lebedev, 2005; Savelyeva-Novoselova, & Savelyev, 2009). It consists of three radially disposed layers of nerve cells and synapses two layers. Simplified diagram of the retina looks as in the fig. 1.

Physiology of the structure of the retina determines the functional relationship between the input photoreceptors (flasks, sticks), horizontal (HC) and bipolar (BC) cells. These bonds form a functional switching layer. This layer distributes the input information signals from the primary photoreceptors.

As a result of the interaction of BC, HC and primary photoreceptors of, BC transmit processed information to the next switching layer of the retina. Synaptic connections between BC, amacrine cells (AC) and ganglion cells (GNC) provides this layer itself. With participation AC after appropriate processing, signals from AK and BC the arrive by inputs GNC. GNC bring together group of signals from the BC and AC, process them and form the output pulse sequences. These pulse sequences come into the optic nerve and the visual cortex of the brain.

Figure 1. A simplified model of the structure of the retina.

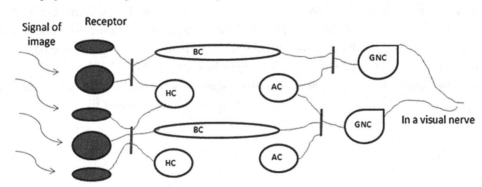

At this time, author do not know the results of research that are devoted to a detailed study of the structure and form of the pulse sequences. Do not described the exact interrelation between the optical signals on photoreceptors and pulse sequences on the outputs of the GNC.

The author took into account the structure of the retina, as well as take into account the physiological principles of its functioning. It was decided that the retina in its structure in a simplified form may be described as the CA (Belan & Belan, 2012). CA is a multilayer structure. Each layer is implemented as a simple CA. At the outputs of the last CA are generated impulses. These pulses are combined in a special pulse sequences by special unit. This unit is working just as GNC.

Since the unknown interconnection between the inputs and outputs of the retina has been proposed time pulse method of image descriptions. This method is implemented on the CA. For the image of an individual object, this method is described in detail in (Belan & Belan, 2012; Roska & Molnar, 2006), and the cell structure of the CA is described in (Belan, 2011). However, the real images are made up of a set of objects that have different shape and location. Together with it the processes of description and forming images as the pulse sequence has a parallel character.

Usually in the real life, we encounter images of complex objects. Visual picture are estimated by quantities of simple objects, their location and the dynamic characteristics. Selection and identification of each object in parallel is important for describe of the complex image. In the subsequently the system takes into account and describes the relationships between objects. After that the system searches for the standard sequence, or creates a new class.

The structure of the system, which carries out the main sequence of actions described in (Belan & Belan, 2013), and the structure and method of recognition of individual objects is presented in (Belan, 2011; Belan & Belan, 2012).

For the description of image the recognition system must perform the following steps.

1. Perform the threshold processing and image binarization.
2. Selects all of the individual objects in the visual picture. Separate binary object is determined by a set of cells in a single condition. This cells is related in a certain neighborhood.
3. The formation of pulse sequences for each of the selected object is carried out.
4. Forming of the general pulse sequence carried out from the formed separate sequences.
5. Processing of the general pulse sequence by threshold processing and by averaging of basic quantitative values.
6. Recognition of images obtained by the pulse sequence.
7. If the image is not recognized then system is forming a new class.

In the second step for the selected binary objects, is set the threshold for the removing of the selected objects. Removes objects, which consist of the amount of cells, that by volume does not exceed the set threshold, on this step. As a result of the threshold processing in the visual scene are remain objects that consist of the number of cells which exceed a predetermined threshold.

In addition, threshold processing is applied to the distances between the selected objects. If distance between objects there is the less set threshold, then there is an integration of them in one object. From this position may be to decrease the number of objects in the scene.

Figure 2. The main stages of the description and recognition of complex images.

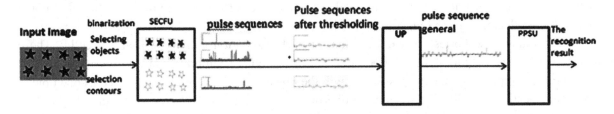

At the same time processing of every separate object performed and pulse sequences are formed. The resulting pulse sequences are also subject to thresholding. Noise pulses are removed and only the information pulses remain. According to their numbers, the amplitudes and the distances between them the system can to identify the object on input of system.

The next step is the formation of a common pulse sequence, which includes the sequences of each object. The order is set by the value of the object. The general sequence describes a scene entirely. Fig. 2 illustrates the processing and the description of complex images.

Since the original image perform the operations pre-processing (Fig. 2) the binarization of image, object selection and the selection of their contours is performed. Next is the formation of pulse sequences for each object. These pulse sequences are combined into a single sequence of pulses with help of unifier device (UP). The generated pulse sequence enters in the unit of search of etalon and the class formation (SECFU). SECFU structure shown in (Belan & Belan, 2012). On its output is a result of recognition. The processing unit of pulse sequences (PPSU) also carries out the threshold processing. The threshold value set for the object, the distance between objects and the amplitudes of the pulses.

SELECTING OBJECTS ON THE VISUAL PICTURE

To select the visual objects in the scene must be determined the cells which are connected with one set of physical properties and merged into one object by value of proximity. Integration into a single object is a connection between the two cells with the same properties through the cells with the same properties.

Assume that there are cells that have properties set S. These cells may be combined into one object. To do this, is performed following conditions apply.

1. Neighboring cells are combined into one object, if they have the same properties S and are located in the immediate neighborhood of the given of cell.
2. Cells were combined in a single object if they have the same properties S and can transmit signals to each other through the cells that has the same properties.

Thus, given these conditions, the object in the visual picture is the set of cells which have the property of S and can transmit to one - another signal through the cell with the same property.

$$Q_S\left(i\right) = \left\{a_{ij}^{S} \Big/ \forall a_{ij}^{S} \ R \forall a_{ij}^{S}\right\}$$

where i – number of object into image; R – the ratio between the image of cells, which indicates that each of these cells can transmit signals to one another through the cells who have the condition S. Sample image of the selected object in Fig. 3 is shown.

Figure 3 shows the shortest route of transmission of the excitation signal from cell A to cell B. These cells are in a single condition, i.e. state S is defined by a single condition (S=1).

After the excitation signal has passed through the object cell, the cells are connected as one object. Objects consisting of cells with identical properties can be many in the scene (for example a binary image). However, the cells of objects can not transmit each - other excitation signals because they have neighbor cells of other conditions.

Another approach to the selection of objects consists in filling cells from the edges. The method consists in the following. Begins to cover the excitation signal from the cells that form the contour of each object. Filling areas carry out inside. An example of such filling on Fig. 4 is shown.

DESCRIPTION OF INDIVIDUAL OBJECTS IN THE SCENE

Each selected object in parallel is described as the pulse sequence. Moreover, the sequence can be formed either simultaneously or with a certain time interval. The process of describing a single binary image by the pulse sequence, and the structure of the CA have been extensively described in the works (Belan, 2011, Belan & Belan, 2012).

Figure 3. Example of an image with the selected object.

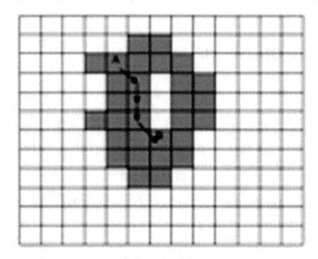

Figure 4. An example of the formation of cell colonies.

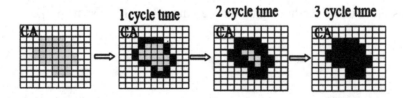

Example simultaneous formation of the pulse sequences shown in Fig. 5,a, when the arbitrary description - Fig. 5,b. In the visual scene shows images of three simple figures.

In an environment the CA begins to move the excitation signal and sets the excited state each cell is on its way. At the same time, the transfer of the excitation signal is specified by active cells. This law provides only transmission of the excitation signal to neighboring cells of contour. When moving from one cell to other cell is forming the impulse excitation signal. Impulse generated in the case where transmission of direction is changing. If the direction is not changed, the impulse is not generated.

For example, for Fig. 5 the pulse sequence shown in general form in Fig. 6. With the simultaneous formation of sequences.

As we see the excitation signal is transmitted to the cells of contour in one direction. However, the excitation signal can spread in two directions of contour. In this case, the sequences will be two for each figure. For our example, the sequences in Fig. 7 are shown.

For real images, the pulse sequences include sets of noise pulses with a small amplitude (fig. 8). These pulse sequences lend themselves thresholding. Noise pulses are deleted. For this is setting amplitude threshold and are deleted pulses with amplitudes less than a predetermined threshold. Pulse amplitudes that greater than a threshold value, proportionally increases to the number of noise pulses are located in front of it and after pulse that not deleted. Thus, the noise pulses are deleted, and the amplitude remain-

Figure 5. Example of the formation of pulse sequences.

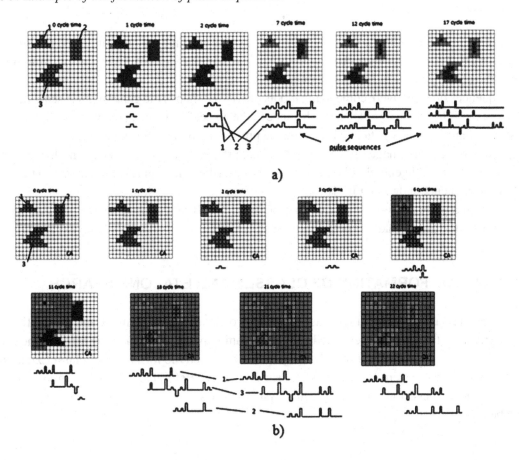

Figure 6. A general view of the sequences is obtained.

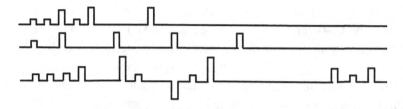

Figure 7. Example of the sequences with bidirectional traffic.

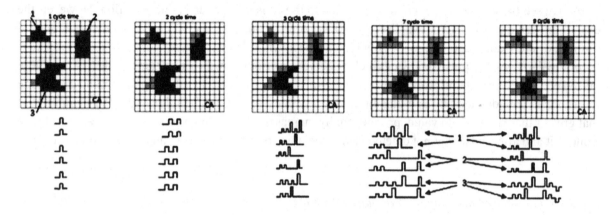

ing pulses are increasing. Also used for the calculation of mean values of amplitude and deleting pulses with amplitudes below the average. Examples of such sequences are obtained by using a program that simulates the above process in Fig. 8 is shown.

The sequences obtained were come to the inputs of UP. UP shapes the general pulse sequence. Taken into account the value of the object and the distance to the object from the object with the highest number of cells. An example of data obtained by the image processing on Fig. 9 is shown.

The numbers near the image of each object indicate the cell number, distance and location. Given these numbers is formed general pulse sequence that describes the visual scene entirely. The example of such pulse sequence shown in Fig. 10.

The generated pulse sequences are easy to process and analyze. These sequences provide an opportunity to reduce the time it takes to process and search for etalons.

PRINCIPLES OF FORMATION OF CLASSES AND ETALONS SEARCH

Known artificial image recognition systems operate in two modes. Learning mode and recognition mode. In most systems, both modes are separated. At the beginning provides learning by forming the learning sample of images and are record it into the system. Is performed the formation of class. Extending the range of classes in the system is performed in learning mode. Beforehand. After learning, the system begins to operate in the recognition mode. Thus, systems with such behavior are limiting class of images that can be recognized.

Figure 8. Examples of sequences after thresholding.

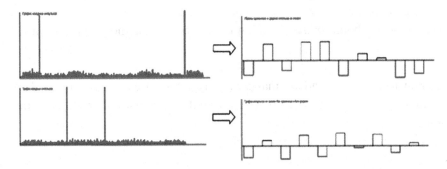

Figure 9. An example of data obtained during processing.

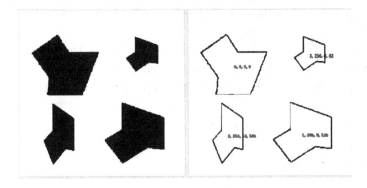

Figure 10. An example of the pulse sequence.

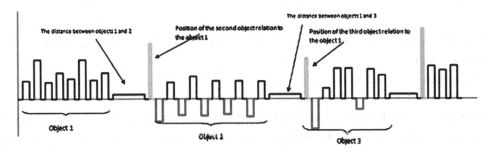

In real biological systems, modes of recognition and learning are not separated. In the process of life activity a biological system recognizes those images, which she learned. If on the input is an image that does not belong to any known her class, a decision on the formation of a new class. Known image is strengthening of the class to which it belongs. Each recognized image may have additional secondary signs. With the secondary features minimized set of attributes that describe the class.

This paper proposes a system in which both modes combined. Images consist of the set of objects. These objects are handled by the system. Such a system simulated on the computer. The system has the following restrictions.

1. Recognition and learning carried out by the geometric characteristics.
2. The image size is pixel 500×500 of format bmp or jpg.
3. Visual scene objects should be separated, not intersected and should not be located inside each other.

Consider the how a class and standard images are created. In (Belan & Belan, 2013) it is shown that for images with these constraints sufficient to determine the three parameters that are described by the following formula.

$$I = \langle Y_i, L_i, \alpha_i \rangle$$

where Y_i – the recognized object in the image, which presented by the pulse sequence; L_i – the minimum distance between the first object and the object i; α_i – the angle of orientation of the object i with relation to the geometric center of the first object.

If the last two values are simple, the first component of Y_i requires decryption. Y_i defines the number of concave and convex vertices, spacing and angles at each vertex.

Formation of the class and standards within a class implemented by the following characteristics.

1. The number of objects in the visual scene.
2. The values of the objects.
3. The distances between objects.
4. Location of object.
5. The relationship between selected values.

Relationships are set for the following values.

1. M_1 R M_i, where M_1 – the number of cells that form the first object; M_i – the number of cells that form the object i.
2. L_i R L_{i+1}, where L_i – distance from the object i to the first object.

The distance is given with the cell size and amount of. Introduction relations in the characteristics of the image allows to define size and also to recognize the scale changes of the object of the same class. Parameter object location allows to take into account the orientation of the object. Exactly the order building of objects in the parameters of the cells takes into account the orientation of the complex images.

Selected figures give an opportunity to build the class code and the pattern. The code consists of the following fields (fig. 11). The first field B denotes the value of the object (the area in number of cells).

However, this structure is difficult to process when determining the orientation and scale changes. Therefore, the fields consistently mixed (fig. 12).

Example code generation in simulation on a computer in Fig. 13 is shown.

However, intuitively it is difficult to set a class in advance. Therefore, the class is formed during the life of the system. Class is given from teacher, and is strengthened during functioning. For example, the class of N-gon contains subclasses, which consist of various forms of (fig. 14).

Figure 11. Structure of the code field.

B	L	α	R

Figure 12. Code structure that forms the etalon.

B_1	$B_2L_2\alpha_2R_2$	$B_3L_3\alpha_3R_3$	....	$B_NL_N\alpha_NR_N$

Figure 13. Example code generation.

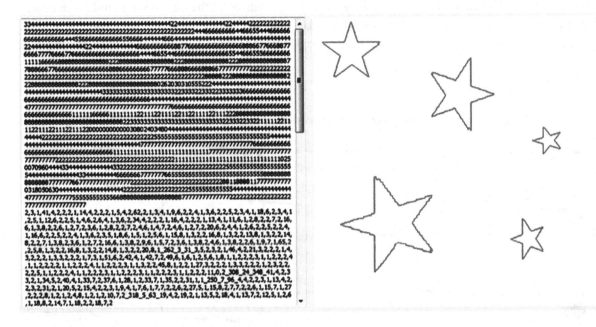

Figure 14. An example of creating subclasses.

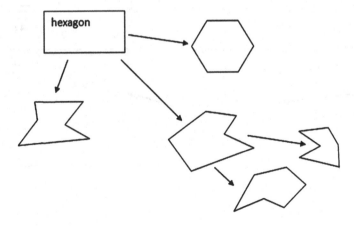

The figure shows that the change in the main parameters leads to the formation of new classes. Among the main parameters are the ones that allow us to judge the differences in their description. This method simulated on a computer. Developed a program that allows to build classes with help of teacher. With this program it is possible to delete objects smaller than a given threshold. According to the number of objects in the visual scene starts forming a new class of. The program allows processing the threshold in size facilities, and pulse sequences. This improves the accuracy of recognition.

Example simulation of system functions for the classification of the individual objects in Fig. 15 is shown. In the initial moment of time or during functioning in system creates classes and subclasses. When appears image of the object on the input of the system are beginning to form pulse sequences which will be passed the threshold processing. Are deleted the smallest pulses with amplitudes equal to 1 or 2. Are deleted pulses that have amplitudes smaller than a threshold value. The resulting pulse sequences are processed by given the number of pulses and their values of the amplitudes and distances between pulses. The data obtained are establish correspondences to the class that includes the object. Fig. 16 shows an example of the formation of subclasses.

For the classification of complex images was created table (Figure 17), which specifies the required parameters.

Figure 15. Example of class formation and classification of simple images.

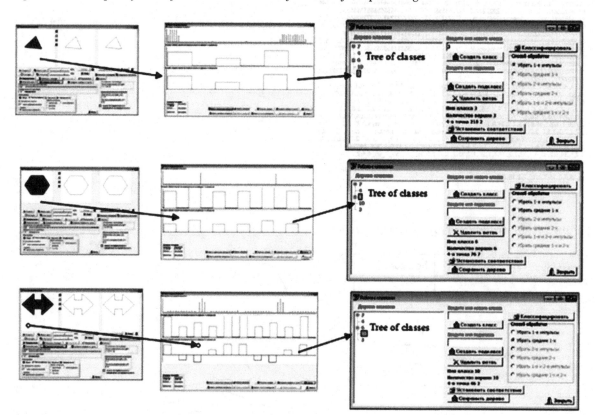

Figure 16. An example of the formation of subclasses.

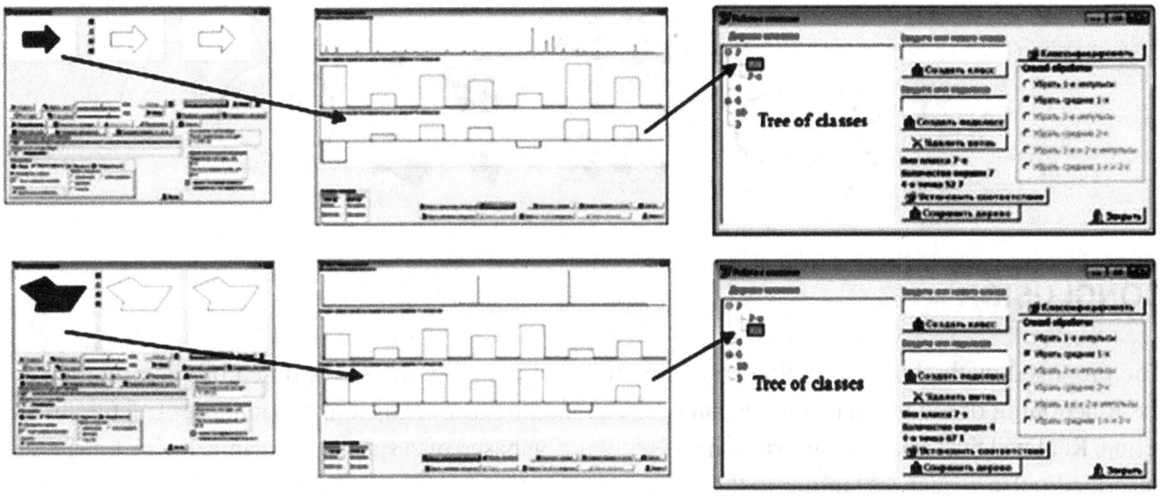

Figure 17. Example of formation of information tables for classifying complex images.

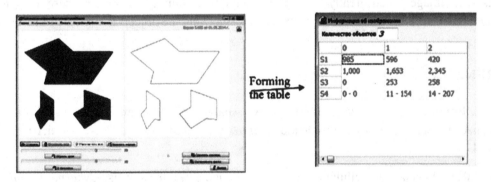

Figure 17 shows the values, which shows in the obtained table S1, S2, S3 and S4, which indicate the lengths of the contours of objects (number of cells), the ratio of the lengths of the contours of the first object to the contour lengths of other objects, the distance from the first object to other objects (number of pixels) and the number of sectors. The angle of rotation relative to north is shown by a dash in the last column. The first parameter that affects the result of the classification is the parameter of area of the object. Research conducted with the participation of the people, showed that in 91% of cases, was called the first object that has the greatest area. Then the, the objects were enumerated with given by the decrease in the area. The remaining parameters are indicated on the topology of the location of other objects, which complex object as a whole are characterize. For example, the topology of the disposition of such objects as the eyes, nose, mouth, an oval face, etc. indicates the relationship of the object to the faces class.

Subject to the limitations were formed images that participated in the experiment. Examples of such images in Fig. 18 are shown.

Figure 18. Examples of images that participated in the experiment.

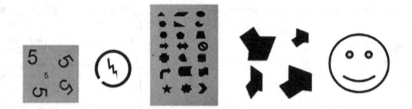

CONCLUSION

The proposed method of description and recognition of complex images is based on the principles of the functioning of the retina of the human eye. The method also takes into account the structure of the retina. Realized the system of description and recognition based on a specially organized CA. Images are described pulse sequences similar to the pulses produced at the output of the retina GNC. The method has allowed to increase the rate of description of complex images. The accuracy of the recognition of complex images as high as 93%. However, there are difficulties in implementing the method of selection of objects in an image which greatly limits the speed description. Furthermore, there are limitations. They do not make it possible to handle objects that intersect, and the objects that are within other objects.

REFERENCES

Bandini, S., Bonomi, A., & Vizzari, G. (2012). An Analysis of Different Types and Effects of Asynchronicity in Cellular Automata update Schemes. *Natural Computing, 11*(2), 277–287. doi:10.100711047-012-9310-4

Belan, S. (2011). Specialized cellular structures for image contour analysis. *Cybernetics and Systems Analysis, 47*(5), 695–704. doi:10.100710559-011-9349-8

Belan, S., & Belan, N. (2012). *Use of Cellular Automata to Create an Artificial System of Image Classification and Recognition. In ACRI 2012, LNCS* (Vol. 7495, pp. 483–493). Heidelberg: Springer.

Belan, S., & Belan, N. (2013). *Temporal-Impulse Description of Complex Image Based on Cellular Automata. In PaCT2013, LNCS* (Vol. 7979, pp. 291–295). Springer-Verlag Berlin Heidelberg.

Belan, S., & Yuzhakov, S. (2013). A Homogenous Parameter Set for Image Recognition Based on Area. *Computer and Information Science, 6*(2), 93–102. doi:10.5539/cis.v6n2p93

Bilan, S. (2017). *Formation Methods, Models, and Hardware Implementation of Pseudorandom Number Generators: Emerging Research and Opportunities*. IGI Global.

Bilan, S., Motornyuk, R., & Bilan, S. (2014). Method of Hardware Selection of Characteristic Features Based on Radon Transformation and not Sensitive to Rotation, Shifting and Scale of the Input Images. *Advances in Image and Video Processing, 2*(4), 12–23. doi:10.14738/aivp.24.392

Bilan, S., & Yuzhakov, S. (2018). *Image Processing and Pattern Recognition Based on Parallel Shift Technology*. Boca Raton, FL: CRC Press.

Bishop, C. (2006). *Pattern Recognition and Machine Learning*. Berlin: Springer.

Gladilin, S. & Lebedev, D. (2005). Neural network reproducing the output signal of a ganglion cell. *Information processes, 5*(3), 258-264.

Ioannidis, K., Andreadis, I., & Sirakoulis, G. (2012). An Edge Preserving Image Resizing Method Based on Cellular Automata. *LNCS, 7495*, 375–384.

Jain, A., Duin, R., & Mao, J. (2000). Statistical pattern recognition: A review. *IEEE Transactions on Pattern Analysis and Machine Intelligence, 22*(1), 4–37. doi:10.1109/34.824819

Lavee, G., Rivlin, E., & Rudzsky, M. (2009). Understanding Video Events: A Survey of Methods for Automatic Interpretation of Semantic Occurrences in Video. *IEEE Transactions on Systems, Man and Cybernetics. Part C, Applications and Reviews, 39*(5), 489–504. doi:10.1109/TSMCC.2009.2023380

Li, J., Robles-Kelly, A., & You, S. (2017). A Frequency Domain Neural Network for Fast Image Super-resolution. *International Joint Conference on Neural Networks*.

Mertoguno, S., & Boubakis, N. (2003). Adigital Retina-Like Low-Level Vision processor. *IEEE Transactions on Systems, Man, and Cybernetics. Part B, Cybernetics, 33*(5), 782–788. doi:10.1109/TSMCB.2003.816925 PMID:18238231

Minicino, J., & Howse, J. (2015). *Computer Vision with Python*. Packt Publishing.

Mohamad, H. (1995). *Fundamentals of Artificial Neural Networks*. MIT Press.

Pratt, W. K. (2016). *Digital Images Processing* (3rd ed.). Wiley.

Roska, B., Molnar, A., & Werblin, F. (2006). Parallel processing in retinal ganglion cells: How integration of space-time patterns of excitation and inhibition form the spiking output. *Journal of Neurophysiology, 95*(6), 3810–3822. doi:10.1152/jn.00113.2006 PMID:16510780

Ryan, Ø. (2019). *Linear Algebra, Signal Processing, and Wavelets - A Unified Approach: Python Version (Springer Undergraduate Texts in Mathematics and Technology)* (1st ed.). Springer.

Savelyeva-Novoselova, N., & Savelyev, A. (2009). Principles of ophthalmic neurocybernetics. In Artificial Intelligence. Intellectual systems. Academic Press.

Xingui, H. & Shaohua, X., (2010). Process Neural Networks: Theory and Applications. *Advanced Topics in Science and Technology in China, 240*.

Chapter 15

Identification System for Moving Objects Based on Parallel Shift Technology

Sergey Yuzhakov

Haisyn Department of the SFS General Directorate in Vinnytsia Region, Ukraine

Stepan Bilan

(iD) https://orcid.org/0000-0002-2978-5556

State University of Infrastructure and Technology, Ukraine

ABSTRACT

There are tasks of automatic identification of the moving stock of the railway, one of which is the automatic identification of rail cars cars by their number plates. Different organizational, legal, moral and ethical, technical, and programmatic methods of automated identification are used to solve this problem. At present little attention is paid to the development of means of automatic identification of moving objects, which would be possible regardless of the orientation and shape of the figure, especially if it concerns the recognition of freely oriented images of number plates. Therefore, many new methods for recognizing of number plates are developing. In the chapter, the system of identification of objects by their number plates in real time is considered. On moving objects (moving stock of a railway), an identifier image is drawn, which is an ordered set of characters. As a rule, these are numbers. But there may be other characters. The work also discusses the method of identification images of number plates with a high percentage of noise.

RELEVANCE OF RESEARCH

At the moment there are many different methods and means of identifying transport objects based on optoelectronic devices, which are mainly aimed at processing stationary objects and use known approaches to implement them on computer systems (Nelson 1992, Teutsch 2015, Soharab at al. 2014, Karasulu at al. 2013).

Widespread this plan have systems built on artificial neural networks (Aggarwal 2018, Nunes da Silva at al. 2017).

DOI: 10.4018/978-1-7998-1290-6.ch015

However, such systems are inertial and require a lot of time for preliminary processing of identifier images. Therefore, to identify moving objects, there is very important to identify moving stock of the railway in real time. Obtaining high positive results in this direction will allow the using of parallel shift technology, which shows high results in the area of image processing and recognition (Belan at al. 2013a, Belan at al. 2013b, Bilan at al. 2014, Bilan at al. 2018).

FORMULATION OF THE PROBLEM

In modern conditions in the identification systems of moving objects in transport, the challenge is to identify in real time. Solving this problem helps automated tools to quickly perform operations that are aimed at performing the necessary transportation of both passengers and cargo. Also, making decisions in real time allows you to increase traffic safety. The chapter aims to identify moving objects in real time using the parallel shift. Images of number plates are used as identifiers.

PRINCIPLES OF IMPLEMENTATION OF PARALLEL SHIFT TECHNOLOGY

The chapter focuses on the use of parallel shift technology (PST) to obtain the main characteristic features when describing certain objects (Belan at al. 2013a, Belan at al. 2013b, Bilan at al. 2018). This technology is based on the interaction of the original object, which needs to be described and its copy, which shifts in some space. The shift of elements occurs in parallel. The number of directions of the shift characterizes the accuracy of the object description.

The area of intersection of the initial image and its copy should be calculated for each iteration during a displacement. A sequence of values of the intersection area is formed for each selected direction. The number of such sets is determined by the number of shift directions. The displacement length is determined by the maximum distance between the extreme points of the initial image, which are located on one straight, corresponding direction of displacement. Each sequence of intersection areas can be turned into a function. Such functions are called the function of the area of intersection (FAI) and can be presented analytically, tabularly or graphically.

The method can be used for all tasks of identifying both stationary and moving objects. It is especially effective for the identification of moving objects, since the image shift occurs in the process of movement of the identification object itself, on which the image of the identifier is depicted.

THE THEORY OF IMAGE DESCRIPTION BASED ON THE FUNCTION OF THE AREA OF INTERSECTION

Pattern Recognition

The function of the area of intersection (FAI (φ)) is determined by the dependence of the values of the intersection area of the figure and its copy, which shifts parallel in the direction of φ at each iteration step (Fig. 1, a) (Belan at al. 2013a, Bilan at al. 2018). The beginning of the shift is the original position of the initial image. Displacement is performed until there is no crossing of both images.

Figure 1. An example of a shift of the image of a sequence of digits 12358 (a) and the function of the area of intersection (b) is obtained

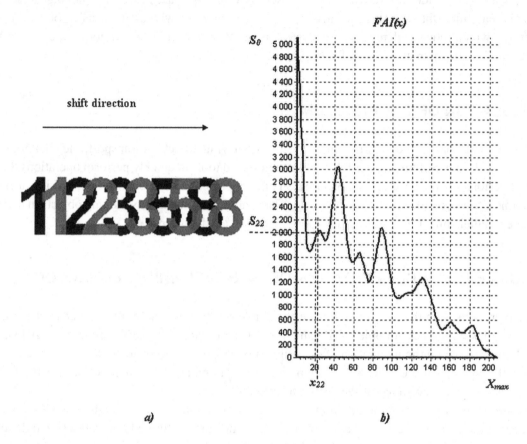

a)   b)

In order to increase the accuracy and detailed identification of the object, shifts copies of the image in additional directions and make the definition of additional FAI for directions $\phi_1 \neq \phi$. Due to additional displacements, the class of Y, which elements $FAI(\varphi_1)$ are identical. The identified image are belongs crossing classes X and Y. Directions of displacement are orthogonal directions.

The input figure (Fig. 2, a) is limited by the function $f_2(x)$ and bottom of the function $f_1(x)$, and on the right by the function $f_5(y)$ and the left by the function $f_4(y)$.

In fig. 3c shows the formation of the image aligned with the bottom edge of fig. 2a This image is bounded below by the 0X axis, and above by the function $f_3(x)$, where

$$f_3(x) = f_2(x) - f_1(x) \tag{1}$$

The process of obtaining the FAI(y) when shifted vertically is shown in Fig. 3d.

In fig. 3a shows the formation of the left-aligned image of fig. 2a. This image is bounded to the left by the 0Y axis, and to the right by the function $f_6(y)$, where

$$f_6(y) = f_5(y) - f_4(y) \tag{2}$$

Figure 2. The original image and its bounding functions

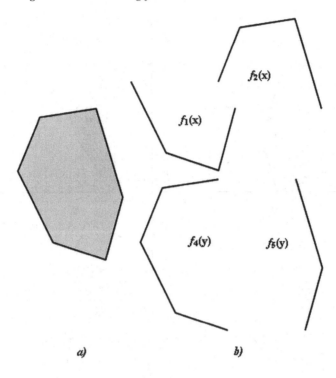

The process of obtaining the FAI(x) when shifted horizontally is shown in fig. 3b.

Taking into account the images from fig. 3, it is possible to express the process of forming the FAIs using formulas.

$$FAI(y) = \int\limits_{x_1}^{x_2} f_3(x)dx - y \cdot (x_2 - x_1),$$ (3)

where $\begin{cases} y = f_3(x_1) \\ y = f_3(x_2) \end{cases}$

$$FAI(x) = \int\limits_{y_1}^{y_2} f_6(y)dy - x \cdot (y_2 - y_1),$$ (4)

where $\begin{cases} x = f_6(y_1) \\ x = f_6(y_2) \end{cases}$

When defining the FAI of the figures which not convex, or those with any outsides inclusions within their image, must take into account such changes that reflect the shape of the figure. With the complication of the image form, FAIs become more complicated, and therefore can serve as criteria for encoding and image recognition.

Figure 3. The process of obtaining the functions of the area of intersection

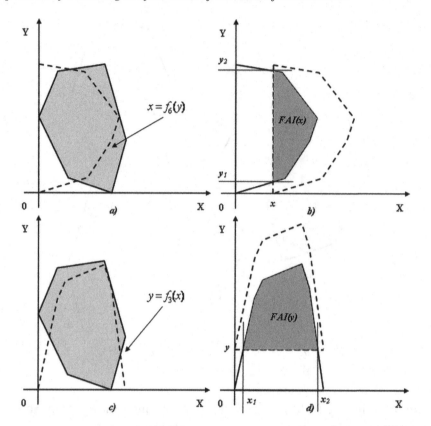

The basic features of the function of the area of intersection in encoding and recognizing images are the initial area of the image (S_0), the maximum shift in the direction φ (X_{max}), the maximum shift in the direction φ_1 (Y_{max}). Determining these parameters is easy to implement by hardware.

Definition of Movement Parameters

In addition to pattern recognition, the parallel shift technology by using functions of the area of intersection also allows you to determine the movement parameters of an object. The main movement parameters are the direction and distance of the object displacement.

The shift of the image copy must be carried out cyclically. When it reaches the edge of the receptor field in the shift direction, this copy should appear at the same level on the other side of the receptor field and continue to move in the original direction (fig. 4a).

The form of the function of the area of intersection during a cyclic shift becomes periodic and symmetric with respect to each of the points of the complete coincidence of the input image, provided that it is no move (fig. 4b).

Figure 4. Example of periodic FAI(x)

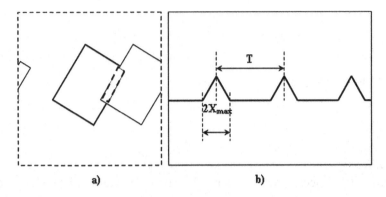

For the immovable object, the following parameters of the function of the are of intersection:

- Period (T) of FAI is the width of the graph when horizontal shift and the height when vertical shift;
- The width of each FAI splash (the section of a function corresponding to nonzero intersection) is $2X_{max}$ or $2Y_{max}$ respectively direction of the shift;
- The maximum amplitude of the FAI is the area of the input image (S_0).

If the initial image moves in the orthogonal direction in the receptor field, then during the cyclic shift in the same direction, the period of function of the area of intersection (T) will vary, depending on the direction of movement of the figure. When the object moves in the direction of the shift of the copy, then the period between the peaks of the function (T_1) will be greater than T in the result of the Doppler effect, and less if the object moves in the reverse direction.

If the image moves not in an orthogonal direction, provided that the copy shift passes so fast that during the intersection the figure does not have time to change strongly in the direction which perpendicular of the shift, then each splash will be symmetrical, but its amplitude is less than that of the immovable input image. Then the function period is defined as the distance between the two neighboring splashes.

We will assume that the copy of the figure moves when determining the FAI(x) to the right, and when determining the FAI(y) to the up, and the center of mass of the figure is at the point of origin. Then the tangent of the angle of the image movement direction (α), if the motion is not orthogonal, will be equal to:

$$tg\alpha = \frac{T_{y1} - T_y}{T_{x1} - T_x},$$
(5)

where

T_{y1} is the period of FAI(y) when object move,
T_y is the period of FAI(y) when immovable object,
T_{x1} and T_x are corresponding periods of FAI(x).

The values of differences at the orthogonal movement of the object:

$$\Delta T_y = T_{y1} - T_y = 0, \tag{6}$$

if the object moves horizontally;

$$\Delta T_x = T_{x1} - T_x = 0, \tag{7}$$

if the object moves vertically.

Other directions of the object movement depending on the values of differences are determined from the data from fig. 5.

The signs of these differences and tgα uniquely determine the direction of movement of the image relative to its original location, and the differences modules are the displacement of the object in the corresponding direction.

The total displacement distance of an object is determined according to the following formula.

$$\Delta T = \sqrt{\Delta T_x^2 + \Delta T_y^2} \tag{8}$$

The capabilities of technical means in responding to movement and determining its basic parameters is limited only to the speed of the cyclic shift of the copy.

The technology of recognition and encoding of images using FAI can be used on rail transport.

Figure 5. The direction of the object movement depending on signs ΔT_x and ΔT_y

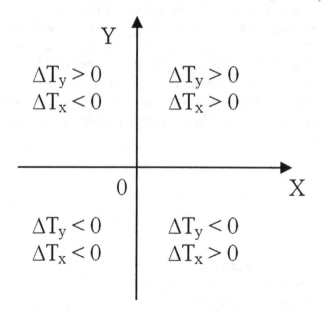

Identification of Moving Objects in Railway Transport

The movement of railway carriages takes place in a horizontal plane. To create a system for identifying the identifiers of the means of this type of transport, they must be recorded and their images must be pre-processed.

The standard means of video perception is a video camera. Each frame of video stream must be stored in memory and separately undergo preliminary processing. For a moving object, the image of the identifier in each frame of the video stream is located in different locations of the optical picture. The image ID field in each subsequent frame is shifted in relation to the image ID field in the previous frame in the horizontal direction. The direction of displacement coincides with the direction of movement of the object. An example location of ID images in a sequence of three frames is shown in fig. 6.

An analysis of this example shows that the object moves to the right side. The speed of this object is determined by the distance of shift from the reference point, the switching time from frame to frame, and the distance from the object to the photodetector. In each subsequent frame, the image of the identifier covers a part of the image field of the previous frame of identifier of video stream. That is, when overlapping two neighboring frames, it is seen that the image field of the image of the previous frame intersects with the image field of the identifier of the next. The area of intersection of the identifiers images is easily calculated.

The identification process consists of two stages. The first stage is directly identification to determine semantic content of the character set. In this case these are the images of number plates of rail transport units. And the second stage is the definition of the movement parameters of the object. These steps can be performed simultaneously.

RECOGNITION OF THE IDENTIFIERS

Selection of the Research Object

In this case, there are four options for selecting a research object for further pre-processing.

1. Choosing the first frame of the video stream and forming on its basis a set of FAIs.
2. Choosing the best frame of the video stream and forming on its basis a set of FAIs.
3. Formation of FAIs for all video stream frames and obtaining a set of average FAIs, which are compared with reference FAIs.
4. Formation of FAI by superimposing of video stream frames on the first frame.

Figure 6. An example location of ID images in a sequence of three frames

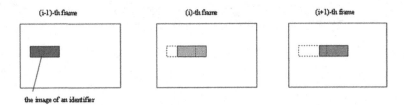

The first way is fastest. However, there may be a case where information from this frame has distorted. This will negatively affect the processes of further processing. In this case, the object of the research is the image from the first frame.

To implement the second approach, there is a need for an additional algorithm that is aimed to find the best frame. Then there must be a frame quality criteria, according to which search of the best frame is made. The implementation of this method takes a lot of time, since all of video stream frames are processed. It is necessary to wait for the formation of all frames. In this case, the object of the research is the image from the best frame.

To implement the third option, all video stream frames are processed. At the same time, as in the second approach, the images formed in each frame are investigated. It also increases the time of selection, but increases the accuracy of recognition. In this case, the object of the research is the average FAI, obtained by the processing of all frames.

The fourth option allows you to form a real-time FAI without the use of additional computing power. However, this approach does not give certainty about the accuracy of the FAI formation. In this case, the object of the research is the FAI, obtained by the processing of all frames.

It is formed as a sequence of (S_i) values of the area of intersection of the image of each frame with the first frame (fig. 7).

In all cases, the final result will be the obtaining of the real image FAI. This function must be compared with the functions of the reference base. The coincidence of their forms allows us to conclude on the identification of the object.

Preprocessing of the Selected Object

In order to preprocess the video stream frames, it is necessary in each of them to perform the control of noise inclusions. This process is proposed to be carried out by the method of removing contour elements. These elements are determined by performing multiple parallel shifts of image. Such a method of noise control has been described in a previous work on this topic (Bilan at al. 2018).

Figure 7. Example of the FAI formation from the frames of the received video stream.

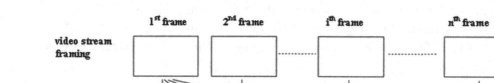

However, in this chapter noise control is proposed that is analogous to the process of "erosion" described in the works on digital image processing (Gonzalez at al. 2004). Removing contour elements not only reduces the amount of noise information, but also distorts the shape of the object. The following combination of actions is proposed to partially restore the image elements.

1. Remove contour elements.
2. Carry out inverting image elements.
3. Remove contour elements.
4. Carry out inverting image elements.

The result will be similar to the process of "dilation". The number of useful elements of the image is increased.

Combinations of actions can be different. Indicate inverting the letter "I", and the removal of contour elements with the letter "D" (from the word "delete"). Then the proposed combination will have the encoding "DIDI", while the prototype describes the combination "D".

The number of noise inclusions will be determined using the percentage of noise (pn). When creating a model noise interference it is the probability with which the elements of the original image inverted. Its relationship with a known characteristic PSNR shown in the following formula.

$$PSNR = 20 \log_{10} \left(\frac{100}{pn} \right) \tag{9}$$

The results of noise removal by various combinations of actions are shown in fig.8.

Table 1 shows the percentage of useful elements of the input image remaining in the receptor field after a certain combination of actions to remove noise inclusions at different noise percentage values.

As can be seen from Table 1, the combination of actions DIDIIDID is the most effective. After removing the noise in all frames, it is necessary to form a FAI for each of them.

Figure 8. The results of noise removal by various combinations of actions

pn (%) / PSNR (dB)	Initial image	"D"	"D-I-D-I"	"I-D-I-D"	"D I D I -I-D-I-D"
2 % / 34 dB	12358	12358	12358	12358	12358
3 % / 30 dB	12358	12358	12358	12358	12358
5 % / 26 dB	12358	12358	12358	12358	12358
10 % / 20 dB	12358	12358	12358	12358	12358
20 % / 14 dB	12358	12358	12358	12358	12358
32 % / 10 dB	12358				

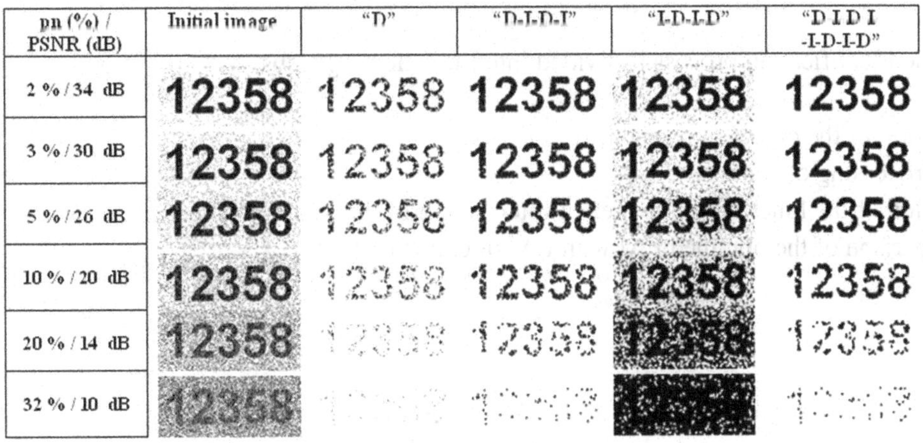

Table 1. Percentage of useful image elements after removal of noise

	D	DIDI	DIDIIDID
pn=2%	0,57	0,93	0,96
pn=5%	0,43	0,84	0,90
pn=10%	0,26	0,68	0,76

Formation of an Etalon Set

Since the movement of research objects can only take place in a horizontal plane, it is enough to keep the reference FAI for one direction for each object. Also, the reference database can be structured. The following is meant.

If the identifier consists of the number of characters equal m, then it makes no sense to find for its equivalent among the etalons that represent the sequence of characters in length not equal to m. If the average area of a single character (S_{symb}) is known, then the number of characters in the identifier is calculated by the following formula.

$$m = round\left(\frac{S_0}{S_{symb}}\right)$$

(9)

The number of characters in the sequence of the identifier may also be explicitly specified.

So, the comparison of an object occurs only with etalons that consist of a certain number of characters. This fact also simplifies the scaling procedure.

In addition, you can create an array of etalons in two ways.

1. Directly fill the database with the functions of the area of intersection of all existing etalons. This approach involves having a memory device.
2. If a known form of characters from which an identifier can be formed, then the patterns can be formed sequentially in the identification system before the comparison. This approach increases the amount of time to identify. This is because time is spent on the creation of etalons FAI.

Thus, the identification process is divided into the following steps.

1. Selection of the object of research.
2. Pre-processing of frames.
3. Creation of the function of the area of intersection of the selected object.
4. Comparison of the obtained FAI with FAI of etalons.

Definition of Movement Parameters

In the theoretical bases of the parallel shift technology the determination of the movement parameters of the object, which is researched, passes by several components. The first one is an object at a zero point in time. The second one is his copy, which shifts cyclically. The third is an object in the i-th time. The technical facilities and analytical system must be available to ensure the research of the mutual movements of these components.

In this case, the direction of момуьуте is in the horizontal plane. Therefore, it is unknown only that the object moves to the right or to the left. Determination of these parameters can be performed in simpler methods, without the use of parallel shift technology. For example, find the mutual location of the mass centers of the identifier on different frames.

With PST can determine the speed of the object. Above mentioned the procedure for determining the number of characters from which the identifier is composed. If the average symbol width (W_{symb}) is known, then the total real length of the object (W) is the next value.

$$W = m W_{symb} \tag{10}$$

The parameter W of the real image can be similar with the maximum shift parameter X_{max} of the function of the area of intersection, which is obtained based on the sequence of frames (fig. 7). Each i-th frame corresponds to the displacement x_i on the FAI. Since the graph of the function has several extremes, the value of S_i can coincide with it at several points (fig. 9).

Knowing the rate of frame formation (t_{frame}) we can calculate all possible speeds (v_{ij}) for each frame. In the given example, j = 3.

$$v_{ij} = \frac{x_{ij}}{i \cdot t_{frame}} \tag{11}$$

At the time of formation of the identifier FAI, we assume that the speed of the object is constant. Then there is the same speed v_{ij} for all frames. We call this speed v_{obj}. Then the real speed of the object (V) will be determined from the following formula.

$$V = \frac{W}{i \cdot t_{frame}} \cdot \frac{x_{ij}}{X_{max}} = \frac{W \cdot v_{obj}}{X_{max}}, \tag{12}$$

where x_{ij} is the shift for $v_{ij} = v_{obj}$.

Figure 9. The coincide of FAI to Si

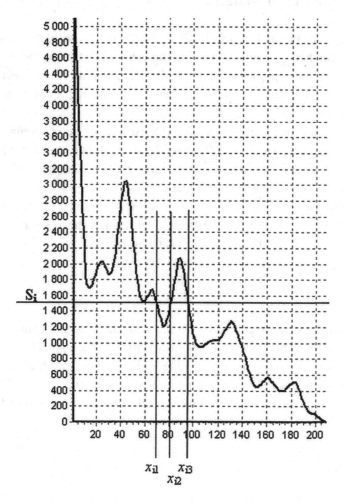

CONCLUSION

In the chapter the analysis and research of modern methods and systems of identification of moving objects with the use of optoelectronic hardware is carried out. The method of identification of moving objects according to their number plates based on the parallel shift technology is proposed.

This system allows you to recognize and encode images for which there are etalons, to determine the speed of the object relative to the plane of the receptor field.

Of course, the existence and best metods that allow the implementation of these functions are possible. But this technology is self-sufficient, allows the complexly to realize these opportunities without the use of other technologies.

REFERENCES

Aggarwal, C. C. (2018). *Neural Networks and Deep Learning: A Textbook*. Springer. doi:10.1007/978-3-319-94463-0

Belan, S., & Yuzhakov, S. (2013a). A Homogenous Parameter Set for Image Recognition Based on Area. Computer and Information Science, 6(2), 93-102. doi:10.5539/cis.v6n2p93

Belan, S., & Yuzhakov, S. (2013b). Machine Vision System Based on the Parallel Shift Technology and Multiple Image Analysis. Computer and Information Science, 6(4), 115-124. doi:10.5539/cis.v6n4p115

Bilan, S., & Yuzhakov, S. (2018). *Image Processing and Pattern Recognition Based on Parallel Shift Technology*. Boca Raton, FL: CRC Press.

Bilan, S., Yuzhakov, S., & Bilan, S. (2014). Saving of Etalons in Image Processing Systems Based on the Parallel Shift Technology. Advances in Image and Video Processing, 2(6), 36-41. doi:10.14738/aivp.26.772

Fathy, S. (2010). *Computer Vision Technologies for Identification of Car License Plates: Investigation and performance evaluation using Morphological Operation*. LAP LAMBERT Academic Publishing.

Gonzalez, R. C., Woods, R. E., & Eddins, S. L. (2004). *Digital Image Processing using MATLAB*. Pearson Prentice Hall.

Karasulu, B., & Korukoglu, S. (2013). *Performance Evaluation Software: Moving Object Detection and Tracking in Videos (SpringerBriefs in Computer Science)*. Springer. doi:10.1007/978-1-4614-6534-8

Murray, T. C. (2002). *The Official License Plate Book 2002: A Complete Plate Identification Resource*. Motorbooks Intl.

Nelson, R. (1992). *Detection, Stabilization, and Identification of Moving Objects by a Moving Observer*. PN.

Nunes da Silva, I., Spatti, D. H., Flauzino, R. A., Bartocci Liboni, L. H., & Franco dos Reis Alves, S. (2017). *Artificial Neural Networks: A Practical Course*. Springer. doi:10.1007/978-3-319-43162-8

Pyrgidis, C. N. (2016). *Railway Transportation Systems: Design, Construction and Operation*. CRC Press. doi:10.1201/b19472

Soharab, H. S., Khalid, S., & Nabendu, C. (2014). *Moving Object Detection Using Background Subtraction (SpringerBriefs in Computer Science)*. Springer.

Teutsch, M. (2015). *Moving Object Detection and Segmentation for Remote Aerial Video Surveillance* (German Edition). KIT Scientific Publishing.

Wilson, F. R. (2012). *Railway-Signalling: Automatic; An Introductory Treatment of the Purposes, Equipment, and Methods of Automatic Signalling and Track-Circuits for Steam ... Students, and Others (Classic Reprint)*. Forgotten Books.

Chapter 16

SOFM for Image Compression Based on Spatial Frequency Band–Pass Filter and Vector Quantization

Shadi M. S. Hilles

iD https://orcid.org/0000-0002-2605-9524

Al-Madinah International University, Malaysia

Volodymyr P. Maidaniuk

iD https://orcid.org/0000-0002-2386-6603

Vinnytsia National Technical University, Ukraine

ABSTRACT

This chapter presents image compression based on SOFM and vector quantization (VQ). The purpose of this chapter is to show the significance of SOFM with bandpass filter in process of image compression to increase compression ratio and to enhance image compression effectiveness. Image compression by SOFM model is presented and consists of three stages: The first is band-pass filter. The result experiments used Lena.bmp, girl256.bmp, and show compression in block image 16x16 given best compression ratio with a small signal-noise ratio (SNR).

INTRODUCTION

Image coding and decoding methods have gain many role internet media and multimedia technology for digital camera, digital TV and web applications where is huge amount of data transmission via internet is needed to increase compression ratio by remove redundant bits to reduce data storage and increase data transmission, however, there are several methods of image compression, there are enhancing new method day by day, especially of included artificial neural network methods, the image compression has two categories, first is lossless compression and second is lossy compression there is a trade-off

DOI: 10.4018/978-1-7998-1290-6.ch016

between the compression and the quality (Raju, S., & Bhairannawar, S. S. 2017), the human conceptual of vision system is not sensitive with some of reducing bit redundancy and with changing in an image intensities, with high compression ratio is allow much loss bits and less image quality. The methods of Image compression which are required for web application does not need high image quality due to recognition of human vision conceptual, and beside that, in example medicine images and satellites are required high accuracy of image quality, included huge storage for images, The big challenges in image compression are how to save image quality after compression process and to get high compression ratio.

in this chapter is describe self-organization feature map SOFM from Kohonen scientific which is un-supervisor learning neural network, however, SOFM is one of the most common unsupervised neural network which has two layers, input and output with weight coefficients in each neuron connection in figure 1 illustrated system architecture of Kohonen map, SOFM model (Hilles, S. M. 2018) and (Huang, Y. H. 2016) and (Wang, J. P., & Cheng, M. S. 2012) and (Park, Y., & Suh, I. H. 2014) and (Hilles, S. M., & Maidanuk, v. P. 2014)

BACKGROUND

The study of Image compression methods and algorithms shows several contributions have been published in order to reduce image redundancy and increase compression ratio. As it has mentioned above there are two categories of image compression method lossy compression methods and lossless compression methods, the first is used for natural images photo gallery such as jpeg which is based on discrete cosine transform DCT, zigzag methods and entropy coding has used Huffman coding method, other example of lossy approach is jpeg 2000 which is based on discrete wavelet transform and adaptive arithmetic coding for entropy, the second category of image compression is lossless which is common used in clip art, comic arts and technical drawings(Jasmi, R. P., Perumal, B., & Rajasekaran, M. P. 2015, . Hilles, S. M., & Hossain, M. A. 2018), presented classification of data compression method such as RLE, arithmetic coding, LZW and Huffman coding as lossless compression methods, it shows and classified lossless methods in image compression model where using transformation such as DCT and DWT and

Figure 1. Simplified performance model of a critical access module Artificial Neural Network of Self-Organization Feature Map SOFM

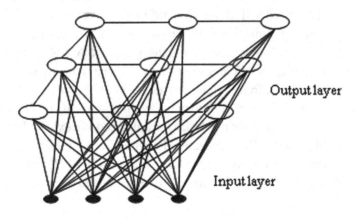

then entropy coding in the last stage, (Han, S., Mao, H., & Dally, W. J. 2015). The deep compression of using neural network presented method for trained quantization, the idea is based on three steps pruning, quantization and Huffman coding, and the quantization is actually comes from weights of neural networks.

Moreover, to use hybrid combination of image compression techniques such as SOFM and vector quantization with Set Partitioning in Hierarchical Trees SPIHT coding, the model shows wavelet transform as first stage of process compression (Rawat, C. S. D., & Meher, S. 2014). SOFM presented and investigated (Hilles, S., & Maidanuk, V. P. 2014), the comparative characteristic of fractal method with SOFM, and by using 16x16 Kohonen map SOFM shows high compression ratio coefficient with small arithmetic operations, the signal noise ratio SNR given small error when compare with JPEG, however, the result shows better performance of compression by using 16x16 Kohonen Map.

In addition, using band-pass filter for analyzing oriented edges to allow many edges as possible in preferred orientation band to pass, (Park, et al., 2014) the result evaluated proposed model with classical filter-based methods.

Image compression is field of Image processing and there are many researches in areas of biometrics, identifications and authorization such as face detection iris and retina (Mady, H. H., & Hilles, S. M. 2017). For real time attendance system and biomedical image processing areas such as automatic brain tumour detection and segmentation (Dong, H., Yang, G., Liu, F., Mo, Y., & Guo, Y. 2017), and combination of image encryption with compression as example encryption based SPIHT compression (Sankaranarayanan, C., & Annadurai, S. 2018) there researcher is focused on using digital watermarked image embedded with un-decimated wavelet transform and then lossless compression method which is presented in SPIHT, therefore, Image compression is needed in many areas of image processing to reduce data size and increase compression ratio, the band-pass filter is presented the characteristics of time frequency localization of band-pass filter and behaviour of three band-biorthogonal wavelet filter bank, the time frequency localization analysis and synthesis such as high pass filter and band-pass filter are localized in the time frequency domain of low pass filter (Bhati, D., Sharma, M., Pachori, R. B., & Gadre, V. M. 2017), the analysis and synthesis of three band filter is compared with standard of two band filter bank, and the result shows that both of analysis and synthesis of two and three band filter banks outperform in the classification of seizure free EEG signal, also it presented multilayer perceptron neural network to implement signal classifier which provide classification accuracy better performance in result of epileptic, study in conceptual of low, high and band-pass filter in graph signals and graph filter, the study is proposed variation of graph signals to frequency on graphs of low, high and band-pass signals filter (Sandryhaila, A., & Moura, J. M. 2014), SOFM model has used in competitive learning there is 173 concrete samples have been used SOFM model in different characteristics (Nikoo, M., Zarfam, P., & Sayahpour, H. 2015), presented optimization SOFM based on genetic algorithms to verify the accuracy model sample, the result shows that is more accuracy in the models of SOFM then predictive compressive of concrete. SOFM has contributed in wireless sensor network, the radio signal and sensor node which is communicated and collected data from neighbours nodes could be done by aggregation technique, clustering techniques is implemented by SOFM to manage amount of data by helping of SOFM (Mittal, M., & Kumar, K. 2016), its allow lifetime of network to be enhanced and extend. Image segmentation and image analysing has used Modified Self-Organization Feature Map MSOFM to classify image pixels of intensity values of image segmentation proposed modification of SOFM NN (Upadhyay, P., & Chhabra, J. K. 2015), vector quantization (Karri, C., & Jena, U. 2016) presented fact vector quantization in image compression the aim of research is to provide the optimization techniques for codebook generations, proposed new algorithm based on Bat algorithm and local binary gradient the performance of vector quantization is related to appropriated codebook generation (Karri, C., & Jena, U. 2016).

In addition, VQ is used in medical image for fuzzy medical image retrieval (Nowaková, J., Prílepok, M., & Snášel, V. 2017) method has been proposed using normalization compression distance 'NCD' to supported system in order to help to determine appropriate healthcare. Image classification presented in image vectors compressed (Sanchez, J., & Perronnin, F. (2014) to extracted local descriptor by generated and having vector elements of mixture model components where is image vector is compressed by VQ algorithm, presented analysing of hybrid scheme combining SOFM based on VQ and SPIHT (Rawat et al. 2014).

Chandan. S. D. Rawat, Sukadev. Meher (2014) analysed a SOFM with SPIHT. The evaluation of result used (PSNR) for decoding upon wavelet for reconstructed image quality with visual information fidelity (VIF) given much effect. Lossy image compression with singular and wavelet decomposition value SVD, WDR proposed technique where is result has been tested by several images and compared with WDR, Discrete cosine transform DCT is the main transformation in JPEG image compression, has used as differential evolution domain for robust image watermarking technique (Ali, M., Ahn, C. W., & Pant, M. 2014) where is DC coefficients from blocks to collected to constructed low-resolution approximation with singular value decomposition.

Gabor filter technique has proposed in approach biometric and identification such as enhancing fingerprint (Liban et al. 2018). However, the efficiency of using Gabor filter is after calculate image pixels and frequency, gabor filter is adjust local orientation and frequency in order to apply image pixel to remove unnecessary noise and recover image correlation of ridge structure with Support Vector Machines SVM methods are wieldy used in image processing in extraction feature and classification

The image contrast, brightness enhancing by using filter such as Gaussian smoothing filter included high pass-filter to produce blur image and sharpen image, The simulation of image compression has implemented and evaluated (O. K. Khorsheed) shows the performance of using multi-bandpass filter, however, the technique focused on periodic image and their experiment to reduced the blurry image significantly to reduce time of compression process(Z. D. Tsai, M. H. Perng), Fractal method in image compression used with combination with wavelet transform DWT and Huffman coding in order to enhance image compression ratio (Jasmi, R. P., Perumal, B., & Rajasekaran, M. P. 2015) the result shows in MSE that fractal algorithm in image compression is provide better performance, (Yen, C. T., & Huang, Y. J. 2016) the result based on digital water-mark recognition which used to protect data for image modification and for copyright, the result of back-propagation neural network combine with DCT watermarking scheme shows suppress the interference affecting watermarks. SOFM technique is contributed and present an efficient indexed color and in genetic algorithm (Nikoo et al. 2015) in the result of SOFM presented that optimized based on genetic algorithm has more accuracy than other models which are based on predicting the compressive strength of concrete.

Similarly, presented principle component analysis PCA technique as unsupervised dimensional reduction which required finding maximum variance of data, PCA technique studied shows that PCA is required to reduce dimension on digital image coding and best feature reduced quality in 35% of achievement file size reduction (Ng, S. C. 2017).

Hybrid neural network predicted-wavelet in novel image compression technique which could be combine with discrete wavelet coding in order to remove intra pixels redundancy, the result after combination of predictive wavelet and discrete wavelet coding shows achieved (Hussain, A. J., Al-Jumeily, D., Radi, N., & Lisboa, P. 2015).

SOFM presented as alternative grid topologies in geometric theory of tessellations, the result presented unsupervised clustering, image segmentation and classification where is different topologies are significant in most cases and optimal topology depending on the problem hand (López-Rubio, E., & Ramos, A. D. 2014).

Combination of DWT and DCT algorithm in hybrid color medical image compression shows that the coding performance is significant improved (Boukli, H. I., & Bessaid, A. 2014). Neural networks based on back-propogation algorithm support image compression in order to enhancing compression ratio, increased performance by reducing compression process (Panda, S. S., Prasad, M. S. R. S., Prasad, M. N. M., & Naidu, C. S. 2012).

Below is proposed conceptual model in image compression based on SOFM and vector quantization, and as preprocessing is used band-pass filter, and for lossless of entropy coding is presented arithmetic coder.

Table 1 shows the summarization the common literature review which have been presented on this chapter and shows the several researches in area of image compression based on neural network and contribution.

IMAGE COMPRESSION BY COMPONENTS

This part is presented image component coding of using 2D analysis of contour-adaptive and synthesis features, image component formulated and analysis in variety of 2D signals which content more details of image inputs in different size.

However, Image component coding consist several apertures in image analysis of different dimensions which districted "positive" and "negative" transparency. Moreover, Discrete Fourier Transform DFT used to summation apertures in image component as a combination of 2D spatial frequency filters. After using synthesis of spatial frequency filters, executed the mathematic operation of distribute function to calculate pixel size of image in order to determine in individual format of apertures, where is largest aperture from a positive transparency which consist 2D low-frequency filter, signal synthesis which generated from aperture is allow to create an image that corresponds to a release initial image. All apertures in positive and negative transparency will be considered in 2D spatial frequency band-pass filters (Hilles M.S., 2018).

Figure 2. SOFM and band-pass filter system architecture

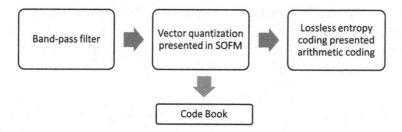

Table 1. Summary of the systems reviewed in image compression using SOFM and band-pass filter

No	Authors Name	Date of Published	Title	Contributions
1.	J. Wang, N. Zheng	2013	A Novel Fractal Image Compression Scheme With Block Classification and Sorting Based on Pearson's Correlation Coefficient	Main contribution is image classification based on fractal image compression, has two blocks of fractal image compression which is equivalent by correlation Coefficient, the result presented high performance and speed up compression process.
2.	Hilles, s. M., & maidanuk, v. P.	2014	Self-organization Feature Map Based on VQ Components to Solve Image Coding Problem.	SOFM has been proposed and investigated to solve image compression problem with arithmetic coding in lossless entropy coding in the last stage, the result shows high compression ratio by using 16x16 SOFM Kohonen compare with jpeg and with less Kohonen map size such as 8x8, 6x6 Kohonen map.
3.	S Raju, SS Bhairannawar	2017	Image Compression using Self Organizing Map and Discrete Wavelet Transform with Error Correction	Proposed image compression method based on SOFM and DWT with error correction, EC block image input vector used is 16x4096, the evaluation result used PSNR and MSE with and without EC, shows error matrix and quantized with arithmetic encoder to obtain compressed error bits, and shows that proposed model is better compared with other technique, the author shows the experiment for evaluation result in lena, mandrill, peppers cameraman as input original image.
4.	Park, Y., & Suh, I. H.	2014	Oriented edge-selective band-pass filtering	proposed oriented edge-selective in band-pass filter, the result shows the performance of proposed model evaluated in classical filter-based methods
5.	Hilles, S. M.	2018	Spatial Frequency Filtering Using SOFM For Image Compression	Image compression model has proposed and investigated as preprocessing is band-pass filter for second stage is SOFM presented and in the last stage arithmetic coding for entropy, the analysis band-pass filter and synthesis shows better performance with 16x16 Kohonen map size, and better compression ratio, the result evaluated with jpg and other Kohonen map size, author contribution also focused on analysis special frequency characters filter for high, low and band-pass in symmetric filter.
6.	K. M. Jeevan, S. Krishnakumar	2014	Compression of images represented in hexagonal lattice using wavelet and Gabor filter	A method presented for image compression performance based on hexagonal wavelet, and compared with square performance, the result by MSE, and PSNR shown the advantages of using hexagonal wavelet, also was proposed Gabor filter for interpolation of hexagonally for image samples.
7.	A. Makandar, B. Halalli	2015	Image Enhancement Techniques using High pass and Low pass Filters	Demonstrated the low pass filter that produced Gaussian smoothing blur image and the high pass filter increased the contrast between bright and dark pixel that produced sharpen image.
8.	Ismail. B. Hacene, A. Bessaid	2014	Hybrid colour medical image compression by CDF wavelet and cosine transforms	Proposed a hybrid compression technique (DWT and DCT). Achieve higher compression rates by applying different compression thresholds for the wavelet of each DWT band.
9.	K. M. Jeevan, S. Krishnakumar	22014	Compression of images represented in hexagonal lattice using wavelet and Gabor filter	A method to reduce high computational complexity and memory usage owing to the high dimensionality of the Gabor filter responses.
10.	Z. D. Tsai, M. H. Perng	22013	Defect detection in periodic patterns using a multi-band-pass filter	Presented a technique for periodic image using a multi-band-pass filter and their experiment reduced the blurry image significantly also computational time.
11.	A. Makandar, B. Halalli	22015	Image Enhancement Techniques using High pass and Low pass Filters	Demonstrated the low pass filter that produced Gaussian smoothing blur image and the high pass filter increased the contrast between bright and dark pixel that produced sharpen image.
12.	Liban, el,	22018	Latent Fingerprint Enhancement Based On Directional Total Variation Model With Lost Minutiae Reconstruction	Gabor filters responses with non-linear kernels and SVM for image extraction and classification.

TWO DIMENSION OF SPATIAL FREQUENCY BAND-PASS FILTER

Present characteristic of band-pass filter and frequency, where low-pass filter is illustrated as active band-pass filter in example:

If there are φ1, φ2....., φn- dimensional low-pass frequency components of image has initial image φ0 and after low-pass filtering, the bandwidth of low-pass filter are presented such as:

$$W1 > W2 > W3 \tag{1}$$

Below shows decomposition of components image presented as follow:

$$\phi = (\phi_n + (\phi_{n-1} - \phi_n) + ... + (\phi_1 - \phi_2) + (\phi_0 - \phi_1)) \tag{2}$$

where $\phi = \phi_0$ each previous component is subtract with next component and sum all components, the process of compression is consist discretization of each component, presented in Kotelnikov theorem (Alexeev, B. V. (2016) time quantization and shannon-nyquist and quantization theorem, variable length coding i Shannon fano and entropy coding which are the fundamental of data coding, data communication transmission and represented data as samples of components φn, and samples of difference components.

IMAGE COMPONENT IMPLEMENTATION

In this section, image component implementation is a technical encoder which is analysis the image based on square apertures on deep analysis with multiples of 2n, however it's significantly reduced the computational cost. Most of appropriate is view of implementation reactions in band pass filters where are difference reactions smoothing filters with different cut-off frequency; smoothing filter consist linear performance. Below is mathematical modulation of differential equation which is described and illustrated in two-dimensional format of low-pass filter:

$$y(n_1, n_2) = \frac{1}{N_1 N_2} \sum_{k_1=0}^{N_1-1} \sum_{k_2=0}^{N_2-1} x(n_1 - k_1, n_2 - k_2) \tag{3}$$

Equation (3) illustrates N1, N2 and analyzing aperture size of each sample values of the original image:

$$x(n_1 - k_1, n_2 - k_2) \tag{4}$$

Correlations of Image analysis shows that the increasing the maximum size of apertures which is 8 to 16 is not appreciable for high aspect ratio of winning. Therefore, the equation (4) which has been described of low-pass filter in 2D with a largest aperture size can be takes as following format of equation to calculate 8 aperture sizes from 64 samples as shown on equation (5):

$$y(n_1, n_2) = \frac{1}{64} \sum_{k_1=0}^{7} \sum_{k_2=0}^{7} x(n_1 - k_1, n_2 - k_2) \qquad (5)$$

Filter of Transferable function can be define as ratio of Z-transformation of output signal to inputs, below shows Z1 and Z2 transform replaced, presented in equation (6):

$$H(Z_1, Z_2) = \frac{1}{64} \sum_{k_1=0}^{7} \sum_{k_2=0}^{7} Z_1^{-k_1}, Z_2^{-k_2}) \qquad (6)$$

where Z1, Z2 transformation of Image representation present delay on line and sampling time, respectively. After Z - transformations, the equation (6) can be represented as:

$$H(Z_1, Z_2) = [\frac{1}{4}(1 + Z_1^{-1})(1 + Z_2^{-1})][\frac{1}{4}(1 + Z_1^{-2})(1 + Z_2^{-2})][\frac{1}{4}(1 + Z_1^{-4})(1 + Z_2^{-4})] \qquad (7)$$

Equation (7) shows that the implementation of the smoothed component for analyzing is the apertures of different sizes; it can use the appropriate smoothing filter taps with the largest aperture of the analyzing. Transfer function of this filter is denoted as:

$$H_3(Z_1, Z_2) = H(Z_1, Z_2) \qquad (8)$$

where is Z transfer functions with smoothing filters 8x8 and 6x6 apertures are according to the equation (7, 8) is illustrated in equation (9) as follow:

$$H_2(Z_1, Z_2) = [\frac{1}{4}(1 + Z_1^{-1})(1 + Z_2^{-1})][\frac{1}{4}(1 + Z_1^{-2})(1 + Z_2^{-2})]$$

$$H_1(Z_1, Z_2) = [\frac{1}{4}(1 + Z_1^{-1})(1 + Z_2^{-1})] \qquad (9)$$

Band-pass filter and his smoothing reactions which is implemented with difference format, shows below:

$$H_3^{'}(Z_1, Z_2) = H_2(Z_1, Z_2) - H_3(Z_1, Z_2);$$

$$H_2^{'}(Z_1, Z_2) = H_1(Z_1, Z_2) - H_2(Z_1, Z_2);$$

$$H_1^{'}(Z_1, Z_2) = H_0(Z_1, Z_2) - H_1(Z_1, Z_2) \qquad (10)$$

In the process of data transformation and representation via internet or on data storage, after sampling and quantization transmitted counts component output filters with transfer functions regarding equations (7) (10). Therefore, implementation of low-pass frequency component in image pixels is decreased concatenation in one-dimensional filters with some delay in element per every second, two seconds or four seconds in rate and one, two and four lines in image. The equations as illustrated below shows the performance of operation which will by shift operations.

However, the disadvantages in given method is because the lack in accuracy of approximation in amplitude with frequency characteristics filters, which allow of increasing quantization levels for each difference components in order to reduce compression ratio, respectively. Amplitude-frequency characteristics filter with symmetric coefficients is defined in equation (11) as:

$$y(n) = \sum_{k_1=-N}^{N} a_k x(n-k) \tag{11}$$

Symmetric coefficients of filter are illustrated as:

$$a_k = a_{-k} = \frac{\Omega_g}{\pi} \frac{\sin k\Omega_g}{k\Omega_g}, \tag{12}$$

$$\Omega_g = 2\pi \frac{f_g}{f_a}, \tag{13}$$

where - f_g - is a limit frequency filter, f_a - frequency sample.

Suppose that - $f_g = W / 8$ and $f_a = 2W$, where is W are band-pass signals, Then we suppose that k = 0 and k = 1, 2 … so the equation can be defined for eight samples:

$$a_0^8 = \frac{1}{8}, \ a_k^8 = a_{-k}^8 = \frac{\sin(k\pi / 8)}{k\pi}, \ k = 1,2... \tag{14}$$

For $f_g = W / 4$ and $f_g = W / 2$ coefficients are defined as follows:

$$a_0^4 = \frac{1}{4}, \ a_k^4 = a_{-k}^4 = \frac{\sin(k\pi / 4)}{k\pi}, \ k = 1,2... \tag{15}$$

$$a_0^2 = \frac{1}{2}, \ a_k^2 = a_{-k}^2 = \frac{\sin(k\pi / 2)}{k\pi}, \ k = 1,2... \tag{16}$$

The approximation filters as selected is shown below:

- N = 15 - filter fg = W/8;

- N = 7 - filter fg = W/4;

- N = 3 - filter fg = W/2.

Differences in equations filters are (k ≠ 0), shows the different size map illustrated by 8, 4 and 2 components as shown below (17, 18 and 19) equations

$$y_8(n) = \frac{1}{8}x(n) + \sum_{k=-15}^{k=15} \frac{\sin(|k|\pi/8)}{k\pi}x(n-k) \tag{17}$$

$$y_4(n) = \frac{1}{4}x(n) + \sum_{k=-7}^{k=7} \frac{\sin(|k|\pi/4)}{k\pi}x(n-k) \tag{18}$$

$$y_2(n) = \frac{1}{2}x(n) + \sum_{k=-3}^{k=3} \frac{\sin(|k|\pi/2)}{k\pi}x(n-k) \tag{19}$$

Band-pass filters and different three components 8, 4 and 2 show in differential equations (20, 21 and 22), shown below:

$$\Delta\, y_4(n) = \frac{1}{8}x(n) + \sum_{k=-7}^{k=7}\left(\frac{\sin(|k|\pi/4)}{k\pi} - \frac{\sin(|k|\pi/8)}{k\pi}\right)x(n-k) \tag{20}$$

$$\Delta\, y_2(n) = \frac{1}{4}x(n) + \sum_{k=-3}^{k=3}\left(\frac{\sin(|k|\pi/2)}{k\pi} - \frac{\sin(|k|\pi/4)}{k\pi}\right)x(n-k) \tag{21}$$

$$\Delta y_0(n) = \frac{1}{2}x(n) - \sum_{k=-3}^{k=3}\left(\frac{\sin(|k|\pi/2)}{k\pi}\right)x(n-k) \tag{22}$$

In addition, we can find evaluation and analysis of amplitude and frequency characteristics filter which is define in equations (20-22) with amplitude and frequency characteristics filter in equations (7,9) as in example the filter of formula (20) and filter in (21), these filters designed to release spectrum of signal only in the range of 0 – W/8.

Figure 3. Amplitude-frequency characteristics filters 1 – Non-recursive symmetric filter, 2 – smoothing linear filter

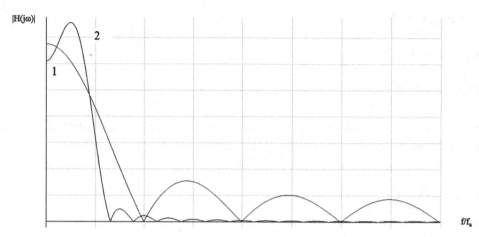

Moreover, to consider one dimension case which of Amplitude-frequency characteristics filter as given on expression (7) is illustrated as shown on Figure 3. Signal (1) as non-recursive symmetric filter

The amplitude and frequency characteristics filter as illustrated on equation (24), the lock domain is an order less Amplitude-frequency characteristics filter in expression (23) transition from zone to zone transmission blocking also occurs abruptly in comparison to the frequency response in accordance with expression (28), which provides a more accurate abutment filter bandwidths for forming an image component.

$$H(j\omega) = \frac{\sqrt{2}}{4}\sqrt{(1 + \cos \omega T_a)(1 + \cos 2\omega T_a)(1 + \cos 4\omega T_a)} \tag{23}$$

Filter which is defined on (13) is illustrated peak signal of amplitude and frequency characteristic filter as shown on Figure. 3, on signal (2) as smoothing linear filter presented in equations (23, 24).

$$H(j\omega) = \left| \frac{1}{8} + 2\sum_{K=1}^{K=15} \frac{\sin(k\pi / 8)}{k\pi} \cos(k\omega T_a) \right| \tag{24}$$

Since the two-dimensional image signal, it is necessary to filter the image first in one direction and then in the other direction, using the expressions (17-22). Further compression in the same order on application of smoothing filters. However, non-recursive filters with symmetrical coefficients more accurately approximate the ideal characteristics of a low pass filter that gives hope to expect an increase in the compression ratio and improve the quality of the synthesized image.

EXPERIMENTAL RESULTS

The result of test experiments is presented and investigated for image compression algorithms based on 2D SOFM. It is shown that, when using SOFM with combination algorithms for image compression it's significantly and important to improve compression performance.

Quality of Image Reconstructed in Critical Rate

Image reconstruction describes the idea of restoring image after compression which is needed to get image from less different with the input image. The extended true image size of compression is calculated by mean square error MSE (Hilles et al. 2014).

Where U_{ij} is a original image value, $\widehat{U}_{ij}$ is reconstructed image value, M, N – image size, E($\bullet$) – expected image value.

The test experiments calculated error from differences image value by using MSE as following equation:

$$e^2 = \frac{1}{M * N} \sum_{i=1}^{N} \sum_{J=1}^{M} E(U_{ij} - \widehat{U}_{ij})^2 \tag{25}$$

Therefore, to determine Signal Noise Ratio SNR is calculated by the following equation:

$$SNR = 10 \lg \frac{255^2}{e^2} \tag{26}$$

Figure 4 is a number of experiments which is executed by several types of images illustrated compression coefficients and hold limits of 3 to 15. For certain images compression coefficient which is override jpeg image format standard at the same brightness.

The values of pixels brightness of high frequency component are concentrated in the area of small image values

A number of experiments, executed by several types of images showed where compression coefficients could be with limits of 3 to 15 is for certain images Figure. 4, 5 of standard experiment lena image and Figure 6, 7 compression coefficient exceeds jpeg image standard format on the same brightness.

Below is comparing between two different SOFM size map of image compression, and based on the result of evaluation above, shows by using 16x16 is gives high compression ratio with the experiment is shows the comparison of two different SOFM size map.

CONCLUSION

This chapter has investigated and evaluated new method of image compression in self-organization feature map SOFM with vector quantization and analysis spatial frequency characteristic filter and presented arithmetic coding for entropy coding of lossless compression, band-pass filter in the first stage of proposed method is preprocessing, the chapter shows that using analysis aperture and synthesis with symmetrical coefficient is much more accurately approximation result and could be arrange in efficiently

Table 2. Result of compression ratio based on SOFM and compared with jpeg image format compression ratio

Compression	Size of Initial File, byte	Size of Compressed File, byte	Compression Ratio	SNR
JPEG & Lena.bmp	1192,054	13106	14,7	0,019
Vector Quantization, 2 bit/px (SOFM 16x16)				
Lena.bmp	1192,054	18034	10,65	0,01975
Girl256.bmp		51458	3,7	0,01936
Vector Quantization 1,5 bit/px (SOFM 8x8)				
Lena.bmp	9192,054	12209	15,7	0,0298
Girl256.bmp		37366	5,14	0,027
Vector Quantization 1 bit/px (SOFM 6x6)				
Lena.bmp	1192,054	8860	21,68	0,041
Girl256.bmp		26236	7,32	0,037

Figure 4. Shows SOFM 16x16 the compression ratio is 9 lena image experiment

Figure 5. Shows SOFM 16x16, the compression ratio is 14.8 lena image experiment

Figure 6. Compression ratio 3.7 – size 16x16 SOFM

Figure 7. Compression ratio 5.14 – Size 8x8 of SOFM

image pixels where is SOFM map size has been tested and evaluated with different size map and shows that 16x16 Kohonen map is high compression ration based on SNR, in chapter provide analysis of low, high and band-pass filters, the experiment result lena.bmp shows different result in compression ratio and image correlation with Kohonen map with 6x6, 8x8 and 16x6 also in the evaluation result and comparison with Jpeg, The jpeg which is lossy image method gives less compression ratio than 16x16 size map of Kohonen, and it has better result in compression ratio based on SNR, in the third stage is arithmetic coding for entropy coding, the result of SOFM with band-pass filter compared with fractal method and shows the advantages of using SOFM with band-pass filter is less mathematic operation which allow much efficiently on process of compression performance, future work is to expand evaluation result with method of image compression based on discrete wavelet transform and with other deep learning method used in image compression approaches.

REFERENCES

Addison, P. S. (2017). *The illustrated wavelet transform handbook: introductory theory and applications in science, engineering, medicine and finance*. CRC Press.

Ali, M., Ahn, C. W., & Pant, M. (2014). A robust image watermarking technique using SVD and differential evolution in DCT domain. *Optik-International Journal for Light and Electron Optics*, *125*(1), 428–434. doi:10.1016/j.ijleo.2013.06.082

Bhati, D., Sharma, M., Pachori, R. B., & Gadre, V. M. (2017). Time–frequency localized three-band biorthogonal wavelet filter bank using semidefinite relaxation and nonlinear least squares with epileptic seizure EEG signal classification. *Digital Signal Processing*, *62*, 259–273. doi:10.1016/j.dsp.2016.12.004

Boukli, H. I., & Bessaid, A. (2014). Hybrid colour medical image compression by CDF wavelet and cosine transforms. *International Journal of Biomedical Engineering and Technology*, *16*(1), 1–13. doi:10.1504/IJBET.2014.065633

Dong, H., Yang, G., Liu, F., Mo, Y., & Guo, Y. (2017, July). Automatic brain tumor detection and segmentation using U-Net based fully convolutional networks. In *Annual conference on medical image understanding and analysis* (pp. 506-517). Springer.

Han, S., Mao, H., & Dally, W. J. (2015). *Deep compression: Compressing deep neural networks with pruning, trained quantization and Huffman coding*. arXiv preprint arXiv:1510.00149

Hilles, S., & Maidanuk, V. P. (2014). Self-organization feature map based on VQ components to solve image coding problem. *Journal of Engineering and Applied Sciences (Asian Research Publishing Network)*, *9*(9), 1469–1475.

Hilles, S. M. (2018, July). Sofm And Vector Quantization For Image Compression By Component. In *2018 International Conference on Smart Computing and Electronic Enterprise (ICSCEE)* (pp. 1-6). IEEE. 10.1109/ICSCEE.2018.8538402

Hilles, S. M. (2018, July). Spatial Frequency Filtering Using Sofm For Image Compression. In *2018 International Conference on Smart Computing and Electronic Enterprise (ICSCEE)* (pp. 1-7). IEEE.

Hilles, S. M., & Hossain, M. A. (2018). Classification on Image Compression Methods. *International Journal of Data Science Research, 1*(1), 1–7.

Hussain, A. J., Al-Jumeily, D., Radi, N., & Lisboa, P. (2015). Hybrid neural network predictive-wavelet image compression system. *Neurocomputing, 151,* 975–984. doi:10.1016/j.neucom.2014.02.078

Jasmi, R. P., Perumal, B., & Rajasekaran, M. P. (2015, January). Comparison of image compression techniques using huffman coding, DWT and fractal algorithm. In *2015 International Conference on Computer Communication and Informatics (ICCCI)* (pp. 1-5). IEEE.

Karri, C., & Jena, U. (2016). Fast vector quantization using a Bat algorithm for image compression. *Engineering Science and Technology, an International Journal, 19*(2), 769-781.

Khorsheed, O. K. (2014). Produce Low-Pass and High-Pass Image Filter in Java. *International Journal of Advances in Engineering and Technology, 7*(3), 712.

López-Rubio, E., & Ramos, A. D. (2014). Grid topologies for the self-organizing map. *Neural Networks, 56,* 35–48. doi:10.1016/j.neunet.2014.05.001 PMID:24861385

Mady, H. H., & Hilles, S. M. (2017). Efficient Real Time Attendance System Based on Face Detection Case Study "MEDIU Staff". *International Journal on Contemporary Computer Research, 1*(2), 21–25.

Mittal, M., & Kumar, K. (2016, April). Data clustering in wireless sensor network implemented on self-organization feature map (SOFM) neural network. In *2016 International Conference on Computing, Communication and Automation (ICCCA)* (pp. 202-207). IEEE. 10.1109/CCAA.2016.7813718

Ng, S. C. (2017). Principal component analysis to reduce dimension on digital image. *Procedia Computer Science, 111,* 113–119. doi:10.1016/j.procs.2017.06.017

Nikoo, M., Zarfam, P., & Sayahpour, H. (2015). Determination of compressive strength of concrete using Self Organization Feature Map (SOFM). *Engineering with Computers, 31*(1), 113–121. doi:10.100700366-013-0334-x

Nowaková, J., Prílepok, M., & Snášel, V. (2017). Medical image retrieval using vector quantization and fuzzy S-tree. *Journal of Medical Systems, 41*(2), 18. doi:10.100710916-016-0659-2 PMID:27981409

Panda, S. S., Prasad, M. S. R. S., Prasad, M. N. M., & Naidu, C. S. (2012). Image compression using back propagation neural network. *International Journal of Engineering Science and Advance Technology, 2,* 74-78.

Park, Y., & Suh, I. H. (2014). Oriented edge-selective band-pass filtering. *Information Sciences, 276,* 80–103. doi:10.1016/j.ins.2014.02.048

Raju, S., & Bhairannawar, S. S. (2017). Image Compression using Self Organizing Map and Discrete Wavelet Transform with Error Correction. *International Journal of Applied Engineering Research, 12*(10), 2509–2516.

Rawat, C. S. D., & Meher, S. (2014). Selection of wavelet for image compression in hybrid coding scheme combining SPIHT-and SOFM-based vector quantisation. *International Journal of Signal and Imaging Systems Engineering, 7*(1), 38–42. doi:10.1504/IJSISE.2014.057937

Rawat, C. S. D., & Meher, S. (2014). Selection of wavelet for image compression in hybrid coding scheme combining SPIHT-and SOFM-based vector quantisation. *International Journal of Signal and Imaging Systems Engineering*, 7(1), 38–42. doi:10.1504/IJSISE.2014.057937

Sanchez, J., & Perronnin, F. (2014). *U.S. Patent No. 8,731,317*. Washington, DC: U.S. Patent and Trademark Office.

Sandryhaila, A., & Moura, J. M. (2014). Discrete signal processing on graphs: Frequency analysis. *IEEE Transactions on Signal Processing*, 62(12), 3042–3054. doi:10.1109/TSP.2014.2321121

Sankaranarayanan, C., & Annadurai, S. (2018). *An Optimized Digital Image Encryption based SPIHT Compression using RC4-Blowfish and UWT Algorithm*. Academic Press.

Tsai, Z. D., & Perng, M. H. (2013). Defect detection in periodic patterns using a multi-band-pass filter. *Machine Vision and Applications*, 24(3), 551–565. doi:10.100700138-012-0425-5

Upadhyay, P., & Chhabra, J. K. (2015). Modified Self Organizing Feature Map Neural Network (MSOFM NN) Based Gray Image Segmentation. *Procedia Computer Science*, 54, 671–675. doi:10.1016/j.procs.2015.06.078

Wang, J., & Zheng, N. (2013). A Novel Fractal Image Compression Scheme With Block Classification and Sorting Based on Pearson's Correlation Coefficient. *IEEE Transactions on Image Processing*, 22(9), 3690–3702. doi:10.1109/TIP.2013.2268977 PMID:23797251

Yen, C. T., & Huang, Y. J. (2016). Frequency domain digital watermark recognition using image code sequences with a back-propagation neural network. *Multimedia Tools and Applications*, 75(16), 9745–9755. doi:10.100711042-015-2718-y

Zhuiko, V. J., Verbitskyi, I. V., & Kyselova, A. G. (2014, June). Kotelnikov double series of modulating signals with limited spectrum. In *2014 IEEE International Conference on Intelligent Energy and Power Systems (IEPS)* (pp. 18-20). IEEE. 10.1109/IEPS.2014.6874177

Compilation of References

Abawajy, J. H., Mukherjea, S., Thampi, S. M., & Ruiz-Martínez, A. (2015). Security in Computing and Communications. *Third International Symposium, SSCC 2015*, Kochi, India.

Adamatzky, A. (1994). *Identification of Cellular Automata*. Taylor and Francis.

Adamatzky, A. (Ed.). (2010). *Game of Life. Cellular Automata*. Springer. doi:10.1007/978-1-84996-217-9

Adamović, S., Šarac, M., Veinović, M., Jevremović, A., & Milosavljević, M. (2013). *An add-on for networking CrypTool 2 simulation environments*. Faculty of computing and informatics, Singidunum University, Belgrade, Serbia. (in Serbian)

Addison, P. S. (2017). *The illustrated wavelet transform handbook: introductory theory and applications in science, engineering, medicine and finance*. CRC Press.

Agarwal, M. K., Gupta, M., Kar, G., Neogi, A., & Sailer, A. (2004). Mining Activity Data for Dynamic Dependency Discovery in e-Business Systems. *IEEE eTransactions on Network and Service Management*, *1*(2), 49–58. doi:10.1109/TNSM.2004.4798290

Aggarwal, C. (2018). Neural Networks and Deep Learning: A Textbook. Springer. doi:10.1007/978-3-319-94463-0

Aghajanian, J., & Prince, S. J. D. (2009). Face pose estimation in uncontrolled environments. *Proceeding of British Machine Vision Conference*, *1*, 1-11.

Ahmad Al-Khoder, A., & Harmouch, H. (2014). Evaluating four of the most popular Open Source and Free Data Mining Tools. *IJASR International Journal of Academic Scientific Research*, *3*(1), 13–23.

Ahmadi, Amjadian, & Pardegi. (2012). New Approach to Bankruptcy Prediction using Genetic Algorithm. *International Journal of Computer Applications*, *44*(4).

Ahmad, I., Abdullah, A., Alghamdi, A., & Hussain, M. (2013). Optimized intrusion detection mechanism using soft computing techniques. *Telecommunication Systems*, *52*(4), 2187–2195.

Ahmad, T., Studiawan, H., Ahmad, H. S., Ijtihadie, R. M., & Wibisono, W. (2014, October). Shared secret-based steganography for protecting medical data. *Proceedings of the 2014 International Conference on Computer, Control, Informatics and Its Applications (IC3INA)* (pp. 87-92). IEEE.

Ahmed, M., & Ward, R. (2002). A Rotation Invariant Rule-Based Thinning Algorithm for Character Recognition. *IEEE Transactions on Pattern Analysis and Machine Intelligence*, *24*(12), 1672–1678. doi:10.1109/TPAMI.2002.1114862

Aizawa, Y., & Nishikawa, I. (1986). *Toward the classification of the patterns generated by one-dimensional cellular automata. In Dinamical Systems and Nonlinear Oscillators* (Vol. 1, pp. 210–222). Advanced Series in Dinamical Systems.

Akashdeep, I. M., & Kumar, N. (2017). A Feature Reduced Intrusion Detection System using ANN Classifier, Elsevier -. *Expert Systems with Applications*, *88*, 249–257. doi:10.1016/j.eswa.2017.07.005

Alavi, S. (2012). Comparison of Some Motion Detection Methods in cases of Single and Multiple Moving Objects. *International Journal of Image Processing*, *6*(5), 389–396.

Albdour, N. (2018). Selection Image Points Method for Steganography Protection of Information. *WSEAS Transactions on Signal Processing*, *14*, 151–159.

Ali, M., Ahn, C. W., & Pant, M. (2014). A robust image watermarking technique using SVD and differential evolution in DCT domain. *Optik-International Journal for Light and Electron Optics*, *125*(1), 428–434. doi:10.1016/j.ijleo.2013.06.082

Alonso-Sanz, R. (2009). *Cellular Automata with Memory*. Old Sity Publishing.

Alonso-Sanz, R. (2006). Elementary cellular automata wiyh elementary memory rules in cell: The case of linear rules. *Journal of Cellular Automata*, *1*(1), 71–87.

Alonso-Sanz, R. (2013). Cellular Automata with Memory and the Density Classification Task. *JCA*, *8*(3-4), 283–297.

Anbalagan, E., Puttamadappa, C., Mohan, E., Jayaraman, B., & Madane, S. (2008). Datamining and Intrusion Detection Using Back-Propagation Algorithm for Intrusion Detection. *International Journal of Soft Computing*, *3*(4), 264–270.

Ansari, A. Q., Patki, T., Patki, A. B., & Kumar, V. (2007). Integrating fuzzy logic and data mining: impact on cyber security. *Proceeding of Fourth International Conference on Fuzzy Systems and Knowledge Discovery*. 10.1109/FSKD.2007.365

Antonio Gulli, A., & Pal, S. (2017). Deep learning with Keras- implement neural networks with Keras on Theano and TensorFlow. Mumbai: Packt Book.

Anuar, N. B., Sallehudin, H., Gani, A., & Zakari, O. (2008). Identifying False Alarm for Network Intrusion Detection System using Hybrid Data Mining and Decision Tree. *Malaysian Journal of Computer Science*, *21*(2), 101–115. doi:10.22452/mjcs.vol21no2.3

Arslan, M. U., & Rehan, M. U. (2018). Using Image Steganography for Providing Enhanced Medical Data security. Proceedings of the *15th IEEE annual consumer communications & networking conference*, Las Vegas, NV. IEEE.

Arun, Ishan, & Sanmeet. (2016). Loan Approval Prediction based on Machine Learning Approach. *IOSR Journal of Computer Engineering*, *18*(3).

Babitha, P. K., Thushara, T., & Dechakka, M. (2015). P. FPGA Based N - bit LFSR to generate random sequence number. *International Journal of Engineering Research and General Science*, *3*(3), 60–10.

Dalashov, E. (1985). Evolutionary synthesis of systems. Radio & Communication, 1(1), 328.

Bandini, S., Bonomi, A., & Vizzari, G. (2012). An Analysis of Different Types and Effects of Asynchronicity in Cellular Automata update Schemes. *Natural Computing*, *11*(2), 277–287. doi:10.100711047-012-9310-4

Bastos, P., Lopes, I., & Pires, L. (2014). Application of data mining in a maintenance system for failure prediction. In Safety, Reliability and Risk Analysis: Beyond the Horizon. Taylor & Francis Group.

Basurto, R., Leon, P. A., Martinez, G. J., & Seck-Tuoh-Mora, J. C. (2013). Logic Gates and Complex Dynamics in a Hexagonal Cellular Automaton: The Spiral Rule. *JCA*, *8*(1-2), 53–71.

Belan, S. (2011). Specialized cellular structures for image contour analysis. *Cybernetics and Systems Analysis, 47*(5), 695-704.

Belan, S. N., & Motornyuk, R. L. (2013a). Extraction of characteristic features of images with the help of the radon transform and its hardware implementation in terms of cellular automata. Cybernetics and Systems Analysis, 49(1), 7-14.

Belan, S., & Belan, N. (2012). Use of Cellular Automata to Create an Artificial System of Image Classification and Recognition. *LNCS, 7495*, 483-493.

Belan, S., & Yuzhakov, S. (2013b). A Homogenous Parameter Set for Image Recognition Based on Area. Computer and Information Science, 6(2), 93-102.

Belan, S., & Yuzhakov, S. (2013b). Machine Vision System Based on the Parallel Shift Technology and Multiple Image Analysis. Computer and Information Science, 6(4), 115-124. doi:10.5539/cis.v6n4p115

Belan, S., & Yuzhakov, S. (2013c). Machine Vision System Based on the Parallel Shift Technology and Multiple Image Analysis. Computer and Information Science, 6(4), 115-124.

Belan, S. (2011). Specialized cellular structures for image contour analysis. *Cybernetics and Systems Analysis*, *47*(5), 695–704. doi:10.100710559-011-9349-8

Belan, S. N., & Motornyuk, R. L. (2013). Extraction of characteristic features of images with the help of the radon transform and its hardware implementation in terms of cellular automata. *Cybernetics and Systems Analysis*, *49*(1), 7–14. doi:10.100710559-013-9479-2

Belan, S., & Belan, N. (2012). Use of Cellular Automata to Create an Artificial System of Image Classification and Recognition, *ACRI2012* [), Springer-Verlag Berlin Heidelberg.]. *LNCS, 7495*, 483–493.

Belan, S., & Belan, N. (2012). *Use of Cellular Automata to Create an Artificial System of Image Classification and Recognition. In ACRI 2012, LNCS* (Vol. 7495, pp. 483–493). Heidelberg: Springer.

Belan, S., & Belan, N. (2013). *Temporal-Impulse Description of Complex Image Based on Cellular Automata. In PaCT2013, LNCS* (Vol. 7979, pp. 291–295). Springer-Verlag Berlin Heidelberg.

Belan, S., & Yuzhakov, S. (2013). A Homogenous Parameter Set for Image Recognition Based on Area. *Computer and Information Science*, *6*(2), 93–102. doi:10.5539/cis.v6n2p93

Berry, J. K. (1993). *Beyond Mapping: Concepts, Algorithms, and Issues in CIS*. Fort Collins, CO: GIS World.

Bhati, D., Sharma, M., Pachori, R. B., & Gadre, V. M. (2017). Time–frequency localized three-band biorthogonal wavelet filter bank using semidefinite relaxation and nonlinear least squares with epileptic seizure EEG signal classification. *Digital Signal Processing*, *62*, 259–273. doi:10.1016/j.dsp.2016.12.004

Bhattacharjee, K., Paul, D., & Das, S. (2016). Pseudorandom Pattern Generation Using 3-State Cellular Automata. In S. El Yacoubi, J. Wąs, & S. Bandini (Eds.), Lecture Notes in Computer Science: Vol. 9863. *Cellular Automata. ACRI 2016* (pp. 3–13). doi:10.1007/978-3-319-44365-2_1

Bilan, S., Yuzhakov, S., & Bilan, S. (2014). Saving of Etalons in Image Processing Systems Based on the Parallel Shift Technology. Advances in Image and Video Processing, 2(6), 36-41.

Bilan, S., Yuzhakov, S., & Bilan, S. (2014). Saving of Etalons in Image Processing Systems Based on the Parallel Shift Technology. Advances in Image and Video Processing, 2(6), 36-41. doi:10.14738/aivp.26.772

Bilan, S. (2017). *Formation Methods, Models, and Hardware Implementation of Pseudorandom Number Generators: Emerging Research and Opportunities*. IGI Global.

Bilan, S., Bilan, M., & Bilan, S. (2015). Novel pseudorandom sequence of numbers generator based cellular automata. *Information Technology and Seqcurity*, *3*(1), 38–50.

Bilan, S., Bilan, M., Motornyuk, R., Bilan, A., & Bilan, S. (2016). Research and Analysis of the Pseudorandom Number Generators Implemented on Cellular Automata. *WSEAS Transactions on Systems, 15*, 275–281.

Bilan, S., Bilan, M., Motornyuk, R., Bilan, A., & Bilan, S. (2016). Research and Analysis of the Pseudorandom Number Generators Implemented on Cellular Automata. *WSEAS TRANSACTIONS on SYSTEMS, 15*, 275–281.

Bilan, S., Motornyuk, R., & Bilan, S. (2014). Method of Hardware Selection of Characteristic Features Based on Radon Transformation and not Sensitive to Rotation, Shifting and Scale of the Input Images. *Advances in Image and Video Processing, 2*(4), 12–23. doi:10.14738/aivp.24.392

Bilan, S., & Yuzhakov, S. (2018). *Image Processing and Pattern Recognition Based on Parallel Shift Technology*. Boca Raton, FL: CRC Press.

BIOMETRY-MobiComBiom. (n.d.). Retrieved December 5, 2019, from http://biometry.com/media/downloads/files/BIOMETRY White Paper.pdf

Bishop, C. (2006). *Pattern Recognition and Machine Learning*. Berlin: Springer.

Black, S., Debar, H., Michael, J., & Wespi, G. A. (2002). US7308689. US Patent Office.

Blokdyk, G. (2019). Steganography (3rd ed.). 5STARCooks.

Bonde, G., & Khaled, R. (1953). *Stock price prediction using genetic algo- rithms and evolution strategies*. New York: McGraw Hill.

Boukli, H. I., & Bessaid, A. (2014). Hybrid colour medical image compression by CDF wavelet and cosine transforms. *International Journal of Biomedical Engineering and Technology, 16*(1), 1–13. doi:10.1504/IJBET.2014.065633

Boyce, R. R., & Wav, C. (1964). The Concept of Shape in Geography. *Geographical Review, 54*, 561–572.

Bracewell, R. N. (1986). *The Hartley transform*. Oxford University Press, Inc.

Bronshteyn, I., & Semendayev, K. (1986). *Mathematics: Moscow, Science*. Academic Press. (in Russian)

Cardell, S. D., & Fúster-Sabater, A. (2016). Linear Models for the Self-Shrinking Generator Based on CA. *JCA, 11*(2-3), 195–211.

Carthy, S. M. (2017). A Practical Implementation of Identity Based Encryption over NTRU Lattices. *Cryptography and Coding, 16th IMA International Conference*, 227-246.

Cattell, K., & Muzio, J.C. (1996). Syntesis one-dimensional linear hybrid cellular automata. IEEE Trans. *On Computer – aided desing of integrated circuits and systems, 15(3)*, 325 – 335.

Chauhan, S., & Sharma, A. (2019). Improved fuzzy commitment scheme. *International Journal of Information Technology*.

Chebrolu, S., Abraham, A., & Thomas, J. P. (2005). Feature deduction and ensemble design of intrusion detection systems. *Computers & Security, 24*(4), 295–307. doi:10.1016/j.cose.2004.09.008

Chen, W.-S., & Huang, R.-H., & Hsieh, L. (2009). Iris recognition using 3D co-occurrence matrix. In *International Conference on Biometrics* (pp. 1122–1131). Springer.

Chen, B., Chen, F., Guan, J., & He, Q. (2016). Glider Collisions in Hybrid Cellular Automata Rule 168 and 133. *JCA, 11*(2-3), 167–194.

Chen, C. H., Rau, L. F., & Wang, P. S. P. (1995). *Handbook of pattern recognition and computer vision*. Singapore: World Scientific Publishing Co. Pte. Ltd.

Chen, N., Chen, X. S., Xiong, B., & Lu, H. W. (2009, September). An anomaly detection and analysis method for network traffic based on correlation coefficient matrix. *Proceedings of the 2009 International Conference on Scalable Computing and Communications; Eighth International Conference on Embedded Computing* (pp. 238-244). IEEE.

Chervonkin, A., Nabokin, P., & Hyppenen, A. (2006). Compact two-coordinate beam guidance device for atmospheric optical communication lines between moving objects. *Optical Journal, 5.*

Cho, S.J., Choi, U. S., Kim, H.D., Hwang, Y.H., Kim, J.G., & Heo, S.H. (2007). "New syntheesis of one-dimensional 90/150 liner hybrid group CA". *IEEE Transactions on comput-aided design of integrated circuits and systems, 25*(9). pp. 1720-1724

Chugunkov, E.V. (2012). *Methods and tools to evaluate the quality of pseudo-random sequence generators, focused on solving problems of information security: Textbook*/M.: NEYAU MIFI, 236.

Ciampa, F., Mahomoodi, P., Pinto, F., & Meo, M. (2018). Recent analysis in active infrared thermography for non-destructive testing of aerospace components. *Sensors (Basel), 18*(609), 1–37. PMID:29462953

Cicala, G., Massaro, A., Velardi, L., Senesi, G. S., & Valentini, A. (2014). Self-assembled pillar-like structures in nanodiamond layers by pulsed spray technique. *ACS Applied Materials & Interfaces, 6*(23), 21101–21109. doi:10.1021/am505974d PMID:25402729

Cook, M. (2008). A Concrete View of Rule 110 Computation. In T. Neary, D. Woods, A.K. Seda, & N. Murphy (Eds.), The Complexity of Simple Programs (pp. 31-55). Academic Press.

Cook, M. (2004). Universality in elementary cellular automata. *Complex Systems, 15*(1), 1–40.

Coronel, C., & Morris, S. (2014). Database Systems: Design, Implementation, and Management. Academic Press.

Czajka, A., & Pacut, A. (2008). Replay attack prevention for iris biometrics. *Proceedings - International Carnahan Conference on Security Technology*, 247–253. 10.1109/CCST.2008.4751309

Dakin, J., & Brown, R. (2017). Handbook of Optoelectronics (2nd ed.). CRC Press. doi:10.1201/9781315157009

Daugman, J. (2009). How iris recognition works. In The Essential Guide to Image Processing. Academic Press.

David, H. K., Hoe, J. Comer, M., Cerda, J. C., Martinez, C. D., & Shirvaikar, M. V. (2012). Cellular Automata-Based Parallel Random Number Generators Using FPGAs. *International Journal of Reconfigurable Computing Volume 2012*, 1-13, Article ID 219028.

Davida, G. I., Frankel, Y., & Matt, B. J. (1998). On enabling secure applications through off-line biometric identification. In *Proceedings. 1998 IEEE Symposium on Security and Privacy (Cat. No. 98CB36186)* (pp. 148–157). IEEE.

de Campos, L. M. L., de Oliveira, R. C. L., & Roisenberg, M. (2012, September). Network intrusion detection system using data mining. *Proceedings of the International Conference on Engineering Applications of Neural Networks* (pp. 104-113). Springer. doi:10.1007/978-3-642-32909-8_11

Deans, S. R., & Roderick, S. (1983). *The Radon Transform and Some of its Applications.* New York: Wiley.

DeMers, M. N. (2008). *Fundamentals of Geographic Information Systems* (4th ed.). Wiley.

Devaraju S. & Ramakrishnan S. (2015). Detection of Attacks for IDS using Association Rule Mining Algorithm. *IETE Journal of Research, 61*(6), 624-633.

Devaraju, S., & Ramakrishnan, S. (2011). Performance Analysis of Intrusion Detection System Using Various Neural Network Classifiers. *IEEE Proceedings of the International Conference on International Conference on Recent Trends in Information Technology (ICRTIT 2011)*, Madras Institute of Technology, Anna University, Chennai, India (pp. 1033-1038). IEEE.

Devaraju, S., & Ramakrishnan, S. (2013). Performance Comparison of Intrusion Detection System using Various Techniques – A Review. *ICTACT Journal on Communication Technology*, 4(3), 802–812. doi:10.21917/ijct.2013.0114

Devaraju, S., & Ramakrishnan, S. (2014). Performance Comparison for Intrusion Detection System using Neural Network with KDD Dataset. *ICTACT Journal on Soft Computing*, 4(3), 743–752. doi:10.21917/ijsc.2014.0106

Dewangan, U., Sharma, M., & Bera, S. (2015). *Devlopment and Analysis of Stego Images Using Wavelet Transform.* Lap Lambert Academic Publishing.

Dewdney, A. K. (1990). Computer recreations. The cellular automata programs that create Wireworld, Rugworld and the diversions. *Scientific American.*

Dkhil, M. B., Wali, A. & Alimi, A. M. (2016). Towards a Real Time Road Moving Object Detection and Tracking System. *Journal of Information Assurance and Security, 11*, 39-47.

Dong, H., Yang, G., Liu, F., Mo, Y., & Guo, Y. (2017, July). Automatic brain tumor detection and segmentation using U-Net based fully convolutional networks. In *Annual conference on medical image understanding and analysis* (pp. 506-517). Springer.

Dottling, N., & Garg, S. (2017). *IDE from Deffie Hellman Assumption.* Retrieved from https://eprint.iacr.org/2017/543.pdf

Dudgeon, D. E., & Mersereau, R. M. (1984). *Multidimensional Digital Signal Processing.* Englewood Cliffs, NJ: Printice-Hall, Inc.

Dutta, N., & Zhang, X. (2018). *Optoelectronic Devices.* World Scientific Publishing Company. doi:10.1142/10894

Ekuakille, A.-L., Durikovic, I., Lanzolla A., Morello, R., De Capua, C., Girao, P. S., ... Van Biesen, L. (2019). Effluents, surface and subterranean waters monitoring: Review and advances. *Measurements, 137*(1), 567-579.

Ell, T. A., Bihan, N. L., & Sangwine, S. J. (2014). *Quaternion Fourier Transforms for Signal and Image Processing (Focus Series)* (1st ed.). Wiley-ISTE.

Ensel, C. (2001). A scalable approach to automated service dependency modeling in heterogeneous environments. *Enterprise Distributed Object Computing Conference, 2001. EDOC '01. Proceedings. Fifth IEEE International.* 10.1109/EDOC.2001.950429

Fan, Y., Nowaczyk, S., & Rögnvaldsson, T. (2015). Incorporating expert knowledge into a self-organized approach for predicting compressor faults in a city bus fleet. *Frontiers in Artificial Intelligence and Applications, 278*(1), 58–67.

Fathy, S. (2010). *Computer Vision Technologies for Identification of Car License Plates: Investigation and performance evaluation using Morphological Operation.* LAP LAMBERT Academic Publishing.

Fernandes, L. A. F., & Oliveira, M. M. (2008). Real-time line detection through an improved Hough transform voting scheme. *Pattern Recognition, 41*(1), 299–314. doi:10.1016/j.patcog.2007.04.003

Floriani, L., Falcidieno, B., Nagy, G., & Pienovi, C. (1991). On sorting triangles in a Delaynay tessellation. *Algorithmica, 6*(6), 522–535. doi:10.1007/BF01759057

Fortune, S. (1987). A sweepline algorithm for Voronoi diagrams. *Algorithmica, 2*(2), 153–174. doi:10.1007/BF01840357

Fraile Ruboi, C., Hernandez Encinas, L., Hoya White, S., & Martin del Rey, A., & Rodrigues Sancher. (2004). The use of Linear Hybrid Cellular Automata as Pseudorandom bit Generators in Cryptography. *Neural Parallel & Scientific Comp., 12*(2), 175–192.

Frascati Manual. (2015). *The Measurement of Scientific, Technological and Innovation Activities- Guidelines for Collecting and Reporting Data on Research and Experimental Development*. OECD.

Fu, Y. (2015). *Face recognition in uncontrolled environments* (PhD thesis). University College London.

Fu, K. S. (1982). *Syntactic pattern recognition and applications*. Prentice-Hall.

Galiano, A., Massaro, A., Barbuzzi, D., Legrottaglie, M., Vitti, V., Pellicani, L., & Birardi, V. (2016). Face recognition system on mobile device based on web service approach. *International Journal of Computer Science and Information Technologies, 7*(4), 2130–2135.

Gardner, M. (1970). The Fantastic Combinations of John Conway's New Solitaire Game "Life". *Scientific American*, (223): 120–123. doi:10.1038cientificamerican1070-120

Gariepy, G., Tonolini, F., Henderson, R., Leach, J., & Faccio, D. (2016). Detection and tracking of moving objects hidden from view. *Nature Photonics, 10*(1), 23–27. doi:10.1038/nphoton.2015.234

Gealow, C., & Sodini, G. (1999). A pixel-parallel image processor usinglogic pitch-matched to dynamic memory. Academic Press.

Genov R., & Cauwenberghs G. (2001). *Charge-Mode Parallel Architecture for Vector–Matrix Multiplication*. Academic Press.

Genov, R., & Cauwenberghs, G. (2002). Stochastic mixed-signal VLSI architecture for high-dimensional kernel machines. *Advances in Neural Information Processing Systems, 14*.

Ghali, N. I. (2009). Feature Selection for Effective Anomaly-Based Intrusion Detection. *International Journal of Computer Science and Network Security, 9*(3), 285–289.

Giraul, B. & Vlassopoulos, N. (2012). Evolution of 2-Dimensional Cellular Automata as Pseudo-random Number Generators./ *Springer-Verlag Berlin Heidelberg, ACRI 2012*, LNCS 7495, 611–622

Gladilin, S. & Lebedev, D. (2005). Neural network reproducing the output signal of a ganglion cell. *Information processes, 5*(3), 258-264.

Golay, M. J. E. (1969). Hexagonal parallel pattern transformations. *IEEE Transactions on Computers, C-18*(8), 733–740. doi:10.1109/T-C.1969.222756

Golomb, S. W. (1967). *Shift register sequences*. Holden-Day.

Gomez-Barrero, M., Rathgeb, C., Galbally, J., Busch, C., & Fierrez, J. (2016). Unlinkable and irreversible biometric template protection based on bloom filters. *Information Sciences, 370*, 18–32. doi:10.1016/j.ins.2016.06.046

Gonzalez, R. C., & Woods, R. E. (2008). *Digital Image Processing* (3rd ed.). Prentice Hall.

Gonzalez, R. C., Woods, R. E., & Eddins, S. L. (2004). *Digital Image Processing using MATLAB*. Pearson Prentice Hall.

Goodman, J. (2017). *Introduction to Fourier Optics* (4th ed.). W. H. Freeman.

GOST 26086–84. (1985). *Lasers. Methods for measuring the beam diameter and the energy divergence of laser radiation*. IPK Publishing House of Standards.

Gribunin, V., Okov, I., & Turiptsev, I. (2002). *Digital steganography.* SOLON-Press.

Guibas, L., & Stolfi, J. (1985). Primitives for the manipulation of general subdivisions and the computation of Voronoi diagrams. *ACM Transactions on Graphics, 4*(2), 74–123. doi:10.1145/282918.282923

Gupta, R., & Sehgal, P. (2018a). A Non-deterministic Approach to Mitigate Replay Attack and Database Attack Simultaneously on Iris Recognition System. In *International Conference on Intelligent Human Computer Interaction* (pp. 239–250). Springer. 10.1007/978-3-030-04021-5_22

Gupta, K. K., Nath, B., & Kotagiri, R. (2010). Layered Approach Using Conditional Random Fields for Intrusion Detection. *IEEE Transactions on Dependable and Secure Computing, 7*(1), 35–49. doi:10.1109/TDSC.2008.20

Gupta, R., & Sehgal, P. (2016). Mitigating Iris based Replay Attack using Cuckoo Optimized Reversible Watermarking. *Seventh International Conference on Advances in Computing, Control, and Telecommunication Technologies.*

Gupta, R., & Sehgal, P. (2018b). Non-deterministic approach to allay replay attack on iris biometric. *Pattern Analysis & Applications,* 1–13.

Gupta, R., & Sehgal, P. (2019). A Complete End-to-End System for Iris Recognition to Mitigate Replay and Template Attack. In *Soft Computing and Signal Processing* (pp. 571–582). Singapore: Springer. doi:10.1007/978-981-13-3600-3_54

Gusev, M., & Evans, D. (1994). A new matrix vector product systolic array. Parallel and Distribute Computing, 22(2), 346-349. doi:10.1006/jpdc.1994.1094

Gutowitz, H. A., Victor, J. D., & Knight, B. W. (1987). Local structure theory for cellular automata. *Physica D. Nonlinear Phenomena, 28*(1-2), 18–48. doi:10.1016/0167-2789(87)90120-5

Hadeler, K. P., & Müller, J. (2017). *Cellular Automata: Analysis and Applications (Springer Monographs in Mathematics)* (1st ed.). Springer. doi:10.1007/978-3-319-53043-7

Hajisalem, V., & Babaie, S. (2018). A hybrid intrusion detection system based on ABC-AFS algorithm for misuse and anomaly detection. *Computer Networks, 136,* 37–50. doi:10.1016/j.comnet.2018.02.028

Hamid, H. A., Rahman, S. M. M., Hossain, M. S., & Almogren, A. (2017). A Security Model for Preserving the Privacy of Medical Big Data in a Healthcare Cloud Using a Fog Computing Facility with Pairing-Based Cryptography. *IEEE Access, 5,* 22313–22328. doi:10.1109/ACCESS.2017.2757844

Hämmerle-Uhl, J., Pschernig, E., & Uhl, A. (2009). Cancelable iris biometrics using block re-mapping and image warping. *Information Security. Springer Berlin Heidelberg,* 135–142. doi:10.1007/978-3-642-04474-8_11

Hammerle-Uhl, J., Pschernig, E., & Uhl, A. (2013). Cancelable iris-templates using key-dependent wavelet transforms. In *2013 International Conference on Biometrics (ICB)* (pp. 1–8). IEEE. 10.1109/ICB.2013.6612960

Hämmerle-Uhl, J., Raab, K., & Uhl, A. (2011). Robust watermarking in iris recognition: Application scenarios and impact on recognition performance. *Applied Computing Review, 11*(3), 6–18. doi:10.1145/2034594.2034595

Han, S., Mao, H., & Dally, W. J. (2015). *Deep compression: Compressing deep neural networks with pruning, trained quantization and Huffman coding.* arXiv preprint arXiv:1510.00149

Hanguang, L., & Yu, N. (2012). Intrusion detection technology research based on apriori algorithm. *Physics Procedia, 24,* 1615–1620.

Hausdorff, F. (1962). *Set theory.* Chelsea Pub. Co.

Hedieh, S. (2012). *Recent Advances in Steganography.* InTech.

Hedlung, G. A. (1969). Endomorphism and Automorphism of the Shift Dynamic System. *Mathematical Systems Theory*, (3): 51–59.

Hegarty, M., & Keane, A., (2018). *Steganography, The World of Secret Communications*. CreateSpace Independent Publishing Platform.

Helgason, S. (2014). *Integral Geometry and Radon Transforms*. Springer.

Hellerstein, J. L., Ma, S., & Perng, C.-S. (2002). Discovering actionable patterns in event data. *IBM Systems Journal*, *41*(3), 475–493. doi:10.1147j.413.0475

Herranz, J. (2016). Attribute-based encryption implies identity based encryption. *IET Information Security Journal*, *11*(6), 2016.

Hertz, J., Krogh, A., & Palmer, R. (1991). *Introduction to the Theory of Neural Computation*. Academic Press.

He, Y., Feng, G., Hou, Y., Li, L., & Micheli-Tzanakou, E. (2011). Iris feature extraction method based on LBP and chunked encoding. In *2011 Seventh International Conference on Natural Computation*, (pp. 1663–1667). IEEE. 10.1109/ICNC.2011.6022302

Hilles, S. M. (2018, July). Sofm And Vector Quantization For Image Compression By Component. In *2018 International Conference on Smart Computing and Electronic Enterprise (ICSCEE)* (pp. 1-6). IEEE. 10.1109/ICSCEE.2018.8538402

Hilles, S. M. (2018, July). Spatial Frequency Filtering Using Sofm For Image Compression. In *2018 International Conference on Smart Computing and Electronic Enterprise (ICSCEE)* (pp. 1-7). IEEE.

Hilles, S. M., & Hossain, M. A. (2018). Classification on Image Compression Methods. *International Journal of Data Science Research*, *1*(1), 1–7.

Hilles, S., & Maidanuk, V. P. (2014). Self-organization feature map based on VQ components to solve image coding problem. *Journal of Engineering and Applied Sciences (Asian Research Publishing Network)*, *9*(9), 1469–1475.

Holland, J. (1966). *Universal Spaces: A Basis for Studies in Adaptation. In Automata Theory* (pp. 218–230). Academic Press.

Horn, B. K. P. (1986). *Robot Vision*. MIT Press.

Hu, J., Yu, X., Qiu, D., & Chen, H.-H. (2009). A simple and efficient hidden Markov model scheme for host- based anomaly intrusion detection. *Journal IEEE Network*, *23*(1), 42–47. doi:10.1109/MNET.2009.4804323

Hussain, A. J., Al-Jumeily, D., Radi, N., & Lisboa, P. (2015). Hybrid neural network predictive-wavelet image compression system. *Neurocomputing*, *151*, 975–984. doi:10.1016/j.neucom.2014.02.078

Hwa, S., L., & Cho, N. I. (2018). Cancelable biometrics using noise embedding. *24th International Conference on Pattern Recognition (ICPR)*. 10.1109/ICPR.2018.8545121

Ioannidis, K., Andreadis, I., & Sirakoulis, G. (2012). An Edge Preserving Image Resizing Method Based on Cellular Automata. *LNCS*, *7495*, 375–384.

Jain, A. (1989). *Fundamentals of Digital Image Processing*. Prentice-Hall.

Jain, A. K., Nandakumar, K., & Nagar, A. (2008). Biometric Template Security. *EURASIP Journal on Advances in Signal Processing*, *579416*(1), 579416. doi:10.1155/2008/579416

Jain, A., Duin, R., & Mao, J. (2000). Statistical pattern recognition: A review. *IEEE Transactions on Pattern Analysis and Machine Intelligence*, *22*(1), 4–37. doi:10.1109/34.824819

Jasmi, R. P., Perumal, B., & Rajasekaran, M. P. (2015, January). Comparison of image compression techniques using huffman coding, DWT and fractal algorithm. In *2015 International Conference on Computer Communication and Informatics (ICCCI)* (pp. 1-5). IEEE.

Jiang, H., & Ruan, J. (2009). The Application of Genetic Neural Network in Network Intrusion Detection. *Journal of Computers*, *4*(12), 1223–1230. doi:10.4304/jcp.4.12.1223-1230

Jiang, M., Gan, X., Wang, C., & Wang, Z. (2011). Research of the Intrusion Detection Model Based on Data Mining, Elsevier. *Energy Procedia*, *13*, 855–863.

Jitcha Shivang, S. S. (2018). Weather prediction for Indian location using Machine learning. *International Journal of Pure and Applied Mathematics*, *118*(22).

Kabir, E., Hu, J., Wang, H., & Zhuo, G. (2018). A novel statistical technique for intrusion detection systems, Elsevier-. *Future Generation Computer Systems*, *79*, 303–318. doi:10.1016/j.future.2017.01.029

Kahn, C. E. Jr, Carrino, J. A., Flynn, M. J., Peck, D. J., & Horii, S. C. (2007). DICOM and Radiology: Past, Present, and Future. *Journal of the American College of Radiology*, *4*(9), 652–657. doi:10.1016/j.jacr.2007.06.004 PMID:17845973

Kamberović, H., Saracevic, M., & Koricanin, E. (2015). The standard for digital imaging and communications in medicine – DICOM. *University Journal of Information Technology and Economics*, *2*(1), 1–4.

Kannammal, A., & Subha, R. S. (2012). DICOM Image Authentication and Encryption Based on RSA and AES Algorithms. In *Trends in Intelligent Robotics, Automation, and Manufacturing*. Berlin: Springer. doi:10.1007/978-3-642-35197-6_39

Karasulu, B., & Korukoglu, S. (2013). *Performance Evaluation Software: Moving Object Detection and Tracking in Videos (SpringerBriefs in Computer Science)*. Springer. doi:10.1007/978-1-4614-6534-8

Karpyk, A. (2004). Methodological and technological bases of geoinformation support of territories. Academic Press.

Karri, C., & Jena, U. (2016). Fast vector quantization using a Bat algorithm for image compression. *Engineering Science and Technology, an International Journal*, *19*(2), 769-781.

Kass, M., Witkin, A., & Terzopoulos, D. (1987). Snakes: Active contour models. *International Journal of Computer Vision*, *1*(4), 321–331. doi:10.1007/BF00133570

KDD Cup 1999 Intrusion Detection Data. (2010). Retrieved from http://kdd.ics.uci.edu/databases/kddcup99/kddcup99.html

Khorsheed, O. K. (2014). Produce Low-Pass and High-Pass Image Filter in Java. *International Journal of Advances in Engineering and Technology*, *7*(3), 712.

Knuth, D. E. (1969). The Art of Computer Programming: Vol. 2. *Seminumerical Algorithms*. Reading, MA: Addison-Wesley.

Knuth, D. E. (1998). The art of computer programming: Vol. 2. *Seminumerical algorithms* (3rd ed.). Reading, MA: Addison-Wesley.

Kobasyar, M.I. & Rusin, B.P. (2001). Detection of curves from binary images by Radon transformation. *Bulletin of the National University "Lviv Polytechnic" "Radioelektronika i telekomunikatsiia"*, (428), 6-9.

Kobayashi, L. O. M., Furuie, S. S., & Barreto, P. S. L. (2009). Providing Integrity and Authenticity in DICOM Images: A Novel Approach. *IEEE Transactions on Information Technology in Biomedicine*, *13*(4), 582–589. doi:10.1109/TITB.2009.2014751 PMID:19244022

Kohonen, T. (1989). Self Organization and Associative Memory (3rd ed.). Academic Press. doi:10.1007/978-3-642-88163-3

Kohonen, T. (2000). *Self-organized Maps* (3rd ed.). Springer.

413

Konheim, A. G. (2009). *Computer Security and Cryptography*. John Wiley & Sons.

Kormanovsky, S., Shvejki, N., & Timchenko, L. (2001). Approach to determining the center of image connectivity. *Bulletin of the FPI*, (4), 71-73.

Kościelny, C., Kurkowski, M., & Srebrny, M. (2013). *Modern Cryptography Primer: Theoretical Foundations and Practical Applications*. Berlin, Germany: Springer. doi:10.1007/978-3-642-41386-5

Kovalev, V., Kalinovsky, A., & Kovalev, S. (2016). Deep learning with Theano, Torch, Caffe, TensorFlow, and deeplearning4j: which one is the best in speed and accuracy? *XIII Int. Conf. on Pattern Recognition and Information Processing*, 99-103.

Kovzel, M., Kutaev, I., & Tymchenko, Y. (2006). Parallel-hierarchical transformation and Q-processing of information for real-time systems. Academic Press.

Kovzel, M., Timchenko, L., Kutaev, Y., Svechnikov, S., Kozhemyako, V., Stasyuk, O., ... Zohoruiko, L. (2006). Parallel - hierarchical transformation and Q-processing of information for real-time systems. Kyiv: KUETT.

Kozemyako, V. (1997). A look at the nature of artificial intelligence. Herald of VPI, 1, 26-30.

Kozemyako, V., Bilan, O., & Kozemyako, A. (2004) Optical-electronic geoinformation and energy system as a global means of harmonious solving of problems of development of civilization. Optoelectronic Information and Energy Technologies, 2(8), 5-10.

Kozemyako, V., Tymchenko, Y., Kutaev, I., & Ivasyuk, I. (1994). Introduction to the algorithmic theory of the hierarchy and parallelism of neural-like computing environments and its application to the transformation of images. Fundamentals of the Theory of Pyramid-Network Image Transformation, 2.

Kozhemyako, V., Bilan, S., & Savaliuk, I. (2001). Optoelectronic self-regulation neural system for treatment of vision information. *SPIE Proceedings, 3055,* 120–126.

Kozhemyako, V., Tymchenko, L., Kutaev, Y., & Yaroviy, A. (2002). Approach for real-time image recognition. *Opto-Electronic Information Technologies*, (1), 110-124.

Kumar, P., (2019). *Steganography using visual cryptography*. Independently published.

Kupchenko, Y. (2003). Home networks on electric wires - time has come? Computer Review, 18-19(387), 24-38.

Kwok, P. A. (1988). thinning algorithm by contour generation. *Univ. of Calgary, 31*(11), 1314–1324.

Lam, L., & Suen, C. Y. (1995). An evaluation of parallel thinning algorithms for characterrecognition. *IEEE Trans. PAMI, 17*(9), 914–919. doi:10.1109/34.406659

Land, M., McConnell, P., & McMahon, M. (2006). US 7,155,676 B2. US Patent Office.

Lang, S. (2012). *Introduction to Linear Algebra*. Springer Science & Business Media.

Lavee, G., Rivlin, E., & Rudzsky, M. (2009). Understanding Video Events: A Survey of Methods for Automatic Interpretation of Semantic Occurrences in Video. *IEEE Transactions on Systems, Man and Cybernetics. Part C, Applications and Reviews, 39*(5), 489–504. doi:10.1109/TSMCC.2009.2023380

Li, J., Robles-Kelly, A., & You, S. (2017). A Frequency Domain Neural Network for Fast Image Super-resolution. *International Joint Conference on Neural Networks*.

Li, W. (2004). Using Genetic Algorithm for network intrusion detection. *Proceedings of the United States Department of Energy Cyber Security Group 2004 Training Conference*. Academic Press.

Li, C., Zhou, W., & Yuan, S. (2015). Iris recognition based on a novel variation of local binary pattern. *The Visual Computer, Springer, 31*(10), 1419–1429. doi:10.100700371-014-1023-5

Li, J., Robles-Kelly, A., & You, S. (2017). A Frequency Domain Neural Network for Fast Image Super-resolution. *International Joint Conference on Neural Networks*.

Lin, S.-W., Ying, K.-C., Lee, C.-Y., & Lee, Z.-J. (2012). An intelligent algorithm with feature selection and decision rules applied to anomaly intrusion detection. *Applied Soft Computing, 12*(10), 3285–3290. doi:10.1016/j.asoc.2012.05.004

Liu, J. (2013). *Radial Basis Function (RBF) Neural Network Control for Mechanical Systems: Design, Analysis and Matlab Simulation*. Springer.

Li, W., & Packard, N. (1990). The Structure of the Elementary Cellular Automata Rule Spase. *Complex Systems, 4*(3), 281–297.

López-Rubio, E., & Ramos, A. D. (2014). Grid topologies for the self-organizing map. *Neural Networks, 56*, 35–48. doi:10.1016/j.neunet.2014.05.001 PMID:24861385

Lu, X., Chen, H., Yeung, S. K., Deng, Z., & Chen, W. (2018). *Unsupervised Articulated Skeleton Extraction from Point Set Sequences Captured by a Single Depth Camera*. Association for the Advancement of Artificial Intelligence.

Mabu, S., Chen, C., Lu, N., Shimada, K., & Hirasawa, K. (2011). An Intrusion-Detection Model Based on Fuzzy Class-Association-Rule Mining Using Genetic Network Programming. *IEEE Transactions on Systems, Man and Cybernetics. Part C, Applications and Reviews, 41*(1), 130–139. doi:10.1109/TSMCC.2010.2050685

Mady, H. H., & Hilles, S. M. (2017). Efficient Real Time Attendance System Based on Face Detection Case Study "MEDIU Staff". *International Journal on Contemporary Computer Research, 1*(2), 21–25.

Mahua, B., Koushik, P., Goutam, G., & .... (2015). Generation of Novel Encrypted Code using Cryptography for Multiple Level Data Security for Electronic Patient Record. *Proceedings of the IEEE International Conference on Bioinformatics and Biomedicine*, Washington, DC (pp. 916-921). IEEE.

Mantos, L. K., & Maglogiannis, I. P. (2016). Sensitive Patient Data Hiding using a ROI Reversible Steganography Scheme for DICOM Images. *Journal of Medical Systems, 40*(6), 1–17. doi:10.100710916-016-0514-5 PMID:27167526

Marić, N., & Pejnović, P. (2004). Digital imaging and communication in medicine. *Proceedings of the IX Scientific Conference - Information Technology - Present and Future*, Montenegro. Academic Press.

Marsaglia, G. (1984). *The Marsaglia Random Number CDROM including the Diehard Battery of Tests of Randomness*. Department of statistics and supercomputer computations and research institute, from http://www.stat.fsu.edu/pub/diehard

Marsaglia, G. (2003). Random number generators. *Journal of Modern Applied Statistical Methods; JMASM, 2*(1), 2–13. doi:10.22237/jmasm/1051747320

Martin, B., & Sole, P. (2008). Pseudorandom Sequences Generations, Prders and Graphs, *Interactions with Computer Science*, Mahdia Tunisia, Nouha editions, 401 - 410.

Mašovic, S., Saracevic, M., Kamberovic, H., & Milovic, B. (2010). Information and communication technology as a tool for establishing e-health. *Proceedings of the 10th International Conference -Research and Development in Mechanical Industry RaDMI 2010* (pp. 624-632). Academic Press.

Massaro, A., Barbuzzi, D., Galiano, A., Vitti, V., & Pellicani, V. (2017). Simplified and efficient face recognition system on real image set and synthesised data. *International Journal of Biometrics, 9*(2), 143–162. doi:10.1504/IJBM.2017.085678

Massaro, A., Ekuakille, A. L., Caratelli, D., Palamara, I., & Morabito, F. C. (2012). Optical performance evaluation of oil spill detection methods: Thickness and extent. *IEEE Transactions on Instrumentation and Measurement, 61*(12), 3332–3339. doi:10.1109/TIM.2012.2210336

Massaro, A., Galiano, A., Meuli, G., & Massari, S. F. (2018). Overview and application of enabling technologies oriented on energy routing monitoring, on network installation and on predictive maintenance. *International Journal of Artificial Intelligence and Applications, 9*(2), 1–20. doi:10.5121/ijaia.2018.9201

Massaro, A., Vitti, V., Maurantonio, G., & Galiano, A. (2018). Sensitivity of a video surveillance system based on motion detection. *Signal and Image Processing: an International Journal, 9*(3), 1–21. doi:10.5121ipij.2018.9301

McCall, J. (2005). Genetic algorithms for modeling and optimization. *Journal of Computational and Applied Mathematics, 184*(1), 205–222. doi:10.1016/j.cam.2004.07.034

Mersereau, R. M. (1979). The Processing of Hexagonally Sampled Two-Dimensional Signals. *Proceedings of the IEEE, 67*(6), 930–949. doi:10.1109/PROC.1979.11356

Mertoguno, S., & Boubakis, N. (2003). Adigital Retina-Like Low-Level Vision processor. *IEEE Transactions on Systems, Man, and Cybernetics. Part B, Cybernetics, 33*(5), 782–788. doi:10.1109/TSMCB.2003.816925 PMID:18238231

Minichino, J., & Howse, J. (2015). *Computer Vision with Python*. Packt Publishing.

Minicino, J., & Howse, J. (2015). *Computer Vision with Python*. Packt Publishing.

Mitchell, A. (1999). *ESRI Guide to GIS Analysis*. Retrieved from www.nanonewsnet.ru

Mittal, M., & Kumar, K. (2016, April). Data clustering in wireless sensor network implemented on self-organization feature map (SOFM) neural network. In *2016 International Conference on Computing, Communication and Automation (ICCCA)* (pp. 202-207). IEEE. 10.1109/CCAA.2016.7813718

Modenova, O. (2010). Steganography and stegoanalysis in video files. *Applied Discrete Mathematics, 3*, 37–39.

Mohamad, H. (1995). *Fundamentals of Artificial Neural Networks*. MIT Press.

Motahari-Nezhad, H. R., Saint-Paul, R., Casati, F., & Benatallah, B. (2011). *Event correlation for process discovery from web service interaction logs*. VLDB. doi:10.100700778-010-0203-9

Mukkamala, S., Sung, A. H., & Abraham, A. (2005). Intrusion detection using an ensemble of intelligent paradigms. *Journal of Network and Computer Applications, 28*(2), 167–182.

Mukkamala, S., Sung, A. H., & Abraham, A. (2007). Hybrid multi-agent framework for detection of stealthy probes. *Applied Soft Computing, 7*(3), 631–641. doi:10.1016/j.asoc.2005.12.002

Müller, A. (2009). *Event Correlation Engine*. ETH. doi:10.1109/45.954656

Muniyandi, A. P., Rajeswari, R., & Rajaram, R. (2012). Network Anomaly Detection by Cascasding K-Means Clustering and C4.5 Decision Tree Algorithm. *Procedia Engineering, 30*, 174-182.

Murray, T. C. (2002). *The Official License Plate Book 2002: A Complete Plate Identification Resource*. Motorbooks Intl.

Mustra, M., Delac, K., & Grgic, M. (2008). Overview of the DICOM Standard. *Proceedings of the 50th International Symposium*, Zadar, Croatia (pp. 39–44). Academic Press.

Nadiammai, G. V., & Hemalatha, M. (2014). Effective Approach toward Intrusion Detection System using Data Mining Techniques. *Elsevier Egyptian Informatics Journal, 15*(1), 37–50. doi:10.1016/j.eij.2013.10.003

Nagesh, S. (2013). Role of data mining in cyber security. *Journal of Exclusive Management Science, 2*(5), 2277–5684.

Natsheh, Q. N., Li, A. B., & Gale, G. (2016). Security of Multi-frame DICOM Images Using XOR Encryption Approach. *Procedia Computer Science, 90,* 175–181. doi:10.1016/j.procs.2016.07.018

Natterer, F. (2001). *The Mathematics of Computerized Tomography (Classics in Applied Mathematics, 32).* Philadelphia, PA: Society for Industrial and Applied Mathematics. doi:10.1137/1.9780898719284

Natterer, F., & Wubbeling, F. (2001). *Mathematical Methods in Image Reconstruction.* Philadelphia, PA: Society for Industrial and Applied Mathematics. doi:10.1137/1.9780898718324

Nefian, A. V., Khosravi, M., & Hayes, M. H. (1997). Real-time detection of human faces in uncontrolled environments. *SPIE Proceeding of Visual Communications and Image Processing, 3024*(1), 211-219.

Nelson, R. (1992). *Detection, Stabilization, and Identification of Moving Objects by a Moving Observer.* PN.

Nessus Vulnerability Scanner. (n.d.). Retrieved July 2, 2018, from http://www.tenable.com/products/nessus-vulnerability-scanner

Neumann, J. (1951). The general and logical theory of automata. In *Cerobral Mechanisms in Behavior, The Hixon Symposium* (pp. 1-31). John Wiley & Sons.

Neumann, J. (1951). The general and logical theory of automata. In L.A. Jefferess, ed., Cerobral Mechanisms in Behavior, *The Hixon Symposium* (pp. 1-31), John Wiley & Sons, New Yirk.

Neumann, J. (1966). *Theory of Self-Reproducing Automata.* University of Illinois Press.

Neumann, J. (1966). *Theory of Self-Reproducing Automata: Edited and completed by A. Burks.* University of Illinois Press.

Neves, S., & Araujo, F. (2014). Lecture Notes in Computer Science: Vol. 8384. *Engineering Nonlinear Pseudorandom Number Generators. Parallel Processing and Applied Mathematics. PPAM 2013* (pp. 96–105).

Ng, S. C. (2017). Principal component analysis to reduce dimension on digital image. *Procedia Computer Science, 111,* 113–119. doi:10.1016/j.procs.2017.06.017

Nicoladie, D. T. (2014). Hexagonal pixel-array for efficient spatial computation for motion-detection pre-processing of visual scenes. *Advances in Image and Video Processing, 2*(2), 26 – 36.

Nie, W., & He, D. (2010). A probability approach to anomaly detection with twin support vector machines. *Journal of Shanghai Jiaotong University (Science), 15*(4), 385–391.

Niitsiima, H., & Maruyama, T. (2004). Real-Time Detection of Moving Objects. *LNCS, 3203,* 1155–1157.

Nikoo, M., Zarfam, P., & Sayahpour, H. (2015). Determination of compressive strength of concrete using Self Organization Feature Map (SOFM). *Engineering with Computers, 31*(1), 113–121. doi:10.100700366-013-0334-x

NIST Special Publications 800-22. (2001). A statistical test suite for random and pseudorandom number generators for cryptographic applications.

Nixon, M. S., & Aguardo, A. S. (2002). *Feature Extraction and Image Processing.* Newnes.

Njemanze, H. S., & Kothari, P. S. (2008). *US7376969B1.* US Patent Office.

NMap Reference Guide. (n.d.). Retrieved July 2, 2018, from http://nmap.org/book/man.html

Nowaková, J., Prílepok, M., & Snášel, V. (2017). Medical image retrieval using vector quantization and fuzzy S-tree. *Journal of Medical Systems*, *41*(2), 18. doi:10.100710916-016-0659-2 PMID:27981409

Nunes da Silva, I., Spatti, D. H., Flauzino, R. A., Bartocci Liboni, L. H., & Franco dos Reis Alves, S. (2017). *Artificial Neural Networks: A Practical Course*. Springer. doi:10.1007/978-3-319-43162-8

Ojala, T., Pietikainen, M., & Maenpaa, T. (2002). Multiresolution gray-scale and rotation invariant texture classification with local binary patterns. *IEEE Transactions on Pattern Analysis and Machine Intelligence*, *24*(7), 971–987. doi:10.1109/TPAMI.2002.1017623

Oliver, N., Rosario, M. B., & Pentland, A. P. (2000). A Bayesian computer vision system for modeling human interactions. *IEEE Transactions on Pattern Analysis and Machine Intelligence*, *22*(8), 831–843. doi:10.1109/34.868684

Orten, B., & Alalan, A. (2005). *Moving Object Identification and Event Recognition in Video Surveillance Systems* (Ms. Thesis). Electric and Electronic Department. METU.

Ouda, O., Tsumura, N., & Nakaguchi, T. (2010a). Tokenless cancelable biometrics scheme for protecting iriscodes. *Proceedings - International Conference on Pattern Recognition*, (1), 882–885. 10.1109/ICPR.2010.222

Panda, S. S., Prasad, M. S. R. S., Prasad, M. N. M., & Naidu, C. S. (2012). Image compression using back propagation neural network. *International Journal of Engineering Science and Advance Technology, 2*, 74-78.

Pandey, Bajpa, & Krishna. (2018). Predictive analysis using resilient and traditional back propagation algorithm. *IACSIT International Journal of Engineering and Technology, 7*(4).

Pan, Z., Hariri, S., & Pacheco, J. (2019). Context Aware Intrusion Detection of Building Automation Systems. *Computers & Security*, *85*, 181–201. doi:10.1016/j.cose.2019.04.011

Park, M. G. (2013). *RAMS management of railway systems integration of RAMS management into railway systems engineering* (Thesis). School of Civil Engineering College of Engineering and Physical Sciences, University of Birmingham.

Park, Y., & Suh, I. H. (2014). Oriented edge-selective band-pass filtering. *Information Sciences*, *276*, 80–103. doi:10.1016/j.ins.2014.02.048

Patel, R. (2009). US20090276843. US Patent Office.

Patil, C. M., & Patilkulkarni, S. (2010). A comparative study of feature extraction approaches for an efficient iris recognition system. In *International Conference on Business Administration and Information Processing* (pp. 411–416). Springer. 10.1007/978-3-642-12214-9_68

Patil, P. M., Suralkar, S. R., & Sheikh, F. B. (2005). Rotation invariant thinning algorithm to detect ridge bifurcations for fingerprint identification. *17th IEEE International Conference on Tools with Artificial Intelligence (ICTAI'05)*, 634-641. 10.1109/ICTAI.2005.112

Peddabachigari, S., Abraham, A., Grosan, C., & Thomas, J. (2007). Modeling intrusion detection system using hybrid intelligent systems. *Journal of Network and Computer Applications*, *30*(1), 114–132.

Pennington, T. (1993). *Performance Comparison of Shearing Interferometer and Hartmann Wave Front Sensors*. PN.

Pianykh, O. S. (2012). *DICOM Security: Digital Imaging and Communications in Medicine*. Berlin, Germany: Springer. doi:10.1007/978-3-642-10850-1

Piprek, J. (2017). Handbook of Optoelectronic Device Modeling and Simulation: Lasers, Modulators, Photodetectors, Solar Cells, and Numerical Methods (vol. 2). CRC Press.

Pratt, W. K. (2016). *Digital Images Processing* (3rd ed.). Wiley.

Pyrgidis, C. N. (2016). *Railway Transportation Systems: Design, Construction and Operation*. CRC Press. doi:10.1201/b19472

Qiao, T., Tang, Y., & Ma, F. (2013). Real-time detection technology based on dynamic line-edge for conveyor belt longitudinal tear. *Journal of Computers*, *8*(4), 1065–1071. doi:10.4304/jcp.8.4.1065-1071

Rajpal, P. S., Shishodia, K. S., & Sekhon, G. S. (2006). An artificial neural network for modeling reliability, availability and maintainability of a repairable system. *Reliability Engineering & System Safety*, *91*(7), 809–819. doi:10.1016/j.ress.2005.08.004

Raju, S., & Bhairannawar, S. S. (2017). Image Compression using Self Organizing Map and Discrete Wavelet Transform with Error Correction. *International Journal of Applied Engineering Research*, *12*(10), 2509–2516.

Ramakrishnan, S., & Devaraju, S. (2017). Attack's Feature Selection-Based Network Intrusion Detection System Using Fuzzy Control Language, Springer-. *International Journal of Fuzzy Systems*, *19*(2), 316–328. doi:10.100740815-016-0160-6

Rana, A. R. A., Wang, X.-Z., Huang, J. Z., Abbas, H., & He, Y.-L. (2017). Fuzziness based semi-supervised learning approach for intrusion detection system. *Information Sciences*, *378*, 484–497. doi:10.1016/j.ins.2016.04.019

Ratha, N. K., Connell, J. H., & Bolle, R. M. (2001). Enhancing security and privacy in biometrics-based authentication systems. *IBM Systems Journal*, *40*(3), 614–634. doi:10.1147j.403.0614

Rathgeb, C., & Uhl, A. (2009). Systematic construction of iris-based fuzzy commitment schemes. *Advances in Biometrics*, 940–949. doi:10.1007/978-3-642-01793-3_95

Rathgeb, C., & Uhl, A. (2009a). An iris-based Interval-Mapping scheme for Biometric Key generation. *2009 Proceedings of 6th International Symposium on Image and Signal Processing and Analysis*, 511–516.

Rathgeb, C., & Uhl, A. (2009b). An iris-based Interval-Mapping scheme for Biometric Key generation. *2009 Proceedings of 6th International Symposium on Image and Signal Processing and Analysis*, 511–516.

Rathgeb, C., & Uhl, A. (2010). Adaptive fuzzy commitment scheme based on iris-code error analysis. In *2010 2nd European Workshop on Visual Information Processing (EUVIP)* (pp. 41–44). IEEE. 10.1109/EUVIP.2010.5699103

Rathgeb, C., & Uhl, A. (2010). Secure iris recognition based on local intensity variations. *Image Analysis and Recognition*, 266–275. doi:10.1007/978-3-642-13775-4_27

Rathgeb, C., Breitinger, F., & Busch, C. (2013). Alignment free cancelable iris biometric templates based on adaptive bloom filters. In *Biometrics (ICB), 2013 International Conference on* (pp. 1–8). IEEE. 10.1109/ICB.2013.6612976

Raval, U. R. & Jani, C. (2016). Implementing & improvisation of K-means clustering algorithm. *International Journal of Computer Science and Mobile Computing*, *5*(5), 191-203.

Rawat, C. S. D., & Meher, S. (2014). Selection of wavelet for image compression in hybrid coding scheme combining SPIHT-and SOFM-based vector quantisation. *International Journal of Signal and Imaging Systems Engineering*, *7*(1), 38–42. doi:10.1504/IJSISE.2014.057937

Reiner, B. (2015). Strategies for Medical Data Extraction and Presentation Part 2: Creating a Customizable Context and User-Specific Patient Reference Database. *Journal of Digital Imaging*, *28*(3), 249–255. doi:10.100710278-015-9794-4 PMID:25833767

Reljin, I., & Gavrovska, A. (2013). Telemedicine. Belgrade, Serbia: Academic Thought. (in Serbian)

Richard, O., Duda, P., & Hart, E. (1972). Use of the hough transformation to detect lines and curves in pictures. *Comm. ACM, 15*(1), 11-15.

Richard, W. (1980). *Hamming. Coding and Information Teory/Englewood Cliffs N.1. 07632*. Prentice-Hall.

Riedl, S. E. (1986). An Electronic Support System for Optical Matrix-Vector Processors. Academic Press.

Rodriguez-Colin, R., Claudia, F., & Trinidad-Blas, G. J. (2007). Data Hiding Scheme for Medical Images. *Proceedings of the 17th International Conference on Electronics, Communications and Computers*, Cholula, Puebla (pp. 32-32). Academic Press.

Rosenfeld, A., & Kak, A. (1982). *Digital Picture Processing* (2nd ed.). New York: Academic Press.

Rosin, P. L. (2005). Training Cellular Automata for Image Processing. *LNCS, 3540*, 195–204.

Roska, B., Molnar, A., & Werblin, F. (2006). Parallel processing in retinal ganglion cells: How integration of space-time patterns of excitation and inhibition form the spiking output. *Journal of Neurophysiology, 95*(6), 3810–3822. doi:10.1152/jn.00113.2006 PMID:16510780

Rossi, P., Mancini, F., Dubbini, M., Mazzone, F., & Capra, A. (2017). Combining nadir and oblique UAV imagery to reconstruct quarry topography: Methodology and feasibility analysis. *European Journal of Remote Sensing, 50*(1), 211–221. doi:10.1080/22797254.2017.1313097

Rubin, B. (2015). *Introduction to Radon Transforms: With Elements of Fractional Calculus and Harmonic Analysis (Encyclopedia of Mathematics and its Applications)* (1st ed.). Cambridge University Press.

Rubio, C. F., & Sanchez, L. H. (2004). The use of Linea Hybrid Cellular Automata as Pseudorandom Bit Generator in Cryptography, *Neural Parallel, Sciens. Comput, 12*(2), 175–192.

Rudresh, D., Dey, S., Singh, R., & Prasad, A. (2017). A privacy-preserving cancelable iris template generation scheme using decimal encoding and look-up table mapping. *Computers & Security, 65*, 373–386. doi:10.1016/j.cose.2016.10.004

Ryan, Ø. (2019). *Linear Algebra, Signal Processing, and Wavelets - A Unified Approach: Python Version (Springer Undergraduate Texts in Mathematics and Technology)* (1st ed.). Springer.

Saba, S. (2018). *Generating all balanced parentheses: A deep dive into an interview question*, Retrieved from https://sahandsaba.com/interview-question-generating-all-balanced

Sadoddin, R., & Ghorbani, A. (2006). Alert Correlation Survey: Framework and Techniques. *Proceedings of the International Conference on Privacy, Security and Trust: Bridge the Gap Between PST Technologies and Business Services*.

Sahasri, M., & Gireesh C. (2017). Object motion detection and tracking for video surveillance. *International Journal of Engineering Trends and Technology*, (1), 161-164.

Sahithi, M., MuraliKrishna, B., Jyothi, M., Purnima, K., Jhansi Rani, A., & Sudha, N.N. (2012). Implementation of Random Number Generator Using LFSR for High Secured Multi Purpose Applications. *International Journal of Computer Science and Information Technologies, 3*(1), 3287–3290.

Salvini, R., Mastrorocco, G., Seddaiu, M., Rossi, D., & Vanneschi, C. (2017). The use of an unmanned aerial vehicle for fracture mapping within a marble quarry (Carrara, Italy): Photogrammetry and discrete fracture network modeling. *Geomatics, Natural Hazards & Risk, 8*(1), 34–52. doi:10.1080/19475705.2016.1199053

Sampaio, R. A., & Jackowski, M. P. (2013). Assessment of Steganographic Methods in Medical Imaging. *Proceedings of the XXVI SIBGRAPI Conference on Graphics Patterns and Images*, Arequipa, Peru. Academic Press.

Sanchez, J., & Perronnin, F. (2014). *U.S. Patent No. 8,731,317*. Washington, DC: U.S. Patent and Trademark Office.

Sandryhaila, A., & Moura, J. M. (2014). Discrete signal processing on graphs: Frequency analysis. *IEEE Transactions on Signal Processing, 62*(12), 3042–3054. doi:10.1109/TSP.2014.2321121

Sanguinetti, B., Martin, A., Zbinden, H., & Gisin, N. (2014). Quantum Random Number Generation on a Mobile Phone. *Physical Review X, 4*(031056), 1–6.

Sankaranarayanan, C., & Annadurai, S. (2018). *An Optimized Digital Image Encryption based SPIHT Compression using RC4-Blowfish and UWT Algorithm*. Academic Press.

Sapegin, A., Jaeger, D., Azodi, A., Gawron, M., Cheng, F., & Meinel, C. (2014). Normalisation of Log Messages for Intrusion Detection. *Journal of Information Assurance and Security, 9*, 167–176.

Saracevic, M., Adamović, S., Miškovic, V., Maček, N., & Šarac, M. (2019). A novel approach to steganography based on the properties of Catalan numbers and Dyck words. *Future Generation Computer Systems, 100*, 186 – 197.

Saracevic, M., Selimi, A., Selimovic, F. (2018). Generation of cryptographic keys with algorithm of polygon triangulation and Catalan numbers. *Computer Science – AGH, 19*(3), 243-256.

Saracevic, M., Adamovic, S., & Bisevac, E. (2018). Applications of Catalan numbers and Lattice Path combinatorial problem in cryptography. *Acta Polytechnica Hungarica: Journal of Applied Sciences, 15*(7), 91–110.

Saracevic, M., Hadzic, M., & Koricanin, E. (2017). Generating Catalan-keys based on dynamic programming and their application in steganography. *International Journal of Industrial Engineering and Management, 8*(4), 219–227.

Saracevic, M., Koricanin, E., & Bisevac, E. (2017). Encryption based on Ballot, Stack permutations and Balanced Parentheses using Catalan-keys. *Journal of Information Technology and Applications, 7*(2), 69–77.

Saracevic, M., Masovic, S., Milosevic, D., & Kudumovic, M. (2013). Proposal for applying the optimal triangulation method in 3D medical image processing. *Balkan Journal of Health Science, 1*(1), 27–34.

Sarasamma, S. T., Zhu, Q. A., & Huff, J. (2005). Hierarchical Kohonen Net for Anomaly Detection in Network Security. *IEEE Transactions on Systems, Man, and Cybernetics, 35*(2), 2, 302–312. PMID:15828658

Savelyeva-Novoselova, N., & Savelyev, A. (2009). Principles of ophthalmic neurocybernetics. In Artificial Intelligence. Intellectual systems. Academic Press.

Schneier, B. (1996). Applied Cryptography, Second Edition: Protocols, Algorthms, and Source Code in C, Wiley Computer Publishing, John Wiley & Sons, Inc, 784.

Schneier, B. (1996). Applied Cryptography. Protocols, Algorthms, and Source Code in C (2nd ed.). Wiley Computer Publishing, John Wiley & Sons, Inc.

Seki, M., Wada, T., Fujiware, H., & Sumi, K. (2003). Background subtraction based on occurence of image variations. *Proceeding of IEEE International Conference on Computer vision and Pattern Recognition, 2*(72), 1-8.

Selvakani Kandeeban, S. & Dr. R.S. Rajesh. (2011). A Genetic Algorithm Based elucidation for improving Intrusion Detection through condensed feature set by KDD 99 data set. *Information and Knowledge Management, 1*(1), 1–9.

Seredynski, F., Bouvry, P., & Zomaya, Y. (2004). Cellular automata computtions and secret rey cryptography. *Parallel Computing, 30*(5-6), 753–766. doi:10.1016/j.parco.2003.12.014

Shack, R. V., & Platt, B. C. (1971). Production and use of a lenticular Hartmann screen. *Journal of the Optical Society of America, 61*, 656.

Shaout, A., & Smyth, C. (2017). Fuzzy zero day exploits detector system. *International Journal of Advanced Computer Research*, *7*(31), 154–163. doi:10.19101/IJACR.2017.730022

Shehab, N. (2012). *Toward a New Steganographic Algorithm for Information Hiding: With our algorithm, Wendy should not be able to distinguish in any way between cover-image and stego-image.* LAP LAMBERT Academic Publishing.

Sheikhan, M., Jadidi, Z., & Farrokhi, A. (2010). Intrusion detection using reduced-size RNN based on feature grouping, Springer-Verlag London Limited. *Neural Computing & Applications*, *21*(6), 1185–1190. doi:10.100700521-010-0487-0

Shelton, J., Roy, K., O'Connor, B., & Dozier, G. V. (2014). Mitigating Iris-Based Replay Attacks. *International Journal of Machine Learning and Computing*, *4*(3), 204–209. doi:10.7763/IJMLC.2014.V4.413

Shelukhin, O., & Kanaev, S. (2017). Steganography. Algorithms and software implementation. RiS.

Shenfield, A., Day, D., & Ayesh, A. (2018). Intelligent intrusion detection systems using artificial neural networks. *ICT Express*, *4*(2), 95–99. doi:10.1016/j.icte.2018.04.003

Siddharth, A., Parneet, K., & Prachi, A. (2013). Economical maintenance and replacement decision making in fleet management using data mining. *The SIJ Transactions on Computer Science Engineering & its Applications*, *1*(2), 37-48.

Simões, G. M. P. (2008). *RAMS analysis of railway track infrastructure (Reliability, Availability, Maintainability, Safety)* (Thesis). Instituto Siperior Tecnico.

Sipper, M., & Tomassini, M. (1996). *Co evolving parallel random number generators. In parallel Problem Solving from Nature – PPSN IV* (pp. 950–959). Berlin: Springer Verlag. doi:10.1007/3-540-61723-X_1058

Sirakoulis, G. Ch. (2016). Parallel Application of Hybrid DNA Cellular Automata for Pseudorandom Number Generation. *JCA*, *11*(1), 63–89.

Smith, D. F., Wiliem, A., & Lovell, B. C. (2015). Face Recognition on consumer devices: Reflections on replay attack. *IEEE Transactions on Information Forensics and Security*, *10*(4), 736–745. doi:10.1109/TIFS.2015.2398819

Soharab, H. S., Khalid, S., & Nabendu, C. (2014). *Moving Object Detection Using Background Subtraction (Springer-Briefs in Computer Science)*. Springer.

Soliman, R. F., Ramadan, N., Amin, M., Ahmed, H. H., El-Khamy, S., & El-Samie, F. E. A. (2018a). Efficient Cancelable Iris Recognition Scheme Based on Modified Logistic Map. In *Proceedings of the National Academy of Sciences, India Section A: Physical Sciences* (pp. 1–7). Academic Press.

Soliman, R. F., Ramadan, N., Amin, M., Ahmed, H. H., El-Khamy, S., & El-Samie, F. E. A. (2018b). Efficient Cancelable Iris Recognition Scheme Based on Modified Logistic Map. In *Proceedings of the National Academy of Sciences, India Section A: Physical Sciences* (pp. 1–7). Academic Press. 10.100740010-018-0555-x

Soliman, R. F., El Banby, G. M., Algarni, A. D., Elsheikh, M., Soliman, N. F., Amin, M., & El-Samie, F. E. A. (2018). Double random phase encoding for cancelable face and iris recognition. *Applied Optics*, *57*(35), 10305–10316. doi:10.1364/AO.57.010305 PMID:30645240

Solomon, C., & Breckon, T. (2011). *Fundamental of Digital Image Processing. A Practical Approach with Examples in Matlab*. Wiley – Blackwell.

Special Publications, N. I. S. T. 800-22. (2010). A statistical test suite for random and pseudorandom number generators for cryptographic applications. Revision 1. NIST.- *National institute of standarts and technology. Computer security division. Computer security resource center.* - Download Documentation and Software, from http://csrc.nist.gov/groups/ST/toolkit/rng/documentation_software.html

Sprott, J. (2019). Elegant Fractals: Automated Generation of Computer Art: Fractals and Dynamics in Mathematics, Science, and the Arts: Theory and Applications. World Scientific Publishing Company.

Stanley, R. (2005). *Catalan addendum to Enumerative Combinatorics*. Massachusetts Institute of Technology. Retrieved from http://www-math.mit.edu/~rstan/ec/catadd.pdf

Staunton, R. C. (1989). Hexagonal image sampling, a practical proposition. *Proceedings of the Society for Photo-Instrumentation Engineers, 1008*, 23–27. doi:10.1117/12.949123

Steeb, W. H. (2014). *The Nonlinear Workbook: Chaos, Fractals, Cellular Automata, Genetic Algorithms, Gene Expression Programming, Support Vector Machine, Wavelets, Hidden ... Java And Symbolicc++ Programs (6th ed.)*. Wspc. doi:10.1142/9084

Sugimura, H., & Takashima, K. (1999). On a fractal approach to actual plant images. *Proc. of Int. Conf. Pattern Recognition and Image Processing'99*, 130-133.

Suhinin, B. M. (2010a). High generators of pseudorandom sequences based on cellular automata, *Applied discrete mathematics, Nº 2*, 34 – 41.

Suhinin, B. M. (2010b). Development of generators of pseudorandom binary sequences based on cellular automata. *Science and education, (9)*: 1–21.

Sun, Z., Tan, T., & Qiu, X. (2006). Graph matching iris image blocks with local binary pattern. In *International Conference on Biometrics* (pp. 366–372). Springer.

Sutner, K. (2009). *Classification of cellular Automata*. In R. A. Meyers (Ed.), *Encyclopedia of Complexty and Systems Science* (pp. 755–768). New York: Springer –Verlag.

Ta-Hsin, L., & Gibson, J. (1997). Time corellation analysis of a class of nonstationarysignals with an application to radar imaging. *IEEE Intl. Conf. Acoust., Speech and Signal Proc. (ICASSP97), 5*, 3765-3769.

Talukder, T., & Maithies, L. (2004). Real-time Detection of Moving Objects from Moving Vehicles using Dense Stereo and Optical Flow. *Intelligent Robots and Systems, 4*, 3718–3725.

Tamanaha, E., Murphy, M., Onorato, M., & Tafralian, J. (2019). US20190088025. US Patent Office.

Tan, C. K., Changwei, N. J., Xu, X., Poh, C. L., & ... . (2011). Security Protection of DICOM Medical Images Using Dual-Layer Reversible Watermarking with Tamper Detection Capability. *Journal of Digital Imaging, 24*(3), 528–540. doi:10.100710278-010-9295-4 PMID:20414697

Tan, X., Chen, S., Zhou, Z.-H., & Zhang, F. (2006). Face recognition from a single image per person: A survey. *Pattern Recognition, 39*(9), 1725–1745. doi:10.1016/j.patcog.2006.03.013

Taylor, M., & Koning, M. (2017). *Blue Windmill Media. The Math of Neural Networks*. Academic Press.

Temir, F., Siap, I., & Arin, H. (2014). On Pseudo Random Bit Generators via Two-Dimentional Hybrid Cellular Automata. *Acta Physica Polonica A, 125*(2), 534–537. doi:10.12693/APhysPolA.125.534

Teutsch, M. (2015). *Moving Object Detection and Segmentation for Remote Aerial Video Surveillance* (German Edition). KIT Scientific Publishing.

Thaseen, I. S., & Kumar, C. A. (2017). Intrusion detection model using fusion of chi-square feature selection and multi class SVM. *Journal of King Saud University-Computer and Information Sciences, 29*(4), 462–472.

Timchenko, L., Kokriatskaia, N., Yarovyy, A., & Denysova, A. (2013). Application of multi-level parallel-hierarchic systems based on gpu in laser beam shaping problems. *Journal of Theoretical and Applied Information Technology.*, *54*(3), 525–534.

Timchenko, L., Kutaev, Y., Gertsiy, A., & Baybak, J. (2000). Coordinate Reference System Of Nonstationary Signals. *Proc. Xth Conference on Laser Optics (LO'2000)*.

Timchenko, L., Kutaev, Y., Zhukov, K., Gertsiy, A., & Shveyki, N. (2000). Coordinate Reference System Of Nonstationary Signals. *Proc. Machine Vision and Three-Dimensional Imaging Systems for Inspection and Metrology SPIE Symposium*, 4189, 211-217.

Toft, P. (1996). *The Radon Transform: Theory and Implementation* (PhD thesis). Dept. of Math. Modelling Section for Digital Signal Processing, Technical Univ. of Denmark.

Tokuo, U., Akiko, O., & Tsutomu, G. (2014). Security Model for Secure Transmission of Medical Image Data Using Steganography. In *Integrating information technology and management for quality of care*. IOS Press.

Tsai, D. M., & Lai, S. C. (2008). Independent component analysis-based background subtraction for indoor surveillance. *IEEE Transactions on Image Processing*, *18*(1), 158–167. doi:10.1109/TIP.2008.2007558 PMID:19095527

Tsai, Z. D., & Perng, M. H. (2013). Defect detection in periodic patterns using a multi-band-pass filter. *Machine Vision and Applications*, *24*(3), 551–565. doi:10.100700138-012-0425-5

Tuchs, K. D., & Jobmann, K. (2001). Intelligent search for correlated alarm events in databases. *2001 7th IEEE/IFIP International Symposium on Integrated Network Management Proceedings: Integrated Management Strategies for the New Millennium*. 10.1109/INM.2001.918040

Tushar, J. & Meenu. (2013). Automation and integration of industries through computer vision systems. *International Journal of Information and Computation Technology*, *3*(9), 963–970.

Tyagur, V. (2017). Optical-electronic system. Academic Press.

Ubardulaev, R. (1989). Fiber optic networks. Engineering Encyclopedia, Electronic Communications Technologies, 1(1), 184.

Ulam, S. (1952) Random Processes and Transformations. *Procedings Int. Congr. Mathem.*, (2), 264-275.

Upadhyay, P., & Chhabra, J. K. (2015). Modified Self Organizing Feature Map Neural Network (MSOFM NN) Based Gray Image Segmentation. *Procedia Computer Science*, *54*, 671–675. doi:10.1016/j.procs.2015.06.078

Vasiliev, V. P., Sumerin, V. V., & Chervonkin, A. P. (2002). The equipment for the optical communication line increased secrecy. *Wuxiandian Gongcheng*, 12.

Walker, J. (2008). *ENT. A Pseudorandom Number Sequence Test Program*. January 28th, from http://www.fourmilab.ch/random

Wang, J., & Zheng, N. (2013). A Novel Fractal Image Compression Scheme With Block Classification and Sorting Based on Pearson's Correlation Coefficient. *IEEE Transactions on Image Processing*, *22*(9), 3690–3702. doi:10.1109/TIP.2013.2268977 PMID:23797251

Wang, M., & Zhao, A. (2012). Investigations of Intrusion Detection Based on Data Mining. *Springer Recent Advances in Computer Science and Information Engineering Lecture Notes in Electrical Engineering*, *124*, 275–279.

Welsh, B. M., Roggemann, M. C., Ellerbroek, B. L., & Pennington, T. L. (1995). Fundamental performance comparison of a Hartmann and a shearing interferometer wave-front sensor. *Applied Optics*, *34*(21), 4186. doi:10.1364/AO.34.004186 PMID:21052244

Werbos, P. (1974). *Beyond Regression: New Tools for Prediction and Analysis in the Behavioral Sciences* (Ph.D. Thesis). Applied Mathematics, Harvard University.

Wilson, F. R. (2012). *Railway-Signalling: Automatic; An Introductory Treatment of the Purposes, Equipment, and Methods of Automatic Signalling and Track-Circuits for Steam ... Students, and Others (Classic Reprint).* Forgotten Books.

Wimmer, H., & Powell, L. M. (2015). A comparison of open source tools for data science. *Proceedings of the Conference on Information Systems Applied Research*, *8*(3651), 1-9.

Windows Security Log Events. (n.d.). Retrieved January 22, 2018, from https://www.ultimatewindowssecurity.com/securitylog/encyclopedia/Default.aspx

Wireshark Vulnerability Scanner. (n.d.). Retrieved July 2, 2018, from https://www.wireshark.org

Wolfram, S. (1986). *Appendix of Theory and Applicat ions of Cellular A utomata.* World Scientific.

Wolfram, S. (1986a). Random Sequence Generation by Cellular Automata. *Advances in Applied Mathematics*, *7*(2), 429–432. doi:10.1016/0196-8858(86)90028-X

Wolfram, S. (1986b). Cryptography with Cellular Automata. *Lecture Notes in Computer Science*, *218*, 429–432. doi:10.1007/3-540-39799-X_32

Wolfram, S. (2002). *A new kind of science.* Wolfram Media.

Woodward, M., & Muir, F. (1984). Hexagonal Sampling. *Stanford Exploration Project*, *SEP-38*, 183–194.

Wu, X., Qi, N., Wang, K., & Zhang, D. (2008a). A novel cryptosystem based on iris key generation. *Proceedings - 4th International Conference on Natural Computation*, *4*, 53–56. 10.1109/ICNC.2008.808

Wu, X., Qi, N., Wang, K., & Zhang, D. (2008b). An iris cryptosystem for information security. *Proceedings - 2008 4th International Conference on Intelligent Information Hiding and Multimedia Signal Processing*, 1533–1536. 10.1109/IIH-MSP.2008.83

Wu, S., Wen, W., Xiao, B., Guo, X., Du, J., Wang, C., & Wang, Y. (2019). An Accurate Skeleton Extraction Approach From 3D Point Clouds of Maize Plants. *Frontiers in Plant Science*, *10*, 1–14. doi:10.3389/fpls.2019.00248 PMID:30899271

Xie, Y., & Yu, S.-Z. (2008). A Large Scale Hidden Semi-Markov model for Anomaly Detection on User Browsing Behaviors. *IEEE/ACM Transactions on Networking*, *17*(1), 1–14.

Xingui, H. & Shaohua, X., (2010). Process Neural Networks: Theory and Applications. *Advanced Topics in Science and Technology in China, 240.*

Xiong, Z., Li, Q., Mao, Q., & Zou, Q. (2017). A 3D laser profiling system for rail surface defect detection. *Sensors (Basel)*, *17*(8), 1–19. doi:10.339017081791 PMID:28777323

Xu, L., Xuegang, Y., & Ke, H. (2011). Towards effective bus lane monitoring using camera sensors. *Wireless Sensor Network*, *3*(5), 174–182. doi:10.4236/wsn.2011.35020

Yahalom, R., Steren, A., Nameri, Y., Roytman, M., Porgador, A., & Elovici, Y. (2019). Improving the effectiveness of intrusion detection systems for hierarchical data. *Knowledge-Based Systems*, *168*, 59–69. doi:10.1016/j.knosys.2019.01.002

Yahya, A. (2019). *Steganography Techniques for Digital Images.* Springer. doi:10.1007/978-3-319-78597-4

Yarovyy, A., Timchenko, L., & Kokriatskaia, N. (2012). Parallel-Hierarchical Computing System for Multi-Level Transformation of Masked Digital Signals. *Advances in Electrical and Computer Engineering*, *12*(3), 13–20. doi:10.4316/aece.2012.03002

Yen, C. T., & Huang, Y. J. (2016). Frequency domain digital watermark recognition using image code sequences with a back-propagation neural network. *Multimedia Tools and Applications*, *75*(16), 9745–9755. doi:10.100711042-015-2718-y

Yuan, C., & Mallot, H. A. (2010). Real-Time Detection of Moving Obstacles from Mobile Platforms. *Workshop on Robotics and Intelligent Transportation System*, 109-113.

Zacerkovnyi, V. (2015). Geoinformation system. Academic Press.

Zhang, L., Sun, Z., Tan, T., & Hu, S. (2009). Robust biometric key extraction based on iris cryptosystem. *Advances in Biometrics,* 1060–1069. doi:10.1007/978-3-642-01793-3_107

Zhang, Y., Venkatachalam, A. S., & Xia, T. (2015). Ground-penetrating radar railroad ballast inspection with an unsupervised algorithm to boost the region of interest detection efficiency. *Journal of Applied Remote Sensing*, *9*(1), 095058. doi:10.1117/1.JRS.9.095058

Zhao, C. (2018). Cyber security issues in online games. *AIP Conference Proceedings*, *1955*(040015), 1–5.

Zhuiko, V. J., Verbitskyi, I. V., & Kyselova, A. G. (2014, June). Kotelnikov double series of modulating signals with limited spectrum. In *2014 IEEE International Conference on Intelligent Energy and Power Systems (IEPS)* (pp. 18-20). IEEE. 10.1109/IEPS.2014.6874177

Zoric´, A. B. (2016). Predicting customer churn in banking industry using Neural Networks. *Interdisciplinary Description of Complex Systems*, *14*(2), 116–124. doi:10.7906/indecs.14.2.1

Zuev, B. (n.d.). *Laser navigation devices*. Academic Press.

Zuev, V. (1971). *Lazernye navigacionnye ustrojstva*. Academic Press.

Zuse, K. (1969). *Rechnender Raum*. Braunschweig: Vieweg. doi:10.1007/978-3-663-02723-2

About the Contributors

Stepan Bilan was born on September 15, 1962 in the Kazatin city, Vinnitsia region, Ukraine. He studied at the Vinnitsa Polytechnic Institute from 1979 to 1984. In 1984 he graduated from Vinnitsa Polytechnic with honors and an engineering diploma specializing in Electronic computing machines. From 1986 to 1989 he studied at the graduate school of the Vinnitsa Polytechnic Institute focusing on Computers, complexes and networks. In 1990 he defended his thesis by specialties: 05.13.13 - computer systems, complexes and networks; 05.13.05 - Elements and devices of computer facilities and control systems. He worked at Vinnytsia State Technical University (now the Vinnytsia National Technical University) from 1991 to 2003. In 1998 he was awarded the academic title of assistant professor of "Computer Science" at Vinnytsia National Technical University. From 2003 to the present time, he works at the State University of Infrastructure and Technology (Kiev, Ukraine).

Saleem Issa Al-Zoubi is an associate professor in Faculty of Sciences and Information Technology at Irbid National University, Irbid, Jordan. He is IT manager in Irbid National University (2014 till present). He got a PhD from Vinnitsa National University/ Ukraine, 2004. His area of interest is Information Technology, Networks, Software Engineering, Neural Networks, Artificial Intelligence, Control Systems, Information Security Systems, data mining and machine learning.

* * *

Andrii Bilan was born on April 18, 1982 in Vinnitsa, Vinnitsa region, Ukraine. In 2005 I graduated from the Free International University of Moldova (ULIM), Faculty of Engineering, specialty Programming and Informatics, specialization Computer systems and networks. Until 2007, he worked at MegaNet as a Web programmer for ASP.Net, C #. From 2007 to 2010, he worked as a PHP, JavaScript, HTML, CSS, MySQL programmer at Vingenio SoftWare. Until 2015, it collaborated with the BusinessSoft company in terms of automating accounting using the Universal Accounting program based on the Oracle database. At the present time, he working as a programmer. He has inventions, publications, and patents in the field of cryptography, steganography, and computing.

Mykola Bilan was born on June 27, 1961 in Kazatin, Vinnytsia region, Ukraine. In 1983 he graduated with honors from the Vinnitsa Polytechnic Institute and has a specialty Automation and Remote Control. Until 1994, he worked as a production master in the final assembly shop at the Tashkent Aviation Production Association. V.P. Chkalov. In 1989 he was the best master of the Association. From 1994 to 2015, he worked at the Radio and Television Center (Moldova Republic of) as an engineer and the head of the dispatch service. Currently, he work as an informatics and physics teacher in a secondary school in the village of Mayak, Moldova Republic of. He has many inventions, publications and patents in the field of cryptography, steganography and computer technology

Sergii Bilan was born on December 11, 1983 in the Vinnitsa city. In 2005, he graduated from the Vinnitsa National Technical University with a degree in "Computerized Optical Information Systems". From 2005 to 2008, he studied in the graduate school of the Kiev University of Economics and Transport Technologies with a degree in Laser and Optoelectronic Technology. Currently working as a Technical Lead in the ONSEO Company, Vinnitsa, Ukraine.

Elena Doynikova is a senior researcher at the Laboratory of Computer Security Problems of the St. Petersburg Institute for Informatics and Automation. She received her PhD degree in computer security in 2017. She is the author of more than 50 publications and has participated as a principal investigator and as a researcher in several Russian and international research projects. Her main research interests are security data analysis, risk analysis and security assessment, as well as security decision support in information systems.

Andrey V. Fedorchenko graduated from St. Petersburg State Electrotechnical University. He is a PhD student at St. Petersburg Institute for Informatics and Automation of the Russian Academy of Sciences (SPIIRAS) and holds a position of junior researcher at the Laboratory of Computer Security Problems of SPIIRAS. He has a experience in the research on computer network security and participated in several projects on developing new security technologies. His primary research interests include network security, intrusion detection and malware analysis.

Richa Gupta is a research scholar in Computer Science Department at Delhi University. She completed her B.Sc and M.Sc degree in Computer Science from Delhi University in 2005 and 2007 respectively. She has worked as Assistant Professor in Delhi University and also holds working experience as Software Engineer. She is interested in pattern recognition, information security and biometrics.

Shadi Hilles is an Associate Professor, Computer Science Department and Project Manager in Research and Innovation in Al-Madinah International University, currently working on Project Industrial Revolution 4.0 Professional Education, research & Innovation". Dr. Shadi was keynote speaker, committee member and advisor committee in several international conference and chairman in Seminar in ICT field and area of IR 4.0 and smart campus and has published in ISI and Scopus indexed journals in computer vision fields and cryptography network security, also published in indexed book chapters in Springer and IGI in area of 5G wireless network, dr. Shadi has presented papers in several conferences included IEEE and was one of track chair of IEEE conference and presented in numerous workshops in field of computer science and He is a main supervisor for PhD and Master students and was examiners for postgraduate students, under his supervision there are four PhD students have graduated in image processing field and wireless networking, six master students in image processing and in cryptography and network security, he is one of research development team and editorial manager in industrial revolution 4.0 Professional Education, Research & Innovation in MEDIU and Professional membership of Institute For Engineering Research and Publication, and also in SPIE-The international Society for Optical Engineering.

Igor Kotenko graduated with honors from St. Petersburg Academy of Space Engineering and St. Petersburg Signal Academy. He obtained the Ph.D. degree in 1990 and the National degree of Doctor of Engineering Science in 1999. He is Professor of computer science and Head of the Laboratory of Computer Security Problems of St. Petersburg Institute for Informatics and Automation. He is the author of more than 350 refereed publications, including 12 textbooks and monographs. Igor Kotenko has a high experience in the research on computer network security and participated in several projects on developing new security technologies. For example, he was a project leader in the research projects from the US Air Force research department, via its EOARD (European Office of Aerospace Research and Development) branch, EU FP7 and FP6 Projects, HP, Intel, F-Secure, etc. The research results of Igor Kotenko were tested and implemented in more than fifty Russian research and development projects.

Alessandro Massaro received the Laurea degree in electronic engineering and the Ph.D. degree in telecommunication engineering from the Università Politecnica delle Marche, Ancona, Italy, in 2001 and 2004, respectively.From 2004 to 2006 he worked as Research Scientist (post-doc) in the Department of Electromagnetism and Bioengineering at Università Politecnica delle Marche. In 2006, he spent one year in Research and Development at medical and industrial optics industry(endoscope design and optical systems). He worked for two years with National Nanotechnology Laboratory of CNR-INFM, Università del Salento, as principal investigator. He is currently team leader in Robotics Lab. 1 of the Center of Bio-Molecular Nanotechnology of Italian Institute Technology (IIT), Arnesano, Lecce, Italy. His research interests are in the design and modeling of photonic band gap circuits, in the development of computer aided design (CAD) tools in the area of integrated optics, MEMS technology and systems, and smart material implementation. Actually he is member of the European Microwave Association (EuMA) and of IEEE .Actually he is R&D chief of Dyrecta Lab srl.

Ruslan Motornyuk was born on June 20, 1976 in the village of Ivankovtsy, Kazatinsky District, Vinnitsa Region, Ukrainian SSR. In 2001 he graduated from the magistracy of Vinnitsa State Technical University and received a master's degree in computer systems and networks. In 2013 he defended his thesis for the degree of candidate of technical sciences in the specialty "Computer systems and components". Currently I work as a leading engineer in the Production Unit "Kiev Department" branch of the Main Information and Computing Center of the JSC "Ukrzaliznytsya".

Selver Pepić is employed as a professor at the Higher Technical Machine School of Professional Studies in Trstenik, Serbia. Graduated in 2004 at the University of Podgorica, Montenegro. In 2008 he defended his master's thesis at the Faculty of information technology – University of Novi Pazar, and completed his PhD at the University of Niš, Faculty of Science and Mathematics in 2012. He authored and co-authored several university textbooks and over 40 scientific papers printed in international and national journals, and proceedings of international and national scientific conferences. He is a member of the editorial board for 2 journals. He worked reviews for 4 international journals, 2 domestic journals and many conferences.

Muzafer H. Saračević, Ph.D., is an Associate Professor at the University of Novi Pazar, Serbia. He graduated in computer sciences (cryptography) at the Faculty of Informatics and Computing in Belgrade, obtained his Master degree from the University of Kragujevac, Faculty of Technical Sciences, and completed his Ph.D. (field of computational geometry) at the University of Niš, Faculty of Science and Mathematics in 2013. Muzafer's research areas are programming, software engineering, computational geometry and cryptography. He authored and co-authored several university textbooks and over 150 scientific papers printed in international and national journals, and proceedings of international and national scientific conferences. He is a member of the editorial board for 8 journals. He worked reviews for 10 international journals, 3 domestic journals and many conferences.

Priti Sehgal is an Associate Professor in the department of Computer Science of Keshav Mahavidyalaya in Delhi University. She completed her PhD in Computer Graphics in 2006 from Delhi University. She has a teaching experience of about 23 years. Her research interests include Computer Graphics, Image Processing, Image retrieval, Biometrics and Computer Vision. She has around 35 publications in national and international Journals and Conferences.

Aybeyan Selimi is employed as a Assistant Professor at the International University Vision, Faculty of Informatics in Gostivar. Graduated in 2004 at the Institute of Mathematics in the Faculty of Natural Science and Mathematics in Skopje. In 2015 he defended his master's thesis entitled at field od optimization at the Institute of Mathematics, the Faculty of Natural Sciences and Mathematics in Skopje. PhD at the University of Novi Pazar, Serbia in 2019. Research interests is on the mathematical programming and computational geometry. He is the author of 30 professional and scientific papers.

Devaraju Sellappan received the B.Sc degree in Chemistry in 1997 from the University of Madras, Chennai, and the M.C.A. degree in Computer Applications in 2001 from the Periyar University, Salem, and the M.Phil. degree in Computer Science in 2004 from Periyar University, Salem and also received M.B.A. degree in Human Resource from Madurai Kamaraj University, Madurai in 2007. He received his Ph.D degree in Science and Humanities from Anna University, Chnnai in 2017. He has 16+ years of teaching experience and 2 years industry experience. He is an Associate Professor, Department of Computer Science and Applications, Sri Krishna Arts and Science College, Coimbatore, Tamil Nadu, India. He has published 10 papers in international journals and conference proceedings. His area of research includes Network Security, Intrusion Detection, Soft Computing, and Wireless Communication.

Ramakrishnan Srinivasan received the B.E. degree in Electronics and Communication Engineering in 1998 from the Bharathidasan University, Trichy, and the M.E. degree in Communication Systems in 2000 from the Madurai Kamaraj University, Madurai. He received his PhD degree in Information and Communication Engineering from Anna University, Chennai in 2007. He has 18 years of teaching experience and 1 year industry experience. He is a Professor and the Head of the Department of Information Technology, Dr.Mahalingam College of Engineering and Technology, Pollachi, India. Dr. Ramakrishnan is an Associate Editor for IEEE Access and Reviewer of 24 International Journals such as IEEE Transactions on Image Processing, IET Journals(Formally IEE), ACM Computing Reviews, Elsevier Science, International Journal of Vibration and Control, IET Generation, Transmission & Distribution, etc. He is in the editorial board of 7 International Journals. He is a Guest Editor of special issues in 3 International Journals including Telecommunication Systems Journal of Springer. He has published 160 papers in international, national journals and conference proceedings. Dr. S. Ramakrishnan has published a book on Wireless Sensor Networks for CRC Press, USA and two Books on Speech Processing for InTech Publisher, Croatia and a book on Pattern Recognition for InTech Publisher, Croatia and a book on Face Recognition for InTech Publisher, Croatia and a book Computational Techniques for Lambert Academic

Publishing, Germany and a book on Modern Fuzzy Control Systems for InTech Publisher, Croatia. He has also reviewed 3 books for McGraw Hill International Edition and 15 books for ACM Computing Reviews. He was the convenor of IT board in Anna University of Technology- Coimbatore Board of Studies(BoS). He has guided 3 PhD scholars and guiding 7 scholars. His biography has been included in Marquis Whos's Who in the World 2012 & 2016 edition. His areas of research include digital image processing, soft computing, human-computer interaction, wireless sensor network and cognitive radio.

Sergey Yuzhakov, from 1992 to 1997, studied computer engineering at Vinnytsia State Technical University. Since 2002, he has been working in the information technology divisions of various state institutions of Ukraine. Since 2002 he has been engaged in research in the field of pattern recognition. In 2014 he received the degree of Ph.D.

Index

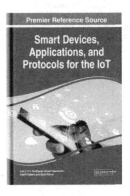

Ensure Quality Research is Introduced to the Academic Community

Become an IGI Global Reviewer for Authored Book Projects

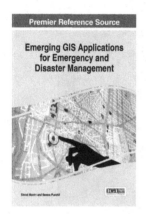

Premier Reference Source

Emerging GIS Applications for Emergency and Disaster Management

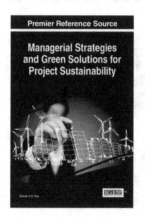

Premier Reference Source

Managerial Strategies and Green Solutions for Project Sustainability

Premier Reference Source

Comparative Approaches to Using R and Python for Statistical Data Analysis

Premier Reference Source

Solutions for High-Touch Communications in a High-Tech World

The overall success of an authored book project is dependent on quality and timely reviews.

In this competitive age of scholarly publishing, constructive and timely feedback significantly expedites the turnaround time of manuscripts from submission to acceptance, allowing the publication and discovery of forward-thinking research at a much more expeditious rate. Several IGI Global authored book projects are currently seeking highly-qualified experts in the field to fill vacancies on their respective editorial review boards:

Applications and Inquiries may be sent to:
development@igi-global.com

Applicants must have a doctorate (or an equivalent degree) as well as publishing and reviewing experience. Reviewers are asked to complete the open-ended evaluation questions with as much detail as possible in a timely, collegial, and constructive manner. All reviewers' tenures run for one-year terms on the editorial review boards and are expected to complete at least three reviews per term. Upon successful completion of this term, reviewers can be considered for an additional term.

If you have a colleague that may be interested in this opportunity, we encourage you to share this information with them.

IGI Global Proudly Partners With eContent Pro International

Receive a 25% Discount on all Editorial Services

Editorial Services

IGI Global expects all final manuscripts submitted for publication to be in their final form. This means they must be reviewed, revised, and professionally copy edited prior to their final submission. Not only does this support with accelerating the publication process, but it also ensures that the highest quality scholarly work can be disseminated.

English Language Copy Editing

Let eContent Pro International's expert copy editors perform edits on your manuscript to resolve spelling, punctuaion, grammar, syntax, flow, formatting issues and more.

Scientific and Scholarly Editing

Allow colleagues in your research area to examine the content of your manuscript and provide you with valuable feedback and suggestions before submission.

Figure, Table, Chart & Equation Conversions

Do you have poor quality figures? Do you need visual elements in your manuscript created or converted? A design expert can help!

Translation

Need your documjent translated into English? eContent Pro International's expert translators are fluent in English and more than 40 different languages.

Hear What Your Colleagues are Saying About Editorial Services Supported by IGI Global

"The service was very fast, very thorough, and very helpful in ensuring our chapter meets the criteria and requirements of the book's editors. I was quite impressed and happy with your service."

– Prof. Tom Brinthaupt,
Middle Tennessee State University, USA

"I found the work actually spectacular. The editing, formatting, and other checks were very thorough. The turnaround time was great as well. I will definitely use eContent Pro in the future."

– Nickanor Amwata, Lecturer,
University of Kurdistan Hawler, Iraq

"I was impressed that it was done timely, and wherever the content was not clear for the reader, the paper was improved with better readability for the audience."

– Prof. James Chilembwe,
Mzuzu University, Malawi

Email: customerservice@econtentpro.com   www.igi-global.com/editorial-service-partners

IGI Global's Transformative Open Access (OA) Model:
How to Turn Your University Library's Database Acquisitions Into a Source of OA Funding

In response to the OA movement and well in advance of Plan S, IGI Global, early last year, unveiled their OA Fee Waiver (Offset Model) Initiative.

Under this initiative, librarians who invest in IGI Global's InfoSci-Books (5,300+ reference books) and/or InfoSci-Journals (185+ scholarly journals) databases will be able to subsidize their patron's OA article processing charges (APC) when their work is submitted and accepted (after the peer review process) into an IGI Global journal.*

How Does it Work?

1. When a library subscribes or perpetually purchases IGI Global's InfoSci-Databases including InfoSci-Books (5,300+ e-books), InfoSci-Journals (185+ e-journals), and/or their discipline/subject-focused subsets, IGI Global will match the library's investment with a fund of equal value to go toward subsidizing the OA article processing charges (APCs) for their patrons.

   Researchers: Be sure to recommend the InfoSci-Books and InfoSci-Journals to take advantage of this initiative.

2. When a student, faculty, or staff member submits a paper and it is accepted (following the peer review) into one of IGI Global's 185+ scholarly journals, the author will have the option to have their paper published under a traditional publishing model or as OA.

3. When the author chooses to have their paper published under OA, IGI Global will notify them of the OA Fee Waiver (Offset Model) Initiative. If the author decides they would like to take advantage of this initiative, IGI Global will deduct the US$ 1,500 APC from the created fund.

4. This fund will be offered on an annual basis and will renew as the subscription is renewed for each year thereafter. IGI Global will manage the fund and award the APC waivers unless the librarian has a preference as to how the funds should be managed.

Hear From the Experts on This Initiative:

"I'm very happy to have been able to make one of my recent research contributions, 'Visualizing the Social Media Conversations of a National Information Technology Professional Association' featured in the *International Journal of Human Capital and Information Technology Professionals*, freely available along with having access to the valuable resources found within IGI Global's InfoSci-Journals database."

– Prof. Stuart Palmer,
Deakin University, Australia

For More Information, Visit:
www.igi-global.com/publish/contributor-resources/open-access or contact IGI Global's Database Team at eresources@igi-global.com.

Printed in the United States
By Bookmasters